AMERICAN GOVERNMENT
POWER & PURPOSE

BRIEF THIRTEENTH EDITION
2014 ELECTION UPDATE

AMERICAN GOVERNMENT
POWER & PURPOSE

Theodore J. Lowi
Cornell University

Benjamin Ginsberg
The Johns Hopkins University

Kenneth A. Shepsle
Harvard University

Stephen Ansolabehere
Harvard University

 W.W. NORTON
NEW YORK · LONDON

W. W. Norton & Company has been independent since its founding in 1923, when William Warder Norton and Mary D. Herter Norton first published lectures delivered at the People's Institute, the adult education division of New York City's Cooper Union. The firm soon expanded its program beyond the Institute, publishing books by celebrated academics from America and abroad. By mid-century, the two major pillars of Norton's publishing program—trade books and college texts—were firmly established. In the 1950s, the Norton family transferred control of the company to its employees, and today—with a staff of four hundred and a comparable number of trade, college, and professional titles published each year—W. W. Norton & Company stands as the largest and oldest publishing house owned wholly by its employees.

Editor: Lisa Camner McKay
Assistant Editor: Sarah Wolf
Project Editor: Christine D'Antonio
Media Editor: Toni Magyar
Editorial Assistant: Samantha Held
Media Editorial Assistant: Cara Folkman
Marketing Manager: Erin Brown
Production Manager: Vanessa Nuttry
Book Designer: Kiss Me I'm Polish LLC, New York
Design Director: Rubina Yeh
Composition: Jouve North America—Brattleboro, VT
Manufacturing: Quad Graphics, Taunton

The Library of Congress has cataloged the full edition as follows:

Library of Congress Cataloging-in-Publication Data

American government : power & purpose / Theodore J. Lowi, Cornell University, Benjamin Ginsberg, The John Hopkins University, Kenneth A. Shepsle, Harvard University, Stephen Ansolabehere, Harvard University. — Thirteenth edition.
     pages cm.
  Includes bibliographical references and index.
  ISBN 978-0-393-26417-3 (hardcover)
  1. United States—Politics and government.   I. Lowi, Theodore J.
JK276.L69 2013
320.473—dc23   2013039130

This edition: **ISBN 978-0-393-26419-7**

W. W. Norton & Company, Inc., 500 Fifth Avenue, New York, NY 10110-0017
wwnorton.com

W. W. Norton & Company Ltd., 15 Carlisle Street,
London W1D 3BS
3 4 5 6 7 8 9 10

For Our Families

Angele, Anna, and Jason Lowi
Sandy, Cindy, and Alex Ginsberg
Rise, Nilsa, and Seth Shepsle
Laurie Gould and Rebecca and
Julia Ansolabehere

Contents

PART 2   INSTITUTIONS

Preface

This book was written for faculty and students who are looking for a little more than just "nuts and bolts" and who are drawn to an analytical perspective—but who also prefer a brief-format text. No fact about American government is intrinsically difficult to grasp, and in an open society such as ours, facts abound. The philosophy of a free and open media in the United States makes information about the government readily available. The advent of the Internet and new communication technologies have expanded further the opportunity to learn about our government. The ubiquity of information in our society is a great virtue. Common knowledge about the government gives our society a vocabulary that is widely shared and enables us to communicate effectively with each other about politics. But it is also important to reach beyond that common vocabulary and to develop a more sophisticated understanding of politics and government. The sheer quantity of facts in our society at times overwhelms us. In a 24/7 news cycle it can be hard to pick out what stories are important and to stay focused on them. The single most important task of the teacher of political science is to confront popular ideas and information and to choose from among them the small number of really significant concepts that help us make better sense of the world. This book aims to help instructors and students accomplish this task.

This Thirteenth Edition continues our endeavor to make *American Government: Power and Purpose* the most authoritative and contemporary introductory text on the market. Those who have used the book in the past know that we have always emphasized the role of American political institutions. We have not strayed from this emphasis. In every chapter we encourage students to think critically and analytically about how well the institutions discussed in that chapter serve the goals of a democratic society.

The major changes in this Thirteenth Edition are intended to deepen the text's analysis of how group politics intersects with the institutions and processes of American government. In addition, the book's organization has been tightened, while new section headings help guide students in their reading. Highlights of the revision include:

- **A new framework in Chapter 4 provides students with a simple but powerful way to analyze civil rights.** Significantly revised, Chapter 4 helps students to understand the contestation over civil rights in terms of *who* has a right and who does not, *what* they have a right to, and *how much* any individual is allowed to exercise that right.

- **Expanded coverage draws on exciting recent research to present students with an analytical perspective on race, gender, and group identity in American politics.** This expansion includes a new section on identity politics in Chapter 9, which analyzes how group identities influence individuals' political opinions and beliefs. Chapter 10 considers the implications of group politics in redistricting battles as well as demographic shifts in who vote and how people vote. Chapter 11 extends the discussion of the group basis of political party identification and allegiance.

- **Four new Analyzing the Evidence units written by expert researchers highlight the political science behind the information in the book,** while the remaining units have been updated with new data and analysis. Each unit poses an important question from political science and presents evidence that can be used to analyze the question. The four new units are:

  "Why Do Congresswomen Outperform Congressmen?" in Chapter 5
  Contributed by Chris Berry, University of Chicago

  "Congressional Design and Control of the Bureaucracy" in Chapter 7
  Contributed by Sean Gailmard, University of California, Berkeley

  "The Contact Hypothesis and Attitudes about Gay Rights" in Chapter 9
  Contributed by Patrick J. Egan, New York University

  "Candidate Religion and Partisan Voting" in Chapter 11
  Contributed by Geoffrey C. Layman, University of Notre Dame; David E. Campbell, University of Notre Dame; John C. Green, University of Akron; and Jeremiah J. Castle, University of Notre Dame

For the Thirteenth Edition we have profited greatly from the guidance of many teachers who have used earlier editions and from the suggestions of numerous thoughtful reviewers. We thank them by name in the Acknowledgments. We recognize that there is no single best way to craft an introductory text, and we are grateful for the advice we have received.

Theodore J. Lowi
Benjamin Ginsberg
Kenneth A. Shepsle
Stephen Ansolabehere

Acknowledgments

Our students at Cornell, Johns Hopkins, and Harvard have already been identified as an essential factor in the writing of this book. They have been our most immediate intellectual community, a hospitable one indeed. Another part of our community, perhaps a large suburb, is the discipline of political science itself. Our debt to the scholarship of our colleagues is scientifically measurable, probably to several decimal points, in the footnotes of each chapter. Despite many complaints that the field is too scientific or not scientific enough, political science is alive and well in the United States. Political science has never been at a loss for relevant literature, and without that literature, our job would have been impossible.

We are pleased to acknowledge our debt to the many colleagues who had a direct and active role in criticism and preparation of the manuscript. The First Edition was read and reviewed by Gary Bryner, Brigham Young University; James F. Herndon, Virginia Polytechnic Institute and State University; James W. Riddlesperger, Jr., Texas Christian University; John Schwarz, University of Arizona; Toni-Michelle Travis, George Mason University; and Lois Vietri, University of Maryland. We also want to reiterate our thanks to the four colleagues who allowed us the privilege of testing a trial edition of our book by using it as the major text in their introductory American Government courses: Gary Bryner, Brigham Young University; Allan J. Cigler, University of Kansas; Burnet V. Davis, Albion College; and Erwin A. Jaffe, California State University–Stanislaus.

For subsequent editions, we relied heavily on the thoughtful manuscript reviews we received from David Canon, University of Wisconsin; Russell Hanson, Indiana University; William Keech, Carnegie Mellon University; Donald Kettl, University of Wisconsin; Anne Khademian, University of Wisconsin; William McLauchlan, Purdue University; J. Roger Baker, Wittenburg University; James Lennertz, Lafayette College; Allan McBride, Grambling State University; Joseph Peek, Jr., Georgia State University; Grant Neeley, Texas Tech University; Mark

Graber, University of Maryland; John Gilmour, College of William and Mary; Victoria Farrar-Myers, University of Texas at Arlington; Timothy Boylan, Winthrop University; Robert Huckfeldt, University of California–Davis; Mark Joslyn, University of Kansas; Beth Leech, Rutgers University; and Charles Noble, California State University, Long Beach.

For the Eighth Edition, we benefited from the comments of Scott Ainsworth, University of Georgia; Thomas Brunell, Northern Arizona University; Daniel Carpenter, Harvard University; Brad Gomez, University of South Carolina; Paul Gronke, Reed College; Marc Hetherington, Bowdoin College; Gregory Huber, Yale University; Robert Lowry, Iowa State University; Anthony Nownes, University of Tennessee; Scott Adler, University of Colorado–Boulder; John Coleman, University of Wisconsin–Madison; Richard Conley, University of Florida; Keith Dougherty, University of Georgia; John Ferejohn, Stanford University; Douglas Harris, Loyola College; Brian Humes, University of Nebraska–Lincoln; Jeffrey Jenkins, Northwestern University; Paul Johnson, University of Kansas; Andrew Polsky, Hunter College–CUNY; Mark Richards, Grand Valley State University; Charles Shipan, University of Iowa; Craig Volden, Ohio State University; and Garry Young, George Washington University.

For the Ninth Edition, we were guided by the comments of John Baughman; Lawrence Baum, Ohio State University; Chris Cooper, Western Carolina State University; Charles Finochiaro, State University of New York–Buffalo; Lisa Garcia-Bellorda, University of California–Irvine; Sandy Gordon, New York University; Steven Greene, North Carolina State University; Richard Herrera, Arizona State University; Ben Highton, University of California–Davis; Trey Hood, University of Georgia; Andy Karch, University of Texas at Austin; Glen Krutz, University of Oklahoma; Paul Labedz, Valencia Community College; Brad Lockerbie, University of Georgia; Wendy Martinek, State University of New York–Binghamton; Nicholas Miller, University of Maryland Baltimore County; Russell Renka, Southeast Missouri State University; Debbie Schildkraut, Tufts University; Charles Shipan, University of Iowa; Chris Shortell, California State University, Northridge; John Sides, University of Texas at Austin; Sean Theriault, University of Texas at Austin; and Lynn Vavreck, University of California, Los Angeles.

For the Tenth Edition, we were grateful for the detailed comments of Christian Grose, Vanderbilt University; Kevin Esterling, University of California–Riverside; Martin Johnson, University of California–Riverside; Scott Meinke, Bucknell University; Jason MacDonald, Kent State University; Alan Wiseman, Ohio State University; Michelle Swers, Georgetown University; William Hixon, Lawrence University; Gregory Koger, University of Miami; and Renan Levine, University of Toronto.

For their advice on the Eleventh Edition, we thank Scott Ainsworth, University of Georgia; Bethany Albertson, University of Washington; Brian Arbour, John Jay College; James Battista, University at Buffalo, State University of New York; Lawrence Becker, California State University, Northridge; Damon Cann, Utah State University; Jamie Carson, University of Georgia; Suzanne Chod, Pennsylvania State University; Michael Crespin, University of Georgia; Ryan Emenaker, College of the Redwoods; Kevin Esterling, University of California–Riverside; Brad Gomez, Florida State University; Sanford Gordon, New York University; Christian Grose, Vanderbilt University; James Hanley, Adrian College; Ryan Hurl, University of Toronto; Josh Kaplan, University of Notre Dame; Wendy Martinek, Binghamton University; Will Miller, Southeast Missouri State University; Evan Parker-Stephen, Texas A&M University; Melody Rose, Portland State University; Eric Schickler, University of California–Berkeley; John Sides, George Washington University; and Lynn Vavreck, University of California–Los Angeles.

For the Twelfth Edition we looked to comments from John M. Aughenbaugh, Virginia Commonwealth University; Christopher Banks, Kent State University; Michael Berkman, Pennsylvania State University; Cynthia Bowling, Auburn University; Matthew Cahn, California State University, Northridge; Damon Cann, Utah State University; Tom Cioppa, Brookdale Community College; David Damore, University of Nevada, Las Vegas; Kevin Esterling, University of California–Riverside; Jessica Feezell, University of California–Santa Barbara; Charle J. Finocchiaro, University of South Carolina; Rodd Freitag, University of Wisconsin, Eau Claire; Richard Glenn, Millersville University; Kevin Jefferies, Alvin Community College; Nancy Jimeno, California State University, Fullerton; Gregory Koger, University of Miami; David E. Lewis, Vanderbilt University; Allison M. Martens, University of Louisville; Thomas M. Martin, Eastern Kentucky University; Michael Andrew McLatchy, Clarendon College; Ken Mulligan, Southern Illinois University, Carbondale; Geoffrey D. Peterson, University of Wisconsin, Eau Claire; Jesse Richman, Old Dominion University; Mark C. Rom, Georgetown University; Laura Schneider, Grand Valley State University; Scot Schraufnagel, Northern Illinois University; Ronald P. Seyb, Skidmore College; Martin S. Sheffer, Tidewater Community College; Charles R. Shipan, University of Michigan; Howard A. Smith, Florida Gulf Coast University; Michele Swers, Georgetown University; Charles Tien, Hunter College; Elizabeth Trentanelli, Gulf Coast State College; and Kenneth C. Williams, Michigan State University.

We also thank the reviewers who advised us on this Thirteenth Edition: Michael M. Binder, University of North Florida; Stephen Borrelli, The University of Alabama; Dan Cassino, Fairleigh Dickinson University; Jangsup Choi, Texas A&M University–Commerce; Martin Cohen, James Madison University; Jeff Colbert, Elon University; Richard S. Conley, University of Florida; Mark Croatti, American University; David Dulio, Oakland University; Andrew M. Essig, DeSales University; Kathleen Ferraiolo, James Madison University; Emily R. Gill, Bradley University; Brad T. Gomez, Florida State University; Paul N. Goren, University of Minnesota; Thomas Halper, Baruch College; Audrey A. Haynes, University of Georgia; Diane J. Heith, St. John's University; Ronald J. Hrebenar, The University of Utah; Ryan Hurl, University of Toronto Scarborough; Richard Jankowski, SUNY Fredonia; Kevin Jefferies, Alvin Community College; Timothy R. Johnson, University of Minnesota; Kenneth R. Mayer, University of Wisconsin–Madison; Mark McKenzie, Texas Tech University; Fiona Miller, University of Toronto Mississauga; Richard M. Pious, Barnard College; Tim Reynolds, Alvin Community College; Martin Saiz, California State University, Northridge; Dante Scala, University of New Hampshire; Sean M. Theriault,

University of Texas at Austin; J. Alejandro Tirado, Texas Tech University; Terri Towner, Oakland University; Nicholas Valentino, University of Michigan; Harold M. Waller, McGill University; Jeffrey S. Worsham, West Virginia University; and Antoine Yoshinaka, American University.

An important contribution to recent editions was made by the authors of the Analyzing the Evidence units. We are grateful to the authors of the new Analyzing the Evidence units in the Thirteenth Edition, who are named in the preface. In addition, Jenna Bednar, Jamie Carson, Andrea Campbell, Kevin Esterling, Beth Leech, David Lewis, Andrew D. Martin, Kenneth Mayer, Kevin M. Quinn, and Joseph Ura contributed to this feature in earlier editions, and much of their work is still reflected in this edition. We also thank Joe Williams, who provided valuable assistance in updating the data figures and tables throughout the book.

We would also like to thank our partners at W. W. Norton & Company, who have continued to apply their talents and energy to this textbook. The efforts of Erin Brown, Christine D'Antonio, Cara Folkman, Lorraine Klimowich, Toni Magyar, Lisa Camner McKay, Vanessa Nuttry, Sarah Wolf, and Kathryn Young kept the production of the Thirteenth edition coherent and in focus. We also thank Roby Harrington, Steve Dunn, and Ann Shin, whose contributions to previous editions remain invaluable.

We are more than happy, however, to absolve all these contributors from any flaws, errors, and misjudgments that this book contains. We wish it could be free of all production errors, grammatical errors, misspellings, misquotes, missed citations, etc. From that standpoint, a book ought to try to be perfect. But substantively we have not tried to write a flawless book; we have not tried to write a book to please everyone. We have again tried to write an effective book, a book that cannot be taken lightly. Our goal was not to make every reader a political scientist. Our goal was to restore politics as a subject of vigorous and enjoyable discourse, releasing it from the bondage of the thirty-second sound bite and the thirty-page technical briefing. Every person can be knowledgeable because everything about politics is accessible. One does not have to be a television anchorperson to profit from political events. One does not have to be a philosopher to argue about the requisites of democracy, a lawyer to dispute constitutional interpretations, an economist to debate public policy. We will be very proud if our book contributes in a small way to the restoration of the ancient art of political controversy.

Theodore J. Lowi
Benjamin Ginsberg
Kenneth A. Shepsle
Stephen Ansolabehere

AMERICAN GOVERNMENT
POWER & PURPOSE

1

Introduction: Making Sense of Government and Politics

American government and politics are extraordinarily complex. The United States has many levels of government: federal, state, county, city, and town— to say nothing of a host of special and regional authorities. Each of these governments operates under its own rules and statutory authority and is related to the others in complex ways. Each level of government, moreover, consists of an array of departments, agencies, offices, and bureaus undertaking a variety of sometimes overlapping tasks. At times this complexity gets in the way of effective governance, as in the case of governmental response to emergencies. America's federal, state, and local public safety agencies seldom share information and frequently use incompatible communications equipment, so they are often not even able to speak to one another. For example, on September 11, 2001, New York City's police and fire departments could not effectively coordinate their responses to the terrorist attack on the World Trade Center because their communications systems were not linked. While communication has improved in the last decade, it is still the case that many security and policy agencies, ranging from the Central Intelligence Agency (CIA) to the National Security Agency (NSA) to the Department of Homeland Security (DHS) to the Federal Bureau of Investigation (FBI), possess separate computer operating systems and databases that inhibit cooperation through sharing.

The complexity of America's government is no accident. Complexity was one element of the Founders' grand constitutional design. The framers of the Constitution hoped that an elaborate division of power among institutions and between the states and the federal government would allow a variety of competing groups, forces, interests, and ideas to have a voice in public affairs—while preventing any single group or coalition from monopolizing power. One set of interests might be active and powerful in some states, other forces would be influential in the national legislature, and still other groups might prevail in the executive branch. The overall pattern would disperse power and opportunity, allowing many groups to achieve at least some of their political goals. In this way, America's political tradition associates complexity with liberty and political opportunity. But does American government work?

America's institutional structure sometimes makes it possible for small groups to prevent the enactment of policies that seem to be favored by the majority. For example, most Americans—75 percent according to some polls—favor ending today's multibillion-dollar tax subsidies for the oil and gas industries, especially at a time when these industries have been earning windfall profits from rising energy prices. However, in 2011, oil and gas backers in the House of Representatives blocked efforts to cut these subsidies. In cases like this, when the government's policies seem inconsistent with popular preferences, we may question whether American government works.

This same institutional structure, on the other hand, makes it possible for minorities to protect their rights against majorities. For example, after the enactment of a restrictive immigration law in Arizona in 2010, most Americans said they supported the idea of arresting individuals who could

CORE OF THE ANALYSIS

→ Government has become a powerful and complex force in the United States.

→ Government is necessary to maintain order, to protect property, and to provide public goods.

→ American government is based on democratic electoral institutions and popular representative bodies.

not prove they were in the United States legally. This effort seemed likely to lead to the harassment of Hispanics, in particular, whether they were in the United States legally or not. Later in 2010, however, a federal judge struck down the most questionable provisions of the Arizona law, and in 2012 the Supreme Court nullified most of the law. When a branch of government blocks action in order to protect rights, we may be tempted to say the government works best when it is prevented from working.

America's complex institutional structure also complicates our politics and places a considerable burden on citizens who might wish to achieve something through political participation. They may not be able to easily discern where particular policies are actually made, who the influential decision makers are, and what forms of political participation are most likely to be effective. This is one of the paradoxes of political life: in a dictatorship, lines of political authority may be simple, but opportunities to influence the use of power are few; in the United States, political opportunities are plentiful, but how they should be used is far from obvious. Indeed, precisely because America's institutional and political arrangements are so complex, many Americans are mystified by government. As we see in Chapter 9, most Americans have difficulty making sense of even the basic features of the Constitution.

For most Americans, the focal point of U.S. politics is the electoral process. As we see in Chapter 10, tens of millions of Americans participate in a host of national, state, and local elections in which they listen to thousands of candidates debate what may seem to be a perplexing array of issues. Candidates fill the air with promises, charges, and countercharges, while an army of pundits and journalists, which we discuss in Chapter 9, adds its own clamor to the din. Politics, however, does not end on Election Day. Long after the voters have spoken, political struggles continue in Congress, the executive branch, and the courts; they embroil political parties, interest groups, and the mass media.

Citizens can hardly be blamed for becoming discouraged, for thinking that our political system is broken when their decisions at the polls seem only to lead to continuing institutional struggle and often fail to produce concrete results. But the framers of the Constitution were wary of making it too easy for shifts in the public's mood to be translated into shifts in policy. The framers believed that new ideas needed time to mature and to be subjected to scrutiny before being written into the law. In 2013, for example, many Americans, including President Obama, were angered at the Senate's refusal to pass gun control legislation proposed by the president and supported by a majority of Americans (including the protesters depicted on page 2). However, the system of government designed by America's framers was not intended to give immediate expression to popular preferences. The framers were wary of government action and thought hasty action was more dangerous than none at all.

MAKING SENSE OF GOVERNMENT AND POLITICS

Can we find order in the complexity and apparent chaos of politics? The answer is that we can, and that is precisely the purpose of our text. It should be noted before we begin that "finding order in the apparent chaos of politics" is precisely what political scientists do. The discipline of political science, and especially the study of American politics, is devoted to identifying patterns and regularities in all the noise and maneuvering of everyday political life. This is motivated by two fundamental questions: What do we observe? And why?

The first question makes clear that political science is an *empirical* enterprise. By this we mean that it aims to identify facts and patterns that are true in the world around us. What do voters decide when they enter the polling booth? What strategies and tactics do candidates employ to capture votes? What decisions do legislators make about how to vote on bills? What groups organize and put pressure on the institutions of government? How do the media report politics? What tools are available to the president to get what he or she wants in dealing with Congress (legislative-executive relations)? How have courts intervened in regulating political life? And how do they come to the decisions they have made (judicial politics)? These and many other questions have been explored by political scientists in an effort to ascertain what is true about the political world and are taken up in more detail in later chapters.

The second question is fundamental to any science. We not only would like to know *that* something is true about the world. We also want to know *why* it is true. Knowing why something is true requires us to create in our minds a theory of how the world works. In this way we not only describe politics, we *analyze* it. One of the most important goals of this book is to provide concepts and tools to help readers critically analyze what they observe in politics and government. In this chapter, we offer a number of concepts that we hope will clarify why American government works the way it does. We conclude with a brief guide to analyzing evidence related to the ways these concepts play out in the American political system.

There is a third type of question that is normative, rather than empirical or analytical. Normative questions focus on "should" issues: What responsibilities should citizens have? How should legislators vote on the motions before them? How should presidents lead? Political science grapples with all three types of questions. In this book, we believe that answers to the empirical and analytical questions help us formulate answers to the normative questions.

Forms of Government

government

The institutions and procedures through which a land and its people are ruled

Government is the term generally used to describe the formal political arrangements by which a land and its people are ruled. Government is composed of institutions and processes that rulers establish to strengthen and perpetuate their power or control over a territory and its inhabitants. A government may be as simple as a tribal council that meets occasionally to advise the chief or as complex as our own vast establishment with its forms, rules, governmental bodies, and bureaucracies. Governments vary in their structure, in their size, and in the way they operate. Two questions are of special importance in determining how governments differ from one another: Who governs? And, how much government control is permitted?

autocracy

A form of government in which a single individual rules

oligarchy

A form of government in which a small group of landowners, military officers, or wealthy merchants controls most of the governing decisions

In some nations, political authority is vested in a single individual. This is called autocracy. When a small group of landowners, military officers, or wealthy merchants control most of the governing decisions, that government is an oligarchy. If many people participate, and if the populace is deemed to have some influence over the leaders' actions, that government is tending toward democracy.

democracy

A system of rule that permits citizens to play a significant part in the governmental process, usually through the selection of key public officials

Governments also vary considerably in how they govern. In the United States and a small number of other nations, governments are severely limited by law as to what they are permitted to control (substantive limits), as well as how they go about it (procedural limits). Governments that are so limited are called constitutional governments. In other nations, including many in Europe, South America, Asia, and Africa, political and social institutions that the government is unable to control—such as an organized church, organized business groups, or organized labor unions—may help keep the government in check, but the law imposes few real limits. Such governments are called authoritarian. In a third group of nations, including the Soviet Union under Joseph Stalin, governments not only are free of legal limits but seek to eliminate those organized social groupings or institutions that might challenge or limit their authority. Because these governments typically attempt to dominate every sphere of political, economic, and social life, they are called totalitarian.

constitutional government

A system of rule in which formal and effective limits are placed on the powers of the government

Foundations of Government

Whatever their makeup, governments historically have included two basic components: a means of coercion, such as an army or police force, and a means of collecting revenue. Some governments, including many in the less-developed nations today, have consisted of little more than an army and a tax-collecting agency. Other governments, especially those in the developed nations such as the United States, attempt to provide services as well as to

authoritarian government

A system of rule in which the government recognizes no formal limits but may nevertheless be restrained by the power of other social institutions

totalitarian government

A system of rule in which the government recognizes no formal limits on its power and seeks to absorb or eliminate other social institutions that might challenge it

collect taxes in order to secure popular consent for control. For some, power is an end in itself. For most, power is necessary to maintain public order.

The Means of Coercion. Government must have the powers to get people to obey its laws and punish them if they do not. Coercion—forcing a person to do something by threats or pressure—takes many forms, and each year millions of Americans are subject to one form of government coercion or another. One aspect of coercion is conscription, whereby the government requires certain involuntary services of citizens. The best-known example of conscription is military conscription, which is called "the draft." Although there has been no draft since 1974, there were drafts during the Civil War, World War I, World War II, the postwar period, and the wars in Korea and Vietnam. With these drafts, the American government compelled millions of men to serve in the armed forces; one-half million of these soldiers made the ultimate contribution by giving their lives in their nation's service. If the need arose, military conscription would probably be reinstituted. Eighteen-year-old men are required to register today, just in case. American citizens can also, by law, be compelled to serve on juries; to appear before legal tribunals when summoned; to file a great variety of official reports, including income tax returns; and to attend school or to send their children to school. Government also has the power to punish those who do not obey its laws.

The Means of Collecting Revenue. Each year American governments on every level collect enormous sums from their citizens to support their institutions and programs. Taxation has grown steadily over the years. In fiscal year 2012, the national government alone collected $1.1 trillion in individual income taxes; $242 billion in corporate income taxes; $845 billion in social insurance taxes; $93 billion in excise, estate, and gift taxes; $30 billion in customs duties; and $106 billion from other sources. The grand total amounted to more than $2.4 trillion, or about $7,700 per person in the United States. But not everyone benefits equally from programs paid for by their tax dollars. One of the perennial issues in American politics is the distribution of tax burdens versus the distribution of program benefits. Every group would like more of the benefits while passing more of the burdens of taxation on to others.

Why Is Government Necessary?

As we have just seen, control is the basis for government. But what forms of government control are justifiable? To answer this question, we begin by examining the ways in which government makes it possible for people to live together.

To Maintain Order. Human beings usually do not venture out of their caves (or the modern counterpart) unless there is a reasonable probability that they can return safely. But for people to live together peacefully, law and order are required, the institutionalization of which is called government. From the standpoint of this definition, the primary purpose of government is to maintain order. But order can come about only by controlling a territory and its people. This may sound like a threat to freedom until you ponder the absence of government, or anarchy—the absence of rule. According to Thomas Hobbes (1588–1679), the author of *Leviathan*, anarchy is even worse than the potential tyranny of government because anarchy, or life outside "the state," is characterized by "continual fear, and danger of violent death . . . [where life is] solitary, poor, nasty, brutish and short."[1] Governmental power can be a threat to freedom, yet we need government to maintain order so that we can enjoy our freedom.

To Protect Property. After safety of persons comes security of a person's labor, which we call property, or private property. Protection of property is almost universally recognized as a justifiable function of government. John Locke (1632–1704), the successor to Hobbes, was the first to assert clearly that whatever we have removed from nature and also mixed our labor with is considered our property. But even Locke recognized that although the right to own what we have produced by our own labor is absolute, it means nothing if someone with greater power than ours decides to take it or trespass on it.

So something we call our own is ours only as long as the laws against trespass improve the probability that we can enjoy it, use it, consume it, trade it, or sell it. In reality, then, property can be defined as all the laws against trespass that permit us not only to call something our own but also to make sure that our claim sticks. In other words, property—that is, private property—is virtually meaningless without a government of laws and policies that makes trespass prohibitive.

J. LOCKE

America's Founders were influenced by the thinking of English philosopher John Locke (1632–1704). Locke asserted the right to private property and the need for a government of laws and policies to protect that right.

To Provide Public Goods. David Hume (1711–76), another successor to Hobbes, observed that although two neighbors may agree voluntarily to cooperate in draining a swampy meadow, the more neighbors there are, the more difficult it will be to cooperate to get the task done. A few neighbors might clear the swamp because they understand the benefits each of them will receive. But as you expand the number of neighbors who benefit from clearing the swamp, many neighbors will realize that all of them can get the same benefit if only a few clear the swamp and the rest do nothing. This is called free riding. A public good (or collective good) is, therefore, a benefit that neighbors or members of a group cannot be kept from enjoying once any individual or a small minority of members have provided the benefit for themselves. The clearing of the swamp is one example; national defense is another. National defense is one of the most important public goods—especially when the nation is threatened by war or terrorism.

free riding
Enjoying the benefits of some good or action while letting others bear the costs

public good
A good that, first, may be enjoyed by anyone if it is provided and, second, may not be denied to anyone once it has been provided

Without government's coercive powers through a policy (backed by taxation) to build a bridge, produce an army, provide a swamp-free meadow, issue "legal tender" (currency), or standardize weights and measures, there is no incentive—in fact, very often there is a disincentive—for even the richest, most concerned members to provide the benefit.[2]

Influencing the Government: Politics

In its broadest sense, the term *politics* refers to conflicts over the character, membership, and policies of any organizations to which people belong. As Harold Lasswell, a famous political scientist, once put it, politics is the struggle over "who gets what, when, how."[3] Although politics is a phenomenon that can be found in any organization, in this book, politics refers to conflicts and struggles over the leadership, structure, and policies of governments. But politics also involves collaboration and cooperation. The goal of politics, as we define it, is to have a share or a say in the composition of the government's leadership, how the government is organized, and what its policies are going to be. Having such a share is called power or influence. Most people are eager to have some "say" in matters affecting them; witness the willingness of so many individuals over the past two centuries to risk their lives for voting rights and representation. In recent years, of course, Americans have become more skeptical about their actual "say" in government, and many do not bother to vote. This skepticism, however, does not mean that Americans no longer want to have a share in the governmental process. Rather, many Americans doubt the capacity of the political system to provide them with influence.

As we see throughout this book, not only does politics influence government but the character and actions of government also influence a nation's politics. The rules and procedures established by political institutions influence what forms political activity may take. We define institutions as the rules and procedures that guide political behavior. The institutions of a constitutional government such as that of the United States are designed to gain popular consent by opening channels for political expression.

politics

Conflict, struggle, cooperation, and collaboration over the leadership, structure, and policies of government

institutions

The rules and procedures that provide incentives for political behavior, thereby shaping politics

FROM COERCION TO CONSENT

Americans have the good fortune to live in a constitutional democracy, with legal limits on what government can do and how it does it. Such democracies were unheard of before the modern era. Prior to the eighteenth and nineteenth centuries, governments seldom sought—and rarely received—the support of their ordinary subjects. But beginning in the seventeenth century, in a handful of Western nations, important changes began to take place in the character and conduct of government.

Limiting Government. The key force behind the imposition of limits on government power, beginning in seventeenth-century Europe, was a new social class, the "bourgeoisie." *Bourgeois* is French for "freeman of the city," or *bourg*. Being part of the bourgeoisie later became associated with being "middle class" and with being in commerce or industry. In order to gain a share of control of government—to join the kings, monarchs, and gentry who had dominated governments for centuries—the bourgeoisie sought to change existing institutions—especially parliaments—into instruments of real political participation. Parliaments had existed for hundreds of years, controlling from the top and not allowing influence from below. The bourgeoisie embraced parliaments as the means by which they could wield their greater numbers and growing economic advantage against their aristocratic rivals.

Although motivated primarily by self-interest, the bourgeoisie advanced many of the principles that became the central underpinnings of individual freedom for *all* citizens—freedom of speech, of assembly, and of conscience, and freedom from arbitrary search and seizure. It is important to note here that the bourgeoisie generally did not favor democracy as such. They were advocates of electoral and representative institutions, but they favored property requirements and other restrictions so as to limit participation to the middle classes. Yet, once the right to engage in politics was established, it was difficult to limit it just to the bourgeoisie.

The Expansion of Democratic Politics. Along with limits on government came an expansion of democratic government. Three factors explain why rulers were forced to give ordinary citizens a greater voice in public affairs: internal conflict, external threat, and the promotion of national unity and development.

First, during the eighteenth and nineteenth centuries, many nations faced intense conflict among the landed gentry, the bourgeoisie, lower-middle-class shopkeepers and artisans, the urban working class, and farmers. Many governments came to the conclusion that if they did not deal with basic class conflicts in some constructive way, disorder and revolution would result. One of the best ways of dealing with such conflict was to extend the rights of political participation, especially voting, to each new group as it grew more powerful.

Another form of internal threat is social disorder. Thanks to the Industrial Revolution, societies had become much more interdependent and therefore much more vulnerable to disorder. As that occurred, and as more people moved from rural areas to cities, disorder had to be managed, and one important approach to that management was to give the masses a bigger stake in the system itself. As one supporter of electoral reform put it, the alternative to voting was "the spoliation of property and the dissolution of social order."[5] In the modern world, social disorder helped to compel East European regimes and the republics of the former Soviet Union to take steps toward democratic reform.

The second factor that helped expand democratic government was external threat. The main external threat to governments' power is the existence of other nation-states. During the past three centuries, more and more tribes and nations—people tied together by a common culture and language—have formed into separate principalities, or nation-states, in order to defend their populations more effectively. But as more nation-states formed, the more likely it was that external conflicts would arise. War and preparation for war became constant rather than intermittent facts of national life, and the size and expense of military forces increased dramatically with the size of the nation-state and the size and number of its adversaries.

The cost of defense forced rulers to seek popular support to maintain military power. It was easier to raise huge permanent armies of citizen-soldiers and induce them to fight more vigorously and to make greater sacrifices if they were imbued with enthusiasm for cause and country. The expansion of participation and representation in government were key tactics used by the European regimes to raise that enthusiasm and support.

The third factor often associated with the expansion of democratic politics was the promotion of national unity and development. In some instances, governments seek to subvert local or regional loyalties by linking citizens directly to the central government via the ballot box. America's Founders saw direct popular election of members of the House of Representatives as a means through which the new federal government could compete with the states for popular allegiance.

The expansion of democratic politics had two historic consequences. First, democracies opened up the possibility that citizens might use government for their own benefit rather than simply watch it being used for the benefit of others. This consequence is widely understood. But the second is not so well understood: once citizens perceived that governments could operate in response to their demands, they became increasingly willing to support the expansion of government. The public's belief in its capacity to control the government's action is only one of the many factors responsible for the growth of government. But at the very least, this linkage of democracy and strong government set into motion a wave of governmental growth that began in the middle of the nineteenth century and has continued to the present day.

DOES AMERICAN DEMOCRACY WORK?

The growth of democracy in the United States has led to wider participation, which in turn has fulfilled the democratic ideals of popular sovereignty and majority rule. Thus, democratization creates the possibility that citizens can use government for their own benefit. But what are the trade-offs involved in democracy? Are there unintended consequences of too much democracy?[6] The answers to these questions are complex. Despite over 200 years of development, American democracy has still not worked out the inconsistencies and contradictions woven in its very fiber by the framers of the Constitution. Similarly, despite all that political scientists and political historians know about American government and politics, puzzles and anomalies reflecting the contradictions within American democracy remain for which we don't have fully satisfactory answers. We conclude this chapter by examining three of them.

Delegating Authority in a Representative Democracy

For over two centuries, we have expanded popular sovereignty to the point where a citizen, from the time she is roughly the age of a college freshman to the time that final breath is taken, can engage in political activity at various levels of government. Yet citizens often find it convenient to delegate many of these activities, sometimes (as when we don't pay attention, or vote, or even register to vote) conceding the field entirely to highly motivated individuals and groups. Ours is a representative democracy for very pragmatic reasons. Most citizens have lives to live and private concerns to attend to, and, therefore, acquiesce in an arrangement enabling them to economize on the effort they must devote to their own governance.

We think of our political representatives as our agents, whom we "hire" to act on our behalf. In this relationship, citizens are the principals—those with the authority—who delegate some of their authority to politicians. This principal-agent relationship means that citizens don't always get what

principal-agent relationship

The relationship between a principal and his or her agent. This relationship may be affected by the fact that each is motivated by self-interest, yet their interests may not be well aligned

Representative democracy entails citizens choosing politicians who they think will promote their interests. This delegation of power gives politicians a level of independence but also makes them accountable to constituents.

they want, despite popular sovereignty, because, inadvertently or not, they allow agents to pursue their own self-interest or to be influenced unduly by those who care more or who have more at stake. Thus, popular sovereignty is qualified (some would say undermined) by our willingness to off-load governance responsibilities on to professional agents.

The Trade-Off between Freedom and Order

If the imperfect fit between popular sovereignty and delegation of governance to a "political class" constitutes one problem, a second involves the trade-off between liberty and coercion. We have taken pains to suggest that governments are necessary to maintain order, to protect property, and to provide public goods. All these activities require a degree of coercion. Laws, regulations, and rulings constrain behavior and restrict the uses of property. Taxes include claims on labor income, on gains in the value of capital, and on the transmission of estates from one generation to another. In short, all of these things constitute limits on liberty. The anomaly here is that liberty is one of the very purposes for which such coercion is necessary in the first place. So a pinch of coercion is one of the ingredients in the stew of liberty. But where to draw the line? And even if we had an answer to this question, there is another: How can we arrange our political life to ensure just the right amount of coercion and no more? As the history of experiments in democratic self-government reveals, coercion is a slippery slope. Especially after the events of September 11, 2001, it is clear that a strong desire for

Does American government work? Congress's inability to agree on budget cuts resulted in automatic cuts to numerous government services and furloughs of some government workers in spring 2013.

public goods such as security from terrorism can lead us to accept extensive limitations on citizens' liberties.

The Instability of Majority Rule

A third puzzle involves the multitude of purposes pursued by different citizens. It is not always easy to add them up into a collective choice without doing damage to the interest of some. As we see in subsequent chapters, majority rule, especially as manifested in the real institutions of constitutional democracies, is vulnerable to the powers of those in a position to influence the political agenda or veto potential courses of action, financial fat cats, and group leaders (political bosses, union heads, corporate CEOs, religious leaders). All democracies struggle with the fact that outcomes, because they entail disproportionate influence by some, are not always fair. In our American democracy, we put a great deal of faith in frequent elections, checks and balances among government institutions, and multiple levels of government. But again we may ask where to draw the line: Elections how frequent? How powerful the checks? How many governmental levels? At what point is something broken enough to need fixing? American political history is filled with instances of decisions, followed by reactions, followed by a revisiting of those decisions, followed by further reactions. The disproportionate influence of some would appear inescapable, despite our efforts to control it. We revisit decisions. We reform institutions. We alter political practices. But still, perfection eludes us.

In all these puzzles and anomalies, normative principles sometimes clash. Popular sovereignty, individual liberty, delegation, and multiple purposes constitute the circle that cannot quite be squared. We noted earlier that making sense of the apparent chaos, puzzles, and contradictions in politics is the goal of political science. Whether they are trying to understand the puzzles we have just discussed or any of the countless other phenomena we observe in American politics, political scientists try to develop theories that can be tested using empirical evidence. The Analyzing the Evidence unit at the end of this chapter describes some of the ways that political scientists analyze and attempt to better understand the patterns and events that shape our political system. With these concepts and tools for analysis in hand, we turn in Chapter 2 to the Founding and the Constitution.

For Further Reading

Selections highlighted in red are included in *Readings in American Politics: Analysis and Perspectives*, Third Edition.

Crenson, Matthew A., and Benjamin Ginsberg. *Downsizing Democracy*. Baltimore: Johns Hopkins University Press, 2002.

Downs, Anthony. *An Economic Theory of Democracy*. New York: Harper, 1957.

Huntington, Samuel P. *Who Are We? The Challenges to America's National Identity*. New York: Simon & Schuster, 2004.

Kiewiet, D. Roderick, and Mathew McCubbins. *The Logic of Delegation*. Chicago: University of Chicago Press, 1991.

Lupia, Arthur, and Mathew D. McCubbins. *The Democratic Dilemma: Can Citizens Learn What They Need to Know?* New York: Cambridge University Press, 1998.

Olson, Mancur, Jr. *The Logic of Collective Action: Public Goods and the Theory of Groups*. Reprinted with new preface and appendix. Cambridge, MA: Harvard University Press, 1971; orig. published 1965.

Tilly, Charles. *Democracy*. New York: Cambridge University Press, 2007.

Tocqueville, Alexis de. *Democracy in America*. Isaac Kramnick, ed. New York: Norton, 2007; orig. published 1835.

Wolfe, Alan. *Does American Democracy Still Work?* New Haven, CT: Yale University Press, 2006.

How Do Political Scientists Know What They Know?

The five principles introduced in this chapter provide a foundation for understanding and explaining political life. However, to make and test arguments about politics, we need more than just an analytical framework; we also need empirical evidence. Political scientists study facts about politics and analyze and interpret these facts to assess different arguments and claims. Typically, we study data, systematically collecting facts and information, and examining the structure of data to see whether they are consistent, or not, with a given line of thinking.

Consider one of the most basic questions about voting: Why do people vote the way they do? In elections, Americans face two main alternatives in the form of the Democratic Party and the Republican Party. These parties have distinctive policy priorities, notably in the important area of economic policy. Since at least the 1930s, the Democratic Party has favored economic policies that redistribute income to poorer segments of society; Republicans, on the other hand, favor lower taxes and little or no redistribution. It is often argued that people vote according to their economic self-interest: people choose the candidate from the party that maximizes their income. On reflection, however, we can see that other factors may also affect voting decisions, including the candidates' personal qualities, important noneconomic issues, and even candidates' appearance or habits. Which factor best explains vote choice?

Table A Vote Cast for President, 2012

VOTE CAST	NUMBER
BARACK OBAMA (Democrat)	65,907,213
MITT ROMNEY (Republican)	60,931,767
Other candidates	2,196,907
Did not vote	90,073,191

What Are Data? Data are systematic measurements or observations that are collected as a source of information about a theoretically defined concept or idea. In our example there is a political behavior that we want to explain, *vote choice*. Vote choice is a general concept, and we can define it before we ever observe an election. The first step in collecting data is to represent the concept that we are interested in as a variable. A variable defines all possible outcomes of a concept that could occur and assigns them a unique label or value. Vote choice, for instance, may take four possible values or outcomes: vote for the Democratic Party candidate, vote for the Republican Party candidate, vote for another party or candidate, or don't vote.

The second step in collecting data is to measure the behavior of interest. This requires the collection of information. Observation of a small set of events can be quite enlightening.

We might, for instance, conduct in-depth interviews with a dozen or so people about how they decided to vote. However, we often require more evidence to support a given claim; a small number of people might not be sufficiently representative.

Censuses and random sample surveys allow social scientists to collect information systematically on a large number of cases. These means of collecting data are staples of social sciences. With a census we observe all individuals in the population at a given moment. Every 10 years, the United States conducts a comprehensive enumeration of all people living in the country, including information on families, education levels, income, race and ethnicity, commuting, housing, and employment. An election is a census, as it is a comprehensive count of all votes cast in a given election. So we can measure a variable such as vote choice by taking count of all electoral votes and nonvotes in the voting-eligible population (Table A).

A survey, on the other hand, consists of a study of a relatively small subset of individuals. We call this subset a sample. We can measure a variable for those individuals in the sample, and extrapolate patterns from the sample to the entire population. One of the most important social science research projects of the second half of the twentieth century is the American National Election Study, or ANES. The ANES is a national survey that has been conducted during every presidential election and most midterm congressional elections since 1948 to gauge how people voted and to understand why. In recent years, the ANES has used a sample of 2,000 Americans to make inferences about the entire voting population of over 100 million. Today, most of the information used by public policy makers, businesses, and academic researchers, including estimates of variables like unemployment and inflation, television and radio ratings, and most demographics of the population, are measured using surveys.

Summarizing Data. Communicating the information in a census or survey requires tools for summarizing data. First, we compute the frequency with which each value of a variable occurs. Frequency may be either the *number of times* that a specific behavior or value of a variable occurs or the percent of the observations in which it occurs.

Second, we construct a graph or statistic that summarizes the frequencies of all values of the variable. The distribution of a variable expresses how often each of the values of the variable occurs. A bar chart displays all possible values of a variable on one axis, usually the horizontal axis; the heights of the bars equal the frequency or *percent* of cases observed for each value (Figure A).

Vote Cast for President, 2012

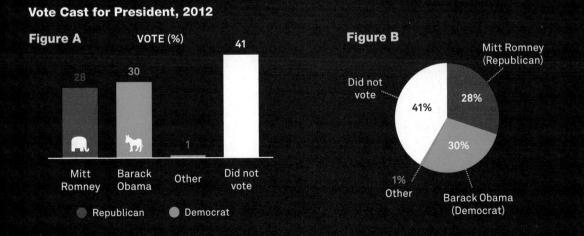

Figure C Party Identification, 1952–2012

PERCENTAGE

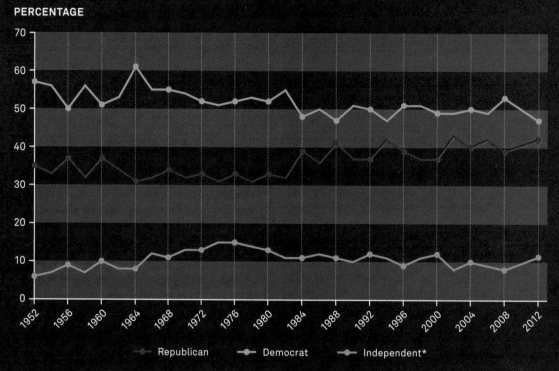

Republican —●— Democrat —●— Independent*

*Independents who said thay leaned toward one party are counted with that party.

In a pie chart, the frequency for each value is depicted as a share of the whole (Figure B). A line graph is often used to show frequency over time (Figure C).

The distribution of income in the United States offers a somewhat different example. This variable takes a range of values, from the smallest household income to the largest household income. For ease of presentation, we can organize this variable into categories. In Figure D, the first category is "less than $10,000," the second category is "$10,000 to $19,999," and so forth up to the top category, "$200,000 or more." All possible income levels are covered in this classification.

Variables such as income can also be characterized with statistics, such as the median or mean. In this example, the median is the value of household income such that half of all households have incomes below the value and half have income above it. Fifty percent of all cases have income above the median value, and 50 percent have income below it; thus the median is also called the 50th percentile. The median household income in the United States in 2011 was $50,054, meaning that half of all households have income below that value and half have income above that amount. The mean is the average value for the variable. In the case of household income, the mean equals the sum of all households' incomes divided by the number of households. Personal income received by households totaled approximately $8.4 trillion in 2011, and there were 121 million households. So the average household income was $69,677.

Figure D Distribution of Household Income in the United States, 2011

PERCENTAGE OF ALL HOUSEHOLDS

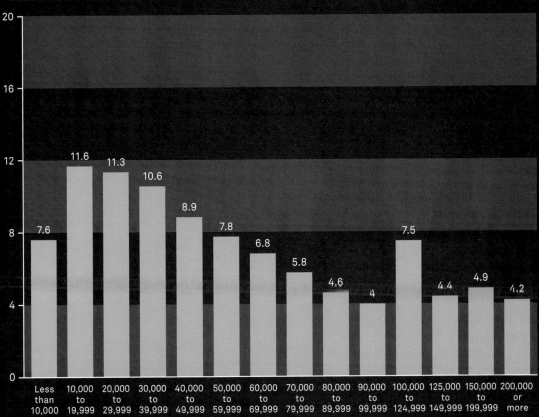

HOUSEHOLD INCOME (U.S. DOLLARS)

Why do the median and mean differ? In calculating the median, every household is equal. We merely count the percent above and below a certain income level. The mean value weights households according to their incomes; consequently, a household with $200,000 income contributes 10 times as much to the calculation of the mean as a household with $20,000. If there were only a small difference in income among households, the mean would be very close to the median. The difference between the median income and the mean income thus provides a way to measure inequality. Only about one-third of households had income above the mean value of $69,677.

Testing Arguments Using Data. Let's return to the idea discussed at the beginning of the section: that people vote their economic self-interest. Is this claim correct?

To test this idea, we need to formulate a hypothesis. In the social sciences, hypotheses often take the form of stating a relationship between two variables, such as income and vote choice.

To test the hypothesis that people vote their economic self-interest, we want to know to what extent voting decisions match up with individuals' income levels. As stated earlier, in the United States today, the Republican Party generally favors lower income taxes and less income redistribution, and the Democratic Party favors higher income taxes and more income redistribution. We therefore want to know if people in high-income households vote Republican more often than people in low-income households. The difference we observe in vote choice between high- and low-income groups is considered to be the effect of income on vote choice.

To see whether the effect of income on the vote is indeed large, we can use the data in Table B to examine the actual voting behavior of different sorts of individuals. The national exit polls in 2012 reveal that 63 percent of voters with income less than $30,000 chose the Democratic candidate, Barack Obama. By comparison, 46 percent of those with income over $100,000 chose Barack Obama. This large difference (17 percentage points) reveals that income is associated with vote choice, but it is not absolutely determinative: not every person of high income voted Republican in this election, and not everyone in low-income groups voted Democrat.

Table B Vote by Level of Income

INCOME	🫏 OBAMA	🐘 ROMNEY
Under $30,000	63%	37%
$30,000–$49,999	57%	43%
$50,000–$99,999	48%	52%
$100,000 or more	46%	54%

As we explore alternative arguments about what determines vote choice, we can make many different comparisons—men versus women, college graduates versus high school graduates, and so forth. Our goal is to find which, if any, of these potential explanations best accounts for the variation in vote choice. Throughout this book, we will consider other political outcomes besides voter behavior, such as the support by members of Congress for different types of legislation and how often the executive succeeds in passing legislation.

Many times we will look for a relationship or association between two variables to see if the predictions from an argument hold true, and if they do, we take that as evidence supporting the argument. A relationship or association between two variables, sometimes called a correlation, should not be taken to mean that one of the variables caused the other to occur. Causation is more difficult to establish. A correlation between two variables X (say X is a measure of education) and Y (say Y is a measure of income) is consistent with a theory that education increases one's earning power. From a simple correlation, however, one cannot tell whether many years of education caused high income or high income led to many years of education. It is also possible that some other variable, say high intelligence, caused both many years of education and high income.

Social scientists design experiments and carefully controlled comparisons in order to measure causal relationships. Observing simple associations and correlations, though, is not the final step in verifying our arguments, ideas, or theories about how politics works.

Be a Savvy Consumer of Quantitative Data. Beyond the figures and tables in this book, which reflect data from sources that we consider reliable and accurate, you will undoubtedly encounter other data about politics in the news and elsewhere. Before you take such data—and whatever argument they seem to support—at face value, it is worth asking a few questions about how the data were gathered and presented.

 What is the source of the data? Is it a respected source like a government office or a major mainstream news organization, which may be relied upon to gather and report data accurately? Or are they from a source that is likely to have a goal other than accurate presentation of the data, like an interest group, a campaign, or an entertainment website?

 When were the data collected and how? What is the date (or date range) for the data? Are the data from a census or sample, and how large is the sample?

 What is being measured? For example, in a poll showing support for a candidate, is it the percent of all Americans? The percentage of likely voters? The percentage of Democrats or Republicans?

 Why are the data presented a certain way? Is this the best way to present these data? Does it distort the data in any way? What relationships and patterns do we observe in the data?

Thinking through the questions above can help you better understand the information in the data figures and tables found throughout this book as well as in other academic writing and in the news. In each of the chapters to follow, you will find an Analyzing the Evidence unit, highlighting arguments and evidence on some of the subjects of that chapter. Many of these sections discuss how political scientists use the basic methodology discussed above to test arguments about American politics.

SOURCES:

Table A U.S. Census Bureau, "The Diversifying Electorate—Voting Rates by Race and Hispanic Origin in 2012 (and Other Recent Elections)," May 2013, www.census.gov/prod/2013pubs/p20-568.pdf (Note: the estimates presented in this report may differ from those based on administrative data or exit polls); CNN, "Election 2012: Results," December 10, 2012, www.cnn.com/election/2012/results/main; Susan Page, "Voter Turnout Higher in Swing States Than Elsewhere," *USA Today*, December 23, 2012, www.usatoday.com/story/news/politics/2012/12/23/voter-turnout-swing-states/1787693/; United States Election Project, "2012 General Election Turnout Rates," March 25, 2013, http://elections.gmu.edu/Turnout_2012G.html (all accessed 6/19/13).

Table B "President Exit Polls," *New York Times*, http://elections.nytimes.com/2012/results/president/exit-polls (accessed 6/19/13); and "Exit Polls 2012: How the Vote Has Shifted," *Washington Post*, November 6, 2012, www.washingtonpost.com/wp-srv/special/politics/2012-exit-polls/table.html (accessed 6/19/13).

Figure C Jeffrey M. Jones, "In U.S., Democrats Re-Establish Lead in Party Affiliation," January 9, 2013, www.gallup.com/poll/159740/democrats-establish-lead-party-affiliation.aspx (accessed 6/19/13); and RTT News, "Poll Shows Democrats Retake Lead in Party Affiliation in 2012," January 9, 2013, www.rttnews.com/2034821/poll-shows-democrats-retake-lead-in-party-affiliation-in-2012.aspx (accessed 6/19/13).

Figure D Linda Levine, "The Distribution of Household Income and the Middle Class," Congressional Research Service, November 13, 2012, http://assets.opencrs.com/rpts/RS20811_20121113.pdf, p. 2.

The Founding and the Constitution

The story of America's Founding and the Constitution is generally presented as something both inevitable and glorious: it was inevitable that the American colonies would break away from England to establish their own country successfully; and it was glorious in that it established the best of all possible forms of government under a new Constitution, which was easily adopted and quickly embraced, even by its critics. In reality, though, America's successful breakaway from England in 1776 was by no means assured, and the Constitution that we revere today as one of the most brilliant creations of any nation was in fact highly controversial. Moreover, its ratification and durability were often in doubt. George Washington, the man venerated as the father of the country and the person chosen to preside over the Constitutional Convention of 1787, thought the document produced that hot summer in Philadelphia would probably last no more than 20 years, at which time leaders would have to convene again to come up with something new.

That Washington's prediction proved wrong is, indeed, a testament to the enduring strength of the Constitution. Nonetheless, the Constitution was not carved in stone. It was a product of political bargaining and compromise, formed very much in the same way political decisions are made today. As this chapter shows, the Constitution reflects political self-interest and high principle, too. It also defines the relationship between American citizens and their government. To understand the character of the American Founding and the meaning of the American Constitution, it is essential to look beyond the myths and rhetoric and explore the conflicting interests and forces at work during the revolutionary and constitutional periods. Thus, we first assess the political backdrop of the American Revolution, and then we examine the Constitution that ultimately emerged as the basis for America's government.

Does the Constitution work? Not every feature of the Constitution has been a success. One of the Constitution's most famous failures was the Eighteenth Amendment (ratified in 1919), which, until its repeal by the Twenty-First Amendment (ratified in 1933), launched America's brief and disastrous experiment with the prohibition of alcoholic beverages. Most scholars agree that the framers did not intend for the amendment process to be used to address substantive social problems normally handled through legislation, but in this case it was. In an example from recent years, the constitutional features intended to leash what James Madison called the "dogs of war" by assigning to Congress rather than the president the power to declare war have been undermined by the expansion of presidential war powers (see Chapter 6).

On the whole, however, we would have to judge the Constitution a success and attribute to it at least some of the credit for America's success as a

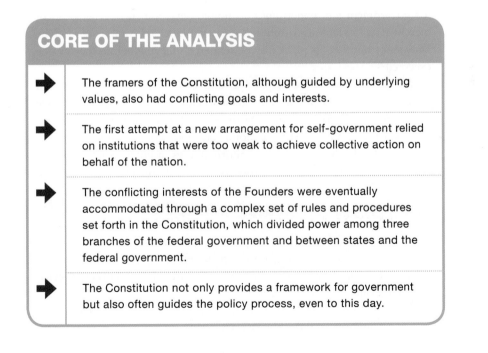

CORE OF THE ANALYSIS

➡ The framers of the Constitution, although guided by underlying values, also had conflicting goals and interests.

➡ The first attempt at a new arrangement for self-government relied on institutions that were too weak to achieve collective action on behalf of the nation.

➡ The conflicting interests of the Founders were eventually accommodated through a complex set of rules and procedures set forth in the Constitution, which divided power among three branches of the federal government and between states and the federal government.

➡ The Constitution not only provides a framework for government but also often guides the policy process, even to this day.

nation. Not only is America a great economic, military, and political power but Americans are relatively free and prosperous. One important way in which the Constitution has contributed to America's success as a nation is by firmly establishing the rule of law.

The rule of law means that a government's actions cannot be arbitrary but must, instead, be based upon a fairly stable body of published, clearly stated statutes that are binding upon government officials as well as citizens. The rule of law is a safeguard for citizens, protecting them from arbitrary action by government officials. At the same time, it enhances the quality of governance and generally promotes the development of a nation's economy. Who would invest in creating a new technology if their property was not protected by the law? Who would purchase a government's bonds if they could not be sure of repayment? Indeed, who would bother to obey any law if the law itself was arbitrarily enforced and constantly changing? The rule of law is the foundation of a successful government.

The framers of the Constitution understood this concept. James Madison's views, expressed in *Federalist 62*, are instructive. Madison writes

> It will be of little avail to the people that the laws are made by men of their own choice if the laws be so voluminous that they cannot be read, or so incoherent that they cannot be understood; if they be repealed or revised before they are promulgated, or undergo such incessant changes that no man, who knows what the law is today, can guess what it will be tomorrow.

Such a state of affairs, according to Madison, reduces popular respect for government and undermines economic development. "What prudent merchant will hazard his fortunes in any new branch of commerce when he knows not but that his plans may be rendered unlawful before they can be executed?"[1]

Similar concerns have inspired a number of regimes, including such authoritarian states as Russia and China, to endeavor to strengthen the rule of law in their domains in recent years. The Chinese leadership has viewed the rule of law as essential to economic development and, in Russia, then-President Dmitri Medvedev said, "Shortcomings in implementing laws . . . are basically macro-economic factors which restrain the growth of national prosperity."[2] In many instances, the strength of a regime and well-being of a nation could be increased if the arbitrary power of rulers and officials were reduced. James Madison understood this principle, but it is one that many rulers, protective of their personal powers and prerogatives, fail to grasp. In China, for example, the central government's efforts to promote legalism as a spur to economic development are often thwarted by local officials accustomed to exercising discretionary power.[3]

The U.S. Constitution, enforced by an independent judiciary, has helped to impose limits upon the arbitrary exercise of governmental power. Under the Constitution, the powers of government officials are defined by law and may only be exercised according to law. The same laws apply to officials and citizens, alike. Those accused of offenses must be treated according to law. These principles safeguard the citizenry and promote the well-being and prosperity of the nation as well. In this chapter, we will explore the institutions and procedures established in the Constitution, and how the framers settled on these features of government.

THE FIRST FOUNDING: INTERESTS AND CONFLICTS

Competing ideals and principles often reflect competing interests, and so it was in Revolutionary America. The American Revolution and the American Constitution were outgrowths of a struggle among economic and political forces within the colonies. Five sectors of society had interests that were important in colonial politics: (1) the New England merchants; (2) the southern planters, (3) the "royalists"—holders of royal lands, offices, and patents (licenses to engage in a profession or business activity); (4) shopkeepers, artisans, and laborers; and (5) small farmers. Throughout the eighteenth century, these groups were in conflict over issues of taxation, trade, and commerce. For the most part, however, the southern planters, the New England merchants, and the royal office and patent holders—groups that together made up the colonial elite—were able to maintain a political alliance that held in check the more radical forces representing shopkeepers, laborers, and small farmers. After 1750, however, British tax and trade policies split the colonial elite, permitting radical forces to expand their political influence and setting into motion a chain of events that culminated in the American Revolution.[4]

Political Strife and the Radicalizing of the Colonists

The political strife within the colonies was the background for the events of 1773–74. In 1773, the British government granted the politically powerful East India Company a monopoly on the export of tea from Britain, eliminating a lucrative form of trade for colonial merchants. Together with their southern allies, the merchants called upon their radical adversaries— shopkeepers, artisans, laborers, and small farmers—for support. The most dramatic result was the Boston Tea Party of 1773, led by Samuel Adams.

The Boston Tea Party was of decisive importance in American history. The merchants hoped to force the British government to rescind the Tea Act, but they did not support any demands beyond this one. They certainly did not seek independence from Britain. Samuel Adams and the other radicals, however, hoped to provoke the British government to take actions that would alienate its colonial supporters and pave the way for a rebellion. This was precisely the purpose of the Boston Tea Party, and it succeeded. By dumping the East India Company's tea into Boston Harbor, Adams and his followers goaded the British into enacting a number of harsh reprisals. The House of Commons closed the port of Boston to commerce, changed the provincial government of Massachusetts, provided for the removal of accused persons to Britain for trial, and added new restrictions on movement to the West—further alienating the southern planters who depended on access to new western lands. These acts of retaliation confirmed the worst criticisms of England and helped radicalize the American colonists.

Thus, the Boston Tea Party set into motion a cycle of provocation and retaliation that in 1774 resulted in the convening of the First Continental Congress—an assembly consisting of delegates from all parts of the country—that called for a total boycott of British goods and, under the prodding of the radicals, began to consider the possibility of independence from British rule. The result was the Declaration of Independence.

The Declaration of Independence

In 1776, the Second Continental Congress appointed a committee consisting of Thomas Jefferson of Virginia, Benjamin Franklin of Pennsylvania, Roger Sherman of Connecticut, John Adams of Massachusetts, and Robert Livingston of New York to draft a statement of American independence from British rule. The Declaration of Independence was written by Jefferson, drawing in part on ideas from the British philosopher John Locke, whose work was widely read in the colonies. Adopted by the Second Continental Congress, the Declaration was an extraordinary document in both philosophical and political terms. Philosophically, the Declaration was remarkable for its assertion—derived from Locke—that certain rights, which it called "unalienable rights"—including life, liberty, and the pursuit of happiness—could not be abridged by governments. In the world of 1776, a world in which some kings still claimed to rule by divine right, this was a dramatic statement. The Declaration was remarkable as a political document because it identified and focused on problems, grievances, aspirations, and principles that might unify the various colonial groups. The Declaration was an attempt to identify and articulate a history and set of principles that might help to forge national unity.[5]

The Revolutionary War

In 1775, even before formally declaring their independence, the colonies had begun to fight the British, most notably at Lexington and Concord, Massachusetts, where colonial militias acquitted themselves well against trained British soldiers. Nevertheless, the task of defeating Britain, then the world's premier military power, seemed impossible. To maintain their hold on the colonies, the British sent a huge expeditionary force composed of British regulars and German mercenaries along with artillery and equipment. To face this force, the colonists relied on inexperienced and lightly armed militias. To make matters worse, the colonists were hardly united in their opposition to British rule. Many colonists saw themselves as loyal British subjects and refused to take up arms against the king. Thousands, indeed, took up arms *for* the king and joined pro-British militia forces.

The war was brutal and bloody with tens of thousands of casualties among the colonists, among British troops, and among the Native Americans who fought on both sides of the conflict. Eventually the revolutionary armies prevailed mainly because the cost to England of fighting a war thousands of miles from home became too great. Colonial militias prevented British forces from acquiring enough food and supplies locally. As a result, these had to be brought from Europe at enormous expense. With the eventual help of Britain's enemy, France, the colonists fought until Britain decided it had had enough of a seemingly endless colonial war. The war ended with the signing of the Treaty of Paris, which officially granted the three American colonies their independence.

The Articles of Confederation

Having declared independence, the colonies needed to establish a government. In November 1777, the Continental Congress adopted the Articles of Confederation and Perpetual Union—the first written constitution of the United States. Although it was not ratified by all the states until 1781, it served as the country's constitution for almost 12 years, until March 1789.

The Articles of Confederation were concerned primarily with limiting the powers of the central government. They created no executive branch. Congress constituted the central government, but it had little power. Execution of its laws was to be left to the individual states. Its members were not much more than messengers from the state legislatures. They were chosen by the state legislature, their salaries were paid out of the state treasuries, and they were subject to immediate recall by state authorities. Each state, regardless of its size, had only a single vote. Furthermore, amendments to the articles required the unanimous agreement of the 13 states.

Articles of Confederation and Perpetual Union
America's first written constitution. Adopted by the Continental Congress in 1777, the Articles of Confederation and Perpetual Union were the formal basis for America's national government until 1789, when they were superseded by the Constitution

Congress was given the power to declare war and make peace, to make treaties and alliances, to coin or borrow money, and to regulate trade with Native Americans. It could also appoint the senior officers of the United States Army. But it could not levy taxes or regulate commerce among the states. Moreover, the army officers it appointed had no army to serve in because the nation's armed forces were composed of the state militias. An especially dysfunctional aspect of the Articles of Confederation was that the central government could not prevent one state from discriminating against other states in the quest for foreign commerce.

In brief, the relationship between Congress and the states under the Articles of Confederation was much like the contemporary relationship between the United Nations and its member states, a relationship in which the states retain virtually all governmental powers. It was called a confederation because, as provided under Article II, "each state retains its sovereignty, freedom and independence, and every Power, Jurisdiction and right, which is not by this confederation expressly delegated to the United States, in Congress assembled." Not only was there no executive, there was also no judicial authority and no other means of enforcing Congress's will. If there was to be any enforcement at all, the states would have to do it.[6] In essence, each state was an independent nation-state.

THE SECOND FOUNDING: FROM COMPROMISE TO CONSTITUTION

The Declaration of Independence and the Articles of Confederation were not sufficient to hold the nation together as an independent and effective nation-state. From almost the moment of armistice with the British in 1783, moves were afoot to reform and strengthen the Articles.

International Standing, Economic Difficulties, and Domestic Turmoil

Many Americans were concerned about the country's international position. Competition among the states for foreign commerce allowed the European powers to play the states against one another, which created confusion on both sides of the Atlantic. At one point during the winter of 1786–87, John Adams, a leader in the independence struggle, was sent to negotiate a new treaty with the British, one that would cover disputes left over from the war. The British government responded that, since the United States under the

Articles of Confederation was unable to enforce existing treaties, it would negotiate with each of the 13 states separately.

At the same time, well-to-do Americans—in particular the New England merchants and southern planters—were troubled by the influence that "populist" forces exercised in the Continental Congress and in the governments of several of the states. The colonists' victory in the Revolutionary War had not only meant the end of British rule but it had also significantly changed the balance of political power within the new states. As a result of the Revolution, one key segment of the colonial elite—the royal land, office, and patent holders—was stripped of its economic and political privileges. In fact, many of these individuals, along with tens of thousands of other colonists who considered themselves loyal British subjects, left for Canada after the British surrender. And as the elite was weakened, the radicals were now better organized than ever before. They controlled such states as Pennsylvania and Rhode Island, where they pursued economic and political policies that struck terror into the hearts of the prerevolutionary political establishment. The central government under the Articles of Confederation was powerless to intervene. Commerce within the states stagnated, and several states borrowed money just to finance the debts they had acquired during the Revolutionary War.

The new nation's weak international position and domestic turmoil led many Americans to consider whether a new version of the Articles might be necessary. In the fall of 1786, delegates from five states met in Annapolis, Maryland, and called on Congress to send commissioners to Philadelphia at a later time to devise adjustments to the Articles. Their resolution took on force as a result of an event that occurred the following winter in Massachusetts: Shays's Rebellion. Daniel Shays led a mob of farmers, who were protesting foreclosures on their land, in a rebellion against the state government. In January 1787, Shays and the rebels attempted to seize a federal armory in Springfield, Massachusetts. The state militia dispersed the mob within a few days, but the threat posed by the rebels scared Congress into action. The states were asked to send delegates to Philadelphia to discuss constitutional revision, and eventually delegates were sent from every state but Rhode Island.

The Constitutional Convention

In May 1787, 29 of a total of 73 delegates selected by the state governments convened in Philadelphia with political strife, international embarrassment, national weakness, and local rebellion fixed in their minds. Recognizing that these issues were symptoms of fundamental flaws in the Articles of Confederation, the delegates soon abandoned the plan to revise the Articles and committed themselves to a second Founding—a second, and ultimately successful, attempt to create a legitimate and effective national system. This effort occupied the convention for the next five months.

The Great Compromise. The proponents of a new government fired their opening shot on May 29, 1787, when Edmund Randolph of Virginia offered a resolution that proposed corrections and enlargements in the Articles of Confederation. His proposal was not a simple motion. It provided for virtually every aspect of a new government. Randolph later admitted it was intended to be an alternative draft constitution, and it was in fact the framework for what ultimately became the Constitution.[7]

The portion of Randolph's motion that became most controversial was known as the Virginia Plan. This plan provided for a system of representation in the national legislature based upon the population of each state or the proportion of each state's revenue contribution, or both. (Randolph also proposed a second branch of the legislature, but it was to be elected by the members of the first branch.) Because the states varied enormously in size and wealth, the Virginia Plan was thought to be heavily biased in favor of the large states that would have greater representation in the proposed system.

While the convention was debating the Virginia Plan, additional delegates arriving in Philadelphia were beginning to mount opposition to it. In particular, delegates from the less populous states, which included Delaware, New Jersey, Connecticut, and New York, asserted that the more populous states, such as Virginia, Pennsylvania, North Carolina, and Massachusetts would dominate the new government if representation were to be determined by population. The smaller states argued that each state should be equally represented in the new regime regardless of its population. The proposal, called the New Jersey Plan (it was introduced by William Paterson of New Jersey), focused on revising the Articles rather than replacing them. Their opposition to the Virginia Plan's system of representation was sufficient to send the proposals back to committee for reworking into a common document.

Great Compromise

An agreement reached at the Constitutional Convention of 1787 that gave each state an equal number of senators regardless of its population but linked representation in the House of Representatives to population

The outcome was the Great Compromise, also known as the Connecticut Compromise. Under the terms of this compromise, in the first branch of Congress—the House of Representatives—the representatives would be apportioned according to the number of inhabitants in each state. This, of course, was what delegates from the large states had sought. But in the second branch—the Senate—each state would have an equal vote regardless of its size; this was to deal with the concerns of the small states. This compromise was not immediately satisfactory to all the delegates. In the end, however, both sets of forces preferred compromise to the breakup of the Union, and the plan was accepted. The Analyzing the Evidence unit for this chapter explores the states' conflicting interests and how these shaped the eventual compromise.

The Question of Slavery: The Three-Fifths Compromise. Many of the conflicts that emerged during the Constitutional Convention were reflections of the fundamental differences between the slave and the nonslave states—differences that pitted the southern planters and the New England merchants against one another. This was the first premonition of a conflict that would almost destroy the Republic in later years. In the midst of debate over large versus small states, Madison observed, "The great danger to our general government is the great southern and northern interests of the continent, being opposed to each other. Look to the votes in Congress, and most of them stand divided by the geography of the country, not according to the size of the states."[8]

Over 90 percent of all slaves resided in five states—Georgia, Maryland, North Carolina, South Carolina, and Virginia—where they accounted for 30 percent of the total population. In some places, slaves outnumbered nonslaves by as much as 10 to 1. Were they to be counted in determining how many congressional seats a state should have? Northerners and southerners eventually reached agreement through the Three-Fifths Compromise. The seats in the House of Representatives would be apportioned according to a "population" in which five slaves would count as three persons. The slaves would not be allowed to vote, of course, but the number of representatives would be apportioned accordingly. This arrangement was supported by

The issue of how to count slaves in determining state populations and apportioning congressional seats nearly prevented the passage of the new constitution. Here, slaves are auctioned in Charleston, South Carolina, around the time of the Founding.

the slave states, which included some of the biggest and some of the smallest states at that time. It was also accepted by delegates from nonslave states who strongly supported the principle of property representation, whether that property was expressed in slaves or in land, money, or stocks.

The issue of slavery was the most difficult one faced by the framers, and it nearly destroyed the Union. Although some delegates believed slavery to be morally wrong, morality was not the issue that caused the framers to support or oppose the Three-Fifths Compromise. Whatever they thought of the institution of slavery, most delegates from the northern states opposed counting slaves in the distribution of congressional seats. But southern

Three-Fifths Compromise

An agreement reached at the Constitutional Convention of 1787 stipulating that for purposes of the apportionment of congressional seats, every slave would be counted as three-fifths of a person

Voting at the Constitutional Convention

Under the Articles of Confederation, there was a unicameral Congress in which each state delegation received a single vote regardless of state population. So Virginia, with roughly 700,000 people, had the same share of votes as Rhode Island, with a population closer to 70,000. Among the issues considered by the framers at the Constitutional Convention, one of the most contentious involved how representation in the Congress would work under the new Constitution.

    The larger states supported the Virginia Plan—because under this plan at least one of the chambers of Congress would be elected with representation proportional to population, giving the more populous states more of a voice in the national government. Given that the smaller, less populous states were poised to lose representation if votes in Congress were based on population, delegates from those states proposed the New Jersey Plan, which called for the creation of a unicameral legislature with one vote per state. Moreover, many of the delegates from the smaller states threatened to leave the Convention if the Virginia Plan were ratified. In an attempt to prevent the smaller states from departing, Roger Sherman proposed the Connecticut Compromise.

Representation in the First Congress

♟ = 30,000 people

♟ Free population

♟ Slave population

States*/Population**	VOTE ON VIRGINIA PLAN	VOTE ON CONNECTICUT COMPROMISE
VIRGINIA 747,550	YES	NO
PENNSYLVANIA 433,611	YES	NO
MASSACHUSETTS 378,556	YES	—
NEW YORK 340,241	NO	—
MARYLAND 319,728	—	YES
NORTH CAROLINA 395,005	YES	YES
SOUTH CAROLINA 249,073	YES	NO
CONNECTICUT 237,655	YES	YES
NEW JERSEY 184,139	NO	YES
GEORGIA 82,548	YES	NO
NEW HAMPSHIRE 141,899	—	—
DELAWARE 59,096	NO	YES
RHODE ISLAND 69,112	—	—

* Maryland's delegates were split equally and thus did not vote. Delegates from New Hampshire never attended at the same time as those from New York, hence their lack of participation. Rhode Island did not send any delegates to attend the Convention.

** Population data are based on the 1790 census and therefore are only approximate with respect to populations in 1787.

This plan called for a bicameral legislature, with representation based on population in the lower house and equal representation of states in the upper house. Although the Virginia Plan received more votes on first consideration, ultimately the Connecticut Compromise was adopted by a 5–4 vote to preserve a union with all 13 original members.

Representation in the First Congress

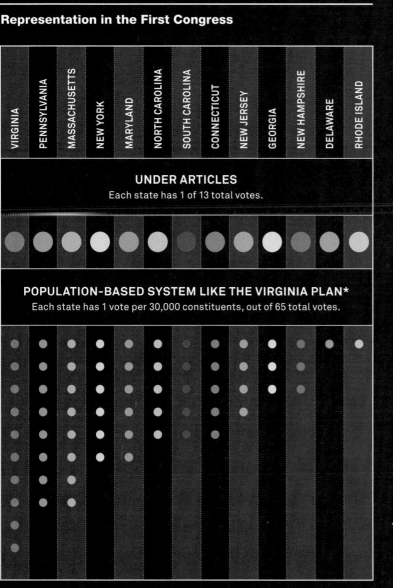

VIRGINIA | PENNSYLVANIA | MASSACHUSETTS | NEW YORK | MARYLAND | NORTH CAROLINA | SOUTH CAROLINA | CONNECTICUT | NEW JERSEY | GEORGIA | NEW HAMPSHIRE | DELAWARE | RHODE ISLAND

UNDER ARTICLES
Each state has 1 of 13 total votes.

POPULATION-BASED SYSTEM LIKE THE VIRGINIA PLAN*
Each state has 1 vote per 30,000 constituents, out of 65 total votes.

If we consider the number of representatives in Congress that each state would receive under the various plans, it becomes clear why individual states voted the way they did. Under the articles and the proposed New Jersey Plan, even the smallest states had 1 out of 13 votes in the Congress.

Under a population-based system like the Virginia Plan, the smaller states would lose voting power in the Congress. For example, in a population-based system with one representative per 30,000 people, Delaware would only have 1 out of 65 votes—significantly less voting power than the 1 out of 13 these states enjoyed under the articles and other arrangements that would give each state equal representation in Congress.

* Note that the framers calculated the number of representatives per state using population estimates. The first census was not taken until 1790.

SOURCES:

Keith L. Dougherty and Jac C. Heckelman, "A Pivotal Voter from a Pivotal State: Roger Sherman at the Constitutional Convention," *American Political Science Review 100* (May 2006): 297–302.

Clinton L. Rossiter, *1787: The Grand Convention* (New York: Macmillan Publishing Company, 1996).

delegates made it clear that if the northerners refused to give in, they would never agree to the new government. This conflict between the southern and the northern delegates was so divisive that many came to question the possibility of creating and maintaining a union of the two, and a compromise that acknowledged the legitimacy of slavery was probably necessary to keep the South from rejecting the Constitution.

THE CONSTITUTION

The political significance of the Great Compromise and the Three-Fifths Compromise was to reinforce the unity of those who sought the creation of a new government. The Great Compromise reassured those who feared that the importance of their own local or regional influence would be reduced by the new governmental framework. The Three-Fifths Compromise temporarily defused the rivalry between the merchants and the planters. Their unity secured, members of the alliance supporting the establishment of a new government moved to fashion a constitutional framework for this government that would be congruent with their economic and political interests.

In particular, the framers sought a new government that, first, would be strong enough to promote commerce and protect property from radical state legislatures such as Rhode Island's. This goal became the basis for the establishment of national control over commerce and finance, as well as the establishment of national judicial supremacy and a strong presidency. Second, the framers sought to prevent what they saw as the threat posed by the "excessive democracy" of the state and national governments under the Articles of Confederation. This led to such constitutional principles as bicameralism (the division of Congress into two chambers), checks and balances, staggered terms in office, and indirect election (the selection of the president by an electoral college rather than by voters directly).

bicameralism

The division of a legislative body into two chambers, or houses

Third, hoping to secure support from the states or the public at large for the new form of government they proposed, the framers provided for direct popular election of representatives and, subsequently, for the addition of the Bill of Rights. Finally, to prevent the new government from abusing its power, the framers incorporated principles such as the separation of powers and federalism into the Constitution. Let us now assess the major provisions of the Constitution to see how each relates to these objectives.

The Seven Articles of the Constitution

I. The Legislative Branch

House: two-year terms, elected directly by the people

Senate: six-year terms (staggered so that only one-third of the Senate changes in any given election), appointed by state legislature (changed in 1913 to direct election)

Expressed powers of the national government: collecting taxes, borrowing money, regulating commerce, declaring war, and maintaining an army and a navy; all other power belongs to the states, unless deemed otherwise by the elastic (necessary and proper) clause

Exclusive powers of the national government: states are expressly forbidden to issue their own paper money, tax imports and exports, regulate trade outside their own borders, and impair the obligation of contracts; these powers are the exclusive domain of the national government

II. The Executive Branch

Presidency: four-year terms (limited in 1951 to a maximum of two terms), elected indirectly by the electoral college

Powers: can recognize other countries, negotiate treaties, grant reprieves and pardons, convene Congress in special sessions, and veto congressional enactments

III. The Judicial Branch

Supreme Court: lifetime terms, appointed by the president with the approval of the Senate

Powers: include resolving conflicts between federal and state laws, determining whether power belongs to national government or the states, and settling controversies between citizens of different states

IV. National Unity and Power

Reciprocity among states: establishes that each state must give "full faith and credit" to official acts of other states and guarantees citizens of any state the "privileges and immunities" of every other state

V. Amending the Constitution

Procedures: requires two-thirds approval in Congress and three-fourths adoption by the states

VI. National Supremacy

The Constitution and national law are the supreme law of the land and cannot be overruled by state law

VII. Ratification

The Constitution became effective when approved by nine states

The Legislative Branch

The first seven sections of Article I of the Constitution provided for a Congress consisting of two chambers—a House of Representatives and a Senate. Members of the House of Representatives were given two-year terms in office and were to be subject to direct popular election—though generally only white males had the right to vote. State legislatures were to appoint members of the Senate (this was changed in 1913 by the Seventeenth Amendment, providing for direct election of senators) for six-year terms. These terms, moreover, were staggered so that the appointments of one-third of the senators would expire every two years. The Constitution assigned somewhat different tasks to the House and Senate. Though the approval of each body was required for the enactment of a law, the Senate alone was given the power to ratify treaties and approve presidential appointments. The House, on the other hand, was given the sole power to originate revenue bills.

The character of the legislative branch was directly related to the framers' major goals. The House of Representatives was designed to be directly responsible to the people in order to encourage popular consent for the new Constitution and, as we saw in Chapter 1, to help enhance the power of the new government. At the same time, to guard against "excessive democracy," the power of the House of Representatives was checked by the Senate, whose members were to be appointed for long (six-year) terms rather than elected directly by the people for short terms.

Staggered terms of service in the Senate were intended to make that body even more resistant to popular pressure. Because only one-third of the senators would be selected at any given time, the composition of the institution would be protected from changes in popular preferences transmitted by the state legislatures. Thus, the structure of the legislative branch was designed to contribute to governmental power, promote popular consent for the new government, and at the same time place limits on the popular political currents that many of the framers saw as a radical threat to the economic and social order.

The Powers of Congress and the States. The issues of power and consent were important throughout the Constitution. Section 8 of Article I specifically listed the powers of Congress, which include the authority to collect taxes, to borrow money, to regulate commerce, to declare war, and to maintain an army and navy. By granting it these powers, the framers indicated very clearly that they intended the new government to be far more influential than its predecessor. At the same time, by giving these important powers to Congress, the framers sought to reassure citizens that their views would be fully represented whenever the government exercised its new powers.

As a further guarantee to the people that the new government would pose no threat to them, the Constitution implied that any powers *not* listed were not granted at all. This is the doctrine of expressed powers. The Constitution grants only those powers specifically *expressed* in its text. But the framers intended to create an active and powerful government, and so they included the necessary and proper clause, sometimes known as the elastic clause, which signified that the enumerated powers were meant to be a source of strength to the national government, not a limitation on it. Each power could be used with the utmost vigor, but no new powers could be seized upon by the national government without a constitutional amendment. Any power not enumerated was conceived to be "reserved" to the states (or the people).

The Executive Branch

The Constitution provided for the establishment of the presidency in Article II. As Alexander Hamilton put it, the presidential article sought "energy in the Executive." It did so in an effort to overcome the natural stalemate that was built into the bicameral legislature as well as into the separation of powers among the legislative, executive, and judicial branches. The Constitution afforded the president a measure of independence from the people and from the other branches of government—particularly Congress.

Some of the framers had argued for a plural executive or executive council in order to avoid the evils that many associated with a monarch.

expressed powers
The powers enumerated in the Constitution that are granted to the federal government

necessary and proper clause
Article I, Section 8, of the Constitution, which enumerates the powers of Congress and provides Congress with the authority to make all laws "necessary and proper" to carry them out; also referred to as the elastic clause

The framers debated whether a plural executive would better protect against tyranny but ultimately decided that the energy required to overcome government stalemates required a single executive. In 1789, George Washington was unanimously elected as America's first president.

In *Federalist 70*, however, Hamilton argued that "energy" required a single rather than a plural executive. While abuse of power should be guarded against by checks and balances and other devices, energy also required that the executive should be provided with "competent powers" to direct the nation's business.[9] These would include the unconditional power to accept ambassadors from other countries; this amounted to the power to "recognize" other countries. He was also given the power to negotiate treaties, although their acceptance required the approval of the Senate. The president was given the unconditional right to grant reprieves and pardons, except in cases of impeachment. And he was provided with the power to appoint major departmental personnel, to convene Congress in special session, and to veto congressional enactments. (The veto power is formidable, but it is not absolute, since Congress can override it by a two-thirds vote.)

At the same time, the framers sought to help the president withstand (excessively) democratic pressures by making him subject to indirect rather than direct election (through his selection by a separate electoral college). The extent to which the framers' hopes were actually realized is the topic of Chapter 6.

The Judicial Branch

Article III established the judicial branch. This provision reflects the framers' concern with giving more power to the national government and checking radical democratic impulses, while guarding against abuse of liberty and property by the new national government itself.

The framers created a court that was to be literally a supreme court of the United States and not merely the highest court of the national government. The Supreme Court was given the power to resolve any conflicts that might emerge between federal and state laws and to determine to which level of government a power belonged. In addition, the Supreme Court was assigned jurisdiction over controversies between citizens of different states. The long-term significance of this was that as the country developed a national economy, it came to rely increasingly on the federal judiciary, rather than on the state courts, for resolution of disputes.

Judges were given lifetime appointments in order to protect them from popular politics and from interference by the other branches. To further safeguard judicial independence, the Constitution also prohibited Congress from reducing the salary of any sitting judge. But they would not be totally immune to politics or to the other branches, for the president was to appoint the judges and the Senate was to approve the appointments. Congress would also have the power to create inferior (lower) courts, to change the jurisdic-

After Congress passed the Affordable Care Act in 2010, opponents of the law asked the federal courts to declare it unconstitutional while supporters of the law asked the courts to uphold it. Although the power of judicial review is not specifically mentioned in the Constitution, the courts have assumed this power.

tion of the federal courts, to add or subtract federal judges, and even to change the size of the Supreme Court.

No specific mention is made in the Constitution of judicial review—the power of the courts to render the final decision when there is a conflict of interpretation of the Constitution or of laws. This conflict could be between the courts and Congress, the courts and the executive branch, or the courts and the states. Scholars generally feel that judicial review is implicit in the very existence of a written Constitution and in the power given explicitly to the federal courts over "all Cases . . . arising under this Constitution, the Laws of the United States, and Treaties made, or which shall be made, under their Authority" (Article III, Section 2). The Supreme Court eventually assumed the power of judicial review. Its assumption of this power, as we see in Chapter 8, was based not on the Constitution itself but on the politics of later decades and the membership of the Court.

judicial review
The power of the courts to declare actions of the legislative and executive branches invalid or unconstitutional. The Supreme Court asserted this power in *Marbury v. Madison* (1803)

National Unity and Power

Various provisions in the Constitution addressed the framers' concern with national unity and power. Article IV provided for comity (reciprocity) among states, which we discuss in more detail in Chapter 3. Each state was also prohibited from discriminating against the citizens of other states in favor of its own citizens, with the Supreme Court being the arbiter in each case.

IN BRIEF

Comparing the Articles of Confederation and the Constitution

	Articles of Confederation	Constitution
✔ **Legislative Branch**	**Power to:** Declare war and make peace. Make treaties and alliances. Coin or borrow money. Regulate trade with Native Americans. Appoint senior officers of the U.S. Army. **Limits on power:** Could not levy taxes, regulate commerce among the states, or create national armed forces	**Power to:** Collect taxes. Borrow money. Regulate commerce. Declare war. Maintain an army and navy. **Limits on power:** All other powers belong to the states
✔ **Executive Branch**	No executive branch was created	**Power to:** Recognize other countries. Negotiate treaties. Grant reprieves and pardons. Appoint major departmental personnel. Convene special sessions of Congress. Veto congressional actions. **Limits on power:** Senate must approve treaties. Congress can override a veto by a two-thirds vote
✔ **Judicial Branch**	No judicial branch was created	**Power to:** Resolve conflicts between state and federal laws. Determine to which level of government a power belongs. Decide conflicts between citizens of different states. **Limits on power:** Judicial appointments are made by the president and approved by the Senate. Congress creates lower courts and can change the jurisdiction of the federal courts. Congress can add or subtract federal judges and can change the size of the Supreme Court

The framers' concern with national supremacy was also expressed in Article VI, in the supremacy clause, which provided that national laws and treaties "shall be the supreme law of the land." This meant that all laws made under the "authority of the United States" would be superior to all laws adopted by any state or any other subdivision, and that the states would be expected to respect all treaties made under that authority. This was a clear effort to keep the states from dealing separately with foreign nations or businesses. The supremacy clause also bound the officials of all state and local as well as federal governments to take an oath of office to support the national Constitution. This meant that every action taken by the U.S. Congress would have to be applied within each state as though the action were, in fact, state law.

Amending the Constitution

The Constitution established procedures for its own revision in Article V. Its provisions are so difficult that Americans have succeeded in the amending process only 17 times since 1791, when the first 10 amendments were adopted. Many other amendments have been proposed in Congress, but fewer than 40 of them have even come close to fulfilling the Constitution's requirement of a two-thirds vote in Congress, and only a fraction have gotten anywhere near adoption by three-fourths of the states. (A breakdown of these figures and further discussion of amending the Constitution appear in Chapter 3.) The Constitution could also be amended by a constitutional convention. Occasionally, proponents of particular measures, such as a balanced-budget amendment, have called for a constitutional convention to consider their proposals. Whatever the purpose for which it was called, however, such a convention would presumably have the authority to revise America's entire system of government.

Ratifying the Constitution

The rules for the ratification of the Constitution of 1787 made up Article VII of the Constitution. This provision actually violated the lawful procedure for constitutional change incorporated in the Articles of Confederation. For one thing, it adopted a nine-state rule in place of the unanimity among the states required by the Articles of Confederation. For another, it provided that ratification would occur in special state conventions called for that purpose rather than in the state legislatures. All the states except Rhode Island eventually did set up state conventions to ratify the Constitution, and none seemed to protest very loudly the extralegal character of the procedure.

Constitutional Limits on the National Government's Power

As we have indicated, though the framers sought to create a powerful national government, they also wanted to guard against possible misuse of that power. To that end, the framers incorporated two key principles into the Constitution—the separation of powers and federalism (see also Chapter 3). A third set of limitations, in the form of the Bill of Rights, was added to the Constitution to help secure its ratification when opponents of the document charged that it paid insufficient attention to citizens' rights.

separation of powers
The division of governmental power among several institutions that must cooperate in decision making

The Separation of Powers. No principle of politics was more widely shared at the time of the 1787 Founding than the principle that power must be used to balance power. The French political theorist Montesquieu (1689–1755) believed that this balance was an indispensable defense against tyranny, and his writings, especially his major work, *The Spirit of the Laws*, "were taken as political gospel" at the Philadelphia Convention.[10] This principle is not stated explicitly in the Constitution, but it is clearly built into Articles I, II, and III, which provide for

federalism
The system of government in which a constitution divides power between a central government and regional governments

1. Three separate branches of government (Figure 2.1).

2. Different methods of selecting the top personnel, so that each branch is responsible to a different constituency. This is intended to produce a "mixed regime," in which the personnel of each department will develop very different interests and outlooks on how to govern, and different groups in society will be assured of some access to governmental decision making.

Bill of Rights
The first 10 amendments to the U.S. Constitution, adopted in 1791. The Bill of Rights ensures certain rights and liberties to the people

3. Checks and balances, a system under which each of the branches is given some power over the others. Familiar examples are the presidential veto power over legislation and the power of the Senate to approve high-level presidential appointments.

checks and balances
The mechanisms through which each branch of government is able to participate in and influence the activities of the other branches

One clever formulation conceives of this system not as separated powers but as "separated institutions sharing power,"[11] thus diminishing the chance that power will be misused.

Federalism. Federalism was a step toward greater centralization of power. The delegates agreed that they needed to place more power at the national governmental level, without completely undermining the power of the state governments. Thus, they devised a system of two sovereigns—the states and the

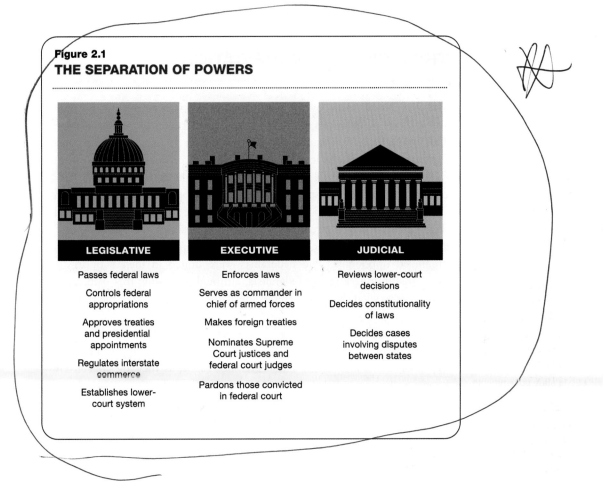

Figure 2.1

THE SEPARATION OF POWERS

LEGISLATIVE	EXECUTIVE	JUDICIAL
Passes federal laws	Enforces laws	Reviews lower-court decisions
Controls federal appropriations	Serves as commander in chief of armed forces	Decides constitutionality of laws
Approves treaties and presidential appointments	Makes foreign treaties	Decides cases involving disputes between states
Regulates interstate commerce	Nominates Supreme Court justices and federal court judges	
Establishes lower-court system	Pardons those convicted in federal court	

nation—with the hope that competition between the two would be an effective limitation on the power of both.

The Bill of Rights. Late in the Philadelphia Convention, a motion was made to include a bill of rights in the Constitution. After a brief debate in which hardly a word was said in its favor and only one speech was made against it, the motion to include it was almost unanimously turned down. Most delegates sincerely believed that since the federal government was already limited to its expressed powers, further protection of citizens was not needed. The delegates argued that the states should adopt bills of rights because their powers needed more limitations than those of the federal government. But almost immediately after the Constitution was ratified, there was a movement to adopt a national bill of rights. This is why the Bill of Rights, adopted in 1791, comprises the first 10 amendments to the Constitution rather than being part of the body of it. We have a good deal more to say about the Bill of Rights in Chapter 4.

THE FIGHT FOR RATIFICATION

The first hurdle faced by the new Constitution was ratification by state conventions of delegates elected by white, propertied males of each state. This struggle for ratification was carried out in 13 separate campaigns. Each was influenced by local as well as national considerations. Two sides faced off throughout all the states, however, taking the names of Federalists and Antifederalists.[12] The Federalists supported the Constitution and preferred a strong national government. The Antifederalists opposed the Constitution and preferred a more decentralized federal system of government; they took on their name by default, in reaction to their better-organized opponents. The Federalists were united in their support of the Constitution. The Antifederalists, although opposing this plan, were divided as to what they believed the alternative should be. (See the In Brief box on page 47.)

Under the name of "Publius," Alexander Hamilton, James Madison, and John Jay wrote 85 articles in the New York newspapers supporting ratification of the Constitution. These *Federalist Papers*, as they are collectively known today, defended the principles of the Constitution and sought to dispel the fears of a national authority.[13] The Antifederalists, however, such as Richard Henry Lee and Patrick Henry of Virginia and George Clinton of New York, argued that the new Constitution betrayed the Revolution and was a step toward monarchy. The Antifederalists wanted a bill of rights to protect against government.

By the end of 1787 and the beginning of 1788, five states had ratified the Constitution. Delaware, New Jersey, and Georgia ratified it unanimously; Connecticut and Pennsylvania ratified it by wide margins. Opposition was overcome in Massachusetts by the inclusion of nine recommended amendments to the Constitution to protect human rights. Ratification by Maryland and South Carolina followed. In June 1788, New Hampshire became the ninth state to ratify. That put the Constitution into effect, but for the new national government to have real power, the approval of both Virginia and New York would be needed. After impassioned debate and a great number of recommendations for future amendment of the Constitution, especially for a bill of rights, the Federalists mustered enough votes for approval of the Constitution in June (Virginia) and July (New York) of 1788. North Carolina joined the new government in 1789, after a bill of rights actually was submitted to the states by Congress, and Rhode Island held out until 1790 before finally voting to become part of the new union.

Federalists ⮞

Those who favored a strong national government and supported the constitution proposed at the American Constitutional Convention of 1787

Antifederalists ⮞

Those who favored strong state governments and a weak national government and who were opponents of the constitution proposed at the American Constitutional Convention of 1787

Federalists versus Antifederalists

	Federalists	Antifederalists
✔ Who were they?	Property owners, creditors, merchants	Small farmers, frontiersmen, debtors, shopkeepers
✔ What did they believe?	Believed that elites were best fit to govern; feared "excessive democracy"	Believed that government should be closer to the people; feared concentration of power in the hands of the elites
✔ What system of government did they favor?	Favored strong national government; believed in "filtration" so that only elites would obtain governmental power	Favored retention of power by state governments and protection of individual rights
✔ Who were their leaders?	Alexander Hamilton James Madison George Washington	Patrick Henry George Mason Elbridge Gerry George Clinton

CHANGING THE FRAMEWORK: CONSTITUTIONAL AMENDMENT

The Constitution has endured for over two centuries as the framework of government. But it has not endured without change. Without change, the Constitution might have become merely a sacred text, stored under glass.

Amendments: Many Are Called, Few Are Chosen

The framers of the Constitution recognized the need for change and provisions for amendment incorporated into Article V. Since 1791, when the first

10 amendments, the Bill of Rights, were added, only 17 amendments have been adopted. And two of them—prohibition of alcohol (Eighteenth) and its repeal (Twenty-First)—cancel each other out, so that for all practical purposes, only 15 amendments have been added to the Constitution since 1791, despite vast changes in American society and its economy.

As Figure 2.2 illustrates, Article V provides for four routes of amendment:

1. Passage in House and Senate by two-thirds vote; then ratification by majority vote of the legislatures of three-fourths (38) of the states.

2. Passage in House and Senate by two-thirds vote; then ratification by conventions called for the purpose in three-fourths of the states.

3. Passage in a national convention called by Congress in response to petitions by two-thirds of the states; ratification by majority vote of the legislatures of three-fourths of the states.

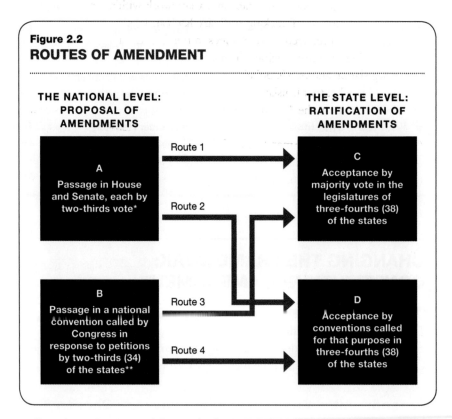

Figure 2.2
ROUTES OF AMENDMENT

THE NATIONAL LEVEL:
PROPOSAL OF
AMENDMENTS

THE STATE LEVEL:
RATIFICATION OF
AMENDMENTS

A
Passage in House and Senate, each by two-thirds vote*

B
Passage in a national convention called by Congress in response to petitions by two-thirds (34) of the states**

Route 1
Route 2
Route 3
Route 4

C
Acceptance by majority vote in the legislatures of three-fourths (38) of the states

D
Acceptance by conventions called for that purpose in three-fourths (38) of the states

*For each amendment proposal, Congress has the power to choose the method of ratification, the time limit for consideration by the states, and other conditions of ratification.
**This method of proposal has never been employed. Thus, amendment routes 3 and 4 have never been attempted.

4. Passage in a national convention, as in route 3; then ratification by conventions called for the purpose in three-fourths of the states.

Because no amendment has ever been proposed by national convention, however, routes 3 and 4 have never been employed. And route 2 has been employed only once (for the Twenty-First Amendment, which repealed the Eighteenth, or Prohibition, Amendment). Thus, route 1 has been used for all the others.

The Twenty-Seven Amendments

The Constitution and its amendments are reproduced at the end of this book. All but two of the Constitution's 27 amendments are concerned with the structure or composition of the government. This is consistent with the concept of a constitution as "higher law," because the whole point and purpose of a higher law is to establish a framework within which government and the process of making ordinary law can take place. Even those who would have preferred more changes in the Constitution would have to agree that there is great wisdom in this principle. A constitution ought to enable legislation and public policies to take place, but it should not attempt to determine what that legislation or those policies ought to be.

The purpose of the 10 amendments in the Bill of Rights was basically to give each of the three branches clearer and more restricted boundaries (Table 2.1). The First Amendment clarified Congress's turf. Although the powers of Congress under Article I, Section 8, would not have justified laws regulating religion, speech, and the like, the First Amendment made this limitation explicit: "Congress shall make no law. . . ." The Second, Third, and Fourth Amendments similarly spelled out limits on the executive branch, a necessity given the abuses of executive power Americans had endured under British rule.

The Fifth, Sixth, Seventh, and Eighth Amendments contain some of the most important safeguards for individual citizens against the arbitrary exercise of government power. And these amendments sought to accomplish their goal by defining the judicial branch more concretely and clearly than had been done in Article III of the Constitution.

Five amendments adopted since 1791 are directly concerned with expansion of the electorate (Table 2.2).[14] The Founders were unable to establish a national electorate with uniform voting qualifications. They decided to evade the issue by providing in the final draft of Article I, Section 2, that eligibility to vote in a national election would be the same as "the Qualification requisite for Elector of the most numerous branch of the state Legislature." Article I, Section 4, added that Congress could alter

Table 2.1

THE BILL OF RIGHTS: ANALYSIS OF ITS PROVISIONS

AMENDMENT	PURPOSE
I	*Limits on Congress*: Congress is not to make any law establishing a religion or abridging the freedom of speech, press, assembly, or the right to petition freedoms.
II, III, IV	*Limits on the Executive*: The executive branch is not to infringe on the right of people to keep arms (II), is not arbitrarily to take houses for a militia (III), and is not to engage in the search for or seizure of evidence without a court warrant swearing to a belief in the probable existence of a crime (IV).
V, VI, VII, VIII	*Limits on the Courts*: The courts are not to hold trials for serious offenses without provision for a grand jury (V), a petit (trial) jury (VII), a speedy trial (VI), presentation of charges, and confrontation of hostile witnesses (VI). Individuals may not be compelled to testify against themselves (V) and are immune from trial more than once for the same offense (V). Neither bail nor punishment can be excessive (VIII), and no property can be taken without just compensation (V).
IX, X	*Limits on National Government*: All rights not enumerated are reserved to the states or the people.

state regulations as to the "Times, Places and Manner of holding Elections for Senators and Representatives," but this meant that any important expansion of the American electorate would almost certainly require a constitutional amendment.

Six more amendments are also electoral in nature, although not concerned directly with voting rights and the expansion of the electorate. These six amendments are concerned with the elective offices themselves or with the relationship between elective offices and the electorate (Table 2.3).

Another five amendments have sought to expand or to limit the powers of the national and state governments (Table 2.4). The Eleventh Amendment protected the states from suits by private individuals and took away from the federal courts any power to take suits by private individuals of one state (or a foreign country) against another state. The other three amendments in Table 2.4 are obviously designed to reduce state power (Thirteenth), to

Table 2.2

AMENDING THE CONSTITUTION TO EXPAND THE ELECTORATE

AMENDMENT	PURPOSE	YEAR PROPOSED	YEAR ADOPTED
XIV	Section 1 provided national definition of citizenship	**1866**	**1868**
XV	Extended voting rights to all races	**1869**	**1870**
XIX	Extended voting rights to women	**1919**	**1920**
XXIII	Extended voting rights to residents of the District of Columbia	**1960**	**1961**
XXIV	Extended voting rights to all classes by abolition of poll taxes	**1962**	**1964**
XXVI	Extended voting rights to citizens ages 18 and over	**1971**	**1971**

reduce state power and expand national power (Fourteenth), and to expand national power (Sixteenth). The Twenty-Seventh put a moderate limit on Congress's ability to raise its own salary.

The Eighteenth, or Prohibition, Amendment underscores the meaning of the rest: this is the only amendment that the country used to try to *legislate*. In other words, it is the only amendment that was designed to deal directly with a substantive social problem. And it was the only amendment ever to have been repealed. Two other amendments—the Thirteenth, which abolished slavery, and the Sixteenth, which established the power to levy an income tax—can be said to have had the effect of legislation. But the purpose of the Thirteenth was to restrict the power of the states by forever forbidding them to treat any human being as property. As for the Sixteenth, it is certainly true that income tax legislation followed immediately; nevertheless, the amendment concerns itself strictly with establishing the power of Congress to enact such legislation. The legislation came later.

Table 2.3

AMENDING THE CONSTITUTION TO CHANGE THE RELATIONSHIP BETWEEN THE ELECTED OFFICES AND THE ELECTORATE

AMENDMENT	PURPOSE	YEAR PROPOSED	YEAR ADOPTED
XII	Created separate ballot for vice president in the electoral college	1803	1804
XIV	Penalized states for depriving freed slaves of the right to vote	1866	1868
XVII	Provided direct election of senators	1912	1913
XX	Shortened the time between election of new Congress and president and their inauguration	1932	1933
XXII	Limited presidential term	1947	1951
XXV	Provided presidential succession in case of disability	1965	1967

DOES THE CONSTITUTION WORK?

The final product of the Constitutional Convention would have to be considered an extraordinary victory for those who wanted a new system of government to replace the Articles of Confederation. The new Constitution laid the groundwork for a government that would be sufficiently powerful to promote trade, to protect property, and to check the activities of radical state legislatures. It established the rule of law to protect citizens and strengthen the government. Moreover, this new government was so constructed through internal checks and balances, indirect selection of officeholders, lifetime judicial appointments, and other similar provisions to preclude the "excessive democracy" feared by many of the Founders. Some of the framers favored

Table 2.4

AMENDING THE CONSTITUTION TO EXPAND OR LIMIT THE POWER OF GOVERNMENT

AMENDMENT	PURPOSE	YEAR PROPOSED	YEAR ADOPTED
XI	Limited jurisdiction of federal courts over suits involving the states	1794	1795
XIII	Eliminated slavery and eliminated the right of states to allow property in persons	1865	1865
XIV	Established due process of law in state courts for all persons. Later used to apply the entire Bill of Rights to the states.	1866	1868
XVI	Established national power to tax incomes	1909	1913
XXVII	Limited Congress's power to raise its own salary	1789	1992

going even further in limiting popular influence, but the general consensus at the Convention was that a thoroughly undemocratic document would never receive the popular approval needed to be ratified by the states.[15]

Though the Constitution was the product of a particular set of political forces, the principles of government it established have a significance that goes far beyond the interests of its authors. Two of these principles, federalism and civil liberties, are discussed in Chapters 3 and 4, respectively. A third important constitutional principle that has affected America's government for the past 200 years is the principle of checks and balances. As we saw earlier, the framers gave each of the three branches of government a means of intervening in and blocking the actions of the others. Often, checks and balances have seemed to prevent the government from getting much done. During the 1960s, for example, liberals were often infuriated as they watched Congress stall presidential initiatives in the area of civil rights. More recently, conservatives were outraged when President Clinton thwarted congressional efforts to enact legislation promised in the Republican "Contract with America." At various times, all sides have vilified the judiciary for invalidating legislation enacted by Congress and signed by the president.

The framers gave each branch of government a means of blocking the other branches. In 2007, President George W. Bush announced that he would veto congressional legislation providing federal funds for stem cell research.

Over time, checks and balances have acted as brakes on the governmental process. Groups hoping to bring about changes in policy or governmental institutions seldom have been able to bring about decisive and dramatic transformations in a short period of time. Instead, checks and balances have slowed the pace of change and increased the need for compromise and accommodation.

Groups able to take control of the White House, for example, must negotiate with their rivals who remain entrenched on Capitol Hill. New forces in Congress must reckon with the influence of other forces in the executive branch and in the courts. Checks and balances inevitably frustrate those who desire change, but they also function as a safeguard against rash action. During the 1950s, for example, Congress was caught up in a nearly hysterical effort to unmask subversive activities in the United States, which might have led to a serious erosion of American liberties if not for the checks and balances provided by the executive branch and the courts. Thus, a governmental principle that serves as a frustrating limitation one day may become a vitally important safeguard the next.

Yet, although the Constitution sought to lay the groundwork for a powerful government, the framers struggled to reconcile government power with freedom. The framers surrounded the powerful institutions of the new regime with a variety of safeguards—a continual array of checks and balances—designed to make certain that the power of the national government could not be used to undermine the states' power and their citizens' freedoms. Thus, the framers were the first Americans to confront head-on the dilemma of coercion and power that we discussed briefly in Chapter 1. Whether their solutions to this dilemma were successful is the topic of the remainder of our chapters.

To Whose Benefit?

Of course, the groups whose interests were served by the Constitution in 1789, mainly the merchants and planters, are not the same groups that benefit from the Constitution's provisions today. Once incorporated into the law, political principles often take on lives of their own and have consequences that were never anticipated by their original champions. Indeed, many of the groups that benefit from constitutional provisions today did not even exist in 1789. Who would have thought that the principle of free speech would influence the transmission of data on the Internet? Who would have predicted that commercial interests that once sought a powerful government might come, two centuries later, to denounce governmental activism as "socialistic"? Perhaps one secret of the Constitution's longevity is that it did not confer permanent advantage on any one set of economic or social forces.

Although they were defeated in 1789, the Antifederalists present us with an important picture of a road not taken and of an America that might have been. Would the country have been worse off if it had been governed by a confederacy of small republics linked by a national administration with severely limited powers? Were the Antifederalists correct in predicting that a government given great power in the hope that it might do good would, through "insensible progress," inevitably turn to evil purposes? Two hundred years of government under the federal Constitution are not necessarily enough to definitively answer these questions. Time must tell.

To What Ends?

The Constitution's framers placed individual liberty ahead of all other political values. Their concern for liberty led many of the framers to distrust both democracy and equality. They feared that democracy could degenerate into a majority tyranny in which the populace, perhaps led by a rabble-rousing demagogue, would trample on liberty. As for equality, the framers were products of their time and place; our contemporary ideas of racial and gender equality would have been foreign to them. The framers concerned primarily with another manifestation of equality: they feared that those without property or position might be driven by what some called a "leveling spirit" to infringe on liberty in the name of greater economic or social equality. Indeed, the framers believed that this leveling spirit was most likely to produce demagoguery and majority tyranny. As a result, the basic structure of the Constitution—separated powers, internal checks and balances, and federalism—was designed to safeguard liberty, and the Bill of Rights created further safeguards for liberty. At the same time, however, many of the Constitution's other key provisions, such as indirect election of senators and the president, as well as the appointment of judges for life, were designed to limit democracy and, hence, the threat of majority tyranny.

By championing liberty, however, the framers virtually guaranteed that democracy and even a measure of equality would sooner or later evolve in the United States. For liberty inevitably leads to the growth of political activity and the expansion of political participation. In James Madison's famous phrase, "Liberty is to faction as air is to fire."[16] Where they have liberty, more and more people, groups, and interests will almost inevitably engage in politics and gradually overcome whatever restrictions might have been placed on their participation. This is precisely what happened in the early years of the American Republic. During the Jeffersonian period, political parties formed. During the Jacksonian period, many state suffrage restrictions were removed, and popular participation greatly expanded. Over time, liberty is conducive to democracy.

Liberty does not guarantee that everyone will be equal. It does, however, reduce the threat of inequality in one very important way. Historically, the greatest inequalities of wealth, power, and privilege have arisen where governments have used their power to allocate status and opportunity among individuals or groups. The most extreme cases of inequality are associated with the most tyrannical regimes. In the United States, however, by promoting democratic politics, over time liberty unleashed forces that militated against inequality. As a result, over the past 200 years, groups that have learned to use the political process have achieved important economic and social gains.

One limitation of liberty as a political principle, however, is that the idea of limits on government action can also inhibit effective government. Take one of the basic tasks of government, the protection of citizens' lives and property. A government limited by concerns over the rights of those accused of crimes may be limited in its ability to maintain public order. For the last decade, the U.S. government has asserted that protecting the nation against terrorists requires law enforcement measures that seem at odds with legal and constitutional formalities. The conflict between liberty and governmental effectiveness is another tension at the heart of the American constitutional system.

For Further Reading

Selections highlighted in red are included in _Readings in American Politics: Analysis and Perspectives_, Third Edition.

Allison, Robert. _The American Revolution: A Concise History_. New York: Oxford University Press, 2011.

Amar, Akhil Reed. _America's Constitution: A Biography_. New York: Random House, 2005.

Bailyn, Bernard. _The Ideological Origins of the American Revolution_. Cambridge, MA: Harvard University Press, 1967.

Beard, Charles A. _An Economic Interpretation of the Constitution of the United States_. New York: Macmillan, 1913.

Breyer, Stephen. _Active Liberty: Interpreting Our Democratic Constitution_. New York: Knopf, 2005.

Chernow, Ron. _Alexander Hamilton_. New York: Penguin, 2004.

Ellis, Joseph. _His Excellency: George Washington_. New York: Knopf, 2004.

Farrand, Max, ed. _The Records of the Federal Convention of 1787_. Rev. ed., 4 vols. New Haven, CT: Yale University Press, 1966.

Hamilton, Alexander, James Madison, and John Jay. _The Federalist Papers_, no. 10 and no. 51. Clinton Rossiter, ed. New York: New American Library, 1961.

Newton, Michael. _Angry Mobs and Founding Fathers: The Fight for Control of the American Revolution_. New York: Eleftheria, 2011.

Storing, Herbert J., ed. _The Complete Anti-Federalist_. 7 vols. Chicago: University of Chicago Press, 1981.

3

Federalism and the Separation of Powers

The great achievement of American politics in the eighteenth century was the fashioning of an effective constitutional structure of political institutions. Although it is an imperfect and continuously evolving work in progress, this structure of law and political practice has served its people well for more than two centuries. Two of America's most important institutional features are federalism and the separation of powers. Federalism seeks to limit government by dividing it into two levels, national and state. Often the two levels must cooperate and jointly plan their efforts, as in the investigation of the 2013 Boston Marathon bombing, when FBI and other federal officials worked with Massachusetts law enforcement. Yet each level is also granted sufficient independence to compete with the other, thereby restraining the power of both.[1] The separation of powers seeks to limit the power of the national government by dividing government against itself—by giving the legislative, executive, and judicial branches separate functions, thus forcing them to share power.

Both federalism and the separation of powers complicate policy making in the United States. If governmental power were arranged neatly and simply in a single hierarchy, decisions could certainly be made more easily and more efficiently. But would they be better decisions? The framers thought that complexity, multiple checks, and institutionalized second-guessing, though messy, would allow more interests to have a voice and would eventually produce better results. And along the way, messy decision processes might preserve liberty and prevent tyranny. Yet, although the constitutional dispersion of power among federal institutions and between the federal government and the states may well protect our liberties, it often seems to make it impossible to get anything done collectively. This lack of decisiveness sometimes appears to negate the most important reason for building institutions in the first place.

Since the adoption of the Constitution, ambitious politicians and decision makers have developed a variety of strategies for overcoming the many impediments to policy change that inevitably arise in our federal system of separated powers. Most commonly, those seeking to promote a new program may try to find ways of dispersing the program's benefits so that other politicians controlling institutional veto powers will be persuaded that it is in their interest to go along. Thus, federalism and the separation of powers have given rise to the federal pork barrel, to the defense subcontracting system, to grants-in-aid, and to other forms of policy that reflect the dispersion of power. For example, if the executive branch hopes to win congressional support for a new weapons system, it generally sees to it that portions of the new system are subcontracted to firms in as many congressional districts as possible. In this way, dispersion of benefits helps

CORE OF THE ANALYSIS

➡ Federalism limits national power by creating two sovereigns: the national government and the state governments.

➡ Under "dual federalism," which lasted from 1789 to 1937, the national government limited itself primarily to promoting commerce, while the states directly coerced citizens.

➡ After 1937, the national government exerted more influence, yet the states maintained many of their traditional powers.

➡ Checks and balances ensure the sharing of power among separate institutions of government. Within the system of separated powers, the framers of the Constitution provided for legislative supremacy.

to overcome the separation of powers between the executive and legislative branches. Similarly, as we see below, federal officials often secure state cooperation with national programs by offering the states funding, called grants-in-aid, in exchange for their compliance. These programs help to overcome the limitations of federalism.

Unfortunately, having to convert needed measures into pork-barrel programs often dilutes or undermines their effectiveness. Take the federal government's effort to enhance the nation's level of readiness for terrorist attacks following September 2001. Under the terms of the 2001 USA PATRIOT Act, Congress appropriated billions of dollars to improve communications, police and fire protection, and intelligence collection at the state and local levels to avert future disasters.

Much of the money—some $40 billion—was not allocated to states and cities on the basis of some assessment of the threat they actually faced. Instead, Congress insisted that every state receive at least 0.75 percent of the funds appropriated during any given year in case terrorists adopted what some politicians dubbed the "heartland strategy," attacking obscure targets in rural and small-town America. Terrorists, of course, had no known interest in the heartland, but members of Congress from heartland states and districts certainly did.

Thus, cities like New York, Los Angeles, and Washington, D.C., which seemed likely to be the main targets for future terrorist attacks, never had enough money for needed preparedness and warning programs. Meanwhile, other localities throughout America that faced virtually no threat of terrorism were happy to receive federal funds for new fire trucks, radio equipment, and educational programs. For example, in 2011, Middleton, Rhode Island, a small city unlikely to attract international terrorists' attention, received $188,000 for fire equipment; in 2005, the 1,600 residents of the tiny hamlet of North Pole, Alaska, were awarded $500,000 in homeland security grants. Other homeland security dollars have gone to states and districts represented by powerful politicians. Nevada, for example, represented by Harry Reid, Senate majority leader from 2007 through 2014, has been a major recipient of homeland security dollars.

In 2011, facing mounting federal deficits, some members of Congress suggested eliminating the homeland security grant program. However, after much debate the program was retained, albeit at a somewhat lower level of funding. Billions of dollars in spending may not have made the nation much safer, but it may have helped enhance the safety of some congressional seats. In this instance, we may wonder if the institutions of federalism worked properly. Would a unitary central government have been better able to spend precious resources where they were needed most? If federalism and the separation of powers work most of the time, what explains the exceptions?

FEDERALISM

Federalism can be defined as the division of powers and functions between the national government and the state governments. As we saw in Chapter 2, the states were individual colonies before independence, and for nearly 13 years they were virtually autonomous units under the Articles of Confederation. In effect, the states had retained too much power relative to the national government, a problem that led directly to the Annapolis Convention in 1786 and the Constitutional Convention in 1787. Under the Articles, disorder within states was beyond the reach of the national government, and conflicts of interest between states were not manageable. For example, states were making their own trade agreements with foreign countries and companies, which might then play one state against another for special advantages. Some states adopted special trade tariffs and further barriers to foreign commerce that were contrary to the interests of another state.[2] Tax and other barriers were also being erected between the states.[3] But even after the ratification of the Constitution, the states continued to be more important than the national government. For nearly a century and a half, virtually all of the fundamental policies governing the lives of American citizens were made by the state legislatures, not by Congress.

Federalism in the Constitution

The United States was the first nation to adopt federalism as its governing framework. With federalism, the framers sought to limit the national government by creating a second layer of state governments. American federalism recognized two sovereigns in the original Constitution and reinforced the principle in the Bill of Rights by granting a few expressed powers to the national government and reserving all the rest to the states.

The Powers of the National Government. As we saw in Chapter 2, the expressed powers granted to the national government are found in Article I, Section 8, of the Constitution. These 17 powers include the power to collect taxes, to coin money, to declare war, and to regulate commerce (which became a very important power for the national government). Article I, Section 8, also contains another important source of power for the national government: the implied powers that enable Congress "to make all Laws which shall be necessary and proper for carrying into Execution the foregoing Powers." Not until several decades after the Founding did

federalism
The system of government in which a constitution divides power between a central government and regional governments

implied powers
Powers derived from the necessary and proper clause (Article I, Section 8) of the Constitution. Such powers are not specifically expressed but are implied through the expansive interpretation of delegated powers

the Supreme Court allow Congress to exercise the power granted in this necessary and proper clause, but, as we see later in this chapter, this doctrine allowed the national government to expand considerably the scope of its authority, although the process was a slow one. In addition to these expressed and implied powers, the Constitution affirmed the power of the national government in the supremacy clause (Article VI), which made all national laws and treaties "the supreme Law of the Land."

The Powers of State Governments. One way in which the framers sought to preserve a strong role for the states was through the Tenth Amendment to the Constitution. The Tenth Amendment states that the powers that the Constitution does not delegate to the national government or prohibit to the states are "reserved to the States respectively, or to the people." The Antifederalists, who feared that a strong central government would encroach on individual liberty, repeatedly pressed for such an amendment as a way of limiting national power. Federalists agreed to the amendment because they did not think it would do much harm, given the powers of the Constitution already granted to the national government. The Tenth Amendment is also called the reserved powers amendment because it aims to reserve powers to the states.

The most fundamental power that is retained by the states is that of coercion—the power to develop and enforce criminal codes, to administer health and safety rules, and to regulate the family via marriage and divorce laws. The states have the power to regulate individuals' livelihoods; if you're a doctor, lawyer, plumber, or a barber, you must be licensed by the state. Even more fundamental, the states have the power to define private property—private property exists because state laws against trespassing define who is and is not entitled to use a piece of property. If you own a car, your ownership isn't worth much unless the state is willing to enforce your right to possession by making it a crime for anyone else to take your car. Similarly, your "ownership" of a house or piece of land means that the state will enforce your possession by prohibiting others from occupying the property against your will. At the same time, however, under its power of eminent domain, the state may seize your property (and compensate you) for virtually anything it deems to be a public purpose.

A state's authority to regulate these fundamental matters is commonly referred to as the police power of the state and encompasses the state's power to regulate the health, safety, welfare, and morals of its citizens. Policing is what states do—they coerce you in the name of the community in order to maintain public order. And this was exactly the type of power that the Founders intended the states to exercise.

In some areas, the states share concurrent powers with the national government, whereby they retain and share some power to regulate commerce and to affect the currency—for example, by being able to charter banks,

reserved powers

Powers, derived from the Tenth Amendment to the Constitution, that are not specifically delegated to the national government or denied to the states; these powers are reserved to the states

eminent domain

The right of the government to take private property for public use, with reasonable compensation awarded for the property

concurrent powers

Authority possessed by both state and national governments, such as the power to levy taxes grant or deny corporate charters, and regulate the quality of products or the conditions of labor. This issue of concurrent versus exclusive power has come up from time to time in our history, but wherever there is a direct conflict of laws between the federal and the state levels, the issue will most likely be resolved in favor of national supremacy.

States' Obligations to One Another. The Constitution also creates obligations among the states. These obligations, spelled out in Article IV, were intended to promote national unity. By requiring the states to recognize actions and decisions taken in other states as legal and proper, the framers aimed to make the states less like independent countries and more like parts of a single nation. Article IV, Section 1, calls for "Full Faith and Credit" among states, meaning that each state is normally expected to honor the "public Acts, Records, and judicial Proceedings" that take place in any other state. So, for example, if a couple is married in Texas—marriage being regulated by state law—Missouri must also recognize that marriage, even though they were not married under Missouri state law.

This full faith and credit clause has recently become entangled in the controversy over same-sex marriage. In 35 states (as of November 2014) individuals of the same gender may marry. A number of other states, though, have passed "defense of marriage acts" that define marriage as a union only between a man and a woman. Eager to show its disapproval of same-sex marriage, Congress passed the federal Defense of Marriage Act (DOMA) in 1996, declaring that states will *not* have to recognize a same-sex marriage legally contracted in another state. DOMA also barred same-sex couples from receiving federal health, tax, social security, and other benefits available to heterosexual couples. In June 2013, the Supreme Court invalidated this section of the law, ruling that in states where same-sex marriage is legal, same-sex married couples are entitled to federal benefits.[4] The case was decided on equal protection grounds (to be discussed in Chapter 5). The ruling, however, is also likely to compel states to recognize same-sex marriages performed in other states.

Article IV, Section 2, known as the "comity clause," also seeks to promote national unity. It provides that citizens enjoying the privileges and immunities clause of one state should be entitled to similar treatment in other states. What this has come to mean is that a state cannot discriminate against someone from another state or give special privileges to its own residents. For example, in the 1970s, when Alaska passed a law that gave residents preference over nonresidents in obtaining work on the state's oil and gas pipelines, the Supreme Court ruled the law illegal because it discriminated against citizens of other states.[5] This clause also regulates criminal justice among the states by requiring states to return fugitives to the states from which they have fled. Thus, in 1952, when an inmate escaped from an Alabama prison and sought to avoid being returned to Alabama on the

full faith and credit clause

The provision in Article IV, Section 1, of the Constitution requiring that each state normally honors the public acts and judicial decisions that take place in another state

privileges and immunities clause

The provision from Article IV, Section 2, of the Constitution that a state cannot discriminate against someone from another state or give its own residents special privileges

The full faith and credit clause establishes that each state must honor the laws and judicial decisions of other states. Should same-sex marriages performed in one state be recognized in other states?

grounds that he was being subjected to "cruel and unusual punishment" there, the Supreme Court ruled that he must be returned according to Article IV, Section 2.[6] This example highlights the difference between the obligations among states and those different countries. In 1997, France refused to return an American fugitive because he might be subject to the death penalty, which does not exist in France.[7] The Constitution clearly forbids states to do something similar.

States' relationships to one another are also governed by the interstate compact clause (Article I, Section 10), which states that "No State shall, without the Consent of Congress . . . enter into any Agreement or Compact with another State." The Court has interpreted the clause to mean that states may enter into agreements with one another, subject to congressional approval. Compacts are a way for two or more states to reach a legally binding agreement about how to solve a problem that crosses state lines. In the early years of the Republic, states turned to compacts primarily to settle border disputes. Today they are used for a wide range of issues but are especially important in regulating the distribution of river water, addressing environmental concerns, and operating transportation systems that cross state lines.[8]

Local Government and the Constitution. Local government, including counties, cities, and towns, occupies a peculiar but very important place in the American system. In fact, the status of American local government is probably unique in world experience. First, it must be pointed out that local government has no status in the American Constitution. *State* legislatures created local governments, and *state* constitutions and laws permit local governments to take on some of the responsibilities of the state governments. Most states amended their own constitutions to give their larger cities home rule—a guarantee of noninterference in various areas of local affairs. But

home rule

The power delegated by the state to a local unit of government to manage its own affairs

Chapter 3: Federalism and the Separation of Powers

local governments enjoy no such recognition in the Constitution. Local governments have always been mere conveniences of the states.[9]

Local governments became administratively important in the early years of the Republic because the states possessed little administrative capability. They relied on local governments—cities and counties—to implement the laws of the state. Local government was an alternative to a statewide bureaucracy.

The Slow Growth of the National Government's Power

Before the 1930s, America's federal system was one of dual federalism, a two-layered system—national and state—in which the states and their local principalities did most of the governing. We refer to it as the traditional system precisely because almost nothing about our pattern of government changed during two-thirds of our history. That is, of course, with the exception of the four years of the Civil War, after which we returned to the traditional system.

But there was more to dual federalism than merely the existence of two tiers. The two tiers were functionally quite different from each other. There have been debates in every generation over how to divide responsibilities between the two tiers. As we have seen in this chapter, the Constitution delegated a list of specific powers to the national government and reserved all the rest to the states. That left a lot of room for interpretation, however, because of the final "elastic" clause of Article I, Section 8. The three formal words *necessary and proper* amounted to an invitation to struggle over the distribution of powers between national and state governments. We confront this struggle throughout the book. However, the most remarkable aspect of the history of American federalism is that federalism remained dual for nearly two-thirds of that history, with the national government remaining steadfastly within a "strict construction" of Article I, Section 8.

The Supreme Court has at times acted as arbiter in the debate over the distribution of powers between national and state governments. The first and most important case favoring national power was *McCulloch v. Maryland*.[10] The issue was whether Congress had the power to charter a bank, in particular the Bank of the United States (created by Congress in 1791 over Thomas Jefferson's constitutional opposition), because no power to create banks was found anywhere in Article I, Section 8. Chief Justice John Marshall, speaking for the Supreme Court, answered that such a power could be "implied" from the other powers in Article I, Section 8, specifically the commerce clause, plus the final clause enabling Congress "to make all Laws which shall be necessary and proper for carrying into Execution the foregoing Powers." Thus the Court created the potential for significant increases in national governmental power.

dual federalism
The system of government that prevailed in the United States from 1789 to 1937 in which most fundamental governmental powers were shared between the federal and state governments, with the states exercising the most important powers

A second question of national power also arose in *McCulloch v. Maryland*: the question of whether Maryland's attempt to tax the bank was constitutional. Once again Marshall and the Supreme Court took the side of the national government, arguing that a legislature representing all the people (Congress) could not be taxed out of business by a state legislature (Maryland) representing only a small portion of the American people. This opinion was accompanied by Marshall's immortal dictum that "the power to tax is the power to destroy." It was also in this case that the Supreme Court recognized and reinforced the supremacy clause: whenever a state law conflicts with a federal law, the state law should be deemed invalid because "the Laws of the United States . . . shall be the supreme Law of the Land." (The concept of federal supremacy was introduced in Chapter 2 and will come up again in Chapter 8.)

This nationalistic interpretation of the Constitution was reinforced by another major case, that of *Gibbons v. Ogden* in 1824. The important but relatively narrow issue was whether the state of New York could grant a monopoly to Robert Fulton's steamboat company to operate an exclusive service between New York and New Jersey. Aaron Ogden had secured his license from Fulton's company. Thomas Gibbons, a former partner of Ogden's, secured a competing license from the U.S. government. Chief Justice Marshall argued that Gibbons could not be kept from competing because the state of New York did not have the power to grant this particular monopoly. At issue was the commerce clause in Article 1, Section 8 of the Constitution, which delegates to Congress the power "to regulate Commerce with foreign nations, and *among the several States* and with Indian tribes" [emphasis added]. In his decision, Marshall insisted that the definition was "comprehensive" but added that the comprehensiveness was limited "to that commerce which concerns more states than one." This opinion gave rise to what later came to be called interstate commerce.[11]

commerce clause ▶

The clause found in Article I, Section 8, of the Constitution, which delegates to Congress the power "to regulate Commerce with foreign Nations, and among the several States and with the Indian Tribes." This clause was interpreted by the Supreme Court to favor national power over the economy

Despite the Supreme Court's expansive reading of national power in the early years of the Republic, between the 1820s and the 1930s federal power grew slowly if at all. During the Jacksonian period, a states' rights coalition developed in the Congress. Among the most important members of this coalition were state party leaders who often had themselves appointed to the Senate where they jealously guarded the powers of the states they ruled. Of course, the senators and members of the House from the southern states had a particular reason to support states' rights. So long as the states were powerful and the federal government weak, the South's "peculiar institution" of slavery could not be threatened.

Aside from the interruption of the Civil War, the states' rights coalition dominated Congress, affected presidential nominations—a matter also controlled by the state party leaders—and influenced judicial appointments, which required senatorial acquiescence, as well. Indeed, the Supreme Court turned sharply away from the nationalistic jurisprudence of John Marshall in favor of a states' rights interpretation of the Constitution. One area in which this interpretation was particularly noticeable was in cases concerning the commerce clause. For many years, any effort by the federal government to regulate commerce in such areas as fraud, the production of impure goods, the use of child labor, or the existence of dangerous working conditions or long hours was declared unconstitutional by the Supreme Court during this period as a violation of the concept of interstate commerce. Regulation in these areas would mean the federal government was entering the factory and the workplace, areas inherently local because the goods produced there had not yet passed into commerce and crossed state lines. Rather, the Court held that regulation of these areas constituted police power, a power reserved to the states. No one questioned the power of the national government to regulate certain kinds of businesses, such as railroads, gas pipelines, and waterway transportation, because they intrinsically involved interstate commerce.[12] But well into the twentieth century, most other efforts by Congress to regulate commerce were blocked by the Supreme Court's interpretation of federalism, with the concept of interstate commerce as the primary barrier.

For example, in the 1918 case of *Hammer v. Dagenhart*, the Supreme Court struck down a statute prohibiting the interstate shipment of goods manufactured with the use of child labor. Congress had been careful to avoid outlawing the production of such goods that took place within states and only prohibited their interstate shipment. The Court, however, declared that the intent of Congress had been to outlaw the manufacture of the products in question and declared that the statutory language was merely a ruse.[13]

After his election in 1932, President Franklin Delano Roosevelt was eager to expand the power of the national government. His "New Deal" depended on governmental power to regulate the economy and to intervene in every facet of American society. Roosevelt's efforts provoked sharp conflicts between the president and the federal judiciary. After making a host of new judicial appointments and threatening to expand the size of the Supreme Court, Roosevelt was able to bend the judiciary to his will. Beginning in the late 1930s, the Supreme Court issued a series of decisions converting the commerce clause from a barrier to a source of national power.

Among the most important of these cases was *National Labor Relations Board v. Jones & Loughlin Steel Company*.[14] At issue was the National Labor Relations Act, known as the Wagner Act, which prohibited corporations from interfering with the efforts of employees to organize into unions, to bargain collectively over wages and working conditions, and to go on strike and engage in picketing. The newly formed National Labor Relations Board (NLRB) had ordered Jones & Loughlin to reinstate workers fired because of their union activities. The appeal reached the Supreme Court because the steel company had made a constitutional issue over the fact

The past 80 years—since Franklin Delano Roosevelt's New Deal—have seen an increase in national government power. Today, some Americans question whether the balance has shifted too far toward federal power.

that its manufacturing activities were local and therefore beyond the government's reach. The Supreme Court rejected this argument, declaring that a large corporation with subsidiaries and suppliers in many states was inherently involved in interstate commerce and hence subject to congressional regulation. In other decisions, the Court upheld minimum wage laws, the Social Security Act and, in the case of *Wickard v. Filburn*, federal rules controlling how much of any given commodity local farmers might grow.[15]

Cooperative Federalism and Grants-in-Aid

cooperative federalism

A type of federalism existing since the New Deal era in which grants-in-aid have been used strategically to encourage states and localities (without commanding them) to pursue nationally defined goals. Also known as intergovernmental cooperation

Roosevelt was able to overcome judicial resistance to expansive New Deal programs. Congress, however, forced him to recognize the continuing importance of the states by crafting a number of programs in such a way as to encourage the states to pursue nationally set goals while leaving them some leeway to administer programs according to local values and needs. If the traditional system of two sovereigns performing highly different functions could be called dual federalism, the system that prevailed after the 1930s could be called cooperative federalism, which generally refers to supportive relations, sometimes partnerships, between national government and the state and local governments. It comes in the form of federal subsidization of special state and local activities; these subsidies are called grants-in-aid. But make no mistake about it: although many of these state and local programs would not exist without the federal grant-in-aid, the grant-in-aid is also an important form of federal influence. (Another form of federal influence, the mandate, will be covered in the next section.)

grants-in-aid

A general term for funds given by Congress to state and local governments

A grant-in-aid is really a kind of bribe or "carrot"—Congress gives money to state and local governments but with the condition that the money will be spent for a particular purpose as designed by Congress. Congress uses grants-in-aid because it does not usually have the direct political or constitutional power to command the cities to do its bidding.

categorical grants-in-aid

Funds given by Congress to states and localities that are earmarked by law for specific categories, such as education or crime prevention

This same approach was applied to cities beginning in the late 1930s. Congress set national goals such as public housing and assistance to the unemployed and provided grants-in-aid to meet these goals. The value of these categorical grants-in-aid increased from $2.3 billion in 1950 to almost $550 billion in 2013 (Figure 3.1). Sometimes Congress requires the state or local government to match the national contribution dollar for dollar; but

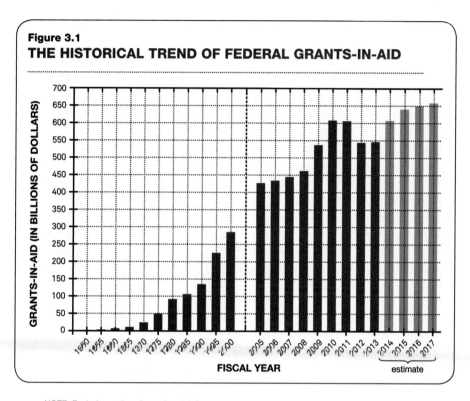

Figure 3.1

THE HISTORICAL TREND OF FEDERAL GRANTS-IN-AID

GRANTS-IN-AID (IN BILLIONS OF DOLLARS)

FISCAL YEAR

estimate

NOTE: Excludes outlays for national defense, international affairs, and net interest.

SOURCE: Office of Management and Budget, *Budget of the U.S. Government, Fiscal Year 2013*, www.whitehouse.gov/omb/budget/historicals (accessed 10/4/12).

for some programs, such as the interstate highway system, the congressional grant-in-aid provides 90 percent of the cost of the program.

For the most part, the categorical grants created before the 1960s simply helped the states perform their traditional functions.[16] In the 1960s, however, the national role expanded and the number of categorical grants increased dramatically. For example, during the 89th Congress (1965–66) alone, the number of categorical grant-in-aid programs grew from 221 to 379.[17] The grants authorized during the 1960s announced national purposes much more strongly than did earlier grants. Central to that national purpose was the need to provide opportunities to the poor.

Many of the categorical grants enacted during the 1960s were project grants, which require state and local governments to submit proposals to federal agencies. In contrast to the older formula grants, which used a formula (composed of such elements as need and state and local capacities) to distribute funds, the new project grants made funding available on a competitive basis. Federal agencies would give grants to the proposals they judged to be the best. In this way, the national government acquired substantial control

project grants

Grant programs in which state and local governments submit proposals to federal agencies and for which funding is provided on a competitive basis

formula grants

Grants-in-aid in which a formula is used to determine the amount of federal funds a state or local government will receive over which state and local governments got money, how much they got, and how they spent it.

The most important scholar of the history of federalism, Morton Grodzins, characterized this as a move from "layer cake federalism" to "marble cake federalism," in which intergovernmental cooperation and sharing have blurred the line between where the national government ends and the state and local governments begin.[18] Figure 3.2 demonstrates the basis of the marble-cake idea. At the high point of grant-in-aid policies in the late 1970s, federal aid contributed about 25–30 percent of the operating budgets of all the state and local governments in the country (Figure 3.3). In 2010, federal aid accounted for more than 35 percent of state and local budgets. This increase was temporary, resulting from the Obama administration's $787 billion stimulus package designed to help state and local governments weather the 2008–10 recession. Briefly, however, federal aid became the single largest source of state revenue, exceeding sales and property tax revenues for the first time in U.S. history.

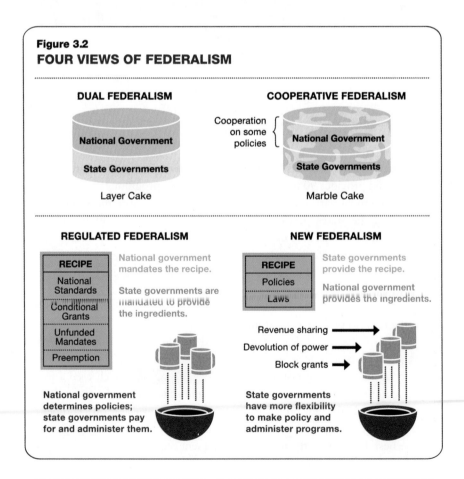

Figure 3.2
FOUR VIEWS OF FEDERALISM

DUAL FEDERALISM

National Government

State Governments

Layer Cake

Cooperation on some policies

COOPERATIVE FEDERALISM

National Government

State Governments

Marble Cake

REGULATED FEDERALISM

RECIPE
National Standards
Conditional Grants
Unfunded Mandates
Preemption

National government mandates the recipe.

State governments are mandated to provide the ingredients.

National government determines policies; state governments pay for and administer them.

NEW FEDERALISM

RECIPE
Policies
Laws

State governments provide the recipe.

National government provides the ingredients.

Revenue sharing →
Devolution of power →
Block grants →

State governments have more flexibility to make policy and administer programs.

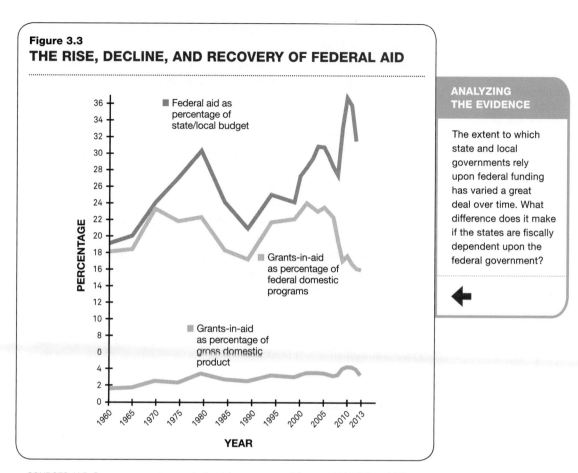

Figure 3.3

THE RISE, DECLINE, AND RECOVERY OF FEDERAL AID

- Federal aid as percentage of state/local budget
- Grants-in-aid as percentage of federal domestic programs
- Grants-in-aid as percentage of gross domestic product

PERCENTAGE (y-axis): 0, 2, 4, 6, 8, 0, 10, 12, 14, 16, 18, 20, 22, 24, 26, 28, 30, 32, 34, 36

YEAR (x-axis): 1960, 1965, 1970, 1975, 1980, 1985, 1990, 1995, 2000, 2005, 2010, 2013

ANALYZING THE EVIDENCE

The extent to which state and local governments rely upon federal funding has varied a great deal over time. What difference does it make if the states are fiscally dependent upon the federal government?

Regulated Federalism and National Standards. Developments from the 1960s to the present have moved well beyond marble-cake federalism to what might be called regulated federalism. [19] In some areas, the national government actually regulates the states by threatening to withhold grant money unless state and local governments conform to national standards. The most notable instances of this regulation are in the areas of civil rights, poverty programs, and environmental protection. In these instances, the national government provides grant-in-aid financing but sets conditions the states must meet in order to keep the grants. The national government refers to these policies as "setting national standards." Important cases of such efforts are in interstate highway use, social services, and education. The net effect of these national standards is that state and local policies are more uniform from coast to coast. However, in a number of other programs the national government engages in regulated federalism by imposing obligations

regulated federalism

A form of federalism in which Congress imposes legislation on the states and localities requiring them to meet national standards

unfunded mandates

National standards or programs imposed on state and local governments by the federal government without accompanying funding or reimbursement

on the states *without providing any funding at all.* These have come to be called unfunded mandates.[20]

These burdens became a major part of the rallying cry that produced the famous Republican Congress elected in 1994, with its Contract with America. One of the first measures adopted by the 104th Republican Congress was an act to limit unfunded mandates—the Unfunded Mandates Reform Act (UMRA). This was considered a triumph of lobbying efforts by state and local governments, and it was "hailed as both symbol and substance of a renewed congressional commitment to federalism."[21] Under this law, a point of order raised on the House or Senate floor can stop any mandate with an uncompensated state and local cost estimated at greater than $50 million a year as determined by the Congressional Budget Office (CBO). This was called a "stop, look, and listen" requirement, forcing Congress to take positive action to own up to the mandate and its potential costs. During 1996, its first full year of operation, only 11 bills included mandates that exceeded the $50 million threshold—from a total of 69 estimates of actions in which mandates were included. Examples included minimum wage increase, parity for mental health and health insurance, mandated use of Social Security numbers on drivers' licenses, and extension of Federal Occupational Safety and Health Administration standards to state and local employees. Most of them were modified in the House to reduce their costs. However, as one expert put it, "The primary impact of UMRA came not from the affirmative blockage of [mandate] legislation, but rather from its effect as a deterrent to mandates in the drafting and early consideration of legislation."[22]

As indicated by the first year of its operation, the effect of UMRA is not revolutionary. UMRA does not prevent congressional members from passing unfunded mandates; it only makes them think twice before they do. Moreover, UMRA exempts several areas from coverage. And states must still enforce antidiscrimination laws and meet other requirements to receive federal assistance. But on the other hand, UMRA is a serious effort to shift power in the national–state relationship a bit further toward the state side.

"New Federalism" and the National–State Tug of War. Presidents Nixon and Reagan called their efforts to reverse the trend toward national standards the new federalism. They helped craft policies to return more discretion to the states. Examples of these policies include Nixon's revenue sharing and Reagan's block grants, which consolidated a number of categorical grants into one larger category, leaving the state (or local) government more discretion to decide how to use the money.

President Barack Obama, on the other hand, seemed to believe firmly in regulated federalism. In 2009, Obama proposed a record-shattering $3 trillion national budget that included hundreds of millions of dollars in grants

block grants

Federal funds given to state governments to pay for goods, services, or programs, with relatively few restrictions on how the funds may be spent to the states for public works and infrastructural improvements as part of his plan to stimulate the nation's faltering economy. Obama told the state governors that he would be watching to see that they spent the money wisely and in a manner consistent with the federal government's purposes. Once again, the national government seemed to view the states as administrative arms more than independent laboratories.

This same idea seemed manifest in the Obama administration's new health care reform law. Under the law, every state is required to establish an insurance exchange where individuals in need of health insurance could shop for the best rate. The law also required states to expand their Medicaid programs, adding as many as 15 million Americans to the Medicaid rolls. Several states were concerned that the costs of the new program would fall on their strained budgets and 12 state attorneys general brought suit, charging that the program's mandates violate the Tenth Amendment. Following conflicting rulings in the lower federal courts, the Supreme Court heard the case in 2012 and upheld major provisions of the legislation, although the Court ruled that the federal government cannot require that Medicaid rolls be expanded. As of November 2014, 27 states had decided to expand their rolls. The Analyzing the Evidence unit for this chapter explores the states' approaches to setting Medicaid eligibility.

The Supreme Court as Referee. For much of the nineteenth century, federal power remained limited. The Tenth Amendment was used to bolster arguments about states' rights, which in their extreme version claimed that the states did not have to submit to national laws when they believed the national government had exceeded its authority. These arguments in favor of states' rights were voiced less often after the Civil War. But the Supreme Court continued to use the Tenth Amendment to strike down laws that it thought exceeded national power, including the Civil Rights Act passed in 1875.

In the early twentieth century, however, the Tenth Amendment appeared to lose its force. Reformers began to press for national regulations to limit the power of large corporations and to preserve the health and welfare of citizens. The Supreme Court approved of some of these laws, but it struck others down, including a law combating child labor. The Court stated that the law violated the Tenth Amendment because only states should have the power to regulate conditions of employment. By the late 1930s, however, the Supreme Court had approved such an expansion of federal power that the Tenth Amendment appeared irrelevant. In fact, in 1941, Justice Harlan Fiske Stone declared that the Tenth Amendment was simply a "truism," that it had no real meaning.[23]

Recent years have seen a revival of interest in the Tenth Amendment and important Supreme Court decisions limiting federal power. Much of the interest in the Tenth Amendment stems from conservatives who believe that a strong federal government encroaches on individual liberties and so

states' rights
The principle that states should oppose increasing authority of the national government. This view was most popular before the Civil War

Health Care Policy and the States

Contributed by
Jenna Bednar
University of Michigan

Responsibility for health care policy and poverty relief is entangled in the 2010 Patient Protection and Affordable Care Act (ACA), an attempt by Congress to standardize access to health care nationally, as well as to contain costs. The primary federalism question in the ACA is what level of government, state or federal, should set Medicaid eligibility criteria. Medicaid is a program to provide health care coverage to the poor and is jointly financed by the federal and state governments. The states set Medicaid eligibility requirements, prescribing an income threshold above which a resident is ineligible to receive Medicaid-funded benefits. States set widely varying thresholds for Medicaid eligibility. The ACA addresses that variation by prescribing a federal minimum income threshold

The first map below shows the 2013 Medicaid eligibility thresholds for working parents of Medicaid-eligible children. (In almost all states, limited-income adults without dependent children are not eligible for Medicaid benefits.) The thresholds are expressed as a percentage of the federal poverty level (FPL), which in 2013 was $23,550 for a family of four. A Minnesota family could earn up to $50,633 (215% of FPL) and the parents would still qualify for Medicaid benefits, while the same family living in Texas would be ineligible if they earned more than $5,888 (25% of FPL). The second map shows the percentage of limited-income adults who lacked health insurance in each state in 2011.

Medicaid Eligibility Thresholds and Percentage Uninsured*

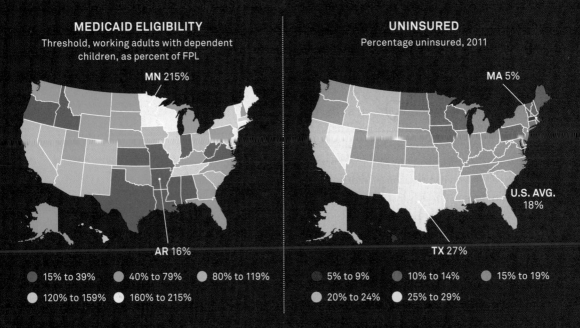

MEDICAID ELIGIBILITY
Threshold, working adults with dependent children, as percent of FPL

MN 215%

AR 16%

- 15% to 39%
- 40% to 79%
- 80% to 119%
- 120% to 159%
- 160% to 215%

UNINSURED
Percentage uninsured, 2011

MA 5%

U.S. AVG. 18%

TX 27%

- 5% to 9%
- 10% to 14%
- 15% to 19%
- 20% to 24%
- 25% to 29%

Rules as of January 1, 2013; FPL criteria from 2013

When public policy is decentralized in a federal system, not only can states set policy according to their own preferences and capacity, as demonstrated by the variation in Medicaid eligibility, but states may innovate to improve policy. For example, in 2006 Massachusetts enacted a law that required residents to obtain insurance but subsidized or offered free coverage for the poor. In the graph below, we see the proportion of the non-elderly Massachusetts adult population without health insurance compared with the proportion of non-elderly adults without health insurance nationwide. Although Massachusetts already had a far lower rate of uninsured than the national average, the introduction of health policy reform further reduced the percentage of uninsured at a time when the national average was increasing.

The ACA is modeled on the Massachusetts plan. Two aspects have been politically controversial: the requirement that all individuals obtain insurance and the standardization of Medicaid eligibility to 133% of FPL, or $31,322 for a family of four (2013). If states comply with the ACA prescription, access to Medicaid benefits will expand considerably, including extending coverage to all limited-income adults regardless of whether they have dependent children, a population that currently lacks access to Medicaid. However, it does so by centralizing authority, reducing the states' control over health care policy and poverty relief.

Although the federal government will pay the lion's share of the costs of the expanded Medicare coverage through at least 2020, many states were unhappy with the dictum from the central government, and 26 states joined lawsuits to challenge Congress's authority. In 2012 the Supreme Court ruled that states cannot be required to conform their Medicaid eligibility thresholds to the national minimum. As of August 2014, 21 states have indicated that they will not raise their Medicaid eligibility thresholds to meet the ACA minimum. Ultimately, the fate of health care responsibility will rest with the American public, as they grow to accept or reject the arguments made on both sides.[1]

Percentage of Population without Health Insurance**

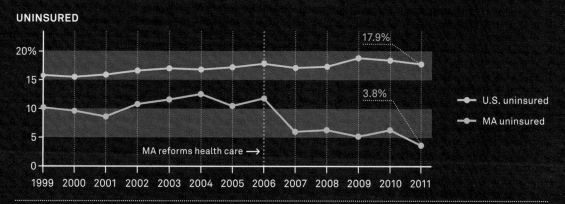

UNINSURED

1 Data and analysis for this unit are from the following sources: 2013 FPL data from the U.S. Department of Health and Human Services, Federal Register Volume 77, Number 57 (Friday, March 23, 2012); *National Federation of Independent Business v. Sebelius,* 567 U.S. ___ (2012); Kaiser Family Foundation, "Status of State Action on the Medicaid Expansion Decision, as of June 20, 2013," http://kff.org/medicaid/state-indicator/state-activity-around-expanding-medicaid-under-the-affordable-care-act/; as well as legislative analysis by the author.

* SOURCE: Kaiser Family Foundation, "Adult Income Eligibility Limits at Application as a Percent of the Federal Poverty Level (FPL)." January 2013, http://kff.org/medicaid/state-indicator/income-eligibility-low-income-adults/; and "Health Insurance Coverage of the Non-Elderly 0-64," http://kff.org/other/state-indicator/nonelderly-0-64/#.

** SOURCE: Compiled from U.S. Census Bureau, Current Population Survey, 2012 Annual Social and Economic Supplement, Health Insurance, Table HI05 (2011, 2010), Table HI A-6.

IN BRIEF

Evolution of the Federal System

1789–1834	**Nationalization:** the Marshall Court interprets the Constitution broadly so as to expand and consolidate national power.
1835–1930s	**Dual federalism:** the functions of the national government are very specifically enumerated. States do much of the fundamental governing that affects citizens' day-to-day life. There is tension between the two levels of government, and the power of the national government begins to increase.
1930s–70s	**Cooperative federalism:** the national government uses grants-in-aid to encourage states and localities to pursue nationally defined goals.
1970s–	**Regulated federalism:** the national government sets conditions that states and localities must meet in order to keep certain grants. The national government also sets national standards in areas without providing funding to meet them.
	New federalism: the national government attempts to return more power to the states through block grants to the states.

state sovereign immunity

A legal doctrine holding that states cannot be sued for violating an act of Congress

power should be returned to the states through the process of devolution. In 1996, the Republican presidential candidate Bob Dole carried a copy of the Tenth Amendment with him to read at rallies.[24] Around the same time, the Court revived the Eleventh Amendment concept of state sovereign immunity. This legal doctrine holds that states are immune from lawsuits by private persons or groups claiming that the state violated a statute enacted by Congress.

The Supreme Court's ruling in *United States v. Lopez* in 1995 fueled further interest in the Tenth Amendment. In that case, the Court, stating that Congress had exceeded its authority under the commerce clause, struck down a federal law that barred handguns near schools.[25] This was the first time since the New Deal that the Court had limited congressional powers in this way. (The New Deal is discussed in Chapter 6.) The Court further limited the power of the federal government over the states in a 1996 ruling based on the Eleventh Amendment that prevented Native Americans from the Seminole tribe from suing the state of Florida in federal court. A 1988 law had given Indian tribes the right to sue a state in federal court if the state did not negotiate in good faith over issues related to gambling casinos on tribal land. The Supreme Court's ruling appeared to signal a much broader limitation on national power by raising new questions about whether individuals can sue a state if it fails to uphold federal law.[26]

Another significant decision involving the relationship between the federal government and state governments was the 1997 case *Printz v. United States* (joined with *Mack v. United States*),[27] in which the Court struck down a key provision of the Brady Bill, enacted by Congress in 1993 to regulate gun sales. Under the terms of the act, state and local law enforcement officers were required to conduct background checks on prospective gun purchasers. The Court held that the federal government cannot require states to administer or enforce federal regulatory programs. This trend continued with the 2006 *Gonzales v. Oregon* case, in which the Court ruled that the federal government could not use federal drug laws to interfere with Oregon's assisted-suicide law.[28] These rulings signaled a move toward greater latitude for the states. In 2012, however, the Court gave indication that it would once again underline the importance of national power in the nation-state tug-of-war. In addition to the Affordable Care Act decision cited earlier, the Supreme Court struck down portions of an Arizona immigration law, declaring that immigration was a federal, not a state, matter.[29] And in its 2013 decision in the case of *Arizona v. Inter Tribal Council of Arizona, Inc.,* the Supreme Court struck down an Arizona law requiring individuals to show documentation of citizenship when registering to vote. The Court ruled that this requirement was preempted by the federal National Voter Registration Act requiring states to use the official federal voter registration form.[30]

THE SEPARATION OF POWERS

As we noted at the beginning of this chapter, the separation of powers gives several different federal institutions the ability to influence the nation's agenda, to affect decisions, and to prevent the other institutions from taking action—dividing agenda, decision, and veto power. This arrangement may be cumbersome, but the Constitution's framers saw it as an essential means of protecting liberty.

In his discussion of the separation of powers, James Madison quoted the originator of the idea, the French political thinker Baron de Montesquieu: "There can be no liberty where the legislative and executive powers are united in the same person . . . [or] if the power of judging be not separated from the legislative and executive powers."[31] Using this same reasoning, many of Madison's contemporaries argued that there was not *enough* separation among the three

The system of checks and balances ensures that political power is shared by the separate institutions. Here, President Obama meets with House Speaker John Boehner.

branches, and Madison had to backtrack to insist that complete separation was not required:

> Unless these departments [branches] be so far connected and blended as to give to each a constitutional control over the others, the degree of separation which the maxim requires, as essential to a free government, can never in practice be duly maintained.[32]

This is the secret of how Americans have made the separation of powers effective: they have made it self-enforcing by giving each branch of government the means to participate in, and partially or temporarily obstruct, the workings of the other branches.

Checks and Balances

The means by which each branch of government interacts with every other branch is known informally as checks and balances. The best-known examples are shown in Figure 3.4. The framers sought to guarantee that the three branches would in fact use these checks and balances as weapons against one another by giving each branch a different political constituency and therefore a different perspective on what the government ought to do: direct, popular election for the members of the House; indirect election of senators (until the Seventeenth Amendment, adopted in 1913); indirect election of the president through the electoral college; and appointment of federal judges for life. All things considered, the best characterization of the separation of powers principle in action is "separated institutions sharing power."[33]

Legislative Supremacy

legislative supremacy

The preeminent position assigned to Congress by the Constitution

Although each branch was to be given adequate means to compete with the other branches, it is also clear that within the system of separated powers the framers provided for legislative supremacy by making Congress the preeminent branch. Legislative supremacy made the provision of checks and balances in the other two branches all the more important.

The most important indication of the intentions of the framers was the provisions in Article I to treat the powers of the national government as powers of Congress. The Founders also provided for legislative supremacy in their decision to give Congress the sole power over appropriations.

Figure 3.4
CHECKS AND BALANCES

LEGISLATIVE

EXECUTIVE OVER LEGISLATIVE

President can veto acts of Congress

President can call a special session of Congress

President carries out, and thereby interprets, laws passed by Congress

Vice president casts tiebreaking vote in the Senate

JUDICIAL OVER LEGISLATIVE

Court can declare laws unconstitutional

Chief justice presides over Senate during hearing to impeach the president

LEGISLATIVE OVER EXECUTIVE

Congress can override presidential veto

Congress can impeach and remove president

Senate can reject president's appointments and refuse to ratify treaties

Congress can conduct investigations into president's actions

Congress can refuse to pass laws or provide funding that president requests

LEGISLATIVE OVER JUDICIAL

Congress can change size of federal court system and number of Supreme Court justices

Congress can propose constitutional amendments

Congress can reject Supreme Court nominees

Congress can impeach and remove federal judges

Congress can amend court jurisdictions

Congress controls appropriations

JUDICIAL OVER EXECUTIVE

Court can declare executive actions unconstitutional

Court has the power to issue warrants

Chief justice presides over impeachment of president

EXECUTIVE OVER JUDICIAL

President nominates Supreme Court justices

President nominates federal judges

President can pardon those convicted in federal court

President can refuse to enforce the courts' decisions

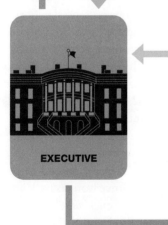

EXECUTIVE

JUDICIAL

Although "presidential government" gradually supplanted legislative supremacy after 1937, the relative power of the executive and legislative branches has varied. The power play between the president and Congress is especially intense during periods of divided government, when one party controls the White House and another controls Capitol Hill, as has been the case almost continuously since 1969.

The Role of the Supreme Court

The role of the judicial branch in the separation of powers has depended on the power of judicial review, a power not provided for in the Constitution but asserted by Chief Justice Marshall in 1803:

> If a law be in opposition to the Constitution; if both the law and the Constitution apply to a particular case, so that the Court must either decide that case conformable to the law, disregarding the Constitution, or conformable to the Constitution, disregarding the law; the Court must determine which of these conflicting rules governs the case: This is of the very essence of judicial duty.[34]

Review of the constitutionality of acts of the president or Congress is relatively rare. For example, there were no Supreme Court reviews of congressional acts in the 50-plus years between *Marbury v. Madison* (1803) and *Dred Scott v. Sandford* (1857). In the century or so between the Civil War and 1970, 84 acts of Congress were held unconstitutional (in whole or in part), but there were long periods of complete Supreme Court deference to Congress, punctuated by flurries of judicial review during periods of social upheaval. The most significant of these was 1935–36, when 12 acts of Congress were invalidated, blocking virtually the entire New Deal program.[35] Then, after 1937, when the Court made its great reversals, no significant acts were voided until 1983, when the Court declared the legislative veto unconstitutional.[36] The Supreme Court became much more activist (that is, less deferential to Congress) after the elevation of Justice William H. Rehnquist to chief justice (1986–2005), and "a new program of judicial activism"[37] seemed to be in place. Between 1995 and 2002, at least 26 acts or parts of acts of Congress were struck down on constitutional grounds.[38]

The Court has been far more deferential toward the president since the New Deal period, with only five significant confrontations. One was the so-called steel seizure case of 1952, in which the Court refused to permit President Truman to use "emergency powers" to force workers back into the steel mills during the Korean War.[39] A second case was *United States v. Nixon*, in which the Court declared unconstitutional President Nixon's refusal to respond to a subpoena to make available the infamous White House tapes as evidence in a criminal prosecution. The Court argued that although executive privilege did protect confidentiality of communications to and from the president, this did not extend to data in presidential files or tapes bearing on criminal prosecutions.[40] During the heat of the scandal over President Clinton's relationship with the intern Monica Lewinsky, the Supreme Court rejected the claim that the pressures and obligations of the office of president were so demanding that all litigation "but the most exceptional cases" should be deferred until his term ended.[41] The Supreme Court also struck down the Line-Item Veto Act of 1996, which would have allowed the president to veto certain portions of bills while accepting others, on the grounds that it violated Article I, Section 7, which prescribed procedures for congressional enactment and presidential acceptance or veto of statutes. Any such change in the procedures of adopting laws would have to be made by amendment to the Constitution, not by legislation.[42] More recently, and of far greater importance, the Supreme Court repudiated the Bush administration's claims about the president's authority to detain enemy combatants without giving detainees an opportunity to defend themselves in an open court.[43]

executive privilege
The claim that confidential communications between a president and the president's close advisors should not be revealed without the consent of the president

DO FEDERALISM AND THE SEPARATION OF POWERS WORK?

Federalism and the separation of powers are two of the most important constitutional principles upon which the United States' system of limited government is based. As we have seen, federalism limits the power of the national government in numerous ways. By its very existence, federalism recognizes the principle of two sovereigns, the national government and the state governments (hence the term *dual federalism*). In addition, the Constitution specifically restrained the power of the national government to regulate the economy. As a result, the states were free to do most of the fundamental governing for the first century and a half of American government. This began to change during and following the New Deal, as the national government began to exert more influence over the states through grants-in-aid and mandates. But even as the powers of the national government grew, so did the powers of the states. In recent decades, we have noticed a countertrend to the growth of national power as Congress has opted to devolve some of its powers to the states.

But the problem that arises with devolution is that programs that were once uniform across the country (because they were the national government's responsibility) can become highly variable, with some states providing benefits not available in other states. To a point, variation can be considered one of the virtues of federalism. But dangers are inherent in

From 1974–87, the federal government set a national maximum speed limit at 55 miles per hour, to help conserve fuel following the oil shortage of the 1970s. Since 1995, the states are free to set their own limits, and in some areas of Texas the speed limit is as high as 85 miles per hour.

large variations and inequalities in the provision of services and benefits in a democracy. For example, the Food and Drug Administration has been under attack in recent years. Could the government address the agency's perceived problems by devolving its regulatory tasks to the states? Would people care if drugs would require "caution" labels in some states but not in others? Devolution, as attractive as it may be, is not an approach that can be applied across the board without analyzing carefully the nature of the program and of the problems it is designed to solve.

A key puzzle of federalism is deciding when differences across states reflect the proper democratic decisions of the states and when such differences reflect inequalities that should not be tolerated. Sometimes a decision to eliminate differences is made on the grounds of equality and individual rights, as in the Civil Rights Act of 1964, which outlawed segregation. At other times, a stronger federal role is justified on the grounds of national interest, as in the case of the oil shortage and the institution of a 55-mile-per-hour speed limit in the 1970s (which improves fuel efficiency). Advocates of a more limited federal role often point to the value of democracy. Public actions can more easily be tailored to fit distinctive local or state desires if states and localities have more power to make policy. Viewed this way, variation across states can be an expression of democratic will.

The second feature of limited government, separation of powers, is manifested in our system of checks and balances, whereby separate institutions of government share power with each other. Even though the Constitution clearly provided for legislative supremacy, checks and balances have functioned well. Some would say this system has worked too well. The last 50 years have witnessed long periods of divided government, when one party controls the White House, while the other party controls Congress. During these periods, the level of conflict between the executive and legislative branches has been particularly divisive, resulting in what some analysts derisively call gridlock.[44]

During President George W. Bush's first six years in office, the separation of powers did not seem to work effectively. Congress gave Bush a free rein in such important matters as the war in Iraq and the war against terrorism. Of course during this period, Congress was controlled by the president's fellow Republicans. In 2006, Democrats won control of both houses and promised to scrutinize the president's actions carefully. With the election of the Democrat Barack Obama to the presidency in 2008, Congress and the presidency were once again controlled by the same party, but in 2010 Republicans took control of the House of Representatives and challenged the president's domestic and foreign policies. At times, the stalemate between Congress and the president became so severe that the government was virtually paralyzed. Then, in November 2014, the Republican Party won control of the Senate while retaining control of the House. This victory seemed to put Republicans in a more favorable position in their contest with the executive.

For Further Reading

Selections highlighted in red are included in *Readings in American Politics: Analysis and Perspectives*, Third Edition.

Bednar, Jenna. *The Robust Federation.* New York: Cambridge University Press, 2008.

Campbell, Tom. *Separation of Powers in Practice.* Palo Alto, CA: Stanford University Press, 2004.

Ferejohn, John A., and Barry R. Weingast, eds. *The New Federalism: Can the States Be Trusted?* Stanford, CA: Hoover Institution Press, 1997.

Fisher, Louis. *Constitutional Conflicts between Congress and the President.* 5th ed., revised. Lawrence: University Press of Kansas, 2007.

LaCroix, Alison L. *The Ideological Origins of American Federalism.* Cambridge, MA: Harvard University Press, 2010.

Noonan, John T. *Narrowing the Nation's Power: The Supreme Court Sides with the States.* Berkeley: University of California Press, 2002.

Riker, William H. *Federalism: Origin, Operation, Significance.* Boston: Little, Brown, 1964.

Robertson, David. *Federalism and the Making of America.* New York: Routledge, 2011.

Samuels, David, and Matthew Shugart, *Presidents, Parties and Prime Ministers: How the Separation of Powers Affects Party Organization and Behavior.* New York: Cambridge University Press, 2010.

Van Horn, Carol E. *The State of the States.* 4th ed. Washington, DC: CQ Press, 2004.

4

Civil Liberties and Civil Rights

The first 10 amendments of the U.S. Constitution, together called the Bill of Rights, are the basis for the freedoms we enjoy as American citizens. The Bill of Rights might well have been entitled the "Bill of Liberties," because the provisions that were incorporated in the Bill of Rights were seen as defining a private sphere of personal liberty, free of governmental restrictions. These freedoms include the right to free speech, the right to the free exercise of religion, prohibitions against unreasonable searches and seizures, and guarantees of due process of law.

As Jefferson had put it, a bill of rights "is what people are entitled to against every government on earth   ." Civil liberties are protections from improper government action. Thus, as we will see in the first sections of this chapter, the Bill of Rights is a series of restraints imposed on government.

Whereas civil liberties are phrased as negatives (what government cannot do), civil rights are obligations (what government must do) to guarantee equal citizenship and protect citizens from discrimination. Civil rights regulate *who* can participate in the political process and civil society and *how* they can participate. They determine such things as who can vote, who can serve in office, who can have a trial or serve on juries, and when and how

civil liberties

The protections of citizens from improper governmental action

civil rights

The legal or moral claims that citizens are entitled to make on the government we can petition the government to take action. Civil rights also define how people are treated in employment, education, and other aspects of American society.

In some nations, citizens have few, if any, civil rights. They have no right to vote, no right to stand for office, and no right to be judged by their peers if accused of a crime. America, on the other hand, began life as a nation with a number of civil rights guaranteed in both federal and state constitutions. The federal Constitution provided such rights as representation in Congress (Article I, Section 2), established who can serve in Congress and become president, and guaranteed the privilege of *habeas corpus* for all people (Article I, Section 9). The Bill of Rights, in addition to defining the major civil liberties, also provides for important civil rights, such as the right of all persons to due process of law, guaranteed in the Fifth Amendment.

Yet America's early conception of civil rights was much narrower than it is today. Originally, the Constitution did not guarantee a general right to vote; it left voting and many other civil rights to the states. The Founders' initial rules permitted widely disparate treatment of different categories of individuals, including women, members of minority racial and ethnic groups, owners of property, and others. The greatest restriction on civil rights at the time of the American Constitution was on black people. Eight of the 13 original states permitted slavery, and slaves came almost entirely from Africa or the Caribbean. Those slaves possessed virtually no civil rights.

The Constitution banned the importation of slaves after 1808, but permitted the practice of slavery to continue. Immediately prior to the Civil War, roughly 4 million African Americans were slaves in the southern states where they were the backbone of the agricultural economy of the region. Slavery was by that time prohibited in most of the northern states, and the

CORE OF THE ANALYSIS

➡ Civil liberties are rules that limit the government's authority to interfere in certain spheres of activity, such as free speech and religion.

➡ Civil rights curb the power of majorities to exclude or harm individuals based on factors such as race, gender, or ethnicity.

➡ Today's conceptions of civil liberties and civil rights have been shaped by their historical development and their interpretation by key political actors, especially the Supreme Court.

issue of whether or not slavery should be allowed in America's western territories bitterly divided the nation. In the 1857 case of *Dred Scott v. Sandford*, involving the fate of a former slave, the Supreme Court ruled that a former slave was not a citizen under Missouri law (the state in question), could not bring suit in court, and was merely his master's personal property. Moreover, said the Court, slavery could not be excluded from the territories.[1] This decision inflamed sectional divisions, infuriated antislavery groups in the North, and helped to provoke the Civil War.

In the aftermath of the Civil War, Congress adopted the Thirteenth, Fourteenth, and Fifteenth amendments to the Constitution to protect civil rights that had been violated by the practice of slavery. The Thirteenth Amendment prohibited slavery and involuntary servitude in the United States. The Fifteenth extended the right to vote to blacks, stating, "The right of citizens of the United States to vote shall not be denied or abridged by the United States or by any State on account of race, color, or previous condition of servitude." The Fourteenth Amendment asserted the idea of civil rights much more broadly for all citizens:

> All persons born or naturalized in the United States, and subject to the jurisdiction thereof, are citizens of the United States and of the State wherein they reside. No State shall make or enforce any law which shall abridge the privileges or immunities of citizens of the United States; nor shall any State deprive any person of life, liberty, or property, without due process of law; nor deny to any person within its jurisdiction the equal protection of the laws.

The last clause of this section, called the equal protection clause, has transformed civil rights in the United States, as it creates the foundation for asserting equal civil rights for all persons.

The words of the equal protection clause launched more than a century of political movements and legal efforts to press for equality. African Americans' quest for civil rights in turn inspired many other groups—including members of other racial and ethnic groups, women, people with disabilities, and gay men and lesbians—to seek new laws and constitutional guarantees of their civil rights. Their struggles were aided by the simplicity of the clause, which offers its guarantee to *any person*.

As we see in this chapter, the enforcement of this guarantee was hard-won, and debates over the extent of the government's responsibility in ensuring equal protection persist. The reason is that the definition of civil rights depends not only on what laws are passed or the interpretation of the words of the Constitution but on the behavior of people in society. How can we understand historical patterns of discrimination? Are there political divisions between whites and racial and ethnic minorities today?

Is there evidence of intentional discrimination in election administration, employment, housing, and other activities? Before we consider these questions, we turn first to civil liberties and the long effort to make personal liberty a reality for every citizen in America.

CIVIL LIBERTIES: NATIONALIZING THE BILL OF RIGHTS

The First Amendment provides that "Congress shall make no law respecting an establishment of religion . . . or abridging freedom of speech, or of the press; or the right of [assembly and petition]." But this is the only amendment in the Bill of Rights that addresses itself exclusively to the national government. For example, the Second Amendment provides that "the right of the people to keep and bear Arms shall not be infringed." The Fifth Amendment says, among other things, that "no person shall . . . be twice put in jeopardy of life or limb" for the same crime; that no person "shall be compelled in any Criminal Case to be a witness against himself"; that no person shall "be deprived of life, liberty, or property, without due process of law"; and that private property cannot be taken "without just compensation."[2]

Because the First Amendment is the only part of the Bill of Rights that is explicit in its intention to put limits on the national government, a fundamental question inevitably arises: Do the remaining amendments of the Bill of Rights put limits on state governments or only on the national government?

Dual Citizenship

The question of whether the Bill of Rights also limits state governments was settled in 1833 in a way that may seem odd to Americans today. The case was *Barron v. Baltimore*, and the facts were simple. In paving its streets, the city of Baltimore had disposed of so much sand and gravel in the water near Barron's wharf that the value of the wharf for commercial purposes was virtually destroyed. Barron brought the city into court on the grounds that it had, under the Fifth Amendment, unconstitutionally deprived him of his property without just compensation. Here, Chief Justice Marshall, in one of the most significant Supreme Court decisions ever handed down, said:

> The Constitution was ordained and established by the people of the United States for themselves, for their own government, and not for the government of the individual States. Each State established a constitution

for itself, and in that constitution provided such limitations and restrictions on the powers of its particular government as its judgment dictated. . . . If these propositions be correct, *the fifth amendment must be understood as restraining the power of the general government, not as applicable to the States.*[3] [Emphasis added]

In other words, if an agency of the national government had deprived Barron of his property, there would have been little doubt about Barron's winning his case. But if the constitution of the state of Maryland contained no such provision protecting citizens of Maryland from such action, then Barron had no legal leg to stand on against Baltimore, an agency of the state of Maryland.

Barron v. Baltimore confirmed dual citizenship—that is, that each American was a citizen of the national government and separately a citizen of one of the states. This meant that the Bill of Rights did not apply to decisions or procedures of state (or local) governments. Even slavery could continue, because the Bill of Rights could not protect anyone from state laws treating people as property. In fact, the Bill of Rights did not become a vital instrument for the extension of civil liberties for anyone until after a bloody Civil War and a revolutionary Fourteenth Amendment intervened. And even so, nearly a second century would pass before the Bill of Rights would truly come into its own.

The Fourteenth Amendment

From a constitutional standpoint, the defeat of the South in the Civil War settled one question and raised another. It probably settled forever the question of whether secession was an option for any state. After 1865, there was more "united" than "states" to the United States. But this left unanswered just how much the states were obliged to obey the Constitution, and in particular, the Bill of Rights. Just reading the words of the Fourteenth Amendment, anyone might think it was almost perfectly designed to impose the Bill of Rights on the states and thereby to reverse *Barron v. Baltimore*. The very first words of the Fourteenth Amendment point in that direction:

> All persons born or naturalized in the United States, and subject to the jurisdiction thereof, are citizens of the United States and of the State wherein they reside.

This provides for a single national citizenship, and at a minimum that means that civil liberties should not vary drastically from state to state. That would seem to be the spirit of the Fourteenth Amendment: to nationalize the Bill of Rights by nationalizing the definition of citizenship.

This interpretation of the Fourteenth Amendment is reinforced by the next clause of the Amendment:

> No state shall make or enforce any law which shall abridge the privileges or immunities of citizens of the United States; nor shall any state deprive any person of life, liberty, or property, without due process of law.

All of this sounds like an effort to extend the Bill of Rights in its entirety to citizens wherever they might reside.[4] But this was not to be the Supreme Court's interpretation for nearly 100 years. Within five years of ratification of the Fourteenth Amendment, the Court was making decisions as though it had never been adopted.[5] Table 4.1 outlines the major developments in the history of the Fourteenth Amendment against the backdrop of *Barron*, citing the particular provisions of the Bill of Rights as they were incorporated by Supreme

Table 4.1

INCORPORATION OF THE BILL OF RIGHTS INTO THE FOURTEENTH AMENDMENT

SELECTED PROVISIONS AND AMENDMENTS	DATE "INCORPORATED"	KEY CASES
Eminent domain (V)	1897	*Chicago, Burlington and Quincy Railroad v. Chicago*
Freedom of speech (I)	1925	*Gitlow v. New York*
Freedom of the press (I)	1931	*Near v. Minnesota ex rel. Olson*
Free exercise of religion (I)	1934	*Hamilton v. Regents of the University of California*
Freedom of assembly (I)	1939	*Hague v. Committee for Industrial Organization*
Freedom from unnecessary search and seizure (IV)	1949	*Wolf v. Colorado*
Freedom from warrantless search and seizure ("exclusionary rule") (IV)	1961	*Mapp v. Ohio*
Freedom from cruel and unusual punishment (VIII)	1962	*Robinson v. California*
Right to counsel in any criminal trial (VI)	1963	*Gideon v. Wainwright*
Right against self-incrimination and forced confessions (V)	1964	*Malloy v. Hogan Escobedo v. Illinois*
Right to privacy (III, IV, and V)	1965	*Griswold v. Connecticut*
Right to remain silent (V)	1966	*Miranda v. Arizona*
Right against double jeopardy (V)	1969	*Benton v. Maryland*
Right to bear arms (II)	2010	*McDonald v. Chicago*

Court decisions into the Fourteenth Amendment as limitations on all the states. This is a measure of the degree of "nationalization" of civil liberties.

The only change in civil liberties during the first 60 years after the adoption of the Fourteenth Amendment came in 1897, when the Supreme Court held that the due process clause of the Fourteenth Amendment did in fact prohibit states from taking property for a public use without just compensation.[6] This effectively overruled the specific holding in *Barron*; henceforth a citizen of Maryland or any state was protected from a "public taking" of property even if the state constitution did not provide such protection. The power of public agencies to seize private property is called eminent domain. According to the Fifth Amendment, private owners must be paid "just compensation" by the government if it decides that it needs their property. But, the Supreme Court had "incorporated" into the Fourteenth Amendment *only* the property protection provision of the Fifth Amendment, despite the fact that the due process clause applied to the taking of life and liberty as well as property.

No further expansion of civil liberties through incorporation occurred until 1925, when the Supreme Court held that freedom of speech is "among the fundamental personal rights and 'liberties' protected by the due process clause of the Fourteenth Amendment from impairment by the states."[7] In 1931, the Supreme Court added freedom of the press to that short list of civil rights protected by the Bill of Rights from state action; in 1939, it added freedom of assembly.[8] For the following two decades, this was as far as the Supreme Court was willing to go in the effort to nationalize more of the rights in the Bill of Rights.

The shadow of *Barron* extended into its second century, despite adoption of the Fourteenth Amendment. At the time of World War II, the Constitution, as interpreted by the Supreme Court, left standing the framework in which the states had the power to determine their own law on a number of fundamental issues. It left states with the power to pass laws segregating the races. It also left states with the power to engage in searches and seizures without a warrant, to indict accused persons without benefit of a grand jury, to deprive persons of trial by jury, to force persons to testify against themselves, to deprive accused persons of their right to confront adverse witnesses, and to prosecute accused persons more than once for the same crime.[9] Few states exercised these powers, but the power was there for any state whose legislative majority chose to use it.

The Constitutional Revolution in Civil Liberties

Signs of change in the constitutional framework came after 1954, in *Brown v. Board of Education*, when the Court found state segregation laws for schools unconstitutional.[10] Even though *Brown* was not a civil liberties case, it indicated rather clearly that the Supreme Court was going to be expansive about civil liberties, because with *Brown* the Court had effectively promised that it would actively subject the states and all actions affecting civil rights and civil liberties to strict scrutiny. In retrospect, this constitutional revolution was given a jump-start in 1954 by *Brown v. Board of Education*, even though the results were not apparent until after 1961, when the number of incorporated civil liberties increased (see Table 4.1).

As we saw in Chapter 3, the constitutional revolution in federalism began when the Supreme Court in 1937 interpreted "interstate commerce" in favor of federal government regulation.[11] Both revolutions, then, were movements toward nationalization, but they required opposite motions on the part of the Supreme Court. In the area of commerce (the first revolution), the Court had to decide to assume a *passive* role by not interfering as Congress expanded the meaning of the commerce clause of Article I, Section 8. This expansion has been so extensive that the national government can now constitutionally reach a single farmer growing 20 acres of wheat or a small restaurant selling barbecue to local "whites only" without being anywhere near interstate commerce routes. In the second revolution—involving the Bill of Rights and the Fourteenth Amendment—the Court had to assume an active role. It required close review of the laws of state legislatures and decisions of state courts in order to apply a single national Fourteenth Amendment standard to the rights and liberties of all citizens.

Table 4.1 shows that until 1961, only the First Amendment and one clause of the Fifth Amendment had been clearly incorporated into the Fourteenth Amendment.[12] After 1961, several other important provisions of the Bill of Rights were incorporated. Of the cases that expanded the Fourteenth Amendment's reach, the most famous was *Gideon v. Wainwright*, which established the right to counsel in a criminal trial, because it became the subject of a best-selling book and a popular movie.[13] In *Mapp v. Ohio*, the Court held that evidence obtained in violation of the Fourth Amendment ban on unreasonable searches and seizures would be excluded from trial.[14] This exclusionary rule was particularly irksome to the police and prosecutors because it meant that patently guilty defendants sometimes go free because the evidence that clearly incriminated them could not be used. In *Miranda*, the Court's ruling required that arrested persons be informed of the right to remain silent and to have counsel present during interrogation.[15] This is the basis of the Miranda rule of reading persons their rights. By 1969, in *Benton v. Maryland*, the Supreme Court had come full circle regarding the rights of the criminally accused, explicitly reversing a 1937 ruling and thereby incorporating double jeopardy.[16]

Beginning in the mid-1950s, the Court also expanded another important area of civil liberties: rights to privacy. In 1958, the Supreme Court recognized "privacy in one's association" in its decision to prevent the state of Alabama from using the membership list of the National Association for the Advancement of Colored People in the state's investigations.[17] As we see later in this chapter, legal questions about the right to privacy have come to the fore in more recent cases concerning birth control, abortion, homosexuality, and assisted suicide.

THE BILL OF RIGHTS TODAY

Because liberty requires restraining the power of government, the general status of civil liberties can never be considered fixed and permanent.[18] Every provision in the Bill of Rights is subject to interpretation, and in any dispute involving a clause of the Bill of Rights, interpretations will always be shaped by the interpreter's interest in the outcome. As we have seen, the Court continuously reminds everyone that if it has the power to expand the Bill of Rights, it also has the power to contract it.[19]

The First Amendment and Freedom of Religion

The Bill of Rights begins by guaranteeing freedom of religion, and the First Amendment provides for that freedom in two distinct clauses: "Congress shall make no law [1] respecting an establishment of religion, or [2] prohibiting the free exercise thereof." The first clause is called the establishment clause, and the second is called the free exercise clause.

Separation between Church and State. The establishment clause and the idea of "no law" regarding the establishment of religion could be interpreted in several possible ways. One interpretation, which probably reflects the views of many of the First Amendment's authors, is that the government is prohibited from establishing an official church. Official state churches, such as the Church of England, were common in the eighteenth century and were viewed by many Americans as inconsistent with a republican form of government. Indeed, many American colonists had fled Europe to escape persecution for having rejected state-sponsored churches. A second possible interpretation is the "nonpreferentialist" or "accommodationist" view, which holds that the government may not take sides among competing religions but is not prohibited from providing assistance to religious institutions or ideas

establishment clause

The First Amendment clause that says, "Congress shall make no law respecting an establishment of religion." This law means that a wall of separation exists between church and state so long as it shows no favoritism. The United States accommodates religious beliefs in a variety of ways, from the reference to God on U.S. currency to the prayer that begins every session of Congress. These forms of establishment have never been struck down by the courts.

The third view regarding religious establishment, which for many years dominated Supreme Court decision making in this realm, is the idea of a "wall of separation" between church and state that cannot be breached by the government. Despite the absolute sound of the phrase *wall of separation*, there is ample room to disagree on how high the wall is or of what materials it is composed. For example, the Court has been consistently strict in cases of school prayer, striking down such practices as Bible reading,[20] non-denominational prayer,[21] a moment of silence for meditation, and pregame prayer at public sporting events.[22] On the other hand, the Court has been quite permissive (and some would say inconsistent) about the public display of religious symbols, such as city-sponsored Nativity scenes in commercial or municipal areas.[23] In 1971, after 30 years of cases involving religious schools, the Court attempted to specify some criteria to guide its decisions and those of lower courts, indicating, for example, in a decision invalidating state payments for the teaching of secular subjects in parochial schools, circumstances under which the Court might allow certain financial assistance. The case was *Lemon v. Kurtzman*; in its decision, the Supreme Court established three criteria to guide future cases, in what came to be called the *Lemon* test. The Court held that government aid to religious schools would be accepted as constitutional if (1) it had a secular purpose, (2) its effect was neither to advance nor to inhibit religion, and (3) it did not entangle government and religious institutions in each other's affairs.[24]

In 2004, the question of whether the phrase "under God" in the Pledge of Allegiance violates the establishment clause was brought before the Court, but the Court ruled that the plaintiff lacked a sufficient personal stake in the case to bring the complaint.[25] This inconclusive decision by the Court left "under God" in the Pledge while keeping the issue alive for possible resolution in a future case.

In two cases in 2005, the Supreme Court ruled, also inconclusively, on government-sponsored displays of religious symbols. Both cases involved displays of the Ten Commandments. In *Van Orden v. Perry*, the Court said in a 5–4 decision that a display of the Ten Commandments in the Texas state capital did not violate the Constitution.[26] However, in *McCreary v. ACLU*, decided at the same time and also by a 5–4 margin, the Court determined that a display of the Ten Commandments inside two Kentucky courthouses was unconstitutional.[27] Justice Breyer, the swing vote in the two cases, intimated that the difference had been the purpose of the displays. Most legal observers, though, could see little difference between the two and assume that the Court will provide further clarification in future cases.

Lemon test

Rule articulated in *Lemon v. Kurtzman* according to which governmental action in respect to religion is permissible if it is secular in purpose, does not lead to "excessive entanglement" with religion, and neither promotes nor inhibits the practice of religion

Chapter 4: Civil Liberties and Civil Rights

Free Exercise of Religion. The *free exercise clause* protects the right to believe and practice whatever religion one chooses; it also protects the right to be a nonbeliever. Although the Supreme Court has been fairly consistent and strict in protecting the free exercise of religious belief, it has taken pains to distinguish between religious beliefs and actions based on those beliefs. In one case, for example, two Native Americans had been fired from their jobs for smoking peyote, an illegal drug. They claimed they had been fired from their jobs illegally because smoking peyote was a religious sacrament protected by the free exercise clause. The Court disagreed with their claim in an important 1990 decision, saying that the state's duty to prevent the use of dangerous drugs should be given more weight than the claimed religious exercise.[28] Congress, however, literally reversed the Court's decision with the enactment of the Religious Freedom Restoration Act (RFRA) of 1993, which forbids any federal agency or state government from restricting a person's free exercise of religion unless the federal agency or state government demonstrates that its action "furthers a compelling government interest" and "is the least restrictive means of furthering that compelling governmental interest." However, in the *City of Boerne* case, the Supreme Court declared the RFRA unconstitutional but on grounds rarely utilized, if not unique, to this case: Congress had violated the separation-of-powers principle, infringing on the powers of the judiciary by going so far beyond its lawmaking powers.[29] The *City of Boerne* case did settle some matters of constitutional controversy over the religious exercise and the establishment clauses of the First Amendment, but it left a lot more unsettled.

The First Amendment and Freedom of Speech and the Press

Because democracy depends on an open political process, freedom of speech and freedom of the press are considered critical. In 1938, freedom of speech (which in all important respects includes freedom of the press) was given extraordinary constitutional status when the Supreme Court established that any legislation that attempts to restrict these fundamental freedoms "is to be subjected to a more exacting judicial scrutiny . . . than are most other types of legislation."[30]

The Court was saying that the democratic political process must be protected at almost any cost. This higher standard of judicial review came to be called strict scrutiny. Strict scrutiny implies that speech—at least some kinds of speech—occupy a "preferred" position and will be protected almost absolutely. In 2011, for example, the Supreme Court ruled 8–1 that the Westboro Baptist Church, a tiny Kansas institution, had a First Amendment right to picket the funerals of American soldiers killed in action while

Different interpretations of the establishment clause have led to debates about the extent to which church and state must be separated. This monument of the Ten Commandments displayed in an Alabama courthouse was declared unconstitutional.

displaying signs reading "Thank God for Dead Soldiers." Members of the church believe that these deaths represent divine punishment for America's tolerance of homosexuality and other matters. In his opinion, Chief Justice John Roberts wrote, "As a nation we have chosen to protect even hurtful speech on public issues to ensure that we do not stifle public debate."[31] But even though we do protect many types of speech with which most Americans strongly disagree, it turns out that only some types of speech are fully protected against restrictions. Many forms of speech are less than absolutely protected—even though they are entitled to strict scrutiny.

Political Speech. Since the 1920s, political speech has been consistently protected by the courts even when it has been deemed "insulting" or "outrageous." Here is the way the Supreme Court put it in one of its most important statements on the subject:

> The constitutional guarantees of free speech and free press do not permit a State to forbid or proscribe advocacy of the use of force or of law violation *except where such advocacy is directed to inciting or producing imminent lawless action and is likely to incite or produce such action.*[32] [Emphasis added]

This statement was made in the case of a Ku Klux Klan leader, Charles Brandenburg, who had been arrested and convicted of advocating "revengent" action against the president, Congress, and the Supreme Court, among others, if they continued "to suppress the white, Caucasian race." Although Brandenburg was not carrying a weapon, some members of his audience were. Nevertheless, the Supreme Court reversed the state courts and freed Brandenburg while declaring Ohio's Criminal Syndicalism Act unconstitutional because it punished persons who "advocate, or teach the duty, necessity, or propriety [of violence] as a means of accomplishing industrial or political reform" or who publish materials or "voluntarily assemble . . . to teach or advocate the doctrines of criminal syndicalism." The Supreme Court argued that the statute did not distinguish "mere advocacy" from "incitement to imminent lawless action." It would be difficult to go much further in protecting freedom of speech. Typically, the federal courts will strike down restrictions on speech if they are deemed to be "overbroad," "vague," or lacking "neutrality" in terms of the content of the speech, as for example, if a statute prohibited the views of the political left but not the political right, or vice versa.

Another area of recent expansion of political speech—the participation of wealthy persons and corporations in political campaigns—was opened up in 1976 with the Supreme Court's decision in *Buckley v. Valeo*.[33] Campaign finance reform laws of the early 1970s, arising out of the Watergate scandal, sought to put severe limits on campaign spending, and a number of important provisions were declared unconstitutional on the basis of a new principle that spending money by or on behalf of candidates is a form of speech protected by the First Amendment. The issue came up again in 2003, after passage of a new and more severe campaign finance law, the Bipartisan Campaign Reform Act of 2002 (BCRA). This time, in *McConnell v. Federal Election Commission*, the majority seriously reduced the area of speech protected by the *Buckley v. Valeo* decision by holding that Congress was well within its power to put limits on the amounts individuals could spend, plus severe limits on the amounts of "soft money" that could be spent by corporations and their PACs and limits on issue advertising prior to Election Day.[34] This decision was the anomaly, however. In 2007, in the case of *Federal Election Commission v. Wisconsin Right to Life*, the Supreme Court struck down a key portion of BCRA, finding that the act's limitations on political advertising violated the First Amendment's guarantee of free speech.[35] In *Citizens United v. Federal Election Commission*, in 2010, the Court ruled that corporate funding of independent electioneering ads could not be limited under the First Amendment.[36] And in 2014, in *McCutcheon v. Federal Election Commission*, the Court struck down aggregate limits on an individual's contributions to candidates for federal office, political parties, and political action committees. The decision stated that such limits do not further the government's interest in preventing corruption and are thus invalid under the First Amendment.[37]

Symbolic Speech, Speech Plus, and the Rights of Assembly and Petition. The First Amendment treats the freedoms of assembly and petition as equal to the freedoms of religion and political speech. Freedom of assembly and freedom of petition are closely associated with speech but go beyond it to speech associated with action. Since at least 1931, the Supreme Court has sought to protect actions that are designed to send a political message. Thus although the Court upheld a federal statute making it a crime to burn draft cards to protest the Vietnam War on the grounds that the government had a compelling interest in preserving draft cards as part of the conduct of the war itself, it considered the wearing of black armbands to school a protected form of assembly. In these sorts of cases, a court will often use the standard it articulated in the draft card case, *United States v. O'Brien*, and now known as the *O'Brien* test.[38] Under the terms of the *O'Brien* test, a statute restricting expressive or symbolic speech must be justified by a compelling government interest and be narrowly tailored toward achieving that interest.

Another example is the burning of the American flag as a symbol of protest. In 1984, at a political rally held during the Republican National Convention in Dallas, a political protester burned an American flag in violation of a Texas statute that prohibited desecration of a venerated object. In a 5–4 decision, the Supreme Court declared the Texas law unconstitutional on the grounds that flag burning is expressive conduct protected by the First Amendment.[39] Further effort in Congress was probably killed by the Supreme Court's 2003 decision striking down a Virginia cross-burning statute.[40] In that case, the Court ruled that states could make cross burning a crime as long as the statute required prosecutors to prove that the act of setting fire to the cross was intended to intimidate.

Closer to the original intent of the assembly and petition clause is the category of speech plus—following speech with physical activity such as picketing, distributing leaflets, and other forms of peaceful demonstration or assembly. Such assemblies are consistently protected by courts under the First Amendment; state and local laws regulating such activities are closely scrutinized and frequently overturned.

Freedom of the Press. For all practical purposes, freedom of speech implies and includes freedom of the press. With the exception of the broadcast media, which are subject to federal regulation, the press is protected under the doctrine prohibiting prior restraint. Beginning with the landmark 1931 case of *Near v. Minnesota*,[41] the Supreme Court has held that except under the most extraordinary circumstances, the First Amendment prohibits government agencies from seeking to prevent newspapers or magazines from publishing whatever they wish.

speech plus ➡
Speech accompanied by activities such as sit-ins, picketing, and demonstrations. Protection of this form of speech under the First Amendment is conditional, and restrictions imposed by state or local authorities are acceptable if properly balanced by considerations of public order

prior restraint ➡
An effort by a government agency to block the publication of material it deems libelous or harmful in some other way; censorship. In the United States, the courts forbid prior restraint except under the most extraordinary circumstances

Chapter 4: Civil Liberties and Civil Rights

Libel, Slander, Obscenity, and Pornography. Some speech is not protected at all. If a written statement is made in "reckless disregard of the truth" and is considered damaging to the victim because it is "malicious, scandalous, and defamatory," it can be punished as libel. If an oral statement of such nature is made, it can be punished as slander.

Today most libel suits involve freedom of the press, and the realm of freedom of the press is enormous. Historically, newspapers were subject to the law of libel, whereby newspapers that printed false and malicious stories could be compelled to pay damages to those they defamed. In recent years, however, American courts have greatly narrowed the meaning of libel and made it extremely difficult, particularly for politicians or other public figures, to win a libel case against a newspaper.

If libel and slander cases can be difficult because of the problem of determining the truth of statements and whether those statements are malicious and damaging, cases involving pornography and obscenity can be even stickier. It is easy to say that pornography and obscenity fall outside the realm of protected speech, but it is impossible to draw a clear line defining where protection ends and unprotected speech begins. All attempts by the courts to define pornography and obscenity have proved impractical because each instance required courts to screen thousands of pages of print material or feet of film alleged to be pornographic.

In recent years, the battle against obscene speech has taken place in the realm of pornography on the Internet. Opponents of this form of expression argue that it should be banned because of the easy access children have to the Internet. The first major effort to regulate the content of the Internet occurred on February 1, 1996, when the 104th Congress passed major telecommunications legislation. Attached to the Telecommunications Act was an amendment, called the Communications Decency Act (CDA), that was designed to regulate the online transmission of obscene material. In the 1997 Supreme Court case of *Reno v. ACLU*, the Court struck down the CDA, ruling that it suppressed speech that "adults have a constitutional right to receive."[42] Congress again tried limiting children's access to Internet pornography with the 2001 Children's Internet Protection Act, which required public libraries to install antipornography filters on all library computers with Internet access. The law was challenged, and in 2003 the Court upheld it, asserting that its provisions did not violate library patrons' First Amendment rights.[43] In 2003, Congress enacted the Prosecutorial Remedies and Other Tools to end the Exploitation of Children Today (PROTECT) Act, which outlawed efforts to sell child pornography via the Internet. The Supreme Court upheld this act in the 2008 case of *United States v. Williams*, in which the majority said that criminalizing efforts to pander child pornography did not violate free-speech guarantees.[44]

libel

A written statement made in "reckless disregard of the truth" and considered damaging to a victim because it is "malicious, scandalous, and defamatory"

slander

An oral statement made in "reckless disregard of the truth" and considered damaging to a victim because it is "malicious, scandalous, and defamatory"

Fighting Words and Hate Speech. Speech can also lose its protected position when it moves toward the sphere of action. "Expressive speech," for example, is protected until it moves from the symbolic realm to the realm of actual conduct—to direct incitement of damaging conduct with the use of so-called fighting words. In 1942, the Supreme Court upheld the arrest and conviction of a man who had violated a state law forbidding the use of offensive language in public. He had called the arresting officer a "goddamned racketeer" and "a damn Fascist." When his case reached the Supreme Court, the arrest was upheld on the grounds that the First Amendment provides no protection for such offensive language because such words "are no essential part of any exposition of ideas."[45] Since that time, however, the Supreme Court has reversed almost every conviction based on arguments that the speaker had used "fighting words." But again, that does not mean this is an absolutely settled area.

fighting words

Speech that directly incites damaging conduct

Many jurisdictions have drafted ordinances banning forms of expression designed to assert hatred toward one or another group, be they African Americans, Jews, Muslims, or others. Such hate speech ordinances seldom pass constitutional muster. The leading Supreme Court case in this realm is the 1992 decision in *R.A.V. v. City of St. Paul.*[46] Here, a white teenager was arrested for burning a cross on the lawn of a black family in violation of a municipal ordinance that banned cross burning. The Court ruled that the ordinance was not content neutral, because it prohibited only cross burning—typically an expression of hatred of African Americans. Since a statute banning all forms of hateful expression would be deemed overly broad, the *R.A.V.* standard suggests that virtually all hate speech is constitutionally protected.

Commercial Speech. Commercial speech, such as newspaper or television advertising, does not have full First Amendment protection because it cannot be considered political speech. Some commercial speech is still unprotected and therefore regulated. For example, the regulation of false and misleading advertising by the Federal Trade Commission is an old and well-established power of the federal government. The Supreme Court long ago upheld the constitutionality of laws prohibiting the electronic media from carrying cigarette advertising.[47] However, the gains far outweigh the losses in the effort to expand the protection commercial speech enjoys under the First Amendment. As the scholar Louis Fisher explains, "In part, this reflects the growing appreciation that commercial speech is part of the free flow of information necessary for informed choice and democratic participation."[48] For example, in a 2001 case, the Court ruled that a Massachusetts ban on all cigarette advertising violated the First Amendment right of the tobacco industry to advertise its products to adult consumers.[49]

In 2008 the Supreme Court ruled that the federal government could not prohibit individuals from owning guns for self-defense in their homes. In 2010 the Supreme Court ruled that the Second Amendment also applies to the states, making it the most recent right to be incorporated.

The Second Amendment and the Right to Bear Arms

The point and purpose of the Second Amendment is the provision for militias; they were to be the backup of the government for the maintenance of local public order. *Militia* was understood at the time of the Founding to be a military or police resource for state governments, and militias were specifically distinguished from armies and troops, which came within the sole constitutional jurisdiction of Congress. Some groups, though, have always argued that the Second Amendment also establishes an individual right to bear arms. In its 2008 decision in the case of *District of Columbia v. Heller*, the Supreme Court ruled that the federal government could not prohibit individuals from owning guns for self-defense in their homes.[50] The case involved a District of Columbia ordinance that made it virtually impossible for residents to possess firearms legally. The District of Columbia is an entity of the federal government, and the Court did not indicate that its ruling applied to state firearms laws. However, in the 2010 case of *McDonald v. Chicago*, the Court struck down a Chicago firearms ordinance and applied the Second Amendment to the states as well.[51]

Rights of the Criminally Accused

Except for the First Amendment, most of the battle to apply the Bill of Rights to the states was fought over the various protections granted to individuals who are accused of a crime, who are suspects in the commission of

due process

Proceeding according to law and with adequate protection for individual rights

a crime, or who are brought before the court as a witness to a crime. The Bill of Rights entitles every American to due process of law. The Fourth, Fifth, Sixth, and Eighth amendments, taken together, are the essence of the due process of law, even though this fundamental concept does not appear until the very last words of the Fifth Amendment.

The Fourth Amendment and Searches and Seizures. The purpose of the Fourth Amendment is to guarantee the security of citizens against unreasonable (that is, improper) searches and seizures. In 1990, the Supreme Court summarized its understanding of the Fourth Amendment brilliantly and succinctly: "A search compromises the individual interest in privacy; a seizure deprives the individual of dominion over his or her person or property."[52]

The exclusionary rule, which prohibits evidence obtained during an illegal search from being introduced in a trial, is the most severe restraint ever imposed by the Constitution and the courts on the behavior of the police. The exclusionary rule is a dramatic restriction because it rules out precisely the evidence that produces a conviction; it frees those people who are *known* to have committed the crime of which they have been accused. Because it works so dramatically in favor of persons known to have committed a crime, the Court has since softened the application of the rule. In recent years, the federal courts have relied on a discretionary use of the exclusionary rule, whereby they make a judgment as to the "nature and quality of the intrusion." It is thus difficult to know ahead of time whether a defendant will or will not be protected from an illegal search under the Fourth Amendment.[53]

grand jury

A jury that determines whether sufficient evidence is available to justify a trial. Grand juries do not rule on the accused's guilt or innocence

The Fifth Amendment. The first clause of the Fifth Amendment, the right to have a grand jury determine whether a trial is warranted, is considered "the oldest institution known to the Constitution."[54] Grand juries play an important role in federal criminal cases. However, the provision for a grand jury is the one important civil liberties provision of the Bill of Rights that was not incorporated by the Fourteenth Amendment to apply to state criminal prosecutions. Thus some states operate without grand juries. In such states, the prosecuting attorney simply files a "bill of information" affirming that sufficient evidence is available to justify a trial.

The Fifth Amendment also provides the constitutional protection from double jeopardy, or being tried more than once for the same crime, and the guarantee that no citizen "shall be compelled in any criminal case to be a witness against himself." This protection against self-incrimination led to the *Miranda* case and the *Miranda* rules that police must follow when questioning an arrested criminal suspect.

Another fundamental clause of the Fifth Amendment is the "takings clause," which extends to each citizen a protection against the taking of private property "without just compensation." Although this part of the amendment is not specifically concerned with protecting persons accused of crimes, it is nevertheless a fundamentally important instance where the government and the citizen are adversaries. As discussed earlier in this chapter, the power of any government to take private property for a public use is called eminent domain.

The Sixth Amendment and the Right to Counsel. Like the exclusionary rule of the Fourth Amendment and the self-incrimination clause of the Fifth Amendment, the "right to counsel" provision of the Sixth Amendment is notable for freeing defendants who seem to the public to be patently guilty as charged. Other provisions of the Sixth Amendment, such as the right to a speedy trial and the right to confront witnesses before an impartial jury, are less controversial in nature.

Gideon v. Wainwright is the perfect case study because it involved a disreputable person who seemed patently guilty of the crime for which he was convicted. In and out of jails for most of his 51 years, Clarence Earl Gideon received a five-year sentence for breaking into and entering a poolroom in Panama City, Florida. While serving time in jail, Gideon became a fairly well-qualified "jailhouse lawyer," made his own appeal on a handwritten petition, and eventually won the landmark ruling on the right to counsel in all felony cases.[55] In 1964, the year after the *Gideon* decision, the Supreme Court ruled in *Escobedo v. Illinois* that suspects had a right to counsel during police interrogations, not just when their cases reached trial.[56] The right to counsel has been expanded further during the past few decades. For example, in 2003 the Supreme Court overturned the death sentence of a Maryland death-row inmate, holding that the defense lawyer had failed to fully inform the jury of the defendant's history of "horrendous childhood abuse."[57]

The Eighth Amendment and Cruel and Unusual Punishment. The Eighth Amendment prohibits "excessive bail," "excessive fines," and "cruel and unusual punishment." Virtually all the debate over Eighth Amendment issues focuses on the last clause of the amendment: the protection from "cruel and unusual punishment." One of the greatest challenges in interpreting this provision consistently is that what is considered "cruel and unusual" varies from culture to culture and from generation to generation. And unfortunately, it also varies by class and race.

By far the biggest issue in the inconsistency of class and race as constituting cruel and unusual punishment arises over the death penalty. In 1972, the Supreme Court overturned several state death-penalty laws not because they were cruel and unusual but because they were being applied in a capricious manner.[58] Since 1976, the Court has consistently upheld state laws providing for capital punishment, although it also continues to review numerous death-penalty appeals each year. The Analyzing the Evidence unit for this chapter examines the debate over the death penalty in greater detail.

Constitutional objections to the death penalty often invoke the Eighth Amendment's protection against punishments that are "cruel and unusual." Yet supporters of the death penalty say it can hardly be considered a violation of this protection, since it was commonly used in the eighteenth century and was supported by most early American leaders.

The Right to Privacy

right to privacy

The right to be left alone, which has been interpreted by the Supreme Court to entail individual access to birth control and abortions

When the Court began to take a more activist role in the mid-1950s and 1960s, the idea of a right to privacy gained traction. The Constitution does not specifically mention a right to privacy, but the Ninth Amendment declares that the rights enumerated in the Constitution are not an exhaustive list. In 1958, the Supreme Court recognized "privacy in one's association" in its decision to prevent the state of Alabama from using the membership list of the NAACP in the state's investigations. The sphere of privacy was drawn in earnest in 1965, when the Court ruled that a Connecticut statute forbidding the use of contraceptives violated the right of marital privacy. Justice William O. Douglas, author of the majority decision in the *Griswold* case, argued that this right of privacy is also grounded in the Constitution because it fits into a "zone of privacy" created by a combination of the Third, Fourth, and Fifth amendments. The right to privacy was confirmed and extended in 1973 in the most important of all privacy decisions and one of the most important Supreme Court decisions in American history: *Roe v. Wade*. This decision established a woman's right to seek an abortion and prohibited states from making abortion a criminal act.[59]

In the last three decades, the right to be left alone began to include the privacy rights of gay men and lesbians. One morning in Atlanta in the mid-1980s, Michael Hardwick was arrested by a police officer who discovered him in bed with another man. Hardwick was charged under Georgia's laws against heterosexual and homosexual sodomy. Hardwick filed a lawsuit against the state, challenging the constitutionality of the Georgia law, and won his case in the federal court of appeals. The state of Georgia, in an unusual move, appealed the court's decision to the Supreme Court. The majority of the Court reversed the lower-court decision, holding against Hardwick on the grounds that "the federal Constitution confers [no] fundamental right upon homosexuals to engage in sodomy" and that there was therefore no basis to invalidate "the laws of the many states that still make such conduct illegal and have done so for a very long time."[60] With *Lawrence v. Texas* in 2003, the Court overturned its 1986 decision in *Bowers v. Hardwick*, and state legislatures no longer had the authority to make private sexual behavior a crime.[61] Drawing from the tradition of negative liberty, the Court maintained, "In our tradition the State is not omnipresent in the home. And there are other spheres of our lives and existence outside the home, where the State should not be a dominant presence." Explicitly encompassing lesbians and gay men within the umbrella of privacy, the Court concluded that the "petitioners are entitled to respect for their private lives. The State cannot demean their existence or control their destiny by making their private sexual conduct a crime." This decision added substance to the Ninth Amendment "right of privacy."

Another area ripe for litigation and public discourse is the so-called right to die. A number of highly publicized physician-assisted suicides have focused attention on whether people have a right to choose their own death and receive assistance in carrying it out. Can this become part of the privacy right, or is it a new substantive right? In the 2006 case of *Gonzales v. Oregon*, the Supreme Court upheld an Oregon law that allowed doctors to use drugs to facilitate the deaths of terminally ill patients who requested such assistance.[62] This decision is not a definitive ruling on the right-to-die question, but it does suggest that the Court is not hostile to the idea.

CIVIL RIGHTS

Civil rights are the rules the government must follow with regard to the treatment of individuals when collective decisions are made. Some civil rights concern who can be involved in collective decisions and how. Other civil rights concern how people are treated in civil society, including who has access to public facilities, such as schools and public hospitals. Increasingly, civil rights have extended to private spheres of life, including the right to work, the right to marry, and the question of whether clubs and organizations can exclude people on the basis of gender or race. Even when no legal right currently exists, civil rights may be asserted as a matter of justice or morality. When there is a demand for new civil rights, society must decide whether and how rights should be extended.

Civil rights can be thought of in terms of three features: who, what, and how much. *Who* has a right and who does not? A right to *what*? And *how much* is any individual allowed to exercise that right? Consider the right to vote. The "what," of course, is the vote. The "who" concerns which persons are allowed to vote. Today in the United States all citizens 18 years of age and older are eligible to vote. There are additional criteria for voting imposed by states, such as requirements in some states that voters show photo IDs or rules prohibiting voting by ex-felons. The "how much" concerns whether

Evaluating
the Death Penalty

Contributed by
Joseph Ura
Texas A&M University

Statistical analysis of the relationship between the availability of the death penalty as a punishment and murder rates produces mixed evidence of the deterrent effect of the death penalty. In general, analysis of national crime data indicates that there is a negative relationship between the use of the death penalty and the murder rate over the last half-century. That is, as the number of executions goes down the rate of murders nationwide goes up, and vice versa. In contrast, analysis that compares murder rates in states with the death penalty to states without it often finds that states that continue to utilize the death penalty have crime rates that are comparable to states that do not utilize the death penalty.

Evaluating the effectiveness of the death penalty deterrent presents substantial challenges for social science. The association between the use of the death penalty and crime rates over time is complicated by the close association between the number of executions and other law enforcement and penal policy changes. For example, increasing numbers of executions during the 1980s and 1990s were part of a larger trend of sending greater numbers of convicted criminals to prison for longer periods of time. Likewise, it is difficult to simply compare crime rates in death penalty states and non–death penalty states, since the comparisons are complicated by economic, social, and demographic differences among states which are associated with variance in state crime rates.

Executions and the Murder Rate

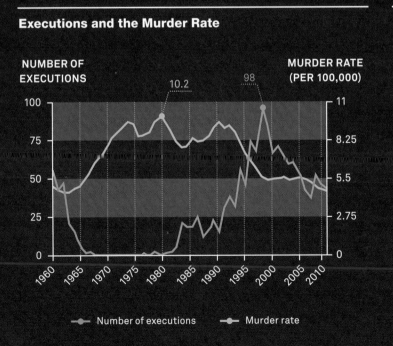

NUMBER OF
EXECUTIONS

MURDER RATE
(PER 100,000)

10.2   98

Number of executions   Murder rate

Over time, there is a reasonably strong negative relationship between the annual number of executions and the murder rate. Murder rates in the United States began to rise dramatically around 1967 and remained high until the mid-1990s. The sharp rise and subsequent decline in the murder rate corresponds to periods of declining and then increasing use of the death penalty. This aggregate correlation supports claims that the use of the death penalty deters potential murders.

SOURCE: Bureau of Justice Statistics, *FBI Uniform Crime Report.*

Incarceration and the Murder Rate

INCARCERATION RATE
(PER 100,000)

MURDER RATE
(PER 100,000)

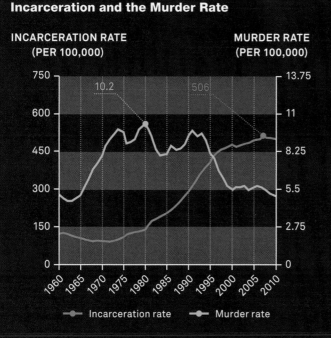

10.2

506

— ● — Incarceration rate — ● — Murder rate

The increased use of the death penalty in the United States during the 1990s was part of a larger trend of increased utilization of the criminal justice system. The rate of incarceration in the United States grew steadily through the 1980s before jumping dramatically during the 1990s. The growth of the penal population in the United States was also coincident with other policy changes designed to reduce crime, including a dramatic increase in the number of police officers, and changes in the American criminal landscape, such as stabilization of the market for illegal drugs. It is therefore difficult to pinpoint the effects of a single causal force out of several reinforcing developments that occurred at more or less the same time.

SOURCE: Sourcebook of Criminal Justice Statistics, www.albany.edu/sourcebook (accessed 5/20/13).

Executions and the Murder Rate per State, 2010

DEATH PENALTY

● At least 1 execution in 2010
● Death penalty legal but no executions in 2010
● Death penalty no longer legal

MURDER RATE
(per 100,000)

● < 2   ● 2.0–3.9
● 4.0–5.9   ● > 6

Across states, the relationship between the use of the death penalty and murder rates provides little evidence of a deterrent effect. In 2010, the murder rate in the 14 states that had abolished the death penalty completely was 4.3 per 100,000 people. Among the states that allow the death penalty but did not carry out an execution in 2010, the murder rate averaged 4.6 per 100,000 people. And, in the 11 states that conducted at least one execution, the murder rate averaged 5.4 per 100,000 people. The 2010 data pattern is typical, which challenges the idea that criminals are deterred from committing murder by the availability of the death penalty.

SOURCE: Bureau of Justice Statistics, *FBI Uniform Crime Report*.

that right can be exercised equally—whether some people's votes count more than others or whether the election laws create greater obstacles for some people and make it easier for other people. For instance, until the mid-1960s, the California State Senate had one senator from Los Angeles County, with 6 million people, and one senator from Inyo County, with 14,000 people. The votes of the 14,000 people translated into the same amount of representation in the California state senate as the votes of the 6 million people. The U.S. Supreme Court ruled that such arrangements violated the equal protection clause and hence the civil rights of those in the more populous counties.

In the course of American history, two principles have emerged that answer "who" enjoys civil rights and "how much." First, civil rights ought to be universal—that is, all persons should enjoy civil rights. Second, civil rights ought to be equal—that is, all people who enjoy a civil right ought to be allowed an equal ability or opportunity to practice that right. However, in practice, these principles have not always been applied.

What civil rights we enjoy and who has them are political decisions. The Constitution sets forth a small number of civil rights. The Bill of Rights created a larger number of legal rights. But, many of the civil rights we enjoy now were not specified explicitly in the Constitution, and instead were left to Congress and the states to determine. In other words, most of the civil rights we enjoy today are the result of legislation, litigation, and administration that took place after the country was founded.

The Struggle for Voting Rights

Some of the most profound political debates and deepest divisions in American society have concerned *who* has civil rights. Who has what civil rights is a source of contention precisely because those who have civil rights, such as the right to vote, are asked to extend those rights to those who do not. At the time of the Founding, most states granted voting rights exclusively to white, male property owners. In 1787, the constitutions and laws of many states also imposed religious criteria, forbidding Catholics or Jews from voting, standing for office, and engaging in other public activities. White, male property owners had disproportionate political power in 1787 because they had voting rights while no one else did. In order to expand voting rights to other groups, those who had power had to decide to remove property qualifications, extend voting rights to women and blacks, and remove other restrictions, such as age and religion.

Religious restrictions on the right to vote were the first to go. Article 1 of the Constitution prohibits religious tests as a qualification for "any office or Public Trust under the United States." Property qualifications fell next. At the time of the Founding, most states required some form of property ownership as a criterion for voting or running for office. Throughout the first half of the nineteenth century, the American states began to shed the requirement that people hold property in order to vote or stand for office, especially as the economy became more industrial and less agricultural, with large numbers of people moving to cities for work. These new city denizens were less likely to own their own property. By 1850, property qualifications were eliminated as a requirement for voting and running for office. Even still, many states had poll taxes well into the twentieth century. Voters would have to pay a nominal amount, such as $2, every time they voted. Poll taxes were found to abridge the civil rights of poor people; in addition, they were often administered so as to discriminate against black people. The Twenty-Fourth Amendment to the Constitution eliminated poll taxes in 1964.

The restrictions on the right to vote based on religion and property were removed with relatively little protest. The struggle to extend the right to vote to women and to racial and ethnic minorities, however, proved much more contentious, fueling two of the greatest struggles in American political history. The conflict over race runs so deep in U.S. politics that we will discuss that matter more broadly in the next section.

Women's Suffrage. At the beginning of the 1800s, few municipalities granted women voting rights. New Jersey explicitly granted women the right to vote in 1790, but the legislature removed that right in 1807. It took an entire century of agitation and activism, of protest and political maneuvering, to guarantee women's voting rights. In the decades prior to the Civil War, attitudes about women's civil rights began to change. The changes came in part because of practical problems of maintaining property, inheritance, and settlement in new states and territories. The United States adapted laws of inheritance and property from Britain, which granted men control over all property, and those laws proved problematic in a country of settlers, rather than established families and classes. It is no coincidence that many of the newer states, such as Indiana and Kentucky, were the first ones to give women economic rights. At about that time, American women began to organize to advance their political and social rights, including the right to vote. In 1848, women and men attending the Seneca Falls Convention issued the "Declaration of Sentiments and Resolutions," asserting that women were entitled to rights in every way equal to those of men.

In 1869, the National Woman Suffrage Association (NWSA) was formed in New York, and it immediately began an effort to amend the U.S. Constitution to allow women to vote. By the 1880s, the issue of voting rights for women was the subject of mass meetings, parades, and protests, and as of 1917, NWSA had 2 million members. By 1918, all of the western states and territories plus Michigan and New York had granted women

It took over a century of activism and protests for women to win the right to vote in national elections. By 1915, when this photo was taken, parades in support of women's suffrage often attracted thousands of participants, as well as onlookers and opponents.

full suffrage. Once a critical mass of states had granted women the right to vote, it was only a matter of time before Congress changed federal law. In 1919, Congress ratified the Nineteenth Amendment granting women the right to vote in federal elections.[63] Two months later, the amendment was ratified by the states, and women across the United States voted in the presidential election of 1920.

The Right to Vote for Black Americans. The struggle to extend full voting rights to racial minorities, especially blacks, cuts to even deeper divisions in American society. It took a full century after the Civil War for Congress to guarantee minorities' voting rights with the Voting Rights Act of 1964, and the battle to protect minority voting rights continues today.

The Fifteenth Amendment to the Constitution, ratified in 1870, gives blacks voting rights, and during the Reconstruction era following the Civil War, the federal government enforced those rights. With the withdrawal of federal troops from the South, however, state legislatures and local governments in the South (and elsewhere) began to enact practices that excluded blacks from elections or weakened their political power. In many states, blacks were excluded from primary elections, a practice called the white primary. Poll taxes, literacy tests, registration list purges, and other tactics were used to keep blacks from voting.[64] District and municipal boundaries were drawn to place blacks in jurisdictions in which they had little or no impact on the election of representatives or the approval of public expenditures.[65]

Blacks had little hope of changing state law because the state legislatures had written the laws and state legislators had benefited electorally from them. Congress was also reluctant to pass federal legislation to enforce the Fifteenth Amendment. At last the Supreme Court intervened. It struck down the white primary in the *Smith v. Allwright* case in 1944, in which it

Chapter 4: Civil Liberties and Civil Rights

asserted the power of the federal government to intervene in the states' conduct of elections in order to protect the voting rights of blacks.[66] The Court acted again in 1961 in the *Gomillion v. Lightfoot* case, this time ruling that state and local governments could not draw the boundaries of election districts so as to discriminate against blacks.[67] In 1965, Congress finally took action with the Voting Rights Act, sweeping aside a large number of state laws and practices that were used to discriminate against blacks. That act has been amended several times to expand who is covered, including Hispanics (1975) and language groups (1982), and what sorts of activities are prohibited, most notably racial gerrymandering (see Chapter 5). In 2013 the Supreme Court declared unconstitutional an important section of the Voting Rights Act in the case of *Shelby County v. Holder*. This section—Section 4(b)—obligated jurisdictions in Alabama, Alaska, Arizona, Georgia, Louisiana, Mississippi, South Carolina, and Texas, as well as municipalities and counties in other states, to obtain approval of any change in election administration procedures from the Department of Justice or the Federal District Court in the District of Columbia—a procedure called *preclearance*. The *Shelby County* case did not gut the Voting Rights Act, however, as other parts of the act still hold.[68]

Thus the fight over minority voting rights continues. New administrative procedures, such as laws requiring that people show a government-issued photo ID, and legislative district maps, drawn every 10 years, are subject to intense scrutiny and debate. There are frequent allegations that these practices affect minorities' voting rights adversely and even embody intentional discrimination. Disputes over these laws often end up in federal courts. Since the 1960s, the courts—and not the legislatures—have become the arena in which minorities, poor people, city dwellers, and many others can argue for the protection of their voting rights.

Racial Discrimination after the Fourteenth Amendment

As we saw at the start of the chapter, the Fourteenth Amendment's equal protection clause guaranteed equal protection of the laws to all Americans. However, the Supreme Court was initially no more ready to enforce the civil rights aspects of the Fourteenth Amendment than it was to enforce the civil liberties provisions discussed earlier. Conflict over race continued.

Plessy v. Ferguson: "Separate but Equal." The Court declared the Civil Rights Act of 1875—a key piece of legislation written to enforce the new constitutional provisions—unconstitutional on the ground that the act sought to protect blacks against discrimination by private businesses, whereas

equal protection clause

The provision of the Fourteenth Amendment guaranteeing citizens "the equal protection of the laws." This clause has served as the basis for the civil rights of African Americans, women, and other groups the Fourteenth Amendment, according to the Court's interpretation, was intended to protect individuals only against discrimination by *public* officials of state and local governments.

In 1896, the Court went still further, in the infamous case of *Plessy v. Ferguson*, by upholding a Louisiana statute that required segregation of the races on trolleys and other public carriers (and by implication in all public facilities, including schools). The Supreme Court held that the Fourteenth Amendment's "equal protection of the laws" was not violated by racial distinction as long as the law applied to both races equally.[69] Many people generally pretended that blacks were treated equally as long as some accommodation existed. What the Court was saying, in effect, was that it was not unreasonable to use race as a basis of exclusion in public matters. This was the origin of the "separate but equal" rule that was not reversed until 1954.

"separate but equal" rule

The doctrine that public accommodations could be segregated by race but still be equal

Challenging "Separate but Equal." The Supreme Court had begun to change its position regarding racial discrimination before World War II by defining more strictly the criterion of equal facilities under the "separate but equal" rule. Notably, in 1938, the Court rejected Missouri's policy of paying the tuition of qualified blacks to out-of-state law schools rather than admitting them to the University of Missouri Law School.[70] After the war, modest progress resumed. In 1950, the Court rejected Texas's claim that its new "law school for Negroes" afforded education equal to that of the all-white University of Texas Law School. Without confronting the "separate but equal" principle itself, the Court's decision anticipated *Brown v. Board of Education* by opening the question of whether *any* segregated facility could be truly equal.[71]

As the Supreme Court was ordering the admission of blacks to all-white state laws schools, it was also striking down the southern practice of white primaries, which legally excluded blacks from participation in the nominating process.[72] The most important pre-1954 decision was probably *Shelley v. Kraemer*, in which the Court ruled against the practice of "restrictive convenants," whereby the seller of a home added a clause to the sales contract requiring the buyer to agree not to resell the home to a non-Caucasian, non-Christian, and so on.[73]

Although none of those cases confronted "separate but equal" and the principle of racial discrimination as such, they were extremely significant to black leaders and gave them encouragement enough to believe that at last they had an opportunity and enough legal precedent to change the constitutional framework itself. By the fall of 1952, plaintiffs had brought cases to the Supreme Court from Kansas, South Carolina, Virginia, Delaware, and the District of Columbia challenging the constitutionality of school segregation. Of these, the Kansas case became the focal point. It seemed to be ahead of the pack in its district court, and it had the special advantage of being located in a state outside the Deep South.[74]

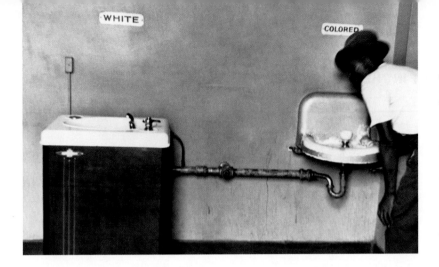

In the infamous 1896 *Plessy* decision, the Supreme Court upheld the "separate but equal" rule that was often used to justify racial segregation. Until the 1960s, laws in many states required separate public facilities—from separate schools to separate drinking fountains—for blacks and whites.

Oliver Brown, the father of three girls, lived in a low-income, racially mixed Topeka neighborhood. Every school-day morning, one of his daughters, Linda Brown, took the school bus to the Monroe School for black children about a mile away. In September 1950, Oliver Brown took Linda to the all-white Sumner School, which was closer to home, to enter her into the third grade in defiance of state law and local segregation rules. When they were refused, Brown took his case to the NAACP, and soon thereafter *Brown v. Board of Education* was born.

In deciding the case, the Court, to the surprise of many, rejected as inconclusive all the scholarly arguments about the intent of the Fourteenth Amendment and committed itself to considering only the consequences of segregation:

> Does segregation of children in public schools solely on the basis of race, even though the physical facilities and other "tangible" factors may be equal, deprive the children of the minority group of equal educational opportunities? We believe that it does. . . . We conclude that in the field of public education the doctrine of "separate but equal" has no place. Separate educational facilities are inherently unequal.[75]

The *Brown* decision altered the constitutional framework in two fundamental respects. First, after *Brown*, the states would no longer have the power to use race as a basis of discrimination in law. Second, the national government would from then on have the power to intervene with strict regulatory policies against the discriminatory actions of state or local governments, school boards, employers, and others in the private sector.

Civil Rights after *Brown v. Board of Education*. Although *Brown v. Board of Education* withdrew all constitutional authority to use race as a criterion of exclusion, this historic decision was merely a small first step. First, most states refused to cooperate until sued, and many ingenious schemes

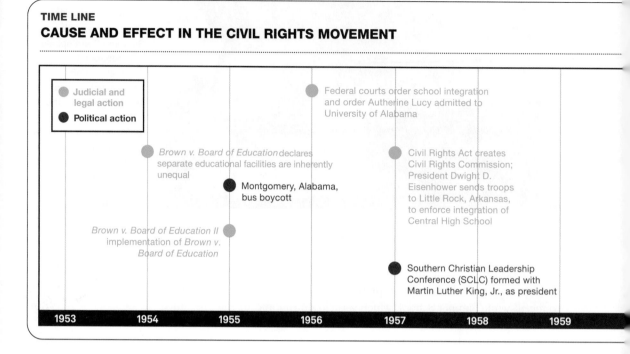

CAUSE AND EFFECT IN THE CIVIL RIGHTS MOVEMENT

● Judicial and legal action

● Political action

Federal courts order school integration and order Autherine Lucy admitted to University of Alabama

Brown v. Board of Education declares separate educational facilities are inherently unequal

● Montgomery, Alabama, bus boycott

Civil Rights Act creates Civil Rights Commission; President Dwight D. Eisenhower sends troops to Little Rock, Arkansas, to enforce integration of Central High School

Brown v. Board of Education II implementation of *Brown v. Board of Education*

● Southern Christian Leadership Conference (SCLC) formed with Martin Luther King, Jr., as president

| 1953 | 1954 | 1955 | 1956 | 1957 | 1958 | 1959 |

de jure segregation

Racial segregation that is a direct result of law or official policy

de facto segregation

Racial segregation that is not a direct result of law or government policy but is, instead, a reflection of residential patterns, income distributions, or other social factors

were employed to delay obedience (such as paying the tuition for white students to attend newly created "private" academies). Second, even as southern school boards began to cooperate by eliminating their legally enforced (de jure) school segregation, extensive actual (de facto) segregation persisted in the North as well as the South. *Brown* could not affect de facto segregation, which was not legislated but happened as a result of racially segregated housing. Third, *Brown* did not directly touch discrimination in employment, public accommodations, juries, voting, and other areas of social and economic activity.

A decade of frustration following *Brown* made it fairly obvious to all that the goal of "equal protection" required positive, or affirmative, action by Congress and by administrative agencies. And given massive southern resistance and a generally negative national public opinion toward racial integration, progress would not be made through courts, Congress, or government agencies without intense, well-organized support.

Organized civil rights demonstrations began to mount slowly but surely after *Brown v. Board of Education*. In an impressive demonstration of collective political action, hundreds of thousands of Americans, both black and white, exercised their right to peaceably assemble and petition the government for a redress of grievances, demanding that the civil rights guaranteed to white Americans now be recognized and protected for black Americans too.

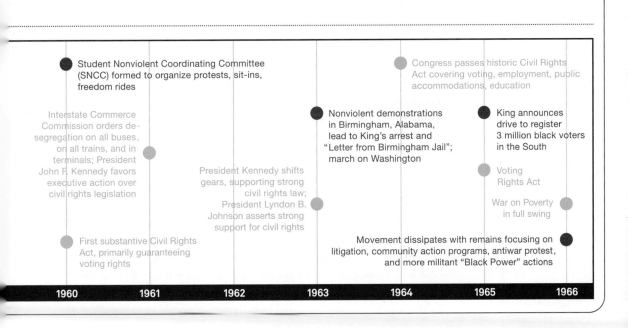

Student Nonviolent Coordinating Committee (SNCC) formed to organize protests, sit-ins, freedom rides

Congress passes historic Civil Rights Act covering voting, employment, public accommodations, education

Interstate Commerce Commission orders desegregation on all buses, on all trains, and in terminals; President John F. Kennedy favors executive action over civil rights legislation

Nonviolent demonstrations in Birmingham, Alabama, lead to King's arrest and "Letter from Birmingham Jail"; march on Washington

King announces drive to register 3 million black voters in the South

President Kennedy shifts gears, supporting strong civil rights law; President Lyndon B. Johnson asserts strong support for civil rights

Voting Rights Act

War on Poverty in full swing

First substantive Civil Rights Act, primarily guaranteeing voting rights

Movement dissipates with remains focusing on litigation, community action programs, antiwar protest, and more militant "Black Power" actions

| 1960 | 1961 | 1962 | 1963 | 1964 | 1965 | 1966 |

By the 1960s, the many organizations that made up the civil rights movement had accumulated experience and built networks capable of launching massive direct action campaigns against southern segregationists. The Southern Christian Leadership Conference, the Student Nonviolent Coordinating Committee, and many other organizations had built a movement that stretched across the South. That movement used the media to attract nationwide attention and support. In the massive March on Washington in 1963, the Reverend Martin Luther King, Jr., staked out the movement's moral claims in his "I Have a Dream" speech. Also in the 1960s, images of protesters being beaten, attacked by police dogs, and set on with fire hoses did much to win broad sympathy for the cause of black civil rights and discredit state and local governments in the South. In this way, the movement created intense pressure for a reluctant federal government to take more assertive steps to defend black civil rights.

Opportunity in Education

Education has been the focus of some of the most important battles over civil rights. An important reason is that Americans believe that everyone should have an equal chance to succeed in life. Inequities in educational opportunities were painfully obvious in the 1950s. Poverty rates of blacks far exceeded those of whites. Equal access to quality education, it was thought, would reduce and perhaps eliminate those inequities over the course of a generation.

School Desegregation. Although the District of Columbia and some of the school districts in the border states began to respond almost immediately to court-ordered desegregation, the states of the Deep South responded with a well-planned delaying tactic. Southern legislatures passed laws ordering school districts to maintain segregated schools and state superintendents to withhold state funding from racially mixed classrooms.

Most of these plans were tested in the federal courts and were struck down as unconstitutional.[76] But southern resistance was not confined to legislation. Perhaps the most serious incident occurred in Arkansas in 1957. On the first day of school a large mob assembled at Little Rock Central High School to protest integration and block black students from attending. Governor Orval Faubus ordered the National Guard to prevent enforcement of a federal court order to integrate the high school. President Eisenhower deployed U.S. troops and placed the city under martial law. Faubus responded by closing all four of the city's public high schools. In December 1959, the Supreme Court of the United States ordered the schools reopened.

As the southern states invented new devices to avoid desegregation, it was becoming unmistakably clear that the federal courts could not do the job alone. At last, in 1964, the U.S. Congress passed the Civil Rights Act of 1964, which outlawed discrimination against racial, ethnic, and religious minorities, and against women. To give the law teeth, it allowed federal agencies to withhold federal grants, contracts, and loans to states and municipalities found to discriminate or obstruct the implementation of the law.

Further progress in the desegregation of schools came in the form of busing[77] and redistricting. Figure 4.1 shows the increase in racial integration in southern schools as a result of such measures. However, further progress is likely to be slow unless the Supreme Court decides to permit federal action against de facto segregation and against the varieties of private schools and academies that have sprung up for the purpose of avoiding integration.[78] A Supreme Court decision handed down in 1995, in which the Court signaled to the lower courts to "disengage from desegregation efforts," dimmed the prospects for further school integration. In 2007, the Court went further, declaring unconstitutional programs put in place by the Louisville and Seattle school districts that used race as a determining factor in admissions in order to achieve racial diversity. Provocatively, Chief Justice John Roberts quoted the counsel for Oliver Brown in his decision for the majority, writing, "We have one fundamental contention which we will seek to develop in the course of this argument, and that contention is that no state has any authority under the equal-protection clause of the Fourteenth Amendment to use race as a factor in affording educational opportunities among its citizens."[79]

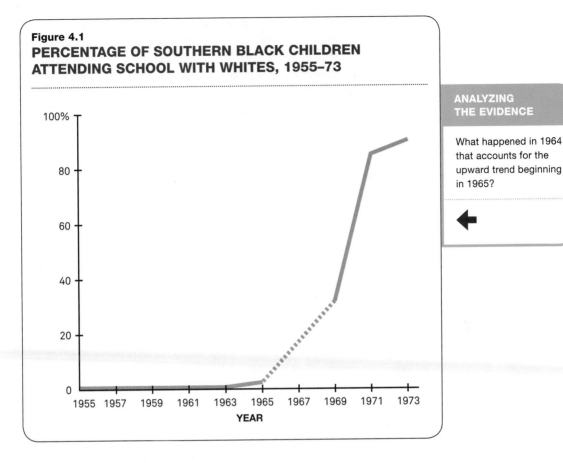

Figure 4.1

PERCENTAGE OF SOUTHERN BLACK CHILDREN ATTENDING SCHOOL WITH WHITES, 1955–73

ANALYZING THE EVIDENCE

What happened in 1964 that accounts for the upward trend beginning in 1965?

NOTE: Dashed line indicates missing data.
SOURCE: Gerald N. Rosenberg, *The Hollow Hope: Can Courts Bring About Social Change?* (Chicago: University of Chicago Press, 1991), pp. 50–1.

Women and Education. Women have also suffered from unequal access to education. Throughout the nineteenth century, relatively few colleges and professional schools admitted women. Even as late as the 1960s, elite universities such as Harvard and Yale did not admit women, and even at colleges that did admit women, women had many fewer opportunities to participate in programs, clubs, and athletics. Congress took an initial step to remedy these inequities with the Civil Rights Act of 1964, but the most significant federal legislation to guarantee women equal access to education is the 1972 Education Act. Title IX of this act forbids gender discrimination in education. The Education Act provided the nudge that many schools needed. By the mid-1970s most universities had become fully coed. But enforcing equality was more difficult.

The Education Act of 1972 provided fairly weak enforcement provisions, but it has proven an effective tool for litigation. Perhaps the most significant step came in 1992, when the Court decided in *Franklin v. Gwinnett County Public Schools* that violations of Title IX could be remedied with monetary damages.[80] The Court's 1992 ruling opened the door for further legal action in the area of education and led to stronger enforcement against sexual harassment, gender inequities in resources (such as lab space, research support for faculty, and athletics), and gender inequities in compensation. In the two years after the *Franklin* case, complaints to the Education Department's Office for Civil Rights about unequal treatment of women's athletic programs nearly tripled. In several high-profile legal cases, some prominent universities have been ordered to create more women's sports programs; many other colleges and universities have begun to add more women's programs in order to avoid potential litigation.[81]

In 1996, the Supreme Court made another important decision about gender and education by putting an end to all-male schools supported by public funds. It ruled that the Virginia Military Institute's policy of not admitting women was unconstitutional.[82] Along with the Citadel, an all-male military college in South Carolina, Virginia Military Institute (VMI) had never admitted women. It argued that the unique educational experience it offered, including intense physical training and the harsh treatment of freshmen, would be destroyed if women were admitted. The Court, however, ruled that the male-only policy denied "substantial equality" to women. Two days after the Court's ruling, the Citadel announced that it would accept women. VMI considered becoming a private institution in order to remain all male, but in September 1996 the school board finally voted to admit women. The legal decisions may have removed formal barriers to entry, but the experience of the female cadets at these schools has not been easy. The first female cadet at the Citadel, Shannon Faulkner, won admission in 1995 under a federal court order but quit after four days. Although four women were admitted to the Citadel after the Supreme Court decision, two of them quit several months later. They charged harassment by male students, including attempts to set the female cadets on fire.[83]

The Politics of Rights

The Nineteenth Amendment, *Brown v. Board of Education*, the Civil Rights Act, and the Voting Rights Act were the signal achievements of the civil rights movements of women and blacks. They helped redefine the meaning of civil rights in America not just for those groups but for all people. The civil rights movements of women and of blacks became models for other groups of people to press civil rights claims, and the strategies of these

Chapter 4: Civil Liberties and Civil Rights

movements have been widely mimicked. The principles behind equality in voting and in education have since been applied to many other areas, including employment, housing, immigration, access to public facilities, and athletics. With the push for rights in these spheres, there has also been a push back. Just how far do civil rights extend?

Outlawing Discrimination in Employment. Despite the agonizingly slow progress of school desegregation, there was some progress in other areas of civil rights during the 1960s and 1970s. Voting rights were established and fairly quickly began to revolutionize southern politics. Service on juries was no longer denied to minorities. But progress in the right to participate in politics and government dramatized the relative lack of economic progress, and it was in this area that battles over civil rights were increasingly fought.

The federal courts and the Justice Department entered the arena of discrimination in employment through Title VII of the Civil Rights Act of 1964. Title VII outlawed job discrimination by all private and public employers, including governmental agencies (such as fire and police departments), that employed more than 15 workers. We have already seen that the Supreme Court gave "interstate commerce" such a broad definition that Congress had the constitutional authority to outlaw discrimination by virtually any local employer.[84] Title VII made it unlawful to discriminate in employment on the basis of color, religion, sex, or national origin, as well as race.

A potential difficulty with Title VII is that the complaining party had to show that deliberate discrimination was the cause of the failure to get a job or a training opportunity. Rarely does an employer explicitly admit discrimination on the basis of race, sex, or any other illegal reason. For a time, courts allowed the complaining parties to make their case if they could show that an employer's hiring practices, whether intentional or not, had the *effect* of exclusion. Employers, in effect, had to justify their actions.[85] In recent years, though, the Supreme Court has placed a number of limits on employment discrimination suits. In 2007, for example, in the case of *Ledbetter v. Goodyear Tire and Rubber Co.*, the court said that a complaint of gender discrimination must be brought within 180 days of the time the discrimination was alleged to have occurred.[86] This blocks suits based on events that might have taken place in the past. In 2009, Congress effectively overturned the Court's decision by enacting legislation greatly extending the amount of time available to workers filing such suits.

Women and Gender Discrimination. Although women succeeded in gaining voting and property rights long ago, women continued to suffer discrimination in a variety of forms, particularly in the realm of employment. Here, women benefited from the civil rights movement, and, especially, from Title VII. Title VII not only provided a valuable tool for the growing women's movement in the 1960s and 1970s but actually fostered the movement's growth.[87] The first major campaign of the National Organization for Women (NOW) involved picketing the Equal Employment Opportunity Commission (EEOC) for its refusal to ban sex-segregated employment advertisements.

Building on these victories and the growth of the women's movement, women's rights activists sought an equal rights amendment (ERA) to the Constitution. The proposed amendment was short: its substantive passage stated that "equality of rights under the law shall not be denied or abridged by the United States or by any State on account of sex." The amendment's supporters believed that such a sweeping guarantee of equal rights was a necessary tool for ending all discrimination against women and for making gender roles more equal. Opponents charged that it would be socially disruptive and would introduce changes—such as coed restrooms—that most Americans did not want. The amendment easily passed Congress in 1972 and won quick approval in many state legislatures but fell three states short of the 38 needed to ratify the amendment by the 1982 deadline for its ratification.[88]

Despite the failure of the ERA, gender discrimination expanded dramatically as an area of civil rights law. In the 1970s, the conservative Burger Court helped to establish gender discrimination as a major and highly visible civil rights issue. Although the Burger Court refused to treat gender discrimination as the equivalent of racial discrimination,[89] it did make it easier for plaintiffs to file and win suits on the basis of gender discrimination by applying an "intermediate" level of review to these cases.[90] This intermediate scrutiny is midway between traditional rules of evidence, which put the burden of proof on the plaintiff, and the doctrine of strict scrutiny, which requires the defendant to show not only that a particular classification is reasonable but also that there is a need or compelling interest for it. Intermediate scrutiny shifts the burden of proof partially onto the defendant, rather than leaving it entirely on the plaintiff.

Elevated awareness of sexual harassment as a form of gender discrimination has also advanced the cause of women's civil rights. Courts began to find sexual harassment a form of sex discrimination during the late 1970s. In 1986, the Supreme Court recognized two forms of sexual harassment—the quid pro quo type, which involves sexual extortion, and the hostile-environment type, which involves sexual intimidation.[91] In its decision, the Court said that sexual harassment may be legally actionable even if the employee did not suffer tangible economic or job-related losses in relation to it. And in 1993, the Court said that sexual harassment may be legally actionable even if the employee did not suffer tangible psychological costs as a result of it.[92] In two 1998 cases, the Court further strengthened the law when it said that whether or not sexual harassment results in economic harm to the employee, an employer is liable for the harassment if it was committed by someone with authority over the employee—by a supervisor, for example.

intermediate scrutiny

The test used by the Supreme Court in gender discrimination cases. Intermediate scrutiny places the burden of proof partially on the government and partially on the challengers to show that the law in question is constitutional

Chapter 4: Civil Liberties and Civil Rights

But the Court also said that an employer may defend itself by showing that it had a sexual harassment prevention and grievance policy in effect.[93]

Latinos. The labels "Latino" and "Hispanic" encompass a wide range of groups with diverse national origins, distinctive cultural identities, and particular experiences. For example, the early political experiences of Mexican Americans were shaped by race and region. In 1898, Mexican Americans were given formal political rights, including the right to vote. In many places, however, and especially in Texas, Mexican Americans were segregated and prevented from voting by such means as the white primary and the poll tax.[94]

The earliest independent Mexican American political organizations, the League of United Latin American Citizens (LULAC) and the American GI Forum, worked to stem discrimination against Mexican Americans in the years after World War II. By the late 1950s, the first Mexican American had been elected to Congress, and four others followed in the 1960s. In the late 1960s, a new kind of Mexican American political movement was born. Inspired by the black civil rights movement, Mexican American students launched boycotts of high school classes in Los Angeles, Denver, and San Antonio. Students in colleges and universities across California joined in as well. Among their demands were bilingual education, an end to discrimination, and greater cultural recognition. In Crystal City, Texas, which had been dominated by Anglo politicians despite a population that was overwhelmingly Mexican American, the newly formed La Raza Unida Party took over the city government.[95]

Discrimination against Mexican Americans and other Latinos in the Southwest was pervasive prior to World War II, with segregated schools common in Texas and California along with housing and employment restrictions. In 1947, LULAC won an important court victory in the case of *Mendez v. Westminster*, which overturned an Orange County, California, policy of school segregation aimed at Mexican Americans.[96] The *Mendez* case was an important precedent for *Brown v. Board of Education* and is now recognized as a major landmark in the civil rights struggle.

In recent years, Latino political strategy has developed along two tracks. One is a traditional ethnic-group path of voter registration and voting along ethnic lines because Hispanic voter registration typically lags far behind the rates at which whites and blacks are registered to vote. This strategy is helped by the enormous growth of the Latino population, resulting in part from immigration. The second is a legal strategy using the various civil rights laws designed to ensure fair access to the political system. The Mexican American Legal Defense and Education Fund (MALDEF) has played a key role in designing and pursuing the latter strategy.

Asian Americans. The early Asian experience in the United States was shaped by a series of naturalization laws dating back to 1790, the first of which declared that only white immigrants were eligible for citizenship. Chinese immigrants had begun arriving in California in the 1850s, drawn by the boom of the gold rush. They were immediately met with hostility. The virulent antagonism toward Chinese immigrants in California led Congress in 1870 to declare Chinese immigrants ineligible for citizenship. In 1882, the first Chinese Exclusion Act suspended the entry of Chinese laborers.

At the time of the Exclusion Act, the Chinese community was composed predominantly of single male laborers, with few women and children. The few Chinese children in San Francisco were initially denied entry to the public schools; only after parents of American-born Chinese children pressed legal action were the children allowed to attend public school. Even then, however, they were made to attend a separate Chinese school. American-born Chinese children could not be denied citizenship, however; this right was confirmed by the Supreme Court in 1898, when it ruled in *United States v. Wong Kim Ark* that anyone born in the United States was entitled to full citizenship.[97] Still, new Chinese immigrants were barred from the United States until 1943; China by then had become a key wartime ally, and Congress repealed the Chinese Exclusion Act and permitted Chinese residents to become citizens.

Immigration climbed rapidly after the 1965 Immigration and Nationality Services Act, which lifted discriminatory quotas. In spite of this and other developments, limited English proficiency barred many Asian Americans and Latinos from full participation in American life. Two developments in the 1970s, however, established rights for language minorities. In 1974, the Supreme Court ruled in *Lau v. Nichols*, a suit filed on behalf of Chinese students in San Francisco, that school districts have to provide education for students whose English is limited.[98] It did not mandate bilingual education, but it established a duty to provide instruction that students could understand. The 1970 amendments to the Voting Rights Act of 1965 permanently outlawed literacy tests as a prerequisite to register to vote and mandated bilingual ballots or oral assistance for those who speak Spanish, Chinese, Japanese, Korean, Native American languages, or Inuit languages.

Immigration and Rights. From its very beginning the United States has struggled to define the rights of immigrants and the notion of citizenship. Waves of immigration have led to contentious questions as to whether immigrants should enjoy the same civil rights as citizens, such as the right to vote and equal access to education, or whether immigrants should enjoy a narrower set of rights. This issue gets to the question of *what rights*, as described earlier in the chapter.

Asian Americans, Latinos, and other groups have been concerned about the impact of immigration laws on their civil rights. Many Asian

In recent years, immigration laws have become a source of debate in American politics. Some people feel that not enough is being done to prevent illegal immigration, while others worry that harsher laws violate immigrants' rights and fundamental American values.

American and Latino organizations opposed the Immigration Reform and Control Act of 1986 because it imposes sanctions on employers who hire undocumented workers. Such sanctions, they feared, would lead employers to discriminate against Latinos and Asian Americans. These suspicions were confirmed in a 1990 report by the General Accounting Office that found employer sanctions had created a "widespread pattern of discrimination" against Latinos and others who appear foreign.[99] Organizations such as MALDEF and the Asian Law Caucus monitor and challenge such discrimination. These groups have turned their attention to the rights of legal and illegal immigrants as anti-immigrant sentiment has grown in recent years.

The Supreme Court has ruled that illegal immigrants are eligible for education and medical care but can be denied other social benefits; legal immigrants, however, are to be treated much the same as citizens. But growing immigration—including an estimated 300,000 illegal immigrants per year—and mounting economic insecurity have undermined these practices. Groups of voters across the country now strongly support drawing a sharper line between immigrants and citizens. Not surprisingly, the movement to deny benefits to noncitizens began in California, which experienced sharp economic distress in the early 1990s and has the highest levels of immigration of any state. In 1994, Californians voted in favor of Proposition 187, which denied illegal immigrants all services except emergency medical care. Supporters of the measure hoped to discourage illegal immigration and pressure illegal immigrants already in the country to leave. Opponents contended that denying basic services to illegal immigrants risked creating a subclass of residents in the United States whose lack of education and poor health would threaten all Americans. In 1994 and 1997, a federal court declared most of Proposition 187 unconstitutional, affirming previous rulings that illegal immigrants should be granted public education.

The question of the rights of legal immigrants points to an even tougher problem. Congress has the power to deny public benefits to this group, but doing so would go against long-standing traditions in American political culture. Legal immigrants have traditionally enjoyed most of the rights and obligations of citizens (such as paying taxes). The Constitution begins with "We the People of the United States"; likewise, the Bill of Rights refers to the rights of *people*, not the rights of citizens. Immigration continues to be a divisive issue in American politics.

Americans with Disabilities. The concept of rights for people with disabilities began to emerge in the 1970s as the civil rights model spread to other groups. The seed was planted in a little-noticed provision of the 1973 Rehabilitation Act that outlawed discrimination against individuals on the basis of disabilities. As in many other cases, the law itself helped give rise to the movement demanding rights.[100] Modeling itself on the NAACP's Legal Defense Fund, the disability movement founded a Disability Rights Education and Defense Fund to press its legal claims. The movement achieved its greatest success with the passage of the Americans with Disabilities Act (ADA) of 1990, which guarantees people with disabilities equal employment rights and access to public businesses. Claims of discrimination in violation of this act are considered by the EEOC. The impact of the law has been far-reaching as businesses and public facilities have installed ramps, elevators, and other devices to meet its requirements.[101]

Gay Men and Lesbians. In less than 50 years, the gay rights movement has become one of the largest civil rights movements in contemporary America. Beginning with street protests in the 1960s, it has grown into a well-financed and sophisticated lobby. The Human Rights Campaign is the primary national political action committee that raises and distributes campaign money to further gay rights; it provides campaign financing and volunteers to work for candidates endorsed by the group. The movement has also formed legal rights organizations, including the Lambda Legal Defense and Education Fund.

The 1990s proved something of a watershed moment in the fight for gay rights, witnessing both the first national anti-gay laws and the first declaration by the Supreme Court protecting the civil rights of gay men and women. In 1993, President Bill Clinton confronted the question of whether gays should be allowed to serve in the military. As a candidate, Clinton had said he favored lifting the ban on gays in the military. The issue set off a huge controversy in the first months of his presidency. After nearly a year of deliberation, the administration enunciated a compromise: its "Don't Ask, Don't Tell" policy, which allowed gay men and lesbians to serve in the military as long as they did not openly proclaim their sexual orientation or engage in homosexual activity. Two years later the gay rights movement experienced a further setback when Clinton signed the Defense of Marriage Act (DOMA), which recognized a marriage as the union of one man and one woman for the purposes of the application of federal laws, such as taxes and benefits.

As in the case of other civil rights movements, it was the Supreme Court that took a major step in protecting gay men and lesbians from discrimination. This marked an important departure from its earlier juris-prudence. The first gay rights case that the Court decided, *Bowers v. Hardwick* (1986), had ruled against a right to privacy that would protect consensual homosexual activity. After the *Bowers* decision, the gay rights movement sought suitable legal cases to test the constitutionality of discrimination against gay men and lesbians, much as the civil rights movement had done in the late 1940s and 1950s. As one advocate put it, "lesbians and gay men are looking for their *Brown v. Board of Education*."[102] Among the cases tested were those stemming from local ordinances restricting gay rights (including the right to marry), job discrimination, and family law issues such as adop-tion and parental rights. Finally, in 1996, in *Romer v. Evans*, the Supreme Court explicitly extended fundamental civil rights protections to gay men and lesbians by declaring unconstitutional a 1992 amendment to the Colo-rado state constitution that prohibited local governments from passing ordi-nances to protect gay rights.[103] The decision's forceful language highlighted the connection between gay rights and civil rights as it declared discrimina-tion against gay people unconstitutional.

Finally, in *Lawrence v. Texas* (2003), the Court overturned *Bowers* and struck down a Texas statute criminalizing certain intimate sexual conduct between consenting partners of the same sex. A victory for lesbians and gay men every bit as significant as *Roe v. Wade* was for women, *Lawrence v. Texas* extends at least one aspect of civil liberties to sexual minorities: the right to privacy. However, this decision by itself does not undo the various exclusions that deprive lesbians and gay men of full civil rights. Another important victory occurred in 2010, when Congress finally repealed Don't Ask, Don't Tell. In 2008, then-candidate Barack Obama promised to repeal the act should he be elected. When he did not do so in the first months of his administration, he was roundly criticized by gay rights activities. After a lengthy study by the Defense Department of the possible consequences of allowing openly gay men and women to serve, Congress voted for the repeal of Don't Ask, Don't Tell.

The focal point for the assertion of gay rights has now become the right to marry. In 2004, the Supreme Judicial Court of Massachusetts ruled that under the state's constitution gay men and lesbians were entitled to marry. The state senate then requested the court to rule on whether a civil union statute (avoiding the word *marriage*) would, as it did in Vermont, satisfy the court's ruling, in response to which the court ruled negatively, asserting that civil unions are too much like the "separate but equal" doctrine that maintained legalized racial segregation from 1896 to 1954. In the decade between 2004 and 2014, same-sex marriage became legal in 35 states. This state-by-state process took place through court order, voter initiative, and legislative enactment. However, as with the women's suffrage movement, these changes faced pushback. In many states, voters and state legislatures had supported constitutional amendments banning same-sex marriage. Some of these bans were struck down by courts, but in November 2014, same-sex marriage remained illegal in 15 states.

The discrepancy between some state laws, which recognized same-sex marriage, and the federal law under DOMA, which did not, ultimately proved to be the act's undoing. The nation's laws extend to everyone equally; that is the meaning of equal protection under the Fifth and Fourteenth amendments. Edith Windsor and Thea Speyer were a same-sex couple who resided in New York but were lawfully married elsewhere. In 2009, Speyer died, leaving her estate to Windsor. Windsor sought the exemption afforded to surviving spouses from federal estate taxes, but under DOMA she was prevented from that benefit. In 2013 the Supreme Court ruled DOMA unconstitutional "as a depravation of liberty of the person protected by the Fifth Amendment."[104]

Affirmative Action

In the past 50 years, the politics of rights not only spread to increasing numbers of groups in society but also expanded its goal. The relatively narrow goal of equalizing opportunity by eliminating discriminatory barriers developed into the far broader goal of affirmative action—compensatory action to overcome the consequences of past discrimination and encourage greater diversity. In 1965, President Lyndon Johnson attempted to inaugurate affirmative action by executive orders directing agency heads and personnel officers to pursue vigorously a policy of minority employment in the federal civil service and in companies doing business with the national government. But affirmative action did not become a prominent goal until the 1970s.

The Supreme Court and the Burden of Proof. As affirmative action spread, it began to divide civil rights activists and their supporters. The whole issue of qualification versus minority preference was addressed in the case of Allan Bakke. Bakke, a white man with no minority affiliation, brought suit

affirmative action
A policy or program designed to redress historic injustices committed against specific groups by making special efforts to provide members of these groups with access to educational and employment opportunities

against the University of California Medical School at Davis on the grounds that in denying him admission the school had discriminated against him on the basis of his race (that year the school had reserved 16 of 100 available slots for minority applicants). He argued that his grades and test scores had ranked him well above many students who had been accepted at the school and that the only possible explanation for his rejection was that the others were black or Hispanic and he was white. In 1978, Bakke won his case before the Supreme Court and was admitted to the medical school, but he did not succeed in getting affirmative action declared unconstitutional. The Court rejected the procedures at the University of California because its medical school had used both a quota *and* a separate admissions system for minorities. The Court agreed with Bakke's argument that racial categorizations are suspect categories that place a severe burden of proof on those using them to show a "compelling public purpose." The Court went on to say that achieving "a diverse student body" was such a public purpose, but the method of a rigid quota of student slots assigned on the basis of race was incompatible with the equal protection clause. Thus the Court permitted universities (and other schools, training programs, and hiring authorities) to continue to take minority status into consideration but limited severely the use of quotas.[105]

For nearly a decade after *Bakke*, the Supreme Court was tentative and permissive about efforts by corporations and governments to experiment with affirmative action programs in employment.[106] But in 1989, the Court returned to the *Bakke* position, ruling that any "rigid numerical quota" is suspect. That same year, the Court ruled that any affirmative action program already approved by federal courts could be challenged by individuals (usually white men) who alleged that the program discriminated against them.[107] In 1995, the Supreme Court's ruling in *Adarand Constructors v. Pena* further weakened affirmative action. This decision stated that race-based policies, such as preferences given by the government to minority contractors, must survive strict scrutiny, placing the burden on the government to show that such affirmative action programs serve a compelling government interest and are narrowly tailored to address identifiable past discrimination.[108] In 1996, a federal court (the U.S. Court of Appeals for the Fifth Circuit) stated that race could never be considered in granting admissions and scholarships at state colleges and universities.[109] This decision effectively rolled back the use of affirmative action permitted by the 1978 *Bakke* case. In 1996, the Supreme Court refused to hear a challenge to the case. This meant that its ruling remains in effect in the states covered by the Fifth Circuit—Texas, Louisiana, and Mississippi—but does not apply to the rest of the country.

This betwixt-and-between status of affirmative action was where things stood in 2003, when the Supreme Court took two cases against the University of Michigan that would clarify legal policy on affirmative action. The first suit, *Gratz v. Bollinger*, alleged that by using a point-based ranking system that automatically awarded 20 points (out of 150) to African American, Latino, and Native American applicants, the university's undergraduate admissions policy discriminated unconstitutionally against white students with otherwise equal or superior academic qualifications. The Supreme Court agreed, 6–3, arguing that something tantamount to a quota was involved because undergraduate admissions lacked the necessary "individualized consideration," employing instead a "mechanical one," based too much on the favorable minority points.[110] The Court's ruling in *Gratz v. Bollinger* was not surprising, given *Bakke*'s holding against quotas and recent decisions calling for strict scrutiny of all racial classifications, even those that are intended to remedy past discrimination or promote future equality.

The second case, *Grutter v. Bollinger*, broke new ground. Barbara Grutter sued the University of Michigan Law School on the grounds that it had discriminated in a race-conscious way against white applicants with grades and law boards equal or superior to those of minority applicants. A precarious vote of 5–4 aligned the majority of the Supreme Court with Justice Lewis Powell's opinion in *Bakke* for the first time. In *Bakke*, Powell had argued that diversity in education is a compelling state interest and that constitutionally race could be considered a positive factor in admissions decisions. In *Grutter*, the Court reiterated Powell's holding and, applying strict scrutiny to the law school's policy, found that its admissions process was narrowly tailored to the school's compelling state interest in diversity because it gave a "highly individualized, holistic review of each applicant's file," in which race counted but was not used in a "mechanical way."[111] This ruling put affirmative action on stronger ground.

CAN RIGHTS AND LIBERTIES BE BALANCED?

As we observed at the beginning of this chapter, the Constitution's Bill of Rights includes both rights and liberties. A liberty is an area such as speech or religious belief into which intrusion by the government is limited. A right, on the other hand, is an obligation imposed upon the government. When citizens have a right, such as the right to vote or to a jury trial, the government must not only respect that right but act vigorously to protect it.

In the real world, of course, nothing is ever neat. Without any regulation speech can lead to riots and violence. As a result, we tolerate a variety of restrictions on speech designed to keep the peace. Liberties and rights may clash. Today, for example, some assert that governmental recognition

Chapter 4: Civil Liberties and Civil Rights

of "gay rights" violates their own deeply held religious beliefs. The courts are constantly asked to adjudicate and balance these and a host of other conflicts among rights and liberties.

Civil rights and civil liberties are among America's most important promises and aspirations. Perfection is impossible, but we must always strive to be better.

For Further Reading

Selections highlighted in red are included in *Readings in American Politics: Analysis and Perspectives*, Third Edition.

Ackerman, Bruce. *Before the Next Attack: Preserving Civil Liberties in an Age of Terrorism*. New Haven, CT: Yale University Press, 2006.

Baer, Judith, and Leslie Goldstein. *The Constitutional and Legal Rights of Women*. Los Angeles: Roxbury, 2006.

Dawson, Michael. *Not in Our Lifetimes: The Future of Black Politics*. Chicago: University of Chicago Press, 2011.

Klarman, Michael. *From Jim Crow to Civil Rights: The Supreme Court and the Struggle for Racial Equality*. New York: Oxford University Press, 2004.

Koppelman, Andrew M. *Same Sex, Different States: When Same-Sex Marriages Cross State Lines*. New Haven, CT: Yale University Press, 2006.

Lewis, Anthony. *Gideon's Trumpet*. New York: Random House, 1964.

Lewis, Anthony. *Freedom for the Thought That We Hate: A Biography of the First Amendment*. New York: Basic Books, 2010.

Rosenberg, Gerald N. *The Hollow Hope: Can Courts Bring About Social Change?* Chicago: University of Chicago Press, 1991.

Tushnet, Mark, and Michael Olivas. *"Colored Men" and "Hombres Aquí:" Hernandez v. Texas and the Emergence of Mexican American Lawyering*. Houston, TX: Arte Público Press, 2006.

Yoshino, Kenji. *Covering: The Hidden Assault on Our Civil Rights*. New York: Random House, 2007.

5

Congress: The First Branch

The U.S. Congress is the "first branch" of government under Article I of the Constitution and is also among the world's most important representative bodies. Most of the world's representative bodies only represent—that is, their governmental functions consist mainly of affirming and legitimating the national leadership's decisions. The U.S. Congress is one of the few national representative bodies that actually possesses powers of governance. It has vast authority over the two most important powers given to any government: the power of force (control over the nation's military forces) and the power over money. Specifically, according to Article I, Section 8, Congress can "lay and collect Taxes," deal with indebtedness and bankruptcy, impose duties, borrow and coin money, and generally control the nation's purse strings. It also may "provide for the common Defence and general Welfare," regulate interstate commerce, undertake public works, acquire and control federal lands, promote science and "useful Arts" (pertaining mostly to patents and copyrights), and regulate the militia.

In the realm of foreign policy, Congress has the power to declare war, deal with piracy, regulate foreign commerce, and raise and regulate the armed forces and military installations. Further, the Senate has the power to ratify treaties (by a two-thirds vote) and to approve the appointment of ambassadors. Capping these powers, Congress is charged to make laws "which shall be necessary and proper for carrying into Execution the foregoing Powers, and all other Powers vested by this Constitution in the Government of the United States, or in any Department or Officer thereof."

It is extraordinarily difficult for a large representative assembly to formulate, enact, and implement the laws. The internal complexities of conducting business within Congress—the legislative process—are daunting. These difficulties are exacerbated by partisanship. For example, the framers of the Constitution viewed bicameralism, or the division of the legislature into two distinct bodies, as a "salutary check on government."[1] James Madison averred that requiring two distinct bodies to agree on legislation would lessen the risk that ambitious politicians could carry out schemes inconsistent with the public good. Bicameralism, however, can sometimes thwart needed legislative action, particularly if the two houses of Congress are controlled by different political parties.

Recent struggles over the federal debt limit have been difficult to resolve in part because of divided control of Congress. On May 16, 2011, the U.S. government reached its legal debt limit of $14.3 trillion, which is the statutory limit on the amount the government can borrow to meet its obligations. Congress created the original debt limit in 1917 but has raised it many times since then. Reaching the debt limit means that the government is no longer able to borrow money to pay its bills. In order to meet the federal government's expected expenses for the fiscal year ending in September 2011, the government would need an additional $738 billion more than its anticipated revenues.

CORE OF THE ANALYSIS

➡ Congress is the most important representative institution in American government.

➡ Constituents hold their representatives to account through elections.

➡ The legislative process is driven by numerous political forces: political parties, committees, staffs, caucuses, rules of lawmaking, and the president.

➡ Congress also makes the law. Before a bill can become law, it must pass through the legislative process, a complex set of procedures.

When the debt limit was reached, the U.S. Treasury announced that it would adopt a number of fiscal measures that would avert a crisis until approximately August 4, 2011. After that date, the government would no longer be able to meet all of its obligations and would need to institute significant spending cuts that could include outlays for federal social and military programs as well as interest payments on U.S. government securities. Each of these types of cuts could have serious consequences. If, for example, the government failed to meet its debt obligations, bond holders, who include foreign governments, might dump U.S. securities, causing interest rates to rise dramatically throughout the economy. The result might then be an extremely severe economic downturn, or even a depression.

As the potential crisis approached, Congress began discussing its options. Usually the debt ceiling is raised as needed without much fanfare, but in 2011, differences between the House and Senate complicated the picture. In that year, the Senate was controlled by Democrats and the House by Republicans, many of whom had been elected in 2010 with Tea Party support on an anti-tax and anti-spending platform. House Republicans declared that they would only agree to an increase in the debt ceiling if Senate Democrats accepted substantial cuts in domestic spending that would bring about long-term reductions in the federal debt. Indeed, Republicans sought $1.7 trillion in cuts by severely reducing spending on such domestic programs as education, food safety, health research, and criminal justice. Senate Democrats, for their part, replied that they, too, saw the need to reduce the federal deficit, but that this could only be accomplished through a mix of spending cuts and what they characterized as tax increases for the wealthy. They vowed to defend certain domestic programs against the GOP's budget axe. House Republicans retorted that they would not allow any new taxes.

Though the potential consequences of a default seemed dire, neither side was anxious to compromise. In late June 2011, House Republican Majority Leader Eric Cantor (R-Va.) denounced the Democrats and walked out of the budget talks organized by Vice President Joseph Biden. In the end, with just one day remaining before a possible U.S. default, the two sides reached an agreement that was widely seen as a victory for the Republicans. The president accepted their formula of spending cuts with no tax increases. Republicans also secured a promise of a vote on a balanced-budget amendment to the U.S. Constitution. Again in the spring of 2013, U.S. borrowing approached the debt ceiling. This time, spending cuts combined with higher government revenue (a result of improved economic conditions as the country emerged from recession) pushed the date by which a new debt ceiling must be negotiated into the future.

Many individuals and institutions have the capacity to influence the legislative process. To exercise its power to make the law, Congress must first bring about something close to an organizational miracle. In this chapter, after a brief consideration of representation, we examine the organization of Congress and the legislative process. Throughout, we point out the connections between these two aspects—the ways in which representation affects congressional operations (especially through the "electoral connection") and the ways in which congressional institutions enhance or diminish representation (especially Congress's division- and specialization-of-labor committee system).

REPRESENTATION

Congress is the most important representative institution in American government. Each member's primary responsibility is to the district, to his constituency, not to the congressional leadership, a party, or even Congress itself. Yet the task of representation is not a simple one. Views about what constitutes fair and effective representation differ, and constituents can make very different kinds of demands on their representatives. Members of Congress must consider these diverse views and demands as they represent their districts (Figure 5.1).

Some legislators see themselves as perfect agents of others: they have been elected to do the bidding of those who sent them to the legislature, and they act as delegates. Others see themselves as having been selected by their fellow citizens to do what they think is "right," and they act as trustees. Most legislators are a mix of these two types. And all, one way or another, need to survive the next election in order to pursue whatever role they formulate for themselves.

Legislators not only represent others; they may be representative *of* others as well. The latter is especially salient today when it comes to gender and race, where is symbolically significant at the very least. Descriptive characteristics permit women members and representatives drawn from minority groups to serve and draw support from those with whom they share an identity, both inside their formal constituency and in the nation at large. (See Table 5.1 for a summary of demographic characteristics of members of Congress.) Descriptive representation for African American and Hispanic minorities has been facilitated by the process of drawing new district boundaries within states every 10 years following the decennial census of the population. Some districts have been created—so-called majority-minority districts—with racial or ethnic minorities in the majority.

As we discussed in Chapter 1, we think of our political representatives as our agents. Agency representation takes place when constituents have the power to hire and fire their representatives. Frequent competitive elections

constituency
The district making up the area from which an official is elected

delegate
A representative who votes according to the preferences of his or her constituency

trustee
A representative who votes based on what he or she thinks is best for his or her constituency

agency representation
The type of representation according to which representatives are held accountable to their constituents if they fail to represent them properly. That is, constituents have the power to hire and fire their representatives

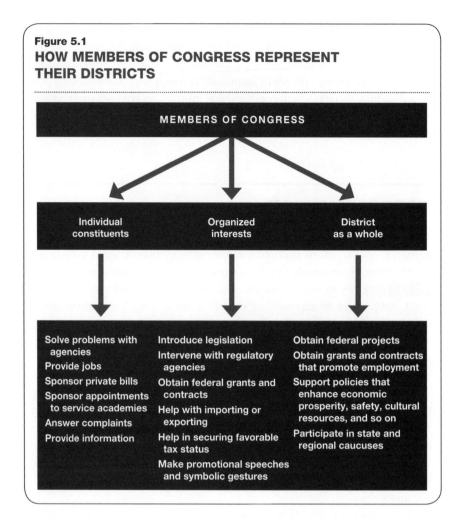

Figure 5.1
HOW MEMBERS OF CONGRESS REPRESENT THEIR DISTRICTS

MEMBERS OF CONGRESS

Individual constituents	Organized interests	District as a whole
Solve problems with agencies	Introduce legislation	Obtain federal projects
Provide jobs	Intervene with regulatory agencies	Obtain grants and contracts that promote employment
Sponsor private bills	Obtain federal grants and contracts	Support policies that enhance economic prosperity, safety, cultural resources, and so on
Sponsor appointments to service academies	Help with importing or exporting	
Answer complaints	Help in securing favorable tax status	Participate in state and regional caucuses
Provide information	Make promotional speeches and symbolic gestures	

constitute an important means by which constituents hold their representatives to account and keep them responsive to constituency views and preferences. The idea of a representative as agent is similar to the relationship of lawyer and client. True, the relationship between the member of Congress and as many as 700,000 "clients" in the district or that between the senator and possibly millions of clients in the state is very different from that of lawyer and client. But the criteria of performance are comparable.

We would expect at the very least that each representative will constantly be seeking to discover the interests of the constituency and will be speaking for those interests in Congress and other centers of government.[2] We expect this because we believe that members of Congress, like politicians everywhere, are ambitious. For many, this ambition is satisfied simply by maintaining a hold on their present office and advancing up the rungs of power in that legislative body. Some may be looking ahead to the next level—to

Table 5.1

DEMOGRAPHICS OF MEMBERS OF THE 113TH CONGRESS

	HOUSE	SENATE
AGE*		
Average	57 years	62 years
Range	30–89 years	39–89 years
OCCUPATION**		
Business	187 representatives	27 senators
Education	77	15
Law	156	55
Public service/politics	184	42
Previous military experience	87	18
EDUCATION†		
High school is highest degree	21	1
College degree	405	99
Law degree	169	57
PhD	20	0
MD	22	3
RELIGION††		
Protestant	247	52
Catholic	136	27
Jewish	22	11
Mormon	8	7
GENDER		
Women	77	20
Men	358	80
RACE/ETHNICITY		
African American	40	2
Hispanic/Latino	34	4
Asian/Pacific Islander	12	1
CONGRESSIONAL SERVICE		
Number serving in first term	75	14
Average length of service	9.1 years (4.6 terms)	10.2 years (1.7 terms)

*Age at time of election (November 6, 2012).

**Most members list more than one occupation.

† Education categories are not exclusive (e.g., a representative with a law degree might also be counted as having a college degree).

†† Ninety-eight percent of members cite a specific religious affiliation. Other affiliations not listed here include Buddhist, Muslim, Hindu, Orthodox Christian, and Unitarian.

SOURCE: Jennifer E. Manning, "Membership of the 113th Congress: A Profile," *Congressional Research Service*, April 11, 2013.

higher legislative office, as when a representative seeks a Senate seat, or to an executive office, as when a legislator returns home to run for the state's governorship, or at the highest level, when a legislator seeks the presidency.[3] (This means that members of Congress may not only be concerned with their present *geographic* constituency. They may want to appeal to a different geographic constituency, for instance, or seek support from a broader gender, ethnic, or racial community.) In each of these cases, the legislator is eager to serve the interests of constituents, either to enhance her prospects of contract renewal at the next election or to improve the chances of moving to another level.[4]

House and Senate: Differences in Representation

bicameral legislature

A legislative assembly composed of two chambers, or houses

money bill

A bill concerned solely with taxation or government spending

The framers of the Constitution provided for a bicameral legislature— that is, a legislative body consisting of two chambers. As we saw in Chapter 2, the framers intended each of these chambers, the House and Senate, to serve a different constituency. Members of the House were to be "close to the people," elected by popular vote every two years. Because they saw the House as the institution closest to the people, the framers gave it a special power. All money bills, that is, bills authorizing new taxes or authorizing the government to spend money for any purpose, were required to originate in the House of Representatives. Until the Seventeenth Amendment (1913) provided for direct popular election of senators, members of the Senate were to be appointed by the state legislatures for six-year terms, were to represent the elite members of society, and were to be attuned more to the interests of property than to those of the population. Today, members of the House and Senate are elected directly by the people. The 435 members of the House are elected from districts apportioned according to population: the 100 members of the Senate are elected by state, with two senators from each.

The House and Senate play different roles in the legislative process. In essence, the Senate is the more deliberative of the two bodies—the forum in which any and all ideas can receive a thorough public airing. The House is the more centralized and organized of the two bodies—better equipped to play a role in the routine governmental process. In part, this difference stems from the different rules governing the two bodies. These rules give House leaders more control over the legislative process and provide for House members to specialize in certain legislative areas. The rules of the much-smaller, more free-wheeling Senate give its leadership relatively little power and discourage specialization.

Both formal and informal factors contribute to differences between the two chambers of Congress. Differences in the length of terms and requirements for holding office specified by the Constitution in turn generate differences in how members of each body develop their constituencies and exercise their powers of office. The result is that members of the House most effectively and frequently are the agents of well-organized local interests with specific legislative agendas—used-car dealers seeking relief from regulation, labor unions seeking more favorable legislation, or farmers looking for higher subsidies. The small size and relative homogeneity of their constituencies and the frequency with which they must seek re-election make House members more attuned to the legislative needs of local interest groups. This, too, was the intent of the Constitution's drafters—namely, that the House of Representatives would be the "people's house" and that its members would reflect and represent public opinion in a timely manner.

Citizens often feel that officials who share their race, gender, or other demographic characteristics will better represent their interests in government. Linda Sanchez and Loretta Sanchez, who are sisters, were elected to the House of Representatives with support from women's and Hispanic groups.

Senators, on the other hand, serve larger and more heterogeneous constituencies. As a result, they are somewhat better able than members of the House to be the agents for groups and interests organized on a statewide or national basis. Moreover, with longer terms in office, senators have the luxury of considering new ideas or seeking to bring together new coalitions of interests, rather than simply serving existing ones. This is what the framers intended when they drafted the Constitution.

For much of the late twentieth century, the House exhibited more intense partisanship and ideological division than the Senate. Because of their diverse constituencies, senators tended to be more inclined to seek compromises that offended as few voters and interest groups as possible. Members of the House, in contrast, typically represented more homogeneous districts in which their own party was dominant. This situation tended to make House members less inclined to seek compromises and more willing than their Senate counterparts to stick to partisan and ideological guns during the policy debates of the past several decades. However, beginning with the presidency of George W. Bush, even the Senate grew more partisan and polarized—especially on social issues and the war in Iraq. During Barack Obama's presidency, many of the president's initiatives dealing with the economic crisis, health care, gay rights, financial rescues, and most other areas received virtually no Republican support.

The Electoral System

In light of their role as agents for various constituencies in their states and districts, and the importance of elections as a mechanism by which principals (constituents) reward and punish their agents, representatives are very much influenced by electoral considerations. Three factors related to the U.S. electoral system affect who gets elected and what he does once in office. The first set of issues concerns who decides to run for office and which candidates have an edge over others. The second issue is the advantage incumbents have in winning re-election. Finally, the way congressional district lines are drawn can greatly affect the outcome of an election. Let us examine more closely the impact these considerations have on who serves in Congress.

Running for Office. Voters' choices are restricted from the start by who decides to run for office. In the past, decisions about who would run for a particular elected office were made by local party officials. A person who had a record of service to the party, or who was owed a favor, or whose "turn" had come up might be nominated by party leaders for an office. Today few party organizations have the power to slate candidates in that way. Instead, the decision to run for Congress is a more personal choice. One of the most important factors determining who runs for office is a person's individual ambition.[5] A potential candidate may also assess whether he or she can attract enough money to mount a credible campaign. The ability to raise money depends on connections to other politicians, interest groups, and the national party organization.

Features distinctive to each congressional district also affect the field of candidates. For any candidate, decisions about running must be made early because once money has been committed to already declared candidates, it is harder for new candidates to break into a race. Thus the outcome of a November election is partially determined many months earlier, when decisions to run are finalized.[6]

Incumbency. Incumbency plays a very important role in the American electoral system and in the kind of representation citizens get in Washington. Once in office, members of Congress are typically eager to remain in office and make politics a career. The career ambitions of members of Congress are helped by an array of tools that they can use to stack the deck in favor of their re-election. Through effective use of these tools, an incumbent establishes a reputation for competence, imagination, and responsiveness—the attributes most principals look for in an agent.

Perhaps the most important advantage of incumbency is the opportunity legislators have to serve on legislative committees. Especially in the House, but often in the Senate as well, incumbent legislators are able to burnish their policy credentials, to develop expertise and, critically, to be in a position to help constituents, either through affecting the legislative agenda or interceding with the bureaucracy. It is here—on committees—that incumbents establish a track record of accomplishments that compares favorably with the mere promises of electoral challengers.

The opportunity to help constituents is a clear advantage that committee membership gives incumbents. But helping constituents—and thus gaining support in the district—goes beyond the particular committees in which a member serves. In establishing an attractive political reputation and a "personal" relationship with her constituents, well over a quarter of a representative's time and nearly two-thirds of the time of her staff members is devoted to constituency service (termed casework). This service includes talking to constituents, providing them with minor services, introducing special bills for them, and attempting to influence decisions by agencies and regulatory commissions on their behalf.

One very direct way in which incumbent members of Congress serve as the agents of their constituencies is through patronage. Patronage refers to a variety of forms of direct services and benefits that members provide for their districts. One of the most important forms of patronage is pork-barrel legislation. Through pork-barrel legislation, representatives seek to capture federal projects and federal funds for their own districts (or states in the case of senators) and thus "bring home the bacon" for their

incumbency

Holding the political office for which one is running

casework

An effort by members of Congress to gain the trust and support of constituents by providing personal services. One important type of casework comprises helping constituents obtain favorable treatment from the federal bureaucracy

patronage

The resources available to higher officials, usually opportunities to make partisan appointments to offices and to confer grants, licenses, or special favors to supporters

pork-barrel legislation

The appropriations made by legislative bodies for local projects that often are not needed but are created so that local representatives can carry their home district in the next election

Alaska's "bridge to nowhere" (shown here in a computer rendering) became an infamous example of pork-barrel legislation after Alaskan members of Congress inserted earmarks for $320 million into a highway bill. The bridge, which would have connected the town of Ketchikan to an almost uninhabited island, was never built.

constituents. A common form of pork barreling is the "earmark," the practice by which members of Congress insert language into otherwise pork-free bills that provides special benefits for their own constituents.[7] By 2010, House Republicans had sworn off earmarks altogether, and their partisan colleagues in the Senate, though less enthusiastically, seemed willing to go along. In one of the last actions taken by the 111th Congress—the lame-duck session following the November 2010 elections—a spending bill funding government operations through March 2011 was stripped of nearly all earmarks. In the most recent Congress any earmark inserted in a bill must be accompanied by the name of the sponsoring legislator. The practice is intended to discourage the more outrageous efforts to direct special benefits to a district.

Finally we should note that all of these incumbent benefits are publicized through another incumbency advantage—the franking privilege. Under a law enacted by the first U.S. Congress in 1789, members of Congress may send mail to their constituents free of charge to keep them informed of government business and public affairs. The franking privilege provides incumbents with a valuable resource for publicizing their activities and making themselves visible to voters.

The incumbency advantage is evident in the high rates of re-election for congressional incumbents: over 90 percent for House members and nearly 90 percent for members of the Senate in recent years (Figure 5.2).[8] Incumbents with their "brand name" are in a position to raise campaign funds

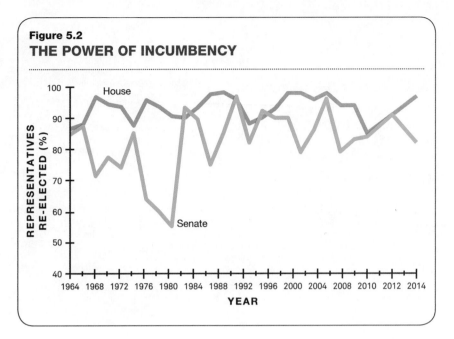

Figure 5.2
THE POWER OF INCUMBENCY

SOURCES: Center for Responsive Politics, www.opensecrets.org/bigpicture/reelect.php (accessed 10/15/13), and author updates.

throughout their term, often in such quantities as to scare off prospective challengers. Thus, the advantage is also evident in what is called sophomore surge—the tendency for candidates to win a higher percentage of the vote when seeking their second term in office than in their initial election victory. Members of Congress almost always are able to outspend their challengers.[9] Over the past quarter-century, and despite many campaign-finance regulations to level the playing field, the gap between incumbent and challenger spending has grown (House) or held steady (Senate). Members of the majority party in the House and Senate are particularly attractive to donors who want access to those in power,[10] not only from an incumbent's warchest advantages but also because challengers fear that the incumbent simply has brought too many benefits to the district, has too much money, or is too well liked or too well known.[11]

The role of incumbency also has implications for the social composition of Congress. For example, the incumbency advantage makes it harder for women to increase their numbers in Congress because most incumbents are men. Women who run for open seats (for which there are no incumbents) are just as likely to win as male candidates.[12] (See the Analyzing the Evidence unit for further discussion of the election of women to Congress.) Supporters of term limits argue that such limits are the best way to get new faces into Congress. They believe that the incumbency advantage and the

Why Do Congresswomen Outperform Congressmen?

Contributed by
Chris Berry
University of Chicago

In January 2015, over 100 women—the largest number ever—were sworn in as members of the U.S. Congress. Despite this achievement, women are still substantially underrepresented in elected offices. As the charts show, women have never held more than 20 percent of the seats in either the House of Representatives or the Senate.

Share of Seats Held by Women

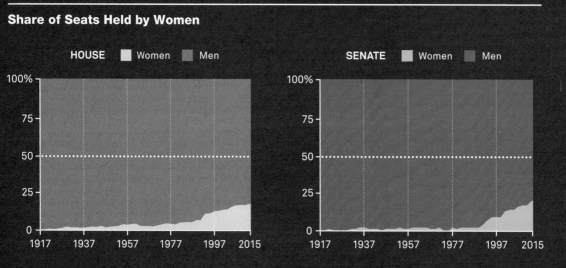

Why are women underrepresented in elected office? One reason is continued discrimination by voters against female candidates. According to a Gallup survey, 11 percent of respondents reported that they would not vote for a female candidate, and another 11 percent would vote for a female "only with reservations." This is a significant hurdle for female politicians to overcome.

Would You Vote for a Candidate Who Was...?

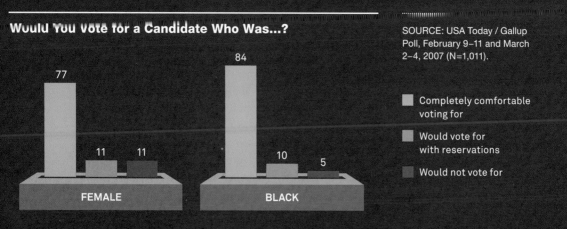

SOURCE: USA Today / Gallup Poll, February 9–11 and March 2–4, 2007 (N=1,011).

When women confront voter bias, only the most talented, politically ambitious females will attempt to run for office, and voters will elect only the most highly capable women. Because of one or both of these factors, the women who *win* a seat will be higher performing than their male colleagues, on average. That individuals facing discrimination must perform better in order to succeed is familiar from the history of minorities in professional sports. A leading example is Jackie Robinson, the first African American to play major league baseball and one of the best players of all time. Researchers have dubbed this phenomenon "The Jackie (and Jill) Robinson Effect."

To measure a legislator's performance on the job, we can look at constituency services, which includes bringing home federal projects, and legislating, which means writing bills and shepherding them through the lawmaking process. The chart below provides evidence that congresswomen outperform congressmen on both dimensions. For each activity, the performance of men is normalized to 1 and the score for women indicates the percentage by which women outperform the men. For example, the score of 1.09 for women in the first bar indicates that a district receives on average 9 percent more spending in the years when a woman represents it. This is equivalent to roughly $50 million per year. Congresswomen also sponsor and cosponsor more bills than congressmen do, and they obtain more cosponsors on their own legislation.

These results are consistent with the idea that women outperform men in logrolling, coalition building, and other deal-making activities that are essential to being a successful legislator. Note, however, that the argument is not that women are innately more talented or harder working than men but that the process by which women are selected into office means that those *who are elected* have to work harder or be more capable. Over time, if voter prejudice against women were eliminated, women's observed performance advantage should evaporate as well.

"The Jackie (and Jill) Robinson Effect"

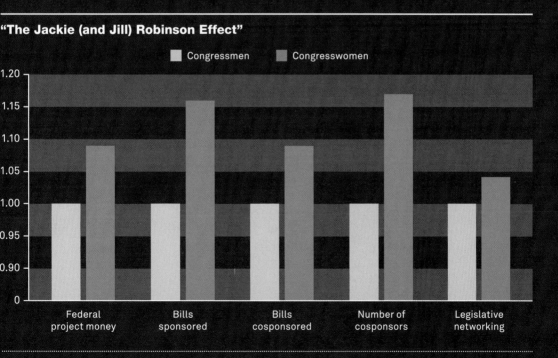

SOURCE: Sarah F. Anzia and Christopher R. Berry, "The Jackie (and Jill) Robinson Effect: Why Do Congresswomen Outperform Congressmen?" *American Journal of Political Science*, 55, no. 3 (2011): 478–93.

tendency of many legislators to view politics as a career mean that very little turnover will occur in Congress unless limits are imposed on the number of terms a legislator can serve.

Congressional Districts. The final factor that affects who wins a seat in Congress is the way congressional districts are drawn. Every 10 years, state legislatures must redraw congressional districts to reflect population changes. In 1929, Congress enacted a law fixing the total number of congressional seats at 435. As a result, when states with fast-growing populations gain districts, they do so at the expense of states with slower population growth. In recent decades, this has meant that the nation's growth areas in the South and West have gained congressional seats at the expense of the Northeast and the Midwest (Figure 5.3). After the 2010 Census, for example, Texas

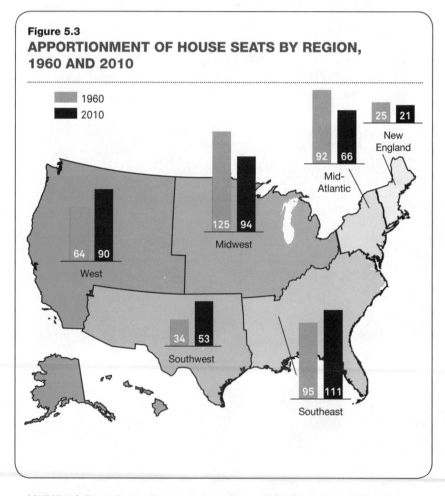

Figure 5.3
APPORTIONMENT OF HOUSE SEATS BY REGION, 1960 AND 2010

SOURCE: U.S. Census Bureau, Congressional Apportionment, 2010 Census Briefs, Table 1, www .census.gov/prod/cen2010/briefs/c2010br-08.pdf (accessed 2/16/13).

Chapter 5: Congress: The First Branch

gained four seats and Florida two, whereas New York and Ohio lost two each. Redrawing congressional districts is a highly political process: in most states, districts are shaped to create an advantage for the majority party in the state legislature, which controls the redistricting process (subject to a possible veto by the governor who may be of a different party). As we see in Chapter 10, gerrymandering can have a major effect on the outcome of congressional elections.

Since the passage of the 1982 amendments to the 1965 Voting Rights Act, race has become a major—and controversial—consideration in drawing voting districts. These amendments, which encouraged creation of districts in which members of racial minorities have decisive majorities, have greatly increased the number of minority representatives in Congress. At the same time, the growing number of majority-minority districts has meant that minority voter proportions in other districts have been diluted, opening up the possibility that representatives from these districts will be less responsive to minority policy concerns. Nonetheless, there is no doubt that descriptive representation has grown. After the 2012 and 2014 elections, the House is more female and minority than ever before.

gerrymandering
The apportionment of voters in districts in such a way as to give unfair advantage to one political party

THE ORGANIZATION OF CONGRESS

We now examine the organization of Congress and the legislative process, particularly the basic building blocks of congressional organization: political parties, the committee system, congressional staff, the caucuses, and the parliamentary rules of the House and Senate. Each of these factors plays a key role in the organization of Congress and in the process through which Congress formulates and enacts laws. We also look at powers Congress has in addition to lawmaking and explore the future role of Congress in relation to the powers of the executive.

Party Leadership and Organization in the House and the Senate

One significant aspect of legislative life is not even part of the *official* organization: political parties. The legislative parties—primarily Democratic and Republican in modern times, but also numerous others over the course of American history—foster cooperation, coalitions, and compromise. They are the vehicles of collective action, both for legislators sharing common policy objectives inside the legislature and for those very same legislators as candidates in periodic election contests back home.[13] In short, political parties in Congress are the fundamental building blocks from which policy coalitions are fashioned to pass legislation and monitor its implementation, thereby providing a track record on which members build electoral support.

Every two years, at the beginning of a new Congress, the members of each party gather to elect their House leaders. This gathering is traditionally called the party caucus, or, in the case of Republicans, the party conference.

The elected leader of the majority party is later proposed to the whole House and is automatically elected to the position of Speaker of the House, with voting along straight party lines. The House majority caucus (or conference) then also elects a majority leader. The minority party goes through the same process and selects the minority leader. Both parties also elect whips to line up party members on important votes and relay voting intentions to the leaders.

At one time, party leaders strictly controlled committee assignments, using them to enforce party discipline. Today, representatives expect to receive the assignments they want and resent leadership efforts to control assignments. The leadership's best opportunities to use committee assignments as rewards and punishments come when more than one member seeks a seat on a committee.

Generally, representatives seek assignments that will allow them to influence decisions of special importance to their districts. Representatives from farm districts, for example, may request seats on the Agriculture Committee.[14] Seats on powerful committees such as Ways and Means, which is responsible for tax legislation, and Energy and Commerce, responsible for health, energy, and regulatory policy, are especially popular.

Within the Senate, the president pro tempore exercises mainly ceremonial leadership. Usually, the majority party designates a member with the greatest seniority to serve in this capacity. Real power is in the hands of the majority leader and minority leader, each elected by party caucus or conference. The majority and minority leaders, together, control the Senate's calendar or agenda for legislation. In addition, the senators from each party elect a whip.

Party leaders reach outside their respective chambers in an effort to augment their power and enhance prospects for their party programs. One important external strategy involves fund-raising. In recent years, congressional leaders have frequently established their own political action committees. Interest groups are usually eager to contribute to these "leadership PACs" to curry favor with powerful members of Congress. The leaders, in turn, use these funds to support the various campaigns of their party's candidates in order to create a sense of obligation.

party caucus, or party conference

A nominally closed meeting of a political or legislative group to select candidates or leaders, plan strategy, or make decisions regarding legislative matters

Speaker of the House

The chief presiding officer of the House of Representatives. The Speaker is elected at the beginning of every Congress on a straight party vote. He or she is the most important party and House leader

majority leader

The elected leader of the party holding a majority of the seats in the House of Representatives or in the Senate. In the House the majority leader is subordinate in the party hierarchy to the Speaker

minority leader

The elected leader of the party holding less than a majority of the seats in the House or Senate

In addition to the tasks of organizing Congress, congressional party leaders may also seek to set the legislative agenda. Since the New Deal, presidents have taken the lead in creating legislative agendas. (This trend will be discussed in the next chapter.) But in recent years, congressional leaders, especially when facing a White House controlled by the opposing party, have attempted to devise their own agendas.

The Committee System

The committee system provides Congress with its second organizational structure, but it is more a division and specialization of labor than the hierarchy of power that determines leadership arrangements.

Six fundamental characteristics define the congressional committee system:

1. *The official rules give each* standing committee *a permanent status*, with a fixed membership, officers, rules, staff, offices, and, above all, a jurisdiction that is recognized by all other committees and usually the leadership as well (Table 5.2).

2. *The jurisdiction of each standing committee is defined according to the subject matter of basic legislation.* Except for the House Rules Committee, all the important committees are organized to receive proposals for legislation and to process them into official bills. The House Rules Committee decides the order in which bills come up for a vote and determines the specific rules that govern the length of debate and the opportunity for amendments. Rules can be used to help or hinder particular proposals.

3. *Standing committees' jurisdictions usually parallel those of the major departments or agencies in the executive branch.* There are important exceptions— Appropriations (House and Senate) and Rules (House), for example— but by and large, the division of labor is self-consciously designed to parallel executive-branch organization.

4. *Bills are assigned to standing committees on the basis of subject matter*, but the Speaker of the House and the Senate's presiding officer have some discretion in the allocation of bills to committees. Most bills "die in committee"—that is, they are not reported out favorably. Ordinarily this ends a bill's life. There is only one way for a legislative proposal to escape committee processing: a bill passed in one chamber may be permitted to move directly to the calendar of the other chamber. Even here, however, the bill has received the full committee treatment before passage in the first chamber.

standing committee

A permanent legislative committee that considers legislation within its designated subject area; the basic unit of deliberation in the House and the Senate

Table 5.2

STANDING COMMITTEES OF CONGRESS, 2013*

HOUSE COMMITTEES	
Agriculture	Intelligence
Appropriations	Judiciary
Armed Services	Natural Resources
Budget	Oversight and Government Reform
Education and the Workforce	Rules
Energy and Commerce	Science and Technology
Ethics	Small Business
Financial Services	Transportation and Infrastructure
Foreign Affairs	Veterans' Affairs
Homeland Security	Ways and Means
House Administration	

SENATE COMMITTEES	
Agriculture, Nutrition, and Forestry	Finance
Appropriations	Foreign Relations
Armed Services	Health, Education, Labor, and Pensions
Banking, Housing, and Urban Affairs	Homeland Security and Governmental Affairs
Budget	
Commerce, Science, and Transportation	Judiciary
	Rules and Administration
Energy and Natural Resources	Small Business and Entrepreneurship
Environment and Public Works	Veterans' Affairs

*These are the committees in the 113th Congress (2013–14). Committee names and jurisdictions change over time, as does the number of committees.

5. *Each standing committee is unique.* No effort is made to compose the membership of any committee to be representative of the total House or Senate membership. Members with a special interest in the subject matter of a committee are expected to seek membership on it. In both the House and the Senate, each party has established a Committee on Committees, which determines the committee assignments of new members and of established members who wish to change committees. Ordinarily, members can keep their committee assignments as long as they like.

6. *Traditionally, each standing committee's hierarchy is based on seniority.* Seniority is determined by years of continuous service on a particular committee, not by years of service in the House or Senate. In general, each committee is chaired by the most senior member of the majority party. The U.S. House operated according to a strict seniority principle from about 1910 (and, informally, even earlier) until the mid-1970s, when most members felt that the burdens of this arrangement were beginning to outweigh its advantages. Committee chairs are now elected by the majority-party members of the full legislature, though there remains a presumption (which may be rebutted) that the most senior committee member will normally assume the chair.

seniority
The priority or status ranking given to an individual on the basis of length of continuous service on a congressional committee

The Staff System: Staffers and Agencies

A congressional institution second in importance only to the committee system is the staff system. Every member of Congress employs a large number of staff members, whose tasks include handling constituency requests and, to a large and growing extent, dealing with legislative details and overseeing the activities of administrative agencies. Increasingly, staffers bear the primary responsibility for formulating and drafting proposals, organizing hearings, dealing with administrative agencies, and negotiating with lobbyists. Indeed, legislators typically deal with one another through staff rather than through direct, personal contact. Representatives and senators together employ nearly 11,000 staffers in their Washington and home offices.

In addition to the personal staffs of individual senators and representatives, Congress also employs roughly 2,000 committee staffers. These individuals are the permanent staff, who stay regardless of turnover in Congress, attached to every House and Senate committee, and who are responsible for organizing and administering the committee's work, including research, scheduling, organizing hearings, and drafting legislation.

Not only does Congress employ personal and committee staffs, but it has also established three *staff agencies* designed to provide the legislative branch with resources and expertise independent of the executive branch. These agencies enhance Congress's capacity to oversee administrative agencies and to evaluate presidential programs and proposals. They are the Congressional Research Service, which performs research for legislators who wish to know the facts and competing arguments relevant to policy proposals or other legislative business; the General Accounting Office, through which Congress can investigate the financial and administrative affairs of any government agency or program; and the Congressional Budget Office, which assesses the economic implications and likely costs of proposed federal programs, such as health care reform proposals and the rescue packages for the failing financial system in 2008 and 2009.

Informal Organization: The Caucuses

In addition to the official organization of Congress, an unofficial organizational structure also exists—the caucuses, formally known as *legislative service organizations* (LSOs). Caucuses are groups of senators or representatives who share certain opinions, interests, or social characteristics. They include ideological caucuses such as the liberal Democratic Study Group and the conservative Democratic Forum. There are also a large number of caucuses composed of legislators representing particular economic or policy interests, such as the Travel and Tourism Caucus, the Steel Caucus, the Mushroom Caucus, and the Concerned Senators for the Arts. Legislators who share common backgrounds or social characteristics have organized caucuses such as the Congressional Black Caucus, the Congressional Caucus for Women's Issues, and the Hispanic Caucus. All these caucuses seek to advance the interests of the groups they represent by promoting legislation, encouraging Congress to hold hearings, and pressing administrative agencies for favorable treatment.

RULES OF LAWMAKING: HOW A BILL BECOMES A LAW

The institutional structure of Congress is one key factor that helps to shape the legislative process. A second and equally important factor is the rules of congressional procedures. These rules govern everything from the introduction of a bill through its submission to the president for signing. Not only do these regulations influence the fate of each and every bill, they also help to determine the distribution of power in Congress (Figure 5.4).

Committee Deliberation

Even if a member of Congress, the White House, or a federal agency has spent months developing and drafting a piece of legislation, it does not become a bill until it is submitted officially by a senator or representative to the clerk of the House or Senate and referred to the appropriate committee for deliberation. No floor action on any bill can take place until the committee with jurisdiction over it has taken all the time it needs to deliberate. During the course of its deliberations, the committee typically refers the bill to one of its subcommittees, which may hold hearings, listen to expert testimony, and amend the proposed legislation before referring it to the full

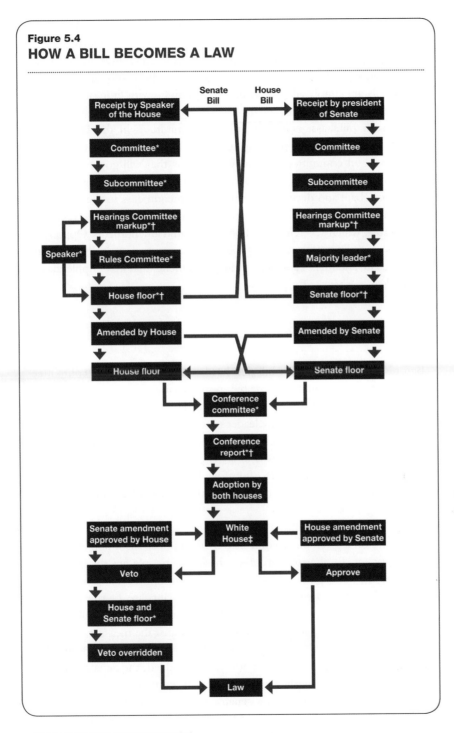

Figure 5.4

HOW A BILL BECOMES A LAW

Senate Bill — House Bill

Receipt by Speaker of the House	Receipt by president of Senate
Committee*	Committee
Subcommittee*	Subcommittee
Hearings Committee markup*†	Hearings Committee markup*†
Speaker* → Rules Committee*	Majority leader*
House floor*†	Senate floor*†
Amended by House	Amended by Senate
House floor	Senate floor

Conference committee*

Conference report*†

Adoption by both houses

Senate amendment approved by House	White House‡	House amendment approved by Senate
Veto		Approve
House and Senate floor*		
Veto overridden		

Law

*Points at which the bill can be amended.
†Points at which the bill can die.
‡If the president neither signs nor vetoes the bill within 10 days, it automatically becomes law.

committee for its consideration. The full committee may accept the recommendation of the subcommittee or hold its own hearings and prepare its own amendments. Or, even more frequently, the committee and subcommittee may do little or nothing with a bill that has been submitted to them. Many bills are simply allowed to die in committee with little or no serious consideration ever given to them.

Once a bill's assigned committee or committees in the House have reported it, the bill must pass one additional hurdle: the Rules Committee. This powerful committee determines the rules that will govern action on the bill on the House floor. In particular, the Rules Committee allots the time for debate and decides to what extent amendments to the bill can be proposed from the floor. A bill's supporters generally prefer what is called a closed rule, which severely limits floor debate and amendments. Opponents of a bill usually prefer an open rule, which permits potentially damaging floor debate and makes it easier to add amendments that may cripple the bill or weaken its chances for passage.

Debate

Before members vote on a bill that has been reported out of committee, supporters and opponents of the bill speak for or against it on the chamber floor. Party control of the agenda is reinforced by the rule giving the Speaker of the House and the majority leader of the Senate the power of recognition during debate on a bill. Usually the chair knows the purpose for which a member intends to speak well in advance of the occasion. Spontaneous efforts to gain recognition are often foiled. For example, the Speaker may ask, "For what purpose does the member rise?" before deciding whether to grant recognition.

In the House, virtually all of the time allotted by the Rules Committee for debate on a given bill is controlled by the bill's sponsor and by its leading opponent. In almost every case, these two people are the committee chair and the ranking minority member of the committee that processed the bill—or those they designate. These two participants are, by rule and tradition, granted the power to allocate most of the debate time in small amounts to members who are seeking to speak for or against the measure.

In the Senate, other than the power of recognition, the leadership has much less control over the floor debate. Indeed, the Senate is unique among the world's legislative bodies for its commitment to unlimited debate. Once given the floor, a senator may speak as long as he wishes. On a number of memorable occasions, senators have used this right to prevent action on legislation that they opposed. Through this tactic, called the filibuster, small minorities or even one individual in the Senate can

---

closed rule

The provision by the House Rules Committee that prohibits the introduction of amendments during debate

open rule

The provision by the House Rules Committee that permits floor debate and the addition of amendments to a bill

filibuster

A tactic used by members of the Senate to prevent action on legislation they oppose by continuously holding the floor and speaking until the majority backs down. Once given the floor, senators have unlimited time to speak, and it requires a cloture vote of three-fifths of the Senate to end a filibuster force the majority to give in to their demands. During the 1950s and 1960s, for example, opponents of civil rights legislation often sought to block its passage by adopting the tactic of filibuster. Sixty votes are needed to end a filibuster. This procedure is called cloture. It should be noted that the modern filibuster is used mostly as a threat. An indication by a senator that she intends to filibuster is often sufficient to induce the majority leader to move on to another topic.

In general, the party leadership in the House has total control over debate. In the Senate, each member has substantial power to block debate. This is one reason that the Senate tends to be a less partisan body than the House. A House majority can override opposition, whereas it takes a three-fifths vote in the Senate; thus the Senate tends to be more accommodating of various views.

Senator Strom Thurmond of South Carolina famously filibustered for over 24 hours in opposition to the Civil Rights Act of 1957. Here, Thurmond speaks to the press after his marathon filibuster.

Conference Committee: Reconciling House and Senate Versions of a Bill

Getting a bill out of committee and through both of the houses of Congress is no guarantee that a bill will be enacted into law. Frequently, bills that began with similar provisions in both chambers emerge with little resemblance to one another. Alternatively, a bill may be passed by one chamber but undergo substantial revision in the other chamber. If the differences cannot be worked out by passing the revised version back to the other chamber and having it accept any changes, a conference committee composed of the senior members of the committees or subcommittees that initiated the bills may be required to iron out differences. Sometimes members or leaders will let objectionable provisions pass on the floor with the idea that they will get the change they want in conference. Usually, conference committees meet behind closed doors. Agreement requires majority support from the two delegations. Legislation that emerges from a conference committee is more often a compromise than a clear victory of one set of political forces over another.

When a bill comes out of conference, it faces one more hurdle. Before a bill can be sent to the president for signing, the House–Senate conference report must be approved on the floor of each chamber. Usually, such approval is given quickly. Occasionally, however, a bill's opponents use approval as one last opportunity to defeat a piece of legislation.

cloture

A rule allowing a supermajority of the members of a legislative body to sat a time limit on debate over a given bill.

conference committee

A joint committee created to work out a compromise on House and Senate versions of a piece of legislation

Presidential Action

veto

The president's constitutional power to turn down acts of Congress within 10 days of their passage while Congress is in session. A presidential veto may be overridden by a two-thirds vote of each house of Congress

pocket veto

A veto that is effected when Congress adjourns during the time a president has to approve a bill and the president takes no action on it

Once adopted by the House and Senate, a bill goes to the president, who may choose to sign the bill into law or veto it. The veto is the president's constitutional power to reject a piece of legislation. To veto a bill, the president returns it within 10 days to the house of Congress in which it originated, along with his objections to the bill. If Congress adjourns during the 10-day period, and the president has taken no action, the bill is also considered to be vetoed. This latter method is known as the pocket veto. The possibility of a presidential veto affects how willing members of Congress are to push for different pieces of legislation at different times. If they think the president is likely to veto a proposal, they might shelve it for a later time. Alternatively, the sponsors of a popular bill opposed by the president might push for passage in order to force the president to pay the political costs of vetoing it.[15]

A presidential veto may be overridden by a two-thirds vote in both the House and the Senate. A veto override says much about the support that a president can expect from Congress, and it can deliver a stinging blow to the executive branch. Presidents will often back down from a veto threat if they believe that Congress will override the veto.

HOW CONGRESS DECIDES

What determines the kinds of legislation that Congress ultimately produces? The process of creating a legislative agenda, drawing up a list of possible measures, and deciding among them is very complex, and a variety of influences from inside and outside government play important roles. External influences include a legislator's constituency and various interest groups. Influences from inside government include party leadership, congressional colleagues, and the president. Let us examine each of these influences individually and then consider how they interact to produce congressional policy decisions.

Constituency

Because members of Congress want to be re-elected, the views of their constituents have a key influence on the decisions that legislators make. Yet constituency influence is not so straightforward. In fact, most constituents do not even know what policies their representatives support. The number of citizens who *do* pay attention to such matters—the attentive public—is usually very small. Nonetheless, members of Congress spend a lot of time worrying about what their constituents think, because these representatives realize that the choices they make may be scrutinized in a future election and used as ammunition by an opposing candidate. Because of this possibility, members of Congress try to anticipate their constituents' policy views.[16] Legislators are more likely to be influenced by their constituents' views if they think that voters will take them into account during elections. In this way, constituents may affect congressional policy choices even when there is little direct evidence of their influence.[17]

Interest Groups

Interest groups are another important external influence on the policies that Congress produces. When members of Congress are making voting decisions, those interest groups that have some connection to constituents in particular members' districts are most likely to be influential. For this reason, interest groups with the ability to mobilize followers in many congressional districts may be especially influential in Congress. The small business lobby, for example, played an important role in defeating President Clinton's proposal for comprehensive health care reform in 1993–94. Because of the mobilization of networks of small businesses across the country, virtually every member of Congress had to take their views into account. In 2009, the Obama administration brought small business groups and the insurance industry to the table on health care very early in the process precisely because of this.

In addition to mobilizing voters, interest groups contribute money. In the 2014 electoral cycle, interest groups and political action committees (PACs) donated many millions of dollars in campaign contributions to incumbent legislators and challengers. What does this money buy? A popular conception is that campaign contributions buy votes. In this view, legislators vote for whichever proposal favors the bulk of their contributors. Although the vote-buying hypothesis makes for good campaign rhetoric, it has little factual support. Empirical studies by political scientists show little evidence that contributions from large PACs influence legislative voting patterns.[18]

If contributions don't buy votes, what do they buy? Our claim is that campaign contributions influence legislative behavior in ways that are difficult for the public to observe and for political scientists to measure. The institutional structure of Congress provides opportunities for interest groups to influence legislation outside the public eye.

Committee proposal power enables legislators, if they are on the relevant committee, to introduce legislation that favors contributing groups. Gatekeeping power enables committee members to block legislation that harms

The National Rifle Association (NRA), an interest group representing gun owners and manufacturers, has been successful in lobbying Congress to resist demands for stronger gun laws. Supporters of gun control protest that the NRA has too much influence.

contributing groups. The fact that certain provisions are *excluded* from a bill is as much an indicator of PAC influence as the fact that certain provisions are *included*. The difference is that it is hard to measure what you don't see. Committee oversight powers enable members to intervene in bureaucratic decision making on behalf of contributing groups.

The point here is that voting on the floor, the alleged object of campaign contributions according to the vote-buying hypothesis, is a highly visible, highly public act, one that could get a legislator in trouble with her broader electoral constituency. The committee system, on the other hand, provides loads of opportunities for legislators to deliver to PAC contributors and other donors "services" that are more subtle and disguised from broader public view. Thus, we suggest that the most appropriate places to look for traces of campaign contribution influence on the legislative process are in the manner in which committees deliberate, mark up proposals, and block legislation from the floor; outside public view, these are the primary arenas for interest-group influence.

Interest groups mobilize voters and contribute campaign finance, but that's not all they do. They also convey information. While it is true that legislators become specialists, acquire expertise, and hire expert staff to assist them, much specialized knowledge, especially about how various aspects of policy will affect local constituencies, is possessed by lobbyists. Informational lobbying is a very important inside-the-beltway activity. Interest-group expenditures on lobbying dwarf money given in campaign contributions.[19]

Party Discipline

In both the House and the Senate, party leaders have a good deal of influence over the behavior of their party members. This influence, sometimes called "party discipline," was once so powerful that it dominated the lawmaking process. At the turn of the century, because of their control of patronage and the nominating process, party leaders could often command the allegiance of more than 90 percent of their members. A vote on which 50 percent or more of the members of one party take a particular position while at least 50 percent of the members of the other party take the opposing position is called a party vote. At the beginning of the twentieth century, most roll-call votes in the House of Representatives were party votes. Today, primary elections have deprived party leaders of the power to decide who receives the party's official nomination. The patronage resources available to the leadership, moreover, have become quite limited. As a result, party-line voting happens less often. It is, however, fairly common to find at least a majority of Democrats opposing a majority of Republicans on any given issue.

Typically, party unity is greater in the House than in the Senate. House rules grant greater procedural control of business to the majority party leaders, which gives them more influence over their members. In the Senate, however, the leadership has few sanctions over its members. Party unity has increased as a consequence of the intense partisan struggles in recent decades (Figure 5.5). In the first term of the Obama administration, party voting in both chambers was strong. Republican votes supporting Obama initiatives were quite rare.

To some extent, party divisions are based on ideology and background. Republican members of Congress are more likely than Democrats to be drawn from rural or suburban areas. Democrats are likely to be more liberal on economic and social questions than their Republican colleagues. This

party vote

A roll-call vote in the House or Senate in which at least 50 percent of the members of one party take a particular position and are opposed by at least 50 percent of the members of the other party. Party votes are less common today than they were in the nineteenth century

roll-call vote

Votes in which each legislator's yes or no vote is recorded

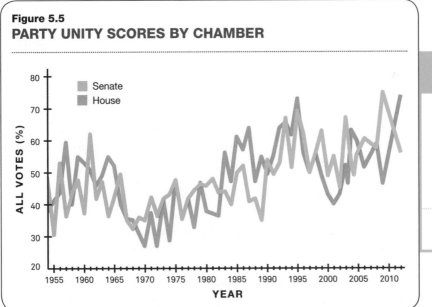

Figure 5.5
PARTY UNITY SCORES BY CHAMBER

ANALYZING
THE EVIDENCE

Party voting increased in the 1970s, peaked in the mid-1990s, and has remained fairly high since then. What contributes to party voting?

NOTE: The scores represent the percentage of recorded votes on which the majority of one party voted against the majority of the other party.
SOURCES: Voteview, http://voteview.com/Party_Unity.htm (accessed 9/16/13).

ideological gap has been especially pronounced since 1980 (Figure 5.6). These differences certainly help to explain roll-call divisions between the two parties. Ideology and background, however, are only part of the explanation of party unity. The other part has to do with organization and leadership.

Although party organization has weakened since the turn of the century, today's party leaders still have some resources at their disposal: (1) committee assignments, (2) access to the floor, (3) the whip system, (4) logrolling, and (5) the presidency. These resources are regularly used and are often very effective in securing the support of party members.

Committee Assignments. Leaders can create debts among members by helping them get favorable committee assignments. These assignments are made early in the congressional careers of most members and cannot be taken from them if they later balk at party discipline. Nevertheless, if the leadership goes out of its way to get the right assignment for a member, this effort is likely to create a bond of obligation that can be called on without any other payments or favors.

Access to the Floor. The most important everyday resource available to the parties is control over access to the floor. With thousands of bills awaiting passage and most members clamoring for access in order to influence a bill or to publicize themselves, floor time is precious. In the House, the Speaker, as head of the majority party (in consultation with the minority leader), allocates large blocks of floor time. More important, the Speaker of the House and the majority leader in the Senate possess the power of recognition. Although this power may not appear to be substantial, it is a formidable authority and can be used to block a piece of legislation completely or to frustrate a member's attempts to speak on a particular issue. Because the power is significant, members of Congress usually attempt to stay on good terms with the Speaker and the majority leader to ensure that they will continue to be recognized.[20]

The Whip System. Some influence accrues to party leaders through the whip system, which is primarily a communications network. Between 12 and 20 assistant and regional whips are selected by zones to operate at the direction of the majority or minority leader and the whip. They take polls of all the members in order to learn their intentions on specific bills. This tells the leaders whether they have enough support to allow a vote, as well as whether the vote is so close that they need to put pressure on a few swing votes. Leaders also use the whip system to convey their wishes and plans to the members, but only in very close votes do they actually exert pressure on a member. In those instances, the Speaker or a lieutenant will go to a few party members

whip system

A communications network in each house of Congress. Whips poll the membership to learn their intentions on specific legislative issues and assist the majority and minority leaders in various tasks

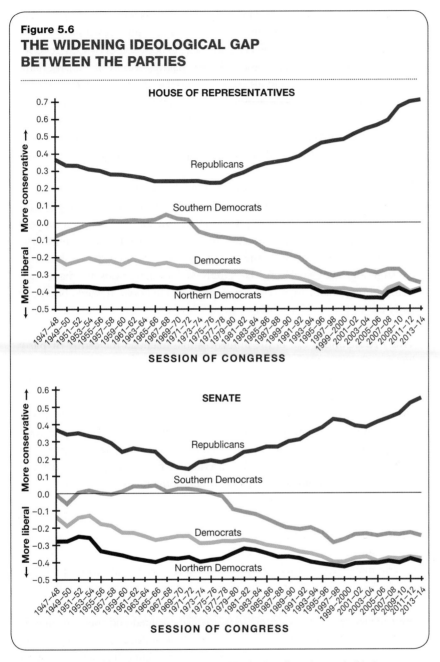

Figure 5.6

THE WIDENING IDEOLOGICAL GAP
BETWEEN THE PARTIES

HOUSE OF REPRESENTATIVES

Republicans

Southern Democrats

Democrats

Northern Democrats

SESSION OF CONGRESS

SENATE

Republicans

Southern Democrats

Democrats

Northern Democrats

SESSION OF CONGRESS

SOURCE: Voteview, The Polarization of Congressional Parties, http://voteview.com/political_
polarization.asp (accessed 12/15/14).

who have indicated they will switch if their vote is essential. The whip system helps the leaders limit pressuring members to a few times per session.

The whip system helps maintain party unity in both houses of Congress, but it is particularly critical in the House of Representatives because of the large number of legislators whose positions and votes must be accounted for. The majority and minority whips and their assistants must be adept at inducing compromise among legislators who hold widely differing viewpoints. The whips' personal styles and their perception of their function significantly affect the development of legislative coalitions and influence the compromises that emerge.

Logrolling. An agreement between two or more members of Congress who have nothing in common except the need for support is called logrolling. The agreement states, in effect, "You support me on bill X, and I'll support you on another bill of your choice." Since party leaders are the center of the communications networks in the two chambers, they can help members create large logrolling coalitions. Hundreds of logrolling deals are made each year. Although there are no official record-keeping books, it would be a poor party leader whose whips did not know who owed what to whom.

The Presidency. Of all the influences that maintain the clarity of party lines in Congress, the influence of the presidency is probably the most important. Indeed, it is a touchstone of party discipline in Congress. Since the late 1940s, under President Truman, presidents each year have identified a number of bills to be considered part of the administration's program. By the mid-1950s, both parties in Congress began to look to the president for these proposals, which became the most significant part of Congress's agenda. The president's support is a criterion for party loyalty, and party leaders in Congress are able to use it to rally some members.

Weighing Diverse Influences

Clearly, many factors affect congressional decisions. But at various points in the decision-making process, some factors are likely to be more influential than others. For example, interest groups may be more effective at the committee stage, when their expertise is especially valued and their visibility is less obvious. Because committees play a key role in deciding what legislation actually reaches the floor of the House or Senate, interest groups can often put a halt to bills they dislike, or they can ensure that the options that do reach the floor are those that the group's members support.

Once legislation reaches the floor and members of Congress are deciding among alternatives, constituent opinion becomes more important. Legislators are also influenced greatly by other legislators: many of their

logrolling

A legislative practice wherein reciprocal agreements are made between legislators, usually in voting for or against a bill. In contrast to bargaining, logrolling unites parties that have nothing in common but their desire to exchange support

Party Discipline

The influence that party leaders have over the behavior of their party members is maintained through a number of sources:

✔ **Committee assignments:** By giving favourable committee assignments to members, party leaders create a sense of debt.

✔ **Access to the floor:** Ranking committee members in the Senate and the Speaker of the House control the allocation of floor time, so House and Senate members want to stay on good terms with these party leaders so that their bills get time on the floor.

✔ **Whip system:** The system allows party leaders to keep track of how many votes they have for a given piece of legislation; if the vote is close, they can try to influence members to switch sides.

✔ **Logrolling:** Members who have nothing in common agree to support one another's legislation because each needs the vote.

✔ **Presidency:** The president's legislative proposals are often the most important part of Congress's agenda. Party leaders use the president's support to rally members.

assessments about the substance and politics of legislation come from fellow members of Congress.

The influence of the external and internal forces described in the preceding section also varies according to the kind of issue being considered. On policies of great importance to powerful interest groups—farm subsidies, for example—those groups are likely to have considerable influence. On other issues, members of Congress may be less attentive to narrow interest groups and more willing to consider what they see as the general interest.

Finally, the mix of influences varies according to the historical moment. The 1994 electoral victory of Republicans allowed their party to control both houses of Congress for the first time in 40 years. That fact, combined with an unusually assertive Republican leadership, meant that party leaders became especially important in decision making. The willingness of moderate Republicans to support measures they had once opposed indicated the unusual importance of party leadership in this period.[21]

BEYOND LEGISLATION: ADDITIONAL CONGRESSIONAL POWERS

In addition to the power to make the law, Congress has at its disposal an array of other instruments through which to influence the process of government. As we saw in Chapter 2, the Constitution gives the Senate the power to approve treaties and appointments. And Congress has drawn to itself a number of other powers through which it can share with the other branches the capacity to administer the laws.

Oversight

oversight

The effort by Congress, through hearings, investigations, and other techniques, to exercise control over the activities of executive agencies

Oversight, as applied to Congress, refers not to something neglected but to the effort to oversee or to supervise how the executive branch carries out legislation. Individual senators and members of the House can engage in a form of oversight simply by calling or visiting administrators, sending out questionnaires, or talking to constituents about programs. But in a more formal sense, oversight is carried out by committees or subcommittees of the Senate or House, which conduct hearings and investigations in order to analyze and evaluate bureaucratic agencies and the effectiveness of their programs. The purpose may be to locate inefficiencies or abuses of power, to explore the relationship between what an agency does and what a law intended, or to change or abolish a program. Most programs and agencies are subject to some oversight every year during the course of hearings on appropriations, that is, the funding of agencies and government programs. Committees or subcommittees have the power to subpoena witnesses, administer oaths, cross-examine, compel testimony, and bring criminal charges for contempt (refusing to cooperate) and perjury (lying).

Hearings and investigations resemble each other in many ways, but they differ on one fundamental point. A hearing is usually held on a specific bill, and the questions asked there are usually intended to build a record with regard to that bill. In an investigation, the committee or subcommittee does not begin with a particular bill, but examines a broad area or problem and then concludes its investigation with one or more proposed bills. One

Congressional hearings and investigations are often conducted to determine how to reform flawed policies and practices. In 2011, Congress heard testimony from economists, mortgage bankers, and public policy groups on the future of the housing finance system following the collapse of the housing market.

example of an investigation is the Senate hearings on the abuse of prisoners in Iraq's Abu Ghraib prison. Many Democrats and some Republicans complained that congressional oversight of the entire Iraq war had been too lax. Reflecting on the prison abuse scandal, Representative Christopher Shays (R-Conn.) stated, "I believe our failure to do proper oversight has hurt our country and the administration. Maybe they wouldn't have gotten into some of this trouble if our oversight had been better."[22]

Advice and Consent: Special Senate Powers

The Constitution has given the Senate a special power, one that is not based on lawmaking. The president has the power to make treaties and to appoint top executive officers, ambassadors, and federal judges—but only "with the Advice and Consent of the Senate" (Article II, Section 2). For treaties, two-thirds of those present must concur; for appointments, a majority is required.

The power to approve or reject presidential requests also involves the power to set conditions. The Senate only occasionally exercises its power to reject treaties and appointments. The Senate has rejected only nine judicial nominees during the past century, whereas many times that number have been approved. In 2009, Republicans criticized President Obama's nominee to the Supreme Court, Sonia Sotomayor, but her nomination was easily approved, thanks in part to a large Democratic majority in the chamber.

More common than Senate rejection of presidential appointees is a senatorial "hold" on an appointment. By Senate tradition, any member may place an indefinite hold on the confirmation of a mid- or lower-level presidential appointment. The hold is typically used by senators trying to wring concessions from the White House on matters having nothing to do with the appointment in question. After George W. Bush took office in January 2001, the Democratic minority in the Senate scrutinized judicial nominations and prevented final confirmation votes on a dozen especially conservative nominees, a matter about which the president frequently complained during the 2004 re-election campaign.

Most presidents make every effort to take potential Senate opposition into account in treaty negotiations and will frequently resort to executive agreements with foreign powers instead of treaties. The Supreme Court has held that such agreements are equivalent to treaties, but they do not need Senate approval.[23] In the past, presidents sometimes concluded secret agreements without informing Congress of the agreements' contents or even their existence. American involvement in the Vietnam War grew in part out of a series of secret arrangements made between American presidents and the South Vietnamese during the 1950s and 1960s. Congress did not even learn of these agreements until 1969.

In 1972, Congress passed the Case Act, which requires that the president inform Congress of any executive agreement within 60 days of its having been reached. This provides Congress with the opportunity to cancel

executive agreement

An agreement between the president and another country that has the force of a treaty but does not require the Senate's "advice and consent" agreements that it opposes. In addition, Congress can limit the president's ability to conduct foreign policy through executive agreement by refusing to appropriate the funds needed to implement an agreement. In this way, for example, Congress can modify or even cancel executive agreements to provide economic or military assistance to foreign governments.

Impeachment

impeachment

The charging of a governmental official (president or other) with "Treason, Bribery, or other high Crimes and Misdemeanors" and bringing him or her before Congress to determine guilt

The Constitution also grants Congress the power of impeachment over the president, vice president, and other executive officials. To impeach means to charge a government official (president or other) with "Treason, Bribery, or other high Crimes and Misdemeanors," and bring him before Congress to determine guilt. The procedure is similar to a criminal indictment in that the House of Representatives acts like a grand jury, voting (by simple majority) on whether the accused ought to be impeached. If a majority of the House votes to impeach, the impeachment trial moves to the Senate, which acts like a trial jury by voting whether to convict and forcibly remove the person from office. (This vote requires a two-thirds majority.)

Controversy over Congress's impeachment power has arisen over the meaning of "high Crimes and Misdemeanors." A strict reading of the Constitution suggests that the only impeachable offense is an actual crime. But a more commonly agreed-on definition is that an impeachable offense is whatever the majority of the House of Representatives considers it to be at a given time. In other words, impeachment, especially the impeachment of a president, is a political decision.

During the course of American history, only two presidents have been impeached. In 1867, President Andrew Johnson, a Southern Democrat who had battled a congressional Republican majority over Reconstruction, was impeached by the House but saved from conviction by one vote in the Senate. In 1998, President Bill Clinton was impeached by the House for perjury and obstruction of justice arising from his sexual relationship with a former White House intern, Monica Lewinsky. At the conclusion of a Senate trial in 1999, Democrats, joined by a handful of Republicans, acquitted the president of both charges.

DOES CONGRESS WORK?

Congress is both a representative assembly and a powerful institution of government. In assessing the effectiveness of Congress, we focus on both its representative character and the efficiency with which Congress is able to get things done.

Congress is the most important representative institution in American government. Each member's primary responsibility is to the district, to her constituency, not to the congressional leadership, a party, or even Congress itself. Yet the task of representation is not a simple one. Views about what defines fair and effective representation differ, and constituents can make very different kinds of demands on their representatives. Members of Congress must consider these diverse views and demands as they represent their districts (see Figure 5.1). A representative claims to act or speak for some other person or group. But how can one person be trusted to speak for another? How do we know that those who call themselves our representatives are actually speaking on our behalf, rather than simply pursuing their own interests?

As we saw earlier in this chapter, legislators vary in the weight they give to personal priorities and the things desired by campaign contributors and past supporters. Some see themselves as delegates, elected to do the bidding of those who sent them to the legislature. Other legislators see themselves as trustees, selected by their fellow citizens to do what the legislator thinks is "right." Most legislators are mixes of these two types. Frequent competitive elections are an important means by which constituents hold their representatives to account and keep them responsive to constituency views and preferences.

Indeed, taking care of constituents explains a lot of the legislation that Congress produces. It is not too much of an exaggeration to suggest the following list of individuals whose support is necessary in order to get a measure through Congress and signed into law:

- A majority of the authorizing subcommittees in the House and Senate (probably including the subcommittee chairs)
- A majority of the full authorizing committees in the House and Senate (probably including committee chairs)
- A majority of the appropriations subcommittees in the House and Senate (probably including the subcommittee chairs)
- A majority of the full appropriations committees in the House and Senate (probably including committee chairs)
- A majority of the House Rules Committee (including its chair)
- A majority of the full House
- A majority—possibly as many as 60 votes, if needed to shut off a filibuster—of the Senate
- The Speaker and majority leader in the House
- The majority leader in the Senate
- The president

This list includes an extraordinarily large number of public officials.

With so many hurdles to clear for a legislative initiative to become a public law, the benefits must be spread broadly. It is as though a bill must travel on a toll road past a number of tollbooths, each one containing a collector with his hand out for payment. Frequently, features of the bill are drafted initially or revised so as to be more inclusive, spreading the benefits widely among members' districts. This is the distributive tendency.

The distributive tendency is part of the American system of representative democracy. Legislators, in advocating the interests of their constituents, are eager to advertise their ability to deliver for their state or district. They maneuver to put themselves in a position to claim credit for good things that happen there and to duck blame for bad things. This is the way they earn trust back home, deter strong challengers in upcoming elections, and defeat those who run against them. This means that legislators must take advantage of every opportunity that presents itself. In some instances, as in our earlier discussion of the pork barrel, the results may seem bizarre. Nevertheless, the distributive tendency is a consequence of how Congress was designed to work.

Another consequence of Congress's design is almost the opposite of the distributive tendency: the tendency toward the status quo. The U.S. Congress has more veto points than any other legislative body in the world. If any of the individuals listed above says no, a bill dies. Some celebrate this design. As a result, the government is unlikely to change in response to superficial fluctuations in public sentiment. Congress's design does mean greater representation of minority interests in the legislative process (at least to say no to the majority). But it also creates the impression of gridlock, leading some to question Congress's effectiveness.

Critics of Congress want it to be both more representative and more effective. On the one hand, Congress is frequently criticized for falling victim to gridlock and failing to reach decisions on important issues such as Social Security reform. (Or, as we saw earlier with the debt ceiling crisis, allowing partisanship to dominate legislative decision making.) This was one reason why, in 1995, the Republican House leadership reduced the number of committees and subcommittees in the lower chamber. Having fewer committees and subcommittees generally means greater centralization of power and more expeditious decision making. On the other hand, critics demand that Congress become more representative of the changing makeup and values of the American populace. In recent years, for example, some reformers have demanded limits on the number of terms that any member of Congress can serve. Term limits are seen as a device for producing a more rapid turnover of members and, hence, a better chance for new political and social forces to be represented in Congress. The problem, however, is that although reforms such as term limits and greater internal diffusion of power may make Congress more representative, they may also make it less efficient and effective. By the same token, reforms that may make Congress better able to act—such as strong central leadership, reduction of the number of committees and subcommittees, and retention of members with seniority and experience—may make

Congress less representative. This is the dilemma of congressional reform. Efficiency and representation are often competing principles in our system of government; we must be wary of gaining one at the expense of the other.

For Further Reading

Selections highlighted in red are included in *Readings in American Politics: Analysis and Perspectives*, Third Edition.

Arnold, R. Douglas. *The Logic of Congressional Action*. New Haven, CT: Yale University Press, 1990.

Binder, Sarah. *Stalemate: Causes and Consequences of Legislative Gridlock*. Washington, DC: Brookings Institution, 2003.

Brady, David W., and Mathew D. McCubbins, eds. *Party, Process, and Political Change in Congress: New Perspectives on the History of Congress*. Palo Alto, CA: Stanford University Press, 2002.

Cox, Gary W., and Mathew D. McCubbins. *Setting the Agenda: Responsible Party Government in the U.S. House of Representatives*. New York: Cambridge University Press, 2005.

Fenno, Richard F., Jr. *Home Style: House Members in Their Districts*. Boston: Little, Brown, 1978.

Fiorina, Morris P. *Congress: Keystone of the Washington Establishment*. 2nd ed. New Haven, CT: Yale University Press, 1989.

Frisch, Scott A., and Sean Q. Kelly. *Committee Assignment Politics in the U.S. House of Representatives*. Norman: University of Oklahoma Press, 2006.

Krehbiel, Keith. *Pivotal Politics: A Theory of U.S. Lawmaking*. Chicago: University of Chicago Press, 1998.

Harbridge, Laurel, and Neil Malhotra. "Electoral Incentives and Partisan Conflict in Congress: Evidence from Survey Experiments." *American Journal of Political Science* 55 (2011): 494–510.

Mayhew, David. *Congress: The Electoral Connection*. New Haven, CT: Yale University Press, 1974.

Sinclair, Barbara. *Unorthodox Lawmaking: New Legislative Processes in the U.S. Congress*. 3rd ed. Washington, DC: CQ Press, 2007.

Stewart, Charles H. *Analyzing Congress*. 2nd ed. New York: Norton, 2012.

6

The Presidency

Presidential power generally seems to increase during times of war. For example, President Abraham Lincoln's 1862 declaration of martial law and Congress's 1863 legislation giving the president the power to make arrests and imprisonments through military tribunals amounted to a "constitutional dictatorship" that lasted through the war and Lincoln's re-election in 1864. But these measures were viewed as emergency powers that could be revoked once the crisis of union was resolved. In less than a year after Lincoln's death, Congress had reasserted its power, leaving the presidency in many respects the same as, if not weaker than, it had been before the war.

During World War II, Franklin Delano Roosevelt, like Lincoln, did not bother to wait for Congress but took executive action first and expected Congress to follow. Roosevelt brought the United States into an undeclared naval war against Germany a year before Pearl Harbor, and he ordered the unauthorized use of wiretaps and other surveillance as well as the investigation of suspicious persons for reasons not clearly specified. The most egregious (and revealing) of these was his segregation and eventual confinement of 120,000 individuals of Japanese descent, many of whom were American citizens. The Supreme Court validated Roosevelt's treatment of the Japanese, on the grounds of military necessity. One dissenter on the Court called the president's assumption of emergency powers "a loaded weapon ready for the hand of any authority that can bring forward a plausible claim of an urgent need."[1]

The "loaded weapon" was seized again on September 14, 2001, when Congress defined the World Trade Center and Pentagon attacks as an act of war and proceeded to adopt a joint resolution authorizing the president to use "all necessary and appropriate force against those nations, organizations or persons he determines planned, authorized, committed or aided the terrorist attacks that occurred on September 11, 2001, or harbored such organizations or persons. . . ."[2] On the basis of this authorization, President George W. Bush ordered the invasion of Afghanistan and began the reorganization of the nation's "homeland security."

The question then arises of whether presidents have too much power. The framers of the Constitution were concerned with what they saw as the tendency of "executive magistrates" to engage in "ambitious intrigues" to enhance their powers and prerogatives.[3] The framers hoped that this threat to citizens' liberties would be mitigated by the system of checks and balances they devised to prevent any branch of government from improperly expanding its power. In recent decades, as we see in this chapter, successive presidents have greatly enhanced the power of the executive branch, expanding presidential war power and devising a host of administrative instruments the framers would hardly recognize.

Even before World War II, President Franklin Delano Roosevelt enhanced the president's control over the federal budget, made executive orders and executive agreements routine instruments of presidential power, and built the Executive Office of the President. Ronald Reagan introduced the use of regulatory review and bolstered presidential war powers. George W. Bush made

CORE OF THE ANALYSIS

➡️ The Constitution endows the president with a limited number of expressed powers. Other presidential powers are delegated by Congress or claimed by presidents without specific statutory authority.

➡️ Since the 1930s, the presidency has been the dominant branch of American government.

➡️ Contemporary presidents have also increased the power of the executive branch through "administrative strategies" that often allow them to achieve policy goals without congressional approval.

signing statements an instrument through which presidents seek to rewrite the law. (We will discuss each of these sources of power in this chapter.)

The framers might not have been familiar with the precise mechanisms of presidential power used today, but they were familiar with the ambition that seems to drive executives, be they kings or presidents. For example, as a senator, Barack Obama was a frequent critic of George W. Bush's expansion of executive authority, claiming that Bush had exceeded his constitutional war powers. In 2007, Senator Obama said, "The president does not have power under the Constitution to unilaterally authorize a military attack in a situation that does not involve stopping an actual or imminent threat to the nation."[4] As president, however, Obama ordered U.S. forces into combat against Libyan leader Mu'ammar Qaddafi, asserting that congressional authorization was not needed for his action, which was undertaken in the context of a NATO effort to oust Qaddafi. In this case, Obama did not hesitate to assert the powers of the executive office.

In this chapter, we examine the foundations of the American presidency and assess the origins and character of presidential power today. National emergencies are one source of presidential power, but presidents are also empowered by democratic political processes and, increasingly, by their ability to control and expand the institutional resources of the office. The Supreme Court, to be sure, can sometimes check presidential power. For example, in the 2006 *Hamdan v. Rumsfeld* decision, the Court invalidated the military tribunals established by President Bush to try terror suspects. And, of course, through legislative investigations and its budgetary powers, Congress can oppose the president. With Democratic majorities in both houses of Congress after the 2006 elections, congressional opposition to President Bush's policies in Iraq and the war on terrorism increased. And President Obama encountered congressional opposition to his economic and foreign policies after the GOP won control of the House in 2010 and the Senate in 2014.

This chapter explains why the American system of government could be described as presidential government and how it got to be that way. We also explore how and why the president, however powerful, is nevertheless vulnerable to the popular will. But first, we begin with a look at the presidential powers provided for in the Constitution.

THE CONSTITUTIONAL ORIGINS AND POWERS OF THE PRESIDENCY

The presidency was established by Article II of the Constitution, which begins by asserting, "The executive power shall be vested in a President of the United States of America." It goes on to describe the manner in which the president is to be chosen and defines the basic powers of the presidency. By vesting the executive power in a single president, the framers were emphatically rejecting proposals for various forms of collective leadership. Some delegates to the Constitutional Convention had argued in favor of a multiheaded executive or an "executive council" in order to avoid undue concentration of power in the hands of one individual. Most of the framers, however, were anxious to provide for "energy" in the executive. They hoped to have a president capable of taking quick and aggressive action. They believed that a powerful executive would help to protect the nation's interests vis-à-vis other nations and promote the federal government's interests relative to the states.

Immediately following the first sentence, Article II, Section 1, defines the manner in which the president is to be chosen. This is an odd sequence, but it does say something about the difficulty the delegates were having over how to give power to the executive and at the same time how to balance that power with limitations. This reflected the twin struggles etched in the memories of the Founding generation—against the powerful executive authority of King George III and of the dismal low energy of the government under the Articles of Confederation. There was disagreement between those delegates who wanted the president to be selected by Congress, and thus responsible to it, and those delegates who preferred that the president be elected directly by the people. Direct popular elections would create a more independent and more powerful presidency. The framers finally agreed on a scheme of indirect election through an electoral college, the electors to be selected by the state legislatures (and close elections would be resolved in the House of Representatives). In this way, the framers hoped to achieve a "republican" solution: a strong president who would be responsible to state and national legislators rather than directly to the electorate.

While Section 1 of Article II explains how the president is to be chosen, Sections 2 and 3 outline the powers and duties of the president. These two sections identify two sources of presidential power. Some presidential powers are specifically established by the language of the Constitution. For example, the president is authorized to make treaties, grant pardons, and nominate judges and other public officials. These specifically defined powers are called the expressed powers of the office and cannot be revoked by the Congress or any other agency without an amendment to the Constitution. Other expressed powers include the power to receive ambassadors and command of the military forces of the United States.

In addition to establishing the president's expressed powers, Article II declares that the president "shall take Care that the Laws be faithfully executed." Since the laws are enacted by Congress, this language implies that Congress is to delegate to the president the power to implement or execute its will. Powers given to the president by Congress are called

expressed powers
The powers enumerated in the Constitution that are granted to the federal government

delegated powers

Constitutional powers assigned to one governmental agency but exercised by another agency with the express permission of the first

delegated powers. In principle, Congress delegates to the president only the power to identify or develop the means to carry out congressional decisions. So, for example, if Congress determines that air quality should be improved, it might delegate to the executive branch the power to determine the best means of improvement as well as the power to implement the cleanup process. In practice, of course, decisions about how to clean the air are likely to have an enormous impact on businesses, organizations, and individuals throughout the nation. As it delegates power to the executive, Congress substantially enhances the importance of the presidency and the executive branch. In most cases, Congress delegates power to executive agencies rather than to the president. As we shall see, however, contemporary presidents have found ways to capture a good deal of this delegated power for themselves.

Presidents have claimed a third source of institutional power beyond expressed and delegated powers. These are powers not specified in the Constitution or the law but said to stem from "the rights, duties and obligations of the presidency."[5] They are referred to as the inherent powers of the presidency and are most often asserted by presidents in times of war or national emergency. For example, after the fall of Fort Sumter and the outbreak of the Civil War, President Abraham Lincoln issued a series of executive orders for which he had no clear legal basis. Without even calling Congress into session, Lincoln combined the state militias into a 90-day national volunteer force, called for 40,000 new volunteers, enlarged the regular army and navy, diverted $2 million in unspent appropriations to military needs, instituted censorship of the U.S. mail, ordered a blockade of southern ports, suspended the writ of *habeas corpus* in the border states, and ordered the arrest by military police of individuals whom he deemed to be guilty of engaging in or even contemplating treasonous actions.[6] Lincoln asserted that these extraordinary measures were justified by the president's inherent power to protect the nation.[7] Subsequent presidents, including Franklin Delano Roosevelt and George W. Bush, have had similar views.

inherent powers

Powers claimed by a president that are not expressed in the Constitution but are inferred from it

Expressed Powers

The president's expressed powers, as defined by Sections 2 and 3 of Article II, fall into several categories including military, judicial, diplomatic, executive, and legislative powers.

commander in chief

The power of the president as commander of the national military and the state national guard units (when called into service)

Military and Domestic Defense Power. The president's military powers are among the most important that the chief executive exercises. The position of commander in chief makes the president the highest military officer in the United States, with control of the entire military establishment.

Though the constitutional power to declare war is given to Congress, the past 60 years have seen the president become the most dominant figure in military affairs. Thus, the public's dissatisfaction with the handling of the war in Afghanistan has been charged mostly against the presidents who oversaw it, George W. Bush and Barack Obama.

The president is also the head of the nation's intelligence hierarchy, which includes not only the Central Intelligence Agency (CIA) but also the National Security Council (NSC), the National Security Agency (NSA), the Federal Bureau of Investigation (FBI), and a host of lesser-known but very powerful international and domestic security agencies.

The president's military powers extend into the domestic sphere. Although Article IV, Section 4, provides that the "United States shall [protect] . . . every State . . . against Invasion . . . and . . . domestic Violence," Congress has made this an explicit presidential power through statutes directing the president as commander in chief to discharge these obligations.[8] The Constitution restrains the president's use of domestic force by providing that a state legislature (or governor when the legislature is not in session) must request federal troops before the president can send them into the state to provide public order. Yet this proviso is not absolute. First, presidents are not obligated to deploy national troops merely because the state legislature or governor makes such a request. And more important, presidents may deploy troops in a state or city without a specific request if they consider it necessary to maintain an essential national service, to enforce a federal judicial order, or to protect federally guaranteed civil rights.

A famous example of the unilateral use of presidential power to protect the states against domestic disorder occurred in 1957 under President Eisenhower. He decided to send troops into Little Rock, Arkansas, against the wishes of the state of Arkansas, to enforce court orders to integrate Little Rock's Central High School. Governor Orval Faubus had posted the Arkansas National Guard at the entrance of the school to prevent the court-ordered admission of nine black students. After an effort to negotiate

Expressed Powers of the Presidency

The Constitution defines certain specific powers of the presidency. These expressed powers fall into the following categories.

1. **Military.** Article II, Section 2, provides for the power as "Commander in Chief of the Army and Navy of the United States, and of the Militia of the several States, when called in to the actual Service of the United States."

2. **Judicial.** Article II, Section 2, also provides the power to "grant Reprieves and Pardons for Offenses against the United States, except in Cases of Impeachment."

3. **Diplomatic.** Article II, Section 3, provides the power to "receive Ambassadors and other public Ministers."

4. **Executive.** Article II, Section 3, authorizes the president to see to it that all the laws are faithfully executed; Section 2 gives the chief executive the power to appoint, remove, and supervise all executive officers and to appoint all federal judges.

5. **Legislative.** Article I, Section 7, and Article II, Section 3, give the president the power to participate authoritatively in the legislative process.

with Governor Faubus failed, President Eisenhower reluctantly sent to Little Rock a thousand paratroopers, who stood watch while the black students took their places in the all-white classrooms. This case makes quite clear that the president does not have to wait for a request by a state legislature or governor before acting as domestic commander in chief.[9] However, in most instances of domestic disorder—whether from human or from natural causes—presidents tend to exercise unilateral power justified by declaring a "state of emergency," thereby making available federal grants, insurance, and direct assistance as well as troops. After hurricanes Katrina and Rita struck the Gulf Coast in fall 2005, President Bush declared a state of emergency, using both state militias and federal troops for rescue operations, the prevention of looting and violence, and the delivery of medical, health, and food services. More recently, in 2010 President Obama sent the Coast Guard and teams from other agencies to participate in the rescue and cleanup operation following the BP *Deepwater Horizon* explosion and oil spill in the Gulf of Mexico.

Military emergencies have typically also led to expansion of the domestic powers of the executive branch. This was true during World Wars I and II and has been true during the "war on terrorism" as well. Within a month of the September 11 attacks, the White House drafted and Congress enacted the USA PATRIOT Act, expanding the power of government agencies to engage in domestic surveillance activities, including electronic surveillance, and restricting judicial review of such efforts. The act also gave the attorney general greater authority to detain and deport immigrants suspected of having terrorist affiliations. The following year, Congress created the Department of Homeland Security, combining offices from 22 federal agencies into one huge new cabinet department responsible for protecting the nation from attack. The White House drafted the reorganization plan, but Congress weighed in to make certain that the new agency's workers had civil service and union protections.

Judicial Power. The presidential power to grant reprieves, pardons, and amnesties as well as to "commute" or reduce the severity of sentences, literally gives the president the power of life and death over individuals. Presidents may use this power on behalf of a particular individual, as did Gerald Ford when he pardoned Richard Nixon in 1974 "for all offenses against the United States which he . . . has committed or may have committed." Similarly, in 2007, President Bush commuted the sentence handed down to Lewis "Scooter" Libby, one of Vice President Cheney's top aides. Libby had been found guilty of perjury and obstruction of justice and was sentenced to several years in prison as well as ordered to pay a steep fine. President Bush declared that Libby would not go to prison, though he would still have to pay the fine.

Diplomatic Power. The president is America's "head of state"—its chief representative in dealings with other nations. As head of state, the president has the power to make treaties for the United States (with the advice and consent of the Senate). When President George Washington received Edmond Genêt ("Citizen Genêt") as the formal emissary of the revolutionary government of France in 1793, he transformed the power to "receive Ambassadors and other public Ministers" into the power to "recognize" other countries. That power gives the president the almost unconditional authority to review the claims of any new ruling groups to determine whether they indeed control the territory and population of their country, so that they can commit it to treaties and other agreements.

In recent years, presidents have expanded the practice of using executive agreements to conduct foreign policy.[10] An executive agreement is like a treaty because it is a contract between two countries, but an executive agreement does not require a two-thirds vote of approval by the Senate (a treaty does

executive agreement

An agreement between the president and another country that has the force of a treaty but does not require the Senate's "advice and consent" require this approval). Ordinarily, executive agreements are used to carry out commitments already made in treaties or to arrange for matters well below the level of policy. But when presidents have found it expedient to use an executive agreement in place of a treaty, Congress has typically acquiesced.

Executive Power. The most important basis of the president's power as chief executive is found in the sections of Article II that stipulate that the president must see that all the laws are faithfully executed and that provide that the president will appoint all executive officers and all federal judges. In this manner, the Constitution focuses executive power and legal responsibility upon the president. The famous sign on President Truman's desk, "The buck stops here," was not merely an assertion of Truman's personal sense of responsibility. It acknowledged his acceptance of the constitutional imposition of that responsibility upon the president.

The president's executive power is not absolute, however, as many presidential appointments, including ambassadors, cabinet officers and other high-level administrators, and federal judges, are subject to a majority approval by the Senate. But these appointments are at the discretion of the president.

Another component of the president's power as chief executive is executive privilege, which is the claim that confidential communications between a president and close advisers should not be revealed without the consent of the president. Presidents have made this claim ever since George Washington refused a request from the House of Representatives to deliver documents concerning negotiations of an important treaty. Washington refused (successfully) on the grounds that, first, the House was not constitutionally part of the treaty-making process and, second, that diplomatic negotiations required secrecy.

Executive privilege became a popular part of the "checks and balances" between the president and Congress, and presidents have usually had the upper hand when invoking it. Although many presidents have claimed executive privilege, the concept was not tested in the courts until the 1971 Watergate affair, during which President Nixon refused congressional demands that he turn over secret White House tapes that congressional investigators thought would establish Nixon's complicity in illegal activities. In *United States v. Nixon*, the Supreme Court ordered Nixon to turn over the tapes.[11] The president complied with the order and resigned from office to avoid impeachment and conviction. *United States v. Nixon* is often seen as a blow to presidential power, but in actuality the Court's ruling recognized for the first time the validity of a claim of executive privilege, although it held that the claim did not apply in this instance. Subsequent presidents have cited *United States v. Nixon* in support of their claims of executive privilege. For example, the administration of George W. Bush invoked executive privilege when it refused to give Congress documents relating to the president's decision to

executive privilege

The claim that confidential communications between a president and the president's close advisers should not be revealed without the consent of the president make use of warrantless wiretaps and when it refused to obey congressional subpoenas demanding materials pertaining to the firing of a number of assistant U.S. attorneys.[12] More recently, in June 2012, the Obama administration appealed to executive privilege in refusing to comply with a subpoena from the House of Representatives for documents related to operation "Fast and Furious," a Justice Department drug-trafficking program.

Legislative Power. The president plays a role not only in the administration of government but also in the legislative process. Two constitutional provisions are the primary sources of the president's power in the legislative arena. Article II, Section 3, provides that the president "shall from time to time give to the Congress Information of the State of the Union, and recommend to their Consideration such Measures as he shall judge necessary and expedient." This first legislative power has been important especially since Franklin Delano Roosevelt began to use the provision to initiate proposals for legislative action in Congress. Roosevelt established the presidency as the primary initiator of legislation.

The second of the president's legislative powers is the "veto power" assigned by Article I, Section 7. The veto power is the president's constitutional power to turn down acts of Congress. This power alone makes the president the most important single legislative leader. No bill vetoed by the president can become law unless both the House and the Senate override the veto by a two-thirds vote. In the case of a pocket veto, Congress does not even have the option of overriding the veto, but must reintroduce the bill in the next session. The president may exercise a pocket veto when presented with a bill during the last 10 days of a legislative session. Usually, if a president does not sign a bill within 10 days, it automatically becomes law. But this is true only while Congress is in session. If a president chooses not to sign a bill within the last 10 days that Congress is in session, then the 10-day limit does not expire until Congress is out of session, and instead of becoming law, the bill is vetoed. Figure 6.1 illustrates the president's veto option. In 1996, a new power was added—the line-item veto—giving the president the power to strike specific spending items from appropriations bills passed by Congress, unless reenacted by a two-thirds vote of both the House and Senate. In 1997, President Clinton used this power 11 times to strike 82 items from the federal budget. But, as we saw in Chapter 5, in 1998 the Supreme Court ruled that the Constitution does not authorize the line-item veto power.[13] Only a constitutional amendment would give this power to the president.

The Games Presidents Play: The Veto. Use of the veto varies according to the political situation that each president confronts. George W. Bush vetoed no bill during his first term, a period in which his party

veto power
The ability to defeat something even if it has made it on to the agenda of an institution

pocket veto
A veto that is effected when Congress adjourns during the time a president has to approve a bill and the president takes no action on it

line-item veto
The power of the executive to veto specific provisions (lines) of a bill passed by the legislature

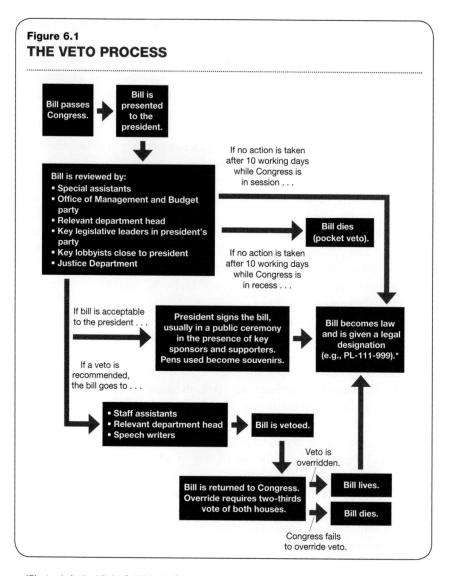

Figure 6.1
THE VETO PROCESS

Bill passes Congress.

Bill is presented to the president.

Bill is reviewed by:
• Special assistants
• Office of Management and Budget party
• Relevant department head
• Key legislative leaders in president's party
• Key lobbyists close to president
• Justice Department

If no action is taken after 10 working days while Congress is in session . . .

Bill dies (pocket veto).

If no action is taken after 10 working days while Congress is in recess . . .

If bill is acceptable to the president . . .

President signs the bill, usually in a public ceremony in the presence of key sponsors and supporters. Pens used become souvenirs.

Bill becomes law and is given a legal designation (e.g., PL-111-999).*

If a veto is recommended, the bill goes to . . .

• Staff assistants
• Relevant department head
• Speech writers

Bill is vetoed.

Veto is overridden.

Bill is returned to Congress. Override requires two-thirds vote of both houses.

Bill lives.

Bill dies.

Congress fails to override veto.

*PL stands for "public law"; 111 is the Congress (e.g., the 111th Congress was in session in 2009–11); 999 is the number of the law.

controlled both houses of Congress. After the Democrats won control of Congress in 2006, Bush's use of the veto increased markedly.[14] In President Obama's first term, with Democratic control of both the House and the Senate, he vetoed only two bills, both in the first two years. He vetoed no bills in the second two years of his first term, after the Democrats lost their House majority and had their Senate majority pared down, nor in the first two years of his second term. This was mainly because the Republican strategy of obstruction produced very little legislation. In general, presidents have used the veto to equalize or upset the balance of power with Congress. Although the power to reject or accept legislation in its entirety might seem like a crude tool for making sure that legislation adheres to a president's preferences, the politics surrounding the veto is complicated, and it is rare that vetoes are used simply as bullets to kill legislation. Instead, vetoes are usually part of an intricate bargaining process between the president and Congress, involving threats of vetoes, repassing legislation, and re-vetoes.[15]

Although presidents rarely veto legislation, this does not mean vetoes and veto bargaining have an insignificant influence over the policy process. In many cases the *threat* of a veto may be sufficient. This means that members of Congress will alter the content of a bill to make it more to a president's liking to discourage a veto. Thus the veto power can be influential even when the veto pen rests in its inkwell, particularly when it comes to the content of legislation.

What about the relationship between mass public support for the president and the use of the veto? At least for the modern presidency, a crucial resource for the president in negotiating with Congress has been his public approval as measured by opinion polls.[16] In some situations, members of Congress pass a bill not because they want to change policy but because they want to force the president to veto a popular bill that he disagrees with in order to hurt his approval ratings.[17] As a result, vetoes may come at a price to the president.

Delegated Powers

Many of the powers exercised by the president and the executive branch are not set forth in the Constitution but are the products of congressional statutes and resolutions. Over the past three-quarters of a century, Congress has voluntarily delegated a great deal of its own legislative authority to the executive branch. To some extent, this delegation of power has been an almost inescapable consequence of the expansion of governmental activity in the United States since the New Deal. Given the vast range of the federal government's responsibilities, Congress cannot execute and administer all the programs it creates and the laws it enacts. Inevitably Congress must turn to the hundreds of departments and agencies in the executive branch or, when necessary, create new agencies to implement its goals. Thus, for example, in 2002, when Congress sought to protect America from terrorist attacks, it established the Department of Homeland Security and gave it broad powers in the realms of law enforcement, public health, and immigration. Similarly, in 1970, when Congress enacted legislation designed to improve the nation's air and water quality, it assigned the task of implementing its goals to the new Environmental Protection Agency (EPA) created by Nixon's executive order. Congress gave the EPA substantial power to set and enforce air- and water-quality standards.

As they implement congressional legislation, federal agencies collectively develop thousands of rules and regulations and issue thousands of orders and findings every year. Agencies interpret Congress's intent, promulgate rules aimed at implementing that intent, and issue orders to individuals, firms, and organizations throughout the nation designed to impel them to conform to the law.

In the nineteenth and early twentieth centuries, Congress typically wrote laws that provided fairly clear principles and standards to guide executive implementation. At least since the New Deal, however, Congress has tended to give executive agencies broad mandates and draft legislation that offers few clear standards or guidelines for implementation by the executive. For example, the 1933 National Industrial Recovery Act, a major piece of New Deal legislation, gave the president the authority to set rules to bring about fair competition in key sectors of the economy without ever defining what the term meant or how it was to be achieved. This pattern of broad delegation became typical in the ensuing decades, and the result is to shift power from Congress to the executive branch.

Inherent Powers

A number of presidential powers are neither expressed explicitly in the Constitution nor delegated by congressional statute or resolution. They are "inherent" in the role of the office. The president exercises these powers through his leadership in proposing ideas for legislation to Congress and by broadly employing the means to execute constitutional and statutory authority.

War and Inherent Presidential Power. The Constitution gives Congress the power to declare war. Presidents, however, have gone a long way toward capturing this power for themselves. Congress has not declared war since December 1941, yet since then American military forces have engaged in numerous campaigns throughout the world under the orders of the president. When North Korean forces invaded South Korea in June 1950, Congress was prepared to declare war, but President Harry S. Truman decided not to ask for congressional action. Instead, Truman asserted the principle that the president and not Congress could decide when and where to deploy America's military might. He dispatched American forces to Korea without a congressional declaration, and in the face of the emergency, Congress felt it had to acquiesce. It passed a resolution approving the president's actions, and this became the pattern for future congressional-executive relations in the military realm. The wars in Vietnam, Bosnia, Afghanistan, and Iraq, as well as a host of smaller-scale conflicts, were all fought without declarations of war.

In 1973, Congress responded to presidential unilateralism by passing the War Powers Resolution over President Nixon's veto. This resolution reasserted the principle of congressional war power, required the president to inform Congress of any planned military campaign, and stipulated that forces must be withdrawn within 60 days in the absence of a specific congressional authorization for their continued deployment. Presidents, however, have generally ignored the War Powers Resolution, claiming inherent executive power to defend the nation. Thus, for example, in 1989, President George H. W. Bush ordered an invasion of Panama without consulting Congress. President Clinton ordered a massive bombing campaign against Serbian forces in the former nation of Yugoslavia without congressional authorization. And, of course, President George W. Bush responded to the 2001 attacks by Islamic terrorists by organizing a major military campaign to overthrow the Taliban regime in Afghanistan, which had sheltered the terrorists. In 2003, Bush ordered a major American campaign against Iraq, which he accused of posing a threat to the United States. In both instances, Congress passed resolutions approving the president's actions, but the president was careful to assert that he did not need congressional authorization. The War Powers Resolution was barely mentioned on Capitol Hill and was ignored by the White House. However, tensions stemming from the separation of powers between the Congress have not ceased. The powers of the purse and investigation give Congress levers with which to constrain the executive. For these reasons, the president often restrains himself to minimize adverse political consequences. Thus in 2013, with public opinion running against him, President Obama sought authorization from Congress for an airstrike on Syria as punishment for its use of chemical weapons, in part to implicate Congress in the action and thereby share accountability.

On September 20, 2001, President George W. Bush addressed Congress and the public with a speech declaring a "war on terror." Congress passed a resolution approving the military campaign in Afghanistan (and, in 2002, the invasion of Iraq), but Bush insisted he did not need congressional authorization to go to war.

War Powers Resolution

A resolution of Congress declaring that the president can send troops into action abroad only by authorization of Congress or if U.S. troops are already under attack or seriously threatened

Legislative Initiative. Although it is not explicitly stated, the Constitution provides the president with the power of legislative initiative. To initiate means to originate, and in government that can mean power. The framers of the Constitution clearly saw legislative initiative as one of the keys to

legislative initiative

The president's inherent power to bring a legislative agenda before Congress executive power. Initiative obviously implies the ability to formulate proposals for important policies, and the president, as an individual with a great deal of staff assistance, is able to initiate decisive action more frequently than Congress, with its large assemblies that have to deliberate and debate before taking action. With some important exceptions, Congress banks on the president to set the agenda of public policy. And quite clearly, there is power in being able to set the terms of discourse in the making of public policy.

For example, in 2009, soon after taking office, President Obama presented Congress with a record-breaking $3 trillion budget proposal that included a host of new programs in such areas as health and human services, transportation, housing, and education. Obama told Congress that he would soon be requesting several hundred billion more for the financial bailout designed to rescue America's banks and revive the nation's credit markets. Not only was Congress responsive to the president's initiatives but lawmakers also expected the president to take the lead in responding to America's financial emergency and other problems.

The president's initiative does not end with policy making involving Congress and the making of laws in the ordinary sense of the phrase. The president has still another legislative role (in all but name) within the executive branch. This is designated as the power to issue executive orders. The executive order is first and foremost simply a management tool, a power possessed by virtually any CEO to make "company policy"—rules-setting procedures, etiquette, chains of command, functional responsibilities, and so on. But evolving out of this normal management practice is a recognized presidential power to promulgate rules that have the effect and the formal status of legislation. Most of the executive orders of the president provide for the reorganization of structures and procedures or otherwise direct the affairs of the executive branch. The power to issue executive orders illustrates that although reputation and persuasion are typically required in presidential policy making, the practice of issuing executive orders, within limits, allows a president to govern without the necessity to persuade.[18]

executive order

A rule or regulation issued by the president that has the effect and formal status of legislation

THE RISE OF PRESIDENTIAL GOVERNMENT

Most of the real influence of the modern presidency derives from the powers granted by the Constitution and the laws made by Congress. Presidential power is institutional. Thus, any person properly elected and sworn in as president will possess all of the power held by the strongest presidents in American history. But what variables account for a president's success in exercising these powers? Why are some presidents considered to be great successes, others colossal failures, and most somewhere in between? The answer relates broadly to the very concept of presidential power. Is that power a reflection of the attributes of the person or is it more a characteristic of the political situations that a president encounters?

The personal view of presidential power dominated political scientists' view for several decades,[19] but recent scholars have argued that presidential power should be analyzed in terms of the strategic interactions that a president has with other political actors. The veto, which we reviewed in the last section, is one example of this sort of strategic interaction, but there are many other "games" that presidents play: the Supreme Court–nomination and treaty-ratification games with the Senate, the executive-order game, the agency-supervision-and-management game with the executive branch. As the political scientist Charles M. Cameron has argued, "Understanding the presidency means understanding these games."[20] Success in these "games" translates into presidential power. With the occasional exception, however, it took more than a century, perhaps as much as a century and a half, before presidents came to be seen as consequential players in these strategic encounters. A bit of historical review will be helpful in understanding how the presidency has risen to its current level of influence.

The Legislative Epoch, 1800–1933

In 1885, a then-obscure political science professor named Woodrow Wilson titled his general textbook *Congressional Government* because American government was just that, congressional government. There is ample evidence that Wilson's description of the national government was consistent not only with nineteenth-century reality but also with the intentions of the framers. Within the system of three separate and competing powers, the clear intent of the Constitution was legislative supremacy. In the early nineteenth century, some observers saw the president as little more than America's chief clerk. Indeed, most historians agree that after Thomas Jefferson and until the beginning of the twentieth century, presidents Andrew Jackson and Abraham Lincoln were the only exceptions to a succession of weak presidents. Both Jackson and Lincoln are considered great presidents because they used their power in momentous ways. But it is important in the history of the presidency that neither of them left his powers as an institutional legacy to his successors. That is to say, once Jackson and Lincoln left office, the presidency reverted to the subordinate role that it played during the nineteenth century.

One reason that so few great men became presidents in the nineteenth century is that there was only occasional room for greatness in such a weak office.[21] As Chapter 3 indicated, the national government of that period was not particularly powerful. Another reason is that during this period, the presidency was not closely linked to major national political and social forces. Federalism had taken very good care of ensuring this by fragmenting political interests and diverting the energies of interest groups toward state and local governments, where most key decisions were being made.

The presidency was strengthened somewhat in the 1830s with the introduction of the national convention system of nominating presidential candidates. Until then, presidential candidates had been nominated by their party's congressional delegates. The national nominating convention arose outside Congress in order to provide some representation for a party's voters who lived in districts where they weren't numerous enough to elect a member of Congress. It was seen as a victory for democracy against the congressional elite. And the national convention gave the presidency a base of power independent of Congress. This independence did not immediately transform the presidency into the office we recognize today, though, because Congress was able to keep tight reins on the president's power. The real turning point came during the administration of Franklin Delano Roosevelt.

The New Deal and the Presidency

The "first hundred days" of the Roosevelt administration in 1933 have no parallel in U.S. history. But this period was only the beginning. The policies proposed by President Roosevelt and adopted by Congress during the first 100 days of his administration so changed the size and character of the national government that they constitute a moment in American history equivalent to the Founding or to the Civil War. The president's constitutional obligation to see "that the laws be faithfully executed" became, during Roosevelt's presidency, virtually a responsibility to shape the laws before executing them.

An Expanded Role for the National Government. Many of the New Deal programs were extensions of the traditional national government approach, which was described in Chapter 3. But the New Deal also adopted policies never before tried on a large scale by the national government. It began intervening into economic life in ways that had hitherto been reserved to the states. For example, during the early days of the New Deal in the throes of the Great Depression, the Roosevelt administration created the Works Progress Administration, seeking to put the able-bodied back to work; the federal government became the nation's largest employer at this time. The Social Security Act, to give another example, sought to improve the economic condition of the most impoverished segment of the population—the elderly. In other words, the national government discovered that it, too, had "police power" and that it could directly regulate individuals as well as provide roads and other services.

The new programs were such dramatic departures from the traditional policies of the national government that their constitutionality was in doubt. The turning point came in 1937 with *National Labor Relations Board v. Jones & Laughlin Steel Corporation*. At issue was the National Labor Relations Act, or Wagner Act, which prohibited corporations from interfering with the efforts of employees to engage in union activities. The newly formed National Labor Relations Board (NLRB) had ordered Jones & Laughlin to reinstate workers fired because of their union activities. The appeal reached the Supreme Court because Jones & Laughlin had made a constitutional issue over the fact that its manufacturing activities were local and therefore beyond the national government's reach. The Court rejected this argument with the response that a big company with subsidiaries and suppliers in many states was innately involved in interstate commerce.[22] Since the end of the New Deal, the Court has never again seriously questioned the constitutionality of an important act of Congress broadly authorizing the executive branch to intervene into the economy or society.

Delegation of Power. The most important constitutional effect of Congress's actions and the Supreme Court's approval of those actions during the New Deal was the enhancement of presidential power. Most major acts of Congress in this period involved significant exercises of control over the economy. But few programs specified the actual controls to be used. Instead, Congress authorized the president or, in some cases, a new agency to determine what the controls would be. Some of the new agencies were independent commissions responsible to Congress. But most of the new agencies and programs of the New Deal were placed in the executive branch directly under presidential authority.

No modern government can avoid the delegation of significant legislative powers to the executive branch. But the fact remains that during the 1930s, the growth of the national government through acts delegating legislative power tilted the American national structure away from a Congress-centered government toward a president-centered government. Congress continues to be the constitutional source of policy, and Congress can rescind these delegations of power or restrict them with later amendments, committee oversight, or budget costs. But since Congress has continued to enact large new programs involving very broad delegations of legislative power to the executive branch, and since the Court has gone along with such actions, we can say that presidential government has become an established fact of American life.

PRESIDENTIAL GOVERNMENT

Presidents have at their disposal a variety of formal and informal resources that enable them to govern. Indeed, without these resources, presidents would lack the tools needed to make much use of the power and responsibility given to them by the Constitution and by Congress. Let us first consider the president's formal or official resources (Figure 6.2). Then, in the section following, we will turn to the more informal resources that affect a president's capacity to govern, in particular the president's popular support.

Formal Resources of Presidential Power

The formal resources of presidential power include the Cabinet, the White House staff, the Executive Office of the President, and the vice presidency.

Cabinet →

The secretaries, or chief administrators, of the major departments of the federal government. Cabinet secretaries are appointed by the president with the consent of the Senate

The Cabinet. In the American system of government, the Cabinet is the traditional but informal designation for the heads of all the major federal government departments. The Cabinet has only a limited constitutional status. Unlike that of England and many other parliamentary countries, where the cabinet *is* the government, the American Cabinet is not a collective body. It meets but makes no decisions as a group. Each appointment must be approved by the Senate, but the person appointed is not responsible to the Senate or to Congress at large. Cabinet appointments help build party and popular support, but the Cabinet is not a party organ. The Cabinet is made up of directors but is not a board of directors.

National Security Council (NSC) →

A presidential foreign-policy advisory council comprising the president, the vice president, the secretaries of State, Defense, and the Treasury, the attorney general, and other officials invited by the president

Some presidents have relied heavily on an "inner cabinet," the National Security Council (NSC). The NSC, established by law in 1947, is composed of the president, the vice president, the secretary of state, the secretary of defense, and other officials invited by the president. It has its own staff of foreign-policy specialists run by the special assistant to the president for national security affairs. Presidents have varied in their reliance on the NSC and other sub-Cabinet bodies, because executive management is inherently a personal matter. However, one generalization can be made: presidents have increasingly preferred the White House staff to the Cabinet as their means of managing the gigantic executive branch.

The White House Staff. The White House staff is composed mainly of analysts and advisers. Although many of the top White House staffers are given the title "special assistant" for a particular task or sector, the types

Figure 6.2
THE INSTITUTIONAL PRESIDENCY, 2013

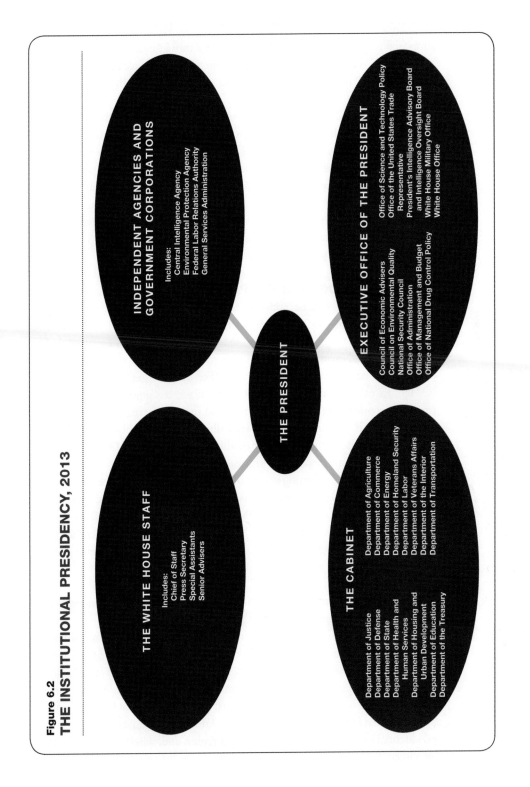

THE WHITE HOUSE STAFF

Includes:
Chief of Staff
Press Secretary
Special Assistants
Senior Advisers

INDEPENDENT AGENCIES AND GOVERNMENT CORPORATIONS

Includes:
Central Intelligence Agency
Environmental Protection Agency
Federal Labor Relations Authority
General Services Administration

THE PRESIDENT

THE CABINET

Department of Justice
Department of Defense
Department of State
Department of Health and
    Human Services
Department of Housing and
    Urban Development
Department of Education
Department of the Treasury
Department of Agriculture
Department of Commerce
Department of Energy
Department of Homeland Security
Department of Labor
Department of Veterans Affairs
Department of the Interior
Department of Transportation

EXECUTIVE OFFICE OF THE PRESIDENT

Council of Economic Advisers
Council on Environmental Quality
National Security Council
Office of Administration
Office of Management and Budget
Office of National Drug Control Policy
Office of Science and Technology Policy
Office of the United States Trade
    Representative
President's Intelligence Advisory Board
    and Intelligence Oversight Board
White House Military Office
White House Office

of judgments they are expected to make and the kinds of advice they are supposed to give are a good deal broader and more generally political than those that come from the Cabinet departments or the Executive Office of the President. The White House staff has grown substantially under recent presidents.

The White House staff is a crucial information source and management tool for the president. But it may also insulate the president from other sources of information. Managing this trade-off between in-house expertise and access to independent outside opinion is a major challenge for the president. Sometimes it is botched, as when President George W. Bush depended too heavily on his staff for information about WMDs in Iraq, leading him to erroneous conclusions. In 2009, President Obama merged the White House Homeland Security staff with the National Security Council staff to create a new National Security staff to deal with all security problems.[23]

The Executive Office of the President. The development of the White House staff can be appreciated only in relation to the still larger Executive Office of the President (EOP). Created in 1939, the EOP is what is often called the "institutional presidency"—the permanent agencies that perform defined management tasks for the president. The most important and the largest EOP agency is the Office of Management and Budget (OMB). Its roles in preparing the national budget, designing the president's program, reporting on agency activities, and overseeing regulatory proposals make OMB personnel part of virtually every conceivable presidential responsibility. The status and power of the OMB within the EOP has grown in importance from president to president.

The process of budgeting was at one time a bottom-up procedure, with expenditure and program requests passing from the lowest bureaus through the departments to "clearance" in OMB and hence to Congress, where each agency could be called in to reveal what its original request had been before OMB got hold of it. Now the process is top-down, with OMB setting the budget guidelines for agencies as well as for Congress.

The Vice Presidency. The Constitution created the vice presidency along with the presidency, and the office exists for two purposes only: to succeed the president in the case of a vacancy and to preside over the Senate, casting the tie-breaking vote when necessary.[24] The main value of the vice presidency as a political resource for the president is electoral. Traditionally, a presidential candidate's most important rule for the choice of a running mate is that she bring the support of at least one state (preferably a large one) not otherwise likely to support the ticket. Another rule holds that the vice-presidential nominee should come from a region and, where possible, from an ideological or ethnic subsection of the party differing from the presidential nominee's. It is very doubtful that John Kennedy would have won in 1960 without his vice-presidential candidate, Lyndon Johnson, and the contribution Johnson made to carrying Texas.

The emphasis has recently shifted away from geographical to ideological balance. George W. Bush's choice of Dick Cheney in 2000 was completely devoid of direct electoral value since Cheney came from one of our least populous states (Wyoming, which casts only three electoral votes). But given Cheney's stalwart right-wing record both in Congress and as President George H. W. Bush's secretary of defense, his inclusion on the Republican ticket was clearly an effort to consolidate the support of the restive right wing of his party. In 2008, Barack Obama chose Senator Joseph Biden of Delaware as his vice-presidential

The vice presidency was long considered a weak office, but recent presidents have often delegated important responsibilities to their vice presidents. Vice President Joseph Biden, shown here with the Russian foreign minister, has played a key role in foreign policy.

running mate. Obama had often been criticized for lacking background in the realm of foreign policy. Biden, the chair of the Senate Foreign Relations Committee, brought considerable foreign-policy experience to the ticket.

As the institutional presidency has grown in size and complexity, most presidents of the past 25 years have sought to use their vice presidents as a management resource after the election. George H. W. Bush, as vice president, was "kept within the loop" of decision making because President Reagan delegated so much power. President Bush did not take such pains to keep Dan Quayle "in the loop," but President Clinton relied greatly on his vice president, Al Gore, who emerged as one of the most trusted and effective figures in the Clinton White House. The presidency of George W. Bush resulted in unprecedented power and responsibility for his vice president, Dick Cheney. For the Obama administration, Vice President Joe Biden has played an important liaison role to Congress and has been an important sounding board on foreign affairs matters.

The Contemporary Bases of Presidential Power

Generally, presidents can expand their power in three ways: party, popular mobilization, and administration. In the first instance, presidents may construct or strengthen national partisan institutions with which to exert influence in the legislative process and through which to implement their programs. Alternatively, or in addition to the first tactic, presidents may use popular appeals to create a mass base of support that will allow them to subordinate their political foes. This tactic has sometimes been called the strategy of "going public" or the "rhetorical" presidency.[25] Third, presidents may seek to bolster their control of established executive agencies or to create new administrative institutions and procedures that will reduce their dependence on Congress and give them a more independent governing and policy-making capability. Presidents' use of executive orders to achieve their policy goals in lieu of seeking to persuade Congress to enact legislation is, perhaps, the most obvious example.

Party as a Source of Power. All presidents have relied on the members and leaders of their own party to implement their legislative agendas. President George W. Bush, for example, worked closely with congressional GOP leaders on such matters as energy policy and Medicare reform, and President Obama depended on Democratic leaders to secure enactment of his budget and his health care and energy proposals. But the president does not control his own party; party members have considerable autonomy. Moreover, in America's system of separated powers, the president's party may be in the minority in Congress and unable to do much for the chief executive's programs (Figure 6.3). Consequently, although their party is valuable to chief executives, it has not been a fully reliable presidential tool. The more unified the president's party is behind his legislative requests, the more unified the opposition party is also likely to be. Unless the president's party majority is very large, he must also appeal to the opposition to make up for the inevitable defectors within the ranks of his own party. Thus the president often poses as being above partisanship to win "bipartisan" support in Congress. But to the extent that he pursues a bipartisan strategy, he cannot throw himself fully into building the party loyalty and the party discipline that would maximize the value of his own party's support in Congress. This is a dilemma for every president, particularly one faced with an opposition-controlled Congress.

Going Public. Popular mobilization as a technique of presidential power has its historical roots in the presidencies of Theodore Roosevelt and Woodrow Wilson and has, subsequently, become a weapon in the political arsenals of most presidents since the mid-twentieth century. During the nineteenth century, it was considered inappropriate for presidents to engage in personal campaigning on their own behalf or in support of programs and policies. When Andrew Johnson broke this unwritten rule and made a series of speeches vehemently seeking public support for his Reconstruction program, even some of Johnson's most ardent supporters were shocked at what they saw as his lack of decorum.

The president who used public appeals most effectively was Franklin Delano Roosevelt. The political scientist Sidney Milkis observes that Roosevelt was "firmly persuaded of the need to form a direct link between the

Chapter 6: The Presidency

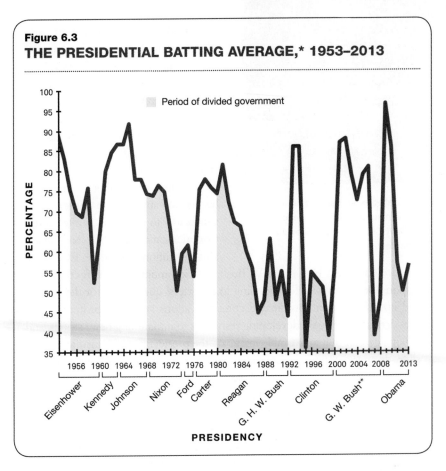

Figure 6.3

THE PRESIDENTIAL BATTING AVERAGE,* 1953–2013

*Percentage of congressional votes in which the president took the position supported by Congress.
**In 2001, the government was divided for only part of the year.
NOTE: Percentages are based on votes on which presidents took a position.
SOURCES: *Congressional Quarterly Weekly Report*, January 3, 2011, pp. 18–24, and authors' update.

executive office and the public.[26] He developed a number of tactics aimed at forging such a link. Like his predecessors, he often embarked on speaking trips around the nation to promote his programs. In addition, Roosevelt made limited but important use of the new electronic medium, the radio, to reach millions of Americans. In his famous "fireside chats," the president, or at least his voice, came into every living room in the country to discuss programs and policies and generally to assure Americans that Roosevelt was aware of their difficulties and working diligently toward solutions.

Roosevelt also made himself available for biweekly press conferences, during which he offered candid answers to reporters' questions and made certain to make important policy announcements that would provide the reporters with significant stories to file with their papers.[27] Roosevelt was especially effective in designating a press secretary (Stephen Early), who

Today, presidents use an array of strategies to reach constituents, shape their image, and attempt to win support for their policies. Nontraditional programs like *The Daily Show with Jon Stewart* appeal to younger Americans in particular.

organized press conferences and made certain that reporters observed the informal rules distinguishing presidential comments that were off the record from those that could be attributed directly to the president.

Every president since Roosevelt has sought to craft a public-relations strategy that would emphasize the incumbent's strengths and maximize his popular appeal. One Clinton innovation was to make the White House Communications Office an important institution within the EOP. In a practice continued by George W. Bush, the Communications Office became responsible not only for responding to reporters' queries but for developing and implementing a coordinated communications strategy—promoting the president's policy goals, developing responses to unflattering news stories, and making certain that a favorable image of the president would, insofar as possible, dominate the news. Consistent with President Obama's successful use of social networking in his 2008 election campaign, the Obama administration's communications office has emphasized social networking techniques, including tweeting, to reach newsmakers and the American people directly. The White House posts several tweets a day on topics as varied as immigration reform, climate change, and the Chicago Blackhawk's Stanley Cup win.

In addition to using the media, recent presidents have reached out directly to the American public to gain its approval (Figure 6.4). This is an expression of the presidency as a permanent campaign for re-election. A study by the political scientist Charles O. Jones shows that President Clinton engaged in campaignlike activity throughout his presidency and was the most-traveled American president in history. In his first 20 months in office, he made 203 appearances outside of Washington, compared with 178 for George H. W. Bush and 58 for Ronald Reagan. Time will tell whether President Obama will challenge Clinton's total record for appearances by a president.

However, popular support has not been a firm foundation for presidential power. To begin with, popular support is notoriously fickle. President George W. Bush maintained an approval rating of over 70 percent for more than a year after the September 11 terrorist attacks. By 2003, however, his approval rating had fallen nearly 20 points as American casualties in Iraq mounted; by the end of 2005 it had fallen almost another 20 points, to the high-30s range. Such declines in popular approval during a president's term in office are nearly inevitable and follow a predictable pattern (Figure 6.5).[28] Presidents generate popular support by promising to undertake important programs that will

Chapter 6: The Presidency

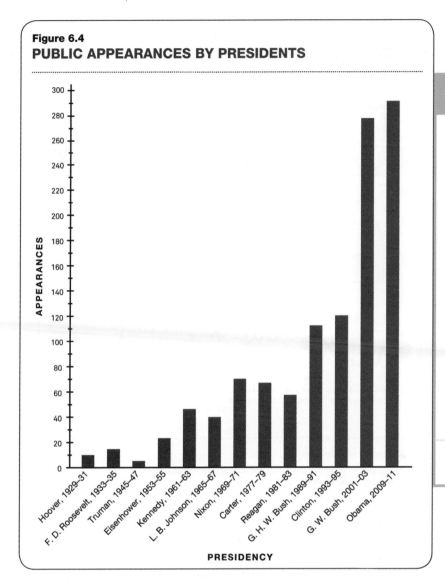

Figure 6.4
PUBLIC APPEARANCES BY PRESIDENTS

(Chart: vertical axis labeled APPEARANCES, 0 to 300; horizontal axis labeled PRESIDENCY with bars for Hoover, 1929–31; F. D. Roosevelt, 1933–35; Truman, 1945–47; Eisenhower, 1953–55; Kennedy, 1961–63; L. B. Johnson, 1965–67; Nixon, 1969–71; Carter, 1977–79; Reagan, 1981–83; G. H. W. Bush, 1989–91; Clinton, 1993–95; G. W. Bush, 2001–03; Obama, 2009–11)

ANALYZING THE EVIDENCE

In the nineteenth century, presidents seldom made public speeches or other public appearances. By the end of the twentieth century, the number of times presidents went public had increased dramatically. What accounts for the growth in public appearances? What do presidents hope to accomplish through speeches and other public events? What risks do presidents take when they seek to develop and use popular support as a political tool?

NOTE: Only the first two years of each term are included, because the last two years include many purely political appearances for the president's re-election campaign.

SOURCES: Kernell, *Going Public*, p.118, Lyn Ragsdale, *Vital Statistics on the Presidency*, 3rd ed. (Washington, DC: CQ Press, 2009), Table 4-9, pp. 202–3; POTUS Tracker, *Washington Post*, http://projects.washingtonpost.com/potus-tracker/ (accessed 8/8/11); and authors' updates.

contribute directly to the well-being of large numbers of Americans. Almost inevitably, presidential performance falls short of those promises and popular expectations, leading to a sharp decline in public support and an ensuing collapse of presidential influence. Reagan and Clinton are the exceptions among modern presidents—leaving office at least as popular as when they arrived.

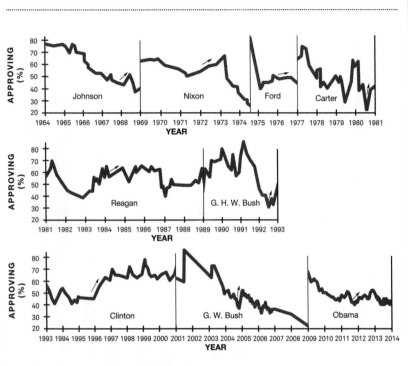

Figure 6.5
PRESIDENTIAL PERFORMANCE RATINGS

In the presidential performance-rating poll, respondents are asked, "Do you approve of the way the president is handling his job?" The graphs show the percentage of positive responses. What factors help explain changes in presidential approval ratings? Does popular approval really affect presidential power? How can popular feelings about the president affect the president's conduct and influence?

NOTE: Arrows indicate preelection upswings.

SOURCES: Gallup, Presidential Job Approval Center, www.gallup.com/poll/124922/presidential–approval–center.aspx (accessed 6/14/13).

Presidents have certainly not abandoned "going public," but they have employed institutionalized public- and media-relations efforts more to create a generally favorable public image than to promote specific policies.[29] Thus, in 2002, President George W. Bush made several speeches to boost the proposed creation of the Homeland Security Department. At the same time, however, the White House Communications Office was engaged in a nonstop, seven-days-a-week effort to promote news and feature stories aimed at bolstering the president's more general public image.

Technological change has also affected the tactics of going public. The growing heterogeneity of media outlets—cable stations, streamed radio, the blogosphere—and the declining viewership and readership of mainstream outlets has fragmented the public. This has necessitated newly crafted approaches—"narrowcasting" to reach targeted demographic categories rather than broadcasting to reach "the public." Instead of going "capital P" public, new approaches seek to appeal to myriad "small p" publics (plural). Shrinking and fragmented audiences have raised the costs and cast doubt on the effectiveness of presidential efforts to educate and mobilize public opinion. The limitations of going public as a route to presidential power have also led contemporary presidents to make use of a third technique: expanding their administrative capabilities.

The Administrative State

Contemporary presidents have increased the administrative capabilities of their office in two important ways. First, they have sought to increase White House control over the federal bureaucracy. Second, they have expanded the role of executive orders and other instruments of direct presidential governance. Taken together, these components of what might be called the White House "administrative strategy" have given presidents the potential to achieve their programmatic and policy goals even when they are unable to secure congressional approval. Indeed, some recent presidents have been able to accomplish quite a bit without much congressional, partisan, or even public support.

Appointments and Regulatory Review. Presidents have sought to increase their influence through bureaucratic appointments and regulatory review. By appointing loyal supporters to top jobs in the bureaucracy, presidents make it more likely that agencies will follow the president's wishes. As the Analyzing the Evidence unit in this chapter shows in more detail, recent presidents have increased the number of political appointees in the bureaucracy. Through regulatory review, presidents have tried to control rule making by the agencies of the executive branch. Whenever Congress enacts a statute, its actual implementation requires the promulgation of hundreds of rules by the agency charged with administering the law and giving effect to the will of Congress. Some congressional statutes are quite detailed and leave agencies with relatively little discretion. Typically, however, Congress enacts a relatively broad statement of legislative intent and delegates to the appropriate administrative agency the power to fill in many important details.[30] In other words, Congress typically says to an administrative agency, "Here is the problem. Deal with it."[31]

The discretion Congress delegates to administrative agencies has provided recent presidents with an important avenue for expanding their power. For example, President Clinton ordered the Food and Drug Administration (FDA) to develop rules designed to restrict the marketing of tobacco products to children. White House and FDA staffers then spent several months preparing nearly 1,000 pages of new regulations affecting tobacco manufacturers and vendors.[32] Republicans denounced Clinton's actions as a usurpation of power.[33] However,

regulatory review
The Office of Management and Budget function of reviewing all agency regulations and other rule making before they become official policy

Presidential Appointees in the Executive Branch

Contributed by
David Lewis
Vanderbilt University

Article II of the Constitution states that "The executive power shall be vested in a President of the United States of America" and details one of the president's most important constitutional roles: leading the executive branch. Today, this means the president must manage 15 cabinet departments and 55–60 independent agencies—and the over 2 million civilian employees who work in the federal government. Given the system of separation of powers, the president often competes with Congress for control of the executive branch. Congress also has a legitimate interest in the actions of executive branch officials since Congress creates programs and agencies and determines their budgets. The stakes of this competition between the branches are increasing. As the scope and complexity of government work have grown, Congress has delegated important policy-making responsibility to government officials working in the executive branch. These officials determine important public policies such as allowable levels of pollutants in the environment, eligibility rules for government benefits like medical care and Social Security, and safety rules in workplaces. Modern presidents have sought to exert more control over these agencies by a number of means, including increasing the number of presidential appointments.

Civil Service Systems

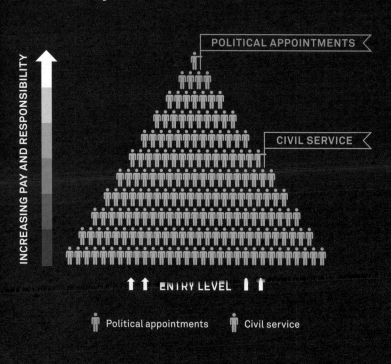

INCREASING PAY AND RESPONSIBILITY

POLITICAL APPOINTMENTS

CIVIL SERVICE

ENTRY LEVEL

Political appointments   Civil service

Government agencies are generally staffed by a mix of two types of employees: civil servants and political appointees. Civil servants staff the lower strata of government agencies and are to be hired, fired, promoted, and demoted on the basis of merit, and they cannot be removed without good cause. Political appointees, however, are generally selected from outside the civil service by the president, and most can be removed at the president's discretion.

SOURCE: David E. Lewis, *The Politics of Presidential Appointments* (Princeton, NJ: Princeton University Press, 2008).

Total Number of Federal Government Appointees and Percentage Appointed*

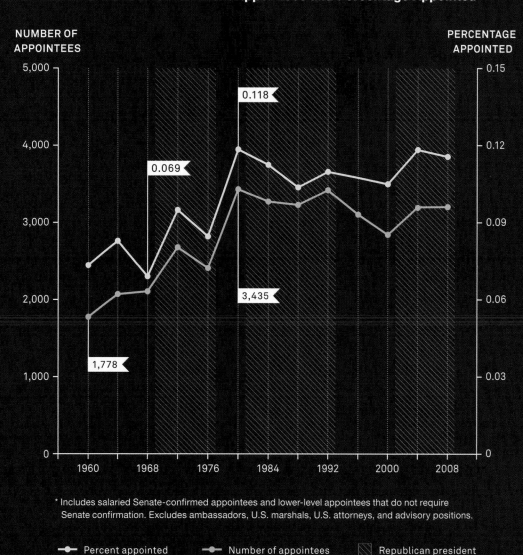

NUMBER OF
APPOINTEES

PERCENTAGE
APPOINTED

5,000 — — 0.15

0.118

0.069

4,000 — — 0.12

— 0.09
3,000 —

3,435

2,000 — — 0.06

1,778

1,000 — — 0.03

0 — — 0

1960 1968 1976 1984 1992 2000 2008

* Includes salaried Senate-confirmed appointees and lower-level appointees that do not require
Senate confirmation. Excludes ambassadors, U.S. marshals, U.S. attorneys, and advisory positions.

Percent appointed   Number of appointees   Republican president

Presidents since the middle of the twentieth century have sought to push down the dividing line between appointees and civil servants in government agencies. The figure above presents the total number of presidential appointees as well as the percentage of appointees in the federal government workforce over the last five decades. First, it should be noted that appointees make up a very small percentage of the federal workforce. However, and interestingly, the proportion of federal employees who are appointees has grown during this time period, as presidents have tried to exert greater influence over the executive branch.

SOURCE: David E. Lewis, "Modern Presidents and the Transformation of the Federal Personnel System," *The Forum* 7(4): Article 6 (2010), www.bepress.com/forum/vol7/iss4/art6 (accessed 10/24/11).

after he took office, President George W. Bush made no move to surrender the powers Clinton had claimed, and Obama has continued the practice.

Executive Orders. Another mechanism through which contemporary presidents have sought to enhance their power to govern unilaterally is through the use of executive orders and other forms of presidential decrees, including executive agreements, national security findings and directives, proclamations, reorganization plans, signing statements, and a host of others.[34] Presidents may not use executive orders to issue whatever commands they please. The use of such decrees is bound by law. If a president issues an executive order, proclamation, directive, or the like, in principle he does so pursuant to the powers granted to him by the Constitution or delegated to him by Congress, usually through a statute. When presidents issue such orders, they generally state the constitutional or statutory basis for their actions. For example, when President Truman ordered the desegregation of the armed services, he did so pursuant to his constitutional powers as commander in chief. In a similar vein, when President Johnson issued Executive Order No. 11246, he asserted that the order was designed to implement the 1964 Civil Rights Act, which prohibited employment discrimination. Where an executive order has no statutory or constitutional basis, the courts have held it to be void. The most important case illustrating this point is *Youngstown Sheet & Tube Co. v. Sawyer*, the so-called steel seizure case of 1952.[35] Here the Supreme Court ruled that President Truman's seizure of the nation's steel mills during the Korean War had no statutory or constitutional basis and was thus invalid.

A number of court decisions, though, have established broad boundaries that leave considerable room for presidential action. By illustration, the courts have held that Congress might approve a presidential action after the fact or, in effect, ratify a presidential action through "acquiescence"—for example, by not objecting for long periods of time or by continuing to provide funding for programs established by executive orders. In addition, the courts have indicated that some areas, most notably the realm of military policy, are presidential in character and have allowed presidents wide latitude to make policy by executive decree. Thus, within the very broad limits established by the courts, presidential orders can be and have been important policy tools (Figure 6.6).

President George W. Bush did not hesitate to use executive orders, issuing more than 40 during his first year in office alone and continuing to employ this device (along with signing statements) regularly during his presidency. During his first months in office, Bush issued orders prohibiting the use of federal funds to support international family-planning groups that provided abortion-counseling services and placing limits on the use of embryonic stem cells in federally funded research projects. Bush also made very aggressive use of executive orders in response to the threat of terrorism, which the president declared to be his administration's most important policy agenda.

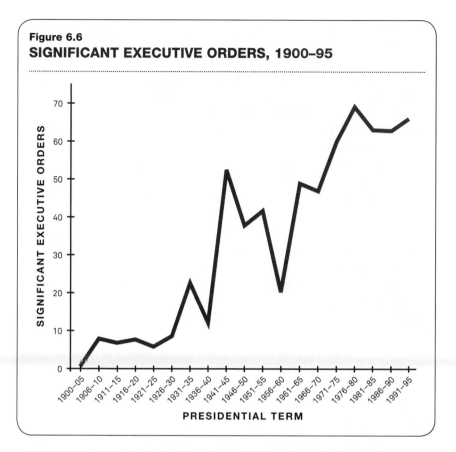

Figure 6.6

SIGNIFICANT EXECUTIVE ORDERS, 1900–95

SOURCE: William G. Howell, "The President's Powers of Unilateral Action: The Strategic Advantages of Acting Alone" (Ph.D. diss., Stanford University, 1999).

In November 2001, for example, Bush issued a directive authorizing the creation of military tribunals to try noncitizens accused of involvement in acts of terrorism against the United States.

President Obama signed four executive orders on his second full day in office. With the stroke of a pen, he changed government policy on detention operations at the naval base at Guantánamo Bay; clarified his administration's stance on the use of torture and/or controversial interrogation techniques; reversed the previous administration's ban on certain types of stem cell research; and reversed the rule restricting federal funding for groups that performed or advocated abortion in other countries as part of family-planning services. Obama continued to use executive orders often, issuing 31 in 2012 and more than 20 in 2013.

Signing Statements. The signing statement has become another instrument of presidential power. To negate congressional actions to which they objected, recent presidents have made frequent and calculated use of presidential signing statements when signing bills into law.[36] A signing statement is an announcement made by the president at the time of signing a congressional enactment into law, sometimes presenting the president's interpretation of the law as well as usually innocuous remarks predicting the many benefits the new law will bring to the nation. Occasionally, presidents have used signing statements to point to sections of the law they deemed improper or even unconstitutional, and to instruct executive branch agencies how they were to execute the law.[37] President Harry Truman, for example, accompanied his approval of the 1946 Hobbs Anti-Racketeering Act with a message offering his interpretation of ambiguous sections of the statute and indicating how the federal government would implement the new law.[38]

Presidents have made signing statements throughout American history, though many were not recorded and so did not become part of the official legislative record. Ronald Reagan's attorney general, Edwin Meese, is generally credited with transforming the signing statement into a routine tool of presidential direct action.[39] With the way paved, Reagan proceeded to use detailed and artfully designed signing statements—prepared by the Department of Justice—to attempt to reinterpret congressional enactments. When he signed the Competition in Contracting Act in 1984, President Reagan declared that portions of the law were unconstitutional and directed executive branch officials not to comply with them. Subsequently, U.S. District Court judge Harold Ackerman upheld the act and decried the notion that the president had the power to declare acts of Congress unconstitutional.[40] The same conclusion was later reached by the Ninth Circuit Court of Appeals, which declared that the president did not have the authority to "excise or sever provisions of a bill with which he disagrees."[41]

Despite these adverse rulings, however, the same tactic of reinterpreting and nullifying congressional enactments was continued by Reagan's successor, George H. W. Bush. Bill Clinton followed the examples set by Reagan and Bush and made extensive use of signing statements both to reinterpret and nullify congressional enactments.

Presidential use of signing statements to challenge legislative provisions increased sharply during the George W. Bush years. President Reagan used signing statements to attack 71 legislative provisions, and President Clinton made 105 significant signing statements. Bush challenged more than 800 legislative provisions with his signing statements, including a number of important domestic and security matters, such as a congressional effort, led by Senator John McCain, to ban the use of torture by American interrogators. Though he had denounced Bush's use of signing statements during the campaign, soon after taking office President Obama began to make use of the same tactic. By the end of his first term, Obama had issued more than two dozen signing statements in which he offered his own interpretation of portions of the bills he signed into law. Still, the legal status of signing statements has not been fully resolved.

The Limits of Presidential Power

Presidents are powerful political actors and have become increasingly so during the past century. This is the take-home point of this chapter. But we would be remiss if we said nothing about the limits of presidential power. Indeed, presidents have had to resort to institutional and behavioral invention—signing statements, executive orders, public appeals—precisely because their official powers are limited. The separation of powers is a mighty constraint—"the president proposes; the Congress disposes." The president cannot always bend the Congress to his will, though it is an easier task when his party controls the two chambers. On the other hand, the agendas of powerful congressional players must obtain the president's consent, as the presentment clause of the Constitution requires. Through his veto power, the president can defeat, but more importantly can influence in advance, congressional aspirations. Presidential power is real, but it is tempered by the necessity of bilateral bargaining with the legislature, by his ability to lead the bureaucracy, and by the permissiveness of the federal judiciary. The growth in presidential power of the last hundred years has required the acquiescence if not the outright support of all the other players in the game.

IS THE PRESIDENCY TOO STRONG?

The framers of the Constitution, as we saw, created a unitary executive branch because they thought this would make the presidency a more energetic institution. At the same time, they checked the powers of the executive branch by creating a system of separated powers. Did the framers' work make the presidency a strong or weak institution?

At one time, historians and journalists liked to debate the question of strong versus weak presidents. Some presidents, such as Lincoln and Franklin Delano Roosevelt, were called "strong" for their leadership and ability to guide the nation's political agenda. Others, such as James Buchanan and Calvin Coolidge, were seen as "weak" for failing to develop significant legislative programs and seeming to observe rather than shape political events. Today, the strong versus weak categorization has become moot. Despite the limits mentioned in the preceding section, *every president is strong*. This strength is not so much a function of personal charisma as it is a reflection of the increasing powers of the institution of the presidency. Of course, as we noted earlier, political savvy in strategic interactions with other politicians and mobilizing public opinion can account for a president's success in exercising these powers. But contemporary presidents all possess a vast array of resources and powers.

Indeed, presidents seek to dominate the policy-making process and claim the inherent power to lead the nation in time of war. The expansion of presidential power over the past century has not come about by accident but as the result of an ongoing effort by successive presidents to expand the power of the office. Some presidential efforts have succeeded and others have failed. One recent president, Richard Nixon, was forced to resign, and others have left office under clouds. Most presidents, nevertheless, have sought to increase the office's power. As the framers of the Constitution predicted, presidential ambition has been a powerful and unrelenting force in American politics. Why has presidential ambition gone virtually unchecked? What are the consequences of such a development?

As is often noted by the media and in the academic literature, popular participation in American political life has declined precipitously since its nineteenth-century apogee. Voter turnout in national presidential elections barely reaches the 60 percent mark; hardly a third of those eligible participate in off-year congressional races. Turnout in state and local contests is typically even lower. These facts are well known, and their implications for the representative character of American government frequently deplored.

The decay of popular political participation, however, also has institutional implications that are not often fully appreciated. To put the matter succinctly, the decline of voting and other forms of popular involvement in American political life reduce congressional influence while enhancing the power of the presidency. For all its faults and foibles, Congress is the nation's most representative political institution and remains the only entity capable of placing limits on unwise or illegitimate presidential conduct. Certainly, the courts have seldom been capable of thwarting a determined president, especially in the foreign-policy realm. Unfortunately, however, in recent decades our nation's undemocratic politics has undermined Congress while paving the way for aggrandizement of power by the executive and the presidential unilateralism that inevitably follows.

The framers of the Constitution created a system of government in which the Congress and the executive branch were to share power. In recent years, however, the powers of Congress have waned while those of the presidency have expanded dramatically. To take one instance of congressional retreat in the face of presidential assertiveness, in October 2002, pressed by President George W. Bush, both houses of Congress voted overwhelmingly to authorize the White House to use military force against Iraq. The resolution adopted by Congress allowed the president complete discretion to determine whether, when, and how to attack Iraq. Indeed, Bush's legal advisers had pointedly declared that the president did not actually need specific congressional authorization to attack Iraq if he deemed such action to be in America's interest. Few members of Congress even bothered to object to this apparent rewriting of the U.S. Constitution.

There is no doubt that Congress continues to be able to harass presidents and even, on occasion, to hand the White House a sharp rebuff. In the larger view, however, presidents' occasional defeats—however dramatic—have to be seen as temporary setbacks in a gradual and decisive shift toward increased presidential power in the twenty-first century.

For Further Reading

Selections highlighted in red are included in *Readings in American Politics: Analysis and Perspectives*, Third Edition.

Canes-Wrone, Brandice. *Who Leads Whom? Presidents, Policy, and the Public.* Chicago: University of Chicago Press, 2006.

Crenson, Matthew, and Benjamin Ginsberg. *Presidential Power: Unchecked and Unbalanced.* New York: Norton, 2007.

Deering, Christopher, and Forrest Maltzman. "The Politics of Executive Orders: Legislative Constraints on Presidential Power." *Political Research Quarterly* 52 (1999): 767–83.

Howell, William, G. *Power without Persuasion: The Politics of Direct Presidential Action.* Princeton, NJ: Princeton University Press, 2003.

Krutz, Glen, and Jeffrey Peake. *Presidential-Congressional Governance and the Rise of Executive Agreements.* Ann Arbor: University of Michigan Press, 2009.

Milkis, Sidney M. *The President and the Parties: The Transformation of the American Party System Since the New Deal.* New York: Oxford University Press, 1993.

Nelson, Michael, ed. *The Presidency and the Political System.* 9th ed. Washington, DC: CQ Press, 2009.

Neustadt, Richard E. *Presidential Power and the Modern Presidents: The Politics of Leadership from Roosevelt to Reagan.* 1960. Rev. ed., New York: Free Press, 1990.

Skowronek, Stephen. *The Politics Presidents Make: Leadership from John Adams to Bill Clinton.* Cambridge, MA: Harvard University Press, 1997.

7

The Executive Branch

The bureaucracies of the executive branch are the administrative heart and soul of government. They are literally where the rubber meets the road—where the policies formulated, refined, and passed into law by elected officials are interpreted, implemented, and ultimately delivered to a nation's citizens. Government touches the life of the ordinary citizen most directly in her interactions with bureaucratic agents—at the Department of Motor Vehicles when obtaining a driver's license; in filing one's income-tax return with the Internal Revenue Service; at the recruiting center when enlisting in one of the armed services; at the Board of Elections when registering to vote.

Public bureaucracies are powerful because legislatures and chief executives—and, indeed, the people—delegate to them vast power to make sure a particular job is done, enabling the rest of us to be freer to pursue our private ends. The public sentiments that emerged after September 11 revealed this underlying appreciation of public bureaucracies. When faced with the challenge of making air travel safe again, the public strongly supported giving the federal government responsibility for airport security even though this meant increasing the size of the federal bureaucracy. In 2008 and 2009, Americans again looked to the federal bureaucracy to help solve the financial crisis. However, Americans have often been more suspicious of bureaucracy.

One reason for this is concern about organizational bias. Bureaucracies are created to give effect to the will of the nation's elected representatives. However, the practices of bureaucratic agencies often reflect their own external or internal interests more than Congress's plans or some broader conception of the public purpose. Two types of organizational interests or biases are especially likely to drive the behavior of bureaucratic agencies. First, agency executives are often concerned with their budget, power, and autonomy vis-à-vis other institutions and political forces.[1] For example, since the creation of the Department of Defense (DOD) and the Central Intelligence Agency (CIA) in 1947, the secretary of Defense and the director of Central Intelligence have engaged in continual bureaucratic struggle over control of the nation's intelligence assets and budgets.

A second type of organizational bias often results from an organization's internal politics. Just as organizations vie with one another, factions within an agency compete with rival groups for money, power, and prestige. A particularly important factor in such internal struggles is the agency's definition of its central mission and core responsibilities. Usually, one or another faction within the organization bases its claim to power and preferment on its particular ability to carry out the agency's core

CORE OF THE ANALYSIS

➡️ The bureaucracy is necessary for the maintenance of order in a large society.

➡️ The size of the federal bureaucracy is large but has not been growing faster than the economy or the population as a whole.

➡️ By implementing the laws and policies passed by elected officials, bureaucrats can be seen as agents of Congress and the presidency. As in any principal-agent relationship, the agent (the bureaucracy) is delegated authority and has a certain amount of leeway for independent action.

➡️ Bureaucrats have their own goals and thus exercise their own influence on policy. Congressional committees use oversight to make the bureaucracy accountable.

mission. A change in mission might threaten that power. For example, when aircraft carriers were developed, the top commanders of many navies resisted their introduction. These officers had generally built their careers on the command of battleships and other surface combatants and feared that a shift in naval missions and tactics would diminish their influence and empower a rival faction of officers, which, indeed, eventually took place.[2] The commitment of a bureaucracy's leaders to the mission that bolsters their own power within the organization is a major reason that bureaucracies often seem reluctant to change their practices and priorities in response to shifts in the external environment. Over time, this mission and associated practices can become so deeply ingrained in the minds of agency executives and staffers that adherence to them becomes a matter of habit and reflex. Students of bureaucracy refer to this set of established practices and beliefs about the organization's role and purpose as the agency's institutional "culture."[3]

The political scientist James Q. Wilson observed, "Every organization has a culture . . . a persistent, patterned way of thinking about the central tasks of and human relationships within an organization. Culture is to an organization what personality is to an individual . . . it is passed from one generation to the next. It changes slowly, if at all."[4] All agencies, civilian as well as military, are almost certain to resist efforts to compel them to undertake activities that are foreign to their institutional cultures and, thus, seem to pose a threat to their institutional autonomy or internal balance of power.

We can shed some systematic light on public attitudes toward government bureaucracy by examining one of the standard questions posed in election years by the American National Election Studies (ANES). As part of its survey of the American public, the ANES asks a range of questions, among which is "Do you think that people in the government waste a lot of money we pay in taxes, waste some of it, or don't waste very much of it?" Although not perfect for eliciting from the public a nuanced assessment of bureaucratic performance, the question allows respondents to register a blunt evaluation. Results from the past several decades are given in Figure 7.1.

We examine the federal bureaucracy in this chapter both as an organizational setting within which policies are interpreted and implemented and as a venue in which politicians (called bureaucrats or bureaucratic agents) pursue their own and public interests. We first seek to define and describe bureaucracy as a social and political phenomenon. Second, we look in detail at American bureaucracy in action by examining the government's major administrative agencies, their role in the governmental process, and their political behavior.

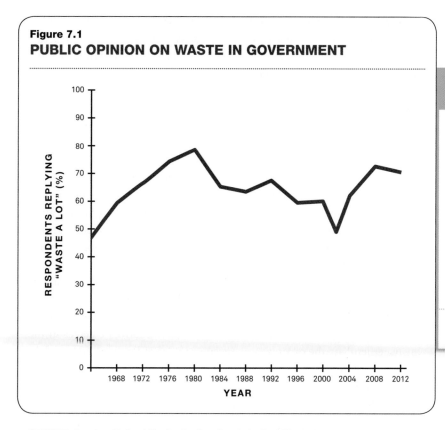

Figure 7.1

PUBLIC OPINION ON WASTE IN GOVERNMENT

SOURCES: American National Election Studies, Cumulative Data File, 1958–2008, www
.electionstudies.org/nesguide/toptable/tab5a_3.htm (accessed 12/7/11), and www.electionstudies
.org/studypages/anes_timeseries_2012/anes2012TS_codebook.pdf (accessed 6/11/13).

ANALYZING THE EVIDENCE

Survey respondents were asked the following question: "Do you think that people in the government waste a lot of the money we pay in taxes, waste some of it, or don't waste very much of it?" What do you think? Is the public justified in its belief that the government wastes a lot of money?

HOW DOES BUREAUCRACY WORK?

Despite the tendency to criticize bureaucracy, most Americans recognize that maintaining order in a large society is impossible without some sort of large governmental apparatus staffed by professionals with some expertise in public administration. When we approve of what a government agency is doing, we give the phenomenon a positive name, administration; when we disapprove, we call the phenomenon bureaucracy.

Although the terms *administration* and *bureaucracy* are often used interchangeably, it is useful to distinguish between the two. Administration is the more general of the two terms; it refers to all the ways human beings might

bureaucracy

The complex structure of offices, tasks, rules, and principles of organization that are employed by all large-scale institutions to coordinate the work of their personnel

rationally coordinate their efforts to achieve a common goal. This applies to private as well as public organizations. Bureaucracy refers to the actual offices, tasks, and principles of organization that are employed by large institutions to coordinate their work.

Bureaucratic Organization Enhances Efficiency

The core of bureaucracy is the division of labor. The key to bureaucratic effectiveness is the coordination of experts performing complex tasks. If each job is specialized in order to gain efficiencies, then each worker must depend on the output of other workers and that requires careful allocation of jobs and resources. Inevitably, bureaucracies become hierarchical, often approximating a pyramid in form. At the base of the organization are workers with the fewest skills and specializations; one supervisor can deal with a relatively large number of these workers. At the next level of the organization, where workers are more highly specialized, the supervision and coordination of work involve fewer workers per supervisor. Toward the top of the organization, a very small number of high-level executives engages in the "management" of the organization, meaning the coordination and oversight of all the tasks and functions, plus the allocation of the appropriate supplies, and the distribution of the outputs of the organization to the market (if it is a "private sector" organization) or to the public.

Bureaucracies Allow Governments to Operate

Bureaucracy, when used pejoratively, conjures up images of endless paperwork, red tape, and lazy, uncaring employees. In fact, the term refers to a rather spectacular human achievement. By dividing up tasks, matching tasks to a labor force that develops appropriately specialized skills, routinizing procedures, and providing the incentive structure and oversight arrangements to get large numbers of people to operate in a coordinated, purposeful fashion, bureaucracies accomplish tasks and missions in a manner that would otherwise be unimaginable. The provision of "government goods" as broad as the defense of people, property, and national borders or as narrow as a subsidy to a wheat farmer, beef rancher, or manufacturer of specialty steel requires organization, routines, standards, and, at the end of the day, the authority for someone to cut a check and put it in the mail. Bureaucracies are created to do these things.

Bureaucracy also consolidates a range of complementary programs and insulates them from the predatory ambitions of out-of-sympathy political forces. Nothing in this world is permanent, but bureaucracies come close. By creating clienteles—in the legislature, the world of interest groups, and public opinion—a bureaucracy establishes a coalition of supporters, some of whom will fight to the end to keep it in place. Clienteles, after all, value consistency, predictability, and durability. It is a well-known rule of thumb that everyone in the political world cares deeply and intensely about a subset of policies and the agencies that produce them, and opposes other policies and agencies but not with nearly the same passion. Opponents, to succeed, must clear many hurdles, whereas proponents, to maintain the status quo, must only marshall their forces at a few veto points. In the final analysis, opponents typically meet obstacle after obstacle and eventually give up their uphill battles and concentrate on protecting and expanding that about which they care most deeply. In a complex political system such as that of the United States, it is much easier to do the latter. Politicians acknowledge this fact of life. Consequently, both opponents and proponents of a particular set of government activities wage the fiercest battles at the time programs are enacted and a bureaucracy is created. Once created, these organizations assume a position of relative permanence.

So, in response to the question of how bureaucracy makes government possible, there is an efficiency part to the answer as well as a credibility part. The creation of a bureau is a way to deliver government goods efficiently and a device by which to "tie one's hands," thereby providing a credible commitment to the long-term existence of a policy.

Bureaucrats Fulfill Important Roles

Bureaucracy conveys to most people a picture of hundreds of office workers shuffling millions of pieces of paper. There is a lot of truth in that image, but we have to look more closely at what papers are being shuffled and why.

Bureaucrats Implement Laws. Bureaucrats, whether in public or in private organizations, communicate with each other in order to coordinate all the specializations within their organization. This coordination is necessary to carry out the primary task of bureaucracy, which is implementation, that is, implementing the objectives of the organization as laid down by its board of directors (if a private company) or by law (if a public agency). In government, the "bosses" are ultimately the legislature and the elected chief executive.

implementation
The efforts of departments and agencies to translate laws into specific bureaucratic routines

Bureaucrats Make and Enforce Rules. When the bosses— Congress, in particular, when it is making the law—are clear in their instructions to bureaucrats, implementation is a fairly straightforward process. Bureaucrats translate the law into specific routines for each of the employees of an agency. But what happens to routine administrative implementation when several bosses disagree as to what the instructions ought

The rules made by bureaucracies have the force of law. Bureaucracies may charge a person or business with violating the law, such as when peanut processing companies were found to have engaged in practices that caused a salmonella outbreak in 2007.

to be? This requires a fourth job for bureaucrats: interpretation. Interpretation is a form of implementation, in that the bureaucrats still have to carry out what they believe to be the intentions of their superiors. But when bureaucrats have to interpret a law before implementing it, they are in effect engaging in lawmaking.[5] Congress often deliberately delegates to an administrative agency the responsibility of lawmaking. Members of Congress often conclude that some area of industry needs regulating or some area of the environment needs protection, but they are unwilling or unable to specify just how that should be done. In such situations, Congress delegates to the appropriate agency a broad authority within which the bureaucrats have to make law, through the procedures of rule making and administrative adjudication.

Rule making is essentially the same as legislation; in fact it is often referred to as quasi-legislation. The rules issued by government agencies provide more detailed and specific indications of what the policy actually will mean. For example, the Forest Service is charged with making policies that govern the use of national forests. Just before President Clinton left office, the agency issued rules that banned new road building and development in the forests. This was a goal long sought by environmentalists and conservationists. In 2005, the Forest Service relaxed the rules, allowing states to make proposals for building new roads within the national forests. Just as the timber industry opposed the Clinton rule banning road building, environmentalists challenged the new ruling and sued the Forest Service in federal court for violating clean-water and endangered-species legislation.

New rules proposed by an agency take effect only after a period of public comment. Reaction from the people or businesses that are subject to the rules may cause an agency to modify the rules they first issue. Public participation takes the form of filing statements and giving testimony in public forums devoted to eliciting public opinion from interested parties. This occurs after a draft rule or regulation is announced but before it becomes official, giving the agency the opportunity to revise its draft. The rule-making process is thus highly political. Once rules are approved, they are published in the *Federal Register* and have the force of law.

Bureaucrats Settle Disputes. Administrative adjudication is very similar to what the judiciary ordinarily does: applying rules and precedents to specific cases in order to settle disputes. In administrative adjudication, the agency charges the person or business suspected of violating the law. The ruling in an adjudication dispute applies only to the specific case being considered. Many regulatory agencies use administrative adjudication to make decisions about specific products or practices. The adjudicative role of the Federal Communications Commission (FCC) in license renewal challenges is one example. In seeking a renewal, a television or radio station may be challenged in its claims to have met all requirements (mainly technical requirements but also those regarding the adequacy of local public service programming). The FCC determines whether the renewing station or the challenger has made the stronger case.

In sum, government bureaucrats do essentially the same things that bureaucrats in large private organizations do. But because of the authoritative, coercive nature of government, far more constraints are imposed on public bureaucrats than on private bureaucrats, even when their jobs are the same. Public bureaucrats are required to maintain a far more thorough paper trail. Public bureaucrats are also subject to a great deal more access from the public. Newspaper reporters, for example, have access to public bureaucrats. Public access has been vastly facilitated in the past half-century; the adoption of the Freedom of Information Act (FOIA) in 1966 gave ordinary citizens the right of access to agency files and agency data to determine whether derogatory information exists in the file about citizens themselves and to learn about what the agency is doing in general.

Bureaucracies Serve Politicians

In principle, the legislature could make all bureaucratic decisions itself, writing very detailed legislation each year, dotting every *i* and crossing every *t*. In some jurisdictions—tax policy, for example—this is in fact done. Tax policy is promulgated in significant detail by the House Ways and Means Committee, the Senate Finance Committee, and the Joint Committee on Taxation. The Internal Revenue Service, the administrative agency charged with implementation, engages in relatively less discretionary activity than many other regulatory and administrative agencies. But this is the exception.

The norm is for statutory authority to be delegated to the bureaucracy, sometimes with specificity but often in relatively vague terms. The bureaucracy is expected to fill in the gaps. This, however, is not a blank check to exercise unconstrained discretion. The bureaucracy will be held to account by the legislature's oversight of bureaucratic performance. The latter is monitored by the staffs of relevant legislative committees, which also serve as repositories for complaints from affected parties.[6] Poor performance or the exercise of discretion inconsistent with the preferences of the important legislators invites sanctions ranging from the browbeating of senior bureaucrats to the trimming of budgets and the clipping of authority.

HOW IS THE EXECUTIVE BRANCH ORGANIZED?

Cabinet departments, agencies, and bureaus are the operating parts of the bureaucratic whole. These parts can be separated into four general types: (1) cabinet departments, (2) independent agencies, (3) government corporations, and (4) independent regulatory commissions.

Although Figure 7.2 is an "organizational chart" of the Department of Agriculture, any other department could have been used as an illustration. At the top is the head of the department, who in the United States is called the "secretary" of the department. Below the department head are several top administrators, such as the general counsel and the chief economist, whose responsibilities cut across the various departmental functions and enable the secretary to manage the entire organization. Of equal status are the assistant and undersecretaries, each of whom has management responsibilities for a group of operating agencies, which are arranged vertically below each of the undersecretaries.

The next tier, generally called the bureau level, is the highest level of responsibility for specialized programs. The names of these bureau-level agencies are often very well known to the public: the Forest Service and the Food Safety and Inspection Service are two examples. Sometimes they are officially called bureaus, as in the Federal Bureau of Investigation (FBI), which is a bureau in the Department of Justice. Nevertheless, *bureau* is also the generic term for this level of administrative agency. Within the bureaus, there are divisions, offices, services, and units—sometimes designating agencies of the same status, sometimes designating agencies of lesser status.

Not all government agencies are part of cabinet departments. Some independent agencies are set up by Congress outside the departmental structure altogether, even though the president appoints and directs the heads of these agencies. Independent agencies usually have broad powers to provide public services that are either too expensive or too important to be left to private initiatives. Some examples of independent agencies are the National Aeronautics and Space Administration (NASA), the Central Intelligence Agency (CIA), and the Environmental Protection Agency (EPA). Government corporations are a third type of government agency, but are more like private businesses performing and charging for a market service, such as transporting railroad passengers (Amtrak).

A fourth type of agency is the independent regulatory commission, given broad discretion to make rules. The first regulatory agencies established by Congress, beginning with the Interstate Commerce Commission in 1887, were set up as independent regulatory commissions because Con-

Figure 7.2

ORGANIZATIONAL CHART OF THE DEPARTMENT OF AGRICULTURE

Secretary

Deputy Secretary

- Director of Communications
- Inspector General
- General Counsel
- Assistant Secretary for Congressional Relations
- Assistant Secretary for Administration
- Assistant Secretary for Civil Rights

- Chief Economist
- Director, National Appeals Division
- Chief Information Officer
- Chief Financial Officer
- Executive Operations

Under Secretary for Natural Resources and Environment
- Forest Service
- Natural Resources Conservation Service

Under Secretary for Farm and Foreign Agricultural Services
- Farm Service Agency
- Foreign Agricultural Service
- Risk Management Agency

Under Secretary for Rural Development
- Rural Utilities Service
- Rural Housing Service
- Rural Business Cooperative Service

Under Secretary for Food, Nutrition, and Consumer Services
- Food and Nutrition Service
- Center for Nutrition Policy and Promotion

Under Secretary for Food Safety
- Food Safety and Inspection Service

Under Secretary for Research, Education, and Economics
- Agricultural Research Service
- National Institute of Food and Agriculture
- Economic Research Service
- National Agricultural Library
- National Agricultural Statistics Service

Under Secretary for Marketing and Regulatory Programs
- Agricultural Marketing Service
- Animal and Plant Health Inspection Service
- Grain Inspection Packers and Stockyards Administration

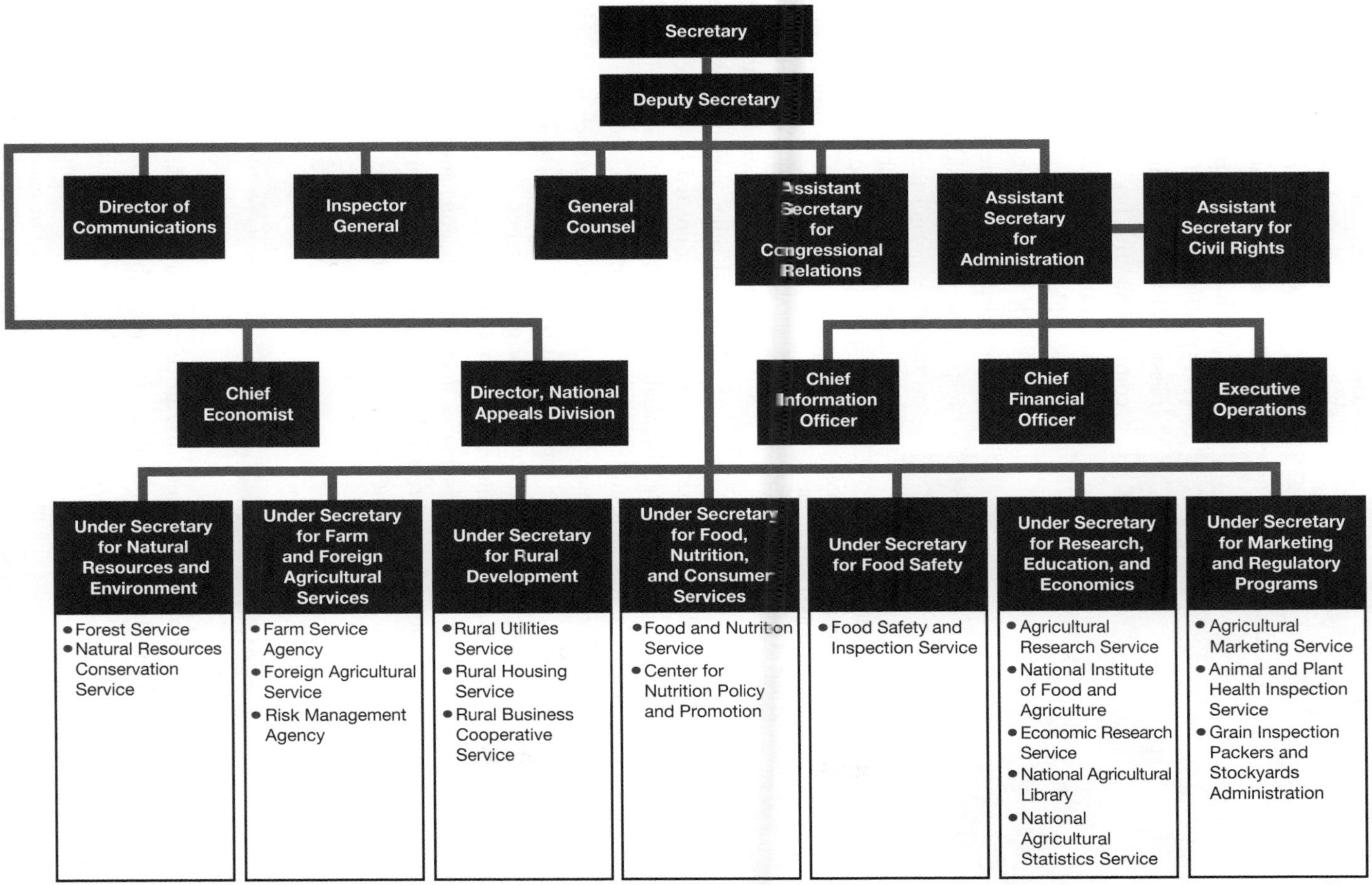

SOURCE: U.S. Department of Agriculture, www.usda.gov/documents/AgencyWorkflow.pdf.

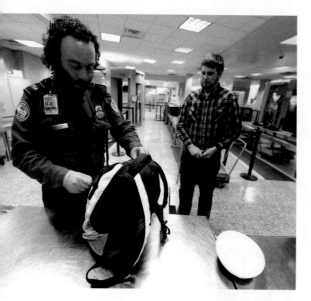

The Transportation Security Administration (TSA) oversees travel safety, including airport security. Created in 2001, the TSA was originally part of the Department of Transportation but became part of the Department of Homeland Security in 2003.

gress recognized that regulatory agencies are "mini-legislatures," whose rules are the same as legislation but require the kind of expertise and full-time attention that is beyond the capacity of Congress. Until the 1960s, most of the regulatory agencies that were set up by Congress, such as the Federal Trade Commission (1914) and the Federal Communications Commission (1934), were independent regulatory commissions. But beginning in the late 1960s and the early 1970s, all new regulatory programs, with two or three exceptions (such as the Federal Election Commission), were placed within existing departments and made directly responsible to the president. Since the 1970s, no major new regulatory programs had been established, independent or otherwise, until the financial crisis of 2008–09. The Dodd-Frank Wall Street Reform and Consumer Protection Act, signed into law by President Obama in 2010, brought major changes to the regulation of banks and other financial institutions. To accomplish a very complex mission, the act created several new regulatory bodies, including the Financial Stability Oversight Council, the Office of Financial Research, and the Bureau of Consumer Financial Protection.

There are too many agencies in the executive branch to identify them all here, so a simple classification of agencies will be helpful. Instead of dividing the bureaucracy into four general types, as we did previously, this classification is organized by the mission of each agency, as defined by its jurisdiction: clientele agencies, agencies for maintenance of the Union, regulatory agencies, and redistributive agencies. We examine each of these types of agencies, focusing on both their formal structure and their place in the political process.

Clientele Agencies

clientele agency
A department or bureau of government whose mission is to promote, serve, or represent a particular interest

The entire Department of Agriculture is an example of a clientele agency. So are the departments of the Interior, Labor, and Commerce. Although all administrative agencies have clienteles, certain agencies are singled out and called by that name because they are specifically directed by law to foster and promote the interests of their clientele. For example, the Department of Commerce and Labor was founded in 1903 as a single department "to foster, promote, and develop the foreign and domestic commerce, the mining, the manufacturing, the shipping, and fishing industries, and the transportation facilities of the United States."[7] It remained a single department until 1913, when the law created the two separate departments of Commerce and Labor, with each statute providing for the same obligation: to support and foster their respective clienteles.[8] The Department of Agriculture serves the many farming interests that, taken together, are one of the United States' largest economic sectors.

Most clientele agencies locate a relatively large proportion of their total personnel in field offices dealing directly with the clientele. The Extension

Service of the Department of Agriculture is among the most familiar, with its numerous local "extension agents" who consult with farmers on farm productivity. These same agencies also seek to foster the interests of their clientele by providing "functional representation"; that is, they try to learn what their clients' interests and needs are and then operate almost as a lobby in Washington on their behalf. In addition to the Department of Agriculture, other clientele agencies include the Department of Interior and five of the newest cabinet departments: Housing and Urban Development (HUD), created in 1966; Transportation (DOT), created in 1966; Energy (DOE), created in 1977; and Education (ED) and Health and Human Services (HHS), both created in 1979.[9]

Agencies for Maintenance of the Union

The Constitution entrusts many of the vital functions of public order, such as the police, to the state governments. But some agencies vital to maintaining national bonds do exist in the national government, and they can be grouped into three categories: (1) agencies for control of the sources of government revenue, (2) agencies for control of conduct defined as a threat to internal national security, and (3) agencies for defending American security from external threats. The most powerful departments in these three areas are Treasury, Justice, Defense, State, and Homeland Security.

Revenue Agencies. The Treasury Department's Internal Revenue Service (IRS) is the most important revenue agency. The IRS is also one of the federal government's largest bureaucracies. Over 100,000 employees are spread through 4 regions, 63 districts, 10 service centers, and hundreds of local offices.

Agencies for Internal Security. As long as the country is not in a state of insurrection, most of the task of maintaining the Union takes the form of legal work, and the main responsibility for that lies with the Department of Justice (DOJ). It is indeed a luxury, and rare in the world, when national unity can be maintained by routines of civil law rather than imposed by an army with guns. The largest and most important agency in the DOJ is the Criminal Division, which is responsible for enforcing all the federal criminal laws except a few specifically assigned to other divisions. Criminal litigation is actually done by the U.S. attorneys. A presidentially appointed U.S. attorney is assigned to each federal judicial district, and he supervises the work of assistant U.S. attorneys. The work or jurisdiction of the Antitrust and Civil Rights Divisions is described by their official names. Although it looms so very large in American folklore, the FBI is simply another bureau of the

DOJ. The FBI handles no litigation but instead is the information-gathering agency for all the other divisions.

In 2002, Congress created the Department of Homeland Security (DHS) to coordinate the nation's defense against the threat of terrorism. The new department is responsible for a number of tasks, including protecting commercial airlines from would-be hijackers. Most visible to the traveling public are the employees of the Transportation Security Administration (TSA). Consisting of 50,000 security officers and employees protecting airports and rail and bus depots, and staffing security screening operations, the TSA is the largest unit of the DHS.

Agencies for External National Security. Two departments occupy center stage here, State and Defense. A few key agencies outside State and Defense also have external national-security functions.

Although diplomacy is generally considered the primary task of the State Department, diplomatic missions make up only one of its organizational dimensions. The State Department is also composed of geographic, or regional, bureaus concerned with all problems within that region of the world; "functional" bureaus, which handle such things as economic and business affairs, intelligence, and research; and international organizations and bureaus of internal affairs, which handle such areas as security, finance and management, and legal issues.

Despite the importance of the State Department in foreign affairs, fewer than 20 percent of all U.S. government employees working abroad are directly under its authority. By far the largest number of career government professionals working abroad are under the authority of the Department of Defense (DOD).

The creation of the DOD by legislation enacted between 1947 and 1949 was an effort to unify the two historic military departments, the War Department and the Navy Department, and integrate into them a new department, the Air Force Department. Real unification did not occur, however. Instead, the DOD added more pluralism to national security.

America's primary political problem with its military has been relatively mundane compared to the experience of many other countries, which have struggled to keep their militaries out of the politics of governing. Rather, the American military problem is that of pork-barrel politics: defense contracts are often incredibly lucrative for local districts, so military spending becomes a matter of parochial interests as well as military need. For instance, President Clinton's long list of proposed military-base closings, a major part of his budget-cutting drive for 1993, caused a firestorm of opposition even in his own party, with some of the opposition coming from members of Congress who otherwise prominently favored significant reductions in the Pentagon budget. Emphasis on jobs rather than strategy and policy means pork-barrel use of the military for political purposes. This is a classic way for a bureaucracy to defend itself politically in a democracy. It is an example of the distributive tendency, in which the bureaucracy ensures political support among elected officials by making sure to distribute things—military bases, contracts, facilities, and jobs—to the states and districts that elected the legislators.

Regulatory Agencies

regulatory agencies

A department, bureau, or independent agency whose primary mission is to eliminate or restrict certain behaviors defined as negative in themselves or negative in their consequences

The United States has many regulatory agencies. Some of these are bureaus within departments, such as the Food and Drug Administration (FDA) in the Department of Health and Human Services, the Occupational Safety and Health Administration (OSHA) in the Department of Labor, and the Animal and Plant Health and Inspection Service (APHIS) in the Department of Agriculture. Other regulatory agencies are independent regulatory commissions. An example is the Federal Trade Commission (FTC). But whether departmental or independent, an agency or commission is regulatory if Congress delegates to it relatively broad powers over a sector of the economy or a type of commercial activity and authorizes it to make rules governing the conduct of people and businesses within that jurisdiction. Rules made by regulatory agencies have the force and effect of legislation; indeed, the rules they make are referred to as administrative legislation. And when these agencies make decisions or orders settling disputes between parties or between the government and a party, they are really acting like courts.

administrative legislation

Rules made by regulatory agencies and commissions

Agencies of Redistribution

Welfare, fiscal, and monetary agencies are responsible for the transfer of hundreds of billions of dollars annually between the public and the private spheres, and through such transfers these agencies influence how people and corporations spend and invest trillions of dollars annually. We call them agencies of redistribution because they influence the amount of money in the economy and because they directly influence who has money, who has credit, and whether people will want to invest or save their money rather than spend it.

Fiscal and Monetary Policy Agencies. Government activity affecting or relating to money may be partitioned into *fiscal* and *monetary* policy. Fiscal policy includes taxing and spending activities. Monetary policies have to do with banks, credit, and currency. (We will discuss these policies in Chapter 13.)

Administration of fiscal policy is primarily performed in the Treasury Department. It is no contradiction to include the Treasury here as well as with the agencies for maintenance of the Union. This indicates that (1) the Treasury is a complex department performing more than one function of government, and (2) traditional controls have had to be adapted to modern economic conditions and new technologies.

Today, in addition to administering and policing income tax and other tax collections, the Treasury is responsible for managing the enormous federal debt. The Treasury Department is responsible for printing the currency that we use, but currency represents only a tiny proportion of the entire money economy. Most of the trillions of dollars used in the transactions that compose the private and public sectors of the U.S. economy exist on printed accounts and computers, not in currency.

Another important fiscal and monetary policy agency is the Federal Reserve System, headed by the Federal Reserve Board. The Federal Reserve System (the Fed) has authority over the credit rates and lending activities of the nation's most important banks. Established by Congress in 1913, the Fed is responsible for adjusting the supply of money to the needs of banks in the different regions and of the commerce and industry in each. It also ensures that the banks do not overextend themselves by having lending policies that are too liberal, out of fear that if there is a sudden economic scare, a run on a few banks might be contagious and cause another terrible stock market crash like the one in 1929. The Federal Reserve Board sits at the top of the pyramid of 12 district Federal Reserve banks, which are "bankers' banks," serving the monetary needs of the hundreds of member banks in the national bank system (see also Chapter 13).

Federal Reserve System (the Fed)
A system of 12 Federal Reserve banks that facilitates exchanges of cash, checks, and credit; regulates member banks; and uses monetary policies to fight inflation and deflation

Welfare Agencies. No single government agency is responsible for all the programs that make up the "welfare state." The largest agency in this field is the Social Security Administration (SSA), which manages the social insurance aspects of Social Security and Supplementary Security Income (SSI). Other agencies in the Department of Health and Human Services administer Temporary Assistance to Needy Families (TANF) and Medicaid, and the Department of Agriculture is responsible for the food stamp program. With the exception of Social Security, these are means-tested programs, requiring applicants to demonstrate that their total annual cash earnings fall below an officially defined poverty line. These public-assistance programs compose a large administrative burden. In 1996, Congress enacted the Personal Responsibility and Work Opportunity Reconciliation Act (PRA), which abolished virtually all national means-tested public-assistance programs, devolving that power to state governments.

THE PROBLEM OF BUREAUCRATIC CONTROL

Two centuries, millions of employees, and trillions of dollars after the Founding, we must return to James Madison's observation that "you must first enable the government to control the governed; and in the next place oblige it to control itself."[10] Today the problem is the same, but the form has changed. Our problem now is the challenge of keeping the bureaucracy accountable to elected political authorities.

Motivational Considerations of Bureaucrats

The economist William Niskanen proposed that we consider a bureau or department of government as analogous to a division of a private firm and conceive of the bureaucrat just as we would the manager who runs that division.[11] In particular, Niskanen stipulated that a bureau chief or department head can be thought of as trying to maximize her budget (just as the private-sector counterpart tries to maximize his division's profits).

There are quite a number of motivational bases on which bureaucratic budget maximizing might be justified. A cynical (though some would say realistic) basis for budget maximizing is that the bureaucrat's own compensation is often tied to the size of her budget. A second, related motivation for large budgets is nonmaterial personal gratification. An individual understandably enjoys the prestige and respect that comes from running a major enterprise. You can't take these things to the bank or put them on your family's dinner table, but your self-esteem and your status are surely buoyed by the conspicuous fact that your bureau or division has a large budget.

But salary and status are not the only forces driving a bureaucrat toward gaining as large a budget as possible. Some bureaucrats, perhaps most, actually *care* about their mission.[12] They initially choose to go into public safety, or the military, or health care, or social work, or education because they believe in the importance of helping people in their community. As they rise through the ranks of a public bureaucracy and assume management responsibilities, they take this mission orientation with them. Thus they try to secure as large a budget as they can to succeed in achieving the mission to which they have devoted their professional lives.

This does not mean that the legislature, which controls the bureau's budget, has to fork over whatever the bureau requests. In making budget allocations, Congress often evaluates a bureau's performance. Legislative committees hold hearings, request documentation on production, assign investigatory staff to various research tasks, and query bureau personnel.

After the fact, the committees engage in oversight; making sure that what the legislature was told at the time when authorization and appropriations were voted on actually holds in practice. The legislature can be much more proactive than the Niskanen budget-maximizing theory gives it credit for.

Before leaving motivational considerations, we should remark that budget maximizing is not the only objective that bureaucrats pursue. It needs to be emphasized and reemphasized that career civil servants and high-level political appointees are politicians. They spend their professional lives pursuing political goals, bargaining, forming alliances and coalitions, solving cooperation and collective action problems, making policy decisions, operating within and interfacing with political institutions—in short, doing what other politicians do. As politicians who are subject to the oversight and authority of others, bureaucrats must be strategic and forward thinking. Whichever party wins control of the House or the Senate, and the presidency, whoever becomes chair of the legislative committee with authorization or appropriation responsibility over their agency, bureau chiefs will have to adjust to the prevailing political winds. To protect and expand authority and resources, bureaucratic politicians seek, in the form of autonomy and discretion, insurance against political change. They don't always succeed in acquiring this freedom, but they do try to insulate themselves from changes in the broader political world.[13] So bureaucratic motivations include budget-maximizing behavior, to be sure, but bureaucrats also seek the autonomy to weather changes in the political atmosphere and the discretion and flexibility to achieve their goals.

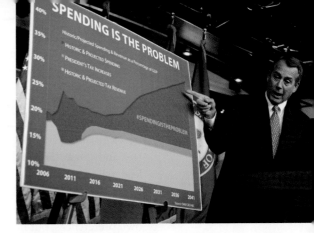

Government agencies depend on Congress to approve their budgets, and bureaucrats work to convince Congress that they are using the funds effectively. When Congress makes cuts to limit spending, some agencies suffer more than others.

The Bureaucracy and the Principal-Agent Problem

How does the principal-agent problem introduced in Chapter 1 apply to the president's and Congress's control of the bureaucracy? Suppose the legislation that created the EPA required that after 10 years new legislation be passed renewing its existence and mandate. The issue facing the House, the Senate, and the president in their consideration of renewal involves how much authority to give this agency and how much money to permit it to spend. Eventually relevant majorities in the House and the Senate and the president agree on a policy reflecting a compromise among their various points of view.

The bureaucrats are not particularly pleased with this compromise because it gives them considerably less authority and funding than they had hoped for. If they flout the wishes of their principals and implement a policy exactly to their liking, they risk the unified wrath of the House, the Senate, and the president. Undoubtedly the politicians would react with new legislation (and they would also presumably find other political appointees and career bureaucrats at the EPA to replace the current bureaucratic leadership). If, however, the EPA implements some policy located between its own preferences and the preferences of its principals, it might be able to get away with it. That is, at the margins, the bureau tilts policy toward its own preferences, but not so far as to stimulate a legislative response.

Thus we have a principal-agent relationship in which a political principal—a collective principal consisting of the president and coalitions in the House and Senate—formulates policy and creates an implementation agent to execute its details. The agent, however, has policy preferences of its own and, unless subjected to further controls, will inevitably implement a policy that drifts toward its ideal.

bureaucratic drift

The oft-observed phenomenon of bureaucratic implementation that produces policy more to the liking of the bureaucracy than faithful to the original intention of the legislation that created it, but without triggering a political reaction from elected officials

A variety of controls might conceivably restrict this bureaucratic drift. Indeed, legislative scholars often point to congressional hearings in which bureaucrats may be publicly rebuked, annual appropriations decisions that may be used to punish out-of-control bureaus, and watchdog agents, such as the Government Accountability Office, that may be used to monitor and scrutinize the bureau's performance. But these all come after the fact and may be only partially credible threats to the agency. The most powerful before-the-fact political weapon is the appointment process. The adroit control of the political stance of a given bureau by the president and Congress, through their joint powers of nomination and confirmation (especially if they can arrange for appointees who closely share the political consensus on policy) is a self-enforcing mechanism for ensuring reliable agent performance. A second powerful before-the-fact weapon is procedural controls. The general rules and regulations that direct the manner in which federal agencies conduct their affairs are contained in the Administrative Procedure Act. This act is almost always the boilerplate of legislation creating and renewing federal agencies. It is not uncommon, however, for an agency's procedures to be tailored to suit particular circumstances.

The President as Manager-in-Chief

In 1937, President Franklin Delano Roosevelt's Committee on Administrative Management gave official sanction to an idea that had been growing increasingly urgent: "The president needs help." The national government had grown rapidly during the preceding 25 years, but the structures and procedures necessary to manage the burgeoning executive branch had not yet been established. The response to the call for help for the president initially took the form of three management policies: (1) all communications and decisions that related to executive policy decisions must pass through the White House; (2) to cope with such a flow, the White House must have an adequate staff of specialists in research, analysis, legislative and legal writing, and public affairs; and (3) the White House must have additional staff to follow through on presidential decisions—to ensure that those decisions are made, communicated to Congress, and carried out by the appropriate agency.

Establishing a management capacity for the presidency began in earnest with Roosevelt, but it did not stop there. The story of the modern presidency can be told largely as a series of responses to the plea for managerial help. Indeed, each expansion of the national government into new policies and programs in the twentieth century was accompanied by a parallel expansion of the president's management authority. This pattern began even before Roosevelt's presidency, with the policy innovations of President Woodrow Wilson between 1913 and 1920. Congress responded to Wilson's policies with the 1921 Budget and Accounting Act, which conferred on the White House agenda-setting power over budgeting. The president, in his annual budget message, transmits comprehensive budgetary recommendations to Congress. Because Congress retains ultimate legislative authority, a president's proposals are sometimes said to be dead on arrival on Capitol Hill. Nevertheless, the power to frame deliberations is potent and constitutes an important management tool. Each successive president has continued this pattern of setting the congressional agenda, creating what we now know as the managerial presidency.

For example, President Clinton inaugurated one of the most systematic efforts to change the way government does business in his National Performance Review. Heavily influenced by the theories of management consultants who prize decentralization, customer responsiveness, and employee initiative, Clinton sought to infuse these new practices into government.[14] George W. Bush was the first president with a graduate degree in business. His management strategy followed a standard business-school dictum: select skilled subordinates and delegate responsibility to them. Bush followed this model closely in his appointment of highly experienced officials to cabinet positions. This was no guarantee of policy success, as doubts emerged about the conduct of the Iraq War, and the administration's mishandling of relief to New Orleans and the Gulf Coast after Hurricane Katrina. Barack Obama's administrative style fell somewhere in between his two predecessors. He selected some highly talented and self-assured manager-politicians, such as Secretary of State Hillary Clinton and her successor, John Kerry. Yet he brought a "Chicago crowd" to the White House, led in his first term by Chief-of-Staff Rahm Emanuel, who choreographed administration policy from the center.

Congress is constitutionally essential to responsible bureaucracy because, in a "government of laws," legislation is the key to government responsibility. When a law is passed and its intent is clear, the president knows what to "faithfully execute," and the agency understands its guidelines. But when Congress enacts vague legislation, everybody, from president to agency to courts to interest groups, gets involved in the interpretation of legislation. In that event, to whom is the agency responsible?

oversight

The effort by Congress, through hearings, investigations, and other techniques, to exercise control over the activities of executive agencies

The answer lies in oversight. The more legislative power Congress delegates to the executive branch, the more power it seeks to regain through committee and subcommittee oversight of executive branch agencies. (See the Analyzing the Evidence unit for a discussion of control of the bureaucracy.) The standing committee system of Congress is well suited for oversight, inasmuch as most congressional committees and subcommittees have jurisdictions roughly parallel to one or more executive departments or agencies. Appropriations committees and authorization committees have oversight powers—and delegate their respective oversight powers to their subcommittees. In addition, there is a committee on government operations both in the House and the Senate, and these committees have oversight powers not limited by departmental jurisdiction. Committees and subcommittees oversee agencies through public hearings. Representatives from each agency, the White House, major interest groups, and other concerned citizens are called as witnesses to present testimony at these hearings.

However, often the most effective and influential lever over bureaucratic accountability is "the power of the purse"—the ability of the House and Senate committees and subcommittees on appropriations to look at agency performance through the microscope of the annual appropriations process. This annual process makes bureaucrats attentive to Congress because they know that Congress has a chance each year to reduce their funding.[15] This may be another explanation for why there may be some downsizing but almost no terminations of federal agencies.

Congressional Oversight: Abdication or Strategic Delegation?

Congress often grants the executive branch bureaucracies discretion in determining certain features of a policy during the implementation phase. Although the complexities of governing a modern industrialized democracy make the granting of discretion necessary, some argue that Congress not only gives unelected bureaucrats too much discretion but also delegates too much policy-making authority to them. By enacting vague statutes that give bureaucrats broad discretion, so the argument goes, members of Congress effectively abdicate their constitutionally designated roles and effectively remove themselves from the policy-making process.

Others claim that even though Congress may possess the tools to engage in effective oversight, it fails to use them, as we do not see Congress actively engaging in much oversight activity.[16] However, Mathew McCubbins and Thomas Schwartz argue that these critics have focused on the wrong type of oversight and have missed a type of oversight that benefits members of Congress in their bids for re-election.[17] McCubbins and Schwartz distinguish between two types of oversight: police patrol and fire alarm. Under the police-patrol variety, Congress systematically initiates investigation into the activity of agencies. Under the fire-alarm variety, members of Congress do not initiate investigations but wait for adversely

Some citizens worry that Congress does not engage in sufficient oversight of bureaucratic agencies until after a problem has emerged. Here, Interior Secretary Ken Salazar testifies before the House Natural Resources Committee in the aftermath of the *Deepwater Horizon* oil spill in 2010.

affected citizens or interest groups to bring bureaucratic perversions of legislative intent to the attention of the relevant congressional committee. To make sure that individuals and groups bring these violations to members' attention—set off the fire alarm, so to speak—Congress passes laws that help individuals and groups make claims against the bureaucracy, granting them legal standing before administrative agencies and federal courts.

McCubbins and Schwartz argue that fire-alarm oversight is more efficient than the police-patrol variety, given the costs and the incentives of elected officials. Why should members spend their scarce resources (mainly time) to initiate investigations without having any evidence that they will reap electoral rewards? Police-patrol oversight can waste taxpayers' dollars too, because many investigations will not turn up any evidence of violations of legislative intent. It is much more cost effective for members to conserve their resources and then claim credit for fixing the problem (and saving the day) after the fire alarms have been sounded.

On the other hand, bureaucratic drift might be contained if Congress spent more of its time clarifying its legislative intent and less of its time on oversight activity. If its original intent in the law were clearer, Congress could then afford to defer to presidential management to maintain bureaucratic responsibility. Bureaucrats are more responsive to clear legislative guidance than to anything else. But when Congress and the president are at odds (or coalitions within Congress are at odds), bureaucrats have an opportunity to evade responsibility by playing one side against the other.

Congressional Design and Control of the Bureaucracy

Contributed by
Sean Gailmard
University of California, Berkeley

Who controls the bureaucracy? Scholars usually argue that political principals try to make bureaucratic agents responsive to their own direction. For example, Congress tries to make agencies choose policies that Congress prefers through oversight and threat of budget reductions. Paradoxically, however, in some cases the best agent for Congress is not one that is controlled by Congress itself but by some other political principal.

When might this be true? On some issues, the president exercises substantially more authority over the direction of public policy than other issues. This is true of foreign policy and defense. The president sets the agenda for U.S. diplomacy, can commit U.S. troops to battle without the prior approval of Congress, and plays an important role in the use of U.S. armed forces as commander in chief.

In order to use this authority effectively, the president needs advice that he trusts. Congress could try to control the bureaucratic agents that advise the president on foreign and defense policy. But if congressional interests conflict with those of the president, such agents might not be effective or trusted advisers to the president. A better alternative for Congress is to let the president control these agents himself. This will build trust and make the agencies' advice more helpful to the president as he exercises his formidable policy authority in foreign affairs and defense. Ultimately, informed use of this policy authority by the president is good for Congress too.[1]

Congress can influence how much control different political principals exert over agencies in its decision about where the agencies are "located" within the executive branch. The location of an agency within the executive branch is determined in the legislation creating that agency.

Organization of the Executive Branch

- President
- Executive office of the president
- Cabinet departments
- Independent agencies

The president's closest advisers (e.g., national security adviser, budget director) are in the executive office of the president (EOP). Senior members serve at the pleasure of the president and help him formulate policy. In cabinet departments (e.g., Department of State, Department of Agriculture), senior staff also serve at the pleasure of the president, and major policy decisions are reviewed by the EOP. Independent agencies (e.g., Securities and Exchange Commission, Federal Communications Commission) are the furthest removed from presidential control. Senior officers cannot be dismissed by the president simply for disagreements over policy, and major policy decisions are not reviewed by the EOP.

If Congress wishes the president to have relatively more control over agencies involved in foreign policy and defense than over agencies involved primarily in domestic affairs, then it should locate those agencies closer to the president within the executive branch. This expectation is borne out.[2]

Percentage of Agencies in Each Sphere of the Executive Branch

For all agencies created in legislation between 1946 and 2000, Congress was twice as likely to locate foreign and defense policy agencies in the EOP than domestic policy agencies. The reverse is true for independent agencies and commissions. Overall, when Congress designs agencies, it appears to consider the effect of bureaucratic structure on the ease of control by the relevant political principals.

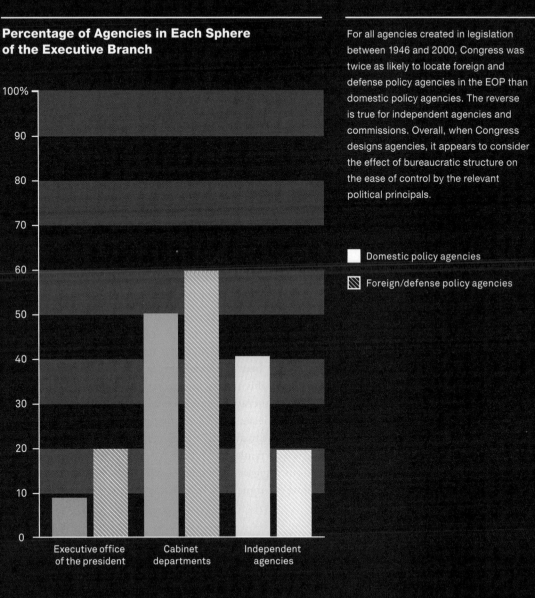

Domestic policy agencies

Foreign/defense policy agencies

1 Sean Gailmard and John W. Patty, *Learning While Governing: Institutions and Accountability in the Executive Branch* (Chicago: University of Chicago Press, 2012).

2 Data are from David E. Lewis, *Presidents and the Politics of Agency Design: Political Insulation in the United States Government Bureaucracy, 1946–1997* (Palo Alto, CA: Stanford University Press, 2003).

REFORMING THE BUREAUCRACY

Americans like to complain about bureaucracy. Americans don't like big government because big government means big bureaucracy, and bureaucracy means the federal service—about 2.8 million civilian and 1.4 million military employees.[18] Promises to cut the bureaucracy are popular campaign appeals; "cutting out the fat" with big reductions in the number of federal employees is held up as a surefire way of cutting the deficit.

Despite fears of excessive bureaucratic growth, however, the federal service has hardly grown at all during the past 35 years; it reached its peak post–World War II level in 1968 with 2.9 million civilian employees plus an additional 3.6 million military personnel (a figure swollen by the Vietnam War). The number of civilian federal executive branch employees has since remained close to that figure. The growth of the federal service is even less imposing when placed in the context of the total workforce and when compared with the size of state and local public employment, which was 14.4 million full- and 4.9 part-time employees in 2012.[19] Figure 7.3 indicates that, since 1950, the ratio of federal service employment to the total workforce has been steady and in fact has declined slightly in the past 25 years. Another useful comparison is to be found in Figure 7.4. Although the dollar increase in federal spending shown by the bars looks very impressive, the horizontal line indicates that even here the national government has simply kept pace with the growth of the economy.

To sum up, the national government is indeed "very large," but the federal service has not been growing any faster than the economy or society. The same is roughly true of the growth pattern of state and local public personnel. Bureaucracy keeps pace with our society, despite our seeming dislike for it, because we can't operate the control towers, the prisons, the Social Security system, and other essential elements without bureaucracy. And we certainly could not have conducted wars in Iraq and Afghanistan without a gigantic military bureaucracy. Nevertheless some Americans continue to argue that bureaucracy is too big and should be reduced.

Termination

The only certain way to reduce the size of the bureaucracy is to eliminate programs. But most agencies have a supportive constituency—people and groups that benefit from the programs—that will fight to reinstate any cuts that are made. Termination is the only way to ensure an agency's reduction, and it is a rare occurrence.

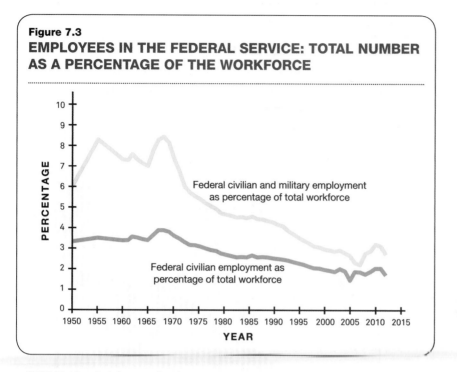

Figure 7.3

EMPLOYEES IN THE FEDERAL SERVICE: TOTAL NUMBER AS A PERCENTAGE OF THE WORKFORCE

Federal civilian and military employment as percentage of total workforce

Federal civilian employment as percentage of total workforce

YEAR

NOTE: Workforce includes unemployed persons.
SOURCES: Tax Foundation, *Facts and Figures on Government Finance* (Baltimore: Johns Hopkins University Press, 1990), pp. 22, 44; Office of Management and Budget, *Budget of the U.S. Government, Fiscal Year 2009*, table 17.5; and U.S. Bureau of Labor Statistics, "Employment Status of the Civilian Population by Sex and Age," *Labor Force Statistics from the Current Population Survey*, http://stats.bls.gov/webapps/legacy/cpsatab1.htm, table A1 (accessed 10/15/13) and authors' update.

The overall lack of success in terminating bureaucracy is a reflection of Americans' love/hate relationship with the national government. As antagonistic as Americans may be toward bureaucracy in general, they grow attached to the services being rendered and protections being offered by particular bureaucratic agencies—that is, they fiercely defend their favorite agencies while perceiving no inconsistency between that defense and their antagonistic attitude toward the bureaucracy in general. A good case in point was the agonizing problem of closing military bases in the wake of the end of the Cold War, when the United States no longer needed so many bases. Since every base is in some congressional member's district, it proved impossible for Congress to decide to close any of them. Consequently, between 1988 and 1990, Congress established a Defense Base Closure and Realignment Commission to decide on base closings, taking the matter out of Congress's hands altogether.[20] And even so, the process has been slow and agonizing.

Elected leaders have come to rely on a more incremental approach to downsizing the bureaucracy. Much has been done by budgetary means,

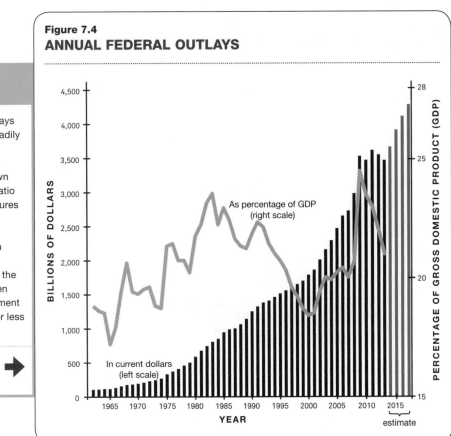

Figure 7.4

ANNUAL FEDERAL OUTLAYS

Annual federal outlays have increased steadily over time. So has the size of the U.S. economy (not shown in figure). But the ratio of federal expenditures to annual GDP has varied over time. What might explain these fluctuations, and what might be the consequences when the federal government contributes more or less to the economy?

As percentage of GDP (right scale)

In current dollars (left scale)

BILLIONS OF DOLLARS

PERCENTAGE OF GROSS DOMESTIC PRODUCT (GDP)

YEAR

estimate

NOTE: Data for 2014–17 are estimated.
SOURCE: Office of Management and Budget, *Budget of the U.S. Government, Fiscal Year 2014*, tables 1.1 and 1.2, and World Bank.

reducing the budgets of all agencies across the board by small percentages and cutting some less-supported agencies by larger amounts. Yet these changes are still incremental, leaving the existence of agencies unaddressed.

An additional approach has been taken to thwart the highly unpopular regulatory agencies, which are so small (relatively) that cutting their budgets contributes virtually nothing to reducing the deficit. This approach is called deregulation, simply defined as a reduction in the number of rules promulgated by regulatory agencies. But deregulation by rule reduction is still incremental and has certainly not satisfied the hunger of the American public in general and Washington representatives in particular for a genuine reduction of bureaucracy.

deregulation

The policy of reducing or eliminating regulatory restraints on the conduct of individuals or private institutions

Devolution

An alternative to genuine reduction of the size of the bureaucracy is devolution—downsizing the federal bureaucracy by delegating the implementation of programs to state and local governments. Indirect evidence for this is seen in Figure 7.5, which shows the increase in state and local government employment against a backdrop of flat or declining federal employment. This evidence suggests a growing share of governmental actions taking place on the state and local levels. Devolution often alters the pattern of who benefits most from government programs. In the early 1990s, a major devolution of transportation policy sought to open up decisions about transportation to a new set of interests. Since

◀ **devolution**

The policy of removing a program from one level of government by delegating it or passing it down to a lower level, such as from the national government to the state and local governments

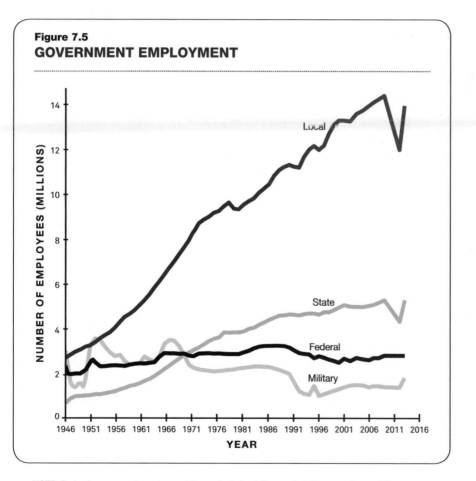

Figure 7.5
GOVERNMENT EMPLOYMENT

NOTE: Federal government employment figures include civilians only. Military employment figures include only active-duty personnel.
SOURCE: U.S. Bureau of the Census, *Statistical Abstract of the United States*, 2011 and 2012 (Washington, DC: Government Printing Office, 2011).

the 1920s, transportation policy had been dominated by road-building interests in the federal and state governments. Many advocates for cities and many environmentalists believed that the emphasis on road building hurt cities and harmed the environment. The 1992 reform, initiated by environmentalists, put more power in the hands of metropolitan planning organizations and lifted many federal restrictions on how the money should be spent. Reformers hoped that these changes would open up the decision-making process so those advocating alternatives to road building, such as mass transit, bike paths, and walking, would have more influence over how federal transportation dollars were spent. Although the pace of change has been slow, devolution has indeed brought new voices into decisions about transportation spending, and alternatives to highways have received increasing attention.

Often the central aim of devolution is to provide more efficient and flexible government services. Yet, by its very nature, devolution entails variation across the states. In some states, government services may improve as a consequence of devolution. In other states, services may deteriorate as the states use devolution as an opportunity to cut spending and reduce services. This has been the pattern in the implementation of the welfare reform passed in 1996, the most significant devolution of federal government social programs in many decades. Some states, such as Wisconsin, have used the flexibility of the reform to design innovative programs that respond to clients' needs; other states, such as Idaho, have virtually dismantled their welfare programs. Because the legislation placed a five-year lifetime limit on receiving welfare, the states will take on an even greater role in the future as existing clients lose their eligibility for federal benefits. Many have praised welfare reform for reducing welfare rolls and responding to the public desire that welfare be a temporary program. At the same time, it has placed more low-income women and their children at risk for being left with no form of assistance at all, depending on the state in which they live.

This variation is the dilemma that devolution poses. Up to a point, variation can be considered a virtue of federalism. But there are dangers inherent in large variations in the provisions of services and benefits in a democracy (see Chapter 3).

Privatization

Privatization, another downsizing option, may seem like a synonym for termination, but that is true only at the extreme. Most of what is called "privatization" is not termination at all but the provision of government goods and services by private contractors under direct government supervision. Except for top-secret strategic materials, virtually all of the production of military hardware, from boats to bullets, is done on a privatized basis by private contractors. Billions of dollars of research services are bought under contract by government; these private contractors are universities as well as ordinary industrial corporations and private "think tanks." Privatization simply means that a formerly public activity is picked up under contract by a private company or companies. But such programs are still very much government programs; they are paid for and supervised by government. Privatization downsizes the government only in that the workers providing the service are no longer counted as part of the government bureaucracy.

Privatization can reduce the costs of certain government activities, but it can also create issues of accountability and transparency. In recent years, the practice has become particularly controversial with regard to security contracting in Iraq and Afghanistan.

The central aim of privatization is to reduce the cost of government. When private contractors can perform a task as well as government but for less money, taxpayers win. Often the losers in such situations are the workers. Government workers are generally unionized and, therefore, receive good pay and benefits. Private-sector workers are less likely to be unionized, and private firms often provide lower pay and fewer benefits. For this reason, public-sector unions have been one of the strongest voices arguing against privatization. Other critics of privatization observe that private firms may not be more efficient or less costly than government. This is especially likely when there is little competition among private firms and when public bureaucracies are not granted a fair chance to bid in the contracting competition. When private firms have a monopoly on service provision, they may be less efficient than government and more expensive. This problem raises important questions about how private contractors can be held accountable. As one analyst of Pentagon spending put it, "The Pentagon is supposed to be representing the taxpayer and the public interest—its national security. So it's really important to have transparency, to be able to see these competitions and hold people accountable."[21] As security has become the nation's paramount concern, new worries about privatization have surfaced. Some Pentagon officials fear that too many tasks vital to national security may have already been contracted out and that national security might best be served by limiting privatization.

The new demands of domestic security have altered the thrust of bureaucratic reform. Despite the strong agreement on the goal of fighting terrorism, the effort to streamline the bureaucracy around a single purpose is likely

privatization
The act of moving all or part of a program from the public sector to the private sector

to face considerable obstacles along the way. Reform of public bureaucracies is always complex because strong constituencies may attempt to block changes that they believe will harm them. Initiatives that aim to improve coordination among agencies can easily provoke political disputes if the proposed changes threaten to alter the access of groups to the bureaucracy. And groups that oppose bureaucratic changes can appeal to Congress to intervene on their behalf.

DOES BUREAUCRACY WORK?

Bureaucracy is one of humanity's most significant inventions. It is an institutional arrangement that allows for division and specialization of labor, harnesses expertise, and coordinates collective action for social, political, and economic purposes. It enables governments to exist and perform. In this chapter, we focused on what public bureaucracies do, how they are organized at the national level in the United States, and how they are controlled (or not) by elected politicians.

At a theoretical level, public bureaucracy is the concrete expression of rational, purposeful, political action. Elected politicians have goals—as broad as defending the realm, maintaining public health and safety, or promoting economic growth; as narrow as securing a post office for Possum Hollow, Pennsylvania, or an exit off the interstate highway for Springfield, Massachusetts. Bureaucracy is the instrument by which political objectives, established by elected legislators and executives, are transformed from ideas, concepts, and intentions into the actual "bricks and mortar" of implemented policies.

At a practical level, this transformation depends upon the motivations of bureaucratic agents and the institutional machinery created when a bureaucratic entity is formed or reformed. Bureaucrats, as we saw above, have their own goals and motives. Elected politicians engage in institutional design in creating agencies. They have their greatest impact at this point. Once an agency is up and running, elected officials only imperfectly control their bureaucratic agents. Institutional arrangements, and simple human nature, provide a certain amount of insulation to agencies, enabling bureaucrats to march to their own drummers, at least some of the time. Of course, bureaucrats are not entirely free agents. But control is a constant and recurring problem for elected officials.

We cannot live without bureaucracy—it is the most efficient way to organize people to get a large collective job done. But we can't live comfortably with bureaucracy either. Bureaucracy requires hierarchy, appointed authority, and professional expertise. Those requirements make bureaucracy the natural enemy of representation, which requires discussion and reciprocity among equals. Yet the task is not to retreat from bureaucracy but to take advantage of its strengths while trying to make it more accountable to the demands that democratic policies and representative government make upon it.

Indeed, as the president and Congress seek to translate the ideal of democratic accountability into practice, they struggle to find the proper balance between administrative discretion and the public's right to know. An administration whose every move is subject to intense public scrutiny may be hamstrung in its efforts to carry out the public interest. On the other hand, a bureaucracy that is shielded from the public eye may wind up pursuing its own interests rather than those of the public. The last century has seen a double movement

Americans' feelings toward bureaucracy are complicated and often vacillate from issue to issue. Some may feel that the government is a poor manager of certain programs, while insisting that it continue to oversee others, such as Social Security.

toward strengthening the managerial capacity of the presidency and making bureaucratic decision making more transparent. The purpose of these reforms has been to create an effective, responsive bureaucracy. But reforms alone cannot guarantee democratic accountability. Presidential and congressional vigilance in the defense of the public interest is essential.

Another approach to bureaucratic accountability is for Congress to spend more of its time clarifying its legislative intent and less of its time on committee or individual oversight. If the intent of the law were clear, Congress could then count on the president to maintain a higher level of bureaucratic responsibility, because bureaucrats are more responsive to clear legislative guidance than to anything else. Nevertheless, this is not a neat and sure solution, because Congress and the president can still be at odds, and when they are at odds, bureaucrats have an opportunity to evade responsibility by playing one branch off against the other.

As to the vast apparatus, bureaucracy is here to stay. The administration of myriad government functions and responsibilities in a large, complex society will always require "rule by desks and offices" (the literal meaning of *bureaucracy*). No "reinvention" of government, however well conceived or executed, can alter that basic fact, nor can it resolve the problem of reconciling bureaucracy in a democracy. President Clinton's National Performance Review accomplished some impressive things: the national bureaucracy has become somewhat smaller, and in the next few years, it will become smaller still; government procedures are being streamlined and are under tremendous pressure to become even more

How the Three Branches Regulate Bureaucracy

The president may	• Appoint and remove agency heads • Reorganize the bureaucracy (with congressional approval) • Make changes in agencies' budget proposals • Initiate or adjust policies that would alter the bureaucracy's activities
Congress may	• Pass legislation that alters the bureaucracy's activities • Abolish existing programs • Investigate bureaucratic activities and force bureaucrats to testify about them • Influence presidential appointments of agency heads and other officials
The judiciary may	• Rule on whether bureaucrats have acted within the law and require policy changes to comply with the law • Force the bureaucracy to respect the rights of individuals through hearings and other proceedings • Rule on the constitutionality of all rules and regulations

efficient. But these efforts are no guarantee that the bureaucracy itself will become more malleable. Congress will not suddenly change its practice of loose and vague legislative draftsmanship. Presidents will not suddenly discover new reserves of power or vision to draw more tightly the reins of responsible management. No deep solution can be found in quick fixes. As with all complex social and political problems, the solution lies mainly in a sober awareness of the nature of the problem. This awareness enables people to avoid fantasies and myths about the abilities of a democratized presidency—or the potential of a reform effort, or the powers of technology, or the populist rhetoric of a new Congress—to change the nature of governance by bureaucracy.

For Further Reading

Selections highlighted in red are included in *Readings in American Politics: Analysis and Perspectives,* Third Edition.

Aberbach, Joel, and Bert A. Rockman. *In the Web of Politics: Three Decades of the U.S. Federal Executive.* Washington, DC: Brookings Institution, 2000.

Downs, Anthony. *Inside Bureaucracy.* Boston: Little, Brown, 1966.

Gailmard, Sean, and John W. Patty. *Learning While Governing: Expertise and Accountability in the Executive Branch.* Chicago: University of Chicago Press, 2013.

Goodsell, Charles. *The Case for Bureaucracy.* 4th ed. Washington, DC: CQ Press, 2003.

Heclo, Hugh. *On Thinking Institutionally.* Boulder, CO: Paradigm, 2007.

Kerwin, Cornelius M., and Scott R. Furlong. *Rulemaking.* 4th ed. Washington, DC: CQ Press, 2010.

Kettl, Donald F. *The Politics of the Administrative Process.* 5th ed. Washington, DC: Brookings Institution, 2011.

Light, Paul C. *The True Size of Government.* Washington, DC: Brookings Institution, 1999.

McCubbins, Mathew, and Thomas Schwartz. "Congressional Oversight Overlooked: Police Patrols versus Fire Alarms." *American Journal of Political Science* 28 (1984): 165–79.

Meier, Kenneth J., and John Bohte. *Politics and the Bureaucracy.* 5th ed. Belmont, CA: Wadsworth, 2007.

Seidman, Harold. *Politics, Position, and Power: The Dynamics of Federal Organization.* 5th ed. New York: Oxford University Press, 1997.

Wilson, James Q. *Bureaucracy: What Government Agencies Do and Why They Do It.* New York: Basic Books, 1989.

8

The Federal Courts

Courts serve an essential and ancient function. When disputes arise, those involved need an impartial arbiter to help settle the matter. When laws must be enforced, justice requires an impartial judge to determine guilt and innocence and, if the accused is found guilty, the appropriate punishment. And when questions arise about the meaning of the laws, we rely on the wisdom of judges to divine what Congress meant and how that applies in a given circumstance. It is not possible, or even wise, to pass a law to cover every contingency. Nearly every nation today has established a system of courts—the judiciary—to satisfy the need for an arbiter and interpreter.

Perhaps the most significant and distinctive feature of the American judiciary is its independence. The Constitution of the United States, as it was written and as it has evolved over time, sets up the courts as a separate entity from the legislature, the executive, and the states, and insulated from electoral politics. As we see in this chapter, four important institutional features of the American judiciary ensure a powerful, independent legal system. First, the Constitution establishes the federal courts as a separate branch of government from Congress and the president. Second, authority among the courts is hierarchical, with federal courts able to overturn state courts and the U.S. Supreme Court as the ultimate authority. Third, the Supreme Court and other federal courts of appeals can strike down actions of Congress, the president, or states if the judges deem those acts to be violations of the Constitution. This is the power of judicial review. Fourth, federal judges are appointed for life. Federal judges are not subject to the pressures of running for re-election and need not be highly responsive to changes in public opinion.[1]

The framers of the Constitution looked to the judiciary not only to resolve legal disputes but also to play an important role in the national system of checks and balances, guarding against the improper expansion of both presidential and congressional power. Yet some question whether the judiciary has balanced these two branches equally. Over the decades, the federal courts have certainly acted against congressional power, striking down approximately 184 acts of Congress (see Figure 8.3 on p. 253). When it comes to presidential power, however, the federal courts have not been so vigilant. For example, only 14 of the thousands of executive orders issued by presidents have been rejected by the Supreme Court, most of these only in part.

Indeed, the growth of presidential power has largely been reinforced, not restrained, by the federal courts. At least since the New Deal and World War II, assertions of presidential power in such realms as foreign policy, war and emergency powers, legislative power, and administrative authority have, more often than not, been upheld by the federal bench. Rather than curb presidential power, the federal judiciary has sometimes taken extraordinary presidential claims made for limited and temporary purposes and rationalized them—that is, converted them into routine and permanent instruments of presidential government. One example is Richard Nixon's sweeping

CORE OF THE ANALYSIS

➡ The power of judicial review makes the Supreme Court not just a judicial agency but also a major lawmaking body.

➡ Judicial decisions are highly constrained by the past, in the form of common law and precedents, but every decision also contributes to the evolution of the law.

➡ The courts maintain their independence from the legislature and executive because federal judges are appointed for life and are not elected. Independence allows the courts to act as a check on the democratically chosen branches of government.

claims of executive privilege. In *United States v. Nixon*, the Court rejected the president's refusal to turn over tapes to congressional investigators. For the first time, though, the justices also recognized the validity of the principle of executive privilege and discussed the situations in which such claims might be appropriate.[2] This judicial recognition of the principle encouraged presidents Bill Clinton and George W. Bush to make broad claims of executive privilege during their terms in office.

The support given the executive branch by the federal courts has often been noted by legal scholars and a number of explanations offered. For example, constitutional historian Edward Corwin thought that the courts tended to defer to the president because presidential exercises of power often produced some change in the world that the judiciary felt powerless to negate.[3] Political scientists Terry Moe and William Howell, on the other hand, point to the dependence of the courts on the good will of the executive branch for enforcement of their decisions.[4] Other scholars emphasize the reluctance of the courts to risk their prestige in disputes with popular presidents.[5]

Another factor that has played an important role in linking the courts to the White House is the process of judicial appointment. While many assume this is due to presidents seeking to appoint judges who will support them, the actual significance of the appointment process as it pertains to presidential power is somewhat more subtle. During the nineteenth century, federal judges were typically drawn from—and often had continuing ties to—the nation's electoral and representative systems. Not only were most judicial nominees active in party politics, but before their appointment to the bench, many district and circuit court judges, and even a number of Supreme Court justices, had run for elective office and had served in the state legislatures. Some had served in the U.S. Congress. Chief Justice John Marshall, for example, served in both the Virginia House of Delegates and the U.S. House of Representatives. His successor, Roger Brooke Taney, served in the Maryland legislature.

Today, hardly any federal judges (fewer than 5 percent) have a legislative background. Most are recruited from the legal profession, the judiciary, and the executive branch. These institutions often look to the highest levels of the executive branch, rather than to Congress and the state legislatures, for leadership. These judges may be more inclined to check Congress but less likely to balance the executive.

In this chapter, we first examine the judicial process, including the types of cases that the federal courts consider. We then assess the organization and structure of the federal court system and consider how judicial review makes the Supreme Court a "lawmaking body." Last, we examine various influences on the Supreme Court and analyze the role and power of the federal courts in the American political process, looking in particular at the growth of judicial power in the United States.

THE COURT SYSTEM

Court cases in the United States proceed under three broad categories of law: criminal law, civil law, and public law.

Cases of criminal law are those in which the government charges an individual with violating a statute that has been enacted to protect the public health, safety, morals, or welfare. In criminal cases, the government is always the plaintiff (the party that brings charges) and alleges that a criminal violation has been committed by a named defendant. Most criminal cases arise in state and municipal courts and involve matters ranging from traffic offenses to robbery and murder. Although the bulk of criminal law is still a state matter, a growing body of federal criminal law deals with such matters as tax evasion, mail fraud, and the sale of narcotics. Defendants found guilty of criminal violations may be fined or sent to prison.

Cases of civil law involve disputes among individuals or between individuals and the government where no criminal violation is charged. But unlike in criminal cases, the losers in civil cases cannot be fined or sent to prison, although they may be required to pay monetary damages for their actions. In a civil case, the one who brings a complaint is the plaintiff and the one against whom the complaint is brought is the defendant. The two most common types of civil cases involve contracts and torts. In a typical contract case, an individual or corporation charges that it has suffered because of another's violation of a specific agreement between the two. For example, the Smith Manufacturing Corporation may charge that Jones Distributors failed to honor an agreement to deliver raw materials at a specified time, causing Smith to lose business. Smith asks the court to order Jones to compensate it for the damage allegedly suffered. In a typical tort case, one individual charges that he or she has been injured by another's negligence or malfeasance. Medical malpractice suits are one example of tort cases.

In deciding cases, courts apply statutes (laws) and legal precedents (prior decisions). State and federal statutes, for example, often govern the conditions under which contracts are and are not legally binding. Jones Distributors might argue that it was not obliged to fulfill its contract with the Smith Corporation because actions by Smith, such as the failure to make promised payments, constituted fraud under state law. Attorneys for a physician being sued for malpractice, on the other hand, may search for prior instances in which courts ruled that actions similar to those of their client did not constitute negligence. Such precedents are applied under the doctrine of *stare decisis*, a Latin phrase meaning "let the decision stand."

A case becomes a matter of the third category, public law, when plaintiffs or defendants in a civil or criminal case seek to show that their case

criminal law
The branch of law that deals with disputes or actions involving criminal penalties (as opposed to civil law)

civil law
A system of jurisprudence, including private law and governmental actions, for settling disputes that do not involve criminal penalties

precedents
Prior cases whose principles are used by judges as the bases for their decisions in present cases

public law
Cases involving the action of public agencies or officials

IN BRIEF

Types of Laws and Disputes

Type of Law	Type of Case or Dispute	Form of Case
Criminal law	Cases arising out of actions that violate laws protecting the health, safety, and morals of the community. The government is always the plaintiff.	*U.S. (or state) v. Jones* *Jones v. U.S. (or state)*, if Jones lost and is appealing
Civil law	"Private law," involving disputes between citizens or between government and citizen where no crime is alleged. Two general types are contract and tort. *Contract cases* are disputes that arise over voluntary actions. *Tort cases* are disputes that arise out of obligations inherent in social life. Negligence and slander are examples of torts.	*Smith v. Jones* *New York v. Jones* *U.S. v. Jones* *Jones v. New York*
Public law	All cases where the powers of government or the rights of citizens are involved. The government is the defendant. *Constitutional law* involves judicial review of the basis of a government's action in relation to specific clauses of the Constitution as interpreted in Supreme Court cases. *Administrative law* involves disputes of the statutory authority, jurisdiction, or procedures of administrative agencies.	*Jones v. U.S. (or state)* *In re Jones* *Smith v. Jones*, if a license or statute is at issue in their private dispute

involves the powers of government or rights of citizens as defined under the Constitution or by statute. One major form of public law is constitutional law, under which a court examines the government's actions to see if they conform to the Constitution as it has been interpreted by the judiciary. Thus, what begins as an ordinary criminal case may enter the realm of public law if a defendant claims that the police violated his or her constitutional rights. Another important arena of public law is administrative law, which involves disputes over the jurisdiction, procedures, or authority of administrative agencies. Under this type of law, civil litigation between an individual and the government may become a matter of public law if the individual asserts that the government is violating a statute or abusing its power under the Constitution. For example, landowners have asserted that federal and state restrictions on land use constitute violations of the Fifth Amendment's restrictions on the government's ability to confiscate private property. Recently, the Supreme Court has been very sympathetic to such claims, which effectively transform an ordinary civil dispute into a major issue of public law.

Most of the important Supreme Court cases we examine in this chapter involve judgments concerning the constitutional or statutory basis of the actions of government agencies. It is in this arena of public law that the Supreme Court's decisions can have significant consequences for American politics and society.

Types of Courts

In the United States, systems of courts have been established both by the federal government and by the governments of the individual states. Both systems have several levels, as shown in Figure 8.1. More than 99 percent

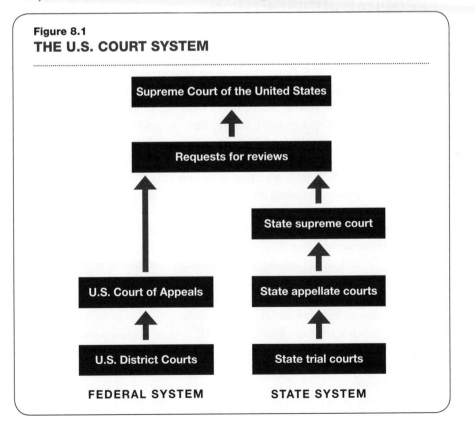

Figure 8.1
THE U.S. COURT SYSTEM

Supreme Court of the United States

Requests for reviews

State supreme court

U.S. Court of Appeals — State appellate courts

U.S. District Courts — State trial courts

FEDERAL SYSTEM   **STATE SYSTEM**

of all court cases in the United States are heard in state courts. The overwhelming majority of criminal cases, for example, involves violations of state laws prohibiting such actions as murder, robbery, fraud, theft, and assault. If such a case is brought to trial, it will be heard in a state trial court, in front of a judge and sometimes a jury, who will determine whether the defendant violated state law. If the defendant is convicted, he may appeal the conviction to a higher court, such as a state court of appeals, and from there to a state's supreme court. Similarly, in civil cases, most litigation is brought in the courts established by the state in which the activity in question took place. For example, a patient bringing suit against a physician for malpractice would file the suit in the appropriate court in the state where the alleged malpractice occurred. The judge hearing the case would apply state law and state precedent to the matter at hand. (It should be noted that in both criminal and civil matters, most cases are settled before trial through negotiated agreements between the parties. In criminal cases, these agreements are called plea bargains.)

trial court

The first court to hear a criminal or civil case

court of appeals (or appellate court)

A court that hears the appeals of trial-court decisions

supreme court

The highest court in a particular state or in the United States. This court primarily serves an appellate function

FEDERAL JURISDICTION

jurisdiction

The domain over which an institution or member of an institution has authority

Cases are heard in the federal courts if they involve federal laws, treaties with other nations, or the U.S. Constitution; these areas are the official jurisdiction of the federal courts. In addition, any case in which the U.S. government is a party is heard in the federal courts. If, for example, an individual is charged with violating a federal criminal statute, such as evading the payment of income taxes, charges would be brought before a federal judge by a federal prosecutor. Civil cases involving the citizens of more than one state and in which more than $75,000 is at stake may be heard in either the federal or the state courts, usually depending on the preference of the plaintiff.

But even if a matter belongs in federal court, how do we know which federal court should exercise jurisdiction over the case? The answer to this seemingly simple question is somewhat complex. The jurisdiction of each federal court is derived from the U.S. Constitution and federal statutes. Article III of the Constitution gives the Supreme Court appellate jurisdiction (the authority to hear appeals) in all federal cases and original jurisdiction (the authority to hear new cases) in cases involving foreign ambassadors and issues in which a state is a party. Article III assigns original jurisdiction in all other federal cases to the lower courts that Congress was authorized to establish. Over the years, as Congress enacted statutes creating the federal judicial system, it specified the jurisdiction of each type of court it established. For the most part, Congress has assigned jurisdictions on the basis of geography. The nation is currently, by statute, divided into 94 judicial districts, including one court for each of three U.S. territories: Guam, the U.S. Virgin Islands, and the Northern Marianas. Each of the 94 U.S. district courts exercises jurisdiction over federal cases arising within its territorial domain. The judicial districts are, in turn, organized into 11 regional circuits and the District of Columbia circuit. Each circuit court exercises appellate jurisdiction over cases heard by the district courts within its region.

Geography is not the only basis for federal court jurisdiction. Congress has also established several specialized courts that have nationwide original jurisdiction in certain types of cases. These include the U.S. Court of International Trade, created to deal with trade and customs issues, and the U.S. Court of Federal Claims, which handles damage suits against the United States. Congress has, in addition, established a court with nationwide appellate jurisdiction. This is the U.S. Court of Appeals for the Federal Circuit, which hears appeals involving patent law and those arising from the decisions of the trade and claims courts.

Cases are heard in federal court if they involve federal law or if the U.S. government is a party in the case. After the Boston Marathon bombing suspect Dzhokhar Tsarnaev was arrested in 2013, he was tried in federal court on federal criminal charges, including using a weapon of mass destruction.

The appellate jurisdiction of the federal courts also extends to cases originating in the state courts. In both civil and criminal cases, a decision of the highest state court can be appealed to the U.S. Supreme Court by raising a federal issue. Appellants might assert, for example, that they were denied the right to counsel or otherwise deprived of the due process guaranteed by the federal Constitution, or they might assert that important issues of federal law were at stake in the case. The U.S. Supreme Court is not obligated to accept such appeals and will accept them only if it believes that the matter has considerable national significance. (We return to this topic later in this chapter.) In addition, in criminal cases defendants who have been convicted in a state court may request a writ of *habeas corpus* from a federal district court. *Habeas corpus* is a court order to the authorities to release a prisoner deemed to be held in violation of her legal rights. Generally speaking, state defendants seeking a federal writ of *habeas corpus* must show that they have exhausted all available state remedies and raise issues not previously raised in their state appeals. Federal courts of appeals and, ultimately, the U.S. Supreme Court have appellate jurisdiction over federal district court *habeas* decisions.

Although the federal courts hear only a small fraction of all the civil and criminal cases decided each year in the United States, their decisions are extremely important. It is in the federal courts that the Constitution and

due process

Proceeding according to law and with adequate protection for individual rights

writ of *habeas corpus*

A court order demanding that an individual in custody be brought into court and shown the cause for detention. *Habeas corpus* is guaranteed by the Constitution and can be suspended only in cases of rebellion or invasion federal laws that govern all Americans are interpreted and their meaning and significance established. Moreover, it is in the federal courts that the powers and limitations of the increasingly powerful national government are tested. Finally, through their power to review the decisions of the state courts, it is ultimately the federal courts that dominate the American judicial system.

Federal Trial Courts

The federal district courts handle most of the cases of original federal jurisdiction. These trial courts have general jurisdiction, and their cases are, in form, indistinguishable from cases in the state trial courts.

There are 89 district courts in the 50 states, plus one in the District of Columbia, one in Puerto Rico, and three territorial courts. These courts are staffed by 678 federal district judges. District judges are assigned to district courts according to the workload; the busiest of these courts may have as many as 28 judges. The routines and procedures of the federal district courts are essentially the same as those of the lower state courts, except that federal procedural requirements tend to be stricter. States, for example, do not have to provide a grand jury, a 12-member trial jury, or a unanimous jury verdict. Federal courts must provide all of these.

Federal Appellate Courts

Roughly 20 percent of all lower-court cases along with appeals from some federal agency decisions are subsequently reviewed by a federal appeals court. The country is divided into 12 judicial circuits, each of which has a U.S. Court of Appeals. A thirteenth appellate court, the U.S. Court of Appeals for the Federal Circuit, is defined by subject matter rather than geographic jurisdiction. This court accepts appeals regarding patents, copyrights, and international trade.

Except for cases selected for review by the Supreme Court, decisions made by the appeals courts are final. Because of this finality, certain safeguards have been built into the system. The most important is the provision of more than one judge for every appeals case. Each court of appeals has 3 to 28 permanent judgeships, depending on the workload of the circuit. Although normally three judges hear appealed cases, in some instances a larger number of judges sit together *en banc*.

Another safeguard is provided by the assignment of a Supreme Court justice as the circuit justice for each of the 11 circuits. The circuit justice deals with requests for special action by the Supreme Court. The most frequent and best-known action of circuit justices is that of reviewing requests for stays of execution when the full Court is unable to do so—mainly during the summer, when the Court is in recess.

The Supreme Court

The Supreme Court is America's highest court. Article III of the Constitution vests "the judicial power of the United States" in the Supreme Court, and this court is supreme in fact as well as form. The Supreme Court is made up of a chief justice and eight associate justices. The chief justice presides over the Court's public sessions and conferences. In the Court's actual deliberations and decisions, however, the chief justice has no more authority than his colleagues. Each justice casts one vote. The chief justice, though, is always the first to speak and to vote when the justices deliberate; voting then proceeds in order of seniority. In addition, if the chief justice has voted with the majority, he decides which of the justices will write the formal opinion for the Court. The character of the opinion can be an important means of influencing the evolution of the law beyond the mere affirmation or denial of the appeal at hand. To some extent, the influence of the chief justice is a function of his own leadership ability. Some chief justices, such as the late Earl Warren, have been able to lead the Court in a new direction. In other instances, a forceful associate justice, such as the late Felix Frankfurter, is the dominant figure on the Court.

chief justice
The justice on the Supreme Court who presides over the Court's public sessions

The Constitution does not specify the number of justices who should sit on the Supreme Court; Congress has the authority to change the Court's size. In the early nineteenth century, there were six Supreme Court justices; later there were seven. Congress set the number of justices at nine in 1869, and the Court has remained that size ever since. In 1937, President Franklin Delano Roosevelt, infuriated by several Supreme Court decisions that struck down New Deal programs, asked Congress to enlarge the Court so that he could add a few sympathetic justices to the bench. Although Congress balked at Roosevelt's "court-packing" plan, the Court gave in to Roosevelt's pressure and began to take a more favorable view of his policy initiatives. The president, in turn, dropped his efforts to enlarge the Court. The Court's surrender to Roosevelt came to be known as "the switch in time that saved nine."

To Six of the Nine

Though Franklin Delano Roosevelt attempted to increase the number of justices in 1937, the size of the Supreme Court has remained at nine since 1869. This political cartoon from 1937 reflects the concern that Roosevelt's strategy threatened the independence of the judiciary.

How Judges Are Appointed

The president appoints federal judges. The nominees are typically the more prominent or politically active members of the legal profession. Many federal judges previously served as state court judges or state or local prosecutors; some were prominent attorneys; others highly regarded law professors. Prior experience as a judge, however, is not necessary, either for appointment or ultimately success. In general, presidents endeavor to appoint judges who possess legal experience and good character and whose partisan and ideological views are similar to theirs. During the presidencies of Richard Nixon, Ronald Reagan, George H. W. Bush, and George W. Bush, most federal judicial appointees were conservative Republicans. Bill Clinton's and Barack Obama's appointees to the federal bench, on the other hand, tended to be liberal Democrats. Following the example of Jimmy Carter, Clinton also made a major effort to appoint women and African Americans to the federal courts. Nearly half his nominees were drawn from these groups. George W. Bush made a strong effort to appoint Hispanics to the federal bench. (See Figure 8.2 on p. 251 for more information on diversity of court appointees.)

The Constitution calls on the Senate to "advise and consent" to federal judicial nominations. This gives the upper chamber of Congress an important check on the president's influence over the judiciary. Before the president makes a formal nomination, the senators from the candidate's own state must indicate that they support the nominee. This is an informal but seldom violated practice called senatorial courtesy. If one or both senators from a prospective nominee's home state belong to the president's political party, the president will almost invariably consult them and secure their blessing for the nomination. Because the president's party in the Senate will rarely support a nominee opposed by a home-state senator from their ranks, this arrangement gives these senators virtual veto power over appointments to the federal bench in their own states. Senators often see this power to grant their support as a way to reward important allies and contributors in their states. If the state has no senator from the president's party, the governor or members of the state's House delegation may make suggestions. Senatorial courtesy is less consequential for appellate court appointments and plays no role in Supreme Court nominations.

Once the president has formally nominated an individual, the appointment must be considered by the Senate Judiciary Committee and confirmed by a majority vote in the full Senate. The politics and rules of the Senate determine the fate of a president's judicial nominees and influence the types of people the president selects for judicial positions. Like any piece of legislation, support for a nomination must be approved by the relevant committee and brought to the floor of the Senate, and to be approved, the nomination must receive a majority of votes. What is more, because this takes place in

senatorial courtesy

The practice whereby the president, before formally nominating a person for a federal district judgeship, finds out whether the senators from the candidate's state support the nomination the Senate, there is always the risk of a filibuster, and cloture of debate requires an affirmative vote of three-fifths of the senators. (See Chapter 5 for discussion of these procedures.) The composition of the Senate Judiciary Committee as well as the Senate as a whole, then, is critical in determining whether a particular nominee will succeed.

Before the 1950s, the Senate Judiciary Committee rarely questioned nominees on their judicial views. Instead, committee inquiries would focus exclusively on qualifications. Since the mid-1950s, however, judicial appointments have become increasingly partisan and, ultimately, ideological. Today, the Judiciary Committee of the Senate subjects nominees for the federal judiciary to lengthy questioning about a wide range of issues, from gun rights to abortion to federal power under the commerce clause. Senators' support for or opposition to specific

Partisan politics tends to play a large role in judicial appointments. Both of President Obama's nominations to the Supreme Court, Sonia Sotomayor and Elena Kagan, were confirmed by the Senate, but with voting following almost entirely along party lines.

nominees turns on the individual's ideological and judicial views as much as on his qualifications. And, for their part, presidents nominate individuals who share their own political philosophy. Presidents Ronald Reagan and George H. W. Bush appointed five Supreme Court justices whom they believed to have conservative perspectives: justices Sandra Day O'Connor, Antonin Scalia, Anthony Kennedy, David Souter, and Clarence Thomas. Reagan also elevated William Rehnquist to the position of chief justice. Reagan and Bush sought appointees who believed in reducing government intervention in the economy and who supported the moral positions taken by the Republican Party in recent years, particularly opposition to abortion. However, not all the Reagan and Bush appointees fulfilled their sponsors' expectations. Bush appointee David Souter, for example, was attacked by conservatives as a turncoat for his decisions on school prayer and abortion rights. Nevertheless, through their appointments, Reagan and Bush were able to create a far more conservative Supreme Court. For his part, President Bill Clinton named Ruth Bader Ginsburg and Stephen Breyer to the Court, hoping to counteract the influence of the Reagan and Bush appointees. But George W. Bush's appointees, John Roberts and Samuel Alito, helped bolster the conservative bloc.

Similarly, President Obama hoped that Sonia Sotomayor and Elena Kagan would add strong voices to the Court's liberal wing. Sotomayor became the first Supreme Court justice of Hispanic origin and thus made judicial history even before participating in the Court's deliberations. (Table 8.1 shows more information about the current Supreme Court justices.)

Table 8.1

SUPREME COURT JUSTICES, 2014

NAME	YEAR OF BIRTH	PRIOR EXPERIENCE	APPOINTED BY	YEAR OF APPOINTMENT
John G. Roberts, Jr. *Chief Justice*	1955	Federal judge	G. W. Bush	2005
Antonin Scalia	1936	Federal judge	Reagan	1986
Anthony M. Kennedy	1936	Federal judge	Reagan	1988
Clarence Thomas	1948	Federal judge	G. H. W. Bush	1991
Ruth Bader Ginsburg	1933	Federal judge	Clinton	1993
Stephen G. Breyer	1938	Federal judge	Clinton	1994
Samuel A. Alito, Jr.	1950	Federal judge	G. W. Bush	2006
Sonia Sotomayor	1954	Federal judge	Obama	2009
Elena Kagan	1960	Solicitor general	Obama	2010

These struggles over judicial appointments reflect the growing intensity of partisanship in the United States today. They also indicate how much importance competing political forces attach to Supreme Court appointments. Because the contending forces see the outcome as critical, they are willing to engage in a fierce struggle when Supreme Court appointments are at stake.

Presidents also try to shape the judiciary through their appointments to the lower federal courts. For example, with a combined total of 12 years in office, Reagan and Bush were able to exercise a good deal of influence on the composition of the federal district and appellate courts. By the end of Bush's term, he and Reagan together had appointed nearly half of all the federal judges, which clearly had a continuing influence on the temperament and behavior of the district and circuit courts. President Clinton promised to appoint more liberal jurists to the district and appellate courts and to increase the number of women and minorities serving on the federal bench. During his years in office, Clinton held to this promise (Figure 8.2).

The increasing role of partisanship or ideology in the nomination process creates a potential danger for the court system. Courts, as we said at the outset,

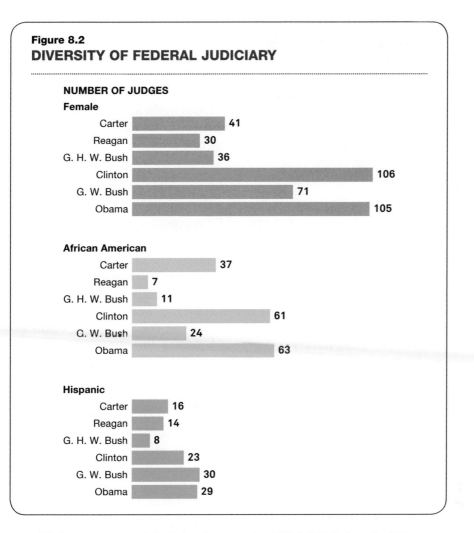

Figure 8.2
DIVERSITY OF FEDERAL JUDICIARY

NUMBER OF JUDGES

Female

President	Number
Carter	41
Reagan	30
G. H. W. Bush	36
Clinton	106
G. W. Bush	71
Obama	105

African American

Carter	37
Reagan	7
G. H. W. Bush	11
Clinton	61
G. W. Bush	24
Obama	63

Hispanic

Carter	16
Reagan	14
G. H. W. Bush	8
Clinton	23
G. W. Bush	30
Obama	29

NOTE: Carter appointed 261 federal judges; Reagan appointed 364; G. H. W. Bush appointed 188; Clinton appointed 372; G. W. Bush appointed 321; and Obama appointed 286 (as of November 2014).

SOURCE: The Federal Judicial Center, History of the Federal Judiciary, www.fjc.gov/history/home.nsf/page/research_categories.html (accessed 11/20/14).

derive much of their authority from their position of political independence, as nonpartisan arbiters in our society. The politics of appointments, which since the civil rights era has grown increasingly focused on ideology, risks tainting judges and the judicial process as little more than extensions of the political views of the people who nominated them. Fortunately, the individuals appointed to the federal judiciary tend to have a strong independent sense of themselves and their mission. Throughout the history of the federal courts are instances of judges who have frustrated the presidents who appointed them.

JUDICIAL REVIEW

judicial review

judicial review
The power of the courts to declare actions of the legislative and executive branches invalid or unconstitutional. The Supreme Court asserted this power in *Marbury v. Madison* (1803)

The phrase judicial review refers to the power of the judiciary to examine and, if necessary, invalidate actions undertaken by the legislative and executive branches. Sometimes the phrase is also used to describe the scrutiny that appeals courts give to the actions of trial courts, but, strictly speaking, this is an improper usage.

Judicial Review of Acts of Congress

Because the Constitution does not give the Supreme Court the power of judicial review of congressional enactments, the Court's exercise of it may be seen as something of a usurpation. Among the proposals debated at the Constitutional Convention was one to create a council composed of the president and the judiciary that would share the veto power over legislation. Another proposal was to route all legislation through both the Court and the president; overruling a veto by either one would have required a two-thirds vote of the House and the Senate. Those and other proposals were rejected by the delegates, and no further effort was made to give the Supreme Court review power over the other branches. This does not prove that the framers of the Constitution opposed judicial review, but it does indicate that "if they intended to provide for it in the Constitution, they did so in a most obscure fashion."[6]

Disputes over the intentions of the framers were settled in 1803 in the case of *Marbury v. Madison*.[7] In that case, William Marbury sued Secretary of State James Madison for Madison's failure to complete Marbury's appointment to a lower judgeship that had been initiated by the outgoing administration of President John Adams. Quite apart from the details of the case, Chief Justice John Marshall, speaking on behalf of the Court, used the case to declare a portion of a law unconstitutional. In effect, he stated that although the substance of Marbury's request was not unreasonable, the Court's jurisdiction in the matter was based on a section of the Judiciary Act of 1789, which the Court declared unconstitutional.

Although Congress and the president have often been at odds with the Court, its legal power to review acts of Congress has not been seriously questioned since 1803. One reason is that judicial power has been accepted as natural, if not intended. Another reason is that during the early years of the Republic, the Supreme Court was careful to use its power sparingly, striking down only two pieces of legislation during the first 75 years

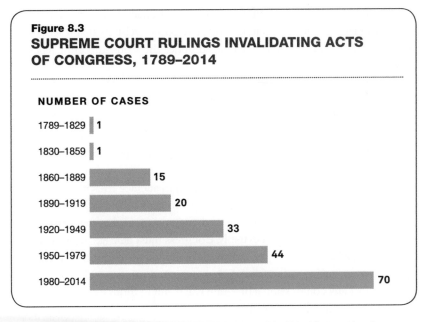

Figure 8.3

SUPREME COURT RULINGS INVALIDATING ACTS OF CONGRESS, 1789–2014

NUMBER OF CASES

Period	Number of Cases
1789–1829	1
1830–1859	1
1860–1889	15
1890–1919	20
1920–1949	33
1950–1979	44
1980–2014	70

SOURCE: U.S. Government Printing Office, "The Constitution of the United States of America: Analysis and Interpretation," www.congress.gov/constitution-annotated (accessed 11/12/14).

of its history. In recent years, with the power of judicial review securely accepted, the Court has been more willing to use it. Between 1980 and 2014, the Supreme Court struck down 70 acts of Congress, in part or in their entirety.[8] (See Figure 8.3.)

Judicial Review of State Actions

The power of the Supreme Court to review state legislation or other state action and to determine its constitutionality is neither granted by the Constitution nor inherent in the federal system. But the logic of the supremacy clause of Article VI of the Constitution, which declares that it and laws made under its authority to be the supreme law of the land, is very strong. Furthermore, in the Judiciary Act of 1789, Congress conferred on the Supreme Court the power to reverse state constitutions and laws whenever they are clearly in conflict with the U.S. Constitution, federal laws, or treaties.[9] This power gives the Supreme Court jurisdiction over all of the millions of cases handled by American courts each year.

The supremacy clause of the Constitution not only established the federal Constitution, statutes, and treaties as the "supreme law of the land" but also provided that "the Judges in every State shall be bound thereby, any Thing in the Constitution or Laws of the State to the Contrary notwithstanding."

supremacy clause
A clause of Article VI of the Constitution that states that all laws passed by the national government and all treaties are the supreme laws of the land and superior to all laws adopted by any state or any subdivision

Under this authority, the Supreme Court has frequently overturned state constitutional provisions or statutes and state court decisions that it feels are counter to rights or privileges guaranteed under the Constitution or federal statutes.

Judicial Review of Federal Agency Actions

Although Congress makes the law, as we saw in Chapters 5 and 7, it can hardly administer the thousands of programs it has enacted and must delegate power to the president and to a huge bureaucracy to achieve its purposes. For example, if Congress wishes to improve air quality, it cannot possibly anticipate all the conditions and circumstances that may arise with respect to that general goal. Inevitably, Congress must delegate to the executive substantial discretionary power to make judgments about the best ways to improve air quality in the face of changing circumstances. Thus, over the years, almost any congressional program will result in thousands of pages of administrative regulations developed by executive agencies nominally seeking to implement the will of the Congress.

The issue of delegation of power has led to a number of court decisions over the past two centuries generally revolving around the question of the scope of the delegation. Courts have also been called on to decide whether the rules and regulations adopted by federal agencies are consistent with Congress's express or implied intent.

As presidential power expanded during the New Deal era, one measure of increased congressional subordination to the executive was the enactment of laws that contained few, if any, principles limiting executive discretion. Congress enacted legislation, often at the president's behest, that gave the executive virtually unfettered authority to address a particular concern. For example, the Emergency Price Control Act of 1942 authorized the executive to set "fair and equitable" prices without offering any indication of what those terms might mean.[10] Although the Court initially challenged these delegations of power to the president during the New Deal, a confrontation with President Franklin Delano Roosevelt caused the Court to retreat from its position. Perhaps as a result, no congressional delegation of power to the president has been struck down as impermissibly broad in more than six decades. In the last two decades in particular, the Supreme Court has found that as long as federal agencies developed rules and regulations "based upon a permissible construction" or "reasonable interpretation" of Congress's statute, the judiciary would accept the views of the executive branch.[11] Generally, the courts give considerable deference to administrative agencies as long as those agencies have engaged in a formal rule-making process and can show that they have carried out the conditions prescribed by the various statutes governing agency rule making. These include the 1946 Administrative Procedure Act, which requires agencies to notify parties affected by proposed rules as well as allow them ample time to comment on such rules before they go into effect.

Judicial Review and Presidential Power

The federal courts are also called on to review the actions of the president. As we saw in Chapter 6, presidents increasingly make use of unilateral executive powers rather than relying on congressional legislation to achieve their objectives. On many occasions, presidential orders and actions have been challenged in the federal courts by members of Congress and by individuals and groups opposing the president's policies. In recent decades, however, assertions of presidential power have been rationalized, upheld, and made standard executive practice. We saw one example of this earlier in the chapter, with the 1974 case *United States v. Nixon*, in which the Court first acknowledged the legitimacy of the executive privilege principle. Executive privilege has also been invoked to protect even the deliberations of the vice president from congressional scrutiny in the case of Dick Cheney's consultations with representatives of the energy industry.

This pattern of judicial deference to presidential authority is also manifest in the Supreme Court's decisions regarding President Bush's war on terrorism. In June 2004, the Supreme Court ruled in three cases involving the president's antiterrorism initiatives and claims of executive power and in two of the three cases appeared to place some limits on presidential authority. But although the Court's decisions were widely hailed as reining in the executive branch, they actually fell far short of stopping presidential power in its tracks.

Perhaps the most important of these cases was *Hamdi v. Rumsfeld*.[12] In June 2004, the Supreme Court ruled that Yaser Esam Hamdi, a prisoner captured in Afghanistan and incarcerated in the United States as an "enemy combatant," was entitled to a lawyer and "a fair opportunity to rebut the government's factual assertions." However, the Supreme Court affirmed that the president possessed the authority to declare a U.S. citizen to be an enemy combatant and to order such an individual held in federal detention. Several of the justices intimated that once designated an enemy combatant, a U.S. citizen might be tried before a military tribunal and the normal presumption of innocence suspended. In 2006, in *Hamdan v. Rumsfeld*, the Court ruled that the military commissions established to try enemy combatants and other detainees violated both the Uniform Code of Military Justice and the Geneva Conventions.[13] Thus, the Supreme Court did assert that presidential actions were subject to judicial scrutiny and placed some constraints on the president's power. But at the same time the Court affirmed the president's single most important claim—the unilateral power to declare individuals, including U.S. citizens, "enemy combatants" who could be detained by federal authorities under adverse legal circumstances.

Judicial Review and Lawmaking

Much of the work of the courts involves the application of statutes to the particular case at hand. Over the centuries, however, judges have developed a body of rules and principles of interpretation that are not grounded in specific statutes. This body of judge-made law is called common law.

The appellate courts are a different realm. Their rulings can be considered laws, but they are laws governing only the behavior of the judiciary. When a court of appeals hands down its decision, it accomplishes two things. First, of course, it decides who wins—the person who won in the lower court or the person who lost in the lower court. But at the same time, it expresses its decision in a manner that provides guidance to the lower courts for handling future cases in the same area. Appellate judges try to give their reasons and rulings in writing so the "administration of justice" can take place most of the time at the lowest judicial level. They try to make their ruling or reasoning clear, so as to avoid confusion, which can produce a surge of litigation at the lower levels. These rulings can be considered laws, but they are laws governing the behavior only of the judiciary. Decisions by appellate courts affect citizens by giving them a cause of action or by taking it away from them. That is, they open or close access to the courts.

THE SUPREME COURT IN ACTION

The Supreme Court plays a vital role in the government as it is part of the structure of checks and balances that prevents the legislative and executive branches from abusing their power. The Court also operates as an institution unto itself with its own internal rules for decision making.

How Cases Reach the Supreme Court

Given the millions of disputes that arise every year, the job of the Supreme Court would be impossible if it were not able to control the flow of cases and its own caseload. The Supreme Court has original jurisdiction in a limited variety of cases defined by the Constitution. The original jurisdiction includes (1) cases between the United States and one of the 50 states,

(2) cases involving two or more states, (3) cases involving foreign ambassadors or other ministers, and (4) cases brought by one state against citizens of another state or against a foreign country. The most important of these cases are disputes between states over land, water, or old debts. Generally, the Supreme Court deals with these cases by appointing a "special master," usually a retired judge, who actually hears the case and presents a report. The Supreme Court then allows the parties involved in the dispute to present arguments for or against the master's opinion.[14]

Rules of Access. Over the years, the courts have developed specific rules that govern which cases within their jurisdiction they will and will not hear. To have access to the courts, cases must meet certain criteria that are initially applied by the trial court but may be reconsidered by appellate courts. These rules of access can be broken down into three major categories: case or controversy, standing, and mootness.

Article III of the Constitution and past Supreme Court decisions define judicial power as extending only to "cases and controversies." This means that the case before a court must be an actual controversy, not a hypothetical one, with two truly adversarial parties (called ripeness). The courts have interpreted this language to mean that they do not have power to render advisory opinions to legislatures or agencies about the constitutionality of proposed laws or regulations. Furthermore, even after a law is enacted, the courts will generally refuse to consider its constitutionality until it is actually applied.

Parties to a case must also have standing, that is, they must show that they have a substantial stake in the outcome of the case. The traditional requirement for standing has been to show injury to oneself; that injury can be personal, economic, or even aesthetic, for example. For a group or class of people to have standing (as in class-action suits), each member must show specific injury. This means that a general interest in the environment, for instance, does not provide a group with sufficient basis for standing.

The Supreme Court also uses a third criterion in determining whether it will hear a case: that of mootness. In theory, this requirement disqualifies cases that are brought too late—after the relevant facts have changed or the problem has been resolved by other means. The criterion of mootness, however, is subject to the discretion of the courts, which have begun to relax the rules of mootness, particularly in cases where a situation that has been resolved is likely to come

ripeness
A case that is ready for litigation and does not depend on hypothetical future events

standing
The right of an individual or an organization to initiate a court case

mootness
A criterion used by courts to avoid hearing cases that no longer require resolution

In 2013, the Supreme Court ruled that opponents of same-sex marriage did not have standing to appeal a lower court decision overturning California's ban on same-sex marriage. Thus same-sex marriages were allowed to continue in the state and original plaintiffs, Sandra Stier and Kristin Perry (pictured here with their son), were able to marry.

up again. In the abortion case *Roe v. Wade*, for example, the Supreme Court rejected the lower court's argument that because the pregnancy had already come to term, the case was moot. The Court agreed to hear the case because no pregnancy was likely to outlast the lengthy appeals process.

Putting aside the formal criteria, the Supreme Court is most likely to accept cases that involve conflicting decisions by the federal circuit courts, cases that present important questions of civil rights or civil liberties, and cases in which the federal government is the appellant.[15] Ultimately, however, the question of which cases to accept can come down to the preferences and priorities of the justices. If a group of justices believes that the Court should intervene in a particular area of policy or politics, they are likely to look for a case or cases that can be vehicles for judicial intervention. For many years, for example, the Court was not interested in considering challenges to affirmative action or other programs designed to provide particular benefits to minorities. In recent years, however, several of the Court's more conservative justices have been eager to push back the limits of affirmative action and racial preference, and have therefore accepted a number of cases that would allow them to do so. In 1995, the Court's decision in *Adarand Constructors v. Peña, Missouri v. Jenkins*, and *Miller v. Johnson* placed new restrictions on federal affirmative action programs, school desegregation efforts, and attempts to increase minority representation in Congress through the creation of "minority districts" (see Chapter 10).[16]

writ of *certiorari*

A formal request by an appellant to have the Supreme Court review a decision of a lower court. *Certiorari* is from a Latin word meaning "to make more certain"

Writs. Most cases reach the Supreme Court through a writ of *certiorari*. *Certiorari* is an order to a lower court to deliver the records of a particular case to be reviewed for legal errors (Figure 8.4). The term *certiorari* is sometimes shortened to *cert*; cases deemed to merit certiorari are referred to as "cert-worthy." An individual who loses in a lower federal court or state court and wants the Supreme Court to review the decision has 90 days to file a petition for a writ of *certiorari* with the clerk of the U.S. Supreme Court. There are two types of petitions, paid petitions and petitions *in forma pauperis* (in the form of a pauper). The former requires payment of filing fees, submission of a certain number of copies, and compliance with a variety of other rules. For *in forma pauperis* petitions, usually filed by prison inmates, the Court waives the fees and most other requirements.

Since 1972, most of the justices have participated in a "*certiorari* pool" in which they pool their law clerks to evaluate the petitions. Each petition is reviewed by one clerk who writes a memo for all the justices participating in the pool. The memo summarizes the facts and issues and makes a recommendation. Clerks for the other justices add their comments to the memo. After they review the memos, any justice may place any case on the "discuss list." This is a list circulated by the chief justice of all the petitions to be talked about and voted on at the Court's conference. If a case is not placed on the discuss list, it is automatically denied *certiorari*. Cases placed on

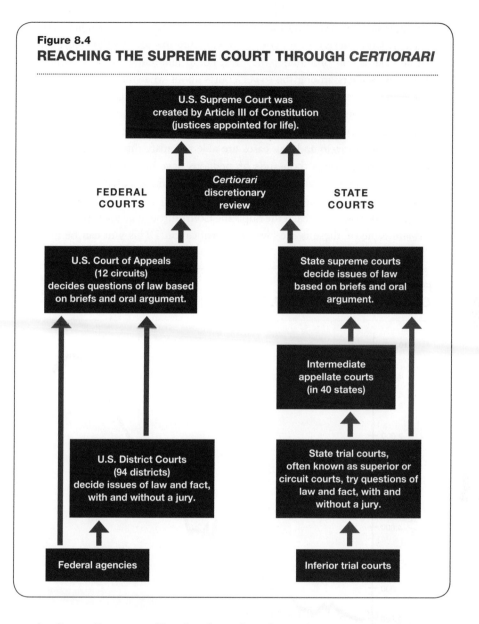

Figure 8.4
REACHING THE SUPREME COURT THROUGH *CERTIORARI*

U.S. Supreme Court was created by Article III of Constitution (justices appointed for life).

FEDERAL COURTS

Certiorari discretionary review

STATE COURTS

U.S. Court of Appeals (12 circuits) decides questions of law based on briefs and oral argument.

State supreme courts decide issues of law based on briefs and oral argument.

Intermediate appellate courts (in 40 states)

U.S. District Courts (94 districts) decide issues of law and fact, with and without a jury.

State trial courts, often known as superior or circuit courts, try questions of law and fact, with and without a jury.

Federal agencies

Inferior trial courts

the discuss list are considered and voted on during the justices' closed-door conference.

For *certiorari* to be granted four justices must be convinced that the case satisfies Rule 10 of the Rules of the U.S. Supreme Court. Rule 10 states that *certiorari* is not a matter of right but is to be granted only where there are special and compelling reasons. These include conflicting decisions by two or more circuit courts; conflicts between circuit courts and state courts of last resort; conflicting decisions by two or more state courts of last resort; decisions by circuit courts on matters of federal law that should be settled by the Supreme

Court; or a circuit court decision on an important question that conflicts with Supreme Court decisions. It should be clear from this list that the Court will usually take action only under the most compelling circumstances—where there are conflicts among the lower courts about what the law should be; where an important legal question has been raised in the lower courts but not definitively answered; and where a lower court deviates from the principles and precedents established by the high court. The support of four justices is needed for *certiorari* and few cases are able to satisfy this requirement. In recent sessions, though thousands of petitions have been filed (Figure 8.5), the Court has granted *certiorari* to fewer than 90 petitioners each year—about 1 percent of those seeking a Supreme Court review.

A handful of cases reach the Supreme Court through avenues other than *certiorari*. One of these is the "writ of certification." This writ can be used

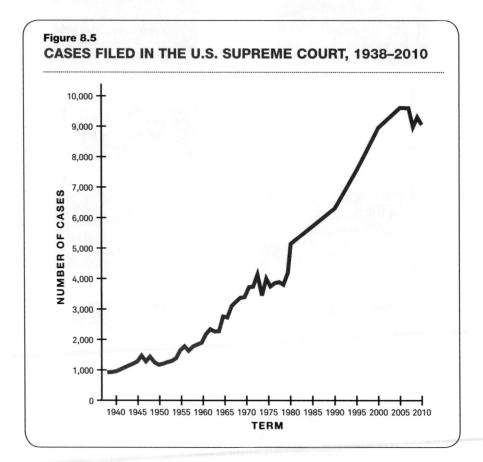

Figure 8.5

CASES FILED IN THE U.S. SUPREME COURT, 1938–2010

NOTE: Graph indicates the number of cases filed in the term beginning in the year indicated.
SOURCES: Years 1938–69: successive volumes of U.S. Bureau of the Census, *Statistical Abstract of the United States* (Washington, DC: Government Printing Office); 1970–79: Office of the Clerk of the Supreme Court; 1980–2010: The 2012 Statistical Abstract, Table 331, www.census.gov /prod/2011pubs/12statab/law.pdf (accessed 6/11/13).

when a U.S. Court of Appeals asks the Supreme Court for instructions on a point of law that has never been decided. A second avenue is the "writ of appeal," used to appeal the decision of a three-judge district court.

Controlling the Flow of Cases: The Role of the Solicitor General

If any single person has greater influence than the individual justices over the work of the Supreme Court, it is the solicitor general of the United States. The solicitor general is third in status in the Justice Department (below the attorney general and the deputy attorney general, who are the government's chief prosecutors) but is the top government defense lawyer in almost all cases before the appellate courts to which the government is a party. Although others can regulate the flow of cases, the solicitor general has the greatest control, with no review of his or her actions by any higher authority in the executive branch. More than half the Supreme Court's total workload consists of cases under the direct charge of the solicitor general.

The solicitor general exercises especially strong influence by screening cases involving the federal government as a party long before they approach the Supreme Court; the justices rely on the solicitor general to "screen out undeserving litigation and furnish them with an agenda to government cases that deserve serious consideration."[17] Agency heads may lobby the president or otherwise try to circumvent the solicitor general, and a few of the independent agencies have a statutory right to make direct appeals, but without the solicitor general's support, these are seldom reviewed by the Court.

The solicitor general can enter a case even when the federal government is not a direct litigant by writing an *amicus curiae* ("friend of the court") brief. A "friend of the court" is not a direct party to a case but has a vital interest in its outcome. Thus, when the government has such an interest, the solicitor general can file an *amicus curiae*, or the Court can invite such a brief because it wants an opinion in writing. Other interested parties may file briefs as well.

amicus curiae
"Friend of the court," an individual or group that is not a party to a lawsuit but seeks to assist the court in reaching a decision by presenting an additional brief

The Supreme Court's Procedures

The Preparation. The Supreme Court's decision to accept a case is the beginning of what can be a lengthy and complex process (Figure 8.6). First, the attorneys on both sides must prepare briefs—written documents in which the attorneys explain why the Court should rule in favor of their client. The document filed by the individual bringing the case is called the petitioner's brief. This brief summarizes the facts of the case and presents the

brief
A written document in which an attorney explains—using case precedents—why a court should rule in favor of his or her client

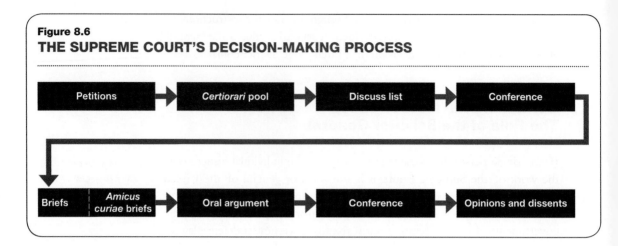

Figure 8.6
THE SUPREME COURT'S DECISION-MAKING PROCESS

Petitions → *Certiorari* pool → Discuss list → Conference →

Briefs | *Amicus curiae* briefs → Oral argument → Conference → Opinions and dissents

legal basis on which the Supreme Court is being asked to overturn the lower court's decision. The document filed by the side that prevailed in the lower court is called the respondent's brief. This brief explains why the Supreme Court should affirm the lower court's verdict. The petitioners will then file a brief answering and attempting to refute the points made in the respondent's brief. This document is called the petitioner's reply brief. Briefs are filled with referrals to precedents specifically chosen to show that other courts have frequently ruled in the same way that the Supreme Court is being asked to rule.

As the attorneys prepare their briefs, they often ask sympathetic interest groups for their help. Groups are asked to file *amicus curiae* briefs that support the claims of one or the other litigant. In a case involving separation of church and state, for example, liberal groups such as the ACLU and Citizens for the American Way are likely to file *amicus* briefs in support of strict separation, whereas conservative religious groups are likely to file *amicus* briefs advocating increased public support for religious ideas. Often, dozens of briefs will be filed on each side of a major case.

oral argument

The stage in Supreme Court proceedings in which attorneys for both sides appear before the Court to present their positions and answer questions posed by the justices

Oral Argument. The next stage of a case is oral argument, in which attorneys for both sides appear before the Court to present their positions and answer the justices' questions. Each attorney has only a half hour to present his or her case, and this time includes interruptions for questions. Certain members of the Court, such as Justice Antonin Scalia, are known to interrupt attorneys dozens of times. Others, such as Justice Clarence Thomas, seldom ask questions. For an attorney, the opportunity to argue a case before the Supreme Court is a singular honor and a mark of professional distinction. It can also be a harrowing experience, as justices interrupt a carefully prepared presentation. Nevertheless, oral argument can be very important to the outcome of a case. It allows justices to better understand the heart of the case and to raise questions that might not have been addressed in the opposing

The oral argument stage of a Supreme Court case is the last opportunity both sides have to present their positions to the Court. In addition to the immediate legal issues at stake, the attorneys may also discuss the larger political and social ramifications of the case.

sides' briefs. It is not uncommon for justices to go beyond the strictly legal issues and ask opposing counsel to discuss the implications of the case for the Court and the nation at large. In oral arguments on the constitutionality of the Defense of Marriage Act in 2013, for example, Justice Kennedy returned frequently to the matter of whether the definition of marriage resided with the states rather than with federal government. Justice Ginsburg took a social perspective, objecting to the fact that the law created "two kinds of marriage: the full marriage, and then this sort of skim milk marriage."[18]

The Conference. Following oral argument, the Court discusses the case in its Wednesday or Friday conference. The chief justice presides over the conference and speaks first; the other justices follow in order of seniority. The Court's conference is secret, and no outsiders are permitted to attend. The justices reach a decision on the basis of a majority vote. While the case is discussed, justices may try to influence or change one another's opinions. At times, this may result in compromise decisions.

Opinion Writing. After a decision has been reached, one of the members of the majority is assigned to write the opinion. This assignment is made by the chief justice or by the most senior justice in the majority if the chief justice is on the losing side. The assignment of the opinion can make a significant difference to the interpretation of a decision. Every opinion of the Supreme Court sets a major precedent for future cases throughout the judicial system. Lawyers and judges in the lower courts will examine the opinion carefully to ascertain the Supreme Court's meaning. Differences in wording and emphasis can have important implications for future litigation.

opinion
The written explanation of the Supreme Court's decision in a particular case

Thus, in assigning an opinion, the justices must give serious thought to the impression the case will make on lawyers and on the public, as well as to the probability that one justice's opinion will be more widely accepted than another's.

One of the more dramatic instances of this tactical consideration occurred in 1944, when Chief Justice Harlan F. Stone chose Justice Felix Frankfurter to write the opinion in the "white primary" case *Smith v. Allwright*. The chief justice believed that this sensitive case, which overturned the Southern practice of prohibiting black participation in nominating primaries, required the efforts of the most brilliant and scholarly jurist on the Court. But the day after Stone made the assignment, Justice Robert H. Jackson wrote a letter to Stone urging a change of assignment. In his letter, Jackson argued that Frankfurter, a foreign-born Jew from New England, would not win the South with his opinion, regardless of its brilliance. Stone accepted the advice and substituted Justice Stanley Reed, an American-born Protestant from Kentucky and a Southern Democrat in good standing.[19]

Once the majority opinion is drafted, it is circulated to the other justices. Some members of the majority may agree with both the outcome and the rationale but wish to emphasize or highlight a particular point and so will draft a concurring opinion for that purpose. In other instances, one or more justices may agree with the majority but may disagree with the rationale presented in the majority opinion. These justices may draft a special concurrence, explaining their disagreements with the majority.

concurrence

An opinion agreeing with the decision of the majority but not with the rationale provided in the majority opinion

dissenting opinion

A decision written by a justice who voted with the minority opinion in a particular case, in which the justice fully explains the reasoning behind his or her opinion

Dissent. Justices who disagree with the majority decision of the Court may choose to publicize the character of their disagreement in the form of a dissenting opinion. A dissenting opinion is generally assigned by the senior justice among the dissenters. Dissenting opinions can be used to signal to defeated political forces in the nation that their position is supported by at least some members of the Court. Ironically, the most dependable way an individual justice can exercise a direct and clear influence on the Court is to write a dissent. Because there is no need to please a majority, dissenting opinions are often more eloquent and less guarded than majority opinions.

The size of the division on the Court, as well as the reasons for dissent, are often taken as an indication of the strength of the position and principles espoused by the majority. A large majority of, say seven or more, indicates that it will be hard to overturn an opinion in the future, but the one-vote margin of a 5–4 decision might be hard to sustain in future cases involving a given question. In recent years, the Supreme Court often splits 5–4, with dissenters writing long and detailed opinions that they hope will help convince a swing justice to join their side on the next round of cases dealing with a similar topic. In 1950, Justice William O. Douglas wrote the dissent in *South v. Peters*, a case challenging the election of the governor of Georgia by a vote of counties rather than a vote of the people.[20] Thirteen years later, Justice Douglas echoed that opinion, but this time writing for the majority in the case of *Gray v. Sanders*.[21] In this opinion, Douglas penned one of the most famous phrases of any court decision. In choosing the representatives of the people, equal protection of the laws means "one person, one vote." More recently, Justice David Souter wrote a 34-page dissent in a 2002 case upholding the use of government-funded school vouchers to pay for parochial school tuition. Souter called the decision "a dramatic departure from basic establishment clause principle" and went on to say that he hoped it would be reconsidered by a future court.[22]

Dissent plays a special role in the work and impact of the Court because it amounts to an appeal to lawyers all over the country to keep bringing cases of the sort at issue. Therefore, an effective dissent influences the flow of cases through the Court as well as the arguments that will be used by lawyers in later cases.

Judicial Decision Making

The judiciary is conservative in its procedures, but its impact on society can be radical. That impact depends on a variety of factors. The first set of factors relates to the individual members of the Supreme Court, their attitudes, and their relationships with each other. The second set of factors includes the other branches of government, particularly Congress.

The Supreme Court Justices. The Supreme Court explains its decisions in terms of law and precedent. But although law and precedent do have an effect on the Court's deliberations and eventual decisions, it is the Supreme Court that decides what laws actually mean and what importance precedent will actually have. Throughout its history, the Court has shaped and reshaped the law. If any individual judges in the country influence the federal judiciary, they are the Supreme Court justices.

From the 1950s to the 1980s, the Supreme Court took an active role in such areas as civil rights, civil liberties, abortion, voting rights, and police procedures. For example, the Supreme Court was more responsible than any other governmental institution for breaking down America's system of racial segregation. The Supreme Court virtually prohibited states from interfering with the right of a woman to seek an abortion and sharply curtailed state restrictions on voting rights. And it was the Supreme Court that placed restrictions on the behavior of local police and prosecutors in criminal cases.

But since the early 1980s, resignations, deaths, and new judicial appointments have led to many shifts in the mix of philosophies and ideologies represented on the Court. In a series of decisions between 1989 and 2001, the conservative justices appointed by Ronald Reagan and George H. W. Bush were able to swing the Court to a more conservative position on civil rights, affirmative action, abortion rights, property rights, criminal procedure, voting rights, desegregation, and the power of the national government.

However, because the Court was so evenly split during this period, the conservative bloc did not always prevail. Among the justices serving at the beginning of 2005, Rehnquist, Scalia, and Thomas took conservative positions on most issues and were usually joined by O'Connor and Kennedy. Breyer, Ginsburg, Souter, and Stevens were reliably liberal. This produced many 5–4 splits. On some issues, though, Justice O'Connor or Justice Kennedy tended to side with the liberal camp, producing a 5–4 and sometimes a 6–3 victory for the liberals.

The departure of Justice Sandra Day O'Connor was widely touted in the media as heralding a shift in the Supreme Court in a much more conservative direction. Justice Samuel Alito, who replaced O'Connor, holds more conservative views than Justice O'Connor. O'Connor's departure, however, moved the pivotal vote on the Court only somewhat, from O'Connor to Kennedy. During the 2007 term, Justice Kennedy found himself the swing voter on numerous 5–4 decisions. One-third of all cases in 2007 were decided by just one vote. The appointments of Sonia Sotomayor and Elena Kagan to replace Souter and Stevens, respectively, did not promise to alter this arithmetic. The Analyzing the Evidence unit on page 268 looks at ideology in the Court.

It should be noted that, while the pattern of a four-person liberal bloc pitted against a four-person conservative bloc with a centrist Justice (O'Connor or Kennedy) swinging between them to create a 5–4 division has prevailed frequently in the last decade or two, this bloc structure is not always predictive, even in important cases. In *National Federation of Independent Business v. Sebelius*, the 2012 case on the constitutionality of Obama's health care law, it was Chief Justice Roberts, a firm member of the conservative bloc who joined the four liberals to uphold the law.[23]

Of course, the meaning of any decision rests not just on which justices vote with the majority but also on the majority's written opinion, which presents the constitutional or statutory rationale for future policy. These options establish the guidelines that govern how federal courts must decide similar cases in the future.

Activism and Restraint. One element of judicial philosophy is the issue of activism versus restraint. Over the years, some justices have believed that courts should interpret the Constitution according to the stated intentions of its framers and defer to the views of Congress when interpreting federal statutes. The late justice Felix Frankfurter, for example, advocated judicial deference to legislative bodies and avoidance of the "political thicket," in which the Court would entangle itself by deciding questions that were essentially political rather than legal in character. Advocates of judicial restraint are sometimes called "strict constructionists," because they look strictly to the words of the Constitution in interpreting its meaning.

The alternative to restraint is judicial activism. Activist judges such as the late chief justice Earl Warren believe that the Court should go beyond the words of the Constitution or a statute to consider the broader societal implications of its decisions. Activist judges sometimes strike out in new directions, promulgating new interpretations or inventing new legal and constitutional concepts when they believe these to be socially desirable. For example, Justice Harry Blackmun's opinion in *Roe v. Wade* was based on a constitutional right to privacy that is not found in the words of the Constitution. Blackmun and the other members of the majority in the *Roe* case argued that other constitutional provisions implied the right to privacy. In this instance of judicial activism, the Court knew the result it wanted to achieve and was not afraid to make the law conform to the desired outcome.

judicial restraint
The judicial philosophy whose adherents refuse to go beyond the text of the Constitution in interpreting its meaning

judicial activism
The judicial philosophy that posits that the Court should see beyond the text of the Constitution or a statute to consider broader societal implications for its decisions

Political Ideology. The second component of judicial philosophy is political ideology. The liberal or conservative attitudes of justices play an important role in their decisions.[24] Indeed, the philosophy of activism versus restraint is, to a large extent, a smoke screen for political ideology. In the past, liberal judges have often been activists, willing to use the law to achieve social and political change, whereas conservatives have been associated with judicial restraint. Interestingly, however, in recent years some conservative justices who have long called for restraint have actually become activists in seeking to undo some of the work of liberal jurists over the past three decades.

Congress. At both the national and state levels in the United States, courts and judges are "players" in the policy game because of the separation of powers. Essentially, this means that the legislative branch formulates policy (defined constitutionally and institutionally by a legislative process); that the executive branch implements policy (according to well-defined administrative procedures, and subject to initial approval by the president or the legislative override of his veto); and that the courts, when asked, rule on the faithfulness of the legislated and executed policy either to the substance of the statute or to the Constitution itself. The courts, that is, may strike down an administrative action either because it exceeds the authority granted in the relevant statute (statutory rationale) or because the statute itself exceeds the authority granted the legislature or executive by the Constitution (constitutional rationale).

Ideological Voting on the Supreme Court

Contributed by
Andrew D. Martin
Washington University in St. Louis
Kevin M. Quinn
UC Berkeley School of Law

Do the political preferences of Supreme Court justices influence their behavior? The starting point for the analysis of the behavior of Supreme Court justices is to look at their votes.[1] For non-unanimous cases, we can compute agreement scores—the fraction of cases in which a pair of justices vote the same way. We display these agreement scores for the Court's 2012–13 term in the first figure below. If you examine this figure, you will see that two groups of justices emerge. Within each group, the justices agree with one another a lot, around 70 to 90 percent of the time. Voting is more structured than we would expect by chance.

One way to represent that structure is by arranging the justices on a line as in the diagram below to the right.[2] Justices who agree a lot should be close to one another; justices who disagree a lot should be far apart.

Does the fact that there are patterns of agreement mean that the justices are deciding based on political ideology? Not necessarily. These patterns are consistent with ideological decision making, but other things might explain the patterns as well. However, when we read the cases and see who wins or loses, there is a great deal of support for the idea that political ideology influences how justices vote.[3]

Agreement Scores for the 2012–13 Term

	Ginsburg	Sotomayor	Kagan	Breyer	Kennedy	Scalia	Roberts	Thomas	Alito
Ginsburg	1	.89	.92	.77	.46	.36	.28	.15	.13
Sotomayor	.89	1	.94	.76	.47	.32	.29	.21	.19
Kagan	.92	.94	1	.81	.43	.35	.3	.19	.14
Breyer	.77	.76	.81	1	.54	.23	.46	.33	.37
Kennedy	.46	.47	.43	.54	1	.59	.72	.54	.63
Scalia	.36	.32	.35	.23	.59	1	.72	.74	.55
Roberts	.28	.29	.3	.46	.72	.72	1	.72	.79
Thomas	.15	.21	.19	.33	.54	.74	.72	1	.76
Alito	.13	.19	.14	.37	.63	.55	.79	.76	1

POSITION

▶ Ginsburg
▶ Sotomayor / Kagan
▶ Breyer
▶ Kennedy
▶ Scalia / Roberts

The figure to the left contains the agreement scores for the 2012–13 term of the U.S. Supreme Court for all non-unanimous cases. These scores are the proportion of cases when each justice agreed with every other justice. Two justices that always disagreed with each other would get a zero; two justices who always agreed would get a one. Red indicates low agreement scores; green indicates high agreement scores. The policy dimension to the right of the figure is one that best represents the patterns in the agreement scores.

This type of analysis can be done for any court, but it becomes more difficult if we are interested in comparing justices across time instead of during just one term. What if we are interested in whether the Supreme Court is becoming more ideologically polarized over time? Or whether individual justices have become more liberal or conservative? Martin-Quinn scores based on a statistical model of voting on the Court help solve this problem.[4]

A number of interesting patterns emerge. Consider the case of Justice Harry Blackmun, who often claimed, "I haven't changed; it's the Court that changed under me."[5] The figure below shows that Justice Blackmun's position did in fact change ideologically over the course of his career. This evidence is consistent with some clear changes in Justice Blackmun's behavior, especially in the area of the death penalty.

We can also look at patterns in the positions of chief justices. While the chief's vote counts just the same as the other justices, he or she plays an important role in organizing the court. Justice Rehnquist was the most conservative justice on the court when he arrived in 1971, but as the figure below shows, after he was elevated in 1986 he, too, drifted more toward the middle. This is what we would expect to see of a justice who was working strategically to build coalitions, as any good chief would.

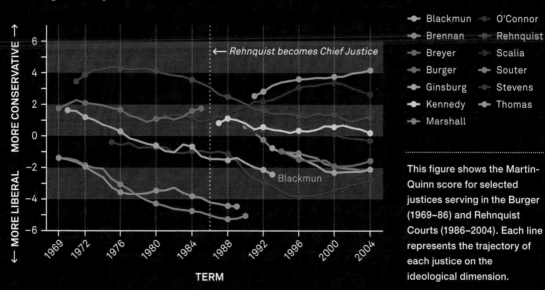

Ideological Trajectories of Selected Justices

JUSTICES

- Blackmun
- Brennan
- Breyer
- Burger
- Ginsburg
- Kennedy
- Marshall
- O'Connor
- Rehnquist
- Scalia
- Souter
- Stevens
- Thomas

This figure shows the Martin-Quinn score for selected justices serving in the Burger (1969–86) and Rehnquist Courts (1986–2004). Each line represents the trajectory of each justice on the ideological dimension.

1   C. Herman Pritchett, *The Roosevelt Court: A Study in Judicial Politics and Values, 1937–1947* (New York: MacMillan Co., 1948).
2   Glendon A. Schubert, *The Judicial Mind: The Attitudes and Ideologies of Supreme Court Justices, 1946–1963* (Evanston, IL: Northwestern University Press, 1965).
3   Jeffry A. Segal and Harold J. Spaeth, *The Supreme Court and the Attitudinal Model* (New York: Cambridge University Press, 1993).
4   Andrew D. Martin and Kevin M. Quinn, "Dynamic Ideal Point Estimation via Markov Chain Monte Carlo for the U.S. Supreme Court, 1953–1999," *Political Analysis* 10, no. 2, (2002): 134–53, http://mqscores.wustl.edu (accessed 10/18/11).
5   Linda Greenhouse, *Becoming Justice Blackmun* (New York: Times Books, 2005).

If the court declares the administrative agent's act as outside the permissible bounds prescribed by the legislation, we suppose the court's majority opinion can declare whatever policy it wishes. If the legislature is unhappy with this judicial action, then it may either recraft the legislation (if the rationale for striking it down was statutory)[25] or initiate a constitutional amendment that would enable the stricken-down policy to pass constitutional muster (if the rationale for originally striking it down was constitutional).

In reaching their decisions, Supreme Court justices must anticipate Congress's response. As a result, judges will not always vote according to their true preferences because doing so may provoke Congress to enact legislation that moves the policy further away from what the judges prefer. By voting for a lesser preference, the justices can get something they prefer to the status quo without provoking congressional action to overturn their decision. The most famous example of this phenomenon is the "switch in time that saved nine," when several justices voted in favor of New Deal legislation, the constitutionality of which they doubted, in order to diminish congressional support for President Roosevelt's plan to "pack" the Court by increasing the number of justices. In short, the interactions between the Court and Congress are part of a complex strategic game.[26]

The President. The president's most direct influence on the Court is the power to nominate justices. Presidents typically nominate judges who they believe are close to their policy preferences and close enough to the preferences of a majority of senators, who must confirm the nomination.

Yet the efforts by presidents to reshape the federal judiciary are not always successful. Often in American history, judges have surprised and disappointed the presidents who named them to the bench. The president must also confront Congress in shaping the judiciary. By using the filibuster (see Chapter 5), both parties have blocked judicial nominees. In 2013, frustration over the Republican strategy of blocking President Obama's federal judicial nominees led Senate Democrats to eliminate the filibuster for most presidential nominees (although the filibuster remains for Supreme Court nominations). As we saw, however, the appointment process has subtly tied the judiciary to the executive and, perhaps, helped to upset the constitutional balance of power.

HOW POWERFUL IS THE JUDICIARY?

Over the past 50 years, the place of the judiciary in American politics and society has changed dramatically. Demand for legal solutions has increased, and the reach of the judiciary has expanded. There are now calls to rein in the power of the courts and the discretion of judges in areas ranging from criminal law and sentencing to property rights to liability and torts. How our society deals with these issues will shape the nature of the judiciary—its independence and effectiveness over the generations to come. All indications now are that even the most conservative justices are reluctant to relinquish their newfound power—authority that, once asserted, has become accepted and, thus, established.

Judges enjoy great latitude because they are not subject to electoral pressures. Judges and justices, more than any other politicians in America, can pursue their own ideas about what is right and their own ideologies. They are, however, constrained by rules governing access to the courts, by other courts, by Congress and the president, by their lack of enforcement powers, and most important, by the past in the form of precedent and common law. For much of its history, the federal judiciary acted very cautiously. The Supreme Court rarely challenged Congress or the president. Instead the justices tended to legitimate laws passed by Congress and the actions of the president. The scope of the Court's decisions was limited only to those individuals granted access to the courts.

Two judicial revolutions have expanded the power and reach of the federal judiciary over the decades since World War II. The first of these revolutions brought about the liberalization of a wide range of public policies in the United States. As we saw in Chapter 4, in certain policy areas—including school desegregation, legislative apportionment, and criminal procedure, as well as obscenity, abortion, and voting rights—the Supreme Court was at the forefront of a series of sweeping changes in the role of the U.S. government and, ultimately, the character of American society. The Court put many of these issues before the public long before Congress or the president were prepared to act.

At the same time that the courts were introducing important policy innovations, they were also bringing about a second, less visible revolution. During the 1960s and 1970s, the Supreme Court and other federal courts instituted a series of institutional changes in judicial procedure that had major consequences by fundamentally expanding the power of the courts in the United States. First, the federal courts liberalized the concept of standing to permit almost any group to bring its case before the federal bench. This change has given the courts a far greater role in the administrative process than ever before. Many federal judges are concerned that federal legislation in areas such as health care reform would create new rights and entitlements that would give rise to a deluge of court cases. "Any time you create a new right, you create a host of disputes and claims," warned Barbara Rothstein, chief judge of the federal district court in Seattle, Washington.[27]

In another institutional change, the federal courts broadened the scope of relief to permit action on behalf of broad categories or classes of persons in "class-action" cases, rather than just on behalf of individuals.[28] A class-action suit permits large numbers of persons with common interests to join together under a representative party to bring or defend a lawsuit.

class-action suit
A lawsuit in which a large number of persons with common interests join together under a representative party to bring or defend a lawsuit, as when hundreds of workers join together to sue a company

Finally, the federal courts began to employ so-called structural remedies, in effect retaining jurisdiction of cases until the court's mandate had actually been implemented to its satisfaction.[29] Perhaps the best known of these instances was the federal judge W. Arthur Garrity's effort to operate the Boston school system from his bench in order to ensure its desegregation. Between 1974 and 1985, Judge Garrity issued 14 decisions relating to different aspects of the Boston school desegregation plan that had been developed under his authority and put into effect under his supervision.[30]

Through these judicial mechanisms, the federal courts paved the way for an unprecedented expansion of national judicial power. Thus, during the 1960s and 1970s, the power of the federal courts expanded in the same way that the power of the executive expanded during the 1930s—through links with constituencies, such as civil rights, consumer, environmental, and feminist groups, that staunchly defended the Supreme Court in its battles with Congress, the executive, or other interest groups.

During the 1980s and 1990s, the Reagan and Bush administrations sought to end the relationship between the Court and liberal political forces. Conservative judges appointed by these Republican presidents modified the Court's position in areas such as abortion, affirmative action, and judicial procedure, though not as completely as some conservative writers and politicians had hoped. Within a one-week window in 2003, for example, the Supreme Court affirmed the validity of affirmative action, reaffirmed abortion rights, strengthened gay rights, offered new protection to individuals facing the death penalty, and issued a ruling in favor of a congressional apportionment plan that dispersed minority voters across several districts—a practice that appeared to favor the Democrats.[31] The Court had made these decisions based on the justices' interpretations of precedent and law, not simply personal belief.

The current Court has not been conservative in another sense. It has not been eager to surrender the expanded powers carved out by earlier Courts, especially in areas that assert the power of the national government over the states. Indeed, the early opponents to the U.S. Constitution (the Antifederalists discussed in Chapter 2) feared the assertion of the national interest over the states through the independent judiciary. Over more than two centuries of U.S. history, the reach and authority of the federal judiciary has expanded greatly, and the judiciary has emerged as a powerful arm of our national politics. Whatever their policy beliefs or partisan orientations, judges and justices understand the new importance of the courts among the three branches of American government and act not just to interpret and apply the law but also to maintain the power of the courts.

For Further Reading

Selections highlighted in red are included in *Readings in American Politics: Analysis and Perspectives*, Third Edition.

Abraham, Henry J. *The Judicial Process: An Introductory Analysis of the Courts of the United States, England, and France*. 7th ed. New York: Oxford University Press, 1998.

Baum, Lawrence. *Judges and Their Audiences: A Perspective on Judicial Behavior*. Princeton, NJ: Princeton University Press, 2006.

Bickel, Alexander M. *The Least Dangerous Branch: The Supreme Court at the Bar of Politics*. Indianapolis, IN: Bobbs-Merrill, 1962.

Epstein, Lee, and Jack Knight. *The Choices Justices Make*. Washington, DC: CQ Press, 1998.

Kahn, Ronald. *The Supreme Court and Constitutional Theory, 1953–1993*. Lawrence: University Press of Kansas, 1994.

Marbury v. Madison, 5 U.S. (1 Cranch) 137, 1803.

O'Brien, David M. *Storm Center: The Supreme Court in American Politics*. 10th ed. New York: Norton, 2014.

Perry, H. W., Jr. *Deciding to Decide: Agenda Setting in the United States Supreme Court*. Cambridge, MA: Harvard University Press, 1991.

Rosenberg, Gerald. *The Hollow Hope: Can Courts Bring About Social Change?* 2nd ed. Chicago: University of Chicago Press, 2008.

Segal, Jeffrey A., and Harold J. Spaeth. *The Supreme Court and the Attitudinal Model Revisited*. New York: Cambridge University Press, 2002.

Silverstein, Mark. *Judicious Choices: The New Politics of Supreme Court Confirmations*. 2nd ed. New York: Norton, 2007.

Toobin, Jeffrey. *The Nine: Inside the Secret World of the Supreme Court*. New York: Knopf, 2008.

Whittington, Keith. *Political Foundations of Judicial Supremacy: The President, the Supreme Court, and Constitutional Leadership in U.S. History*. Princeton, NJ: Princeton University Press, 2008.

9

Public Opinion and the Media

In the United States, as in other democracies, citizens expect their government to pay close attention to popular preferences. Most Americans believe that the government does listen to popular opinion most or at least some of the time. This view is bolstered by a number of scholarly studies that have identified a reasonable correlation between national policy and public opinion over time. The political scientist Alan D. Monroe, for example, found that in a majority of cases, changes in public policy followed shifts in popular preferences. Conversely, in most cases, if opinion did not change, neither did policy.[1] In a similar vein, Benjamin I. Page and Robert Y. Shapiro found that much of the time, significant shifts in public opinion were followed by changes in national policy in a direction that seemed to follow opinion.[2] These findings are certainly affirmed by hosts of politicians who not only claim to be guided by the will of the people in all their undertakings, but seem to poll assiduously to find out what that will is.

But does public opinion influence policy as much as we think? Though there is some measure of congruence or consistency between public opinion and public policy, we should not take this to mean that the public's preferences always control the government's conduct. Most citizens do not have strong and autonomous preferences with regard to most public issues. And many lack the basic information that might help them to understand and evaluate policy choices and governmental processes. For example, 40 percent of the Americans responding to a recent survey did not know that each state has two senators; 43 percent did not know what an economic recession is; 68 percent did not know that a two-thirds majority in each house is required for a congressional override of a presidential veto; and 70 percent did not know that the term of a U.S. House member is two years.[3] These findings should give us pause when we examine poll data concerning as complicated a topic as the 2011 debt limit debate, the ongoing debate on immigration reform, or the issue of how to address economic inequality. Many Americans did not have a good understanding of the economic and political implications of the various plans put forward and probably took their cues from politicians they admired. Hence, most Democrats supported the president while most Republicans found merit in the GOP's position.

Indeed, many Americans' knowledge of contemporary political issues is limited to a fact or claim they saw in an ad or heard on a newscast. And, once they acquire a piece of information, many individuals will retain it long after it ceases to be relevant. In a 2005 Harris poll, for example, more than a third of the respondents believed that Iraq possessed weapons of mass destruction at the time of the American invasion—despite the fact that even President Bush had long since acknowledged that no such weapons had existed.

Lack of information and basic political knowledge makes many Americans quite vulnerable to manipulation by politicians and advocates wielding

CORE OF THE ANALYSIS

➡️ Public opinion is the aggregation of individuals' views. It expresses the range of attitudes and beliefs and on which side of any question a majority of people fall.

➡️ There are a wide range of interests at stake in any question that the government must decide, as well as differing preferences, beliefs, and opinions about what ought to be done.

➡️ Politicians follow public opinion as part of the representative process. They take signals from polls and other indicators of public sentiment to gauge whether a particular decision might affect their prospects at the next election.

➡️ The media are an important influence in shaping public opinion.

the instruments of advertising, publicity, and measurement. Their goal, as researchers Lawrence Jacobs and Robert Shapiro note, is to "simulate responsiveness," by developing arguments and ideas that will persuade citizens to agree with their own policy goals.[4] This effort begins with polling. As Clinton pollster Dick Morris affirmed, "you don't use a poll to reshape a program, but to reshape your argumentation for the program so the public supports it."[5] The effort continues with advertising, publicity, and propaganda, making use of the information gleaned from the polls.

Thus, for example, a coalition of forces that succeeded in bringing about the elimination of the estate tax in 2001 first made extensive use of polling and publicity over the course of several years to persuade the public that what they labeled the "death tax" was unfair and un-American. As Michael Graetz and Ian Shapiro show in their research, while the federal estate tax actually affected only the wealthiest 2 percent of the populace, the intensive campaign for its repeal seemed to persuade many Americans that the tax actually affected them. One poll taken in the wake of the repeal campaign suggested that 77 percent of the populace believed the tax affected all Americans, and several polls indicated that more than one-third of the public believed they themselves would have to pay the tax.[6] When the tax was finally annulled by Congress, its elimination was supported by public opinion. But, does this mean that a change in public opinion brought about this change in policy? Hardly. Instead, a particular set of political forces engineered a shift in opinion that helped them to persuade Congress to change national policy. A similar pattern was also observed by political scientists Jacob Hacker and Paul Pierson when they studied recent changes in tax policy. Citizens, they say, "proved vulnerable to extensive manipulation," as political elites framed a discussion that generated popular support for policy changes that served the interests of a small minority of wealthy Americans.[7]

In this chapter, we examine further the role of public opinion in American politics, including the questions raised above: Do Americans know enough to form meaningful opinions about important policy issues? What factors account for differences in opinion? To what extent can the government manipulate popular sentiment? How do the media influence public opinion? Then we take a closer look at one of the most important influences on public opinion, the media.

WHAT IS PUBLIC OPINION?

public opinion

Citizens' attitudes about political issues, personalities, institutions, and events

Public opinion is the aggregation of many citizens' views and interests. It encompasses assessments of those in office, attitudes toward political organizations and social groups, and preferences about how government ought to address important problems. The term sometimes gives the impression that the public has a single opinion on a given matter; however, that is rarely the case.

Americans do hold common views on questions vital to governance and society. There is consensus on the legitimacy of the U.S. Constitution and trust in the rule of law—that is, the principle that no one is above the law. There is consensus that we are a democratic society and that the outcomes of elections, whether or not a person likes the winners, determine who governs. These commonly held opinions and values are essential to maintaining a well-functioning democracy in the United States. They ensure peaceful transitions of government after each election and respect for laws produced by a legitimately chosen government.

There is also wide agreement on fundamental political values, such as equality of opportunity, liberty, and democracy.[8] Nearly all Americans agree that all people should have equal rights, regardless of race, gender, or social standing. Americans hold a common commitment to freedom. People who live in the United States are free to live where they want, travel where they want, work where they want, say what they want, and practice whatever religion they wish, including no religion at all. And Americans have an undying belief in democracy, that whenever possible public officials should be chosen by majority vote.[9] It makes sense to think of the American public as having a single opinion on these elemental questions.

On most matters that come before the government, however, the public does not hold a single view. Usually, opinions are divided between those who support the government or a proposed action and those who do not. Politicians are still attuned to public opinion when it is divided, but what matters most are the balance and direction of opinion. What do the majority of constituents want? Which way is opinion trending? Is it possible to find a popular middle ground?

People express their views to those in power in a variety of ways. Constituents contact their members of Congress directly through letters, phone calls, e-mails, and even personal visits to their representatives' offices. Most questions before Congress elicit little reaction from the public, but some questions start a maelstrom of objections. During the fall of 2008, Congress considered a $700 billion bailout of financial institutions. The volume of e-mail on this bill was so great that at one point the House of Representatives had to limit incoming e-mail to keep its computers from crashing.[10]

People also express their opinions more publicly, through blogs, letters to newspapers and op-ed pieces, and conversations with others. They express their support for candidates with lawn signs and bumper stickers; by working on campaigns; giving money to candidates, groups, and party organizations; and, most simply, by voting.

Expressions of opinions and preferences are not always easy to interpret. If a constituent votes against a member of Congress, did the voter do so because of a controversial decision that the legislator made in Congress, or because the voter decided to vote against all politicians from the legislator's party? Or for some other reason?

Political scientists and political consultants try to provide more refined and structured descriptions of public opinion using surveys. On any important issue, the government may pursue different policies. Public opinion on a given issue can often be thought of as the distribution of opinion across the different options. Likewise, public opinion may represent the division of support for a leader or party. We try to gauge where majority support lies and how intensely or firmly citizens across the spectrum hold their views. More and more, politicians rely on opinion polls to anticipate the effects of their decisions, to identify opportunities, and to develop ways to blunt the objections to controversial decisions. Answering a survey, then, can also be a form of political action, because it may influence political decisions.

ORIGINS AND NATURE OF PUBLIC OPINION

To understand the meaning and origins of the public's opinions, we must have some sense of the basis for individuals' preferences and beliefs. An individual's opinions are the products of his or her personality, social characteristics, and interests. They mirror who a person is, what she wants, and the manner in which she is embedded in a family and community, and the broader economy and society. But opinions are also shaped by institutional, political, and governmental forces that make it more likely that an individual will hold some beliefs and less likely that he will hold others.

Foundations of Preferences

At a foundational level, individual opinion is shaped by several factors, including self-interest, values about what is right and wrong, and the process of socialization.

Self-Interest. Individuals' preferences about politics and public policy are rooted partly in self-interest. Laws and other governmental actions directly affect people's interests—their disposable income, the quality of public services and goods, and personal safety, to give just a few examples. It is not surprising, then, that when people express their political opinions, they react to the effects that government actions have on them personally.

Economic interests are perhaps the most salient preferences when it comes to people's opinions. Virtually every American has an interest in the government's role in the nation's economy and strong preferences about tax rates and expenditure priorities. Public opinion about taxes and spending reflects these preferences. Given the enormous influence of the federal government in the macro economy, assessments of the president and the party in power often correspond to how well the nation's economy performs.

Individuals' attitudes toward government reflect other forms of self-interest as well. Laws affect families, the status of civic and religious organizations, and communities. Zoning laws and urban redevelopment programs shape the nature of neighborhoods, including the mix of commercial and residential housing and the density of low-income housing in an area. Family law affects how easy it is for families to stay together, what happens when they break down, and what rights and responsibilities parents have. Individuals have a personal stake in decisions bearing on their own communities and families. Proposed changes in such laws bring immediate reaction from those affected.

Values. Much of what individuals want from their government is rooted in values about what is right or wrong and our philosophies about morality, justice, and ethics. Most of us have values systems—principles of right and wrong that we apply to new problems and circumstances. Such values systems originate in many places—families, religion, education, groups, and so forth—and they shape what we want. Values regarding what is right and wrong may determine an individual's preferences about how government and society distribute or redistribute income. Americans generally adhere to a belief in equal opportunity. So long as all people have an equal opportunity, an equal chance to excel, we have a just society. That idea has driven our society to try to root out discrimination in employment, housing, and education. It has also led us to create a universal public education system. In some states, such as New Hampshire, Ohio, and California, courts have invoked this principle of equality to insist that the states try to equalize public school expenditures per pupil across districts.

Values also shape our notions of what is a crime and what is a suitable punishment. One of the most morally laden debates in American history is the debate over capital punishment. Does the government have the right to take the life of an individual if that individual has taken the life of someone else? An ancient sense of justice seems to call for exactly that: an eye for an eye. Other ideas of morality speak against capital punishment, advising that we should turn the other cheek. In addition, our values about government and its appropriate powers say that people must be protected against arbitrary and capricious acts of government. The death penalty is irreversible, and the possibility of a governmental error has led some to claim that the government can never have the power to take the life of an individual. In 1972, the U.S. Supreme Court ruled just that in *Furman v. Georgia*, though it validated the death penalty in certain cases just four years later.

Our values also reflect established social norms of our community, analogous to common law. What, for example, is marriage? One might argue that marriage is an economic convenience, as defined by laws that tie taxes and inheritance to marital status. Most people, however, express more complex ideas of marriage, and those principles dictate whether they think that same-sex marriages ought to be allowed. Such norms change over time.

At a societal level, conflicting values are particularly difficult to resolve. Unlike economic interests, it is hard to bargain over our differences when the differences strike at fundamental principles of right and wrong. By the same token, there are many values that unite us. Probably no nation, and certainly no democracy, could survive if its citizens did not share some fundamental beliefs. If Americans had few common values or perspectives, it would be very difficult for them to reach agreement on particular issues. Over the past half-century, political philosophers and political scientists have reflected on what those values are and settled on three important precepts. Americans almost universally agree with (1) the democracy principle (that majority rule is a good decision rule), (2) the equal opportunity principle, and (3) the principle that the government is best that governs least.

Social Groups. Another source of political preferences is social groups. People use race, religion, place, language, and many other characteristics to describe and define themselves. These descriptors tap fundamental psychological attachments that go beyond self-interest and values, though they are often reinforced by our interests and values.

Membership in a social group may affect individual opinion. For example, many Latinos oppose harsh immigration laws, even if they are not personally directly affected by the laws.

The process through which our social interactions and social groups change our perspectives and preferences is called socialization. Most eighteen-year-olds already have definite political attitudes even though they have not yet voted, and they have learned those opinions and attitudes from their parents and grandparents, their friends, their teachers and religious leaders, and others in their social groups and networks. Of course, socialization does not end upon leaving home. We learn about politics and even what we should think about complex political questions from our family members, coworkers, and others we see and speak with daily.

Socialization works many different ways. One way is simply to provide information. Social groups are one of the main ways that people stay abreast with what is going on in their community and even in national politics. Socialization also takes the form of education or instruction. Parents teach their children how to think about a problem, what is a right or wrong choice or action, and even how to participate in politics. There is nothing wrong with this; indeed, it is how we as humans have learned to survive and adapt. But it does mean that we have, by the time we are adults, already learned much about what we want government to do, what sorts of people we want in government, and even whether it is worth our while to participate.

▶ **socialization**
A process through which individuals assimilate community preferences and norms through social interactions

Political Ideology

An ideology is a comprehensive way of understanding political or cultural situations. It is a set of assumptions about the way the world and society works that helps us to organize our beliefs, information, and new situations. It ascribes values to different alternatives (this is good, that is bad).

In America today, people often describe themselves as liberals or conservatives. Liberalism and conservatism are political ideologies that include beliefs about the role of government, ideas about public policies, and notions about which groups in society should properly exercise power. In earlier times, these terms were defined somewhat differently. As recently as the nineteenth century, a liberal was an individual who favored freedom from state control, whereas a conservative was someone who supported the use of governmental power and favored continuation of the influence of the church and the aristocracy in national life.

Today, in the United States, the term liberal has come to imply support for political and social reform; government intervention in the economy; the expansion of federal social services; more vigorous efforts on behalf of the poor, minorities, and women; and greater concern for consumers and the environment. In social and cultural areas, liberals generally support abortion rights and oppose state involvement with religious institutions and religious expression. In international affairs, liberal positions usually include support for arms control, opposition to the development and testing of nuclear weapons, support for aid to poor nations, opposition to the use of American troops to influence the domestic affairs of developing nations, and support for international organizations such as the United Nations. Of course, liberalism is not monolithic. For example, among individuals who view themselves as liberal, many support American military intervention when it is tied to a humanitarian purpose, as in the case of America's military action in Kosovo in 1998–99. Most liberals initially supported President George W. Bush's war on terrorism even when some of the president's actions seemed to curtail civil liberties.

By contrast, the term conservative today is used to describe those who generally support the social and economic status quo, favor markets as solutions to social problems, and are suspicious of government involvement in the economy. Conservatives believe that a large and powerful government poses a threat to citizens' freedom. Thus in the domestic arena conservatives generally oppose the expansion of governmental activity, asserting that solutions to social and economic problems can be developed in the private sector. Conservatives in particular oppose efforts to impose government regulation on business, pointing out that such regulation is frequently economically inefficient and costly and can ultimately lower the entire nation's standard of living. As for social and cultural positions, many conservatives oppose abortion and support school prayer. In international affairs, conservatism has come to mean support for the maintenance of American military power. Like liberalism, conservatism is far from a monolithic ideology. Some conservatives support many government social programs. Other conservatives oppose efforts to outlaw abortion, arguing that government intrusion

liberal ➡

A liberal today generally supports political and social reform; governmental intervention in the economy; the expansion of federal social services; more vigorous efforts on behalf of the poor, minorities, and women; and greater concern for consumers and the environment

conservative ➡

Today this term refers to one who generally supports the social and economic status quo and is suspicious of efforts to introduce new political formulae and economic arrangements. Many conservatives believe that a large and powerful government poses a threat to citizens' freedoms in this area is as misguided as government intervention in the economy. The real political world is far too complex to be seen in terms of a simple struggle between liberals and conservatives.

There are many other ideologies besides liberal and conservative. Some people seek to expand liberty above all other principles and wish to minimize government intervention in the economy and society. Such a position is sometimes called libertarian. Other ideologies seek a particular outcome, such as environmental protection. Such a stance may emphasize certain issues, such as economic growth, and de-emphasize other issues, such as abortion. Communism and fascism are ideologies that involve government control of all aspects of the economy and society. These ideologies dominated politics in many European countries from the 1920s through the 1940s. Political discourse in the United States, however, has revolved around the division between liberals and conservatives for most of the last century.

Political scientists often think of liberal and conservative ideologies as anchors on a spectrum of possible belief systems. Our own values and interests might make us adhere to many of the tenets and policy positions of one of these ideologies but not all. The Pew Center on People and the Press offers just such a classification in its American Values Survey, conducted annually since 1987.[11] The Pew survey asks respondents about a wide range of political, social, and cultural preferences, behaviors, and beliefs. Classifying people this way, the Pew Center finds that a large plurality of Americans are in fact very moderate—having as many conservative views as liberal views.

Identity Politics

Ideology offers one lens through which people can discern where their interests and values lie in political choices. Identity provides an alternative simplification of the political world. Political identities are distinctive characteristics or group associations that individuals carry, reflecting individuals' social connections or common values and interests with others in that group. A harm or benefit to any individual with a given identity is viewed as a harm or benefit to all people of that identity.

Identities are both psychological and sociological. At the psychological level they are attachments felt by individuals, and at the sociological level they function at the collective level, such as racial groups, genders, or language groups. Unlike ideological politics, identities are absolutes, and identity politics are often zero-sum: one group wins and another loses. The term *identity politics* is sometimes used today to refer to groups that have been oppressed and that seek to assert their rights. But the concept is much broader. *Political identity* is not just a term that describes the situation of groups that have suffered some harm; it applies to any collective identity. In fact, political identity often has a very positive side, as the glue that holds society together and as another way to overcome problems of collective action.[12]

Identity politics are quite obvious in the United States today. All citizens of the United States and even many noncitizens identify themselves as Americans. During international sporting competitions, we root for athletes representing the United States because we identify with that country, and when those athletes win, Americans feel happy and proud. We may feel similarly when an American wins a Nobel Prize or makes a significant scientific discovery. The same is true of people from any country: we feel pride in the accomplishments of others from our country.

One of the most salient political identities in the United States is political party. The authors of *The American Voter*, a now classic work of political science research on the social and psychological foundations of electoral behavior in the United States, characterize party identification as a stable psychological attachment usually developed in childhood and carried throughout one's adult life. Party identifications are, of course, shaped by interests and values as well as by current events, but partisanship also has deep roots in family, local culture, and other factors that shape identities. It is common, for example, for people to rely on their partisan identities in filtering information. Partisan identifiers who watch presidential debates overwhelmingly think their candidate won the debate, regardless of what actually transpired. Party also has its own unique hold on our voting behavior. Even after taking into account self-interests, moral values, and other identities, partisanship continues to be one of the best predictors of how someone will vote. (See the discussion of party voting in Chapters 10 and 11.) This is not to say that party does not reflect ideological choices or self-interest. It does. But it is certainly also the case that party functions as a social identity.

People who hold a specific identity often express strong affinity for others of the same identity. You might vote for someone of the same national background or ethnicity quite apart from, or in spite of, the sorts of laws that politicians promise to enact. Political scientists call this preference for like types of people "descriptive representation." The preference for people of the same identity is an important subject in the area of race and elections. The Voting Rights Act tries to protect African Americans, Hispanics, and other racial and ethnic groups against discriminatory electoral practices that prevent those voters from electing their preferred candidates. Since the Voting Rights Act was passed in 1965, the percentage of members of Congress who are African American or Hispanic increased from 0 to about 15 to 20 percent. Race, gender, social class, and place all create strong identities that shape voting behavior.

People have a wide range of social, cultural, and political identities. Gender and race are obvious, especially because of physical characteristics. Religions, regions of the country, sexual orientations, occupations, and many other distinctive characteristics of people also function as identities. Americans have identities based on who they are, where they live, and how they live, and these identities can have a large impact on individuals' preferences and political behavior.

Blacks. The practice of slavery in the colonies and early American states created a deep, lasting divide in our society between whites and blacks. That division is reflected in a staggering number of statistics, from wages and education levels to poverty levels to neighborhood integration to political ideals. There are, for example, stark differences between blacks and whites in their beliefs about the basic responsibilities of government for providing shelter, food, and other basic necessities to those in need.[13] Blacks and whites also differ in their views of equality of opportunity in the United States, which can impact their preferences for policies that address perceived disadvantages (Figure 9.1).

More striking still, race seems to affect how other factors, like income and education, shape preferences. Among whites, there is a definite correlation between conservatism and income. Higher-income whites tend to support more conservative policies and are more likely to identify with the Republican Party, while lower-income whites tend to favor more liberal economic policies and align with the Democratic Party. Nearly all African Americans, on the other hand, side with the Democrats and support liberal economic policies, regardless of income. Why are high-income African Americans not as supportive of Republicans as their white counterparts? There are many other such instances, including differences across religious groups, between men and women, and between young and old. Some of these differences may be traced to self-interest, but most cannot. The explanations for differences in opinions and voting behaviors among social groups surely have something to do with the nature of such groups in American society.

Latinos. Latinos are another major American subgroup with distinctive opinions on some public issues. For instance, in a 2014 poll, 60 percent of Hispanic voters approved of the Affordable Care Act, while 61 percent of non-Hispanic whites disapproved—a significant disparity.[14] In addition, Hispanic voters routinely identify immigration as one of their top concerns, while the issue ranks lower in priority among non-Hispanic white voters.

Hispanic political identities have a different character than political identities of blacks. Hispanic and Latino group identities are often rooted in particular immigrant communities such as Mexican Americans, Cubans, and Puerto Ricans.[15] And, Hispanic and Latino political identities are strongly tied to particular issues of immigration.[16] These differences have led to

Although America's
system of legally
mandated racial
segregation ended
nearly half a century
ago, its effects
continue to linger. In
contemporary America,
blacks and whites have
different perspectives
on race relations. Do
you think that black–
white differences
have increased or
decreased in the past
few decades? Are these
differences of opinion
important?

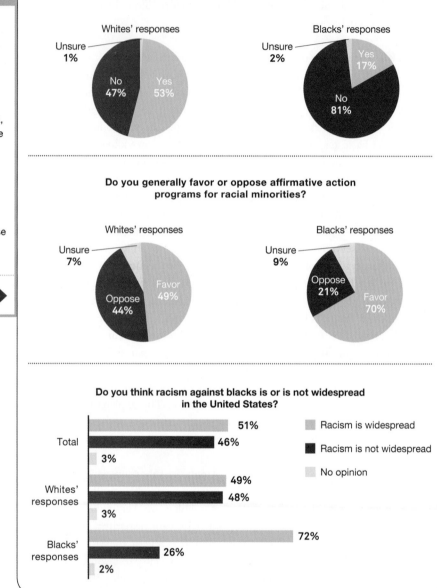

Figure 9.1
DISAGREEMENT AMONG BLACKS AND WHITES

**Do you feel that racial minorities in this country have
equal job opportunities as whites, or not?**

Whites' responses

Unsure 1%
No 47%
Yes 53%

Blacks' responses

Unsure 2%
Yes 17%
No 81%

**Do you generally favor or oppose affirmative action
programs for racial minorities?**

Whites' responses

Unsure 7%
Oppose 44%
Favor 49%

Blacks' responses

Unsure 9%
Oppose 21%
Favor 70%

**Do you think racism against blacks is or is not widespread
in the United States?**

Total — 51% / 46% / 3%

Whites' responses — 49% / 48% / 3%

Blacks' responses — 72% / 26% / 2%

- Racism is widespread
- Racism is not widespread
- No opinion

NOTE: Percentages may not sum to 100 due to rounding.
SOURCES: Gallup polls, June 8–25, 2006, June 12–15, 2003, and October 16–19, 2009, gallup.com.

Table 9.1

CHANGING PARTY AFFILIATION IN THE LATINO COMMUNITY

BACKGROUND	2004		2008		2012	
	DEM. (%)	REP. (%)	DEM. (%)	REP. (%)	DEM. (%)	REP. (%)
Cuban	17	52	53	20	51	37
Mexican	47	18	50	18	64	18
Puerto Rican	50	17	61	11	74	10

SOURCE: Pew Hispanic Center, "2008 National Survey of Latinos" and "2012 National Survey of Latinos," www. pewhispanic.org (accessed 11/13/14).

heterogeneity in opinion among Latinos on certain issues. Among Latinos, Cuban Americans were long disproportionately Republican, while those of Mexican, Puerto Rican, and Central American descent identify more often as Democrats (Table 9.1). That difference traces to Cuban Americans' relationship with their homeland and the long-standing policy differences between the Republicans and Democrats over Cuba. Interestingly, that difference had largely vanished by 2008; surveys during the presidential campaign found that Cuban American were nearly as Democratic as other Hispanic groups.

As with blacks, Latino identity tempers the way other demographic characteristics translate into political identities and values. Although higher-income Latinos are more Republican than lower-income Latinos, the differences are not as stark as among whites, and low-income Latinos are much more Democratic than low-income whites. Latinos' identity mutes the political effects of other characteristics.

Gender. Men and women express differing political opinions as well. Women tend to be less militaristic than men on issues of war and peace, more likely than men to favor measures to protect the environment, and more supportive than men of government social- and health-care programs (Table 9.2). Perhaps because of these differences on issues, women are more likely than men to vote for Democratic candidates, whereas men have become increasingly supportive of Republicans.[17] This tendency for men's and women's opinions to differ is called the gender gap. The gender gap in voting first emerged quite clearly in the 1980 election and has persisted, averaging about 8 percentage points.

gender gap
A distinctive pattern of voting behavior reflecting the differences in views between women and men

Table 9.2

DISAGREEMENTS AMONG MEN AND WOMEN ON ISSUES OF WAR AND PEACE

GOVERNMENT ACTION	APPROVE OF ACTION (%)	
	MEN	WOMEN
Support U.S. missile strikes against Syria (2013)	43	30
Use U.S. troops to attack a terrorist camp (2012)	71	55
Support withdrawal of troops from Iraq (2008)	70	52
Use U.S. troops to intervene in a genocide or civil war (2008)	53	42
Go to war against Iraq (2003)	66	50
Broker a cease-fire in Yugoslavia instead of using NATO air strikes (1999)	44	51
End the ban on homosexuals in the military (1993)	34	51
Go to war against Iraq (1991)	72	53

SOURCES: Gallup polls, 1991, 1993, and 1999; *Washington Post*, 2003; Cooperative Congressional Election Study, 2008 and 2012; Langer Research, 2013.

Why the gender gap emerged 30 years ago and persists today is something of a puzzle. Many speculate that reproductive rights and abortion politics lie at the root of this division. Yet surprisingly, the gender gap has virtually vanished on the abortion issue. An August 2006 Pew Research Center poll indicated that men and women are nearly identical—52 percent versus 51 percent—on the issue of allowing abortion in general or on a limited basis, and 46 percent of both men and women believe abortion should always or almost always be illegal.[18] Rather, the gender gap appears to be more clearly attributable to wages, inheritance, and other differences between the ways that men and women are treated in the economy and society, and to the sense among women that they have a shared objective of ensuring equal treatment for all women.[19]

Religion. Religion shapes peoples' values and beliefs and, thus, political ideologies, but it also serves as a strong identity quite apart from what values are at play. One of the clearest examples was the attachment of Catholics to the Democratic Party. This began in 1924 with the nomination of Al Smith, a Catholic, for president of the United States by the Democratic Party. When Democrat John Kennedy became the country's first Catholic president in 1961, that bond was strengthened.[20] The lesson of the Kennedy election is quite sharp: people are much more likely to vote for candidates of the same religion, even after controlling for ideology, party, and other measures of value. This pattern held true for born-again Christians and Jimmy Carter in 1976 and for Mormons and Mitt Romney in 2012.

Geography. Where we live also molds our sense of identity. People pick up on subtle cues, such as another person's accent or how a person dresses or even wears his hair as an indicator of where that person is from. People from different regions of the country, even from specific states, often have a strong identification with others from that region or state. They are more likely to trust someone of the same region or state as them, and they are more likely to vote for that person. And, people often hold negative stereotypes of people from other regions. An unfortunate consequence of the Civil War is a lasting discomfort that many people from the North and South still feel around one another—and that conflict was 150 years ago. Yet to this day Americans contest the symbols of that conflict, such as whether a southern state should have a Confederate battle flag as part of its state's symbol or flying in the statehouse.

Other geographic identities are tied to the type of community one lives in (or prefers to live in). The division between those in urban and rural areas often reflects self-interest—who gets what from the government. For instance, people from states that have predominantly agricultural economies express stronger support for government farm subsidies. But geography also reflects different ways of living, and we tend to identify with people who live like us. Such differences are cultural. Where we shop, what restaurants we frequent, what we like to do in our spare time, and so forth—all are aspects of our local culture. They shape our identification with others of like backgrounds, experiences, and ways of living.

Residential segregation can also strengthen other aspects of identity politics. People segregate according to income, which might strengthen social class identities, and race and ethnicity, which reinforces racial and ethnic identities. Those who live in highly segregated neighborhoods have much stronger identities with their own racial groups, and they also express much stronger prejudices against other groups.[21]

Outgroups. Some groups are defined not by who they are but by who they are not; they are the outgroups in society. Discrimination is one manifestation of the treatment of an outgroup. If a group is well organized, it can achieve higher success but usually at the expense of those defined not to be in that group. Often an outgroup is clearly identifiable and ostracized, leading to systematic discrimination or persecution. When the discrimination is intense, systematic, and long held, the outgroup can itself develop a particular psychology. Social psychologist James Sidanius expresses this as a social dominance relationship and argues that more numerous groups in all societies systematically discriminate against less numerous groups. The less numerous groups develop a common identity, and they come to see their own situation in the treatment of others of their group.[22] Writing about the particular psychology of African Americans in the United States, Professor Michael Dawson calls this the "linked fate" of African Americans. Groups that have experienced severe discrimination over very long periods of time are most likely to feel a sense of linked fate, which helps account for the persistence of a sense of common identity that remains strong in some groups.[23]

Political, social, and economic discrimination is not limited to race and ethnicity. As we discussed in Chapter 4, the United States has witnessed struggles for equity for many different groups including women, Catholics, Jews, homosexuals, divorced fathers, and even people in urban areas. In all of these cases, people who were part of these groups had to assert themselves politically in order to establish or protect their rights to property, to vote, and to equal protection of the laws. It is exceedingly difficult for those with diminished political rights to work inside the legislative process, and so these people often had to pursue outsider strategies including protests, propaganda, and litigation. The reason that they had their rights abrogated was because they were treated as a class or group, and their identity was the target of discrimination. That very same identity, however, served as a source of power, as it ultimately led these groups to organize and to defend their political rights and identities.

KNOWLEDGE AND INSTABILITY IN PUBLIC OPINION

People are constantly confronted with new political events, issues, and personalities as they watch television, surf the web, talk to friends and family, or read the news. In our democracy we expect every citizen to have views about the major problems of the day as well as opinions about who should be entrusted with the nation's leadership, and we expect people to cast informed votes that convey their preferences about what government ought to do. Issues, however, come and go, and people are continually learning about new issues the nation faces.

Political Knowledge and Democracy

Some Americans know quite a bit about politics, and many have general views and hold opinions on several issues. Few Americans, though, devote sufficient time, energy, or attention to politics to really understand or evaluate the myriad issues with which they are bombarded on a regular basis. Since the advent of polling in the 1930s, studies have repeatedly found that the average American appears to know little about current events or even basic facts of American government.[24]

Why do people seem to know so little, and what might be the consequence of low levels of information about current events and political institutions for the long-run health of democracy? Attending to the day-to-day goings-on in Washington or the state capital or city council is costly; it means spending time at the very least, and often money as well, to collect, organize, and digest political information.[25] Balanced against this cost to an individual is the very low probability that he or she will, on the basis of this costly information, take an action that would not otherwise have been taken and that such a departure in behavior would make a beneficial difference to him or her and that such a difference, if it existed, would exceed the cost of acquiring the information in the first place. Because individuals anticipate that informed actions they take will rarely make much difference and that the costs of informing oneself are often not trivial, it may be rational to remain ignorant. In other words, the rationality principle suggests that many people should more profitably devote their personal resources—particularly their time—to more narrowly personal matters. This idea is in turn suggested by the collective action principle, in which the bearing of burdens— such as the cost of becoming informed—is not likely to have much impact in a mass political setting. A more moderate version of "rational" ignorance recognizes that some kinds of information are inexpensive to acquire, such as sound bites from the evening news, or can be pleasant, such as reading the front page of the newspaper while drinking a cup of coffee. In such cases, an individual may become partially informed, but usually not in detail.

Precisely because becoming truly knowledgeable about politics requires a substantial investment of time and energy, many Americans seek to acquire political information and to make political decisions on the cheap, using shortcuts, labels, and stereotypes, rather than following current events closely. One "inexpensive" way to become informed is to take cues from trusted others—the local minister, the television commentator or newspaper editorialist, an interest-group leader, friends, and relatives.[26] A common shortcut for political evaluation and decision making is to assess new issues and events through the lenses of one's general beliefs and orientation. Thus if a conservative learns of a plan to expand federal social programs, she might express opposition to the endeavor without needing to pore over the specifics of the proposal.

These shortcuts are handy, but not perfect. Taking cues from others may lead individuals to accept positions that they would not support if they had more information. And general ideological orientations can be coarse guides to decision making on concrete issues. For example, what position should a liberal take on immigration? Should a liberal favor keeping America's borders open to poor people from all over the world, or should he be concerned that America's open borders create a pool of surplus labor that permits giant corporations to drive down the wages of poor American workers? Many other issues defy easy ideological characterization.

Although understandable and perhaps inevitable, widespread inattentiveness to politics weakens American democracy in two ways. First, those who lack political information might not truly understand where their interests lie, and they might not effectively defend their political interests. Second, the presence of large numbers of politically inattentive or ignorant individuals means that the political process can be more easily manipulated by the various institutions and forces that seek to shape public opinion.

As to the first of these problems, in our democracy millions of ordinary citizens take part in political life, at least to the extent of voting in national elections. Those with little knowledge of the election's issues, candidates, or procedures can find themselves acting against their own preferences and interests. One example is U.S. tax policy. Over the past several decades, the United States has substantially reduced the rate of taxation for its wealthiest citizens.[27] Tax cuts signed into law by President Bush in 2001 and mostly maintained throughout the decade provided a tax break mainly for the top 1 percent of the nation's wage earners, and further tax cuts proposed by the president offered additional benefits to this privileged stratum. Polling data show that millions of middle-class and lower-middle-class Americans who did not stand to benefit from the president's tax cuts seemed to favor them nonetheless. Their support for these taxes might have been based on principle. Opinion in favor of the 2001 tax cuts among middle-and lower-income people might also have arisen out of ignorance or by following the wrong cue-givers.[28] Millions of individuals who were unlikely to derive much advantage from President Bush's tax policy thought they would.[29] Knowledge may not always translate into political power, but lack of knowledge is almost certain to translate into political weakness.

Campaigns and other forums for public discourse can change public attitudes on issues by altering the nature of the choices or informing the public about the effects of policies. Continued debate of the tax issue throughout the 2008 and 2012 presidential campaigns brought about changes in public attitudes toward taxes, especially on the wealthiest segment of the population. During the 2008 presidential election campaign, Barack Obama seized on the tax issue at a time when the economy was worsening and people's economic prospects looked bleak. He returned to that theme during the 2012 election, promising to raise taxes on the top 2 percent of income earners, those who make at least $250,000 a year. That promise was instrumental in both of President Obama's successful election campaigns. In January 2013, staring at potential automatic tax increases on all Americans, Obama was able to outmaneuver the Republican leadership in Congress and increase taxes on income over $400,000 per year, a tax increase that affected only 1 percent of the population, but nearly failed to make it through the Congress.

Instability in Opinion

There is great stability to public opinion in the United States. What people want government to do on specific issues and who people want to have in charge usually changes little from election to election. On most issues and political attitudes, aggregate public opinion is quite stable. Consider party identification. Almost all people who identify with a party in one election remain with that party in the next election. Indeed, a large fraction of the American public remains Republican for life or Democrat for life. Such stability is also observed in other aspects of people's political preferences. Individuals' notions of what is right and wrong are often formed in childhood and remain fairly stable throughout their lives. Our racial and ethnic identities, gender identities, and other cultural identities are also formed early in life and are quite stable. Our occupations and educational achievement also shape our economic interests, and those tend to be constant throughout our adult lives. Interests, identities, and values, in turn, influence attitudes about when and how government should act.

But it is also clear that public opinion is not static. At times in American history, the majority of Americans' opinions have changed dramatically and rapidly. Between 1945 and 1965, public opinion toward federal action to promote racial equality swung from majority opposition to majority support for the Civil Rights Act and Voting Rights Act as well as for integration of schools and public conveyances. During the late 1960s, public attitudes about taxation changed. Up until that time, most Americans supported high taxes because they believed they promoted the common good. Since the early 1970s, the nation has been divided over the question of taxes, especially income taxes.[30] And since the mid-1990s there has been a near about-face in public attitudes toward same-sex marriage. In 1996, Congress passed the Defense of Marriage Act, which defined marriage as a union between one man and one woman for the purpose of federal benefits. A CNN/USA Today/Gallup poll in 1996 showed that 68 percent of Americans opposed same-sex marriage and only 27 percent supported it. By 2014, a Gallup poll found that 55 percent of Americans supported same-sex marriage and 42 percent opposed it. (The Analyzing the Evidence unit in this section considers the shift in public opinion on same-sex marriage.)

In each of these cases, public attitudes changed quickly—within the span of one or two decades. How and why does public opinion change? In part, the answer lies in the evolving positions of the political choices and elite discourse. As party leaders, celebrities, and other elites debate an issue, the public often follows cues and takes sides. The answer also surely lies with public learning. As the public learns about an issue, the implications of government action and inaction become clearer, as does the right thing to do. In turn, such evolutions in public opinion influence public policy, which is fairly responsive to shifts in public opinion.

SHAPING OPINION: POLITICAL LEADERS, PRIVATE GROUPS, AND THE MEDIA

The fact that many Americans are inattentive to politics and lack even basic political information means that there is a place for public debate and political discourse. Controversy educates us. Through debate, the average person learns what is important and the information needed to make sensible decisions. The lack of information also creates opportunities to influence how the public thinks. Although direct efforts to manipulate opinion often don't succeed, three forces play especially important roles in shaping opinion. These are the government, private groups, and the news media.

Government and Political Leaders

All governments attempt, to a greater or lesser extent, to influence, manipulate, or manage their citizens' beliefs. But the extent to which public opinion is actually affected by governmental public relations efforts is probably limited. The government—despite its size and power—is only one source of information and evaluation in the United States. Very often, governmental claims are disputed by the media, by interest groups, and at times by opposing forces within the government itself.

Influences on Public Opinion

Government

Political leaders try to present their initiatives and accomplishments in a positive light and to generate positive media coverage. However, their claims are often disputed by the media, interest groups, and opposing forces within the government.

Private Groups

Interest groups work to draw attention to issues and ideas that will further their cause.

The Media

The mass media are Americans' main source of information about government and politics. They influence opinion by bringing attention to particular issues (the agenda-setting effect), priming the public to take a certain view of a political actor, and framing issues and events in a certain way.

Often, too, governmental efforts to manipulate public opinion backfire when the public is made aware of the government's tactics. Thus, in 1971, the U.S. government's efforts to build popular support for the Vietnam War were hurt when CBS News aired its documentary *The Selling of the Pentagon*, which revealed the extent and character of government efforts to sway popular sentiment. In this documentary, CBS demonstrated the techniques, including planted news stories and faked film footage, that the government had used to misrepresent its activities in Vietnam. These revelations, of course, had the effect of undermining popular trust in all government claims.

A hallmark of the Clinton administration was the steady use of campaign techniques such as those used in election campaigns to bolster popular enthusiasm for White House initiatives. The president established a "political war room" in the Executive Office Building similar to the one that operated in his campaign headquarters. Representatives from all departments met in the war room every day to discuss and coordinate the president's public-relations efforts. Many of the same consultants and pollsters who directed the successful Clinton campaign were employed in the selling of the president's programs.[31]

The Contact Hypothesis and Attitudes about Gay Rights

Contributed by
Patrick J. Egan
New York University

Americans' attitudes toward gay rights have evolved significantly over the past 20 years. In 1996, opponents of gay marriage in the United States greatly outnumbered supporters by 65 to 27 percent. By 2012, Americans favored gay marriage by 49 to 40 percent.

Americans' Attitudes toward Same-Sex Marriage, 1996–2012

SOURCE: Pew Research Center, 2012.

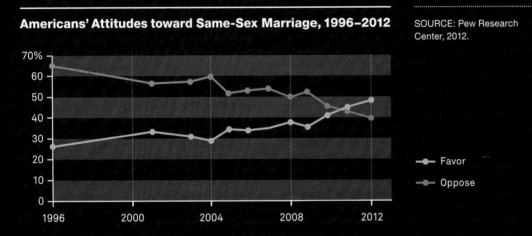

What explains this change in American attitudes? A theory from social psychology known as the *contact hypothesis* holds that contact between in-group and out-group members reduces the stigma directed toward the out-group. In this case, are straight people (the in-group) who know openly gay people (the out-group) more supportive of gay rights? The graphs show that support for gay rights has increased at the same time that growing shares of Americans have reported knowing gays and lesbians.

Americans' Contact with Gays and Lesbians, 1984–2008

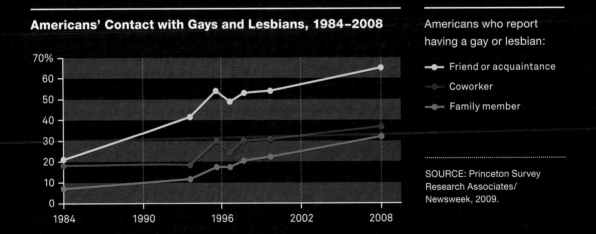

Americans who report having a gay or lesbian:

- Friend or acquaintance
- Coworker
- Family member

SOURCE: Princeton Survey Research Associates/ Newsweek, 2009.

Furthermore, those who report having gay friends are indeed significantly more supportive of gay rights than those who do not. We can see this by creating a composite score for survey respondents based on their opinions on such issues as gay marriage, adoption, and job discrimination. A score of 100 is fully supportive of all gay rights. Those with gay friends score an estimated 43 on the scale; those who report having no gay friends score only 36 (see graph below).

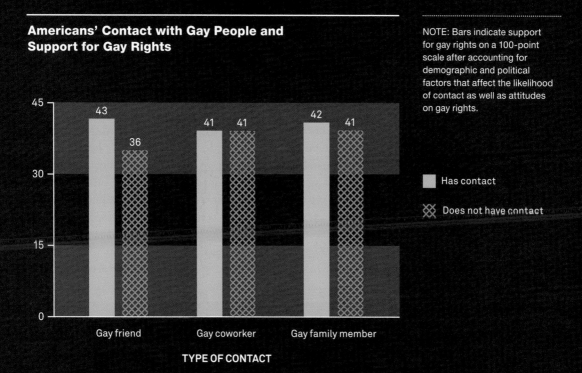

Americans' Contact with Gay People and Support for Gay Rights

NOTE: Bars indicate support for gay rights on a 100-point scale after accounting for demographic and political factors that affect the likelihood of contact as well as attitudes on gay rights.

Has contact

Does not have contact

TYPE OF CONTACT

But can we be sure that contact with gay people is actually *causing* increased support for gay rights? One concern is selection bias. Gay people may be selective about disclosing their identity to those friends whom they already know to be supportive, and straight people who hold more tolerant attitudes may be more likely to select gay people as friends.

To further explore this question, we can examine types of contact that are governed less by selection. While we typically do chose our friends, coworkers and family members are essentially chosen for us. These types of contact thus offer much cleaner tests of the contact hypothesis. As shown in the bar graph above, in these contexts the effect of contact on attitudes is essentially zero (i.e., individuals with gay coworkers or gay family members are no more supportive of gay rights than those without).

This evidence thus runs counter to the contact hypothesis. But it does not entirely settle the question, and some political scientists have presented results in support of the hypothesis. When political scientists find evidence against a hypothesis, they consider different theories. For example, it may be that it is not the *type* but the *quality* of contact that changes attitudes. Definitive answers to these questions await discovery through additional research.

The Obama White House has sought to make the most of new technologies in communicating with the public and promoting the president's agenda. These strategies have included weekly podcasts.

After he assumed office in 2001, President George W. Bush asserted that political leaders should base their programs on their own conception of the public interest rather than the polls. This, however, did not mean that Bush ignored public opinion. Bush relied on the pollster Jan van Lohuizen to conduct a low-key operation, sufficiently removed from the limelight to allow the president to renounce polling while continuing to make use of survey data.[32] At the same time, the Bush White House developed an extensive public-relations program to bolster popular support for the president's policies. These efforts included presidential speeches, media appearances by administration officials, numerous press conferences, and thousands of press releases presenting the administration's views. The White House also made a substantial effort to sway opinion in foreign countries, even sending officials to present the administration's views on television networks serving the Arab world.

Not all political media strategies work. President Obama, attempting to maintain the political momentum from his 2008 election campaign, attempted to use social media to keep up the same buzz about his legislative agenda. He brought Macon Philips, who developed the campaign's social media strategy, into the White House team to organize the effort. The White House maintains a newsy website, a blog, a YouTube channel, a Facebook page, and a Twitter account. But many have criticized the low level of actual engagement with the people. Each of these new media is being used like the old media—to talk at people rather than with them, to disseminate information to the press rather than respond to reporters' questions. Indeed, many White House reporters feel that the Obama press office is less accessible than its predecessors.[33]

Private Groups

We have already seen how the government tries to shape opinion. But the ideas that become prominent in political life are also developed and spread by important economic and political groups searching for issues that will advance their causes. In some instances, private groups espouse values in which they truly believe in the hope of bringing others over to their side. Take, for example, the campaign against so-called partial birth abortion that resulted in the Partial Birth Abortion Ban Act of 2003. Proponents of the act believed that prohibiting particular sorts of abortions would be a first step toward eliminating all abortions—something they viewed as a moral imperative.[34] In other cases, groups will promote principles designed mainly to further hidden agendas of political and economic interests. One famous example is the campaign against cheap, imported handguns—the so-called Saturday night specials—covertly financed by domestic manufacturers of more expensive firearms. The campaign's organizers claimed that cheap handguns posed a grave risk to the public and should be outlawed. The real goal, though, was not safeguarding the public but protecting the economic well-being of the domestic gun industry. A more recent example is the campaign against the alleged "sweatshop" practices of some American companies manufacturing products in Third World countries. This campaign is mainly financed by U.S. labor unions seeking to protect their members' jobs by discouraging American firms from manufacturing products abroad.

Typically, ideas are best marketed by groups with access to financial resources, public or private institutional support, and sufficient skill or education to select, develop, and draft ideas that will attract interest and support. Thus, the development and promotion of conservative themes and ideas in recent years has been greatly facilitated by the millions of dollars that conservative corporations and business organizations, such as the Chamber of Commerce and the Public Affairs Council, spend each year on public information and what is now called in corporate circles "issues management." In addition, conservative businesses have contributed millions of dollars to such conservative institutions as the Heritage Foundation, the Hoover Institution, and the American Enterprise Institute.[35]

Although they often do not have access to financial assets that match those available to their conservative opponents, liberal intellectuals and professionals have ample organizational skills, access to the media, and practice in creating, communicating, and using ideas. During the past three decades, the chief vehicle through which liberal intellectuals and professionals have advanced their ideas has been public interest groups, organizations that rely heavily on voluntary contributions of time, effort, and interest on the part of their members. Through groups such as Common Cause, the National Organization for Women, the Sierra Club, Friends of the Earth, and Physicians for Social Responsibility, intellectuals and professionals have been able to use their organizational skills and educational resources to develop and promote ideas.[36]

The Media

The communications media are among the most powerful forces operating in the marketplace of ideas. Most Americans say that their primary source of information about public affairs is news media—newspapers, broadcast and cable news, radio, and Internet news providers. The alternative sources of political information are direct contact with politics, information provided by groups, and information conveyed by other individuals, such as family members or coworkers. Certainly few people actually go to Washington to find out what's going on in American politics, and the broad access people have to media outlets dwarfs the number of households that receive direct mail from organizations and elected officials. Personal conversation is also an important source for information, but people tend to avoid controversial political topics in casual conversation.

The mass media, as the term suggests, can be thought of as mediators. They are the conduits through which information flows. Through newspapers, radio, television, magazines, and the Internet we can learn about what's going on in our world and in our government. As we see in the following section, providing this opportunity to learn about the world and about politics is the most important way in which the media contribute to public opinion.

THE MEDIA AS AN INSTITUTION

People rely on the media, rather than other sources of information, to find out what's going on in politics and public affairs because it is easy to do so. Media outlets are ubiquitous. More households in the United States have television than have indoor plumbing. Almost every community has a newspaper, with 1,500 daily newspapers published throughout the United States. The number of news programs and the availability of news has also expanded tremendously in recent decades. In the 1960s there were only three television news outlets—CBS, NBC, and ABC. They aired evening and nightly news programs and allowed a half-hour slot for news from local affiliates. The rise of cable television in the 1980s brought a 24-hour news station, CNN; expanded news programming through the Public Broadcasting System (PBS); and created a network devoted exclusively to broadcasting proceedings of Congress and government agencies, C-SPAN. Important competitors to the big three networks emerged, including Fox, UPN, WB, and the Spanish-language networks Univision and Telemundo. There is, today, no shortage of televised news programming available at all hours.[37]

Technological innovations continue to push change in political communication in the United States. Today, more than 75 percent of Americans have Internet access.[38] To put that in historical perspective, Internet penetration in the United States today is comparable to television penetration in the late 1950s. This technology, then, has yet to reach its full power and potential. Nevertheless, the rise of the Internet has already opened the flow of communication further. Conventional media have moved much of their content online, provided for free. Internet users can gain access not only to U.S. media but also to media from around the world. The Internet has also changed the traditional media, leading to the development of interactive graphics and reader forums. We have also witnessed the rise of new forms of communication, most notably blogs, which provide a platform for anyone to have their say. Several websites, such as Google News and realclearpolitics .com, are clearinghouses for traditional media, newswire stories, and blogs. The new, highly competitive media environment has put increased financial pressures on traditional media, and it has radically changed the flow and nature of communication in the United States and the availability of information to the public.

Types of Media

Americans obtain their news from three main sources: broadcast media (radio and television), print media (newspapers and magazines), and, increasingly, the Internet. Each of these sources has distinctive institutional characteristics that help to shape the character of their coverage of political events.

Broadcast Media. Television news reaches more Americans than any other single news source. Tens of millions of individuals watch national and local news programs every day. Television news, however, covers relatively few topics and provides little depth of coverage. Television news is more like a series of newspaper headlines connected to pictures. It serves the extremely important function of alerting viewers to issues and events but provides little else.

The 24-hour news stations such as Cable News Network (CNN) offer more detail and commentary than the networks' half-hour evening news shows. In 2003, at the start of the war in Iraq, CNN, Fox, and MSNBC provided 24-hour-a-day coverage of the war, including on-the-scene reports from embedded reporters, expert commentary, and interviews with government officials. In this instance, these networks' depth of coverage rivaled that of the print media. Normally, however, CNN and the others offer more headlines than analysis, especially during their prime-time broadcasts.

Table 9.3

TRENDS IN NEWS CONSUMPTION, 1994–2012

	1994 (%)	1996 (%)	1998 (%)	2000 (%)	2002 (%)	2004 (%)	2006 (%)	2008 (%)	2010 (%)	2012 (%)
Watched news on TV	72	59	59	56	54	60	57	57	58	55
Read a daily newspaper	49	50	49	47	41	42	40	34	31	29
Listened to news on radio	47	44	48	43	41	40	36	35	34	33
Got news online	–	–	–	–	–	24	23	29	34	39
Got news from any digital platform	–	–	–	–	–	–	–	–	42	50

SOURCE: Pew Research Center for People and the Press, "In Changing News Landscape. Even Television Is Vulnerable." September 27, 2012, www.people-press.org/2012/09/27/section-1-watching-reading-and-listening-to-the-news-3 (accessed 12/10/12).

In recent years, cable has been growing in importance as a news source (Table 9.3).

Radio news is also essentially a headline service without pictures. In the short time—usually five minutes per hour—that they devote to news, radio stations announce the day's major events without providing much detail. In major cities, all-news stations provide a bit more coverage of major stories, but for the most part these stations fill the day with repetition rather than detail. All-news stations such as WTOP (Washington, D.C.) and WCBS (New York City) assume that most listeners are in their cars and that, as a result, the people who constitute the audience change markedly throughout the day as they reach their destination. Thus, rather than use their time to flesh out a given set of stories, these stations repeat the same stories each hour to present them to new listeners.

In recent years, much of the content of the news, especially local news, has shifted away from politics and public affairs toward "soft news"—coverage focusing on celebrities, health tips, advice to consumers, and other topics more likely to provide entertainment than enlightenment. Even a good deal of political coverage is soft. For example, media coverage of the 2008 presidential inauguration devoted nearly as much attention to the dresses worn by President Obama's wife and daughters as it did to the content of the president's address.

Print Media. Newspapers remain an important source of news even though they are not the primary news source for most Americans. The print media are important for three reasons. First, as we see later in this chapter, the broadcast media rely on leading newspapers such as the *New York Times* and the *Washington Post* to set their news agenda. The broadcast media engage in very little actual reporting; they primarily cover stories that have been "broken," or initially reported, by the print media. For example, sensational charges that President Bill Clinton had an affair with a White House intern were reported first by the *Washington Post* and *Newsweek* before being trumpeted around the world by the broadcast media. It is only a slight exaggeration to observe that if an event is not covered in the *New York Times*, it is not likely to appear on the *CBS Evening News*. One important exception, obviously, is the case of "breaking" news, which can be carried by the broadcast media as it unfolds or soon after, while the print media are forced to catch up later in the day. Recall the dramatic real-time videos of the collapsing Twin Towers seen by tens of millions of Americans. Second, the print media provide more detailed and more complete information, offering a better context for analysis. Third, the print media are also important because they are the prime source of news for educated and influential individuals. The nation's economic, social, and political elites rely on the detailed coverage provided by the print media to inform and influence their views about important public matters. The print media may have a smaller audience than their cousins in broadcasting, but they have an audience that matters.

Today, however, the newspaper industry is in serious economic trouble. The rise of websites advertising jobs, items for sale, and personal ads has dramatically reduced newspapers' revenues from traditional advertising, such as "help wanted" and personal ads. For example, the *Rocky Mountain News* in Denver closed in 2008, and the *Seattle Post-Intelligencer* switched to an online format only. Major newspapers serving dozens of large U.S. cities and metropolitan areas have announced that they face serious financial difficulties. It is widely believed that the shakeout at these papers is just the beginning of a wider transformation of the print media in the United States, which may leave the country with few or no print newspapers—the traditional "press"—by 2020. The great unknown is whether other venues can adequately replace newspapers, especially in the provision of news about local area politics and public affairs.[39]

The Internet. The Internet emerged as a major form of communication in the mid-1990s. As with radio in the 1920s and television in the 1950s, over the span of a decade the Internet grew from a curiosity into one of the dominant modes of communication. Internet news providers now stand as a significant competitor to traditional media outlets. Every day tens of millions of Americans scan one of many news sites on the Internet for coverage of current events. The main newspapers and television outlets—such as the *Wall Street Journal* and the *New York Times*, Reuters and the Associated Press, CNN and Fox News—are mainstays of the Internet. All have websites that they use to attract audiences to their traditional media and that they use to sell advertising. The Internet, however, has revolutionized how content is provided and what content is accessible to audiences. Look at the website of one of the traditional media outlets, such as the *New York Times* or CNN. There you will see a reproduction of the content on the newspaper or headline news from television that resembles a traditional newspaper, but there is also streaming video such as can be found on television or audio like on radio, and there you will also find commentary from many different sources, like an opinion magazine or news journal such as *Time* magazine. Along similar lines, President Obama's press office developed White House Live, a service that streams video of events live and keeps an archive of past events. A typical day will have live video of two or three events, such as the president touring a natural disaster, holding a press conference, or meeting with other world leaders.

The Internet differs from traditional outlets in another important way: it allows people to get involved directly. Individual citizens can more easily help create the news and interpret it. Public-access television and radio has always been a source of citizen journalism, but the World Wide Web has expanded greatly the space available for news, commentary, and debate. Most news sites provide space for people to post their own photos, video, and blogs of important events. Individuals who are at the scene of a natural disaster or important political event can provide more (and sometimes even better) coverage of a story and may do so more quickly than a reporter.

Regulation of the Media

In most countries, the government controls media content and owns the largest media outlets. In the United States, the government neither owns nor controls the communications networks, but it does regulate the content and ownership of the broadcast media. The print media, on the other hand, are essentially free from government interference.

equal time rule

The requirement that broadcasters provide candidates for the same political office an equal opportunity to communicate their messages to the public

Broadcast Media. American radio and television are regulated by the Federal Communications Commission (FCC), an independent regulatory agency established in 1934. Radio and TV stations must renew their FCC licenses every five years. Through regulations prohibiting obscenity, indecency, and profanity, the FCC has also sought to prohibit radio and television stations from airing explicit sexual and excretory references between 6 A.M. and 10 P.M., the hours when children are most likely to be in the audience. The FCC has enforced these rules haphazardly. Since 1990, nearly half the

Chapter 9: Public Opinion and the Media

$5 million in fines levied by the agency have involved Howard Stern, the "shock jock" whose programs are often built around sexually explicit material. To avoid such regulations, he moved his show to Sirius Satellite Radio.

For more than 60 years, the FCC also sought to regulate and promote competition in the broadcast industry, but in 1996 Congress passed the Telecommunications Act, a broad effort to do away with most regulations in effect since 1934. The act loosened restrictions on media ownership and allowed for telephone companies, cable television providers, and broadcasters to compete with each other for the provision of telecommunication services. Following the passage of the act, several mergers between telephone and cable companies and among different segments of the entertainment media produced an even greater concentration of media ownership.

The sheer number of news outlets has ensured that different perspectives are well represented in the media. Popular political commentators such as Sean Hannity and Rachel Maddow, for example, offer clear conservative and liberal viewpoints, respectively.

The federal government has used its licensing power to impose several regulations that can affect the political content of radio and TV broadcasts. The first of these is the equal time rule, under which broadcasters must provide candidates for the same political office equal opportunities to communicate their messages to the public. The second regulation affecting the content of broadcasts is the right of rebuttal, which requires that individuals be given the opportunity to respond to personal attacks. For many years, a third important federal regulation was the fairness doctrine—under which broadcasters who aired programs on controversial issues were required to provide air time for opposing views. In 1985, the FCC stopped enforcing the fairness doctrine on the grounds that there were so many radio and television stations—to say nothing of newspapers and newsmagazines—that in all likelihood many different viewpoints were being presented even without the requirement that each station present all sides of an argument.

right of rebuttal
An FCC regulation giving individuals the right to have the opportunity to respond to personal attacks made on a radio or TV broadcast

fairness doctrine
An FCC requirement that broadcasters who air programs on controversial issues provide time for opposing views

prior restraint
An effort by a government agency to block the publication of material it deems libelous or harmful in some other way; censorship. In the United States, the courts forbid prior restraint except under the most extraordinary circumstances

Freedom of the Press. Unlike the broadcast media, the print media are not subject to federal regulation. Indeed, the great principle underlying the federal government's relationship with the press is the doctrine against prior restraint. Beginning with the landmark 1931 case of *Near v. Minnesota*, the U.S. Supreme Court has held that, except under the most extraordinary circumstances, the First Amendment of the Constitution prohibits government agencies from seeking to prevent newspapers or magazines from publishing whatever they wish.[40]

Even though newspapers may not be restrained from publishing whatever they want, they may be subject to sanctions after the fact. Historically, newspapers have been subject to the law of libel, which provides that newspapers that print false and malicious stories can be compelled to pay damages to those they defame. In recent years, however, American courts have greatly narrowed the meaning of libel and made it extremely difficult, particularly for politicians and other public figures, to win a libel case against a newspaper.

Sources of Media Influence

The power of the media to affect political knowledge and public opinion stems from several sources. Learning through mass media occurs both actively and passively. Active learning occurs when people search for a particular type of program or a particular type of information. If you turn on the nightly news to find out what has happened in national and international affairs, you are engaged in active learning. If you search the web for information about your member of Congress, you are engaged in active learning. Passive learning may be just as important. Many entertainment programs discuss current affairs and issues, such as social issues or an election. When that occurs, learning takes a passive form. You watch the program for entertainment but gain information about politics. One study of information gain among voters found that people learned as much from Oprah as from the evening news.[41] Political advertising is perhaps the most common form of passive information. During the last month of national political campaigns, it is not uncommon to see three or four political advertisements during one commercial break in a prime-time television program.

Mass media are our primary source for information about current affairs. They influence how Americans understand politics not just through the volume of information available but also through what is presented and how. Editors, reporters, and others involved in preparing the content of the news must ultimately decide what topics to cover, what facts to include, and whom to interview. Journalists usually try to present issues fairly, but it is difficult, perhaps impossible, to be perfectly objective.

What the media cover and how news is presented and interpreted can affect public opinion. Psychologists have identified two potential pathways through which media coverage shapes what people think. First, the news sets the public's agenda. Through this agenda-setting effect, the media cues people to think about some issues rather than others; it makes some considerations more salient than others. Suppose, for example, that the local news covers crime to the exclusion of all else. When someone who watches the local news regularly thinks about the mayoral election, crime is more likely

agenda-setting effect

The power to bring attention to particular issues and problems to be his or her primary consideration, compared with someone who does not watch the local news. Psychologists call this priming.

Second, news coverage of an issue frames the way the issue is defined. News coverage of crime, to continue the example, may include a report on every murder that happens in a large city. Such coverage would likely make it seem that murder occurs very often and is much more common than it actually is. This in turn might heighten viewers' sense of insecurity or threat, leading to an exaggerated sense of risk of violent crime and increased support for tough police practices.[42] Framing refers to the media's power to influence how events and issues are interpreted.

Priming and framing are often viewed as twin evils. One can distract us from other important problems, and the other can make us think about an issue or a politician in a biased way. The cumulative effects of priming and framing on public opinion depend ultimately on the variety of issues covered and the diversity of perspectives represented. That, after all, is the idea behind the guarantee of a free press in the First Amendment to the Constitution. Free and open communication media allow the greatest likelihood that people will learn about important issues, that they will gain the information they need to distinguish good ideas from bad ones, and that they will learn which political leaders and parties can best represent their interests.

In this regard, the most significant framing effects take the form of the balance in the information available to people. Those in politics—elected officials, candidates, leaders of organized groups—work hard to influence what the news covers. A competitive political environment usually translates into a robust flow of information. However, some political environments are not very competitive. Only one view gets expressed and only one view is reflected in the media. Congressional elections are a case in point. Incumbent politicians today are able to raise much more money than their challengers (an advantage of about 3 to 1). As a result, House elections often have a significant imbalance in the amount of advertising and news coverage between the two campaigns, that of the incumbent member of Congress and that of the challenger. This will likely affect public opinion, because voters hear the incumbent's views and message more often than the challenger's.

A further example of an imbalance in news coverage arises with the president and Congress. Presidential press conferences and events receive much more coverage than the press events of the leaders of the House or Senate. This gives the president the upper hand in setting the public agenda through the media, because members of the public are more likely to hear the president's arguments for a particular policy. That opportunity and power, of course, must be used wisely. A president who pursues an ill-advised policy can easily squander the advantage that is gained from disproportionate attention from the media. If a policy fails, the president's media advantage can be short-lived. President George W. Bush convinced

priming
The process of preparing the public to take a particular view of an event or a political actor

framing
The power of the media to influence how events and issues are interpreted

the nation that Iraq was developing weapons of mass destruction and the United States needed to topple the regime of Saddam Hussein immediately. The invasion occurred and Hussein's regime quickly fell, but large caches of chemical and nuclear weapons were never found, and the United States remained in Iraq for a decade. The backlash against these policies cost the Republicans support among the public, control of Congress in the 2006 election, and ultimately the presidency in 2008. The power of the president is the power to persuade, but control of information for political aims is a power to be used with caution.

Today, it is easy to learn about public affairs and to hear different opinions—even when we don't want to. Furthermore, it is widely conjectured that the new media have facilitated learning and muted some of the biases that may emerge through priming and framing. No one voice or perspective dominates our multifaceted media environment and competitive political system. And biases in the media often reflect not the lack of outlets or restrictive editorial control but failures of political competition.

DOES GOVERNMENT POLICY FOLLOW PUBLIC OPINION?

In democratic nations, leaders should pay attention to public opinion, and most evidence suggests that they do. There are many instances in which public policy and public opinion do not coincide, but in general the government's actions are consistent with citizens' preferences. One study, for example, found that between 1935 and 1979, in about two-thirds of all cases, significant changes in public opinion were followed within one year by changes in government policy consistent with the shift in the popular mood.[43] Other studies have come to similar conclusions about public opinion and government policy at the state level.[44] Do these results suggest that politicians pander to the public? The answer is no. Elected leaders don't always pander to the results of public-opinion polls, but instead use polling to sell their policy proposals and shape the public's views.[45]

In addition, there are always areas of disagreement between opinion and policy. For example, the majority of Americans favored stricter government control of handguns for years before Congress finally adopted the modest restrictions on firearms purchases embodied in the 1994 Brady Bill and the Crime Control Act. More recently, despite the support of large majorities of Americans for some form of screening of prospective gun owners in the wake of mass shootings in Aurora, Colorado, and Newtown, Connecticut, Congress has not been responsive. Similarly, most Americans—blacks as

Chapter 9: Public Opinion and the Media

Public outrage over major air travel delays spurred Congress to action in spring 2013. Congress quickly passed a bill to offset the automatic spending cuts that were causing problems at the Federal Aviation Administration. However, government does not always respond immediately to public preferences.

well as whites—oppose school busing to achieve racial balance, yet such busing continues to be used extensively throughout the nation. Most Americans are far less concerned with the rights of the accused than the federal courts seem to be. Most Americans oppose U.S. military intervention in other nations' affairs, yet interventions continue to take place and often win public approval after the fact.

Several factors can contribute to a lack of consistency between opinion and government policy. First, the nominal majority on a particular issue may not be as intensely committed to its preference as the adherents of the minority viewpoint. An intensely committed minority may often be more willing to commit its time, energy, efforts, and resources to the affirmation of its opinions than an apathetic, even if large, majority. In the case of firearms, for example, although the proponents of gun control are in the majority by a wide margin, most do not regard the issue as one of critical importance to themselves and are not willing to commit much effort to advancing their cause. The opponents of gun control, by contrast, are intensely committed, well organized, and well financed, and as a result are usually able to carry the day.

A second important reason that public policy and public opinion may not coincide has to do with the character and structure of the American system of government. The framers of the American Constitution, as we saw in Chapter 2, sought to create a system of government that was based on popular consent but that did not invariably and automatically translate shifting popular sentiments into public policies. As a result, the American governmental process includes arrangements such as an appointed judiciary that can produce policy decisions that may run contrary to prevailing popular sentiment—at least for a time.

Perhaps the inconsistencies between opinion and policy could be resolved if broader use were made of the initiative and referendum. This procedure allows propositions to be placed on the ballot and voted into law by the electorate, thereby eliminating most of the normal machinery of representative government. In recent years, important propositions affecting public policy have been enacted by voters in the states.[46] In 2014, for example, voters in four states (Arkansas, South Dakota, Nebraska, and Alaska) approved measures to increase their state's minimum wage. California's voters approved a measure reducing sentences for certain nonviolent drug and property crimes, Oregon's voters approved a bill legalizing recreational marijuana, and Georgia's voters approved new limits on the state's income tax.

Initiatives such as these seem to provide the public with an opportunity to express its will. The major problem, however, is that government by initiative offers little opportunity for reflection and compromise. Voters are presented with a proposition, usually sponsored by a special interest group, and are asked to take it or leave it. Perhaps the true will of the people, not to mention their best interest, might lie somewhere between the positions taken by various interest groups. Perhaps, for example, California voters might have preferred legalization of same-sex unions in some form other than "marriage." In a representative assembly, as opposed to a referendum campaign, a compromise position might have been achieved that was more satisfactory to all the residents of the state. This is one reason the framers of the U.S. Constitution strongly favored representative government rather than direct democracy.

When all is said and done, however, there can be little doubt that in general the actions of the American government do not remain out of line with popular sentiment for very long. A major reason for this is, of course, the electoral process, to which we turn next.

For Further Reading

Selections highlighted in red are included in *Readings in American Politics: Analysis and Perspectives*, Third Edition.

Ansolabehere, Stephen, Jonathan Rodden, and James M. Snyder, Jr., "Purple America," *Journal of Economic Perspectives* 20, no. 2 (Spring 2006): 97–118.

Bartels, Larry. *Unequal Democracy: The Political Economy of the New Gilded Age.* Princeton, NJ: Princeton University Press, 2008.

Erikson, Robert S., and Kent L. Tedin. *American Public Opinion: Its Origins, Content, and Impact.* 8th ed. New York: Pearson, 2010.

Fiorina, Morris, Samuel Abrams, and Jeremy Pope. *Culture War?* 3rd ed. New York: Pearson, 2010.

Hamilton, James. *All the News That's Fit to Sell.* Princeton, NJ: Princeton University Press, 2004.

Lee, Taeku. *Mobilizing Public Opinion.* Chicago: University of Chicago Press, 2002.

Kinder, Donald, and Cindy Kam. *Us against Them: Ethnocentric Foundations of American Opinion.* Chicago: University of Chicago Press, 2010.

Lupia, Arthur, and Mathew D. McCubbins. *The Democratic Dilemma: Can Citizens Learn What They Need to Know?* New York: Cambridge University Press, 1998.

Stimson, James A. *Public Opinion in America: Moods, Cycles, and Swings.* 2nd ed. Boulder, CO: Westview Press, 1999.

Zaller, John R. *The Nature and Origins of Mass Opinion.* New York: Cambridge University Press, 1992.

10 Elections

Most Americans think that voting gives them a measure of control over the government and its policies. This belief, like the more general idea that public opinion is important, is regularly affirmed by politicians, taught in the public schools, and frequently reiterated by the mass media. The idea that elections provide citizens with an important measure of political influence certainly seems plausible. Democratic elections, after all, permit ordinary citizens to select and depose powerful public officials. This electoral sanction compels candidates for office to vie with one another for popular approval and forces the nation's leaders to pay heed to citizens' wishes and welfare if they wish to retain their positions. As James Madison observed in *Federalist 57*, "the restraint of frequent elections" induces public officials to "anticipate the moment when their power is to cease . . . unless a faithful discharge of their trust shall have established their title to a renewal of it."[1]

This view of elections certainly has merit. But it is also the case that elections might displace other forms of political activity that could influence politics to an equal, or perhaps even greater, degree. Elections offer a formal and institutional channel to take the place of the more impromptu tactics, including protest and violence, that might be employed by citizens, such as participants in the Occupy Wall Street movement, seeking to force a government to listen to them. Despite official efforts to suppress popular agitation, the citizenry is seldom politically impotent in the absence of elections. Perhaps some regimes are sufficiently powerful and ruthless to stamp out most vestiges of popular dissent. But no government is all-powerful all the time. In recent years, much-feared authoritarian regimes as in Libya and Algeria, seemingly protected by enormous armies and powerful security forces, disappeared almost overnight. Often, it is precisely because clandestine or spontaneous forms of popular political activity are having too great an impact, that governments seek to introduce electoral mechanisms or to expand existing voting rights and to persuade citizens of their value. As the late Walter Lippman observed, "New numbers were enfranchised because they had power, and giving them the vote was the 'least disturbing way' of letting them exercise their power."[2]

An example from recent American history appears to illustrate Lippman's proposition. This is the case of the Twenty-Sixth Amendment, added to the Constitution in 1971, which lowered the U.S. voting age from 21 to 18. This amendment was adopted during a period of civil strife and disorder during which young people—college students in particular—engaged in sometimes violent protests over the Vietnam War, military conscription, race relations, social policy, and other aspects of American politics and society. While student protestors made many demands, their agenda did not include voting rights for young people. But, even though students may not have been especially

CORE OF THE ANALYSIS

➡ The United States holds frequent elections as a means of keeping politicians close to the preferences of a majority of the people.

➡ The institutional features of American elections regulate who votes, what form the ballot takes, how voting districts are drawn, and what it takes to win an election.

➡ The United States uses a system of plurality rule in which the candidate with the most votes wins the electoral district. Plurality rule creates a strong pressure toward two-party politics.

➡ Voters who identify with a political party vote with that party nearly all of the time. Issues and candidate characteristics also influence voters' decisions.

➡ Campaigns try to mobilize their candidate's supporters and persuade undecided voters.

interested in voting, many political leaders seemed eager to give them the right to do so.

Senate Judiciary Committee hearings on the subject indicated a belief among Democrats and Republicans alike that the right to vote would channel students' political activities from the street into the polling places. For example, the late senator Jacob Javits (R-N.Y.) said, "I am convinced that self-styled student leaders who urged such acts of civil disobedience would find themselves with little or no support if students were given a more meaningful role in the political process. In short, political activism . . . is all happening outside the existing political framework. Passage of [the voting rights resolution] would give us the means, sort of the famous carrot and the stick, to channel this energy into our major political parties."[3] In a similar vein, Senator Birch Bayh (D-Ind.) said, "This force, this energy, is going to continue to build and grow. The only question is whether we should continue to ignore it, perhaps leaving this energy to dam up and burst and follow less-than-wholesome channels, or whether we should let this force be utilized by society through the pressure valve of the franchise."[4] Three years later, the resolution under discussion became a constitutional amendment.

Electoral institutions also offer the government benefits in the form of increased popular support from lawful citizen participation. Denying citizens an opportunity to participate in political life tends to alienate those who have political interests and ambitions. Providing those who wish to participate with a lawful outlet for their political energies, on the other hand, is likely to have the opposite effect, generating support for rather than opposition to the regime. A good deal of evidence suggests that an opportunity to participate in the decision-making processes of the institutions that rule them affords many individuals enormous psychic gratification that is not dependent upon their approval of the specific decisions that ultimately result.[5]

In this chapter, we look at how citizens might benefit from voting and how the institutional features of American elections shape the way citizens' goals and preferences are reflected in their government. Then we will consider how voters decide among the candidates and questions put before them on the ballot. We should, however, not lose sight of the fact that voting serves the government as well as the citizenry.

INSTITUTIONS OF ELECTIONS

We have suggested that the relationship between citizens and elected politicians is an instance of a principal-agent relationship. There are two basic approaches to this relationship: the consent approach and the agency approach. The consent approach emphasizes the historical reality that the right of the citizen to participate in his or her own governance, mainly through the act of voting or other forms of consent, arises from an existing governmental order aimed at making it easier for the governors to govern by legitimating their rule. By giving their consent, citizens provide this legitimation. The agency approach treats the typical citizen as someone who would much rather devote scarce time and effort to his or her own private affairs than spend that time and effort on governance. He or she therefore chooses to delegate governance to agents—politicians—who are controlled through elections. In this approach, the control of agents is emphasized.

Whether they are seen as a means to control delegates (the agency approach) or to legitimate governance by politicians (the consent approach), elections allow citizens to participate in political life on a routine and peaceful basis. Indeed, American voters have the opportunity to select and, if they so desire, remove some of their most important leaders. In this way, Americans have a chance to intervene in and influence the government's programs and policies. Yet it is important to recall that elections are not spontaneous affairs. Instead, they are formal governmental institutions. Although elections allow citizens a chance to participate in politics, they also allow the government a chance to exert a good deal of control over when, where, how, and which of its citizens will participate. Electoral processes are governed by a variety of rules and procedures that provide those in power with a significant opportunity to regulate the character—and perhaps also the consequences—of mass political participation.

Four features of U.S. election laws deserve particular emphasis:

- First, *who*. The United States provides for universal adult suffrage—all citizens over the age of 18 have the right to vote.[6]

- Second, *how*. Americans vote in secret and choose among candidates for office using a form of ballot called the Australian ballot.

- Third, *where*. The United States selects almost all elected offices through single-member districts that have equal populations.

- Fourth, *what* it takes to win. For most offices in the United States, the candidate who wins the most votes among all of those competing for a given seat wins the election.

Each of these rules has substantial effects on elections and representation. Before we explore each of these rules in more detail, it is important to note that the rules governing elections are not static. The features of American electoral institutions have evolved over time through legislation, court decisions, administrative rulings of agencies, and public agitation for electoral reform. The nation has gradually converged to our present system of universal suffrage with secret voting and to the use of single-member districts with plurality rule. But this is only one era, and the future will likely bring further innovations in voting and elections. This presents new questions about secrecy and about the form of the ballot; it also provides new opportunities for reform and modes of voting (such as instant runoff voting). Such changes rarely come about through carefully planned federal legislation. Typically, new election institutions emerge out of the experiences and experiments of local election officials and state laws. Let us take a closer look at the key institutional features of American elections.

Who Can Vote: Defining the Electorate

Over the course of American history the electorate has expanded greatly. As discussed in Chapter 4, the United States has gradually extended the right to vote, both on paper and in practice. At the beginning of the Republic, voting rights in most states were restricted to white men over 21 years of age, and many states further required that those people own property. Today, all citizens over 18 years of age are allowed to vote, and the courts, the Department of Justice, and activist organizations work to ferret out discrimination in elections.[7]

While the right to vote is universal, the exercise of this right is not. In a typical U.S. presidential election, approximately 60 percent of those eligible to vote in fact do so. The rate of voting is lower still in midterm elections for Congress, with typically around 45 percent of the eligible electorate voting. And in local elections the percentage of people who vote can be quite low: some city elections conducted in odd-numbered years attract only 10 to 20 percent of the eligible electorate. Some of the most basic questions concerning the functioning and health of our democracy concern the exercise of the franchise. Who votes and why? How does nonparticipation affect election outcomes, and would election outcomes be different if everyone voted? Does low voter turnout threaten the legitimacy of government?

Voting in the United States is a right, not a requirement. Voting, like most other activities in our society, is voluntary. If we do not feel strongly about government, we do not have to participate. If we want to send a message of dissatisfaction, one way to do so is not to vote. While most democracies view voting as a right and a voluntary act, some also treat it as a responsibility of citizenship. In Mexico and Australia, for example, adult citizens are required to vote in national elections, and if they fail to vote they must either receive a medical exemption or pay a fine. That guarantees turnout rates in the range of 90 percent of the eligible electorate and it makes election results a reflection of the preferences of all people. Making voting a requirement is not viewed favorably in the United States, however. Those who don't vote don't want to face a potential fine, and those who do vote may not want the "nonvoters" diluting their power. And most Americans simply do not like the notion that the government can compel us to do something. Even without being compelled to participate, the United States is one of the most participatory democracies in the world. There are many other ways that we can participate in electoral politics, such as blogging and speaking with others, joining organizations, giving money, and of course voting. On nearly all of these activities, Americans participate in politics at much higher rates than people in nearly every other country.[8]

That said, levels of voter participation in the latter half of the twentieth century were quite low in the United States, as compared with voter participation in other Western democracies.[9] And voter participation was low compared to earlier eras of American history, especially the late nineteenth century (Figure 10.1).[10] Over the five decades after World War II there was a steady erosion of voter turnout in the United States. Voter participation in presidential elections in the United States fell below 50 percent in 1996. That decline alarmed many observers and even stirred Congress to reform voter registration rules in the mid-1990s. Turnout rates have grown since then, in response to legal changes and in response to the observation by the political parties and candidates that there was an opportunity to influence elections by bringing people back to the polls. In 2012, 56.5 percent of adult citizens in the United States voted.

The question "Who votes?" is partly explained by the behavior of individuals and partly explained by the laws of democracy, which are the institutions of elections. Later in this chapter we will discuss the correlates of voting to understand who chooses to vote. We discuss here the institutions and how they define and constrain behavior.

People who register to vote are highly likely to turn out and actually vote on Election Day, so getting new voters into the registration system is one way to increase voter participation. Here, members of the Florida Immigrant Coalition prepare to canvass potential voters and help them register.

Measuring Voter Turnout and the Effects of Restrictions on Voting. It is worth a brief detour to explain one term—the turnout rate. It is simple to define, but worth understanding some of the subtleties, especially when making comparisons over time or across countries. The turnout rate is the number of people who vote in a given election divided by the number of people who are allowed to vote. The first part of this ratio is relatively uncontroversial—it is the number of individuals who cast ballots in the election, at polling stations or through absentee ballots.[11] The appropriate baseline in the turnout ratio is more difficult to define. Most commonly, the turnout rate presented for the United States (and other countries) is turnout as a percentage of the voting-*age* population (all adults). This understates the true turnout rate, because it includes noncitizens and people who

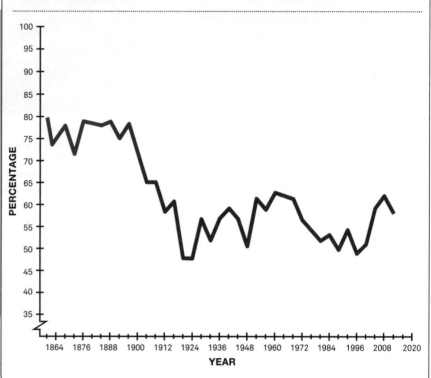

Figure 10.1

VOTER TURNOUT IN U.S. PRESIDENTIAL ELECTIONS

NOTE: Data reflect the population of eligible voters; the percentage of the voting-age population that voted would be smaller.

SOURCES: For 1860–1928, U.S. Bureau of the Census, *Historical Statistics of the United States, Colonial Times to 1970*, pt. 2, p. 1071, www.census.gov/prod/www/abs/statab.html (accessed 6/17/08); for 1932–92, U.S. Bureau of the Census, *Statistical Abstract of the United States*, 1993 (Washington, DC: Government Printing Office, 1993), p. 284; for 1996–2012, U.S. Census Bureau data.

ANALYZING THE EVIDENCE

Voter turnout for American presidential elections was significantly higher in the nineteenth century than in the twentieth. What institutional change caused the sharp decline in turnout between 1890 and 1910? Why did this change have such a dramatic effect? Did it have any positive outcomes?

are institutionalized or not allowed to vote in some states because they are ex-felons. It is difficult to get reliable figures on the populations of institutionalized people and noncitizens, so calculating the voting-*eligible* population can be controversial. Following the usual conventions, we focus here on the voting-age population. However, it is worth understanding the size of the eligible electorate and the effects of current restrictions on the franchise.[12]

How big is the U.S. electorate? There are approximately 319 million people in the United States today. But not all of them are allowed to vote. First, children under 18 are not allowed to vote. Second, noncitizens are not allowed to vote. Third, people in prison are not allowed to vote, and in most states ex-felons are not allowed to vote. The biggest restriction on the size of the electorate is age. There are approximately 77 million people

under age 18 in the United States. Citizenship reduces the eligible electorate further, by another 13 million adults.[13] Finally, the total ineligible prison
and felon population is approximately 2 million persons. Hence, the eligible
electorate is approximately 227 million persons, or about two-thirds of the
people living in the United States.

To put the changes in election laws in perspective, suppose that the
restrictive rules of the nineteenth century were in place today, and that only
white male citizens over 21 were allowed to vote. If that were the law of
the land in 2014, the eligible electorate would total only about 75 million
persons. That is, only about 1 in 4 people in the United States today would
be eligible to vote if the nineteenth-century restrictions on voting remained
in place today. Those restrictions surely would have made for a very different electorate in terms of its interests, values, and preferences; they would
have altered the strategies of the political parties; and they would have surely
resulted in very different election outcomes.

The Registration Requirement. Other restrictions on the franchise
arise from the ways that local election officials run elections. As Figure 10.1
indicates, voter turnout declined markedly in the United States between
1890 and 1910. These years coincided with two changes in the institutions
of elections. First, many states imposed rules such as literacy tests to keep
immigrants, blacks, and other groups out of the electorate. Second, many
states began to create formal registration systems and lists, so that people
had to be on a formal list of eligible voters in order to establish that they
were allowed to vote on Election Day. Personal registration was one of several "progressive" reforms of political practices initiated at the beginning
of the twentieth century. The ostensible purpose of registration was to discourage fraud and corruption. At that time, "corruption" was also code
language that referred to machine politics in large cities, where political parties had organized immigrant and ethnic populations. Election reforms not
only tried to reign in corruption but to weaken the power of urban factions
within parties and keep immigrants and blacks from voting.

Over the years, voter registration restrictions have been modified somewhat to make registration easier. In 1993, for example, Congress approved and
President Bill Clinton signed the "motor voter" bill to ease voter registration
by allowing individuals to register when they applied for driver's licenses, as
well as in public-assistance and military-recruitment offices.[14] In many jurisdictions, casting a vote automatically registers the voter for the next election. In
Europe, there is typically no registration burden on the individual voter; voter
registration is handled automatically by the government. This is one reason
that voter turnout rates in Europe are higher than those in the United States.

The mere requirement that people register in order to vote has a significant effect on turnout rates. Studies of contemporary voter registration

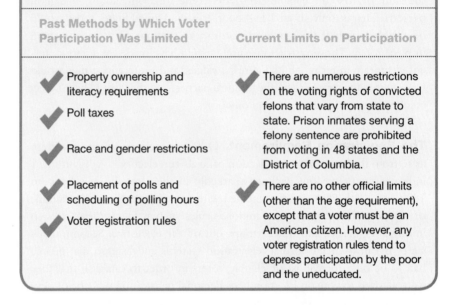

IN BRIEF

Determining Who Votes

Manipulation of the electorate's composition is a device used to regulate voting and its consequences. As we saw in Chapter 4, most restrictions on adult voters have been removed.

Past Methods by Which Voter Participation Was Limited	Current Limits on Participation
✓ Property ownership and literacy requirements	✓ There are numerous restrictions on the voting rights of convicted felons that vary from state to state. Prison inmates serving a felony sentence are prohibited from voting in 48 states and the District of Columbia.
✓ Poll taxes	
✓ Race and gender restrictions	
✓ Placement of polls and scheduling of polling hours	✓ There are no other official limits (other than the age requirement), except that a voter must be an American citizen. However, any voter registration rules tend to depress participation by the poor and the uneducated.
✓ Voter registration rules	

lists find that almost 90 percent of registered voters in fact vote, but only about 80 percent of the eligible electorate is currently registered to vote. In other words, the eligible electorate is really only about 182 million people—the number who are actually registered to vote. There are approximately 45 million eligible voters who have not yet registered. They are disproportionately those ages 18–29. Getting those people into the registration system, and keeping them on the rolls, is viewed by many as an important way to increase the turnout rate. If you are not registered to vote, you cannot vote.[15]

Why, then, have a registration system? Registration systems contain a fairly reliable list of all people who are interested in voting. Local election offices and campaigns use the registration lists to communicate with voters about when, where, and how to vote. Campaigns also use these lists to prepare grassroots' organizing efforts and direct-mail campaigns.

Registration lists are also the basis for administering elections. Local election offices rely on their registration databases to format ballots, set up precincts, determine which voters should vote in which place, and communicate with people. Any given area contains many overlapping election jurisdictions, creating many different combinations of unique sets of offices. For example, one voter might reside in Congressional District 1, State Senate District 7, State Representative District 3, City Council District 1, and so forth. Variations in district boundaries may mean that a few blocks away, another voter lives in Congressional District 2, State Senate District 4, State Representative District 12, City Council District 6, and so forth. Although they live in the same city, these voters live in very different sets of political districts and must vote on different ballots. The first voter is not supposed to vote in Congressional District 2, for instance. Registration lists have become vitally important in sorting out where and on which ballots people should vote.

Efforts to get rid of or reform registration requirements must confront this very practical problem. Some states, such as Minnesota and Wisconsin, allow registration at the polls on Election Day (called same-day registration or Election Day registration). These states have noticeably higher turnout but also must recruit additional poll workers to handle the new registrants in the precincts. In other states, electronic voting equipment now makes it possible to program many different ballots on a single machine. The voter need only key in his or her address to get the appropriate ballot and vote. Innovations such as these may lead ultimately to an election system that does not require or rely heavily on registration before Election Day, but the United States today relies heavily on registration to run elections, even though it creates a hurdle to voting.

Over the past decade, there has been a push to create new ways of authenticating voters at the polls. Half of all states require that voters provide some form of identification when voting, such as a driver's license. Some states now require that all voters show government-issued photo identification. Such rules have been adopted out of fear of voter fraud. The other half of states either have no such formal requirement or prohibit election officials from asking for photographic identification. Legislators and voters in these states either do not judge the risk of voter fraud as great or they view the potential barrier to voting or potentially discriminatory effects of such laws as greater than any possible fraud. Social scientists have tended to find minimum levels of fraud, minimal effects of such laws on voter turnout, and minimal effects on people's confidence in the electoral system.[16]

Laws alone, however, cannot explain the variations observed in turnout. Perhaps the biggest, systematic differences in turnout are between election years. When the president is on the ticket, turnout exceeds 60 percent of the eligible electorate. But, in midterm elections, when the president is not on the ticket, turnout plummets. This pattern of surge and decline in turnout is a function of the election calendar, but it is certainly also a function of the activities of the campaigns and the interests of the voters in the outcomes of the elections. These are behavioral matters, which we will discuss later in this chapter.

How Americans Vote: The Ballot

The way Americans cast their votes reflects some of our most cherished precepts about voting rights. Most people today view voting as a private matter. They may tell others how they voted, but that is their prerogative. Polling places provide privacy for voters and keep an individual's vote secret. In some respects, the secret ballot seems incongruous with voting, because elections are a very public matter. Indeed, for the first century of the Republic, voting was conducted in the open. Public voting led to vote buying and voter intimidation. American history is full of lore involving urban party workers paying poor voters for their support or intimidating members of the opposing party to prevent them from voting. The secret ballot became widespread at the end of the nineteenth century in response to such corrupt practices.

Australian ballot

An electoral format that presents the names of all the candidates for any given office on the same ballot. Introduced at the end of the nineteenth century, the Australian ballot replaced the partisan ballot and facilitated split-ticket voting

With the secret ballot came another innovation, the Australian ballot. The Australian ballot lists the names of all candidates running for a given office and allows the voter to select any candidate for any office. This way of offering choices to voters was first introduced in Australia in 1851, and in the United States today it is universal. Before the 1880s Americans voted in entirely different ways. Some voted in public meetings; others voted on paper ballots printed by the political parties or by slates of candidates distributed to the voters. Voters chose which ballot they wished to submit—a Republican ballot, a Democratic ballot, a Populist ballot, a Greenback ballot, and so forth. The ballots were often printed on different-colored paper so that voters could distinguish among them—and so that the local party workers could observe who cast which ballots. With these party ballots, voters could not choose candidates from different parties for different offices; they had to vote the party line. Under the Australian form, all ballots are identical, making it difficult to observe who votes for which party. More important, voters could choose any candidate for any office, breaking the hold of parties over the vote. The introduction of the Australian ballot gave rise to the phenomenon of split-ticket voting, whereby voters select candidates from different parties for different offices.[17]

The secret and Australian ballot creates the opportunity for voters to choose candidates as well as parties and, as we discuss in more depth later, created a necessary condition for the rise of the personal vote and the incumbency advantage in American electoral politics. (See the discussion of the incumbency advantage in Congress

One change under way in American electoral rules involves the rise of "convenience voting"—voting early or voting by mail. Here, thousands of absentee ballots cast in 2012 are organized for counting.

in Chapter 5.) The possibility of split-ticket voting also created greater fragmentation in the control of government in the United States. With the party ballot, an insurgent party could more readily be swept to power at all levels of government in a given election. A strong national tide toward one of the parties in the presidential election would change not just the presidency but also political control of every state and locality that gave a majority of its votes to that presidential candidate's party. The party ballot thus reinforced the effect of elections on party control of government and public policy. In contrast, because the Australian ballot permitted voters to choose for each office separately, it lessened the likelihood that the electorate would sweep an entirely new administration into power. Thus, ticket splitting led to increasingly divided control of government as well as the rise of personal voting.

Where: Electoral Districts

Elected officials in the United States represent places as well as people. Today, the president, representatives, senators, governors, and many other state officers, state legislators, and most local officers are elected by the people through geographic areas called electoral districts. Generally speaking, the United States employs single-member districts with equal populations. This means that the U.S. House of Representatives, almost all state legislatures, and almost all local governments have their own districts and elect one representative per district, and all of the districts for a given legislative body must have equal populations.

Elections for the U.S. Senate and the presidency are the odd cases. In the U.S. Senate, the states are the districts. Senate districts, then, have multiple members and unequal populations. In presidential elections, every state is allocated votes in the electoral college equal to its number of U.S. senators (two) plus its number of House members. The states are the districts, and each state chooses all of its electors in a statewide vote. The electors commit to casting their votes for a certain candidate in the electoral college.[18] Within the political parties, the nomination process in most states allocates delegates to the parties' national conventions on the basis of House districts and their populations. However, some states choose their delegates on a statewide basis, with all districts selecting multiple delegates to the party conventions.

The U.S. Senate and the electoral college remain the two great exceptions to the requirements of single-member districts with equal populations. The apportionment of Senate seats to states makes that chamber inherently unequal. California's 38 million people have the same number of senators as Wyoming's 575,000 people. The allocation of electoral college votes creates a population inequity in presidential elections, with larger states selecting

single-member district

An electorate that is allowed to elect only one representative from each district—the typical method of representation in the United States

electoral college

The presidential electors from each state who meet in their respective state capitals after the popular election to cast ballots for president and vice president fewer electors per capita than smaller states. In the 1960s, the Supreme Court let stand the unequal district populations in the Senate and the electoral college, because the representation of states in the Senate is specified in the Constitution. The reason lies in the politics of the Constitutional Convention (see Chapter 2). That convention, as you may recall, consisted of delegations of states, each of which held equal numbers of votes under the Articles of Confederation. In order to create a House of Representatives to reflect the preferences of the population, the large states had to strike a deal with the smaller states, which stood to lose representation with the initial plan of a single chamber that reflected population. That deal, the Connecticut Compromise, created the U.S. Senate to balance representation of people with representation of places and led to a clause in Article V of the Constitution that guarantees equal representation of the states in the Senate.

Even though they have unequal populations and select multiple representatives, the Senate and the electoral college share the salient feature of elections for the House and other elections in the use of districts to select representatives. All elections in the United States and all elected officials are tied to geographically based constituencies rather than to the national electorate as a whole. This is certainly true for the House and Senate. It applies also to presidential elections, in which candidates focus on winning key states in the electoral college rather than on winning a majority of the popular vote.

Drawing Electoral Districts. House and state legislative districts are not static. In order to comply with the dictum of equal population representation, they must be remade every decade. Responsibility for drawing new district boundaries rests, in most states, with the state legislatures and the governors, with the supervision of the courts and sometimes with the consultation of commissions (Figure 10.2). Every 10 years, the U.S. Census updates the official population figures of the states, as well as population counts, to a fine level of geographic detail. The politicians, their staffs, party consultants, and others with a stake in the outcome use the census data to craft a new district map; ultimately, the legislatures must pass and the governors must sign a law defining new U.S. House and state legislative districts. This job is forced on the legislatures by their constitutions and by the courts. As the history of unequal representation suggests, most legislatures would, if left to their own devices, leave the existing boundaries in place. Periodic redistricting, although it corrects one problem, invites another. Those in charge of redistricting may try to manipulate the new map to increase the likelihood of a particular outcome, such as the election of a majority of seats for one party or social interest. This problem arose with some of the

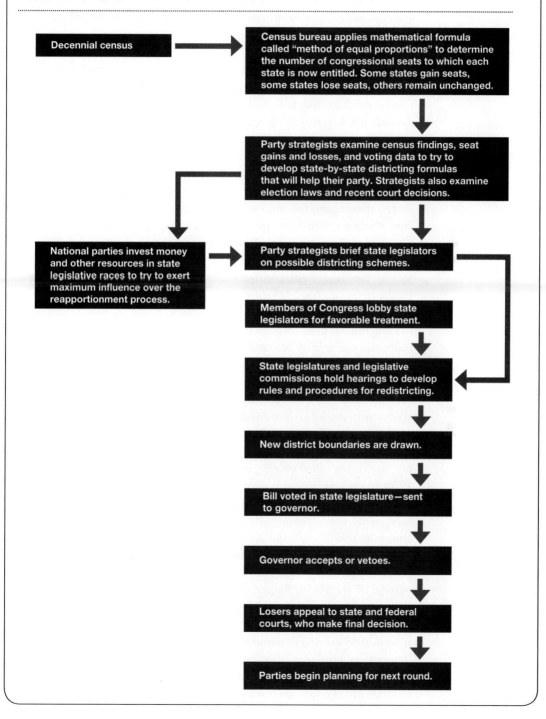

Figure 10.2

CONGRESSIONAL REDISTRICTING

Decennial census

Census bureau applies mathematical formula called "method of equal proportions" to determine the number of congressional seats to which each state is now entitled. Some states gain seats, some states lose seats, others remain unchanged.

Party strategists examine census findings, seat gains and losses, and voting data to try to develop state-by-state districting formulas that will help their party. Strategists also examine election laws and recent court decisions.

National parties invest money and other resources in state legislative races to try to exert maximum influence over the reapportionment process.

Party strategists brief state legislators on possible districting schemes.

Members of Congress lobby state legislators for favorable treatment.

State legislatures and legislative commissions hold hearings to develop rules and procedures for redistricting.

New district boundaries are drawn.

Bill voted in state legislature—sent to governor.

Governor accepts or vetoes.

Losers appeal to state and federal courts, who make final decision.

Parties begin planning for next round.

earliest congressional district maps. A particularly egregious map of the 1812 Massachusetts House districts drawn with the imprimatur of Governor Elbridge Gerry prompted an editorial writer in the *Boston Gazette* to dub a very strangely shaped district the "Gerry-Mander." The term stuck, and gerrymandering refers broadly to any attempt at creating electoral districts for political advantage.

gerrymandering

The apportionment of voters in districts In such a way as to give unfair advantage to one political party

It is easy to draw an intentionally unfair electoral map, especially with the sophisticated software and data on local voting patterns and demographics that are available today. To facilitate districting, the Census Bureau divides the nation into very small geographic areas, called census blocs, which typically contain a few dozen people. U.S. House districts contain over 700,000 people. Political mapmakers combine various local areas, down to census blocs, to construct legislative districts. Those seeking political advantage try to make as many districts as possible that contain a majority of their own voters, maximizing the number of seats won for a given division of the vote. There are constraints on political cartography: the district populations must be equal, and all parts of the district must touch (be contiguous). Even with those constraints, the number of possible maps that could be drawn for any one state's legislative districts is extremely large.[19] The Analyzing the Evidence unit on page 328 shows how this works, using a hypothetical state to explain some basic strategies that parties and politicians might implement to influence elections through the manipulation of district lines, as well as a real-world example of how redistricting affects election outcomes.

Politicians can use gerrymandering to dilute the strength not only of a party but also of a group. Until recently, many state legislatures employed gerrymandering to dilute the strength of racial minorities. One of the more common strategies involved redrawing congressional district boundaries in such a way as to divide and disperse a black population that would have constituted a majority within the original district. This form of gerrymandering, sometimes called *cracking*, was used in Mississippi during the 1960s and 1970s to prevent the election of black candidates to Congress. Historically, the black population of Mississippi was clustered in the western half of the state, along the Mississippi River Delta. From 1882 until 1966, the Delta constituted one congressional district. Although blacks were a clear majority within this district, discrimination against them in voter registration and at the polls guaranteed the continual election of white congressmen. With the passage of the Voting Rights Act in 1965, this district would almost surely be won by a black candidate or one favored by the black majority. To prevent that from happening, the Mississippi state legislature drew new House districts in 1965 in order to minimize the voting power of the black population. Rather than a majority of a single district that encompassed the Delta, the black population was split across three districts and constituted a majority in none. Mississippi's gerrymandering scheme was preserved in the state's redistricting plans in 1972 and 1982 and helped prevent the election of any black representative until 1986, when Mike Espy became the first African American since Reconstruction to represent Mississippi in Congress.

Continuing controversies about the legislatures' involvement in drawing their own districts have raised deep concerns about the fairness of the process. Many states have created commissions to draw plans or appointed "special masters" to draw the maps. California and Arizona conducted their redistricting in 2012 using independent commissions. Both of these procedures were adopted via ballot measures, not by the state legislatures. Political scientists' analyses of the underlying electoral bias indicate that these commissions produced very fair maps. Other states have opened the redistricting process up to input from the public. Now, new developments in GIS software and provision of census data make it possible for anyone to draw credible district maps. Opening up the process, it is hoped, will lessen the extent and effect of gerrymandering.

What It Takes to Win: Plurality Rule

The fourth prominent feature of U.S. electoral law is the criterion for winning. Americans often embrace majority rule as a defining characteristic of democracy. However, that is not quite right. The real standard is plurality rule. The candidate who receives the most votes in the relevant district or constituency wins the election, even if that candidate doesn't receive a majority of votes. Suppose, for example, three parties nominate candidates for a seat and divide the vote such that one wins 34 percent and the other two each receive 33 percent of the vote. Under plurality rule, the candidate with 34 percent wins the seat. There are different types of plurality systems. The system currently used in the United States combines plurality rule with single-member districts and is called *first past the post*. The electoral college is a plurality system in which the candidate who receives the most votes wins all of the delegates: winner take all.[20] Some states set an even higher standard and require a candidate to receive at least 50 percent of all votes in order to win. This is majority rule. Louisiana and Georgia, for instance, require a candidate to receive an outright majority in an election in order to be declared the winner. If no candidate receives a majority in an election, a runoff election is held about one month later between the two candidates who received the most votes in the first round. Other ways of voting also use plurality- and majority-rule criteria. For instance, some city councils still have multimember districts. The top vote getters win the seats. If there are, say, seven seats to fill, the seven candidates who win the most votes each win a seat.

Plurality rule is often criticized for yielding electoral results that do not reflect the public's preferences. The votes for the losing candidates seem

plurality rule
A type of electoral system in which victory goes to the individual who gets the most votes in an election, but not necessarily a majority of the votes cast

majority rule
A type of electoral system in which, to win a seat in a representative body, a candidate must receive a majority (50 percent plus one) of all the votes cast in the relevant district

The Electoral Impact of Congressional Redistricting

District boundaries can have subtle but significant effects on the partisan division of a legislature. If a party can control the districting process, it may be able to craft the lines in such a way that the party wins more seats for the same number of Republican and Democratic votes.

Drawing District Lines

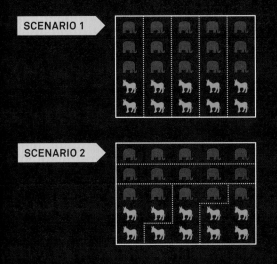

SCENARIO 1

SCENARIO 2

Consider a hypothetical state where Republicans represent 60 percent of voters and Democrats represent the remaining 40 percent of voters. As a result of population changes during the preceding decade, this state now has five congressional districts. A state legislature controlled by a Republican majority could draw congressional districts in such a way that Republicans are 60 percent of voters in each seat and expected to win every seat.

Now suppose that the Democrats are in control of the state legislature. With the same distribution of voters in the state, they could draw the districts to favor the Democrats as much as possible (with Democratic voters dominating three of the districts).

U.S. House Districts, Texas, 2011

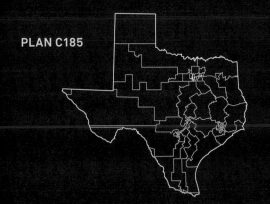

PLAN C185

Consider a real-world example. Reapportionment following the 2010 census allotted Texas four new districts, and the shifting demographics of the state required considerable redrawing of the congressional district lines. The Democrats and Republicans in the Texas state legislature each proposed new district plans. The Republican-controlled legislature passed the Republican plan (Plan C185), and Republican governor Rick Perry signed that plan into law.

In a state of 25 million people, comparing different districting plans is more complicated than in our simple models, but comparing the Republican plan (C185) and the main Democratic plan (C166) in Texas revealed a significant difference. Political scientists started by calculating each party's share of the two-party vote in statewide and federal elections over the decade from 2002 to 2010: the average was 42.3 percent Democratic and 57.7 percent Republican. This average is called the normal vote. Using the normal vote as the measure of the Democratic and Republican strength in each area, Democrats comprise 42.3 percent of the electorate, and they are the majority in 27.8 percent of districts (10 seats) and Republicans the majority 72.2 percent of districts (26 seats).

Political scientists analyzing this case also estimated the bias toward one party or the other. A districting plan is said to be unbiased if when the parties each win 50 percent of the votes statewide, they also each win 50 percent of the legislative seats. A plan is biased in favor of one party if that party wins *more* than half of the seats in an election in which it wins just half of the votes. A plan is biased against the party if it wins *less* than half of the seats when it wins half of the votes. Of course, most elections do not end up with each party winning 50 percent of the vote. More generally, a districting plan is unbiased if a party wins half of its seats by the same margin that it wins the statewide vote, and the plan is biased in favor of a party if it wins more than half of its seats by the margin it wins the statewide vote. Hence, if a party wins 60 percent of the vote statewide, one expects, under an unbiased plan, that the party will win half of its seats with at least 60 percent of the vote. If the map is biased in favor of that party, it will win more than half of its seats by at least 60 percent.

Expected Share of Seats: Democrats

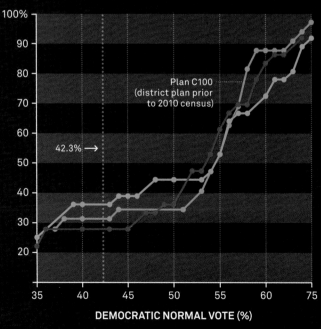

EXPECTED
DEMOCRATIC SEATS

Plan C100
(district plan prior
to 2010 census)

42.3% →

DEMOCRATIC NORMAL VOTE (%)

Plan C185 (Republican)
Plan C166 (Democratic)
Plan C100 (Previous district plan)

The graph shows the expected Democratic share of Texas U.S. House seats won at 42.3 percent and for percentages of the statewide vote above and below that, including at the 50 percent point. We can see the partisan biases of each plan in the graph by looking at the expected Democratic seat share at 50 percent of the vote. The plan passed into law (the red line) has a 13-point bias: under Texas's new districts, Democrats are expected to win 37 percent of seats if they win half of the vote statewide (the difference between 37 and 50 is the partisan bias). Under the Democrats' own plan (the blue line), the bias is just 5 points.

SOURCE: Texas Legislative Council, www.tlc.state.tx.us/redist/redist.html (accessed 10/31/11) and author calculations.

wasted, because they do not translate directly into representation. Indeed, as the example of the three-candidate race above suggests, it is possible that a majority of voters wanted someone other than the winner. In the aggregate, plurality rule with single-member districts tends to inflate the share of seats won by the largest party and deflate the others' shares. A striking example of the effects of plurality rule comes from Great Britain. In 2005, the British Labour Party won 35 percent of the vote and 55 percent of the seats; the Conservatives finished second, with 31 percent of the vote and 31 percent of the seats; the Liberal Democrats garnered 22 percent of the popular vote, but won just 8 percent of the seats. Nevertheless, plurality rule offers certain advantages. It gives voters the ability to choose individuals to represent them personally, not just political parties, and it picks a definite winner without the need for runoff elections.

proportional representation

A multiple-member district system that awards seats based on the percentage of the vote won

Among the democracies of the world, the main alternative to plurality rule is proportional representation, also called PR for short. Under proportional representation, competing parties win legislative seats in proportion to their share of the popular vote. For example, if three parties running for seats in the legislature divide the vote such that one wins 34 percent and the other two receive 33 percent of the vote, the first party received 34 percent of the seats and the other two receive 33 percent.

PR is used rarely in the United States. The most substantial elections in which it is employed are the Democratic presidential primary elections. During the 1988 primary season, Jesse Jackson routinely won 20 percent of the vote in the primaries but ended up with only about 5 percent of the delegates. To make the Democratic National Convention and the party more representative of its disparate voting groups, Jackson negotiated with other party leaders to change the delegate allocation rules so that delegates within congressional districts would be assigned on a proportional basis. If a district elects five delegates, a candidate wins a delegate if the candidate receives at least 20 percent of the vote in the district, two delegates if the candidate wins at least 40 percent of the vote, and so forth. Prior to this rule change the Democratic Party awarded all delegates from a given congressional district to the candidate who won a plurality of the vote. Like any districted system with plurality rule, this created a strong majoritarian tendency.

Plurality rule in single-member districts has a very important consequence. This is the reason for two-party politics in the United States. Around the world, countries with plurality rule in single-member districts have far fewer political parties than other nations. Typically, elections under plurality rule boil down to just two major parties that routinely compete for power, with one of them winning a majority of legislative seats outright. Proportional representation systems, on the other hand, tend to have many more than two parties. Rarely does a single party win a majority of seats. Governments form as coalitions of many different parties.

How votes are cast and counted, and what it takes to win a seat, then, have very substantial consequences for American politics. Plurality rule with single-member districts creates strong pressures toward two-party politics and majority rule in the legislature.

Direct Democracy: The Referendum and Recall

In addition to voting for candidates, voters in some states also vote on referenda. Referendums may come about two ways. First, some state constitutions and laws require that certain types of legislation (such as bonds or property tax increases) be approved by popular vote. Second, people may get a measure put on the ballot by obtaining enough signatures of registered voters to a petition. The referendum process allows citizens to vote directly on proposed laws or other governmental actions. In recent years, voters in several states have voted to set limits on tax rates, to define marriage, and to prohibit social services for illegal immigrants. Although it involves voting, a referendum is not an election. The election is an institution of representative government. Through an election, voters choose officials to act for them. The referendum, by contrast, is an institution of direct democracy; it allows voters to govern directly without intervention by government officials. The validity of referenda results, however, is subject to judicial action. If a court finds that a referendum outcome violates the state or national constitution, it can overturn the result. For example, in 2008 California voters passed

referendum
A measure proposed or passed by a legislature that is referred to the vote of the electorate for approval or rejection

Proposition 8, which stated, "only marriage between a man and a woman is valid and recognized in California." A federal district court in California ruled Proposition 8 unconstitutional in 2010, and the Supreme Court let stand the district court's ruling in 2013.[21]

Referendums are by far the most common way that issues are placed on the ballot for public consideration, but there are other means as well. Twenty-four states permit various forms of the initiative. Whereas the referendum process described above allows citizens to affirm or reject a policy produced by legislative action, the initiative provides citizens with a way forward in the face of legislative inaction. This is done by placing a policy proposal (legislative or state constitutional amendment) on the ballot to be approved or disapproved by the electorate. In order to reserve a place on the ballot, a petition must be accompanied by a minimum number of voter signatures—a requirement that varies from state to state—that are certified by the state's secretary of state.

Ballot propositions often involve policies the state legislature cannot (or does not want to) resolve. Like referendum issues, these are often highly emotional and, consequently, not always well suited to resolution in the electoral arena. On the other hand, one of the "virtues" of the initiative is that it may force action. Legislative leaders can induce recalcitrant legislators to move ahead on controversial issues in the knowledge that a possibly worse outcome will result from inaction.[22]

Eighteen states also have legal provisions for recall elections. The recall is an electoral device introduced by Populists at the turn of the twentieth century to allow voters to remove governors and other state officials from office prior to the expiration of their terms. Federal officials such as the president and members of Congress are not subject to recall. Generally, a recall effort begins with a petition campaign. For example, in California, the site of a tumultuous recall battle in 2003, if 12 percent of those who voted in the last general election sign petitions demanding a special recall election, the state board of elections must schedule one. Such petition campaigns are relatively common, but most fail to garner enough signatures to bring the matter to a statewide vote. In the California case, however, a conservative Republican member of Congress, Darrell Issa, led a successful effort to recall the Democratic governor Gray Davis. Voters were unhappy about the state's economy, dissatisfied with Davis's performance, and blamed Davis for the state's $38 billion budget deficit. Issa and his followers were able to secure enough signatures to force a vote, and in October 2003 Davis became the second governor in American history to be recalled by his state's electorate (the first was North Dakota's governor Lynn Frazier, who was recalled in 1921). Under California law, voters in a special recall election are also asked to choose a replacement for the official whom they dismiss. Californians in 2003 elected the movie star Arnold Schwarzenegger to be their governor.

initiative

A process by which citizens may petition to place a policy proposal on the ballot for public vote

recall

The removal of a public official by popular vote

Direct democracy, even if it is not used aggressively, can change legislative, executive, and even judicial decision making. The referendum, initiative, and recall all entail shifts in agenda-setting power. The referendum gives an impassioned electoral majority the opportunity to reverse legislation that displeases them, thus affecting the initial strategic calculations of institutional agenda setters (who want to get as much of what they want without its being subsequently reversed). The initiative has a similar effect on institutional agenda setters, but here it inclines them toward action rather than inaction. Combining the two, an institutional agenda setter is caught on the two horns of an institutional dilemma: Do I act, risking a reversal via referendum, or do I maintain the status quo, risking an overturn via initiative? The recall complements both of these, keeping institutional agenda setters on their toes to avoid being ousted. As the institution principle implies, these arrangements do not just provide citizens with governance tools. They also affect the strategic calculations of institutional politicians—legislators and governors.

HOW VOTERS DECIDE

An election expresses the preferences of millions of individuals about whom they want as their representatives and leaders. Electoral rules and laws—the institutional side of elections—impose order on that process, but ultimately, elections are a reflection of the people, the aggregation of many millions of individuals' expressions of their preferences about politics.

The voter's decision can be understood as really two linked decisions: whether to vote and for whom. Social scientists have examined both facets of the electoral decision by studying election returns, survey data, and experiments conducted in laboratories as well as field experiments conducted during actual elections. Out of generations of research into these questions, a broad picture emerges of how voters decide. First, the decision to vote or not to vote correlates very strongly with the social characteristics of individuals, especially age and education, but it also depends on the electoral choices and context. An individual who does not know anything about the candidates or dislikes all of the choices is unlikely to vote. Second, which candidates or party voters choose depends primarily on three factors: partisan loyalties, issues, and candidate characteristics. Partisan loyalties have been found to be the strongest single predictor of the vote, though party attachments also reflect issues and experience with candidates. Party, issues, and candidates act together to shape vote choice.

Voters and Nonvoters

As we saw earlier, turnout in modern American presidential elections ranges from 50 to 60 percent of the voting-age population. In 2012, 62 percent of citizens of voting age turned out; thus, almost 40 percent of those who could have voted did not. Why do so many people not vote?

This phenomenon has long puzzled social scientists and motivated reformers. A general explanation is elusive, but what social scientists do know about this phenomenon is that a few demographic characteristics routinely prove to be strong predictors of who votes. The most important of these characteristics are age, education, and residential mobility. Other factors, such as gender, income, and race also matter, but to a much smaller degree. According to the 2012 Current Population Survey, only 41 percent of those under age 25 voted that year, fully 20 points below the population average. By comparison, 71 percent of those over 65 years of age voted. The difference between these groups was 30 percentage points, and the effect of age on voting surely translated into an electoral difference. The interests of retirees are much more likely to receive attention by the government than are the interests of people in college or just entering the labor force.

Education shows similarly large differences. Those without a high school diploma voted at half the rate of those with a college education. More than three in four people with a college education voted, and the rate was 81 percent among those with a professional degree. In contrast, slightly fewer than 40 percent of those without a high school diploma voted and 52 percent of those with only a high school diploma voted. Finally, consider residency and mobility. Only 51 percent of people who lived in their current residence less than a year reported voting, compared with 76 percent of people who lived in their residence at least five years. Those who own their home or apartment voted at a 67 percent rate, but only 49 percent of those who rent voted.[23] Politicians listen to those who vote, and those who vote are disproportionately older, better educated, and more rooted in their communities.

As discussed earlier, election laws have historically had a large effect on the size and character of the electorate. Those interested in encouraging greater participation today have focused on voter registration requirements, which are thought to create an unnecessary hurdle and thus to depress turnout. The decision to vote itself consists of two steps—registration and turnout. In 2012, 87 percent of those who reported that they registered said they voted. Weakening registration requirements may increase participation. One approach to minimizing such requirements is Election Day registration. As of 2014, 10 states plus the District of Columbia allow people to register on Election Day at the polls or at a government office. The three states with the longest experience with same-day registration—Minnesota, Wisconsin, and Maine—do have higher turnout than most other states, and most studies suggest that in a typical state, adopting such a law would increase turnout by about 3 to 5 percent.[24]

Demographics and laws are only part of what accounts for voting and nonvoting. The choices presented to the voters are also quite important. The problem is not that many people have a hard time making up their minds, but that many people do not feel engaged by current elections, or dislike politics altogether. People who are disinterested, "too busy to vote," or do not like the candidates tend not to vote. The Census Bureau survey asks registered nonvoters why they did not vote. The top four reasons are "too busy," "sick or disabled," "not interested," and "did not like the choices."

Partisan Loyalty

The single strongest predictor of how a person will vote is that individual's attachment to a political party. The American National Election Studies (ANES), exit polls, and media polls have found that even in times of great political change in the United States, the overwhelming majority of Americans identifies with one of the two major political parties and votes almost entirely in accordance with that identity. Survey researchers ascertain party identification with simple questions along the following lines: Generally speaking, do you consider yourself to be a Democrat, a Republican, an independent, or what?[25] Survey researchers further classify people by asking of those who choose a party whether they identify strongly or weakly with that party, and by asking independents whether they lean toward one party or another.

party identification

An individual's attachment to a particular political party, which might be based on issues, ideology, past experience, or upbringing

Party identifications capture voters' predisposition toward their party's candidates. Many of these predispositions are rooted in public policies, such as the parties' positions on taxes or civil rights. Those long-standing policy positions lead to divisions in party identifications and voting patterns among different demographic groups. Large majorities of African Americans and Hispanics, for example, identify and vote with the Democratic Party. Women also tend to identify more and vote more with the Democrats than men do. In 2012, Barack Obama received 55 percent of the vote of women, but only 45 percent of the vote among men. That difference is not as large as the difference across racial groups, but it is significant because women now comprise a majority of voters (53 percent).

Although specific features of the choices and context matter as well, party identifications express how voters would likely vote in a "neutral" election. Party identifications are extremely good predictors of voting behavior in less prominent elections, such as for state legislature or lower-level statewide offices, about which voters may know relatively little. Even in presidential elections, with their extensive advertising and very thorough news coverage, party predispositions predict individual voting behavior. Figure 10.3 displays the percentages of Democratic identifiers, Republican identifiers, and self-described independents who voted for Mitt Romney, Barack Obama, or someone else in 2012. Approximately 92 percent of party identifiers voted for their own party's standard bearer. Independents (including independents who lean toward either party) broke 50 to 45 for Romney. The 2012 election was typical in that partisan loyalty is usually in the range of 90 percent. Sometimes, the independent vote decides the election. However, because more Americans are Democrats than Republicans, in this case Obama still won the election.

There are three distinct views about what party identification is. They are not necessarily exclusive of one another, but they point to very different understandings of the nature of party identification and its effect on elections.[26] Debate over the meaning of party identity cuts to the heart of the meaning of elections.

First, party identification is a psychological attachment that individuals hold, often throughout their adulthood, to one of the parties. Individuals learn as children and adolescents from parents, other adults, and even peers about politics, and as part of that socialization they develop attachments to a party, not unlike religion and community. Party identifications continue to form into early adulthood. The first few presidential elections that an individual experiences as an adult are thought to have particularly

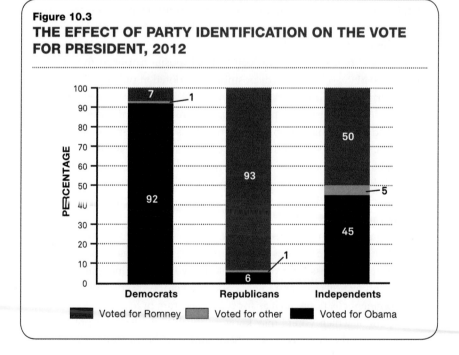

Figure 10.3

THE EFFECT OF PARTY IDENTIFICATION ON THE VOTE FOR PRESIDENT, 2012

　　Chapter 10: Elections

profound influence on that individual's understanding of the parties and politics. And as different cohorts come into politics, their experiences carry forward throughout their lives. Those who were 18 to 24 years old in 1984, for example, identify overwhelmingly with the Republican Party, because those elections marked the triumph of Ronald Reagan's presidency and political philosophy, the rise of a revitalized Republican Party, and the beginning of the end of the Cold War. Those 18 to 24 years old in 2008, on the other hand, identify disproportionately with the Democratic Party, because the Obama campaign galvanized young voters around a new vision for the future. However it is developed, an individual's psychological affinity for a party makes that person want that party to win and want to support that party, even when he or she disagrees with the party on important policies or disapproves of the party's nominees for office.

Of course, the Democratic and Republican parties are quite different entities today than they were 40 years ago or 80 years ago. On matters of race relations, for example, the Democratic Party has moved over the past century from supporting segregation to spearheading civil rights. The Republican Party, once a bastion of economic protectionism, now champions free trade. However strong generational transmission of party identifications may be, the dissonance between identities and issues must surely weaken the pull of party, which suggests a second theory of party. This second idea is that party identifications reflect underlying ideologies of voters and policy positions of parties. Parties in government, as we discussed in Chapter 5, are meaningful organizations for producing public policies. The relatively high degree of party loyalty in Congress and other branches of government means that voters can reasonably anticipate how politicians will act in office. Citizens identify with parties that pursue public policies more to their liking. For example, a union worker will feel a stronger attachment to the Democratic Party because the Democrats have historically protected union interests. A high-income earner may feel a strong pull toward the Republican Party because that party pushes lower taxes overall, whereas the Democrats promote higher tax rates for higher-income households. As mentioned in the introduction to this chapter, elections present an informational problem of adverse selection. The party labels act as brand names and help voters choose the candidates that will best match their preferences. Voters need not know the details of an individual candidate's voting record or campaign promises in order to understand how that politician will likely behave on important matters. As such, party labels provide an informational shortcut for voters. Party identification means, in part, that a voter feels that party represents his interests better than other parties; hence, an identifier is highly likely to vote for that party.[27]

A third explanation is that party identification reflects experiences with political leaders and representatives, especially the presidents from each of the parties. As the political scientist Morris Fiorina put it, party identifications are running tallies of experience. Americans hold their presidents, and to a lesser extent Congress, accountable for the economic performance of the country and success in foreign affairs. A bad economy or a disastrous military intervention will lead voters to disapprove of the president and to lower their assessment of the president's party's ability to govern. Parties are, by this account, teams seeking to run the government. They consist of policy experts, managers, and leaders who will conduct foreign policy, economic policy, and domestic policies (such as environmental protection and health care). When things go well, voters infer that the incumbent party has a good approach to running national affairs, but when things go badly, they infer that the party lacks the people needed to run the government competently or the approach needed to produce economic prosperity, international peace, and other outcomes desired by the public. With each successive presidency and their experience of it, individuals update their beliefs about which party is better able to govern.

Psychological attachments, ideological affinities, and past experiences add up to form an individual's current party identifications. But party is not the only factor in voting. Some partisans do defect, especially in elections when voters are dissatisfied with the incumbent party or are especially drawn to a particular candidate.

Issues

Issues and policy preferences constitute a second factor influencing voters' decisions. Voting on issues and policies cuts to the core of our understanding of democratic accountability and electoral control over government. A simple, idealized account of issue voting goes as follows. Governments make policies and laws on a variety of issues that affect the public. Voters who disagree with those policies and laws on principle or who think those policies have failed will vote against those who made the decisions. Voters who support the policies or like the outcomes that government has produced will support the incumbent legislatures or party. It is important to note that politicians choose what kinds of laws to enact and what kinds of administrative actions to take with the express aim of attracting electoral support. Voters choose the candidates and parties that produce the best results or most preferred laws. Even party identifications reflect the policy preferences of the voters and the policies pursued by the parties and candidates.

Voters' issue choices usually involve a mix of their judgments about the past behavior of competing parties and candidates and their hopes and fears about candidates' future behavior. Political scientists call choices that

issue voting

An individual's propensity to select candidates or parties based on the extent to which the individual agrees with one candidate more than others on specific issues focus on future behavior prospective voting, while those based on past performance are called retrospective voting. To some extent, whether prospective or retrospective evaluation is more important in a particular election depends on the strategies of competing candidates. Candidates always endeavor to define the issues of an election in terms that will serve their interests. Incumbents running during a period of prosperity will seek to take credit for the economy's happy state and define the election as revolving around their record of success. This strategy encourages voters to make retrospective judgments. In contrast, an insurgent running during a period of economic uncertainty will tell voters it is time for a change and ask them to make prospective judgments. Thus, Barack Obama focused on the need for change in 2008, but the White House repeatedly stressed the need to stay the course in 2010 and 2012. In 2014, Obama's popularity had fallen because of uneven economic growth and other issues, and the Republicans campaigned against the president's handling of these issues.

Economic voting is one way that voters solve the information problems inherent in representative democracy. They cannot monitor every policy that the government initiates. They do, however, have a rudimentary way to hold the government accountable—staying the course when times are good and voting for change when the economy sours. Richard Nixon, Ronald Reagan, Bill Clinton, and George W. Bush won re-election easily in the midst of favorable economies. Jimmy Carter in 1980 and George H. W. Bush in 1992 ran for re-election in the midst of economic downturns, and both lost. Over the past quarter-century, the Consumer Confidence Index, calculated by the Conference Board, a business research group, has been a fairly accurate predictor of presidential outcomes. It would appear that a generally rosy view, indicated by a score greater than 100, augurs well for the party in power. An index score of less than 100, suggesting that voters are pessimistic about the economy's trend, suggests that incumbents should worry about their job prospects (Figure 10.4). In 2012, the index was only 72.2, but had been rising steadily for the past several months.

prospective voting
Voting based on the imagined future performance of a candidate

retrospective voting
Voting based on the past performance of a candidate

Candidate Characteristics

Candidates' personal attributes always influence voters' decisions. Some analysts claim that voters prefer tall candidates to short candidates, candidates with shorter names to candidates with longer names, and candidates with lighter hair to candidates with darker hair. Perhaps these rather frivolous criteria do play some role. But the more important candidate characteristics that affect voters' choices are race, ethnicity, religion, gender, geography, and social background. Voters presume that candidates with similar backgrounds

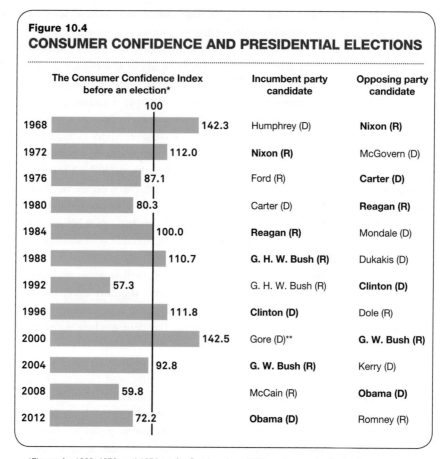

Figure 10.4

CONSUMER CONFIDENCE AND PRESIDENTIAL ELECTIONS

The Consumer Confidence Index before an election*	Incumbent party candidate	Opposing party candidate
1968 — 142.3	Humphrey (D)	**Nixon (R)**
1972 — 112.0	**Nixon (R)**	McGovern (D)
1976 — 87.1	Ford (R)	**Carter (D)**
1980 — 80.3	Carter (D)	**Reagan (R)**
1984 — 100.0	**Reagan (R)**	Mondale (D)
1988 — 110.7	**G. H. W. Bush (R)**	Dukakis (D)
1992 — 57.3	G. H. W. Bush (R)	**Clinton (D)**
1996 — 111.8	**Clinton (D)**	Dole (R)
2000 — 142.5	Gore (D)**	**G. W. Bush (R)**
2004 — 92.8	**G. W. Bush (R)**	Kerry (D)
2008 — 59.8	McCain (R)	**Obama (D)**
2012 — 72.2	**Obama (D)**	Romney (R)

*Figures for 1968, 1972, and 1976 are for October; from 1980 on, they are for September.
**Gore won the popular vote, but Bush was elected by the Electoral College.
NOTE: A score above 100 means people are optimistic about the economy. A score below 100 means most people are pessimistic about the economy. The candidate who won the election appears in bold.
SOURCE: *Bloomberg Markets*.

to their own are likely to share their views. Moreover, they may be proud to see someone of their background in a position of leadership. This is why politicians seek to "balance the ticket" by including members of as many important groups as possible.

A candidate's personal characteristics may attract some voters, but they may repel others. Many voters are prejudiced against candidates of certain ethnic, racial, or religious groups. And many voters—both men and women—continue to be reluctant to support the political candidacies of women, although this appears to be changing.

Voters also pay attention to candidates' personality characteristics, such as their "competence," "honesty," and "vigor." Voters want these skills and attributes because the politicians who have them are more likely to produce good outcomes, such as laws that work, fair and honest administration of government, and the ability to address crises. Candidates, in turn, emphasize certain qualities that they think all voters will value. An excellent example arose in the 2008 primary election between Hillary Clinton and Barack Obama. Clinton ran an ad that intended to show her experience and ability to solve crises. "It's 3 A.M. and your children are safely asleep. But there's a phone in the White House and it's ringing. Something's happening in the world. Your vote will decide who answers that call. . . . Whether it's someone tested and ready to lead in a dangerous world. . . ." Whether this ad had a lasting effect on perceptions of Obama is impossible to know, but it was designed to tap the voters' belief in the need for a certain set of competencies in the White House.

One of the most distinctive features of American politics is the apparent advantage that incumbents have, as we saw in Chapter 5. Why the incumbency advantage has emerged and grown remains something of a puzzle. Redistricting is almost certainly not the explanation: incumbency effects are

IN BRIEF

How Voters Decide

Partisan Loyalty

Most Americans identify with either the Democratic or Republican Party and will vote for candidates accordingly. Party loyalty rarely changes and is most influential in less visible electoral contests, such as on the state or local level, where issues and candidates are less well known.

Issues

Voters may choose a candidate whose views they agree with on a particular issue that is very important to them, even if they disagree with the candidate in other areas. It is easier for voters to make choices based on issues if candidates articulate very different positions and policy preferences.

Candidate Characteristics

Voters are more likely to identify with and support a candidate who shares their background, views, and perspectives; therefore, race, ethnicity, religion, gender, geography, and social background are characteristics that influence how people vote. Personality characteristics such as honesty and integrity have become more important in recent years.

as large in gubernatorial elections, where there are no districts, as in House elections. It is thought that about half of the incumbency advantage reflects the activities of the legislator in office; it is the result of voters rewarding incumbents for their performance. The other half of the incumbency advantage evidently reflects not the incumbents but their opponents.[28] The typical challenger in U.S. elections may not have the personal appeal of the typical incumbent; after all, the typical incumbent has already won office once. Moreover, challengers usually lack the experience and resources that the incumbent has for running a campaign. This is critical. The ability to communicate with the voters can give a politician the edge in close elections.

Although party, issues, and candidate characteristics are perhaps the three most important factors shaping voting decisions, there is much debate among political scientists as to the relative importance of each. Problems of measurement and the limitations of research methods have made it exceedingly difficult to parse the relative importance of these factors in voters' thinking. Recent scholarship suggests that they have roughly equal weight in explaining the division of the vote in national elections.[29] Part of the difficulty in understanding their importance is that the extent to which these factors matter depends on the information levels of the electorate. In the absence of much information, most voters rely almost exclusively on party cues. A highly informed electorate relies more heavily on issues and candidate characteristics.[30]

CAMPAIGNS: MONEY, MEDIA, AND GRASS ROOTS

American political campaigns are freewheeling events with few restrictions on what candidates may say or do. Candidates in hotly contested House and Senate races spend millions of dollars to advertise on television and radio, as well as direct mail and door-to-door canvassing. Those seeking office are in a race to become as well known and as well liked as possible and to get more of their supporters to vote. Federal laws limit how much an individual or organization may give to a candidate but, with the exception of presidential campaigns, place no restrictions on how much a candidate or party committee may spend.

Adding to the freewheeling nature of campaigns is their organizational structure. Most political campaigns are temporary organizations. They form for the sole purpose of winning the coming elections and disband shortly afterward. To be sure, political parties in the United States have a set of permanent, professional campaign organizations that raise money, strategize, recruit candidates, and distribute resources. These are, on the Republican side of the aisle, the Republican National Committee, the National Republican Senatorial Committee, and the National Republican Congressional Committee. On the Democratic side of the aisle are the Democratic National Committee, the Democratic Senatorial Campaign Committee, and the Democratic Congressional Campaign Committee. They account for roughly one-third of the money in politics and have considerable expertise. But most campaigns are formed by and around individual candidates, who often put up the initial cash to get the campaign rolling and rely heavily on family and friends as volunteers. Thousands of such organizations are at work during an election. The two presidential campaigns operate 50 different state-level operations, with other campaigns competing for 34 Senate seats, 435 House seats, dozens of gubernatorial and other statewide offices, and thousands of state legislative seats. There is relatively little coordination among these myriad campaigns, though they all simultaneously work toward the same end—persuading as many people as possible to vote for their candidate on Election Day.

What It Takes to Win. All campaigns, big and small, face similar challenges—how to bring people in, how to raise money, how to coordinate activities, what messages to run, and how to communicate with the public. There is no one best way to run a campaign. There are many tried-and-true approaches, especially building up a campaign from many local connections, from the grass roots. Candidates have to meet as many people as possible and get their friends and their friends' friends to support them. In-person campaigning becomes increasingly difficult in larger constituencies. Candidates continually experiment with new ways of communicating with the public and new ways of organizing in order to more efficiently reach large segments of the electorate. In the 1920s, radio advertising eclipsed handbills and door-to-door canvassing, as broadcasting captured economies of scale. In the 1960s, television began to eclipse radio. In the 1980s and 1990s, cable television and innovations in marketing (especially phone polling and focus groups) allowed candidates to target very specific demographic groups through the media. The great innovation of the Obama campaign was to meld Internet networking tools with old-style organizing methods to develop a massive communications and fund-raising network that came to be called a "netroots" campaign.

It has become an assumption of American elections and election law that candidates and parties will mount competitive campaigns to win office. They will spend millions, even billions, of dollars, to persuade people to vote and how to vote. And because of those efforts voters will understand better what choices they face in the elections. In short, campaigns inform voters, and they do so through competition. In addition to being costly, American political campaigns are long, often spanning years. Campaigns for the presidency officially launch a year and a half to two years in advance of Election Day. Serious campaigns for the U.S. House of Representatives begin at least a year ahead of the general-election date and often span the better part of two years. To use the term of the Federal Election Commission, an election is a two-year *cycle*, not a single day or even the period between Labor Day and Election Day loosely referred to as "the general election."

The long campaigns in the United States are due in large part to the effort required to mount a campaign. There are roughly 319 million people in the United States, and the voting-age population exceeds 242 million people. Communicating with all of those people is an expensive and time-consuming enterprise. A simple calculation reveals the challenge. Suppose you ran for president of the United States. Sending one piece of mail to each household in the United States would cost approximately $100 million dollars, and that is probably the minimum imaginable campaign effort. How long would it take to raise $100 million and mobilize such an effort to communicate with the American people? In the 2012 election cycle, the Barack Obama campaign and allied committees spent $1.2 billion; Mitt Romney's campaign and allied committees spent $1.25 billion—almost $2.5 billion total. Approximately half of that sum was spent to purchase airtime for television advertisements. That money was raised through personal and political networks that the campaigns built up over months, even years of effort. It takes extensive operations to reach out to so many people and to raise such vast sums. Simply putting such an organization in place takes months.

The campaign season is further extended by the election calendar. American elections proceed in two steps: the party primary elections and the general election. General elections for federal offices are set by the U.S. Constitution to take place on the first Tuesday after the first Monday in November. The first presidential caucuses and primaries come early in January and last through the beginning of June. State and congressional primaries do not follow the same calendar, but most occur in the spring and early summer, with a handful of some states waiting to hold their nominating elections until September of the election year. The immediate result of this yearlong calendar of elections is to stretch the campaigns over the entire election year.

Campaign Finance. The expense, duration, and chaos of American campaigns have prompted many efforts at reform, including attempts to limit campaign spending, shorten the campaign season, and restrict what candidates and organizations may say in advertisements. The most sweeping campaign reforms came in 1971, when Congress passed the Federal Elections Campaign Act (or FECA). It limited the amounts that a single individual could contribute to a candidate or party to $1,000 per election for individuals and $5,000 for organizations (these limits have since been increased, as

Table 10.1 indicates). It further regulated how business firms, unions, and other organizations could give money, prohibiting donations directly from the organization's treasury and requiring the establishment of a separate, segregated fund—a political action committee (PAC). It established public funding for presidential campaigns and tied those funds to expenditure limits. And it set up the Federal Election Commission (FEC) to oversee public disclosure of information and to enforce the laws.[31] Congress has amended the act several times, most importantly in the Bipartisan Campaign Reform Act of 2002 (BCRA, also called the McCain-Feingold Act, after senators John McCain and Russell Feingold, its primary sponsors in the Senate). The McCain-Feingold Act prohibited unlimited party spending (called *soft money*) and banned certain sorts of political attack advertisements from interest groups in the last weeks of a campaign. See Table 10.1 for a summary of some of the rules governing campaign finance in federal elections.

The FECA also established public funding for presidential campaigns. If a candidate agrees to abide by spending limits, that candidate's campaign is eligible for matching funds in primary elections and full public funding in the general election. Until 2000, nearly all candidates bought into the system. George W. Bush chose to fund his 2000 primary election campaign outside this system and spent $500 million to win the Republican nomination. Barack Obama and Hillary Clinton ignored the public-financing system in their 2008 primary contest, and Obama opted out of the public system in the general election as well, allowing him to spend several hundred million more dollars than the Republican nominee, John McCain. In 2012, neither Obama nor the Republican candidates for president used public funding.

FECA originally went much further than the law that survives today. Congress originally passed mandatory caps on spending by House and Senate candidates and prohibited organizations from running their own independent campaigns on behalf of or in opposition to a candidate (and not coordinated with any candidate). James Buckley, a candidate for U.S. Senate in New York, challenged the law, arguing that the restrictions on spending and contributions limited his rights to free speech and that the FEC had excessive administrative power. In the 1976 landmark case *Buckley v. Valeo*, the U.S. Supreme Court agreed in part.[32] The Court ruled that "money is speech," but the government also has a compelling interest in protecting elections from corrupt practices, such as bribery through large campaign donations. The justices declared the limits on candidate spending unconstitutional because they violated free speech rights of candidates and groups. However, the need to protect the integrity of the electoral process led the justices to leave contribution limits in place. The presidential public-funding system was also validated because it is voluntary. Candidates can opt into the system, but they are not required to; hence, there is no violation of free speech. What survived *Buckley* is a system in which candidates, groups, and

political action committee (PAC)

A private group that raises and distributes funds for use in election campaigns

Table 10.1

FEDERAL CAMPAIGN FINANCE CONTRIBUTION LIMITS

	To each candidate or candidate committee per election	To national party committee per calendar year	To state, district, and local party committee per calendar year	To any other political committee per calendar year
Individual may give	$2,600*	$32,400*	$10,000 (combined limit)	$5,000
National party committee may give	$5,000	No limit	No limit	$5,000
State, district, and local party committee may give	$5,000 (combined limit)	No limit	No limit	$5,000 (combined limit)
PAC (multicandidate) may give**	$5,000	$15,000	$5,000 (combined limit)	$5,000
PAC (not multicandidate) may give	$2,600*	$32,400*	$10,000 (combined limit)	$5,000
Authorized campaign committee may give	$2,000†	No limit	No limit	$5,000

*These contribution limits are increased for inflation in odd-numbered years.

**A multicandidate committee is a political committee with more than 50 contributors that has been registered for at least six months and, with the exception of state party committees, has made contributions to five or more candidates for federal office.

†A federal candidate's authorized committee(s) may contribute no more than $2,000 per election to another federal candidate's authorized committee(s).

SOURCE: Federal Election Commission, www.fec.gov/pages/brochures/contriblimits.shtml (accessed 7/17/13).

parties may spend as much as they like to win office, but donations must come in small amounts. In an expensive election, campaigns must accumulate their resources from large numbers of individuals and groups. This is a more democratic process of campaign finance, but it increases the effort and time needed to construct a campaign.

In 2010, the Supreme Court reinforced its reasoning in *Buckley v. Valeo* in the case *Citizens' United v. Federal Election Commission*.[33] In *Citizens' United* the

Justices ruled that the BCRA of 2002 had erred in imposing restrictions on independent spending by corporations. It overturned key components of the BCRA and reversed its ruling in the case that had upheld BCRA, *McConnell v. Federal Election Commission.*[34] The majority opinion struck down limits on independent expenditures from corporate treasuries but kept in place limits on direct contributions from corporations and other organizations to candidates. The majority opinion went further than past decisions, however, in solidifying corporations' right to free political speech, on par with the right to free speech of individuals. In the wake of this decision, two sorts of organizations formed—501c(4) organizations, which derive their title from the section of the tax code that allows such entities, and Super PACs. Each can raise and spend unlimited amounts on campaigns, though Super PACs are subject to more disclosure laws. Super PACs spent a total of approximately $546.5 million in 2012, most of that on the presidential election. However, independent expenditures from other organizations decreased, so the increase in total independent spending was about $300 million (or $2 per voter) from 2008 to 2012. In 2014, Super PACs spent $339.4 million, substantially more than all independent spending in 2010, the prior midterm election.

Congressional Campaigns. Congressional campaigns share a number of important features with presidential campaigns, but they are also distinctive. One of the salient features of congressional campaigns is the incumbency advantage. While there is an incumbency advantage for sitting presidents, the two-term limit on the president means that incumbency is a more important feature for congressional representatives, who have no term limits. In recent decades, the incumbency advantage has grown both in magnitude and in importance in U.S. elections. Today, almost every elective office at the state and federal level exhibits an incumbency advantage. Those advantages have ranged from about 5 percent in state legislative elections to 10 percent for U.S. House, U.S. Senate, and governor. A 10 percent incumbency advantage is a massive electoral edge. It turns a competitive race into a blowout for the incumbent.[35]

Congressional incumbents' advantages arise in spending as well as votes. Like presidential campaigns, congressional campaigns have witnessed increasing amounts of spending over time. The average U.S. House incumbent in 2012 spent $1.6 million, to the $260,000 spent by the typical challenger.

Once a campaign has enough money to initiate operations, it begins to communicate with the voters, often starting small by attending meetings with various groups. A successful campaign builds on early successes, bringing in more supporters and volunteers and culminating with intensive advertising campaigns in the final months or weeks before Election Day. Although the Democratic and Republican parties may help campaigns that have a good shot of succeeding, they typically come in late. Every campaign for Congress or president is built by the individual candidates and their close friends and associates from the ground up. The personal style of political campaigning that Americans have come to appreciate reflects an enormous investment of time and resources, an investment that takes the better part of a year to grow. Incumbent members of Congress have particular advantages in campaign fund-raising. They have already been tested; they have their campaign organizations in place; and they have connections in their constituencies, as well as in Washington, D.C.

THE 2012 AND 2014 ELECTIONS

In the fall of 2012, more than 132 million Americans went to the polls to select a president, members of Congress, governors, and numerous other officials. Voters re-elected Barack Obama to the presidency and confirmed the Democratic Party's control of the Senate and the Republican Party's majority in the House of Representatives. Obama won 65 million votes, roughly 51 percent, while his Republican challenger, Mitt Romney, received about 61 million votes, or 47 percent. Though the president's margin of victory was about 5 percentage points less than in 2008, it was enough to give him 332 electoral votes, 62 more than the 270 needed to win a majority in the Electoral College (Figure 10.5). The president's margin of victory was built on a coalition of women, working-class voters, and minority voters in several key battleground states. Despite the billions of dollars spent by candidates and the hoopla of the campaign, the 2012 election was decided more by demographic realities than by political rhetoric.

Generally speaking, incumbent presidents have a substantial advantage when they seek re-election to a second term. During the course of American history, incumbent presidents standing for re-election have won about 70 percent of the time. Despite this advantage of incumbency, the re-election of President Barack Obama in 2012 was never a foregone conclusion. Although Obama scored major legislative successes early in his first term, these accomplishments, especially the Affordable Care Act, were controversial. To make matters worse, unemployment remained high throughout Obama's first four years. The combination of controversial legislation and a weak economic record made the incumbent vulnerable coming into the 2012 election season.

In his 2008 campaign, Obama energized legions of young supporters who saw in the senator from Illinois a charismatic and energetic politician who would pursue a progressive social agenda and bring an end to America's wars in the Middle East. Once in office, Obama was keen to make good on his promise of change. He worked to end the war in Iraq and wind down the war in Afghanistan, partly in order to shift the nation's spending priorities from the military to domestic social needs. In the realm of domestic policy,

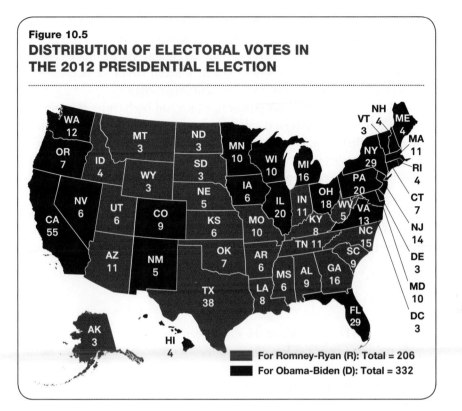

Figure 10.5

DISTRIBUTION OF ELECTORAL VOTES IN THE 2012 PRESIDENTIAL ELECTION

For Romney-Ryan (R): Total = 206
For Obama-Biden (D): Total = 332

between 2008 and 2010, with both chambers of Congress controlled by the Democrats, the president succeeded in passing a $700 billion economic stimulus bill, a law that guaranteed equal pay for women, new financial regulations, and an extensive overhaul of the nation's health care laws. The Affordable Care Act, which came to be known as "Obamacare," became a flashpoint for the 2010 and 2012 elections. The law sought to make access to health care universal: it required individuals without insurance to purchase insurance, it required businesses to provide insurance, it set up insurance pools to allow those without care to purchase inexpensive insurance, it required states to extend their Medicaid coverage, and it forbade insurance companies to exclude people from coverage for preexisting conditions.

These successes came at a cost, and the opportunity for a corrective came at the 2010 midterm election. It is often the case that the president's party loses some seats in the midterm elections, but in 2010 the Democrats lost a whopping 64 seats and ceded control of the House to the Republicans. Many Americans saw Obamacare as a costly government takeover of a major industry and an unwarranted intrusion into the lives of all Americans. Many people also saw financial reform and economic stimulus as policies that would impose too much regulation or create mounting debt problems. The backlash against Obama's early legislative successes took the form of a loose but broad conservative movement called the Tea Party, whose organizations sponsored rallies and protests and recruited candidates to run for office. Against this background of dissatisfaction and dissent, the 2010 midterm elections left the president with a Republican House of Representatives that vowed to block any new presidential initiatives.

All the while, the nation's economy, which had been battered by recession in 2007 and 2008, showed only tepid signs of recovery. For much of the president's first term, unemployment remained in the uncomfortably high 8–9 percent range, with hundreds of thousands of recent college graduates finding themselves unemployed or underemployed; the housing market was weak; and a number of major financial institutions seemed on the edge of failure. As a result, President Obama's re-election hardly seemed assured. However, the Republicans needed to find a candidate who could defeat the president and appeal to the various factions of their party.

The 2012 Republican Nomination

Although the Democratic and the Republican parties have become increasingly polarized over the last 40 years, the fact remains that neither party is ideologically uniform. In 2012, the Republican nomination battle took place among 10 candidates representing different factions within the party. Gradually, candidates who found themselves unable to attract much support dropped out of the race, and by February 2012, only four remained: Newt Gingrich, Ron Paul, Mitt Romney, and Rick Santorum. From the beginning, Romney's superior organization and financial base made him the front-runner. The GOP's social and religious conservatives, though, were unenthusiastic about the former Massachusetts governor. Some saw him as a liberal in Republican clothing, while others, particularly evangelical Protestants, were unhappy about the idea of a member of the Mormon faith leading the party. These groups gave their support to Rick Santorum, who eventually carried 11 states and more than 20 percent of the primary vote. By April 2012, though, Romney had clearly won the delegate votes needed for the nomination, and Santorum suspended his campaign.

Having won the Republican nomination, Romney moved to reassure the party's social conservatives that he was worthy of their enthusiastic support in the general election. One of the biggest challenges facing candidates is motivating likely supporters to actually vote come Election Day. Conservatives would not jump to the Obama camp, but anything less than enthusiastic participation in the campaign by social conservatives would doom the GOP's ticket to defeat. Accordingly, Romney endorsed a party platform that would appeal to this group. Its provisions included a constitutional amendment to ban abortion; elimination of government-funded family planning programs, with the exception of abstinence-only education; and a program of detention for "dangerous" aliens. Other provisions included repealing the Affordable Care Act and reducing federal taxes. As icing on the conservative cake, Romney chose as his vice-presidential running mate Congressman Paul Ryan of Wisconsin. Ryan had vigorously opposed Democratic fiscal and social policies and was enthusiastically supported by the GOP's social and fiscal conservatives.

The 2012 General Election

U.S. presidential elections are shaped by fundamental forces: the economy, foreign conflicts, the underlying partisanship and composition of the electorate, and the approval rating of the incumbent president. The 2012 election was no exception. But, the fundamentals in 2012 pointed in conflicting directions. Barack Obama was a fairly popular incumbent who boasted significant foreign-policy successes; however, he also had to defend a record of four years of slow economic growth and, in some parts of the country, economic stagnation. No president has been re-elected with an unemployment rate exceeding 8 percent, but no president with an approval rating of 50 percent has failed to win re-election. Political scientists' and economists' forecasts based on these fundamentals predicted a very tight election, with a slight edge to the president.

In recent years, the bedrock base of GOP support has consisted of reasonably affluent, educated, middle-aged, middle-class white men living in suburban and rural areas. The Democrats, on the other hand, have been able to rely upon the votes of a majority of women, less affluent Americans, urban residents, younger voters, African Americans, and, increasingly, Latino voters. While there are certainly poor Republicans and affluent Democrats, this split approaches a classic division between the "have mores" and "have lesses." Mitt Romney alluded to this division when he said, in what he thought to be a closed-door meeting with Republican donors, that 47 percent of Americans paid few taxes, depended on government handouts, and would never vote for him. When news of Romney's comments leaked, Republicans sought to contain the damage but did not necessarily dispute the accuracy of Romney's analysis.

Battleground States. While America, of course, comprises 50 states, presidential elections are usually fought in only a handful of "battleground" states. This is so because some states are solidly Republican (sometimes called the red states) while others are solidly Democratic (known as the blue states). In 2012, opinion polls indicated that only 8 of the 50 states were actually toss-ups. These were Colorado, Florida, Iowa, Nevada, New Hampshire, Ohio, Virginia, and Wisconsin. A handful of other states, including

In 2012, Mitt Romney tried to put Barack Obama on the defensive regarding the nation's sluggish economy. However, Obama's success among working-class voters, minorities, and women won him the election.

Michigan, Minnesota, New Mexico, and Pennsylvania, were seen as leaning toward Obama, while Arizona, Indiana, and North Carolina were viewed as leaning toward Romney. The remaining 35 states seemed to be solidly in either the Democratic or the Republican camp.

Thus, the 2012 presidential race was waged in a handful of battleground states. Here the Obama and Romney campaigns and their various supporters matched each other dollar for dollar in an unprecedented amount of political advertising. All told, Team Obama and allied groups spent over $400 million on televised advertising across the United States, and Team Romney and allied groups spent almost $500 million on television advertising. In places like Denver, Colorado, and Columbus, Ohio, the campaigns bought over 30,000 TV ads. In places like Los Angeles, California, and New York, New York, they bought none.

Campaign Tactics and Outcomes. In its battleground state advertisements, the Obama campaign's speeches and campaign commercials labeled Romney a multimillionaire who was out of touch with ordinary Americans and who sent American jobs overseas. These efforts succeeded in shoring up Obama's support among working-class Americans. According to exit polls, the president won 63 percent of the votes of those whose family incomes were less than $30,000 per year and 57 percent of those who earned between $30,000 and $49,000 per year.

The Obama campaign also redoubled its efforts among women voters. In recent years, women have tended to give a majority of their votes to the Democrats, producing a so-called gender gap in the electoral arena. Democratic ads reminded women that it was the Democratic Party that supported such issues as equal pay. Foolish remarks on rape and abortion by GOP senatorial candidates in Indiana and Missouri were highlighted by the Democrats to underscore Republican insensitivity to women. On Election Day, 55 percent of women voters supported Obama, while Obama received the votes of only 45 percent of America's men.

Finally, Obama campaign workers were determined to ensure high levels of turnout among minority voters, who potentially could be decisive in several battleground states. African American voters were a loyal Democratic constituency and could be counted upon to turn out for the president. Obama took 93 percent of the African American vote. But the Democrats had been making enormous efforts to bring Asian and, especially, Latino voters into their camp, too. Latinos are the most rapidly growing group in the American population and were responsible for about 10 percent of the votes cast in 2012. The Democratic Party had made a major effort to court Latinos on such issues as immigration, and, in 2012, Democrats pushed for ballot initiatives in a number of states that offered undocumented young Latinos who had been raised in the United States the opportunity to attend public colleges at the in-state tuition rate. This strategy proved extremely successful. Obama won approximately 70 percent of the Latino vote across the country.

Taken together, working-class voters, women, and minority constituents gave Obama the votes he needed for victory. Astonishingly, President Obama carried all eight battleground states, and in each one, exit polls suggested that the critical margin was provided by low-income groups, minorities, and women (Figure 10.6).

The 2014 Midterms—and Beyond

The 2014 election left the U.S. government divided, with President Obama facing Republican majorities in both chambers of Congress. In the House elections, Republicans picked up 13 seats, increasing their majority to 247 seats—the largest Republican majority in the House since 1946. The GOP also gained control of the Senate in the 2014 midterm elections, picking up nine seats previously held by Democrats—thus the party holds 54 seats. Republicans also picked up a net of three governorships—gaining seats from the Democrats in Arkansas, Illinois, Maryland, and Massachusetts, but losing control in Pennsylvania.

The 2014 elections followed a historical pattern: the incumbent president's party tends to do poorly in the sixth year of an eight-year presidency.

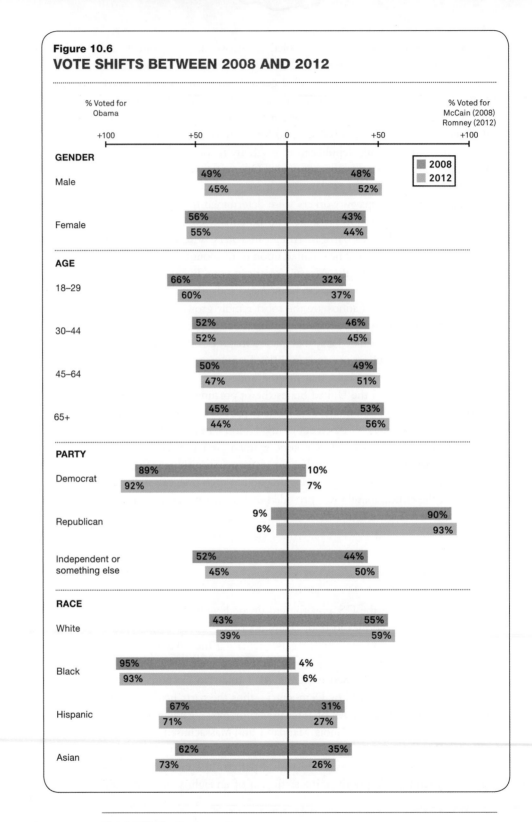

Figure 10.6

VOTE SHIFTS BETWEEN 2008 AND 2012

% Voted for Obama

% Voted for McCain (2008) Romney (2012)

+100 +50 0 +50 +100

■ 2008
■ 2012

GENDER

Male
- 49% | 48%
- 45% | 52%

Female
- 56% | 43%
- 55% | 44%

AGE

18–29
- 66% | 32%
- 60% | 37%

30–44
- 52% | 46%
- 52% | 45%

45–64
- 50% | 49%
- 47% | 51%

65+
- 45% | 53%
- 44% | 56%

PARTY

Democrat
- 89% | 10%
- 92% | 7%

Republican
- 9% | 90%
- 6% | 93%

Independent or something else
- 52% | 44%
- 45% | 50%

RACE

White
- 43% | 55%
- 39% | 59%

Black
- 95% | 4%
- 93% | 6%

Hispanic
- 67% | 31%
- 71% | 27%

Asian
- 62% | 35%
- 73% | 26%

Figure 10.6 (continued)

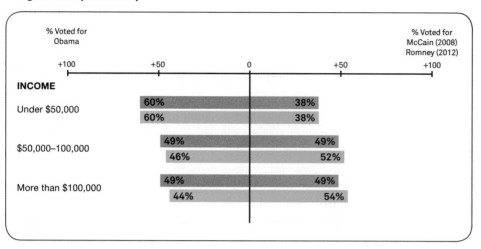

SOURCE: "Exit Polls 2012: How the Vote Has Shifted," *Washington Post*, November 6, 2012, www
.washingtonpost.com/wp-srv/special/politics/2012-exit-polls/table.html (accessed 11/28/12).

By that time in a presidency, the administration may have run out of new
policy initiatives; there are often increasing stresses on the coalition that
helped elect the president; and voters are looking for something new. In
the aftermath of the 2014 elections, it was clear that several factors contributed to Democratic losses. Just 36 percent of the adult population voted
in 2014, the lowest turnout rate in a federal election since 1942.[36] There
were few national issues to energize the electorate. President Obama's popularity had dipped into the low 40s, and ongoing civil conflict in Iraq and
Syria dragged the administration down, especially because the administration had to reverse course on its policy to withdraw from the conflicts in
the Middle East. Democratic candidates tried to distance themselves from
the president and to keep the elections local, but Republicans campaigned
strenuously against Obama and the Democrats, without offering a national
policy agenda. Both parties, it appeared, needed a national message in 2014,
and the electorate was especially demanding of such leadership from the
Democrats because they held the White House. The lack of a clear message
and vision for the next two years hurt Democrats nationwide.

The 2014 midterms set the stage for 2016. The election boosted the
profile of several Republican presidential hopefuls—especially those aligned
with the Tea Party faction within the Republican Party, such as Wisconsin
governor Scott Walker and Kentucky senator Rand Paul. The defeat of several Democratic senators and governors also narrowed the pool of Democratic presidential hopefuls, which seemed to leave the field open to Hillary
Clinton. The strengthening of the Tea Party faction seemed likely to shape the
issues pushed by the Republican Congress in the run-up to 2016—especially

tightening rules governing immigration, repealing the Affordable Care Act, and reducing federal spending and federal income taxes. Immediately after the election, the Obama administration promised to use the administrative and executive powers of the presidency to address policy areas where Obama expected to get little cooperation from Congress, such as immigration and greenhouse gas emissions. Just two weeks after the election, the president announced that the administration would not seek to deport 5 million illegal immigrants who had family in the United States who were citizens or legal residents. These will be the policy legacies inherited by the parties' standard-bearers heading into the 2016 presidential election. The conflict over immigration promises to be especially important for future elections, as Hispanic voters are an increasingly important segment of the electorate and rank immigration policy as one of their top issues.

DO ELECTIONS ENSURE ACCOUNTABILITY?

Elections are not the only form of popular political action but they are the most peaceful means of linking citizens and governments—providing governments with popular support and citizens with a measure of influence.

The institutions of American elections are designed to facilitate majority rule. Single-member districts and plurality rule create strong pressures toward a two-party system and majority rule. Even in elections in which one party wins a plurality but not a majority, that party typically wins an outright majority of legislative seats. The election itself, then, determines the government. Other systems often produce multiparty outcomes, resulting in a period of negotiation and coalition formation among the parties in order to determine who will govern.

The significance of elections derives not only from law but also from the preferences of voters. Voting behavior depends in no small part on habit and the tendency to vote for a given party as a matter of ingrained personal identity. If that were all there is to voting behavior, then it is not clear that elections would provide a meaningful way of governing. Elections would be reduced to little more than a sporting event, in which people merely rooted for their own team. However, voters' preferences are as strongly rooted in the issues at hand as in the choices themselves, the candidates. Voting decisions reflect individuals' assessments about whether it makes sense to keep public policies on the same track or to change direction, whether those in office have done a good job and deserve to be re-elected, or whether they have failed and it is time for new representation. The aggregation of all voters' preferences responds collectively to fluctuations in the economy, to differences in the ideological and policy orientations of the parties, and to the personal abilities of the candidates.

For Further Reading

Selections highlighted in red are included in *Readings in American Politics: Analysis and Perspectives,* Third Edition

Ansolabehere, Stephen, and James M. Snyder, Jr. *The End of Inequality: One Person, One Vote and the Transformation of American Politics.* New York: Norton, 2008.

Brady, David W. *Critical Elections and Congressional Policy Making.* Palo Alto, CA: Stanford University Press, 1988.

Carmines, Edward G., and James A. Stimson. *Issue Evolution: Race and the Transformation of American Politics.* Princeton, NJ: Princeton University Press, 1989.

Conway, M. Margaret. *Political Participation in the United States.* 3rd ed. Washington, DC: CQ Press, 2000.

Fowler, Linda L. *Candidates, Congress, and the American Democracy.* Ann Arbor: University of Michigan Press, 1994.

Gelman, Andrew. *Red State, Blue State, Rich State, Poor State: Why Americans Vote the Way They Do.* Princeton, NJ: Princeton University Press, 2008.

Ginsberg, Benjamin, and Martin Shefter. *Politics by Other Means: Politicians, Prosecutors, and the Press from Watergate to Whitewater.* 3rd ed. New York: Norton, 2002.

Green, Donald, and Alan Gerber. *Get Out the Vote!: How to Increase Voter Turnout.* 2nd ed. Washington, DC: Brookings Institution, 2008.

Jacobson, Gary C. *The Politics of Congressional Elections.* 8th ed. Boston: Pearson, 2013.

McCarty, Nolan, Keith Poole, and Howard Rosenthal. *Polarized America: The Dance of Ideology and Unequal Riches.* Cambridge, MA: MIT Press, 2006.

Morton, Rebecca B. *Analyzing Elections.* New York: Norton, 2006.

Rosenstone, Steven, and John Mark Hansen. *Mobilization, Participation, and Democracy in America.* New York: Macmillan, 1993.

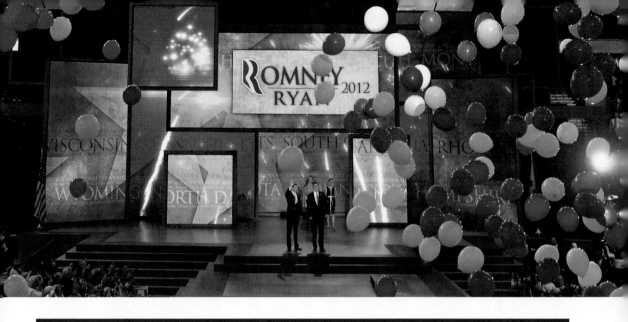

11

Political Parties

Political parties are defined as teams of politicians, activists, and voters whose goal is to win control of government. They do so by recruiting and nominating candidates to run for office; by accumulating the resources needed to run political campaigns, especially manpower and money; and by pursuing a policy agenda that can appeal to large numbers of voters and secure electoral majorities. As we saw in Chapter 5, once in office, parties organize the legislature and attempt to put their stamp on the laws passed by Congress and the president. Their potential political power is immense.

We often refer to the United States as a nation with a "two-party system." By this we mean that in the United States the Democratic and Republican parties compete for office and power. Most Americans believe that party competition contributes to the health of the democratic process. Certainly, we are more than just a bit suspicious of those nations that claim to be ruled by their people but do not tolerate the existence of opposing parties.

The idea of party competition was not always accepted in the United States. In the early years of the Republic, parties were seen as threats to the social order. In his 1796 "Farewell Address," President George Washington warned his countrymen to shun partisan politics:

Let me warn you in the most solemn manner against the baneful effects of the spirit of party generally. This spirit exists under different shapes in all government, more or less stifled, controlled, or repressed, but in those of the popular form it is seen in its greater rankness and is truly their worst enemy.

Often, those in power viewed the formation of political parties by their opponents as acts of treason that merited severe punishment. Thus, in 1798, the Federalist party, which controlled the national government, in effect sought to outlaw its Jeffersonian Republican opponents through the infamous Alien and Sedition acts, which, among other things, made it a crime to publish or say anything that might tend to defame or bring into disrepute either the president or the Congress. Under this law, 25 individuals—including several Republican newspaper editors—were arrested and convicted.

Over the past 200 years, our conception of political parties has changed considerably—from subversive organizations to bulwarks of democracy. In some instances, however, such as the 2011 struggle over increasing the nation's debt limit, the two parties seemed ready to send the nation's economy over a precipice as they struggled for partisan advantage. Rather than contribute to democratic governance, the parties seemed about to cause democratic collapse.

One concern that has become especially acute in recent years is ideological polarization. At one time, each party included liberal, moderate, and

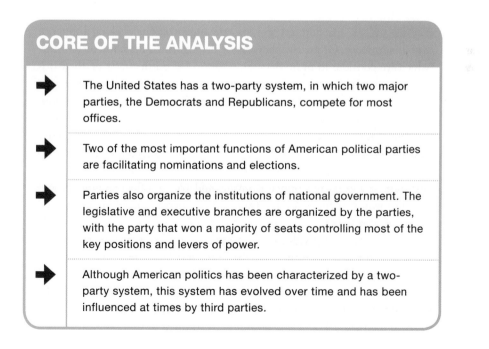

CORE OF THE ANALYSIS

➡ The United States has a two-party system, in which two major parties, the Democrats and Republicans, compete for most offices.

➡ Two of the most important functions of American political parties are facilitating nominations and elections.

➡ Parties also organize the institutions of national government. The legislative and executive branches are organized by the parties, with the party that won a majority of seats controlling most of the key positions and levers of power.

➡ Although American politics has been characterized by a two-party system, this system has evolved over time and has been influenced at times by third parties.

conservative factions. Today, there are few conservative Democrats and hardly any liberal Republicans. Moreover, within each party, the most ideologically motivated groups are also most likely to vote, especially in primary elections. This polarization makes it difficult for the parties to achieve compromise solutions to the nation's problems.

Throughout this chapter we highlight some of the general functions of parties in any democracy, but we are especially attentive to party politics in the United States.

FUNCTIONS OF THE PARTIES

It is difficult to imagine how American politics and government would work without political parties. Our inability to conceive of democracy without parties is not a failure of our imaginations or an accident of American history. Rather, it reflects a law of democratic politics. Parties form to solve key problems in a democracy. Throughout this chapter we highlight some of the general functions of parties in any democracy, but we are especially attentive to party politics in the United States.

Why Do Political Parties Form?

political party

An organized group that attempts to influence the government by electing its members to important government offices

Political parties, like interest groups, are organizations seeking influence over government. Ordinarily, they can be distinguished from interest groups (which we consider in more detail in Chapter 12) on the basis of their orientation. A party seeks to control the entire government by electing its members to office, thereby controlling the government's personnel. Interest groups, through campaign contributions and other forms of electoral assistance, are also concerned with electing politicians—in particular, those who are inclined in their policy direction. But interest groups ordinarily do not sponsor candidates directly, and between elections they usually accept government and its personnel as givens and try to influence government policies through them. They are *benefit seekers*, whereas parties are composed largely of *office seekers*.[1]

Parties are mainly involved in nominations and elections—recruiting the candidates for office, getting out the vote, and facilitating mass electoral choice. They also influence the institutions of government—providing the leadership and organization of the various congressional committees. The political parties in the United States were, ultimately, formed by politicians to serve their aims. Politicians do not need to form or join political parties, and some don't. But parties make easier the basic tasks of political life—running for office, organizing one's supporters, and forming a government.

Recruiting Candidates

One of the most important but least noticed party activities is the recruitment of candidates for local, state, and national office. Each election year, candidates must be found for thousands of state and local offices as well as congressional seats. Where an incumbent is not running for re-election or where an incumbent in the opposing party appears vulnerable, party leaders attempt to identify strong candidates and to interest them in entering the campaign.

The recruiting season begins early, because the dates by which candidates must file for office come as early as January in some states. Candidate recruitment in the spring shapes the parties' message and fortunes in the November general election. In 2006 and 2008, Democrats recruited a number of Iraq War veterans, who became the spokespeople for opposition to the war and helped the party capitalize on public frustration with the conduct of the war after 2005. In 2010 and 2012, Republicans capitalized on public anger and opposition to President Obama's health care law, which contributed to the emergence of the Tea Party movement, and managed to recruit a very strong class of candidates.[2] The biggest challenge for parties is when they fail to recruit anyone to run for a seat. You can't beat somebody with nobody. In 2014, a weak economy and low popularity ratings for the president made it difficult for Democrats to recruit candidates for congressional races.

An ideal candidate will be charismatic, organized, knowledgeable, and an excellent debater; have an unblemished record; and possess the ability to raise enough money to mount a serious campaign. Party leaders are usually not willing to provide financial backing to candidates who are unable to raise substantial funds on their own. For a House seat, this can mean between $500,000 and $1 million; for a Senate seat, a serious candidate must be able to raise several million dollars. Often, party leaders have difficulty finding attractive candidates and persuading them to run. Candidate recruitment is problematic in an era when political campaigns often involve mudslinging, and candidates must assume that their personal lives will be intensely scrutinized in the press.[3]

Nominating Candidates

Nomination is the process of selecting one party candidate to run for each elective office. The nominating process can precede the election by many months, as it does when the many candidates for the presidency are eliminated from consideration through a grueling series of debates and state primaries

nomination
The process by which political parties select their candidate for election to public office

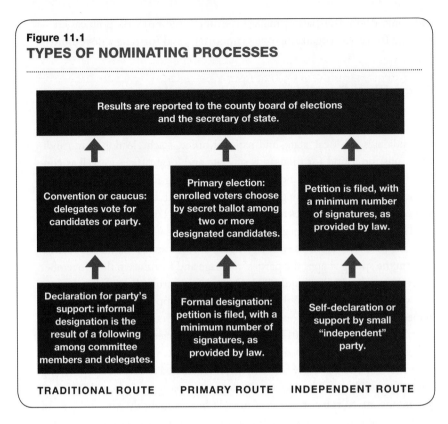

Figure 11.1

TYPES OF NOMINATING PROCESSES

Results are reported to the county board of elections and the secretary of state.

| Convention or caucus: delegates vote for candidates or party. | Primary election: enrolled voters choose by secret ballot among two or more designated candidates. | Petition is filed, with a minimum number of signatures, as provided by law. |

| Declaration for party's support: informal designation is the result of a following among committee members and delegates. | Formal designation: petition is filed, with a minimum number of signatures, as provided by law. | Self-declaration or support by small "independent" party. |

TRADITIONAL ROUTE   **PRIMARY ROUTE**   **INDEPENDENT ROUTE**

until there is only one survivor in each party—that party's nominee. Figure 11.1 summarizes the types of nominating processes described below.

Nomination by Convention. A nominating convention is a formal caucus bound by a number of rules that govern participation and nominating procedures. Conventions are meetings of delegates elected by party members from the relevant county (county convention) or state (state convention). Delegates to each party's national convention (which nominates the party's presidential candidate) are chosen by party members on a state-by-state basis; there is no single national delegate-selection process.

Nomination by Primary Election. In primary elections, party members select the party's nominees directly rather than selecting convention delegates who then select the nominees. Primaries are far from perfect replacements for conventions, since it is rare that more than 25 percent of enrolled voters participate in them. Nevertheless, they have replaced conventions as the dominant method of nomination.[4]

Primary elections fall mainly into two categories: closed and open. In a closed primary, participation is limited to individuals who have declared

closed primary

A primary election in which only those voters who registered with the party a specified period before the primary election day can participate their affiliation by registering with the party prior to the primary. In an open primary, individuals declare their party affiliation on the actual day of the primary election—they simply go to the polling place and ask for the ballot of a particular party. The open primary allows each voter an opportunity to consider candidates and issues before deciding whether to participate and in which party's contest to participate. Open primaries, therefore, are less conducive than closed contests to strong political parties. But in either case, primaries are more open than conventions or caucuses to new issues and new types of candidates.

open primary
A primary election in which voters can choose on the primary election day which party's primary to vote in

Getting Out the Vote

The election period begins immediately after the nominations. Historically, this has been a time of glory for the political parties, whose popular base of support is fully displayed. All the paraphernalia of party committees and all the committee members are activated into local party workforces.

The first step in the electoral process involves voter registration. This aspect of the process takes place all year round. There was a time when party workers were responsible for virtually all of this kind of electoral activity, but they have been supplemented (and in many states virtually displaced) by civic groups such as the League of Women Voters, unions, and chambers of commerce.

Those who have registered have to decide on Election Day whether to go to the polling place, stand in line, and actually vote for the various candidates and referenda on the ballot. Political parties, candidates, and campaigning can make a big difference in convincing the voters to vote. Because it is costly for voters to participate in elections and because many of the benefits that winning parties bestow are public goods (that is, parties cannot exclude any individual from enjoying them), people will often free ride by enjoying the benefits without incurring the costs of electing the party that provided the benefits. This is the *free-rider problem* (see Chapter 1), and parties are important because they help overcome it by mobilizing the voters to support the candidates.

In recent years, the parties themselves and not-for-profit groups have registered and mobilized large numbers of people to vote and raised millions of dollars to devote to election organizing and advertising. Legions of workers, often volunteers, have proved especially effective at using new technologies to build networks of supporters and communicate through those networks. They are the "netroots" organizations of politics. To comply with federal election and tax law, these groups must maintain their independence from the political parties, although they have the same objectives as the parties and work very hard to elect politicians from a particular party. Such organizations act as shadow appendages of the two parties, with some groups mobilizing Democratic supporters and others mobilizing Republicans. The netroots have become integral to campaign organizations, and with the advent of these new forms of direct campaigning, there has been a noticeable uptick in turnout in the United States.

Facilitating Electoral Choice

Parties make the electoral choice much easier for voters. It is often argued that we should vote for the best person regardless of party affiliation. But on any general-election ballot, there are likely to be only a handful of candidates who are well known to the voters, namely, some of the candidates for president, U.S. Senate, U.S. House, and governor. As one moves down the ballot, voters' familiarity with the candidates declines. Without party labels, voters would be constantly confronted by a bewildering array of new names and new choices, causing them considerable difficulty making informed decisions. Without a doubt, candidates' party affiliations help voters make reasonable choices.

Parties lower the information costs of participating in elections by providing a recognizable "brand name." Without knowing a great deal about a candidate for office, voters can infer from party labels how the candidate will likely behave once elected. Individuals know about the parties through their past experience with those parties in state and federal office and from the actions of prominent political leaders from both parties. In the United States, the Democratic Party is associated with a commitment to more extensive government regulation of the economy and a larger public sector; the Republican Party favors a limited government role in the economy and reduced government spending paired with tax reductions. The Democrats favor aggressive protection of civil rights and a secular approach to religion in public life. The Republicans generally want to ban abortion and favor government participation in expanding the role of religious organizations in civil society. The parties' positions on the economy were cemented in the 1930s, and their division over civil society emerged during the 1960s and 1970s. The Democratic positions are loosely labeled liberal and those of the Republicans conservative.

Party labels provide a "brand name" and help voters make choices even when they are less familiar with the candidates. Voters can infer from party labels what principles and policies the candidate is likely to support.

Party labels also benefit the politicians. By having simple, recognizable labels, candidates running in most districts and states are spared the great expense of educating voters about what they stand for. The labels Democrat and Republican are usually sufficient. The content of the labels is sustained because like-minded people sort themselves into the respective organizations. People who broadly share the principles espoused by a party and who wish to participate on a high level in politics will attend party meetings, run for leadership positions in local and state party organizations, attend state and national conventions, and even run for elected office. Each party, then, draws on a distinct pool for activists and candidates. Each successive election reinforces the existing division between the parties.

Influencing National Government

One of the most familiar observations about American politics is that the two major parties are "big tents." They position themselves to bring in as many groups and ideas as possible. The parties make such broad coalitions as a matter of strategy, much as businesses purchase other companies to expand their market share. Positioning themselves as broad coalitions prevents effective national third parties from emerging and guarantees that the Democrats and Republicans vie for control of Congress.

The coalitions that come together in the Democratic and Republican parties shape the parties' platforms on public policy. The political coalitions that party leaders assemble determine which interests and social groups align with the parties and also what sorts of issues can emerge. The Democratic Party today embraces a philosophy of active government intervention in the economy, based on the premise that regulation is necessary to ensure orderly economic growth, prevent the emergence of monopolies, and address certain costs of economic activity, such as pollution, poverty, and unemployment. In addition, the Democratic Party pushes for aggressive expansion and protection of civil rights, especially for women and racial minorities. The Republican Party espouses a philosophy of laissez-faire economics and a minimal government role in the economy. The coalition that Ronald Reagan built in the late 1970s paired this vision of limited government intervention in the economy with an expanded role for religion in society and strong opposition to immigration, affirmative action, and abortion.

The American major parties appeal to distinctly different core constituencies. The Democratic Party at the national level seeks to unite organized labor, the poor, members of racial minorities, and liberal upper-middle-class professionals. The Republicans, by contrast, appeal to business, upper-middle- and upper-class groups in the private sector, and social conservatives. Often, party leaders will seek to develop issues they hope will add new groups to their party's constituent base. During the 1980s, for example, under the leadership of Ronald Reagan, the Republicans devised a series of "social issues," including support for school prayer, opposition to abortion, and opposition to affirmative action, designed to cultivate the support of white southerners. This effort was extremely successful in increasing Republican strength in the once solidly Democratic South. In the 1990s, under the leadership of Bill Clinton, who called himself a "new Democrat," the Democratic Party sought to develop new social programs designed to solidify the party's base among working-class and poor voters, and new, somewhat more conservative economic programs aimed at attracting middle- and upper-middle-class voters.

As these examples suggest, parties do not always support policies because they are favored by their constituents. Instead, party leaders can play the role of policy entrepreneurs, seeding ideas and programs that will expand their party's base of support while eroding that of the opposition. In recent years, for example, leaders of both major political parties have sought to develop ideas and programs they hoped would appeal to America's most rapidly growing electoral bloc: Latino voters. President George W. Bush recommended a number of proposals designed to help Latinos secure U.S. residence and employment. Democrats, for their part, have proposed education, social service programs, and immigration reform designed to appeal to the needs of Latino families. Latino votes split nearly evenly between the parties in the 2004 presidential election. But, since 2005, many Republican leaders at the local, state, and federal levels began to take a hard line on immigration, especially from Latin America. Those policies were very popular among the Republican party base and worked well in Republican primaries, but they alienated many Latino voters in general elections. Exit polls revealed that Obama won 66 percent of the Hispanic vote in 2008, a huge swing from 2004, and he added to that margin in 2012, winning 70 percent of Latino votes.

Both parties translate their general goals into concrete policies through the members they elect to office. Republicans, for example, implemented tax cuts, increased defense spending, cut social spending, and enacted restrictions on abortion during the 1980s and 1990s. Democrats were able to defend consumer and environmental programs against Republican attacks and sought to expand domestic social programs in the late 1990s. In 2009, President Obama and a Democratic-controlled Congress created a national health insurance system that guarantees all people access to health care, a key item on the Democratic Party's platform since the 1940s.

PARTIES IN GOVERNMENT

Parties operate in three spheres: elections, political institutions, and government. The ultimate test of a political party is its influence on the institutions of government and the policy-making process. We begin there.

Most parties originate inside the government. Political parties form as those who support the actions of the government and those who do not; in the United Kingdom, these groups are called Government and Opposition.[5] In the American context, parties vie to control and to oppose those who control both Congress and the presidency.

The Parties and Congress

The two major political parties have a profound influence on the organization and day-to-day operation of Congress. The Speaker of the House, perhaps the most powerful person in Congress, holds a party office. All the members of the House take part in the election of the Speaker. But the actual selection is made by the majority party. When the majority party caucus presents a nominee to the entire House, its choice is then invariably ratified in a straight party-line vote.

The committee system of both houses of Congress is also organized by the parties. Although the rules organizing committees and the rules defining the jurisdiction of each committee are adopted like ordinary legislation by the whole membership, party leadership and caucuses shape all other features of the committees. For example, each party is assigned a quota of members for each committee, depending on the percentage of total seats held by the party. On the rare occasions when an independent or third-party candidate is elected, the leaders of the two parties must agree against whose quota this member's committee assignments will count.

The assignment of individual members to committees is a party decision. Each party has a "committee on committees" to make such decisions. Moreover, advancement up

majority party
The party that holds the majority of legislative seats in either the House or the Senate

The Speaker of the House, who has enormous influence over committee assignments and other congressional activity, is selected by the majority party. Here, Speaker John Boehner and the House Republican leadership meet with reporters to push their legislative agenda.

the committee ladder toward the chair is a party decision. Since the late nineteenth century, most advancements have been automatic—based upon the length of continual service on the committee. This seniority system has existed only because of the support of the two parties, and either party can depart from it by a simple vote. During the 1970s, both parties reinstituted the practice of reviewing each chair—voting anew every two years on whether each chair would be continued. In 2001, Republicans lived up to their 1995 pledge to limit House committee chairs to three terms. Existing chairpersons were forced to step down but were replaced generally by the most senior Republican member of each committee.

President and Party

The presidency is, in many ways, the focal point of the party system in the United States. As we saw earlier, the president carries the mantle of his party, and the electoral fortunes of the parties rise and fall with the success of the president. During midterm congressional elections, when the president is not on the ballot, voters hold the president's party accountable for current problems. When the economy does poorly, Americans will punish the party of the president, even when the opposing party controls Congress.

The president of the United States also relies heavily on his fellow party members in organizing the executive and passing legislation. Unlike parliamentary governments, such as in the United Kingdom, the heads of executive departments are not sitting members of the legislature. With few exceptions, heads of the executive departments and other key presidential appointments are people loyal to the president and his or her political party. Most are politicians who have served as governors of states or members of Congress or are close advisers who have worked with the president on political campaigns or in offices the president previously held.

The president and White House staff also work closely with congressional party leaders to shepherd legislation through Congress. The president cannot introduce legislation and must rely on members of Congress to do so. (There are a few exceptions, such as nominations and treaties.) Nearly all of the president's legislative initiatives are proposed as bills by fellow party members in the House and Senate. As discussed in Chapter 6, when the president's party controls both chambers of Congress, there is the opportunity to get a large majority of the president's legislative agenda passed. The leadership of the president's party also helps to negotiate with individual members of Congress to construct a majority behind a White House–sponsored bill. Sometimes the president will reach out to individual legislators to try to persuade a member of Congress to support a particular bill.

The president's ability to prevail in Congress depends strongly on which party controls the House and Senate. When the president's party enjoys majorities in the House and Senate, the president's legislative agenda succeeds most of the time. A typical president will win in excess of 80 percent of the time on bills if his party controls the House and Senate. Barack Obama, during his first year in office, had the highest degree of support for a president since World War II, with a majority of Congress supporting his position 96 percent of the time.[6] When another party controls at least one chamber of Congress, however, the White House has a much more difficult time getting new laws passed. After Republicans took control of the House in 2011, a majority of the House voted in support of the position President Barack Obama had taken on legislation only 32 percent of the time. In the Senate, by contrast, Democrats retained control after the 2010 and the 2012 elections, and a majority of the Senate voted in line with Obama's preferred outcome 85 percent of the time.

PARTIES IN THE ELECTORATE

Political parties are more than just political leaders; they are made up of millions of people and organizations such as labor unions, corporations, and other interest groups. This large-scale membership helps parties organize and influence elections.

Party Identification

As we saw in Chapter 11's discussion of elections, individual voters tend to develop party identification with one of the political parties. Party identification partly reflects a psychological attachment developed in childhood or adolescence and carried throughout life. Party identification also has a rational component, rooted in evaluations of the performance of the parties in government, the policies they will pursue, and an individual's interest and ideology.[7] Voters generally form attachments to parties that reflect their views and interests. Once those attachments are formed, however, they are likely to persist and even be handed down to children unless some very strong factors convince individuals that their party is no longer an appropriate object of their affections. In some sense, party identification is similar to brand loyalty in the marketplace: consumers choose a brand of automobile for its appearance or mechanical characteristics and stick

party identification

An individual's attachment to a particular political party, which might be based on issues, ideology, past experience, or upbringing with it out of loyalty, habit, and unwillingness to reexamine their choices constantly, but they may eventually switch if the old brand no longer serves their interests.

Although the strength of partisan ties in the United States seems to have declined in the 1960s and 1970s, most Americans continue to identify with either the Republican Party or the Democratic Party (Figure 11.2). The Party identification gives citizens a stake in election outcomes that goes beyond the race at hand. This is why strong party identifiers (that is, people who identify strongly with one party) are more likely than other Americans to go to the polls and, of course, are more likely than others to support the party with which they identify. Party activists are drawn from the ranks of the strong identifiers. Activists are those who not only vote but also contribute their time, energy, and effort to party affairs. Activists ring doorbells, stuff envelopes, attend meetings, and contribute money to the party cause. No party could succeed without the thousands of volunteers who undertake the mundane tasks needed to keep the organization going. It is worth noting that attachment to a party does not guarantee voting for that party's candidates, though it does reflect a tendency. Strong identifiers do so almost always, and weak identifiers do so most of the time.

party activist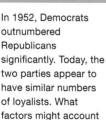

A partisan who contributes time, energy, and effort to support a party and its candidates

ANALYZING THE EVIDENCE

In 1952, Democrats outnumbered Republicans significantly. Today, the two parties appear to have similar numbers of loyalists. What factors might account for this partisan transformation?

Figure 11.2
AMERICANS' PARTY IDENTIFICATION

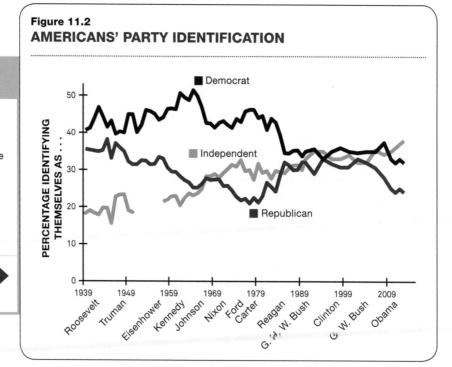

NOTE: Independent data not available for 1951–56.
SOURCES: Pew Research Center. "Party Identification," www.pewresearch.org/data-trend/political-attitudes/party-identification/(accessed 11/13/14).

Group Basis of Politics

One view of political parties, a Pluralist view, is that they consist of coalitions of many organized groups. The leaders of organizations may choose to side with a party to try to influence what government does by influencing the policy orientation of one of the major parties. A group can offer resources to the party, such as campaign workers, contributions, and votes, and the party, in exchange, can pursue policies in line with what the groups want. Once aligned with a party, a group's leaders can then signal to members for whom they should vote. The more disciplined the group and the more resources it can offer, the more power it will have in the party. Party leaders try to build coalitions consisting of many different groups, each of which wants a distinct policy or political benefit. The challenge for political parties is how to build coalitions that can win majorities in elections and do not create too many conflicting demands.[8]

Unorganized social groups are also important. In the United States today, a variety of group characteristics are associated with party identification. These include race and ethnicity, gender, religion, class, and age.

Race and Ethnicity. Since the 1930s and Franklin Delano Roosevelt's New Deal, African Americans have been overwhelmingly Democratic in their party identification. More than 90 percent of African Americans describe themselves as Democrats and support Democratic candidates in national, state, and local elections. Approximately 25 percent of the Democratic Party's support in presidential races comes from African American voters.

Latino and Hispanic voters comprise people whose ancestors came from many different countries, with disparate political orientations. Mexican Americans are the single largest group. They have historically aligned with the Democratic Party, as have Puerto Ricans and Central Americans. Historically, Cuban Americans have voted heavily and identified as Republican. Over the past five years, however, Cubans have exhibited a rapid shift toward the Democratic Party. Asian Americans have been somewhat divided as well. Japanese, Chinese, Filipino, and Korean communities have been long established in the United States and have influential business communities. Higher-income Asians tend to be as Republican as higher-income whites. It is not clear whether newer Asian immigrant groups, such as the Hmong, the Vietnamese, Thais, and Indians, will follow the same trajectory as the Japanese and Chinese communities.

Gender. Women are somewhat more likely to support Democrats, and men are somewhat more likely to support Republicans, in surveys of party identification and voting. This difference is known as the gender gap. In the 2012 election, Barack Obama won 55 percent of the women's vote and 45 percent of the men's vote, a 10-point gap.

gender gap
A distinctive pattern of voting behavior reflecting the differences in views between women and men

---

Religion. Jews are among the Democratic Party's most loyal constituent groups and have been since the New Deal. Nearly 90 percent of all Jewish Americans describe themselves as Democrats, although the percentage is declining among younger Jews. Catholics were once a strongly pro-Democratic group as well but have been shifting toward the Republican Party since the 1970s, when the Republicans began to focus on abortion and other social issues deemed important to Catholics. More religiously conservative Protestant denominations tend to identify with the Republicans, while Protestants who are religiously liberal, such as Unitarians and Episcopalians, tend to identify as Democrats. Protestant fundamentalists, in particular, have been drawn to the Republicans' conservative stands on social issues, such as school prayer and abortion. (See the Analyzing the Evidence unit on page 374 for a discussion of candidate religion and partisan voting.)

Class. Upper-income Americans are considerably more likely to affiliate with the Republicans, whereas lower-income Americans are far more likely to identify with the Democrats. Middle-class voters tend to split evenly between Democrats and Republicans. This divide reflects the differences between the two parties on economic issues. In general, the Republicans support cutting taxes and social spending—positions that reflect the interests of the wealthy. The Democrats, however, favor increased social spending, even if this requires increasing taxes—a position consistent with the interests of less affluent Americans.

Age. Age is another factor associated with partisanship. There is nothing about a particular numerical age that leads to a particular party loyalty. Instead, individuals from the same age cohort are likely to have experienced a similar set of events during the period when they formed their party loyalties. Thus Americans between the ages of 50 and 70 came of political age during the Cold War, the Vietnam War, and the civil rights movement, and those older than 70 are the product of the Great Depression and World War II. Apparently among voters whose initial perceptions of politics were shaped during these periods, more responded favorably to the role played by the Democrats than to the actions of the Republicans. It is interesting that among the youngest group of Americans, a group that came of age during an era of political scandals that tainted both parties, the plurality describe themselves as independents.

Figure 11.3 indicates the relationship between party identification and a number of social criteria. Race, religion, income, and ideology seem to have the greatest influence on Americans' party affiliations. None of these social characteristics is inevitably linked to partisan identification, however. There are union Republicans and business Democrats, Democrats in Utah, and Republicans in Rhode Island. The general party identifications just discussed are broad tendencies that both reflect and reinforce the issue and

Figure 11.3
PARTY IDENTIFICATION BY SOCIAL GROUP, 2012

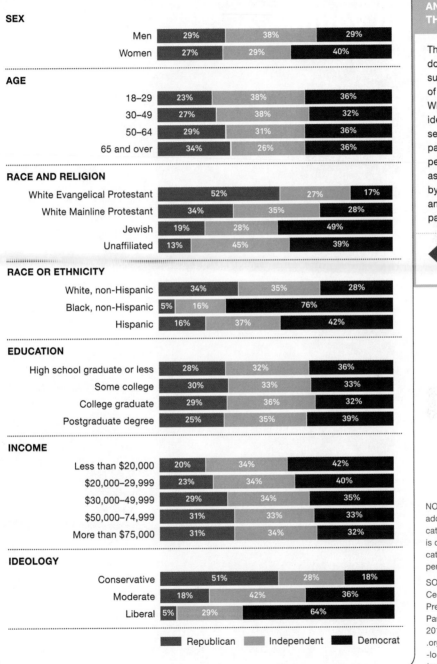

SEX

	Republican	Independent	Democrat
Men	29%	38%	29%
Women	27%	29%	40%

AGE

	Republican	Independent	Democrat
18–29	23%	38%	36%
30–49	27%	38%	32%
50–64	29%	31%	36%
65 and over	34%	26%	36%

RACE AND RELIGION

	Republican	Independent	Democrat
White Evangelical Protestant	52%	27%	17%
White Mainline Protestant	34%	35%	28%
Jewish	19%	28%	49%
Unaffiliated	13%	45%	39%

RACE OR ETHNICITY

	Republican	Independent	Democrat
White, non-Hispanic	34%	35%	28%
Black, non-Hispanic	5%	16%	76%
Hispanic	16%	37%	42%

EDUCATION

	Republican	Independent	Democrat
High school graduate or less	28%	32%	36%
Some college	30%	33%	33%
College graduate	29%	36%	32%
Postgraduate degree	25%	35%	39%

INCOME

	Republican	Independent	Democrat
Less than $20,000	20%	34%	42%
$20,000–29,999	23%	34%	40%
$30,000–49,999	29%	34%	35%
$50,000–74,999	31%	33%	33%
More than $75,000	31%	34%	32%

IDEOLOGY

	Republican	Independent	Democrat
Conservative	51%	28%	18%
Moderate	18%	42%	36%
Liberal	5%	29%	64%

■ Republican ■ Independent ■ Democrat

ANALYZING THE EVIDENCE

The political parties do not draw equal support from members of each social stratum. What patterns in party identification do you see? How might these patterns influence which people are selected as political candidates by political parties and which policies the parties support?

←

NOTE: Percentages do not add to 100 because the category "Other/don't know" is omitted. In this survey, this category was always 2–5 percent of respondents.

SOURCE: Pew Research Center for the People and the Press, "A Closer Look at the Parties in 2012," August 23, 2012, www.people-press.org/2012/08/23/a-closer-look-at-the-parties-in-2012/ (accessed 12/10/12).

Candidate Religion and Partisan Voting

Contributed by

Geoffrey C. Layman
University of Notre Dame

John C. Green
University of Akron

David E. Campbell
University of Notre Dame

Jeremiah J. Castle
University of Notre Dame

Individuals identify with a political party for many reasons, one of which is their own social group memberships as well as their feelings toward other social groups.[1] To what extent do the social group characteristics of political candidates affect the connection between citizens' party identifications and their support for those candidates? One important social group for many people is religion. In recent decades, the American public has come to view the Republican Party as the party of religious people and the Democratic Party as the party of nonreligious people.[2]

Public Perception of Religious Groups' Party Ties

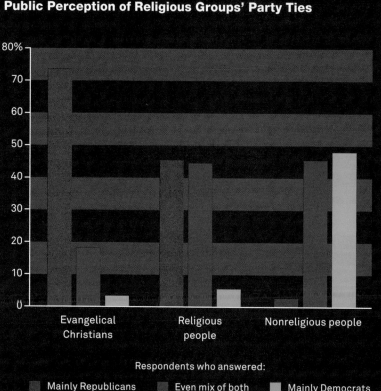

Respondents who answered:

▮ Mainly Republicans   ▮ Even mix of both   ▮ Mainly Democrats

We asked survey respondents whether they considered Evangelical Christians, religious people, and nonreligious people to be "mainly Republicans, mainly Democrats, or a pretty even mix of both." Americans overwhelmingly view Evangelicals as Republican, tend to view religious people as Republican, and generally perceive nonreligious people as Democrats.

SOURCE: 2007 Candidate Religion Survey (conducted online by YouGov/Polimetrix).

1 Angus Campbell, Philip E. Converse, Warren E. Miller, and Donald E. Stokes, *The American Voter* (Chicago: University of Chicago Press); Donald Green, Bradley Palmquist, and Eric Schickler, *Partisan Hearts and Minds* (New Haven, CT: Yale University Press, 2002).

2 Geoffrey Layman, *The Great Divide: Religious and Cultural Conflict in American Party Politics* (New York: Columbia University Press, 2001); John C. Green, *The Faith Factor: How Religion Influences American Elections* (Westport, CT: Praeger, 2007).

How does the public's perception of political parties' social group profiles affect the connection between individuals' party ties and their voting decisions? To find out, we presented survey respondents with descriptions of candidates that were identical except for what they said about the candidate's religion.[3] We found that the support of Republican and Democratic identifiers for the candidate changed markedly with the candidate's religious profile. Our findings suggest that because voters make assumptions about candidates' political orientations based on their social characteristics, these characteristics are quite important for electoral behavior.

The Electoral Impact of Candidate Religiosity

PERCENTAGE "VERY LIKELY"
TO SUPPORT CANDIDATE

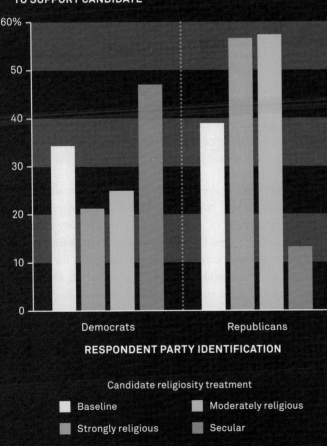

RESPONDENT PARTY IDENTIFICATION

Candidate religiosity treatment

Baseline
Strongly religious
Moderately religious
Secular

We randomly varied what we told survey respondents about the religiosity of a hypothetical state legislative candidate with a nonpartisan issue profile (focusing on goals such as good jobs, a strong economy, and efficient government) and no identified party affiliation. In the baseline (or control) condition, no mention was made of the candidate's religious orientation. When we told respondents that the candidate was moderately religious ("a man of faith") or strongly religious (a "deeply religious" person with a "personal relationship with God"), support decreased among Democrats and increased among Republicans. When we described the candidate as a secular critic of religion in public life (a "man of science" belonging to Americans United for the Separation of Church and State), support strongly increased among Democrats and strongly decreased among Republicans.

SOURCE: 2009 Cooperative Congressional Election Study (conducted online by YouGov/Polimetrix).

3 David E. Campbell, John C. Green, and Geoffrey C. Layman, "The Party Faithful: Partisan Images, Candidate Religion, and the Electoral Impact of Party Identification," *American Journal of Political Science* 55, no. 1 (2011): 42–58; and Jeremiah J. Castle, Geoffrey C. Layman, David E. Campbell, and John C. Green, "Candidate Religiosity and Electoral Support: An Experimental Assessment," 2012. Presented at the Annual Meeting of the Southern Political Science Association, New Orleans.

policy positions the two parties take in the national and local political arenas. They reflect the general tendency of groups—organized and unorganized—to sort into partisan camps.

PARTIES AS INSTITUTIONS

Political parties in the United States today are not tightly disciplined, hierarchical organizations. Indeed, they never have been. Rather, the American parties consist of extensive networks of politicians, interest groups, activists and donors, consultants, and, ultimately, voters.

Contemporary Party Organizations

In the United States, party organizations exist at virtually every level of government (Figure 11.4). These organizations are usually committees made up of a number of active party members. State law and party rules prescribe how such committees are constituted. Usually, committee members are elected at local party meetings—called caucuses—or as part of the regular primary election. The best-known examples of these committees are at the national level—the Democratic National Committee and the Republican National Committee.

caucus (political)
A normally closed meeting of a political or legislative group to select candidates, plan strategy, or make decisions regarding legislative matters

The National Convention. At the national level, the party's most important institution is the quadrennial national convention. The convention is attended by delegates from each of the states; as a group, they nominate the party's presidential and vice-presidential candidates, draft the party's campaign platform for the presidential race, and approve changes in the rules and regulations governing party procedures. Before World War II, presidential nominations occupied most of the time, energy, and effort expended at the national convention. The nomination process required days of negotiation and compromise among state party leaders and often required many ballots before a nominee was selected. In recent years, however, presidential candidates have essentially nominated themselves by winning enough delegate support in primary elections to win the official nomination on the first ballot. The actual convention has played little or no role in selecting the candidates.

The convention's other two tasks, establishing the party's rules and platform, remain important. Party rules can determine the relative influence of competing factions within the party and can also increase or decrease the party's chances for electoral success. In 1972, for example, the Democratic National Convention adopted a new set of rules favored by the party's liberal wing. Under these rules, state delegations to the Democratic convention

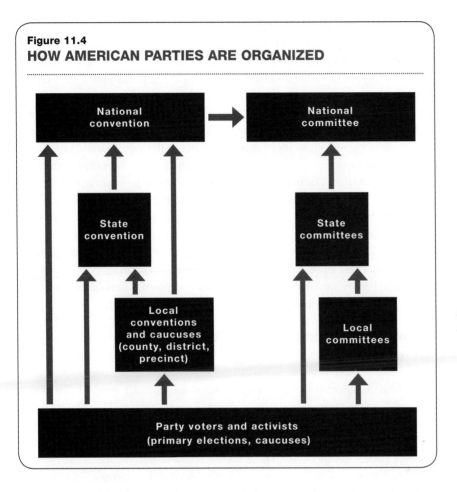

Figure 11.4

HOW AMERICAN PARTIES ARE ORGANIZED

National convention → National committee

State convention

State committees

Local conventions and caucuses (county, district, precinct)

Local committees

Party voters and activists (primary elections, caucuses)

were required to include women and members of minority groups in rough proportion to those groups' representation among the party's membership in that state. Liberals correctly calculated that women and African Americans would generally support liberal ideas and candidates. The convention also approves the party platform. Platforms are often dismissed as documents filled with platitudes that are seldom read by voters. Furthermore, the parties' presidential candidates make little use of the platforms in their campaigns; usually they prefer to develop and promote their own themes. Nonetheless, the platform should be understood as a "treaty" in which the various factions attending the convention state their terms for supporting the ticket.

The National Committee. Between conventions, each national political party is technically headed by its national committee. For the Democrats and Republicans, these are called the Democratic National Committee (DNC) and the Republican National Committee (RNC), respectively. These national committees raise campaign funds, head off factional disputes within the party, and endeavor to enhance the party's media image. Since 1972, the size of staff and the amount of money raised have increased substantially for both national committees. The work of each national committee is overseen by its chairperson. Other committee members are generally major party contributors or fund-raisers and serve in a largely ceremonial capacity.

For the party that controls the White House, the national committee chair is appointed by the president. Typically, this means that that party's national committee becomes little more than an adjunct to the White House staff. For a first-term president, the committee devotes the bulk of its energy to the re-election campaign. The national committee chair of the party not in control of the White House is selected by the committee itself and usually takes a broader view of the party's needs, raising money and performing other activities on behalf of the party's members in Congress and in the state legislatures. Barack Obama's 2008 and 2012 presidential campaigns were based on a 50-state strategy. Obama developed extensive grassroots organizations in every state, which registered many new Democratic voters in traditionally Republican areas, a change that will likely benefit the Democrats for years to come.

Congressional Campaign Committees. Each party forms House and Senate campaign committees to raise funds for the House and Senate election campaigns. The Republicans call their House and Senate committees the National Republican Congressional Committee (NRCC) and the National Republican Senatorial Committee (NRSC), respectively. The Democrats call their House and Senate committees the Democratic Congressional Campaign Committee (DCCC) and the Democratic Senatorial Campaign Committee (DSCC), respectively. These organizations also have professional staff devoted to raising and distributing funds, developing strategies, recruiting candidates, and conducting on-the-ground campaigns. These organizations, however, are accountable to the caucuses inside the House and Senate. The chairs of these committees come from within the respective chambers and rank high in the party leadership hierarchy. The national committees and the congressional committees are sometimes rivals. Both groups seek donations from the same pool of people but for different candidates: the national committee seeks funds primarily for the presidential race, while the congressional campaign committees focus on House and Senate seats.

State and Local Party Organizations. Each of the two major parties has a central committee in each state. The parties traditionally also have county committees and, in some instances, state senate district committees, judicial district committees, and, in the case of larger cities, citywide party committees and local assembly district "ward" committees as well. Congressional districts also may have party committees.

State and local party organizations are very active in recruiting candidates and conducting voter-registration drives. Under current federal law, state and

Local party organizations are important in conducting voter registration drives and getting out the vote.

local party organizations can spend unlimited amounts of money on "party-building" activities such as voter-registration and get-out-the-vote drives (though in some states such practices are limited by state law). As a result, for many years the national party organizations, which have enormous fund raising abilities but were restricted by law in how much they could spend on candidates, transferred millions of dollars to the state and local organizations. The state and local parties, in turn, spent these funds, sometimes called *soft money*, to promote the candidacies of national, as well as state and local, candidates. In this process, as local organizations have become linked financially to the national parties, American political parties became somewhat more integrated and nationalized than ever before. At the same time, the state and local party organizations came to control large financial resources and play important roles in elections despite the collapse of the old patronage machines.[9]

The Contemporary Party as Service Provider to Candidates.

Party leaders have adapted parties to the modern age. Parties as organizations are more professional, better financed, and more organized than ever before.[10] Political parties have evolved into "service organizations," which, though they no longer hold a monopoly over campaigns, still provide services to candidates. Without such services, it would be extremely difficult for candidates to win and hold office. For example, the national organizations of the political parties collect information, ranging from lists of likely supporters and donors in local areas to public-opinion polls in states and legislative districts, and they provide this information directly to their candidates for state and federal offices. They also have teams of experienced campaign organizers and managers who provide assistance to local candidates who are in tight races but are understaffed. Parties have not declined but have simply adapted to serve the interests of political actors.[11]

Parties in Government

- Parties organize in support of and in opposition to government actions and policies.

- Parties select leaders in the House and Senate and make committee assignments.

- Politicians who are in the same party often support one another's legislation.

Parties in the Electorate

- Many voters identify with a political party that reflects their views and interests. Once formed, this identification usually persists.

- Voters use parties as a "shortcut" to decide whom to vote for in elections.

- Some people develop strong attachments to a party and become party activists, organizing local campaign efforts on behalf of a party's candidates.

Parties as Institutions

- Parties comprise networks of politicians, activists, interest groups, donors, consultants, and voters.

- Parties recruit candidates to run for office and organize caucuses, primary elections, and conventions to select one candidate to compete against the other party's candidate.

- Parties raise money and perform other activities on behalf of their members in Congress and in state legislatures.

PARTY SYSTEMS

Our understanding of political parties would be incomplete if we considered only their composition and roles. America's political parties compete with one another for offices, policies, and power. The struggle between the major parties for control of government shapes the policies that the parties put forth, the coalitions of interests that they represent, and the ability of the parties, indeed the government, to respond to the demands of the time and age. In short, the fate of each party is inextricably linked to that of its major rival.

Political scientists often call the constellation of parties that are important at any given moment a nation's party system. The most obvious feature of a party system is the number of major parties competing for power. Usually the United States has had a two-party system, meaning that only two parties have had a serious chance to win national elections. Of course, we have not always had the same two parties, and minor parties have often put forward candidates. The term *party system*, however, refers to more than just the number of parties competing for power. It also connotes the organization of the parties, the balance of power between and within party coalitions, the parties' social and institutional bases, and the issues and policies around which party competition is organized.

The character of a nation's party system changes as the parties realign their electoral coalitions and alter their public philosophies. Such realignment sometimes comes subtly and sometimes suddenly. Today's American party system is very different from the party system of 1950, even though the Democrats and the Republicans continue to be the major competing forces (Figure 11.5). Over the course of American history, changes in political forces and alignments have produced six party systems, each with distinctive political institutions, issues, and patterns of political power and participation. Of course, some political phenomena have persisted across party systems. Conflicts over the distribution of wealth, for example, are an enduring feature of American political life. But even such phenomena manifest themselves in different ways during different political eras.

The First Party System: Federalists and Democratic-Republicans

Although George Washington and, in fact, many other leaders of the time deplored partisan politics, the two-party system emerged early in the history of the new Republic. Competition in Congress between northeastern mercantile and southern agrarian factions led Alexander Hamilton and the northeasterners to form a cohesive voting bloc within Congress. The southerners, led by Thomas Jefferson and James Madison, responded by attempting to organize a popular following to change the balance of power within Congress. When the northeasterners replied to this southern strategy, the result was the birth of America's first national parties—the Democratic-Republicans, whose primary base was in the South, and the Federalists, whose strength was greatest in the New England states. The Federalists spoke mainly for New England mercantile groups and supported protective tariffs to encourage manufacturers, the

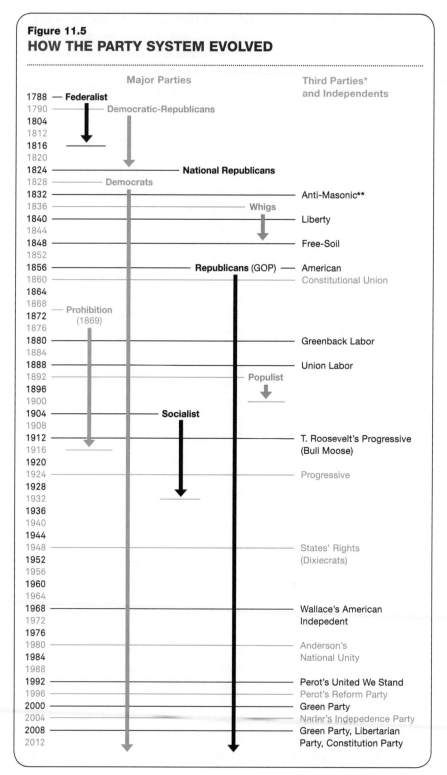

Figure 11.5

HOW THE PARTY SYSTEM EVOLVED

Major Parties

Third Parties* and Independents

Year	Major Parties	Third Parties and Independents
1788	Federalist	
1790	Democratic-Republicans	
1804		
1812		
1816		
1820		
1824	National Republicans	
1828	Democrats	
1832		Anti-Masonic**
1836	Whigs	
1840		Liberty
1844		
1848		Free-Soil
1852		
1856	Republicans (GOP)	American
1860		Constitutional Union
1864		
1868		
1872	Prohibition (1869)	
1876		
1880		Greenback Labor
1884		
1888		Union Labor
1892		Populist
1896		
1900		
1904	Socialist	
1908		
1912		T. Roosevelt's Progressive (Bull Moose)
1916		
1920		
1924		Progressive
1928		
1932		
1936		
1940		
1944		
1948		States' Rights (Dixiecrats)
1952		
1956		
1960		
1964		
1968		Wallace's American Independent
1972		
1976		
1980		Anderson's National Unity
1984		
1988		
1992		Perot's United We Stand
1996		Perot's Reform Party
2000		Green Party
2004		Nader's Independence Party
2008		Green Party, Libertarian Party, Constitution Party
2012		

*In some cases, there was even a fourth party. Most of the parties listed here existed for only one term.
**The Anti-Masonics not only had the distinction of being the first third party but also were the first party to hold a national nominating convention and the first to announce a party platform.

assumption of the states' Revolutionary War debts, the creation of a national bank, and resumption of commercial ties with England. The Democratic-Republicans opposed these policies, favoring instead free trade, the promotion of agrarian over commercial interests, and friendship with France.

The rationale behind the formation of both parties was primarily that they would be a means by which to institutionalize existing voting blocs in Congress around a cohesive policy agenda. Although the Federalists and the Democratic-Republicans competed in elections, their ties to the electorate were loose. In 1800, the American electorate was small, and deference was an important political factor, with voters generally expected to follow the lead of local political and religious leaders and community notables. Nominations were informal, without rules or regulations. Local party leaders would simply gather the party elites, and they would agree on the person, usually one of them, who would be the candidate. The meetings where candidates were nominated were generally called caucuses. In this era, before the introduction of the secret ballot, many voters were reluctant publicly to defy the views of influential members of their community. In this context, the Democratic-Republicans and the Federalists organized political clubs and developed newspapers and newsletters designed to mobilize elite opinion; they also relied on local elites to bring along their followers. In the election of 1800, Jefferson defeated the incumbent Federalist president, John Adams, and led his party to power. Over the ensuing years, the Federalists gradually weakened. The party disappeared altogether after the pro-British sympathies of some Federalist leaders during the War of 1812 led to charges that the party was guilty of treason.

The Second Party System: Democrats and Whigs

From the collapse of the Federalists until the 1830s, America had only one political party, the Democratic-Republicans. This period of one-party politics is sometimes known as the Era of Good Feeling, to indicate the absence of party competition. Throughout this period, however, there was intense factional conflict within the Democratic-Republican Party, particularly between the supporters and opponents of General Andrew Jackson, America's great military hero of the War of 1812. Jackson was one of five significant candidates for president in 1824 and won the most popular and electoral votes but a majority of neither, throwing the election into the House of Representatives. Jackson's opponents united to deny him the presidency, but Jackson won election in 1828 and again in 1832.

Jackson was greatly admired by millions of ordinary Americans living on the nation's farms and in its villages, and the Jacksonians made the most of the general's appeal to the common people by embarking on a program of suffrage expansion that would give Jackson's impecunious but numerous supporters the right to vote. To bring growing numbers of voters to the polls, the Jacksonians built political clubs and held mass rallies and parades, laying the groundwork for a new and more popular politics. Jackson's vice president and eventual successor, Martin Van Buren, was the organizational genius behind the Jacksonian movement, establishing a central party committee, state party organizations, and party newspapers. In response to widespread complaints about cliques of party leaders dominating the nominations at party caucuses and leaving no place for other party members who wanted to participate, the Jacksonians also established the state and national party conventions as the forums for nominating presidential candidates. The conventions gave control of the presidential nominating process to the new state party organizations that the Jacksonians had created and expected to control.

The Jacksonians, whose party came to be known as the Democratic Party, were not without opponents, however, especially in the New England states. During the 1830s groups opposing Jackson for reasons of personality and politics united to form a new political force—the Whig Party—thus giving rise to the second American party system. During the 1830s and 1840s, the Democrats and the Whigs built party organizations throughout the nation, and both sought to enlarge their bases of support by expanding the suffrage through the elimination of property restrictions and other barriers to voting—at least voting by white men. This would not be the last time that party competition paved the way for expansion of the electorate. Support for the new Whig Party was stronger in the Northeast than in the South and the West and stronger among mercantile groups than among small farmers. Hence to some extent the Whigs were the successors of the Federalists. Many, though not all, Whigs favored a national bank, a protective tariff, and federally sponsored internal improvements. The Jacksonians opposed all three policies. In 1840, the Whigs won their first presidential election under the leadership of General William Henry Harrison, a military hero known as Old Tippecanoe. The 1840 election marked the first time in American history that two parties competed for the presidency in every state in the Union.

In the late 1840s and early 1850s, conflicts over slavery produced sharp divisions within both the Whig and the Democratic parties, despite the efforts of party leaders such as Henry Clay and Stephen A. Douglas to develop sectional compromises that would bridge the widening gulf between the North and the South. By 1856, the Whig Party had all but disintegrated under the strain. The Kansas-Nebraska Act of 1854 gave each territory the right to decide whether to permit slavery. Opposition to this policy led to the formation of a number of antislavery parties, with the Republicans emerging as the strongest of the new forces.[12] In 1856, the party's first presidential candidate, John C. Frémont, won one-third of the popular vote and carried 11 states.

The early Republican platforms appealed to commercial as well as anti-slavery interests. The Republicans favored homesteading, internal improvements, the construction of a transcontinental railroad, and protective tariffs, as well as the containment of slavery. In 1858, the Republican Party won control of the House of Representatives; in 1860, the Republican presidential candidate, Abraham Lincoln, was victorious. Lincoln's victory strengthened southern calls for secession from the Union and led, soon thereafter, to all-out civil war.

The Third Party System: Republicans and Democrats, 1860–96

During the course of the war, President Lincoln depended heavily on Republican governors and state legislatures to raise troops, provide funding, and maintain popular support for a long and bloody military conflict. The secession of the South had stripped the Democratic Party of many of its leaders and supporters, but the Democrats nevertheless remained politically competitive throughout the war and nearly won the 1864 presidential election due to war weariness on the part of the northern public. With the defeat of the Confederacy in 1865, some congressional Republicans sought to convert the South into a Republican bastion through Reconstruction, a program that enfranchised newly freed slaves while disenfranchising many white voters and disqualifying many white politicians from seeking office. Reconstruction collapsed in the 1870s as a result of divisions within the Republican Party in Congress and violent resistance to the program by southern whites. With the end of Reconstruction, the former Confederate states regained full membership in the Union and full control of their internal affairs. Throughout the South, African Americans were deprived of political rights, including the right to vote, despite post–Civil War constitutional guarantees to the contrary. The post–Civil War South was solidly Democratic in its political affiliation, and with a firm southern base, the national Democratic Party was able to confront the Republicans on a more or less equal basis. From the end of the Civil War to the 1890s, the Republican Party remained the party of the North, with strong business and middle-class support, while the Democratic Party was the party of the South, with support from working-class and immigrant groups in the North. Republican candidates campaigned by waving the "bloody shirt" of the Civil War and urging their supporters to "vote the way you shot." Democrats emphasized the issue of the tariff, which they claimed was ruinous to agricultural interests.

The Fourth Party System, 1896–1932

During the 1890s, profound and rapid social and economic changes led to the emergence of a variety of protest parties, including the Populist Party, which won the support of hundreds of thousands of voters in the South and the West. The Populists appealed mainly to small farmers but also attracted western mining interests and urban workers. In the 1892 presidential election, the Populist Party carried four states and elected governors in eight states. In 1896, the Democrats in effect adopted the Populist Party platform and nominated William Jennings Bryan, a Democratic senator with pronounced Populist sympathies, for the presidency. The Republicans nominated the conservative senator William McKinley. In the ensuing campaign, northern and midwestern business made an all-out effort to defeat what it saw as a radical threat from the Populist-Democratic alliance. When the dust settled, the Republicans had won a resounding victory. In the nation's metropolitan regions, especially in the Northeast and upper Midwest, workers became convinced that the Populist-Democratic alliance threatened the industries that provided their jobs, while immigrants were frightened by the nativist rhetoric employed by some Populist orators and writers. The Republicans had carried the northern and midwestern states and confined the Democrats to their bastions in the South and the Far West. For the next 36 years, the Republicans were the nation's majority party, carrying 7 of 9 presidential elections and controlling both houses of Congress in 15 of 18 contests. The Republican Party of this era was very much the party of American business, advocating low taxes, high tariffs, and a minimum of government regulation. The Democrats were far too weak to offer much opposition. Southern Democrats, moreover, were more concerned with maintaining the region's autonomy on issues of race to challenge the Republicans on other fronts.

The Fifth Party System: The New Deal Coalition, 1932–68

Soon after the Republican candidate Herbert Hoover won the 1928 presidential election, the nation's economy collapsed. The Great Depression, which produced economic hardship on a scale never seen before, stemmed from a variety of causes. From the perspective of millions of Americans, though, the Republican Party had not done enough to promote economic recovery. In 1932, Americans elected Franklin Delano Roosevelt and a solidly Democratic Congress. Roosevelt developed a program for economic recovery that he dubbed the New Deal, under the auspices of which the size and reach of America's national government were substantially increased.

Chapter 11: Political Parties

The federal government took responsibility for economic management and social welfare to an extent that was unprecedented in American history. Roosevelt designed many of his programs specifically to expand the political base of the Democratic Party. He rebuilt the party around a nucleus of unionized workers, upper-middle-class intellectuals and professionals, southern farmers, Jews, Catholics, and northern African Americans (few blacks in the South could vote) that made the Democrats the nation's majority party for 36 years. Republicans groped for a response to the New Deal but often wound up supporting popular New Deal programs such as Social Security in what was sometimes derided as "me-too" Republicanism.

The New Deal coalition was severely strained during the 1960s by conflicts over President Lyndon Johnson's Great Society initiative, civil rights, and the Vietnam War. A number of Johnson's Great Society programs, designed to fight poverty and racial discrimination, involved the empowerment of local groups that were often at odds with established city and county governments. These programs touched off battles between local Democratic political machines and the national administration that split the Democratic coalition. For its part, the struggle over civil rights initially divided northern Democrats, who supported the civil rights cause, and white southern Democrats, who defended the system of racial segregation. Subsequently, as the civil rights movement launched a northern campaign aimed at securing access to jobs and education and an end to racial discrimination in such realms as housing, northern Democrats also experienced a split, often along class lines, with blue-collar workers tending to vote Republican. The struggle over the Vietnam War further divided the Democrats, with upper-income liberal Democrats strongly opposing the Johnson administration's decision to send U.S. forces to fight in Southeast Asia. These schisms within the Democratic Party provided an opportunity for the Republicans to return to power, which they did in 1968 under the leadership of Richard Nixon.

The Sixth Party System

In the 1960s, conservative Republicans argued that "me-tooism" was a recipe for continual failure and sought to reposition the party as a genuine alternative to the Democrats. In 1964, for example, the Republican presidential candidate, Barry Goldwater, author of a book titled *The Conscience of a Conservative*, argued in favor of substantially reduced levels of taxation and spending, less government regulation of the economy, and the elimination of many federal social programs. Although Goldwater was defeated by Lyndon Johnson, the ideas he espoused continue to be major themes of the Republican Party. The Goldwater message, however, was not enough to lead Republicans to victory. As discussed in Chapter 10, it took Richard Nixon's "southern strategy"

The most recent party system was initiated by the shift of Southern Democrats to the Republican Party. The 1968 campaigns of Republican Richard Nixon and Independent Alabama governor George Wallace (right) appealed to disaffected white southerners, cementing this shift.

to give the Republicans the votes they needed to end Democratic dominance of the political process. Nixon appealed strongly to disaffected white southerners and, with the help of the independent candidate and former Alabama governor George Wallace, sparked the shift of voters that eventually gave the once-hated "party of Lincoln" a strong position in all the states of the former Confederacy. In the 1980s, under the leadership of Ronald Reagan, Republicans added another important group to their coalition: religious conservatives who were offended by Democratic support of abortion rights as well as alleged Democratic disdain for traditional cultural and religious values.

While Republicans built a political base with economic and social conservatives and white southerners, the Democratic Party maintained its support among unionized workers and upper-middle-class intellectuals and professionals. Democrats also appealed strongly to racial minorities. The 1965 Voting Rights Act had greatly increased the participation of black voters in the South and helped the Democratic Party retain some congressional and Senate seats in that region. And while the Republicans appealed to social conservatives, the Democrats appealed strongly to Americans concerned about abortion rights, gay rights, feminism, environmentalism, and other progressive social causes. The results have been something of a draw. Democrats have won the presidency 5 out of the 12 elections since the passage of the Voting Rights Act and held at least one chamber of Congress for most of that time. That apparent stalemate masked dramatic changes in the regional bases of the parties. Republicans surged in the South, making the southern states the foundation of their presidential and congressional victories. Those gains came at the expense of the old-line Republicans in the Northeast. New England, once the bedrock of the Republican Party, had only two Republican U.S. House members (of 22 seats) after the 2014 election.

The shift of much of the South from the Democratic to the Republican camp, along with the other developments mentioned earlier, meant that each political party became ideologically more homogeneous after the 1980s. Today, as we've noted before, there are few liberal Republicans or conservative Democrats. One consequence of this development is that party loyalty in Congress, which had been weak between the 1950s and the 1970s, became a more potent force. The 1990s witnessed a dramatic resurgence of party-line voting in Congress. A simple measure of party developed by Professor Stuart Rice in the 1920s and tracked by *Congressional Quarterly* since the 1950s is the party unity score. This is the percentage of bills on which a majority of one party votes against a majority of the other party. Between the 1950s and the 1970s, unity hovered around 70 percent. Since the 1980s it has regularly exceeded 90 percent.[13]

American Third Parties

Although the United States is said to possess a two-party system, we have always had more than two parties. Typically, third parties in the United States have represented social and economic protests that, for one reason or another, were not given voice by the two major parties.[14] Such parties have had a good deal of influence on ideas and elections in the United States. The Populists, a party centered in the rural areas of the West and the Midwest during the late nineteenth century, and the Progressives, spokesmen for the urban middle classes in the late nineteenth and early twentieth centuries, are among the most important examples. More recently, Ross Perot, who ran in 1992 and 1996 as an independent, impressed some voters with his folksy style in the presidential debates and garnered almost 19 percent of the votes cast in the 1992 presidential election. Earlier, the independent candidate George Wallace received almost 10 percent of the vote in 1968, and John Anderson received about 5 percent in 1980.

Table 11.1 lists all the parties that offered candidates in one or more states in the presidential election of 2012. The third-party and independent candidates together polled about 2.25 million votes, and they gained no electoral votes for president. Third-party candidacies also arise at the state and local levels. In New York, the Liberal and Conservative parties have been on the ballot for decades. In 1998, Minnesota elected a third-party governor, the former professional wrestler Jesse Ventura.

Although it is difficult for third parties to survive, it is worth noting that the two major parties today themselves started as third parties. The Democrats emerged at the beginning of the nineteenth century as an alternative to the Federalists and their opponents, loosely, the Anti-federalists. The Federalist Party, a party organized largely around the ideas and policies of Alexander Hamilton, itself gave way to the Whig Party, which was replaced by the Republicans. In some sense, then, the two major parties today started as alternative parties, as third parties. They have reinvented themselves ideologically to change with the times

Table 11.1
PARTIES AND CANDIDATES, 2012

ANALYZING THE EVIDENCE

Though the Democrats and the Republicans are America's dominant political forces, many minor parties nominate candidates for the presidency. Why are there so many minor parties? Why don't these parties represent much of a threat to the major parties?

➡

CANDIDATE	PARTY	VOTE TOTAL	PERCENT OF VOTE
Barack Obama	Democrat	65,907,213	51.06
Mitt Romney	Republican	60,931,767	47.21
Gary Johnson	Libertarian	1,275,804	0.99
Jill Stein	Green	469,501	0.36
Virgil Goode	Constitution	122,001	0.09
Roseanne Barr	Independent	67,278	0.05
Rocky Anderson	Justice Party	43,111	0.03
Tom Hoefling	America's Party	40,586	0.03
Richard Duncan	Independent	12,557	0.01
Others		217,669	0.17

SOURCE: Federal Election Commission, www.fec.gov.

and to co-opt supporters of emerging parties. The Democratic Party, for example, became a great deal more liberal when it adopted most of the Progressive program early in the twentieth century. In the 1930s, many socialists felt that Roosevelt's New Deal had adopted most of their party's program, including old-age pensions, unemployment compensation, an agricultural marketing program, and laws guaranteeing workers the right to organize into unions.

The ability of the major parties to evolve explains the short lives of third parties. Their causes are usually eliminated by the ability of the major parties to absorb their programs and draw their supporters into the mainstream. There are, of course, additional reasons for the short duration of most third parties. One is the typical limitation of their electoral support to one or two regions. Populist support, for example, was primarily midwestern. The 1948 Progressive Party, with Henry Wallace as its candidate, drew nearly half its votes from the state of New York. The American Independent Party polled nearly 10 million popular votes and 45 electoral votes for George Wallace in 1968—the most electoral votes ever

In 2012 numerous candidates from third parties ran for president, including the Constitution Party's Virgil Goode (left) and the Green Party's Jill Stein (right). Although they may have little chance of winning seats in Washington, D.C., minor parties can influence national politics by drawing attention to their causes, which may then be taken up by the major parties.

polled by a third-party candidate. But all of Wallace's electoral votes and the majority of his popular vote came from the states of the Deep South. Americans usually assume that only the candidates nominated by one of the two major parties have any chance of winning an election. Thus a vote cast for a third-party or an independent candidate is often seen as a wasted vote. For instance, there is evidence in the 2000 race between Al Gore, the Democrat, and George W. Bush, the Republican, that the third-party candidate Ralph Nader did better in those states where either Bush or Gore was nearly certain of winning, whereas his support dwindled in more closely contested states. Third-party candidates must struggle—usually without success—to overcome the perception that they cannot win.

As many scholars have pointed out, third-party prospects are also hampered by America's single-member-district plurality election system. In many other nations, several individuals can be elected to represent each legislative district. This is called a system of multiple-member districts. With this type of system, the candidates of weaker parties have a better chance of winning at least some seats. For their part, voters are less concerned about wasting ballots and usually more willing to support minor-party candidates.

Reinforcing the effects of the single-member district (as noted in Chapter 10), plurality-voting rules generally have the effect of setting what could be called a high threshold for victory. To win a plurality race, candidates usually must secure many more votes than they would need under most European systems of proportional representation. For example, to win an American plurality election in a single-member district with only two candidates, a politician must win more than 50 percent of the votes cast. To win a seat in a European multimember district under proportional-representation rules, a candidate may need to win only 15 or 20 percent of the votes cast. This high threshold in American elections discourages minor parties and encourages the various political factions that might otherwise form minor parties to minimize their differences and remain within the major-party coalitions.[15]

It would nevertheless be incorrect to assert (as some scholars have maintained) that America's single-member plurality election system guarantees that only two parties will compete for power in all regions of the country. All that can be said is that American election law depresses the number of parties likely to survive over long periods of time in the United States. There is nothing magical about two.

DO PARTIES ENHANCE DEMOCRACY?

Political parties help make democracy work. We often do not appreciate that democratic government is a contradiction in terms. Government implies policies, programs, and decisive action. Democracy, on the other hand, implies an opportunity for all citizens to participate fully in the governmental process. Full participation by everyone is inconsistent with getting things done in an efficient and timely manner. How can we balance the ideals of democracy and efficiency in government? How can we make certain that popular participation will result in a government capable of making decisions and developing needed policies? At what point should participation stop and government begin? Strong political parties are a partial antidote to the inherent contradiction between participation and governance. Strong parties can both encourage popular involvement and convert participation into effective government. However, as we have seen, the parties' struggle for political advantage can also lead to the type of intense partisanship that cripples the government's ability to operate efficiently and in the nation's best interest.

Parties also simplify the electoral process. They set the electoral agenda by laying out party platforms, recruiting candidates, accumulating and distributing campaign resources, and registering and mobilizing people to vote. Party control of the nominating process and the pressures toward two-party politics in the United States mean that most voters must decide between just two meaningful or plausible choices in any election. This, in turn, facilitates voters' decision making. Voters can reasonably expect what sorts of policies a candidate who has a party's endorsement will pursue if elected. Even before a given candidate has received the nomination, most voters have already sorted themselves into one of the two competing camps, Democratic or Republican. They know for whom they will vote before the election begins. This may seem like a gross simplification of politics. It reduces the many complex interests in our society to just two competing teams whose policy platforms must be watered down to accommodate the many subtle

Chapter 11: Political Parties

differences or ideological nuances among the groups inside the party. It further reduces politics into warring factions that have little hope of finding compromise or common ground. However, the two-party system does give meaning to the vote. It empowers the voter to say, I want to stay the course with the party in power, or I want to go in a new direction.

For Further Reading

Selections highlighted in red are included in *Readings in American Politics: Analysis and Perspectives*, Third Edition.

Aldrich, John H. *Why Parties? A Second Look.* Chicago: University of Chicago Press, 2011.

Campbell, Angus, Philip E. Converse, Warren E. Miller, and Donald E. Stokes. *The American Voter.* Chicago: University of Chicago Press, 1980.

Chambers, William N., and Walter Dean Burnham, eds. *The American Party Systems: Stages of Political Development.* 2nd ed. New York: Oxford University Press, 1975.

Cox, Gary W., and Mathew D. McCubbins. *Legislative Leviathan: Party Government in the House.* Berkeley: University of California Press, 1993.

Cox, Gary W., and Mathew D. McCubbins. *Setting the Agenda: Responsible Party Government in the U.S. House of Representatives.* New York: Cambridge University Press, 2005.

Hershey, Marjorie R. *Party Politics in America.* 15th ed. New York: Pearson, 2013.

Hofstadter, Richard. *The Idea of a Party System: The Rise of Legitimate Opposition in the United States, 1780–1840.* Berkeley: University of California Press, 1969.

Mayhew, David. *Electoral Realignments: A Critique of an American Genre.* New Haven, CT: Yale University Press, 2007.

Miller, Gary, and Norman Schofield. "The Transformation of the Republican and Democratic Party Coalitions in the U.S." *Perspectives on Politics* (September 2008): 433–50.

Groups and Interests

Democratic politics in the United States does not end with elections. Federal, state, and local governments provide many additional avenues through which individuals and organizations can express their preferences. People may, for example, contact elected officials, their staffs, and bureaucrats directly about a particular decision or problem. They may participate in public meetings about legislation or administrative rulings; some private citizens are even selected to serve on special government commissions because of their expertise or particular concerns. They may file lawsuits to request that a government agency take a particular action or to prevent it from doing so. They may express their opinions in newspapers, on television and the Internet, or through other venues, and even hold public protests, without fear of persecution. Individuals, organizations, and even governments make frequent use of these many points of access. Many of these encounters with government are episodic, as when someone contacts an agency to solve a particular problem. But a substantial amount of political activity in the United States occurs through enduring, organized efforts that bring many individuals into collective action to seek a common goal. These efforts are largely coordinated by interest groups.

Americans often worry about the power of special interests. Many believe that organized groups, following special agendas, dominate the governmental and policy-making processes. The late Senator Edward Kennedy once said that Americans feel they have the "best Congress money can buy." Certainly a good deal of what Americans see and read about their nation's politics seems to confirm this pessimistic view. For example, after spending millions in campaign contributions and lobbying fees, corporations succeeded in bringing about the enactment of pension legislation that allowed them to sharply cut the amount they are required to contribute to their employees' pension funds. The savings to major corporations amounted to nearly $160 billion between 2006 and 2009.[1] Similarly, the health care reform program enacted by Congress in 2010 contains many provisions to benefit insurance and pharmaceutical companies that lobbied relentlessly for their inclusion in the act.

Most of the time, elected officials have every incentive to pay a good deal of attention to the organized interests that fund their campaigns and far less attention to mere voters. Politicians follow the political golden rule: those who have the gold make the rules.[2] Often enough, voters are not aware that their elected officials are giving them the short end of the stick. How many voters understand the intricacies of the law governing taxation of profits earned abroad or energy tax credits or Medicare reimbursement rates? When it comes to these matters, politicians can serve corporate interests without even considering the views of ordinary citizens. Most citizens can safely be assumed to have no views on these topics. But even when it comes to matters that citizens do care about, such as taxes, unemployment, and overall spending, politicians will often still follow the golden rule.

CORE OF THE ANALYSIS

➡ Interest groups are organized to influence government decisions.

➡ There is a clear orientation of interest groups toward those segments of society with better education or more economic resources, and those most directly affected by government actions, especially corporations.

➡ Interest groups use various strategies to promote their goals, including lobbying, gaining access to key decision makers, using the courts, going public, and influencing electoral politics.

The framers of the Constitution feared the power that could be wielded by organized interests and that the public good would be "disregarded in the conflict of rival [factions]."[3] Yet they believed that interest groups thrived because of freedom—the freedom that all Americans enjoyed to organize and express their views. To the framers, this problem presented a dilemma of freedom versus power. If the government were given the power to regulate or in any way to forbid efforts by organized interests to interfere in the political process, the government would in effect have been given the power to suppress freedom. The solution to this dilemma was presented by James Madison:

> . . . Take in a greater variety of parties and interest [and] you make it less probable that a majority of the whole will have a common motive to invade the rights of other citizens. . . . [Hence the advantage] enjoyed by a large over a small republic.[4]

According to Madisonian theory, a good constitution encourages multitudes of interests so that no single interest can ever tyrannize the others. The basic assumption is that competition among interests will produce balance and compromise, with all the interests regulating one another.[5] Today, this Madisonian principle of regulation is called pluralism.

pluralism

The theory that all interests are and should be free to compete for influence in the government. The outcome of this competition is compromise and moderation

There are tens of thousands of organized groups in the United States, but the huge number of interest groups competing for influence does not mean that all interests are fully and equally represented in the American political process. As we will see, the political deck is heavily stacked in favor of those interests able to organize and to wield substantial economic, social, and institutional resources on behalf of their cause. This means that within the universe of interest group politics, it is political power—not some abstract conception of the public good—that is likely to prevail. Moreover, this means that interest group politics, taken as a whole, is a political format that works more to the advantage of some types of interests than others. In general, a politics in which interest groups predominate is a politics with a distinctly upper-class bias.

In this chapter we examine interest group politics in the United States. We analyze the group basis of politics, the challenges groups face in getting individuals to act collectively, and some solutions to these problems. We seek to understand the character and balance of the interests promoted through the pluralistic political system in the United States. We further examine the tremendous growth of interest groups in their number, resources, and activity in recent American political history, especially the emergence of public interest groups. Finally, we examine the strategies that groups use to influence politics and whether their influence in the political process has become excessive.

THE CHARACTERISTICS OF INTEREST GROUPS

An interest group is an organized group of people that makes policy-related appeals to government. Individuals form groups in order to increase the chance that their views will be heard and their interests treated favorably by the government. Interest groups are organized to influence governmental decisions. They are often referred to as lobbies.

Interest groups are sometimes confused with political action committees (see Chapter 10). The difference is that PACs focus on influencing elections, whereas interest groups focus on influencing elected officials. Another distinction that we should make is that interest groups are also different from political parties: interest groups tend to concern themselves with the *policies* of government; parties tend to concern themselves with the *personnel* of government.

◀ **interest group**
An organized group
of individuals or
organizations that makes
policy-related appeals to
government

Enhancing Democracy

There is an enormous number of interest groups in the United States, and millions of Americans are members of one or more groups, at least to the extent of paying dues or attending an occasional meeting. By representing the interests of such large numbers of people and encouraging political participation, organized groups can and do enhance American democracy. Organized groups educate their members about issues that affect them. Groups lobby members of Congress and the executive, engage in litigation, and generally represent their members' interests in the political arena. Groups mobilize their members for elections and grassroots lobbying efforts, thus encouraging participation. Interest groups also monitor government programs to make certain that their members are not adversely affected by these programs. In all these ways, organized interests can be said to promote democratic politics. But because not all interests are represented equally, interest group politics works to the advantage of some and the disadvantage of others.

What Interests Are Represented

When most people think about interest groups, they immediately think of groups with a direct economic interest in governmental actions (Table 12.1). These groups are generally supported by groups of producers

Table 12.1

WHO IS REPRESENTED BY ORGANIZED INTERESTS?

ANALYZING THE EVIDENCE

What types of interests are most likely to be represented by interest groups? If interest group politics is biased in favor of the wealthy and the powerful, should we curb group politics?

ECONOMIC ROLE OF THE INDIVIDUAL	U.S. ADULTS (%)	ORGS. (%)	TYPE OF ORG. IN WASHINGTON	RATIO OF ORGS. PER ADULT
Managerial/ administrative	7	71.0	Business association	10.10
Professional/ technical	9	17.0	Professional association	1.90
Student/teacher	4	4.0	Educational organization	1.00
Farmworker	2	1.5	Agricultural workers' organization	0.75
Unable to work	2	0.6	Organization for the disabled	0.30
Other non-farmworkers	41	4.0	Union	0.10
Homemaker	19	1.8	Women's organization	0.09
Retired	12	0.8	Senior citizens' organization	0.07
Looking for work	4	0.1	Unemployment organization	0.03

NOTE: This study has not been repeated since the 1980s, but a perusal of the Directory of Washington Representatives—the lobbyists' phonebook—reveals that little has changed.
SOURCE: Kay Lehman Schlozman and John T. Tierney, *Organized Interests and American Democracy* (New York: Harper & Row, 1986).

or manufacturers in a particular economic sector. Examples of this type of group include the American Fuel & Petrochemical Manufacturers, the American Farm Bureau Federation, and the National Federation of Independent Business, which represents small business owners. At the same time that broadly representative groups such as these are active in Washington, specific companies—such as Disney, Shell Oil, IBM, and Microsoft—may be active on certain issues that are of particular concern to them.

Labor organizations, although fewer in number and more limited in their financial resources, are extremely active lobbyists. The AFL-CIO, the United Mine Workers, and the Teamsters' union are all groups that lobby on behalf of organized labor. In recent years, lobbies have arisen to further the interests of public employees, the most significant among these being the American Federation of State, County, and Municipal Employees (AFSCME).

Professional lobbies such as the American Bar Association and the American Medical Association have been particularly successful in furthering their own interests in state and federal legislatures. The "gun lobby," comprising the representatives of firearms manufacturers and dealers as well as gun owners, is represented by the National Rifle Association (NRA). The NRA mobilized furiously in 2012 and 2013 to thwart gun control efforts introduced in Congress in the wake of the December 2012 shooting of 20 first graders in a Connecticut elementary school. Financial institutions, represented by organizations such as the American Bankers Association and the National Savings & Loan League, although frequently less visible than other lobbies, also play an important role in shaping legislative policy.

Recent years have witnessed the growth of a powerful "public interest" lobby purporting to represent interests whose concerns are not likely to be addressed by traditional lobbies. These groups have been most visible in the consumer protection and environmental policy areas, although public interest groups cover a broad range of issues, from nuclear disarmament to civil rights to abortion. The National Resources Defense Council, the Union of Concerned Scientists, the National Association for the Advancement of Colored People, the Christian Coalition of America, and Common Cause are all examples of public interest groups.

The perceived need for representation on Capitol Hill has generated a public-sector lobby, including the National League of Cities and the "research" lobby. The latter group comprises think tanks and universities that have an interest in obtaining government funds for research and support, and it includes such prestigious institutions as Harvard University, the Brookings Institution, and the American Enterprise Institute. Indeed, many universities have expanded their lobbying efforts even as they have reduced faculty positions and course offerings and increased tuition.[6] Even with the great expansion in the number of interests, the lion's share of organizations involved in politics in Washington, D.C., and in the state capitals represents economic interests.

The "Free Rider" Problem

Whether organizations need individuals to volunteer or merely to write checks, all must recruit and retain members. Yet many groups find this difficult, even with regard to those who agree strongly with the group's goals.

The reason is that, as the economist Mancur Olson explains, the benefits of a group's success are often broadly available and cannot be denied to non-members.[7] Such benefits are called *collective goods*. This term is usually associated with certain government benefits, but it can also be applied to beneficial outcomes of interest group activity.

To follow Olson's theory, suppose a number of private property owners live near a mosquito-infested swamp. Each owner wants this swamp cleared. But if one or a few of the owners were to clear the swamp alone, their actions would benefit all the other owners as well, without any effort on the part of those other owners. Each of the inactive owners would be free riding on the efforts of the ones who cleared the swamp. Thus, there is a disincentive for any of the owners to undertake the job alone.

Since the number of concerned owners is small in this particular case, they might eventually be able to organize themselves to share the costs as well as enjoy the benefits of clearing the swamp. But suppose the numbers of interested people are increased. Suppose the common concern is not the neighborhood swamp but polluted air or groundwater involving thousands of residents in a region or in fact millions of residents in a whole nation. National defense is the most obvious collective good whose benefits are shared by every resident, regardless of the taxes they pay or the support they provide. As the number of involved persons increases, or as the size of the group increases, the free-rider phenomenon becomes more of a problem. Individuals do not have much incentive to become active members and supporters of a group that is already working more or less on their behalf. The group would no doubt be more influential if all concerned individuals were active members—if there were no free riders. But groups will not reduce their efforts just because free riders get the same benefits as dues-paying activists. In fact, groups may try even harder precisely because there are free riders, with the hope that the free riders will be encouraged to join in.

free riding

Enjoying the benefits of some good or action while letting others bear the costs

Organizational Components

Although there are many interest groups, most share certain key organizational components. First and most important, all groups must attract and keep members. Somehow, groups must overcome the free-rider problem and persuade individuals to invest the money, time, energy, or effort required to take part in the group's activities. Members play a larger role in some groups than in others. In membership associations, group members actually serve on committees and engage in projects. In the case of labor unions, members may march on picket lines, and in the case of political or ideological groups, members may participate in demonstrations and protests. In another set of groups, staff organizations, a professional staff conducts most of the group's

activities; members are called on only to pay dues and make other contributions. Among the well-known public interest groups, some—such as the National Organization for Women (NOW)—are membership groups; others—such as Defenders of Wildlife and the Children's Defense Fund—are staff organizations.

Usually, groups appeal to members not only by promoting political goals or policies they favor but also by offering them direct informational, material, or solidary benefits. This removes the free-riding option for certain benefits, making participation more attractive. Thus, for example, AARP (formerly the American Association for Retired Persons), which promotes the interests of senior citizens, offers members information, insurance benefits, and commercial discounts. Many organizations provide information through conferences, training programs, and newsletters and other periodicals sent automatically to those who have paid membership dues. Material benefits can be discount purchasing, shared advertising, and perhaps most valuable of all, health and retirement insurance. Solidary benefits may include opportunities for social interaction, networking, and good fellowship. Thus, the local chapters of many national groups provide their members with a congenial social environment while collecting dues that finance the national office's political efforts.

Another kind of benefit involves the appeal of an interest group's purpose. The best examples of such purposive benefits are those of religious interest groups. The Christian right is made up of a number of interest groups that offer virtually no material benefits to their members, depending almost entirely on the religious identifications and affirmations of their members. Many religion-based interest groups have arisen throughout American history, such as those that drove abolition and Prohibition.

The second component shared by all groups is that each one must build a financial structure capable of sustaining an organization and funding the group's activities. Most interest groups rely on annual membership dues and voluntary contributions from sympathizers. Many also sell some ancillary services, such as insurance and vacation tours, to members.

Third, every group must have a leadership and decision-making structure. For some groups, this structure is very simple. For others, it can be quite elaborate and involve hundreds of local chapters that are melded into a national apparatus.

Last, most groups include an agency that actually carries out the group's tasks. This may be a research organization, a public-relations office, or a lobbying office in Washington or a state capital.

In addition to promoting shared political goals, interest groups may offer their members informational and material benefits. The AARP offers its members information as well as insurance benefits and commercial discounts.

informational benefits

Special newsletters, periodicals, training programs, conferences, and other information provided to members of groups to entice others to join

material benefits

Special goods, services, or money provided to members of groups to entice others to join

solidary benefits

Selective benefits of group membership that emphasize friendship, networking, and consciousness raising

purposive benefits

Selective benefits of group membership that emphasize the purpose and accomplishments of the group

The Characteristics of Members

Membership in interest groups is not randomly distributed in the population. People with higher incomes, higher levels of education, and management or professional occupations are much more likely to become members of groups than those who occupy lower rungs on the socioeconomic ladder.[8] Well-educated, upper-income professionals are more likely to have the time and the money and to have acquired through the educational process the concerns and skills needed to play a role in a group or association. Moreover, for business and professional people, group membership may provide personal contacts and access to information that can help advance their careers. At the same time, of course, corporate entities—businesses and the like—usually have ample resources to form or participate in groups that seek to advance their causes.

The result is that interest group politics in the United States tends to have a very pronounced upper-class bias. Certainly, many interest groups and political associations have a working-class or lower-class membership—labor organizations or welfare-rights organizations, for example—but the great majority of interest groups and their members are drawn from the middle and upper-middle classes. In general, the "interests" served by interest groups are the interests of society's "haves." Even groups associated with a progressive political agenda and support for the rights of the poor tend, in their own membership, to reflect the interests of the middle and upper-middle classes. When interest groups take opposing positions on issues and policies, the conflicting positions they espouse usually reflect divisions among upper-income strata rather than conflicts between the upper and lower classes.

In general, to obtain adequate political representation, forces from the bottom rungs of the socioeconomic ladder must be organized on the massive scale associated with political parties. Parties can organize and mobilize the collective energies of large numbers of people who, as individuals, may have very limited resources. Interest groups, on the other hand, generally organize smaller numbers of the better-to-do. Thus, the relative importance of political parties and interest groups in American politics has far-ranging implications for the distribution of political power in the United States.

Response to Changes in the Political Environment

If interest groups and our concerns about them were a new phenomenon, we would not have begun this section with James Madison. As long as there is government, as long as government makes policies that add value or impose costs, and as long as there is liberty to organize, interest groups will abound.

And if government expands, so will interest groups. There was, for example, a spurt of growth in the national government during the 1880s and 1890s, arising largely from the first government efforts at economic intervention to fight large monopolies and regulate some aspects of interstate commerce. In the latter decade, a parallel spurt of growth occurred in national interest groups, including the imposing National Association of Manufacturers and numerous other trade associations. Many groups organized around specific agricultural commodities as well. This period also marked the beginning of the expansion of trade unions as interest groups. Later, in the 1930s, interest groups with headquarters and representation in Washington began to grow significantly, concurrent with that decade's expansion of the national government.

Over recent decades, there has been an enormous increase both in the number of interest groups seeking to play a role in the American political process and in the extent of their opportunity to influence that process. The total number of interest groups in the United States today is not known. There are certainly tens of thousands of groups at the national, state, and local levels. One indication of the proliferation of such groups' activity is the growth over time in the number of political action committees (PACs) attempting to influence U.S. elections. Nearly 10 times as many PACs operated in 2012 as in the 1970s, increasing from fewer than 500 to more than 7,000. A *New York Times* report, for example, noted that during the 1970s, expanded federal regulation of the automobile, oil, gas, education, and health care industries impelled each of these interests to substantially increase its efforts to influence the government's behavior. These efforts, in turn, had the effect of spurring the organization of other groups to augment or counter the activities of the first.[9] The rise of PACs exhibits one of the most common features of business political activity: businesses are reactive. They are usually drawn into politics in response to regulations, rather than to create a new program.

Similarly, federal social programs have occasionally sparked political organization and action by clientele groups seeking to influence the distribution of benefits and, in turn, the organization of groups opposed to the programs or their cost. AARP, perhaps the largest membership organization in the United States, owes its emergence to the creation and expansion of Social Security and Medicare. Once older Americans had guaranteed retirement income and health insurance, they had a clear stake in protecting and even expanding these benefits. AARP formed and grew in response to attempts to pare back the program.[10]

Another factor accounting for the explosion of interest group activity in recent decades was the emergence of new social and political movements. The civil rights and antiwar movements of the 1960s and the reactions against them created a generation of upper-middle-class professionals and intellectuals who have seen themselves as a political force in opposition to the public policies and politicians associated with the nation's postwar regime. Such groups sought change in social behavior and public policy, usually through civil disobedience. More recent social movements include the antitax Tea Party movement and the Occupy movement of 2011–12 protesting corporate power in the United States.

Members of the new political movements of the 1960s constructed or strengthened public interest groups such as Common Cause, the Sierra Club, the Environmental Defense Fund, Physicians for Social Responsibility, the National Organization for Women, and the various organizations formed by

political action committee (PAC)

A private group that raises and distributes funds for use in election campaigns

Innovations in technology and social media have played a role in the increase in number and influence of interest groups. Today, groups can use Facebook pages and Twitter feeds to reach and mobilize sympathizers.

the consumer activist Ralph Nader. These groups were able to influence the media, Congress, and even the judiciary and enjoyed a remarkable degree of success during the late 1960s and early 1970s in securing the enactment of policies they favored. Activist groups also played a major role in securing the enactment of environmental, consumer, and occupational health and safety legislation.

Among the factors contributing to the rise and success of public interest groups was technology. Computerized direct-mail campaigns in the 1980s were perhaps the first big innovation that allowed organizations to identify and reach out to potential members efficiently and effectively. Today, Facebook, Twitter, and other new media have allowed public interest groups to reach hundreds of thousands of potential sympathizers and contributors. Relatively small groups can efficiently identify and mobilize their adherents throughout the nation. Individuals with perspectives that might be in a small anonymous minority everywhere can become conscious of each other and mobilize for national political action through the social networking tools that were unheard of even 30 years ago.

Of course, many individuals who share a common interest do not form interest groups. For example, college students could be said to share an interest in the cost and quality of education, but they have not organized to demand lower tuition, better facilities, or a more effective faculty. Students could be called a "latent group." American society is filled with such latent groups. In many instances, the failure of a latent group to organize reflects the ability of individuals to achieve their goals without participating in an organized effort. Individual students, for example, are free to choose among colleges; this, in turn, forces colleges to compete for patronage. Where the market or other mechanisms allow individuals to achieve their goals without joining groups, they are less likely to do so.

STRATEGIES FOR INFLUENCING POLICY

Interest groups work to improve the probability that they and their policy interests will be heard and treated favorably by all branches and levels of the government. The quest for political influence and power takes many forms. We can roughly divide these strategies into "insider strategies" and "outsider strategies."

Insider strategies include gaining access to key decision makers and using the courts. Of course, influencing policy through traditional political institutions requires understanding how those institutions work. A lobbyist who wishes Congress to address a problem with legislation will try to find a sympathetic member of Congress, preferably on a committee with jurisdiction over the problem, and will work directly with the member's staff. If an organization decides to bring suit in the courts, it may want to sue in a jurisdiction where it has a good chance of getting a judge favorable to the case or where the immediate appellate courts are likely to support its case. Gaining access is not easy. Legislators and bureaucrats have little time and many requests to juggle; courts have full dockets. Interest groups themselves have limited budgets and staff. They must choose their battles well and map out the strategy most likely to succeed.

Outsider strategies include going public and using electoral tactics. Just as politicians can gain an electoral edge by informing voters, so too can groups. A well-planned public-information campaign or targeted campaign activities and contributions can have as much influence as working the corridors of Congress.

Many groups employ a mix of insider and outsider strategies. For example, environmental groups such as the Sierra Club lobby members of Congress and key congressional staff members, participate in bureaucratic rule making by offering comments and suggestions to agencies on new environmental rules, and bring lawsuits under various environmental acts such as the Endangered Species Act, which authorizes groups and citizens to come to court if they believe the act is being violated. At the same time, the Sierra Club attempts to influence public opinion through media campaigns and to influence electoral politics by supporting candidates who it believes share its environmental views and opposing candidates who it views as foes of environmentalism. The Analyzing the Evidence unit on page 408 considers the relative influence of different groups.

Direct Lobbying

Lobbying is an attempt by an individual or a group to influence the passage of legislation by exerting direct pressure on members of the legislature. The First Amendment to the Constitution provides for the right to "petition the Government for a redress of grievances." But as early as the 1870s, *lobbying* became the common term for petitioning.

lobbying
An attempt by a group to influence the policy process through persuasion of government officials

The 1946 Federal Regulation of Lobbying Act defines a lobbyist as "any person who shall engage himself for pay or any consideration for the purpose of attempting to influence the passage or defeat of any legislation to the Congress of the United States." According to the 1995 Federal Lobbying Disclosure Act, any person who makes at least one lobbying contact with either the legislative or executive branch in a year, any individual who spends 20 percent of his or her time in support of such activities, or any firm that devotes 10 percent of its budget to such activities must register as a lobbyist. They must report what topics they discussed with the government, though not which particular individuals or offices they contacted. The Analyzing the Evidence unit in this chapter looks at the major types of interest groups and their influence on government.

Lobbying involves a great deal of activity on the part of someone speaking for an interest. Lobbyists badger and buttonhole legislators, administrators, and committee staff members with facts about pertinent issues and facts or claims about public support of them.[11] Lobbyists can serve a useful purpose in the legislative and administrative process by providing this kind of information. However, within each industry, there are a great many different individuals and organizations involved in government advocacy, and they usually do not speak with a common voice. Rather each advocates and defends its own particular interests, often in conflict with other firms in the same industry. What the leading organization or peak association of an industry may advocate may be undercut by the activities of individual firms. The Entertainment Software Association, which spent roughly $5.2 million on lobbying in 2013, likely wants a different set of regulations than Microsoft or Google.

Lobbying Members of Congress. Interest groups have substantial influence in setting the legislative agenda and in helping craft the language

Interest Group Influence

Contributed by
Beth L. Leech
Rutgers University

Which interest groups have the most influence over political outcomes? It is generally accepted among those who study interest groups that business and economic interests predominate. Economic interests are more likely to form organized groups, are more likely to be active, and on average spend more money and more time on political issues than are noneconomic interests like citizen groups or "public interest" groups. When we look at interest groups' involvement in the policy-making process, however, the sheer number of groups or dollars may not directly equal the amount of influence that those groups have. While numbers and dollars are important indicators of which interests are represented, it would be preferable to try to measure which groups actually were influential in politics. To address this question, the political scientist Frank Baumgartner and his colleagues interviewed 315 lobbyists and government officials about 98 randomly selected policy issues. Citizen groups were more likely to be mentioned as being important in the debates than any other type of group, despite the fact that they spent less and they made up a smaller part of the overall group population.

Why were citizen groups seen as so influential despite their relative lack of resources? It may be that those groups have important ties to constituents, granting them greater legitimacy in the eyes of members of Congress, or it could be that some members of Congress already supported the policies that the citizen groups were advocating. Whatever the reason, it is clear that citizen groups have greater voice in Washington than the dollar counts might suggest.

Types of Interest Groups Registered to Lobby

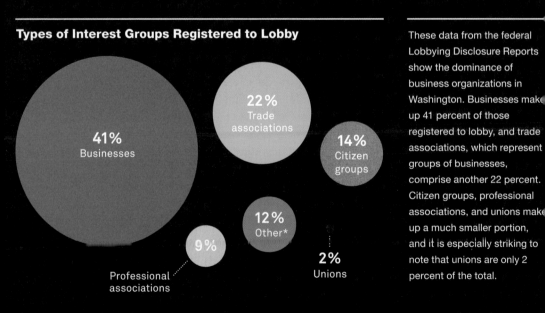

These data from the federal Lobbying Disclosure Reports show the dominance of business organizations in Washington. Businesses make up 41 percent of those registered to lobby, and trade associations, which represent groups of businesses, comprise another 22 percent. Citizen groups, professional associations, and unions make up a much smaller portion, and it is especially striking to note that unions are only 2 percent of the total.

41%
Businesses

22%
Trade associations

14%
Citizen groups

12%
Other*

9%
Professional associations

2%
Unions

*Includes governmental groups, think tanks, universities, and hospitals

Average Spending on Lobbying and Campaign Contributions

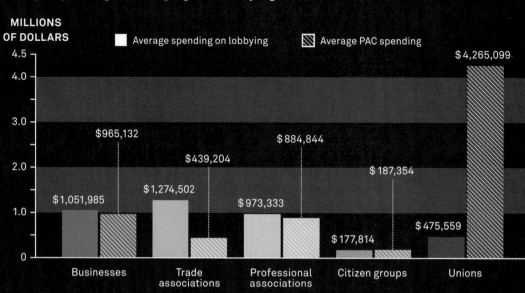

The graph above shows the average amounts spent on lobbying or campaign contributions by interest groups that played a major role in 98 randomly selected issues studied by Baumgartner et al. Citizen groups on average spent much less on lobbying and campaign contributions than other types of groups. Unions on average spent more on campaign contributions than any other type of group, but that spending is tempered by the fact that there are fewer unions.

Who Is Seen as Important in Policy Making?

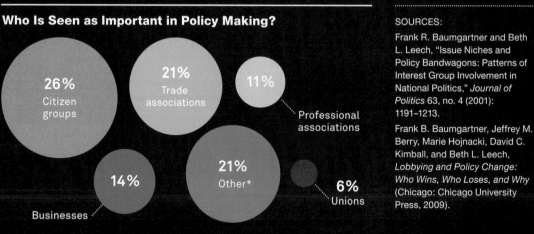

*Includes coalitions, governmental associations, and think tanks.

SOURCES:

Frank R. Baumgartner and Beth L. Leech, "Issue Niches and Policy Bandwagons: Patterns of Interest Group Involvement in National Politics," *Journal of Politics* 63, no. 4 (2001): 1191–1213.

Frank B. Baumgartner, Jeffrey M. Berry, Marie Hojnacki, David C. Kimball, and Beth L. Leech, *Lobbying and Policy Change: Who Wins, Who Loses, and Why* (Chicago: Chicago University Press, 2009).

Although the overall population of interest groups has fewer citizen groups than business groups, as seen in the figure to the left, not all groups are equally influential. Baumgartner and his colleagues interviewed 315 lobbyists and government officials about 98 randomly selected policy issues. Citizen groups were more likely to be mentioned as being important in the debate than any other type of group. More than a quarter of the interest groups seen as being influential were citizen groups.

of legislation (Figure 12.1). Today sophisticated lobbyists win influence by providing information about policies to busy members of Congress. As one lobbyist noted, "You can't get access without knowledge. . . . I can go in to see John Dingell [former chairman of the House Committee on Energy and Commerce], but if I have nothing to offer or nothing to say, he's not going to want to see me."[12]

Providing access is only one of the many services lobbyists perform. Lobbyists often testify on behalf of their clients at congressional committee and agency hearings; lobbyists sometimes help their clients identify potential allies with whom to construct coalitions; lobbyists provide research and information to government officials; lobbyists often draft proposed legislation or regulations to be introduced by friendly lawmakers; lobbyists talk to

ANALYZING
THE EVIDENCE

Interest groups can influence members of Congress in a variety of ways. They may seek to mobilize popular support in the form of grassroots campaigns; they may try to generate publicity favorable to their cause; they may work through congressional staffers; or they may seek to lobby members of Congress directly. How might these various strategies work together? What pitfalls might an interest group encounter in trying to influence members of Congress?

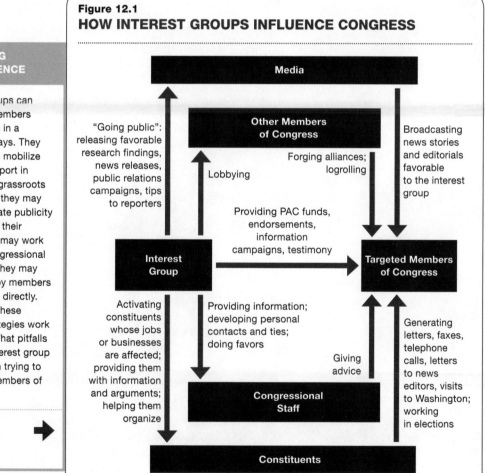

Figure 12.1
HOW INTEREST GROUPS INFLUENCE CONGRESS

reporters, place ads in newspapers, and organize letter-writing, e-mail, and telegram campaigns. Lobbyists also play an important role in fund-raising, helping to direct clients' contributions to members of Congress and presidential candidates. In recent years, interest groups have also begun to build broader coalitions and comprehensive campaigns around particular policy issues.[13] Lobbyists, seeing an opportunity to harness the enthusiasm of political amateurs, now organize and even launch comprehensive campaigns that combine simulated grassroots activity with information and campaign funding for members of Congress.[14]

Some interest groups go still further. They develop strong ties to individual politicians or policy communities within Congress by hiring ex-staffers, ex-members of Congress, or even relatives of sitting members of Congress. The rotation of those in positions of power into lobbying jobs has become sufficiently common as to have its own term in Washington circles: revolving-door politics. The revolving door of congressional and executive staff joining the ranks of lobbying firms is driven by the continual turnover of staff, of lobbyists, and even of the political parties in Washington. Lobbying firms must stay current and connected to Congress in order to offer the best service to their clients. This means that most of the larger lobbying firms in Washington have strong ties to both the Democrats and the Republicans on Capitol Hill. This revolving door has been cause for concern among some policy makers, and a number of states have put restrictions on how quickly ex-lawmakers can return as lobbyists. Seventeen states have one-year restrictions, and seven have two-year bans.[15]

Lobbying the President. So many individuals and groups clamor for the president's time and attention that only the most skilled and well-connected members of the lobbying community can hope to influence presidential decisions. When running for president, Barack Obama laid down a bold promise to "free the executive branch from special interest influence." No political appointee, the Obama team promised, "will be permitted to work on regulations or contracts directly and substantially related to their prior employer for two years." That promise proved exceedingly difficult to keep as many on the Obama transition team, including the nominee for the position of Health and Human Services secretary, former Senate majority leader Thomas Daschle, had close ties to lobbyists or had worked for lobbying firms.[16] One of President Obama's first executive orders created an ethics standard and pledge for all executive branch appointments, and the administration imposed further restrictions on those receiving funds from the Emergency Economic Stabilization Act and the American Recovery and Reinvestment Act. Anyone wishing to receive funds from the nearly $700 billion authorized for the economic stimulus bills had to show that they did not have conflicting interests and were not involved in lobbying the government.[17]

The most powerful interests are able to access, and sometimes influence, presidential decisions. During the economic crisis that began in 2008, President Obama met with CEOs from several of the biggest financial companies to discuss policies that would aid economic recovery.

Lobbying the Executive Branch. Even when an interest group is very successful at getting its bill passed by Congress and signed by the president, the prospect of full and faithful implementation of that law is not guaranteed. Often, a group and its allies do not pack up and go home as soon as the president turns their lobbied-for new law over to the appropriate agency. On average, 40 percent of interest group representatives regularly contact both legislative and executive branch organizations, whereas 13 percent contact only the legislature and 16 percent only the executive branch.[18]

In some respects, interest group access to the executive branch is promoted by federal law. The Administrative Procedure Act, first enacted in 1946 and frequently amended in subsequent years, requires most federal agencies to provide notice and an opportunity for comment before implementing proposed new rules and regulations. So-called notice and comment rule making is designed to allow interests an opportunity to make their views known and to participate in the implementation of federal legislation that affects them. In 1990, Congress enacted the Negotiated Rulemaking Act to encourage administrative agencies to engage in direct and open negotiations with affected interests when developing new regulations. These two pieces of legislation—which have been strongly enforced by the federal courts— have played an important role in opening the bureaucratic process to interest-group influence. Today, few federal agencies would consider attempting to implement a new rule without consulting affected interests.[19]

Regulation of Lobbying. As a result of the constant access to important decision makers that lobbyists seek out and require, stricter guidelines regulating the actions of lobbyists have been adopted. For example, as of 1993, businesses may no longer deduct from their taxes the cost of lobbying.

Trade associations must report to members the proportion of their dues that goes to lobbying, and that proportion may not be reported as a business expense. The most important attempt to limit the influence of lobbyists was the 1995 Lobbying Disclosure Act, which significantly broadened the definition of people and organizations that must register as lobbyists. According to the filings under this act, almost 11,000 lobbyists were working the halls of Congress in 2014.

Congress also chose to restrict interest group influence by passing legislation in 1996 that limited gifts from a single source to $50 and no more than $100 annually. It also banned the practice of honoraria, which special interests had used to supplement congressional salaries. But Congress did not limit the travel of representatives, senators, their spouses, or congressional staff members. Interest groups can pay for congressional travel as long as a trip is related to legislative business and is disclosed on congressional reports within 30 days. On these trips, meals and entertainment expenses are not limited to $50 per event and $100 annually. The rules of Congress allow its members to travel on corporate jets as long as they pay an amount equal to first-class airfare.

In 2007, congressional Democrats secured the enactment of a package of ethics rules designed to fulfill their 2006 campaign promise to bring an end to lobbying abuses. The new rules prohibited lobbyists from paying for most meals, trips, parties, and gifts for members of Congress. Lobbyists were also required to disclose the amounts and sources of small campaign contributions they collected from clients and "bundled" into large contributions. And interest groups were required to disclose the funds they used to rally voters to support or oppose legislative proposals. As soon as these new rules were enacted, lobbyists and politicians hurried to find ways to circumvent them, and these reforms have had little impact. Executive rulings and memoranda issued by President Obama in 2009 further strengthened these rules and made it much more difficult for lobbying firms to influence executive decision making either through direct lobbying or indirectly by hiring people with direct access to decision makers.

Using the Courts

Interest groups sometimes turn to the courts to augment other avenues of access. A group can use the courts to affect public policy in at least three ways: (1) by bringing suit directly on behalf of the group itself; (2) by financing suits brought by individuals; or (3) by filing a companion brief as *amicus curiae* (literally "friend of the court") to an existing court case.

Among the most significant modern illustrations of the use of the courts as a strategy for political influence are those that accompanied the "sexual revolution" of the 1960s and the emergence of the movement for women's

rights. Beginning in the mid-1960s, a series of cases was brought into the federal courts in an effort to force definition of a right to privacy in sexual matters. The case began with a challenge to state restrictions on obtaining contraceptives for nonmedical purposes, a challenge that was effectively made in *Griswold v. Connecticut*, where the Supreme Court held that states could neither prohibit the dissemination of information about nor prohibit the actual use of contraceptives by married couples. That case was soon followed by *Eisenstadt v. Baird*, in which the Court held that the states could not prohibit the use of contraceptives by single persons any more than they could prohibit their use by married couples. One year later, the Court held, in the 1973 case of *Roe v. Wade*, that states could not impose an absolute ban on voluntary abortions. Each of these cases, as well as others, was part of the Court's enunciation of a constitutional doctrine of privacy.[20]

The 1973 abortion case sparked a controversy that brought conservatives to the fore on a national level. These conservative groups made extensive use of the courts to whittle away the scope of the privacy doctrine. They obtained rulings, for example, that prohibit the use of federal funds to pay for voluntary abortions. And in 1989, right-to-life groups used a strategy of litigation that significantly undermined the *Roe v. Wade* decision in the case of *Webster v. Reproductive Health Services*, which restored the right of states to place restrictions on abortion.[21]

Another extremely significant set of contemporary illustrations of the use of the courts as a strategy for political influence is found in the history of the NAACP. The most important of these court cases was, of course, *Brown v. Board of Education of Topeka*, in which the U.S. Supreme Court held that legal segregation of the schools was unconstitutional.[22]

Business groups are also frequent users of the courts because of the number of government programs applied to them. Litigation involving large businesses is most mountainous in such areas as taxation, antitrust cases, interstate transportation, patents, and product quality and standardization. Major corporations and their trade associations pay tremendous fees each year to the most prestigious Washington law firms. Some of this money is expended in gaining access. A great proportion of it, however, is used to keep the best and most experienced lawyers prepared to represent the corporations in court or before administrative agencies when necessary.

The forces of the new politics movement made significant use of the courts during the 1970s and 1980s, and judicial decisions were instrumental in advancing their goals. Facilitated by changes in the rules governing access to the courts (these rules of standing were discussed in Chapter 8), the new politics agenda was clearly visible in court decisions handed down in several key policy areas. In the environmental policy area, new politics groups were able to force federal agencies to pay attention to environmental issues, even when the agencies were not directly involved in activities related to

environmental quality. By the 2000s, the courts often were the battleground on which those in the new political movements waged their fights. Perhaps the most dramatic cases were a string of lawsuits spanning 20 years (from 1986 to 2006) in which antiabortion protest organizations, such as Pro-Life Action Network and Operation Rescue, and the National Organization of Women repeatedly took each other to court to establish the rules governing clinic protests. Ultimately, the U.S. Supreme Court sided with the antiabortion organizations, but not before deciding three separate cases on the matter, at extremely high cost to both sides.[23]

Mobilizing Public Opinion

Organizations try to bring pressure to bear on politicians through a variety of methods designed to mobilize public opinion. This strategy is known as going public. When groups go public, they use their various resources to try to persuade large numbers of people to pay attention to their concerns. They hope that greater visibility and public support will help underline the importance of such issues to those in power. Advertising campaigns, protests, and grassroots lobbying efforts are all examples of going public. An increased use of this kind of strategy is traced to the rise of modern advertising at the beginning of the twentieth century. As early as the 1930s, political analysts distinguished between the "old lobby" of direct group representatives attempting to influence Congress and the "new lobby" of public-relations professionals addressing the public at large in order to reach Congress indirectly.[24] Going public differs from other strategies that interest groups use to influence public policy. The "new lobby" techniques are designed to change the way people think, rather than just change the actions of insiders.

going public
The act of launching a media campaign to build popular support

One way that groups often go public is conventional advertising. For example, a casual scan of major newspapers, magazines, and websites will immediately reveal numerous examples of expensive, well-designed ads by major companies and industry associations, such as those from the oil and gas, automobile, and health and pharmaceutical industries. Such ads are often intended to show what the firms do for the country, not merely the products they develop. Their purpose is to create and maintain a strongly positive association between the organization and the community at large in the hope that the organization can draw on the community's favorable feelings as needed in specific political controversies later.

Sometimes groups advertise expressly to shift public opinion on a question. One of the most famous such advertising campaigns was run by the Health Insurance Association of America in 1993 and 1994 in opposition to President Bill Clinton's proposed national health insurance plan. These ads featured a couple—Harry and Louise (played by the actors Harry Johnson

and Louise Caire Clark)—sitting at their kitchen table disparaging the excessive red tape and bureaucratic problems that they would face under Clinton's plan. The Harry and Louise ads are widely credited with turning public opinion against Clinton's plan, which never even got off the ground in Congress. A decade later, when President Barack Obama proposed an extensive overhaul of the health insurance industry in the United States, a trade group representing drug makers brought the same actors back and remade the Harry and Louise spot but this time fully supporting the administration's plan. In the new advertisements, Harry and Louise are once again in their kitchen, and Louise pours over medical bills and forms. "Having choices we don't like," says a worried Louise, "is no choice at all." Louise concludes the ad saying, "A little more cooperation, a little less politics, and we can get the job done this time."[25]

A second strategy that groups use to bring public pressure to bear is grassroots lobbying. Grassroots lobbying entails many of the same organizing methods one sees in political campaigns—developing lists of supporters and having those supporters voice their concern with an issue and recruit others to do so. It is common today to send direct mail that includes a draft letter that recipients can adapt and then send to their representatives in Congress or to send e-mails urging people to contact their members of Congress regarding a particular bill or controversy. A grassroots campaign can cost anywhere from $40,000 to sway the votes of one or two crucial members of a committee or subcommittee to millions of dollars to mount a national effort aimed at Congress as a whole. Such grassroots campaigns are often organized around controversial, prominent legislation or appointments, such as nominees to the U.S. Supreme Court.

Grassroots lobbying has become more prevalent in Washington over the last couple of decades because the adoption of congressional rules limiting gifts to members has made traditional lobbying more difficult. This circumstance makes all the more compelling the question of whether grassroots campaigning has reached an intolerable extreme. One case in particular may have tipped it over the edge: in 1992, 10 giant companies in the financial services, manufacturing, and high-tech industries began a grassroots campaign and spent millions of dollars over the next three years to influence a decision in Congress to limit the ability of investors to sue for fraud. Retaining an expensive consulting firm, these corporations paid for the use of specialized computer software to persuade Congress that there was "an outpouring of popular support for the proposal." Thousands of letters from individuals flooded Capitol Hill. Many of those letters were written and sent by people who sincerely believed that investor lawsuits are often frivolous and should be curtailed. But much of the mail was phony, generated by the Washington-based campaign consultants; the letters came from people who had no strong feelings or even no opinion at all about the issue. More and

grassroots lobbying

A lobbying campaign in which a group mobilizes its membership to contact government officials in support of the group's position

more people, including leading members of Congress, are becoming quite skeptical of such methods, charging that these are not genuine grassroots campaigns but instead represent "Astroturf lobbying" (a play on the name of an artificial grass used on many sports fields). Such "Astroturf" campaigns have increased in frequency in recent years as members of Congress grow more skeptical of Washington lobbyists and far more concerned about demonstrations of support for a particular issue by their constituents. But after the firms mentioned above spent millions of dollars and generated thousands of letters to members of Congress, they came to the somber conclusion that "it's more effective to have 100 letters from your district where constituents took the time to write and understand the issue," because "Congress is sophisticated enough to know the difference."[26]

Finally, groups often organize protests as a means of bringing attention to an issue or pressure on the government. Protests, in fact, are the oldest means of going public. Those who lack other resources, such as money, contacts, and expertise, can always resort to protest as a means of making their concerns public. Indeed, the right to assembly is protected in the First Amendment to the Constitution.

Protests may have many different consequences, depending on how they are managed. One basic consequence of a well-run protest is that it attracts attention. Organized protests also create a sense of community and common interest among those involved and raise the consciousness of people outside the protest. In addition, protests often attempt to impose costs on others by disrupting traffic or commerce, thereby forcing people to strike a bargain with protestors.

Using Electoral Politics

In addition to attempting to influence members of Congress and other government officials, interest groups also seek to use the electoral process to elect the right legislators in the first place and to ensure that those who are elected will owe them a debt of gratitude for their support. To put matters into perspective, groups invest far more resources in lobbying than in electoral politics. Nevertheless, financial support and campaign activism can be important tools for organized interests.

Political Action Committees. By far the most common electoral strategy that interest groups employ is that of giving financial support to the parties or to particular candidates. But such support can easily cross the threshold into outright bribery. Therefore, Congress has occasionally made an effort to regulate this strategy. One effort was the Federal Election Campaign Act of 1971 (amended in 1974), which we discussed in Chapter 10.

One way organized groups attempt to mobilize popular opinion is by holding protests that generate media attention. Here, the head of a teachers' union speaks to teachers, students, and other citizens at a rally against proposed education budget cuts.

This act limits campaign contributions and requires that each candidate or campaign committee itemize the full name and address, occupation, and principal business of each donor who contributes more than $100. These provisions have been effective up to a point, considering the rather large number of embarrassments, indictments, resignations, and criminal convictions in the aftermath of the Watergate scandal.

The Watergate scandal itself was triggered by the illegal entry of Republican workers into the office of the Democratic National Committee in the Watergate building. But an investigation revealed numerous violations of campaign finance laws, involving millions of dollars in unregistered cash from corporate executives to President Nixon's re-election committee.

Reaction to Watergate produced further legislation on campaign finance in 1974 and 1976, but the effect has been to restrict individual rather than interest group campaign activity. Individuals may now contribute no more than $2,600 to any candidate for federal office in any primary or general election. A PAC, however, can contribute $5,000, provided it contributes to at least five different federal candidates each year. Beyond this, the laws permit corporations, unions, and other interest groups to form PACs and to pay the costs of soliciting funds from private citizens for those PACs.

Electoral spending by interest groups has increased steadily despite the campaign finance reforms that followed the Watergate scandal: total PAC contributions increased from nearly $260 million in 2000 to over $1 billion in the 2012 election cycle.

Interest groups focus their direct contributions on Congress, especially the House. Because of the enormous cost of running modern political campaigns (see Chapter 10), most politicians are eager to receive PAC contributions. A typical U.S. House incumbent receives half of his campaign funds

from interest groups. There is little evidence that interest groups buy roll-call votes or other favors from members of Congress with their donations. Group donations do, however, help to keep those who are sympathetic to groups' interests and views in office.[27]

The potential influence of interest group campaign donations over the legislature has prompted frequent calls from reformers to abolish PACs or limit their activities. The challenge is how to regulate the participation of groups without violating their members' rights to free speech and free association. In 1976, the U.S. Supreme Court weighed in on this matter in the case *Buckley v. Valeo*, which questioned the constitutionality of the 1974 Federal Elections Campaign Act.[28] In its decision to let the act stand, the majority on the Court ruled that donors' rights of expression were at stake but that these rights had to be weighed against the government's interest in limiting corruption, or the perception of corruption. The Court has repeatedly upheld the key tenets of its decision: (1) that money is a form of speech; but (2) that speech rights must be weighed against concerns about corruption.

As we saw in Chapter 10, Congress sought in 2002 to impose significant limits on independent campaign expenditures in the Bipartisan Campaign Reform Act (BCRA). BCRA restricted donations to nonfederal (for example, state party) accounts as a necessary reform to limit corruption, and it imposed limits on the types of campaign commercials that could be aired by groups within 60 days of an election. It also raised the limits on direct campaign contributions for the first time since 1976, as inflation had seriously squeezed the value of contributions.

In 2010, the Supreme Court struck down the restrictions on independent advertising in the case *Citizens United v. Federal Election Commission*.[29] The case involved a political movie critical of then-senator and presidential candidate Hillary Clinton created by an organization called Citizens United. The movie aired on cable television inside the blackout date for independent political advertising stipulated by BCRA. A 5–4 majority on the Court ruled that such blackout dates imposed by BCRA restricted the rights to free speech of corporations and other associations. This decision firmly established the right of business corporations and labor unions to engage in political advocacy and opened the gates to the flood of money in the political arena. This flood was evident during the 2012 national elections, in which independent expenditures amounted to some $1.1 billion (Figure 12.2), and in the 2014 midterms, as initial estimates put the total at $786 million.

Campaign Activism. Financial support is not the only way in which organized groups seek influence through the electoral process. Sometimes activism can be even more important. Perhaps the most notable instance of such activism occurs on behalf of the Democratic Party and candidates

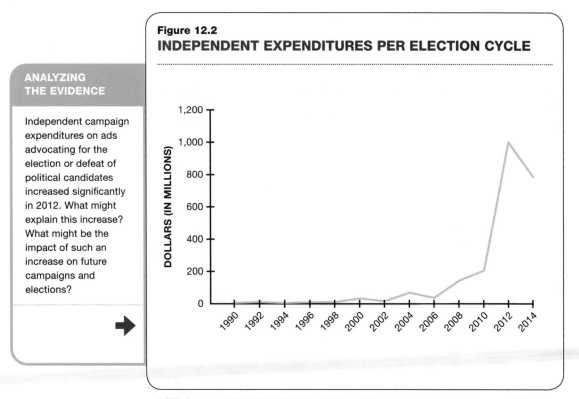

Figure 12.2
INDEPENDENT EXPENDITURES PER ELECTION CYCLE

NOTE: The years 1992, 1996, 2000, 2004, 2008, and 2012 were presidential election years; 2014 data are estimated.
SOURCE: Center for Responsive Politics, www.opensecrets.org/outsidespending/ (accessed 11/13/14).

ANALYZING THE EVIDENCE

Independent campaign expenditures on ads advocating for the election or defeat of political candidates increased significantly in 2012. What might explain this increase? What might be the impact of such an increase on future campaigns and elections?

through unions. Labor unions regularly engage in massive get-out-the-vote drives during political campaigns. The largest such activities are those of the Service Employees International Union (SEIU), which represents workers ranging from hotel and restaurant workers to clerical staff, and the United Auto Workers (UAW). SEIU, for instance, spent in excess of $14.4 million to support Democratic candidates in 2012. Other sorts of groups routinely line up behind the Democratic and Republican campaigns. The National Rifle Association, for example, spent $9.5 million in the 2012 election cycle, and all but $7,000 was in support of Republican candidates.

The cumulative effect of such independent campaign activism is difficult to judge. One important research initiative within political science seeks to measure systematically the marginal effectiveness of campaign contact. Professors Alan Gerber and Donald Green have developed a program of field experiments in which campaigns agree to assign direct campaign activity randomly to some neighborhoods but not others. They have been able to measure the marginal effect of an additional piece of mail, a direct canvasser, or a phone call. In a typical election context, it

IN BRIEF

Interest Group Strategies

✔ **Lobbying**

Influencing the passage or defeat of legislation

✔ **Access**

Development of close ties to decision makers on Capitol Hill and bureaucratic agencies

✔ **Litigation**

Taking action through the courts, usually in one of three ways:

- Filing suit against a specific government agency or program
- Financing suits brought by individuals against the government
- Filing companion briefs as *amicus curiae* (friend of the court) to existing court cases

✔ **Going Public**

Especially via advertising; also through boycotts, strikes, rallies, marches, and sit-ins, generating positive news coverage

✔ **Electoral Politics**

Giving financial support to a particular party or candidate

Congress passed the Federal Election Campaign Act of 1971 to try to regulate this practice by limiting the amount of funding interest groups can contribute to campaigns

---

costs about $40 to get an additional voter to the polls. Professors Gerber and Green further find that campaign activism can have an initially large impact, but after six or so attempted contacts, the effects diminish dramatically. This important empirical research has given campaigns and reformers some sense of the effectiveness of campaign activism in stimulating turnout and possibly influencing elections. Especially in low-turnout elections, such as those for city councils or state legislatures, get-out-the-vote activities by interest groups can have very large effects on who wins. But as other money enters the scene, especially candidates'

own campaign expenditures, the effects of interest groups' direct campaign activities becomes muted.[30]

The Initiative. Another political tactic that interest groups sometimes use is sponsorship of ballot initiatives at the state level. The initiative, a device adopted by a number of states around 1900, allows laws proposed by citizens to be placed on the general-election ballot and submitted directly to the state's voters. This procedure bypasses the state legislature and governor. The initiative was originally promoted by late nineteenth-century Populists as a mechanism that would allow the people to govern directly. Populists saw the initiative as an antidote to interest group influence in the legislative process.

Ironically, many studies have suggested that most initiative campaigns today are actually sponsored by interest groups seeking to circumvent legislative opposition to their goals. In recent years, for example, initiative campaigns have been sponsored by the insurance industry, trial lawyers' associations, and tobacco companies.[31] The role of interest groups in initiative campaigns should come as no surprise, because such campaigns can cost millions of dollars.

ARE INTEREST GROUPS EFFECTIVE?

Do interest groups have an effect on government and policy? A clean answer is difficult to find among the mountains of research on this question. A survey of dozens of studies of campaign contributions and legislative decision making found that in only about 1 in 10 cases was there evidence of a correlation between contributors' interests and legislators' roll-call voting.[32]

Earmarks are a good case in point. Earmarks are expenditures on particular projects in specific districts or states, and they are usually included in a bill late in the legislative process to help secure enough votes for passage. Millions of dollars in earmarks are written into law every year. John de Figueiredo of UCLA and Brian Silverman of the University of Toronto examined the effectiveness of lobbyists to obtain "earmarks" for colleges and universities on whose behalf they are working.[33] The authors discovered that lobbying had a limited impact. The more money schools spent on lobbying activities, the larger the total quantity of earmarked funds they received. However, the magnitude of the effect depended greatly on institutional factors. For most schools, every $1 spent on representation gained about $1 more on earmarks—hardly worth it. In a handful of cases, though, there appear to be exceedingly high returns. Schools in states with a senator on the Senate Appropriations Committee received $18 to $29 in earmarks

for every $1 spent on lobbying. Schools in congressional districts whose representative served on the House Appropriations Committee received between $49 and $55 for every $1 spent on lobbying. Having a legislator on the relevant committee then is a precursor to having influence and explains most of the observed influence.[34]

These results suggest that, as is so often the case, institutions and politics are profoundly related. Schools without access to members of Congress in a position to help them cannot gain much from lobbying. Schools with such access still need to lobby to take advantage of the potential that representation on the Senate and House Appropriations committees can give them. But if they do so, the potential return from lobbying is substantial.

Do Interest Groups Foster or Impede Democracy?

The institutions of American government embrace an open and democratic process in order to ensure that government is responsive to the public's preferences and needs to the society. The Bill of Rights provides for free speech, freedom of the press, and freedom of assembly. The laws of the land have only further cemented this commitment, providing for open meetings, citizen advisory commissions, lobbying, direct contact from constituents, contributions from interested individuals and groups, an open legal system, protests, and many other routes through which individuals and groups may advocate for their interests. Through these many points of access, representatives and government officials learn how their decisions affect groups and individuals. Politics is the arena in which these many interests compete for the attention and imprimatur of the government.

Such a system creates an opportunity for those who have the willingness and capacity to use their resources to represent their interests before the government. Problems of collective action and free riding prevent many latent interests from developing permanent political organizations capable of bringing concerted pressure on the government. Businesses, unions, and professional and industry associations usually have less trouble overcoming the obstacles to organization and group maintenance that many volunteer associations may face. Consequently, interest group politics in Washington, D.C., and state legislatures tends to reflect the interests of and conflicts among those engaged in economic activity around the country.

Although firms, unions, and other organizations can solve the collective action problem, they do not necessarily succeed in the political arena. They often find politics unfamiliar, even hostile, terrain in which to pursue organizational goals. Unlike economic activity, politics involves power derived from the ability to vote on measures, to introduce legislation or rules, or to block actions from happening. Interest groups are necessarily outsiders and can do none of these things directly. Nonetheless, these organizations find

that they can make gains by seeking out the appropriate institutions in which to find support, such as a court with a sympathetic judge or a subcommittee of Congress whose chairperson holds similar views to those of the group. And the way to success is usually quite subtle. Typically, groups succeed not by bringing pressure but by providing expertise to the government and by learning from those in office about the impact of new rules and regulations.

Increasingly over the past 30 to 40 years, interest groups have found that the best route to power is through public action and public opinion. It is not enough for a group to hire a lobbyist to advocate on its behalf. Real pressure can be brought on politicians by shaping what other individuals think. Through advertising, protests, and grassroots networks, interest groups have increasingly brought their issues to the attention of the public and through public pressure have been able to influence politics. Tens of thousands of organizations now compete in the political sphere.

Interest group politics at the beginning of the twenty-first century does not neatly fit stereotypical notions. There are certainly as many lobbyists as ever, but the backroom dealings of the "old lobby" are an anachronism. Interest group politics is diffuse, spread across all branches of government and involving many different interests vying for the attention of politicians in an increasingly crowded and active interest group ecology. Those who are organized gain advantages from pooling resources, but an interest group's political action today is only one aspect of the debate over any given political issue or decision. Other interests and voices making competing claims may very well cancel out a given organization's efforts. And the activities of all groups amount to just one facet of legislators', judges', and executives' deliberations. Those who must ultimately make political decisions and be held accountable for those decisions weigh other voices as well, especially the opinions and preferences of their constituents. Perhaps a better contemporary characterization is that the organized and disorganized interests participating in politics today are really contributing to a much broader sphere of political discourse and debate. That debate takes place inside the institutions of government—Congress, courts, executives, and elections. It also takes place in another arena, the media. That forum is the final part of our discussion of democracy in America, and to that subject we next turn.

For Further Reading

Selections highlighted in red are included in *Readings in American Politics: Analysis and Perspectives*, Third Edition.

Abramoff, Jack. *Capitol Punishment: The Hard Truth about Washington Corruption from America's Most Notorious Lobbyist*. New York: WND Books, 2011.

Ainsworth, Scott. *Analyzing Interest Groups*. New York: Norton, 2002.

Alexander, Robert, ed. *The Classics of Interest Group Behavior*. New York: Wadsworth, 2005.

Ansolabehere, Stephen, John M. de Figueiredo, and James M. Snyder, Jr. "Why Is There So Little Money in U.S. Politics?" *Journal of Economic Perspectives* 17, no. 1 (2003): 105–30.

Birnbaum, Jeffrey H. *The Money Men*. New York: Crown, 2000.

Cigler, Allan J., and Burdett A. Loomis, eds. *Interest Group Politics*. 8th ed. Washington, DC: CQ Press, 2011.

Esterling, Kevin. *The Political Economy of Expertise*. Ann Arbor: University of Michigan Press, 2004.

Gilens, Martin. *Affluence and Influence: Economic Inequality and Political Power in America*. New York and Princeton, NJ: Russell Sage Foundation and Princeton University Press, 2012.

Herrnson, Paul, Christopher Deering, and Clyde Wilcox. *Interest Groups Unleashed*. Washington, DC: CQ Press, 2012.

Moe, Terry M. *The Organization of Interests: Incentives and the Internal Dynamics of Political Interest Groups*. Chicago: University of Chicago Press, 1980.

Nownes, Anthony. *Total Lobbying: What Lobbyists Want and How They Try to Get It*. New York: Cambridge University Press, 2006.

Olson, Mancur, Jr. *The Logic of Collective Action: Public Goods and the Theory of Groups*. Reprinted with new preface and appendix. Cambridge, MA: Harvard University Press, 1965.

Rosenthal, Alan. *The Third House: Lobbyists and Lobbying in the States*. Washington, DC: CQ Press, 2001.

13

Introduction to Public Policy

public policy

A law, rule, statute, or edict that expresses the government's goals and provides for rewards and punishments to promote their attainment

Public policy is an officially expressed intention backed by a sanction; that sanction can be a reward or a punishment. Thus public policy may be a law, a rule, a statute, an edict, a regulation, or an order. Its purpose is to provide incentives, whether carrotlike rewards or sticklike punishments, to induce people to change what they are currently doing and do something else or to do more or less of what they are currently doing.

Many policy analysts assert that government action is often required to correct what they call "market failure." This concept refers to inequities, inefficiencies, or harmful effects produced by the operations of private markets. The presumption underlying this idea is that government agencies and officials are motivated mainly by a concern for the public's welfare and will intervene in the private sector in ways that are likely to promote broad public interests.

But does government policy always serve the general interest? In reality, political processes are hardly guaranteed to produce fair and equitable results. Policy makers are often driven by self-interest, partisan predispositions, institutional concerns, and the demands of powerful constituency groups. Often, too, public programs are developed or administered by

bureaucracies, courts, private contractors, and other entities whose decision-making processes lack transparency and are open to only a narrow range of participants.[1] Though, of course, every governmental program is touted by its proponents and sponsors as serving the public interest, the unfortunate truth is that many, albeit not all, such programs serve particularistic rather than general interests.

One way in which public programs may benefit narrow groups at the expense of the broader public is through *mobilization bias*. Well-organized groups with substantial resources and a high stake in a particular policy are more likely than ordinary individuals to engage in successful efforts to pressure officials to enact the policies they favor.[2] Generally, mobilization biases are most likely to occur when the costs of an interest group's favored program are distributed so widely that no set of potential opponents will have much of an incentive to work against it. There are many well-known examples of this sort of program—direct subsidies to farmers, tax benefits for favored classes of business enterprises, and so forth. In other cases, an interest group may be able to design a self-serving program so cleverly that those who pay for it actually believe themselves to be beneficiaries.

Examples of a second type of bias, *stealth benefits*, are less obvious. An important one is the mortgage-interest tax deduction, which has been an element of America's tax code since the introduction of the federal income tax in 1913 and whose espoused purpose is to encourage home ownership. However, nearly 80 percent of the benefits provided by the mortgage-interest deduction and other housing tax credits accrue to the wealthiest 20 percent

CORE OF THE ANALYSIS

➡ Public policies create incentives for people to alter their behavior.

➡ In economic policy, government can play an important role in establishing the rules and institutions that allow a market economy to function.

➡ Government has numerous tools with which to affect the economy, but there is considerable political conflict over which tools to use, how to use them, and when to use them.

➡ After the Great Depression and the New Deal, the national government assumed greater responsibility for social policies related to broadening opportunity and addressing poverty.

of Americans. Less than 5 percent of these tax benefits are received by the bottom 60 percent of Americans. About half of all families with residential mortgages receive no tax benefit at all.[3] In other words, those families most likely to own homes without government help receive most of the government's largesse, while families that struggle to afford their homes receive little or no assistance from government subsidies.

Despite its dubious value as a tool for promoting home ownership, the mortgage-interest deduction is politically almost untouchable, as becomes evident every time its repeal or modification is proposed. In 2005, the presidentially appointed Advisory Panel on Federal Tax Reform proposed eliminating the mortgage-interest deduction and replacing it with a "home credit" that would allow families to reduce their taxes by a flat 15 percent of the interest they paid on their mortgage, regardless of their own income. This proposal was revived in 2013 but made no headway against the lobbying power of the mortgage and real estate industries that protect the deduction. Had the proposal been adopted, its effect would have been to provide mortgage assistance to less affluent families that currently receive none while reducing the tax break available to wealthier homeowners. This change would certainly seem consistent with the government's avowed goal of expanding home ownership opportunities.

Nevertheless, the panel's proposal generated a storm of protest from the housing and home-lending industries and was ultimately defeated. Vehement industry opposition to the idea of eliminating the mortgage-interest tax deduction is not difficult to understand. Any cut in the mortgage-interest deduction would threaten their lucrative markets in second homes and home equity lines of credit for wealthier Americans and might have a negative impact on home sales and prices, thereby reducing builders', realtors', and lenders' profits.

What is counterintuitive is that surveys indicate that as many as 85 percent of all Americans oppose elimination or modification of the deduction, while only 6 percent favor such an action.[4] Poll numbers like these helped the housing industry stop the 2005 panel's proposal in its tracks. Most Americans, even those who are not currently eligible for the mortgage-interest deduction, seem to think that they can benefit from its provisions—if not now, then at some future time. They overwhelmingly support a program they think benefits them, but actually their taxes pay for a program to reward a wealthy industry.

This is one example of public policy not correcting, and possibly even exacerbating, a market failure, though in other instances government policy does ensure effective and efficient markets. In this chapter, we examine several prerequisites for a market economy that are especially important. We then turn to some of the ways government uses social policies to address poverty and broaden opportunity.

HOW DOES GOVERNMENT MAKE A MARKET ECONOMY POSSIBLE?

There are myriad ways in which governments at all levels in our federal system undergird, manage, protect, and sometimes undermine markets. A market economy does not just happen. It is a complex set of arrangements that is fostered by political provisions that both nourish and protect.

Conditions Required for a Market Economy

In this section, we explore the conditions required for a functioning market economy and the role of government in providing them.

Establishing Law and Order. The first condition necessary for a market economy is actually inherent in the very idea of government. There must be a minimal degree of predictability about the basic rules of social interaction. In other words, there must be a system of law and order. Participants in the market must be able to assume not only that they can get to the market safely—that they won't be robbed on the way—but also that, having arrived, the people with whom they are dealing will behave predictably and will be bound by some number of calculable laws.

Defining Rules of Property and Its Exchange. The second condition that encourages people to participate in the market has to do with defining and dealing with property. If the market involves exchanges of ownership, there must be clear laws about what constitutes property. Property may be many things—your labor or your ideas or the bed you sleep in—but the very concept of property is inconceivable without laws that define what you can call your own.

The existence of property ownership means that we can exercise dominion over something that we have declared our own, and it is defined by laws that enable us to exercise that dominion. Something is not our own unless we can be reasonably certain that someone else cannot walk away with it. Trespass laws, for example, give concrete meaning to what constitutes property: a trespass law confers on us a legal right to keep others away from certain kinds of property. It is clear, then, that laws or rules that define property are an essential part of the political economy. Before we can enter a market and participate in an exchange, we must be able to expect not only that we can lay claim to something but also that those around us will respect that claim. In this sense, private property has a public component.

The probability of enjoying property would be remote without laws that were widely enforced and accepted.

A market exists only when exchanges occur, and there must be rules governing exchange itself. Laws of exchanges structure how, when, and under what conditions you can sell your property. You might think that once the laws of property have defined what you own, you ought to be able to transfer it, but that transfer is surrounded by rules that govern the transfer itself. Certain kinds of exchanges are deemed off-limits altogether. For example, you own your own body, but under what conditions can you sell it? Laws about prostitution limit the selling or renting of one's body.

Enforcing Contracts. A third condition that must be met before a market economy can operate involves rules governing the enforcement of contracts. There are, of course, societies that do not have a recognizable concept of contract, but Western economies are highly dependent on such notions.

Contracts are closely related to property in that they facilitate exchanges of property, broadly construed. A contract is a voluntary agreement between two or more private persons that governs future conduct. And although the agreement may be private, it has a distinctively public component: a contract must be enforceable, or it is meaningless. If contracts were meaningless, the economy would grind to a halt. Businesses would not sell goods to one another if they could not count on the other's promise to provide the agreed-upon good, service, or payment. Similarly, lenders would not offer loans to home buyers without a legally binding promise to repay the loan. What makes these contracts enforceable is the role of the courts in arbitrating disputes between parties in a contract. If a homeowner fails to repay her home loan, for instance, the lending institution can follow a legal procedure to demand payment or take possession of the house.

Setting Market Standards. The fourth condition necessary for the emergence of the modern free market is related to defining property and the conditions for its exchange. When people engage in exchanges that are not face to face—where they can't point to a good and say, "I want that tomato or that fish"—both parties must have some way of understanding what the goods are that they are bargaining over. To do that, terminology must be standardized, and one of the essential acts of any government is to establish standard weights and measures.

public good

A good that, first, may be enjoyed by anyone if it is provided and, second, may not be denied to anyone once it has been provided

Providing Public Goods and Ameliorating Externalities. A fifth condition necessary to the operation of a market economy involves the provision of public goods. The term *public good* refers to a facility that the government may provide because no single participant can afford or is

willing to provide it herself. The provision of public goods extends from supplying the physical marketplace itself—like the common in New England towns, the agora in ancient Greece, or the suk in the Muslim countries of North Africa and the Middle East—to building and maintaining an interstate highway system to stimulate first and foremost continental development and, in the modern era, support for the automobile and trucking industries. The provision of public goods is essential to market operation, and the manner in which the government provides those goods affects the market's character.

Closely related to providing public goods, a sixth prerequisite critical to creating the conditions for a market economy is the provision for allocating responsibility when the social cost of some behavior far exceeds the private cost. For instance, the cost of driving a gas-guzzling car may be more than the total of the monthly payments, insurance, and gasoline, because the social cost also includes the widely distributed impact of smog and the effects of carbon monoxide emissions. External effects, such as pollution, that can result from market activities are called externalities. When individuals or firms engage in private behavior that has broad social consequences, these externalities provide government with an additional rationale for regulating the economy.

A lighthouse is a classic example of a public good: its benefits can be enjoyed by everyone and cannot be denied to anyone. By providing public goods, the government helps make a market economy possible.

externalities
The differences between the private cost and the social cost of economic behavior

Creating a Labor Force. A seventh condition necessary for the emergence of a market economy is the creation of a labor force. Every society has provisions that enable and encourage, or sometimes force, people to work. One example of an enabling provision is the requirement for universal compulsory education: in the United States, people are educated so that they can learn the skills necessary to function in the market. Long before education laws, however, we had poorhouses, vagrancy laws, and other more police-oriented means of forcing people to work; these rules meant that people might starve or suffer punishment if they failed to earn their own keep. Our welfare system today includes provisions that serve the same purpose: the government adjusts the welfare system in cycles to be sure that the support given is uncomfortable enough that people will prefer work to the low income they get from welfare.

Promoting Competition. Finally, once markets emerge, they must be maintained. This means that it should be reasonably easy for a producer to enter and freely compete in the market. If this is not the case, as when one company has established a monopoly, the efficiency of the market and the equitable distribution of its benefits are threatened. Decreased competition provides government with another reason for getting involved in the economy: to function as a watchdog over potential monopoly control.

monopoly

The existence in a market of a single firm that provides all the goods and services of that market; the absence of competition

GOALS OF ECONOMIC POLICY

The last section surveyed some prerequisites for a market economy. They are necessary components—means to an end, so to speak. But to what end? Government intervenes in the economy not only to buttress the conditions for a market economy but also to achieve other concrete goals. These include promoting economic stability, stimulating economic growth, and promoting business development.

Promoting Stable Markets

One of the central reasons for government involvement in the economy is to protect the welfare and property of individuals and businesses. Because the threats to welfare and property change as the economy grows and new technologies emerge, government actions are constantly being updated and adapted to meet new conditions. Generally, governments seek to maintain a measure of stability and predictability in the marketplace so that investors, lenders, and consumers will feel confident in engaging in economic activity.

Maintenance of law and order is one of the most important ways that government can protect welfare and property. The federal government has also enacted laws designed to protect individuals and businesses in economic transactions. Federal antiracketeering laws, for example, aim to end criminal efforts to control businesses through such illegal means as extortion and kickbacks.

Another way in which the government promotes economic stability is by regulating competition. Beginning in the nineteenth century, as many sectors of the national economy flourished, certain companies began to exert monopolistic control over those sectors. Decreased competition threatened the efficiency of the market and the equitable distribution of its benefits. As a result, the national government stepped in to "level the playing field."

Another major reason that Congress began to adopt national business regulatory policies was that the regulated companies themselves felt bur-

dened by the inconsistencies among the states. These companies often pre-ferred a single national regulatory authority, no matter how burdensome, because it would ensure consistency throughout the United States; the companies could thereby treat the nation as a single market.[5]

Political shifts and advances in technology make the regulation of com-petition a moving target. In 1913, when telephone service was becoming widely available, the federal government sanctioned AT&T's status as a publicly regulated monopoly. It believed that a single company—publicly regulated—could provide the best service in this industry. By the 1980s, views about the necessity and effectiveness of such monopoly control had changed, and the federal government moved to break up AT&T and open the field to new competitors. Creating competition in the telephone indus-try, the government hoped, would reduce prices and make the industry more responsive to consumers. And indeed, although consumers have many com-plaints about telephone companies, prices dropped dramatically as competi-tors arose. In the late 1990s, there was considerable concern about emerging monopolies in high technology. A federal lawsuit charged that Microsoft Corporation's monopoly position would stifle future innovation in software. The subsequent settlement, however, did little initially to alter Microsoft's market dominance. In the subsequent two decades, however, the public has enjoyed massive innovation of new technologies by new market entrants, such as Google, Facebook, and Twitter. So while this first goal surely involves providing a stable framework, governments also promote stable market opportunities. And this might involve, from time to time, markets being shaken up by a new technology or new entrant.

Promoting Economic Prosperity

In addition to setting the basic conditions that allow markets to function, gov-ernments may actively intervene in the economy to promote economic growth. Although the idea that government should stimulate economic growth can be traced back to Alexander Hamilton's views about promoting industry, it was not until the twentieth century that the federal government assumed a central role in promoting economic growth. There had long been a suspicion of cen-tralized political power, and this persistent suspicion tended to privilege state and local governments in engaging with the private economy. By the end of the nineteenth century, circumstances began to change as states found them-selves unable to deal with the massive growth in interstate economic activity.

Since the 1930s, the federal government has carefully tracked national economic growth. Economic growth is measured in several different ways. The two most important measures are the gross national product (GNP), which is the market value of the goods and services produced in the

economy, and the gross domestic product (GDP), the same measure but excluding income from foreign investments. In the late 1990s, the American economy grew at a rate of over 4 percent a year, a rate considered high by modern standards. Growth fell to 0.5 percent during the recession in 2001 and remained modest in the first decade of the 2000s, dipping below zero during the economic crisis years of 2008 and 2009. From 2010 to 2013, growth hovered around 1.5–2.5 precent.

Strong investment is an important factor in economic growth. The most fundamental way that government affects investment is by promoting business, investor, and consumer confidence. When businesses fear political instability, unpredictable government action, or widespread disregard of the law, they are unlikely to invest. When consumers are insecure about the future, they are unlikely to spend. Government officials monitor surveys of business and consumer confidence as they devise economic policy. After the terrorist attacks of 2001, the federal government moved quickly to reassure the financial markets, businesses, and consumers. The Federal Reserve responded with interest-rate cuts aimed at promoting spending and investment. In 2008, the federal government enacted a $700 billion rescue plan in order to restore investor confidence after several large banks failed. This was followed in 2009 with a $787 billion stimulus package and financial support to Chrysler and General Motors to allow them the breathing room to reorganize as profitable enterprises.

Promoting Business Development

During the nineteenth century, the national government was a promoter of markets. National roads and canals were built to tie states and regions together. National tariff policies promoted domestic markets by restricting imported goods; a tax on an import raised its price and weakened its ability to compete with similar domestic products. The national government also heavily subsidized the railroad system. Subsidies promote business by making it cheaper for firms to produce their goods. Until the 1840s, railroads were thought to be of limited commercial value. But between 1850 and 1872, Congress granted over 100 million acres of public domain land to railroad interests, and state and local governments pitched in an estimated $280 million in cash and credit. Before the end of the century, the United States had 35,000 miles of track—almost half the world's total at the time.

Railroads were not the only clients of federal support aimed at fostering the expansion of private markets. Many sectors of agriculture also received federal subsidies during the nineteenth century. Agriculture remains highly subsidized. In 2001, an environmental group caused a stir by putting the

exact amounts of subsidies received by individual farmers on a widely publicized website.[6] The top recipient of government aid in Texas, for example,
received $1.3 million in 2001. One of the many criticisms of the farm-subsidy
program is that it disproportionately supports large-scale farmers rather
than small family farmers. The list of farm-subsidy recipients includes many
large corporations.

In the twentieth century, traditional promotional techniques were
expanded, and some new ones were invented. For example, a great proportion of the promotional activities of the national government are now done
indirectly through categorical grants-in-aid (see Chapter 3). The national
government offers grants to states on the condition that the state (or local)
government undertakes a particular activity. Thus to use motor transportation to improve national markets, a national highway system of 900,000
miles was built during the 1930s, based on a formula whereby the national
government would pay 50 percent of the cost if the state would provide the
other 50 percent. And then for over 20 years, beginning in the late 1950s, the
federal government constructed over 45,000 miles of interstate highways.
This project came about through a program whereby the national government agreed to pay 90 percent of the construction costs on the condition
that each state provide for 10 percent of the costs of any portion of a
highway built within its boundaries.[7] More recently, the federal government
has been involved in the subsidization of urban mass transit, airport construction and modernization, and port improvements—a combination of
promotional and security concerns at work.

TOOLS OF ECONOMIC POLICY

The current state and structure of the U.S. economy is no accident; it is the
result of specific policies that have expanded American markets and sustained massive economic growth. As it works to meet the multiple goals of
economic policy outlined above, the federal government relies on a broad
set of tools that has evolved over time. Let us now turn to the actual tools
designed to accomplish the goals of economic policy.

Monetary Policies

Monetary policies manipulate the growth of the entire economy by controlling the availability of money to banks. America's most powerful institution
in the area of monetary policy is the Federal Reserve Board.

monetary policy
Policies to regulate the
economy through the
manipulation of the
supply of money, the
price of money (interest
rate), and the availability
of credit

But banks did not become the core of the American economic system without intense political controversy. The Federalist majority in Congress, led by Alexander Hamilton, did in fact establish a Bank of the United States in 1791, but it was vigorously opposed by the agrarian interests, led by Thomas Jefferson, based on the fear that the interests of urban, industrial capitalism would dominate such a bank. The Bank of the United States was finally terminated during the administration of Andrew Jackson, but the fear of a central, *public* bank still existed eight decades later, when Congress in 1913 established an institution—the Federal Reserve System—to integrate private banks into a single system. The Federal Reserve System did not become a central bank in the European tradition but rather is composed of 12 Federal Reserve banks, each located in a major commercial city. The Federal Reserve banks are not ordinary banks but banker's banks: they make loans to other banks, clear checks, and supply the economy with currency and coins. They also play a regulatory role in relation to the member banks. Every national bank must be a member of the Federal Reserve System; each must follow national banking rules and must purchase stock in the Federal Reserve System (which helps make the system self-financing). State banks and savings and loan associations may also join if they accept the national rules. At the top of the system is the Federal Reserve Board (the Fed), made up of 7 members appointed by the president (with Senate confirmation) for 14-year terms. The chairman of the Fed is selected by the president from among the 7 members of the board for a 4-year term. In all other concerns, however, the Fed is an independent agency inasmuch as its members cannot be removed during their terms except "for cause," and the president's executive power does not extend to them or their policies.

Federal Reserve System

A system of 12 Federal Reserve banks that facilitates exchanges of cash, checks, and credit; regulates member banks; and uses monetary policies to fight inflation and deflation

The major advantage of belonging to the federal system is that each member bank can borrow money from the Fed, using as collateral the notes on loans already made. This privilege enables them to expand their loan operations continually, as long as there is demand for new loans. The ability of a member bank to borrow money from the Fed is a profoundly important monetary policy. The Fed charges interest, called a discount rate, on its loans to member banks.

If the Fed significantly decreases the discount rate—that is, the interest it charges member banks when they apply for credit—that can be a good shot in the arm for a sagging economy. Manipulating interest rates is the Fed's most powerful tool. During 2001, the Fed cut interest rates 11 times to combat the combined effects of recession and the terrorist attacks. As the economy began to sag in late 2007, all eyes were on the Fed to reduce interest rates. By March 2008, the Fed had cut rates 6 times from their high in September 2007. By 2009, the discount rate had been pushed down nearly to zero in an effort to stimulate recovery from the deepest recession since the Great Depression of the 1930s; it has remained there for several

The chair of the Fed, who is appointed by the president but has considerable autonomy as the leader of an independent agency, determines U.S. monetary policy. Former Fed chair Ben Bernanke played a major role in the government's response to the 2008 financial crisis.

years. If the Fed adopts a policy of higher discount rates, it will put a brake on the economy if the economy is expanding too fast, because the higher rate pushes up the interest rates charged by leading private banks to their customers.

Other monetary policies implemented by the Fed include increasing or decreasing the reserve requirement, which sets the proportion of deposited money that a bank must keep "on demand" as it makes all the rest of its deposits available for new loans. A third important technique used by the Fed is open-market operations—the buying and selling of Treasury securities to absorb excess dollars or to release more dollars into the economy. Finally, a fourth power is derived from one of the important services rendered by the Federal Reserve System, which is the opportunity for member banks to borrow from each other. This exchange is called the federal funds market, and the interest rate charged by one bank to another, the federal funds rate, can be manipulated just like the discount rate, to expand or contract credit.

The federal government also provides insurance to foster credit and encourage private capital investment. The Federal Deposit Insurance Corporation (FDIC) protects bank deposits up to $250,000. Another important promoter of investment is the federal insurance of home mortgages provided by the Department of Housing and Urban Development (HUD). This system began to unravel in the first decade of the 2000s with the growth of the subprime market for lending. This market made home loans available to people who could not otherwise afford to buy a home. At the same time, however, it created new instabilities in the market by offering risky loans that would become costlier due to adjustable interest rates. The slowing housing market in 2007 set off a wave of foreclosures when many homeowners discovered that they could not pay back their loans. Some analysts predicted that as many as 2 million homeowners could lose their homes by the end of

reserve requirement

The amount of liquid assets and ready cash that the Federal Reserve requires banks to hold to meet depositors' demands for their money

open-market operations

The process whereby the Open Market Committee of the Federal Reserve buys and sells government securities, etc., to help finance government operations and to reduce or increase the total amount of money circulating in the economy

federal funds rate

The interest rate on loans between banks that the Federal Reserve Board influences by affecting the supply of money available

2009. The foreclosure crisis in turn sent shock waves through the financial system, as investment banks found themselves holding worthless loans.

Fiscal Policies

Fiscal policies include the government's taxing and spending powers.

fiscal policy

Policies to regulate the economy through taxing and spending powers

Taxation. On the tax side of the ledger, personal and corporate income taxes raise most government revenues (Table 13.1). Although the direct purpose of a tax is to raise revenue, each tax has a different impact on the economy, and the government can plan for that impact.

After passing major tax cuts in 2001, President Bush proposed and Congress passed a sweeping new round of cuts in 2003. Bush's plan was intended to promote investment by reducing taxes on most stock dividends, to spur business activity by offering tax breaks to small businesses, and to stimulate the economy by reducing the tax rates for all taxpayers. In 2006, Congress extended the rate reductions on dividends and capital gains. The Bush administration tax cuts were criticized on several grounds. Many Democrats argued that the tax cuts were simply a giveaway to the wealthy and to corporations, that had grown even wealthier relative to ordinary Americans in recent years. There has been concern that the tax cuts are responsible for the large federal deficits: the federal budget moved from running surpluses in 2000 to steep deficits throughout the next decade.

progressive taxation

Taxation that hits the upper income brackets more heavily

A tax is called progressive if the rate of taxation goes up with each higher income bracket. The decision to make the income tax progressive was one of the most important policy choices Congress made. A tax is called regressive if people in lower income brackets pay a higher proportion of their income in taxes than people in higher income brackets. For example, a sales tax is deemed regressive because everybody pays at the same rate, so that the proportion of total income paid in sales tax goes down as the total income goes up (assuming, as is generally the case, that as total income goes up, the amount spent on taxable purchases increases at a lower rate).

regressive taxation

Taxation that hits the lower income brackets more heavily

As we noted earlier, taxes were a controversial issue during the George W. Bush administration. President Bush made tax reduction the centerpiece of his administration and enacted major tax cuts.[8] These tax breaks were scheduled to expire in 2010. As the economy dipped into recession in early 2008, Bush urged making the cuts permanent.[9] Democratic politicians, on the other hand, argued that the tax cuts benefited the rich too much, increasing inequality (see the Analyzing the Evidence unit on page 440). They argued that moving back to higher tax rates on the wealthy would help fund crucial public programs. In 2010, as the clock ticked on the expiring Bush rates, the Republicans sought to make all the rates permanent, while

Table 13.1

FEDERAL REVENUES BY TYPE OF TAX AS PERCENTAGE OF TOTAL RECEIPTS, 1960–2014

FISCAL YEAR	INDIVIDUAL INCOME TAXES	CORPORATION INCOME TAXES	SOCIAL INSURANCE/ RETIREMENT RECEIPTS	EXCISE TAXES	OTHER
1960	44.0	23.2	15.9	12.6	4.2
1970	46.9	17.0	23.0	8.1	4.9
1980	47.2	12.5	30.5	4.7	5.1
1990	45.2	9.1	36.8	3.4	5.4
2000	49.6	10.2	32.2	3.4	4.5
2002	46.3	8.0	37.8	3.6	4.3
2003	44.5	7.4	40.0	3.8	4.3
2004	43.0	10.1	39.0	3.7	4.2
2005	43.1	12.9	36.9	3.4	3.8
2006	43.4	14.7	34.8	3.1	4.0
2007	45.3	14.4	33.9	2.5	3.9
2008	45.4	12.1	35.7	2.7	4.2
2009	43.5	6.6	45.3	3.0	4.7
2010	41.5	8.9	40.0	3.1	6.5
2011	47.4	7.9	35.5	3.1	6.1
2012	46.2	9.9	34.5	3.2	6.2
2013	47.4	9.9	34.2	3.0	5.5
2014*	46.0	11.1	34.0	3.1	5.6

*Estimated

SOURCE: Office of Management and Budget, "Historical Tables" table 2.2, www.whitehouse.gov/omb /budget/historicals (accessed 11/22/14).

ANALYZING THE EVIDENCE

The federal government collects revenue from a variety of different taxes. Most important is the individual income tax. Since 1960, revenues from the corporation income tax have fallen significantly. At the same time, taxes for social insurance and retirement programs have grown substantially. Does the federal government draw more of its revenue from progressive taxes or from regressive taxes?

The Income Gap

Examined carefully, data often raise more questions than they answer. When viewing a table or figure, especially in the context of policy debates, it is usually prudent to make a list of the questions raised by the data presented rather than to accept as a given the interpretation offered by the analyst presenting the data. Take, for example, the so-called income gap that has become a major issue in contemporary American politics. As indicated by the graph below, in the last several years the share of America's income going to the richest Americans has increased, and the share going to the poorest segments of the population has decreased. Many Democrats blame Republican tax cuts for making the rich richer and the poor poorer and assert that major changes in tax policy are needed to restore a measure of equality to American society.

The Portion of Money Income Going to Each Fifth of the Population, 1929–2010*

PORTION OF INCOME
(CUMULATIVE)

- Highest fifth
- Fourth fifth
- Third fifth
- Second fifth
- Lowest fifth

These data may indicate an emergent social problem in the United States, but at least two questions would have to be answered before we can draw any meaningful conclusions from them and certainly before we can make policy recommendations. First, the data deal with portions among income groups. They do not show the absolute income of any group. It is possible that all income groups are better off today than they were in prior years.

* Data for 1929–44 are not strictly comparable to later data because of differences in calculating procedures.

Income in Constant (2010) Dollars, 1950–2010

THOUSANDS OF
DOLLARS

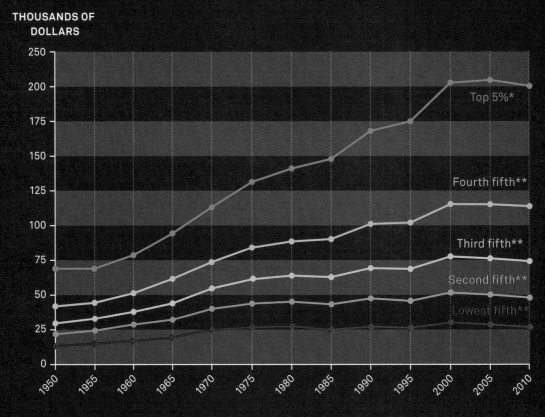

*Average income   ** Income at upper limit of each fifth

If everyone is better off, perhaps we do not want to change our tax policies even if they tend to increase income inequality. This possibility is at least partially borne out by census data. Since 1950, the average incomes of every income group increased — though the incomes of the wealthiest Americans increased more sharply than those of any others.

A second consideration is that the data showing a growing income gap deal with aggregates, not individuals. We cannot know from the data presented whether families are generally locked in to a particular income quartile or are likely to move from year to year. If the latter, then the apparent increase in inequality shown in the first table is at least mitigated by social mobility. Thus in considering the income gap, we may want to consider whether policies designed to reduce inequality might also interfere with social mobility.

SOURCES:
Data for 1929–44, Allan Rosenbaum "State Government, Political Power, and Public Policy" (PhD diss., University of Chicago, 1974), chs. 10–11; data for 1950–2010, U.S. Census Bureau, Historical Income Tables, Table F-2. U.S. Census Bureau, Historical Income Tables, Table F-1.

the Democrats wanted only lower- and middle-class tax rates protected. In a last-minute compromise, all rates were protected but only for two more years. The issue surfaced again in 2012 as the nation approached what some economists called a "fiscal cliff," when the tax cuts would expire at the same time that mandatory cuts in spending would go into effect. Many people feared that this situation would throw the nation back into recession. Following additional negotiations, the parties reached a compromise in which the GOP agreed to rate increase for the wealthiest taxpayers.

Spending and Budgeting. The federal government's power to spend is one of the most important tools of economic policy. Decisions about how much to spend affect the overall health of the economy. They also affect aspects of American life, from the distribution of income through the availability of different modes of transportation to the level of education in society. It is not surprising that the fight for control over spending is one of the most contentious in Washington, as interest groups and politicians strive to determine the priorities and appropriate levels. Decisions about spending are made as part of the annual budget process. During the 1990s, when the federal budget deficit became a major political issue and parties were deeply split on spending, the budget process became the focal point of the entire policy-making process. During the Bush era, the costs of the wars in Iraq and Afghanistan helped to produce new deficits (Figure 13.1).

budget deficit

The amount by which government spending exceeds government revenue in a fiscal year

The president and Congress have each created institutions to assert control over the budget process. The Office of Management and Budget (OMB), in the Executive Office of the President, is responsible for preparing the president's budget. This budget contains the president's spending priorities and the estimated costs of the president's policy proposals. It is viewed as the starting point for the annual debate over the budget. When different parties control the presidency and Congress, the president's budget may have little influence on the budget that is ultimately adopted. Members of the president's own party may also have different priorities.

Congress has its own budget institutions. It created the Congressional Budget Office in 1974 so that it could have reliable information about the costs and economic impact of the policies it considers. At the same time, Congress set up a budget process designed to establish spending priorities and consider individual expenditures in light of the entire budget. A key element of the process is the annual budget resolution, which designates broad targets for spending. By estimating the costs of policy proposals, Congress hoped to control spending and reduce deficits. When the congressional budget process proved unable to hold down deficits in the 1980s, Congress instituted stricter measures to control spending, including spending caps that limit spending on some types of programs. Even these stricter restrictions have proven ineffective. For one thing, when actual spending

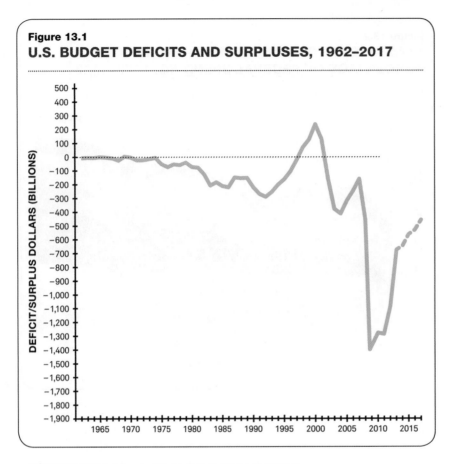

Figure 13.1

U.S. BUDGET DEFICITS AND SURPLUSES, 1962–2017

NOTE: 2014–2017 deficits are estimates (indicated with a dashed line).
SOURCE: Office of Management and Budget, Table 1.1, www.whitehouse.gov/omb/budget /Historicals (accessed 11/12/14).

bills arrive on the legislative floor in violation of spending caps, appropriators seek, and often are granted, waivers of the restriction, permitting the out-of-compliance measure to be taken up. It is evident that small patches to amend the spending process are not up to the task. Whether legislators have the internal fortitude to address wholesale rearranging is an open question.

A very large and growing proportion of the annual federal budget takes the form of mandatory spending, expenditures that are, in the words of the OMB, "relatively uncontrollable." Interest payments on the national debt, for example, are determined by the size of the national debt. Legislation has mandated payment rates for such programs as retirement under Social Security, retirement for federal employees, unemployment assistance, Medicare, and farm price supports (Figure 13.2). These payments increase with the cost of living; they increase as the average age of the population goes

mandatory spending

Federal spending that is made up of "uncontrollables," budget items that cannot be controlled through the regular budget process. Some uncontrollables, such as the interest on the debt, are beyond the power of Congress because the terms of payments are set in contracts

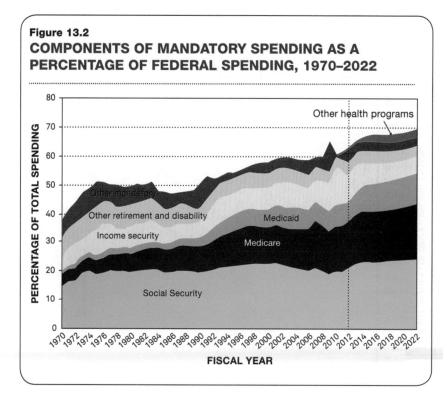

Figure 13.2

COMPONENTS OF MANDATORY SPENDING AS A PERCENTAGE OF FEDERAL SPENDING, 1970–2022

NOTE: 2013–22 percentages are projections.
SOURCE: D. Andrew Austin and Mindy R. Levit, "Mandatory Spending since 1962," *Congressional Research Service*, 7-5700, March 23, 2012.

up; they increase as national and world agricultural surpluses go up. In 1970, 38.6 percent of the total federal budget was made up of these uncontrollables; in 1975, 52.5 percent fell into that category; and by 2012, around 65 percent was in the uncontrollable category. This means that the national government now has very little discretionary spending with which to counteract fluctuations in the business cycle.

This has a profound political implication. With mandatory or relatively uncontrollable spending on the rise, there is less scope for the exercise of discretion. If a budget has to be cut and categories of mandatory spending are taken off the table, then the cuts will fall disproportionately on what remains. With the pain of cutting "available" programs, the prospects for distributing the cuts in a manner acceptable to all interested parties grow dim. Thus the politics will be more intense and dirtier; groups will be more highly mobilized and energized—they will be at one another's throats; Congress and the president will be eyeball to eyeball as they seek to protect their different constituencies; and political partisans will not be in the mood to compromise.[10]

Government spending as a fiscal policy works fairly well when deliberate deficit spending is used to stop a recession and speed up the recovery period

discretionary spending

Federal spending on programs that are controlled through the regular budget process

as we witnessed during the financial crisis of 2008–10. But it does not work very well in fighting either inflation or deficits, because elected politicians are politically unable to make the drastic expenditure cuts necessary to balance the budget, much less to produce a budgetary surplus.

Subsidies and Contracting

Subsidies and contracting are the carrots of economic policy. Their purpose is to encourage people to do something they might not otherwise do or to get people to do more of what they are already doing. Sometimes the purpose is merely to compensate people for something done in the past.

Subsidies. Subsidies are simply government grants of cash or other valuable commodities, such as land. Although subsidies are often denounced as "give-aways," they have played a fundamental role in the history of government in the United States. Subsidies were the dominant form of public policy of the national government and the state and local governments throughout the nineteenth century. They continue to be an important category of public policy at all levels of government. The first planning document ever written for the national government, Alexander Hamilton's *Report on Manufactures*, was based almost entirely on Hamilton's assumption that American industry could be encouraged by federal subsidies and that these were not only desirable but constitutional.

The thrust of Hamilton's plan was not lost on later policy makers. Subsidies in the form of land grants were given to farmers and to railroad companies to encourage western settlement. Substantial cash subsidies have traditionally been given to shipbuilders to help build the commercial fleet and to guarantee the use of their ships as military personnel carriers in time of war. Policies using the subsidy technique continued to be plentiful in the twentieth century, in spite of widespread public and official hostility toward subsidies. Crop subsidies for farmers, for example, from all levels of government amounted to more than $240 billion in 2012. Of this total between $10 billion and $30 billion is distributed to more than 800,000 farmers by the U.S. Department of Agriculture. An additional $5 billion comes as an indirect subsidy in the form of federally sponsored agricultural research and collection of production data.

Politicians have always favored subsidies because subsidies can be treated as benefits that can be spread widely in response to many demands that might otherwise produce profound political conflict. Subsidies can, in other words, be used to buy off the opposition.

Contracting. Like any corporation, a government agency must purchase goods and services by contract. The law requires open bidding for

subsidy
A government grant of cash or other valuable commodities, such as land, to an individual or organization; used to promote activities desired by the government, to reward political support, or to buy off political opposition

a substantial proportion of these contracts because government contracts are extremely valuable to businesses in the private sector and because the opportunities and incentives for abuse surrounding contracting are very great. But contracting is more than a method of buying goods and services. Contracting is also an important technique of policy because government agencies are often authorized to use their contracting power as a means of encouraging corporations to improve themselves, as a means of helping to build up whole sectors of the economy, and as a means of encouraging certain desirable goals or behavior, such as equal employment opportunity. For example, the infant airline industry of the 1930s was nurtured by the national government's lucrative contracts to carry airmail. A more recent example is the use of government contracting to encourage industries, universities, and other organizations to engage in research and development on a wide range of issues in basic and applied science.

contracting power

The power of government to set conditions on companies seeking to sell goods or services to government agencies

Military contracting has long been a major element in government spending. So tight was the connection between defense contractors and the federal government during the Cold War that as he was leaving office, President Eisenhower warned the nation to beware of the powerful "military-industrial complex." After the Cold War, as military spending and production declined, major defense contractors began to look for alternative business activities to supplement the reduced demand for weapons. For example, Lockheed Martin, the nation's largest defense contractor, began to bid on contracts related to welfare reform. After the terrorist attacks of 2001, however, the military budget was awash in new funds: President Bush increased the Pentagon budget by more than 7 percent a year, requesting so many weapons systems that one observer called the budget a "weapons smorgasbord."[11] Military contractors geared up to produce not only weapons for foreign warfare but also surveillance systems to enhance domestic security.

During the financial crisis the Obama administration, as part of its stimulus package to fight the recession, invited businesses, state and local governments, universities, and laboratories to submit "shovel-ready" and "beaker-ready" project proposals. These were funded on an expedited basis in order to generate economic activity in a timely fashion. Tens of billions of dollars were pumped into the economy in the form of contracts to repair roads and bridges, National Institutes of Health grants for research projects, Army Corps of Engineers and Reclamation Bureau activities, and so on.

The government's growing use of contractors can sometimes illustrate the dark side of the principal-agent relationship. We are the principals, and our governmental institutions are the agents. Inherent in all such delegations is the possibility that the agent will not act in the interest of the principal. Legislative institutions, for example, may enact laws desired by lobbyists rather than programs demanded by public opinion. Our system of govern-

ment includes numerous checks—such as frequent elections—to compel agents to pay attention to the wishes of the principals.

The principal-agent problem is compounded in the case of government contracting. Here, our agent—the U.S. Congress—has delegated power to a secondary agent, a government bureaucracy, which has, in turn, delegated power to a tertiary agent—a private contractor. Thus, the agent of the agent of our agent undertakes actions on behalf of the citizens of the United States. We often discover that these tertiary agents are hardly controlled by the bureaucracies that employ them, much less by Congress or the citizenry. Military contractors, for example, were responsible for a number of acts of violence against Iraqi civilians that helped to turn Arab opinion against the United States. President Obama has declared that the government will rely less on contractors and more on civil servants to carry out its responsibilities. The government's dependence on contractors is so great, however, that it seems unlikely that the role of these agents of our agents' agents will truly be diminished.

THE WELFARE SYSTEM AS FISCAL AND SOCIAL POLICY

Government involvement in the relief of poverty and dependency was insignificant until the twentieth century because of Americans' antipathy to government and because of their confidence that all of the deserving poor could be cared for by private efforts alone. This traditional approach crumbled in 1929 in the wake of the Great Depression, when some misfortune befell nearly everyone. Americans finally confronted the fact that poverty and dependency could be the result of imperfections of the economic system itself, rather than a result of individual irresponsibility. Americans held to their distinction between the deserving and undeserving poor but significantly altered these standards regarding who was deserving and who was not. And once the idea of an imperfect system was established, a large-scale public approach became practical not only to alleviate poverty but also to redistribute wealth and to manipulate economic activity through fiscal policy.

The architects of the original Social Security system in the 1930s were probably well aware that a large welfare system can be good *fiscal* policy. When the economy is declining and more people are losing their jobs or are retiring early, welfare payments go up automatically, thus maintaining consumer demand and making the "downside" of the business cycle shorter and shallower. Conversely, during periods of full employment or high levels

The Great Depression helped establish the ideas that unemployment and poverty reflected problems with America's economic system, not just individual irresponsibility, and that the government should take an active role in shaping fiscal and social policy.

of government spending, when inflationary pressures can mount, welfare taxes take an extra bite out of consumer dollars, tending to damp inflation, flattening the "upside" of the economy.

However, the authors of Social Security were more aware of the *social* policy significance of the welfare system. They recognized that a large proportion of the unemployment, dependency, and misery of the 1930s was due to the imperfections of a large, industrial society and occurred through no fault of the victims of these imperfections. They also recognized that opportunities to achieve security, let alone prosperity, were unevenly distributed in our society. This helps explain how the original Social Security laws came to be called—both by supporters and by critics—"the welfare state." The 1935 Social Security Act provided for two separate categories of welfare—*contributory* and *noncontributory*.

contributory program ➡

A social program financed in whole or in part by taxation or other mandatory contributions by its present or future recipients. The most important example is Social Security, which is financed by a payroll tax

Social Security

Social Security ➡

A contributory welfare program into which working Americans contribute a percentage of their wages and from which they receive cash benefits after retirement

Contributory programs are financed by taxation in a way that can be called "forced savings." These programs are what most people have in mind when they refer to Social Security or social insurance. Under the original old-age insurance program, the employer and the employee were each required to

pay equal amounts, which in 1937 were set at 1 percent of the first $3,000 of wages, to be deducted from the paycheck of each employee and matched by the same amount from the employer. This percentage has increased over the years; the total employee contribution is now 6.2 percent on the first $117,000 of income for the Social Security benefits and an additional 1.45 percent on all earnings for Medicare. Employers pay another 6.2 percent for Social Security and 1.45 percent for Medicare.[12] Individuals must pay an additional 0.9 percent on earnings over $200,000 for Medicare.

Social Security is a rather conservative approach to welfare. In effect, the Federal Insurance Contributions Act (FICA) tax, as Social Security is formally known, sends a message that people cannot be trusted to save voluntarily to take care of their retirement needs. But in another sense, it is quite radical. Social Security is not real insurance: workers' contributions do not accumulate in a personal account as an annuity does. Consequently, contributors do not receive benefits in proportion to their contributions, and this means that there is a redistribution of wealth. In brief, contributory Social Security mildly redistributes wealth from higher- to lower-income people, and it significantly redistributes wealth from younger workers to older retirees. Since 1972, Social Security benefits and costs have been adjusted through indexing, whereby benefits paid out under contributory programs are modified annually by cost-of-living adjustments (COLAs) based on changes in the Consumer Price Index, so that benefits increase automatically as the cost of living rises. And to pay for these automatic adjustments, Social Security taxes (contributions) also increased. These changes made Social Security, in the words of one observer, "a politically ideal program. It bridged partisan conflict by providing liberal benefits under conservative financial auspices."[13] In other words, conservatives could more readily yield to the demands of the well-organized and expanding constituency of elderly voters if benefit increases were guaranteed and automatic, and liberals could cement conservative support by agreeing to finance the expanded benefits through increases in the regressive Social Security tax rather than through general revenues from the more progressive income tax.

indexing
The process of periodically adjusting social benefits or wages to account for increases in the cost of living

The Politics of Reforming Social Security. In 2014, some 59 million Americans received around $863 billion in Social Security benefits. For more than half of all American workers, Social Security is their only pension plan. And if there were no Social Security, half of all senior citizens would be living below the poverty line.

Clearly, then, the Social Security program makes a real difference to many people's lives. The program, however, faces demographic pressure as the ratio between contributing workers and retirees has declined, from a comfortable 16 contributors to 1 retiree in the 1950s downward toward 3 contributors to 1 retiree today. With the record-breaking retirement of the baby boomers

beginning around 2010, the ratio of contributors to workers will drop even further in coming years. Fear is therefore growing in all circles that contributions today will not pay for the retirements of tomorrow. Until recently, the system has run a surplus. But the low ratio of contributors to retirees coupled with projected higher life expectancies could stress the system—that is, without reform. Figure 13.3 shows the actual and projected cost of Social Security and Medicare as a percent of U.S. gross domestic product.

Reforms to safeguard Social Security funds have been proposed but tossed aside. One of the best ideas—and certainly the earliest, going back to the 1940s, when the system was just beginning to take hold—was to safeguard the reserve (the trust fund) by having the Treasury invest the contributions in private securities, earning interest and at the same time keeping the reserve safely away from politics and government. One of the elder statesmen of that time retorted, "Why, that would be socialism!" A more recent reform, on which Al Gore staked his 2000 presidential campaign, was simply to respect the trust fund by keeping it in interest-bearing government securities but in a "locked box," unavailable to serve as a hidden part of the national debt. Gore's position was ridiculed.

Most experts believe that Social Security taxes must be increased and the retirement age raised to maintain the program's solvency. When Social Security was first introduced in 1935, a retirement age of 60 seemed reasonable. Indeed, the average life expectancy for American workers was barely 60. Today, Americans can expect to live longer and healthier lives than their forebears. Rather than view increasing the national retirement age as some sort of national failure, we should see it as a sign of our success.

Medicare

Medicare

National health insurance for the elderly and for the disabled

The biggest single expansion in contributory programs since 1935 was the establishment in 1965 of Medicare, which provides substantial medical services to elderly persons who are already eligible to receive old-age, survivors', and disability insurance under the original Social Security system. Medicare provides hospital insurance and allows beneficiaries to choose whether to participate in a government-assisted insurance program to cover doctors' fees. A major role is guaranteed to the private health care industry by essentially limiting Medicare to a financing system. Program recipients purchase all their health services in the free market. The government's involvement is primarily payment for these services. As a result, there is little government control over the quality of the services provided and the fees that health care providers charge.

Like Social Security, Medicare is not means tested. The benefits are available to all former workers and their spouses over the age of 65—over

Figure 13.3

THE INCREASING COST OF ENTITLEMENT PROGRAMS

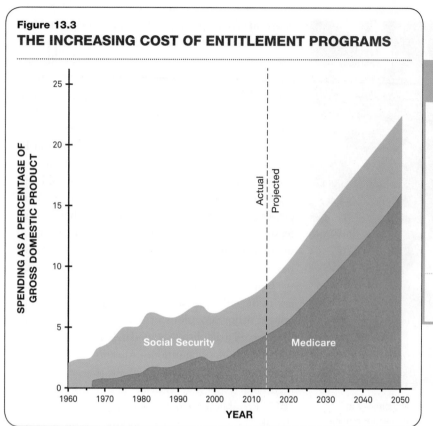

SOURCE: Congressional Budget Office, Budget and Economic Outlook (2014).

ANALYZING THE EVIDENCE

Under current eligibility requirements, federal spending on entitlement programs, particularly Medicare, will grow enormously in the future. What accounts for this growth? What are the arguments for and against the welfare state?

45 million people today—whether they are poor or not. Spending on Medicare has proved difficult to control in recent years, in part because of the growing numbers of people eligible for the programs but also because of rising health care costs. Health care expenditures, especially the cost of prescription drugs, have risen much more sharply than inflation in recent years. In 2003, Congress added a prescription drug benefit to the package of health benefits for the elderly. The high cost of prescription drugs is an issue of growing concern to millions of older Americans.

In 2010, the Obama administration brought about a major expansion of federal health care policy. The Patient Protection and Affordable Care Act, popularly known as "Obamacare," was designed to ensure that tens of millions of Americans who could not afford health insurance would have access to at least basic coverage. Among other things, the act requires individuals to maintain health insurance—the so-called individual mandate—and compels the states to establish insurance exchanges through which individuals and small employers can obtain low-cost and in some cases federally subsidized

The new federal health care policy passed in 2010 requires individuals to obtain either private or government-subsidized health insurance. Opponents have questioned whether this expansion of federal power in Americans' lives is constitutional.

health insurance policies. The act also expands Medicaid and children's health insurance programs and imposes a number of regulations upon health care providers aimed at cutting health care costs. Indeed, the administration claimed that the new law would ultimately lower health care costs by imposing greater efficiencies on providers and reducing fraud.

The act passed despite vehement opposition by Republicans in Congress, who charged that Obamacare would be enormously expensive and would represent a huge expansion of the federal government's power over the lives of Americans. Republicans also feared that an enormous new entitlement program might substantially expand the Democratic Party's base of support as Social Security had in the 1930s.

Opponents of Obamacare challenged the new law in the federal courts. In 2012, the Supreme Court upheld major provisions of the act, but Republicans have vowed to abolish or amend it. In 2013, the Obama administration, citing various problems, delayed implementation of a key provision of the act—the requirement that employers provide health insurance—to 2015. Republicans cited this delay as further proof that the act was unworkable, and they continued their efforts to dismantle Obamacare by attempting to strip it of government funding.

Public Assistance Programs

noncontributory program

A social program that assists people based on demonstrated need rather than contributions they have made. Also known as a public assistance program

Temporary Assistance to Needy Families (TANF)

Federal funds for children in families that fall below state standards of need

Programs to which beneficiaries do not have to contribute—noncontributory programs—are also known as public assistance programs or, derisively, as welfare. Until 1996, the most important noncontributory program was Aid to Families with Dependent Children (AFDC, originally called Aid to Dependent Children, or ADC), which was founded in 1935 by the original Social Security Act. In 1996, Congress abolished AFDC and replaced it with the Temporary Assistance to Needy Families (TANF) block grant. Eligibility for public assistance is determined by means testing, a procedure that requires applicants to show a financial need for assistance. Between 1935 and 1965, the government created programs to provide housing assistance, school lunches, and food stamps to other needy Americans.

Like contributory programs, the noncontributory public assistance programs also made their most significant advances in the 1960s and 1970s.

The largest single category of expansion was the establishment in 1965 of Medicaid, a program that provides extended medical services to all low-income persons who have already established eligibility through means testing under AFDC or TANF. Noncontributory programs underwent another major transformation in the 1970s in the level of benefits they provide. Besides being means tested, noncontributory programs are federal rather than national; grants-in-aid are provided by the national government to the states as incentives to establish the programs (see Chapter 3). Thus, from the beginning there were considerable disparities in benefits from state to state. The national government sought to rectify the disparities in levels of old-age benefits in 1974 by creating the Supplemental Security Income (SSI) program to augment benefits for the aged, the blind, and the disabled. SSI provides uniform minimum benefits across the entire nation and includes mandatory COLAs. States are allowed to be more generous if they wish, but no state is permitted to provide benefits below the minimum level set by the national government. As a result, 25 states increased their own SSI benefits to the mandated level.

The TANF program is also administered by the states, and as with the old-age benefits just discussed, benefit levels vary widely from state to state. For example, in 2013 the states' monthly TANF benefits for a family varied from $170 in Mississippi to $923 in Alaska. Even the most generous TANF payments fall well below the federal poverty line, however. In 2013, the poverty level for a family of three was $19,530 or $1,627 a month.[14]

The number of people receiving AFDC benefits expanded in the 1970s, in part because new welfare programs had been established in the mid-1960s: Medicaid (discussed earlier) and food stamps (now called SNAP, or Supplemental Nutrition Assistance Program), which are now debit cards used to buy food at most grocery stores. These programs provide what are called in-kind benefits—noncash goods and services that would otherwise have to be paid for in cash by the beneficiary. In addition to simply adding on the cost of medical services and food to the level of benefits given to AFDC recipients, the possibility of receiving Medicaid benefits provided an incentive for poor Americans to establish their eligibility for AFDC, which would also establish their eligibility to receive Medicaid. At the same time, the government significantly expanded its publicity efforts to encourage the dependent unemployed to establish their eligibility for these various programs.

Another more complex reason for the growth of AFDC in the 1970s was that it became more difficult for the government to terminate people's AFDC benefits for lack of eligibility. In the 1970 case of *Goldberg v. Kelly*, the Supreme Court held that the financial benefits of AFDC could not be revoked without due process—that is, a hearing at which evidence is presented, and so on.[15] This ruling inaugurated the concept of the

means testing

A procedure that determines eligibility for government public-assistance programs. A potential beneficiary must show a need and an inability to provide for that need

Medicaid

A federally financed, state-operated program providing medical services to low-income people

Supplemental Security Income (SSI)

A program providing a minimum monthly income to people who pass a means test and who are 65 years old or older, blind, or disabled. Financed from general revenues that are not Social Security contributions

food stamps

The largest in-kind benefits program, administered by the Department of Agriculture for individuals and families who satisfy a means test. Food stamps can be used to buy food at most grocery stores

in-kind benefits

Goods and services provided to needy individuals and families by the federal government, as contrasted with cash benefits. The largest in-kind federal welfare program is food stamps

entitlement

The eligibility for benefits by virtue of a category of benefits defined by law. Categories can be changed only by legislation; deprivation of individual benefits can be determined only through due process in court

entitlement, a class of government benefits with a status similar to that of property (which, according to the Fourteenth Amendment, cannot be taken from people "without due process of law"). *Goldberg v. Kelly* did not provide that the beneficiary had a "right" to government benefits; it provided that once a person's eligibility for AFDC was established, and as long as the program was still in effect, that person could not be denied benefits without due process. The decision left open the possibility that Congress could terminate the program and its benefits by passing a piece of legislation. If the welfare benefit were truly a property right, Congress would have no authority to deny it by a mere majority vote.

Thus the establishment of in-kind benefit programs and the legal obstacles involved in terminating benefits contributed to the growth of the welfare state. Together, these programs have significantly increased the security of the poor and the vulnerable and must be included in a genuine assessment of the redistributive influence and the cost of the welfare system today. It is also important to note that real federal spending on AFDC itself did not rise after the mid-1970s. Unlike Social Security, AFDC was not indexed to inflation; without cost-of-living adjustments, the value of AFDC benefits fell by more than one-third. Moreover, the largest noncontributory welfare program, Medicaid, actually devotes less than one-third of its expenditures to poor families; the rest goes to the disabled and the elderly in nursing homes.[16]

Welfare Reform

The most dramatic reform of means-tested welfare policy was the 1996 Personal Responsibility and Work Opportunity Act (PRA). The new law replaced the 61-year-old program of AFDC and its education–work training program, known as JOBS, with block grants to the states over a five-year period for Temporary Assistance to Needy Families (TANF). The act not only imposed the five-year time limit on the TANF benefits but also required work after two years of benefits. It also required community service after two months of benefits, unless the state administrators agreed to an exemption of the rule. Many additional requirements for eligibility were spelled out in the law. And the states were under severe obligation to impose all these requirements lest they lose their TANF federal grants.

Since this new welfare law was enacted, the number of families receiving assistance has dropped by 61 percent.[17] Some observers take this as a sign that welfare reform is working; indeed, former welfare recipients have

been more successful at finding and keeping jobs than many critics of the new law predicted.

As Congress prepared to reauthorize the welfare law in 2002, two perspectives emerged. Democrats proposed changes that would make the welfare law "an antipoverty weapon."[18] They sought to increase spending on child care, allow more education and training, and relax time limits for those working and receiving welfare benefits. Republicans, by contrast, proposed stricter work requirements and advocated programs designed to promote marriage among welfare recipients.[19] Neither party challenged the basic features of the 1996 reform. Nonetheless, as caseloads began to rise again in 2001 as a result of the combined effects of the recession and the terrorist attacks, both sides were attentive to new problems. Because of the nation's economic downturn, welfare rolls surged in 2009, straining many state welfare budgets. To cope with the crisis, the federal government made $5 billion in stimulus funds available to the states to help meet welfare needs and extended unemployment benefits. In 2011, President Obama proposed making welfare benefits available to a large number of poor Americans, but congressional Republicans expressed strong opposition to the idea.

WHAT IS THE ROLE OF PUBLIC POLICY IN DEMOCRACY?

Without government to maintain law and order, define rules of property and exchange enforce contracts, and exchange and provide public goods, no market economy could function. Too much or poorly fashioned government intervention, however, in the form of burdensome regulations, improperly designed monetary and fiscal policies, and public policies serving private interests at the public's expense, can stifle a market economy.

What is the proper balance between government intervention and free enterprise? There is no one answer to this question. In the United States, as in other liberal democracies, however, we have a political process designed to allow every American to weigh in on his question. If this process sometimes seems stalemated, perhaps it is because Americans have not reached any consensus and hope they can have both strong government and maximum individual freedom.

For Further Reading

Selections highlighted in red are included in *Readings in American Politics: Analysis and Perspectives*, Third Edition.

Bartels, Larry. *Unequal Democracy: The Political Economy of the New Gilded Age.* Princeton, NJ: Princeton University Press, 2008.

Béland, Daniel. *Social Security: History and Politics from the New Deal to the Privatization Debate.* Lawrence: University Press of Kansas, 2007.

Gilbert, Neil. *Transformation of the Welfare State.* New York: Oxford University Press, 2004.

McCarty, Nolan, Keith Poole, and Howard Rosenthal. *Polarized America: The Dance of Ideology and Unequal Riches.* Cambridge, MA: MIT Press, 2006.

Mettler, Suzanne. *The Submerged State: How Invisible Government Policies Undermine American Democracy.* Chicago: University of Chicago Press, 2011.

Murray, Charles. *In Our Hands: A Plan to Replace the Welfare State.* Washington, DC: American Enterprise Institute Press, 2006.

Schick, Allen. *The Federal Budget.* 3rd ed. Washington, DC: Brookings Institution, 2007.

Shipler, David. *The Working Poor.* New York: Vintage, 2005.

Skocpol, Theda. *The Missing Middle: Working Families and the Future of American Social Policy.* New York: Norton, 2000.

Starr, Paul. *Remedy and Reaction: The Peculiar American Struggle over Health Care Reform.* New Haven, CT: Yale University Press, 2011.

Weir, Margaret, ed. *The Social Divide: Political Parties and the Future of Activist Government.* Washington, DC: Brookings Institution, 1998.

Wells, Donald. *The Federal Reserve System.* Jefferson, NC: McFarland, 2004.

14 Foreign Policy

The term *foreign policy* refers to the programs and policies that determine America's relations with other nations and foreign entities. Foreign policy includes diplomacy, military and security policy, international human rights policies, and various forms of economic policy, such as trade policy and international energy policy. Of course, foreign policy and domestic policy are not completely separate categories but are closely interwined. Take security policy, for example. Defending the nation requires the design and manufacture of tens of billions of dollars worth of military hardware. The manufacture and procurement of this military equipment involve a host of economic policies, and paying for it shapes America's fiscal policies.

Much recent debate has centered on the efficacy of current U.S. foreign policy and whether government actually can—and should attempt to—end violence elsewhere in the world. Many Americans believe that international conflict and violence are among the most important problems facing our government. Some believe that our government is too quick to make use of armed violence and should seek peaceful means of solving international differences. Such individuals adhere to two main schools of thought, the

Hobbesian and the Kantian. For Hobbes, the solution to the problem of violence was the creation of a powerful sovereign authority that will put an end to strife and violent conflict. For Kant, the solution was an increase in the number of republican governments, a type of regime that, in his view, was extremely reluctant to engage in acts of armed aggression. Thus, modern-day neo-Hobbesians favor the construction of supra-national organizations and the dilution of national sovereignty, while modern-day neo-Kantians count upon the spread of liberal democracy to bring about a "democratic peace."

The main problem faced by the neo-Hobbesians is that the establishment and maintenance of a sovereign powerful enough to suppress violence are most likely to be accepted by states or other actors that already have few or relatively manageable antagonisms toward one another and see submission to a single authority as a means of advancing their mutual interests. The thirteen American states in 1789 or the economically advanced western European states today are examples. The imposition of some sort of sovereign authority over mutually antagonistic states and political forces is likely to require considerable violence and a continuing regime of coercion. In other words, it would entail an imperial project that seems more a recipe than a cure for violence.

As for the neo-Kantians, the statistical evidence concerning the peaceful proclivities of liberal democracies is a bit equivocal. It is interesting to note that the United States, the world's premier liberal democracy, is also among the most bellicose nations on earth. Since the Civil War, American forces have been deployed abroad on hundreds of occasions for major conflicts

CORE OF THE ANALYSIS

➡ The goals of American foreign policy include security, economic prosperity, and—to a lesser extent—humanitarian objectives.

➡ Foreign policy is shaped by domestic actors—such as the president, the bureaucracy, Congress, and interest groups—and through strategic interactions with other foreign actors.

➡ The instruments that the government uses to implement foreign policy may include economic, diplomatic, institutional, or military means. These instruments are deployed strategically to serve the interests of the United States.

as well as minor skirmishes. Writing in 1989, historian Geoffrey Perret commented that no other nation "has had as much experience of war as the United States."[1] America has not become less warlike in the years since Perret published his observation. Between 1989 and the present, American forces have fought two wars in the Persian Gulf and a war in Afghanistan, while engaging in lesser military actions in Panama, Kosovo, Somalia, and elsewhere. Every year, America's military arsenal and defense budget dwarf those of other nations. America currently spends more than $600 billion per year on its military and weapons programs—a figure that represents more than one-third of the world's total military expenditure and nearly six times the amount spent by the Chinese People's Republic, the nation that currently ranks second to the United States in overall military outlays. Perhaps ironically, America has justified many of its wars, including the 2002 Iraq War, by the claim that its goal was to transform its adversary into a peaceful liberal democracy.

Often, citizens and political actors denounce the use of force by some groups or nations while casting a tolerant eye at the use of violence by others. Politically progressive groups typically denounce military actions by the United States, while accepting the need for Third World regimes to resort to violence. Politically conservative groups generally take the opposite view. The moral implications of American foreign policy are further complicated by important concerns about America's security and interests and by the difficult reality that not intervening abroad with violent force may mean effectively condemning some peoples to live under tyranny.

How should our government respond to international violence? Are there peaceful means of solving problems? We also need to remember that many current international threats do not seem soluble by military means. How can military force deal with global climate change, emergent diseases, and energy shortages? In this chapter, we will consider the goals and tools of American foreign policy, as well as the various makers and shapers of foreign policy decisions. Finally, we will turn to the question of America's role in the world today.

THE GOALS OF FOREIGN POLICY

Although U.S. foreign policy has a number of purposes, three main goals stand out. These are security, prosperity, and the creation of a better world. These goals are, of course, closely intertwined and can never be pursued fully in isolation from one another.

Security

To many Americans, the chief purpose of the nation's foreign policy is protection of America's security in an often hostile world. Traditionally, the United States has been concerned about threats that might emanate from other nations, such as Nazi Germany during the 1940s and then Soviet Russia until the Soviet Union's collapse in the late 1980s. Today, American security policy is concerned not only with the actions of other nations but also with the activities of terrorist groups and other hostile non-state actors.[2] To protect the nation's security from foreign threats, the United States has built an enormous military apparatus and a complex array of intelligence-gathering institutions, such as the Central Intelligence Agency (CIA), charged with evaluating and anticipating challenges from abroad.[3] While all nations are concerned with security, American power and global commitments give U.S. foreign policy a unique focus on security issues.

Security is, of course, a broad term. Policy makers must be concerned with Americans' physical security. The September 11 terrorist attacks killed and injured thousands of Americans; the government constantly fears that new attacks could be even more catastrophic. Policy makers must also be concerned with such matters as the security of America's food supplies, transportation infrastructure, and energy supplies. Many of our foreign policy efforts in the Middle East, for example, are aimed at ensuring continuing American access to vital oil fields. In recent years, cyberspace has become a new security concern. The nation's dependence on computers means that the government must be alert to efforts by hostile governments, groups, or even individual "hackers" to damage computer networks.

During the eighteenth and nineteenth centuries, the United States believed that its security was based on its geographic isolation. We were separated by two oceans from European and Asian powers, and many Americans thought that our security would be best preserved by remaining aloof from international power struggles. This policy was known as isolationism. In his 1796 farewell address, President George Washington warned Americans to avoid permanent alliances with foreign powers, and in 1823, President James Monroe warned foreign powers not to meddle in the Western Hemisphere. Washington's warning and what came to be called the Monroe Doctrine were the cornerstones of the U.S. foreign policy of isolationism until the end of the nineteenth century. The United States saw itself as the dominant power in the Western Hemisphere and, indeed, believed that its "manifest destiny" was to expand from sea to sea. The rest of the world, however, should remain at arm's length.

Deterrence during the Cold War. In the twentieth century, technology made oceans less of a barrier to foreign threats, and the world's growing

non-state actor
A group other than a nation-state that attempts to play a role in the international system. Terrorist groups are one type of non-state actor

isolationism
The desire to avoid involvement in the affairs of other nations

economic interdependence meant that the United States could no longer ignore events abroad. At the beginning of the twentieth century, despite its isolationist sentiments, the United States entered World War I on the side of Great Britain and France when the Wilson administration concluded that America's economic and security interests would be adversely affected by a German victory. In 1941, America was drawn into World War II when Japan attacked the U.S. Pacific fleet anchored at Pearl Harbor, Hawaii. Even before the Japanese attack forced America to fight, the Roosevelt administration had already concluded that the United States must act to prevent a victory by the German-Japanese-Italian Axis alliance. Until the Japanese attack, however, President Franklin Delano Roosevelt had not been able to overcome proponents of American isolationism, who declared that our security was best served by leaving foreigners to their own devices. With their attack, the Japanese proved that the Pacific Ocean could not protect the United States from foreign foes and effectively discredited isolationism as a security policy.

In the aftermath of World War II, the United States developed a new security policy known as containment to check the growing power of the Soviet Union. This policy was articulated by George F. Kennan, Director of Policy Planning at the State Department, who said the United States must contain the Soviet Union's expansionist tendencies with the patient application of counter-pressure where the Soviets sought to expand their geopolitical sphere.

By the end of the 1940s, the Soviets had built a huge empire and enormous military forces. Most threatening of all, the Soviet Union had built nuclear weapons and intercontinental bombers capable of attacking the United States. The United States was committed to maintaining its own military might as a means of deterrence, to discourage the Soviets from attacking the United States or its allies. Containment and deterrence remained the cornerstone of American policy towards the Soviet Union for the duration of the Cold War. Some Americans argued that we should attack the Soviets before it was too late. This policy is known as preventive war. Others said that we should show our peaceful intentions and attempt to placate the Soviets. This policy is called appeasement.

The policies that the United States actually adopted, deterrence and containment, could be seen as midway between preventive war and appeasement. A nation pursuing a policy of deterrence, on the one hand, signals its peaceful intentions, but on the other hand indicates its willingness and ability to fight if attacked. Thus, during the era of confrontation with the Soviet Union, known as the Cold War, the United States frequently asserted that it had no intention of attacking the Soviet Union. At the same time, however, the United States built a huge military force, including an arsenal of nuclear weapons and intercontinental missiles, and frequently asserted

containment

A policy designed to curtail the political and military expansion of a hostile power

deterrence

The development and maintenance of military strength as a means of discouraging attack

preventive war

The policy of striking first when a nation fears that a foreign foe is contemplating hostile action

appeasement

The effort to forestall war by giving in to the demands of a hostile power

Cold War

The period of struggle between the United States and the former Soviet Union between the late 1940s and about 1990

that in the event of a Soviet attack, it had the ability and will to respond with overwhelming force. The Soviet Union announced that its nuclear weapons were also intended for deterrent purposes. Eventually the two sides possessed such enormous arsenals of nuclear missiles that each potentially had the ability to destroy the other in the event of war. This heavily armed stand-off came to be called a posture of mutually assured destruction. During the 1962 Cuban missile crisis, the United States and the USSR came to the brink of war when President Kennedy declared that the Soviet Union must remove its nuclear missiles from Cuba and threatened to use force if the Soviets refused. After an extremely intense several weeks, the crisis was defused by a negotiated compromise in which the Soviets agreed to remove their missiles in exchange for a U.S. guarantee that it would not invade Cuba. The two superpowers had come so close to nuclear war that the leaders of both nations sought ways of reducing tensions. This effort led to a period of détente in which a number of arms control agreements were signed and the threat of war was reduced.

The dissolution of the Soviet Union began in 1985, and the final collapse occurred in 1991, partly because its huge military expenditures undermined its creaky and inefficient centrally planned economy. The new Russia, though still a formidable and sometimes unfriendly power, seemed to pose less of a threat to the United States. Americans celebrated the end of the Cold War and believed that the enormous expense of America's own military forces might be reduced. Within a few years of the Soviet collapse, however, a new set of security threats emerged, requiring new policy responses.

New Security Threats. The September 11 terrorist attacks demonstrated a threat against which some security scholars had long warned. The threat was that non-state actors and so-called rogue states might acquire significant military capabilities, including nuclear weapons, and would not be affected by America's deterrent capabilities. To counter these new security threats, the George W. Bush administration shifted from a policy of deterrence to one of preemption. Preemption is often used as another name for preventive war or willingness to strike first in order to prevent an enemy attack. The United States declared that it would not wait to be attacked but would, if necessary, take action to disable terrorist groups and rogue states before they could do us harm. The Bush administration's "global war on terror" is an expression of this notion of preemption, as was the U.S. invasion of Iraq. The United States has also refused to rule out the possibility that it would attack North Korea or Iran if it deemed those nations' nuclear programs to be an imminent threat to American security interests. Accompanying this shift in military doctrines has been an enormous increase in overall U.S. military spending (see the Analyzing the Evidence unit).

preemption
The willingness to strike first in order to prevent an enemy attack

Cutting Defense Spending?

Contributed by
Kenneth Mayer
University of Wisconsin

What will happen to the defense budget in the next decade? With the war in Iraq over and most troops in Afghanistan scheduled to come home by the end of 2014, defense spending will come down from the levels seen at the height of the "war on terror." That height reached $705 billion in 2011, which was twice what the United States spent on defense in 2001.

In addition, further cuts may occur as a result of the budget agreement reached during the summer of 2011, when President Obama and Congress committed to automatic cuts (sequestration) if they could not agree on long-term deficit reduction strategies. Those cuts, which are to be split between defense and nondefense discretionary spending, went into effect in 2013, and if they stay in place will require cuts of about $55 billion in the defense budget each year for the next decade.

In his 2014 budget, President Obama proposed overall defense spending of $627 billion, with declining spending through 2018, when the defense budget is projected to be $592 billion. Some of these savings will come from the continued drawdown of U.S. forces in Afghanistan, although funding for some ongoing activities in Iraq and Afghanistan (Overseas Contingency Operations) will likely continue.

Long-range defense planning is inherently uncertain, as it is difficult to identify concrete threats and to predict the likelihood of action by potential adversaries. Critics of the planned reductions (and sequester cuts) argue that the cuts will jeopardize defense capabilities. A number of expensive programs (the F-35 aircraft and ballistic missile defense especially) will put pressure on defense budgets for years to come.

U.S. Budget, 2012 (in billions of dollars)

SOURCE: Bipartisan Policy Center and Congressional Budget Office.

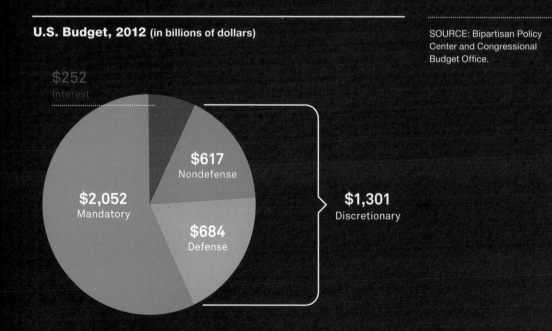

$252
Interest

$617
Nondefense

$2,052
Mandatory

$684
Defense

$1,301
Discretionary

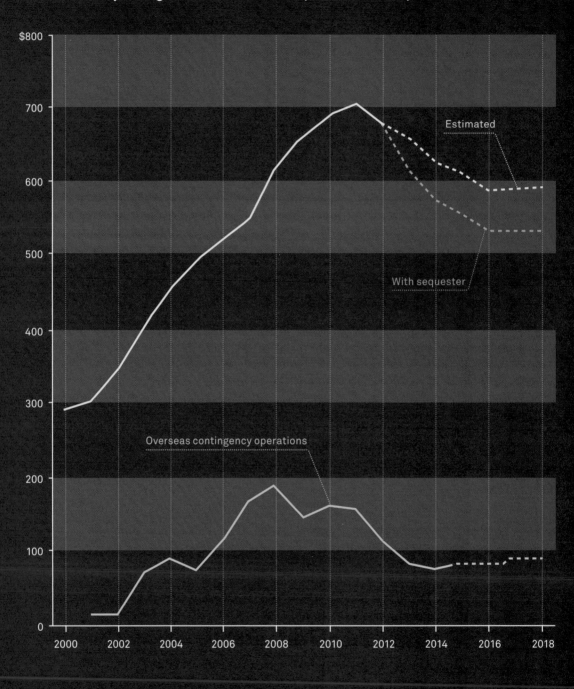

U.S. Defense Spending Fiscal Years 2000–18 (in billions of dollars)

Estimated

With sequester

Overseas contingency operations

SOURCE: FY 2014 Budget, Historical Perspectives table 3-1, Spending by Function and Subfunction; Congressional Budget Office, *Final Sequestration Report for Fiscal Year 2013* (March 2013); Congressional Budget Office, *Updated Budget Projections: Fiscal Years 2013–23* (May 2013).

When President Obama met with Chinese president Xi Jinping in 2013, they discussed security, economic, and humanitarian issues. The United States pursues numerous foreign policy goals in each of these areas.

After Obama was elected in 2008, his administration took a different tone, declaring that it would endeavor to establish constructive dialogues with North Korea, Iran, and other hostile states. However, Obama did not necessarily renounce the Bush Doctrine for those states that declined to become constructively engaged. Furthermore, President Obama did not immediately hasten the departure of American troops from Iraq and Afghanistan, as many Democrats had expected. Instead, Obama initially chose to step up America's military effort in Afghanistan and keep U.S. forces in Iraq. This policy was finally reversed, and the United States withdrew from both countries. However, both regions remain unstable and have required U.S. attention. In 2014, for instance, the military success of the Islamic State in Iraq and Syria led President Obama to send troops back to Iraq to help defend the Iraqi national government.

U.S. foreign policy makers also continue to express concern over Iran and North Korea. In 2013 the North Korean regime continued to test missiles that might soon be able to reach U.S. shores. The Obama administration responded by positioning additional antimissile batteries to protect America's west coast. For its part, Iran continued to work toward the development of nuclear weapons, despite global economic sanctions and President Obama's repeated demands that Iranian nuclear work be halted.

Economic Prosperity

A second major goal of U.S. foreign policy is promoting American prosperity. America's international economic policies are intended to expand employment opportunities in the United States, to maintain access to foreign energy supplies at a reasonable cost, to promote foreign investment in the United States, and to lower the prices Americans pay for goods and services.

Among the most visible and important elements of U.S. international economic policy is trade policy. The promotion and advertising of American goods and services abroad are long-standing goals of U.S. trade policy and are major obligations of the Department of Commerce. Yet modern trade policy involves a complex arrangement of treaties, tariffs, and other mechanisms of policy formation. For example, the United States has a long-standing policy of granting most favored nation status to certain countries—that is, the United States offers to another country the same tariff rate it already gives to its most favored trading partner, in return for trade (and sometimes other) concessions. In 1998, to avoid any suggestion that "most favored nation" implied some special relationship with an undemocratic country (China, for example), President Clinton changed the term from "most favored nation" to "normal trade relations."[4]

The most important international organization for promoting free trade is the World Trade Organization (WTO), which officially came into being in 1995. The WTO grew out of the General Agreement on Tariffs and Trade (GATT). Following World War II, GATT had brought together a wide range of nations for regular negotiations designed to reduce barriers to trade. Such barriers, many believed, contributed to the breakdown of the world economy in the 1930s and helped to cause World War II. The WTO has 159 members worldwide; decisions about trade are made by the Ministerial Conference, which meets every two years. Similar policy goals are pursued in regional arrangements, such as the North American Free Trade Agreement (NAFTA), a trade treaty among the United States, Canada, and Mexico.

For over a half century, the United States has led the world in supporting free trade as the best route to growth and prosperity. Yet the American government, too, has sought to protect domestic industry when it is politically necessary. Subsidies, as we have seen, have long boosted American agriculture, artificially lowering the price of American products on world markets. Trade was also an issue in the 2012 election. Throughout the campaign, the Republican candidate, Mitt Romney, accused President Obama of remaining silent as hundreds of thousands of American factory jobs disappeared in the face of what he called China's unfair trade practices. "It's time to stand up to cheaters," Romney campaign ads declared. For its part, the Obama campaign charged that Romney had run a private equity firm that invested in a Chinese firm that exploited low-wage labor and cost Americans their jobs.

International Humanitarian Policies

A third goal of American policy is to make the world a better place for all its inhabitants. The main forms of policy that address this goal are international environmental policy, international human rights policy, and international

most favored nation status
An agreement to offer a trading partner the lowest tariff rate offered to other trading partners

World Trade Organization (WTO)
The international trade agency promoting free trade that grew out of the General Agreement on Tariffs and Trade

General Agreement on Tariffs and Trade (GATT)
The international trade organization, in existence from 1947 to 1995, that set many of the rules governing international trade

North American Free Trade Agreement (NAFTA)
A trade treaty among the United States, Canada, and Mexico to lower and eliminate tariffs among the three countries

peacekeeping. America's wealth often makes the United States the major source of funding for such endeavors. The United States also contributes to international organizations such as the World Health Organization that work for global health and against hunger. These policies are often seen as secondary to the other goals of American foreign policy, forced to give way if they interfere with security or foreign economic policy. Moreover, although the United States spends billions annually on security policy and hundreds of millions on trade policy, it spends relatively little on environmental, human rights, and peacekeeping efforts. Some critics charge that America has the wrong priorities, spending far more to make war than to protect human rights and the global environment. Nevertheless, a number of important American foreign policy efforts are, at least in part, designed to make the world a better place.

In the realm of international environmental policy, the United States supports a number of international efforts to protect the environment. These include the United Nations Framework Convention on Climate Change, an international agreement to study and ameliorate harmful changes in the global environment, and the Montreal Protocol, an agreement signed by more than 150 countries to limit the production of substances potentially harmful to the world's ozone layer. Other nations have severely criticized the United States for withdrawing from the 1997 Kyoto Protocol, an agreement setting limits on emissions of greenhouse gases from industrial countries. The United States has asserted that the Kyoto Protocol would be harmful to American economic interests. Although the United States is concerned with the global environment, national economic interests took precedence in this case. In preparation for the expiration of the Kyoto agreement at the end of 2012, world leaders gathered in Copenhagen, Denmark, in 2009 to begin the process of negotiating a new climate treaty. The Copenhagen climate summit, however, failed to produce a binding international agreement and ended with the United States, Europe, and China blaming one another for the lack of concrete results.

The same national priorities seem apparent in the area of human rights policy. The United States has a long-standing commitment to human rights and is a signatory to many major international agreements concerning human rights. These include the International Covenant on Civil and Political Rights, the International Convention against Torture, the Convention on the Elimination of All Forms of Racial Discrimination, and various agreements to protect children. The State Department's Bureau of Democracy, Human Rights, and Labor works cooperatively with international organizations to investigate and focus attention on human rights abuses. In 1998, the United States enacted the International Religious Freedom Act, which calls on all governments to respect religious freedom. The act lists a number of

sanctions that the United States and other signatories may employ to punish nations found to be in violation.

Although the United States is committed to promoting human rights, this commitment has a lower priority in American foreign policy than the nation's security concerns and economic interests. Thus, the United States is likely to overlook human rights violations by its major trading partners, such as China, and remain silent in the face of human rights violations by such allies as Saudi Arabia. Nevertheless, human rights concerns do play a role in American foreign policy. For example, beginning in 2007, the United States has made available several million dollars annually in small grants to pay medical and legal expenses incurred by individuals who have been the victims of retaliation in their own countries for working against their governments' repressive practices. In this small way, the United States is backing its often-asserted principles.

Another form of U.S. policy designed to improve the condition of the world is support for international peacekeeping efforts. At any point in time, a number of border wars, civil wars, and guerrilla conflicts flare somewhere in the world, usually in its poorer regions. These wars often generate humanitarian crises in the form of casualties, disease, and refugees. In cooperation with international agencies and other nations, the United States funds a number of efforts to keep the peace in volatile regions and to deal with the health care and refugee problems associated with conflict. In 2007, the United States provided more than $1 billion in funding for United Nations peacekeeping operations in Bosnia, Kosovo, Sierra Leone, Lebanon, the Democratic Republic of Congo, and East Timor. As the world's wealthiest nation, the United States also recognizes an obligation to render assistance to nations facing crises and emergencies. In 2010, for example, the United States sent medical aid, food relief, and rescue teams to Haiti when that impoverished island nation was struck by a devastating earthquake. In 2011, the United States backed a NATO effort to support rebel forces seeking to overthrow Libyan leader Mu'ammar Qaddafi. In 2012, the U.S. government offered sympathy, but not support, to antigovernment forces in Syria. As the civil war in Syria dragged on and the world learned that the Syrian government had used chemical weapons, constituencies in the United States took different views as to whether and how the United States should intervene.

America's humanitarian policies are important. Without American efforts and funding, many international humanitarian programs would be far less successful than they are today. In general, though, security and economic interests take precedence in the eyes of U.S. policy makers over humanitarian concerns. The U.S. government is far more likely to decry abuses of religious freedom in Iran—an adversary—than in Saudi Arabia— an ally.

WHO MAKES AND SHAPES FOREIGN POLICY?

As we have seen, domestic policies are made by governmental institutions and influenced by a variety of interest groups, political movements, and even the mass media. The same is true in the realm of foreign policy.

The President

The president is the dominant actor in the realm of American foreign policy. The president exercises substantial control over the nation's diplomatic and military institutions and, as a result, is in a position to decide with whom, when, and how the United States will engage in the international arena. Since World War II, for example, American military forces have fought numerous engagements throughout the world—Korea, Indo-China, the Middle East, Kosovo, Panama, and others. In every instance, the decision to commit troops to battle was made by the president, often with little or no consultation with Congress. When, following the September 11 terrorist attacks, President Bush ordered American troops into Iraq and Afghanistan, Congress voiced its approval, but the president made it clear that he did not

The president's power in the realm of foreign policy has increased since World War II, especially in recent administrations. In a recent example, the 2011 attack on Osama bin Laden's compound in Pakistan was initiated by President Obama without broad congressional consultation.

believe he needed Congress's permission. In 2011, when President Obama ordered American warplanes into action against Libyan rebels, he made no effort to consult with Congress. And when Obama ordered special operations soldiers to attack Osama bin Laden's compound in Pakistan, members of Congress learned of the operation and bin Laden's death from news broadcasts—just like other Americans.

The president's foreign policy powers, particularly in the military realm, are far greater than the Constitution's framers had thought wise. The framers gave the power to declare war to Congress and made the president the nation's top military commander if and when Congress chose to go to war.[5] Today, presidents command the troops and decide when to go to war.

The Bureaucracy

The major foreign policy players in the bureaucracy are the secretaries of the departments of State, Defense, and the Treasury; the Joint Chiefs of Staff (JCOS), especially the chair of the JCOS; and the director of the Central Intelligence Agency (CIA). A separate unit in the bureaucracy comprising these people and a few others is the National Security Council (NSC), whose main purpose is to iron out the differences among the key players and to integrate their positions in order to confirm or reinforce a decision the president wants to make in foreign policy or military policy. The secretary of commerce has also become an increasingly important foreign policy maker with the rise and spread of economic globalization.

To this group another has been added: the Department of Homeland Security. The department has four main divisions: Border and Transportation Security; Emergency Preparedness and Response; Chemical, Biological, Radiological, and Nuclear Countermeasures; and Information Analysis and Infrastructure Protection.

Coordinating the diverse missions of a single agency is a challenge; coordinating the efforts of multiple agencies is especially problematic. The NSC and now the Department of Homeland Security attempt to keep the various players on the same page. But will these agencies—each with its own authority, interests, and priorities—follow the same protocol?

In addition to top cabinet-level officials, key lower-level staff members have policy-making influence as strong as that of the cabinet secretaries. Some may occasionally exceed cabinet influence. These include the two or three specialized national security advisers in the White House, the staff of the NSC (headed by the national security adviser), and a few other career bureaucrats in the departments of State and Defense whose influence varies according to their specialty and to the foreign policy issue at hand.

Congress

For most of American history, the Senate was the only important congressional foreign-policy player because of its constitutional role in reviewing and approving treaties. The treaty power is still the primary entrée of the Senate into foreign policy making. But since World War II and the continual involvement of the United States in international security and foreign aid, while the president has been the dominant actor, Congress as a whole has continued to exercise influence because most modern foreign policies require financing, which requires approval from both the House of Representatives and the Senate. Congress has also become increasingly involved in foreign-policy making because of the increasing use by the president of executive agreements to conduct foreign policy. Executive agreements have the force of treaties but do not require prior approval by the Senate. They can, however, be revoked by action of both chambers of Congress.

Other congressional players are the foreign policy, military policy, and intelligence committees: in the Senate these are the Foreign Relations Committee, the Armed Services Committee, and Homeland Security; in the House, these are the Foreign Affairs Committee, the Armed Services Committee, and the Homeland Security and Governmental Affairs Committee. Usually, a few members of these committees who have spent years specializing in foreign affairs become trusted members of the foreign policy establishment and are influential makers of foreign policy. In fact, several members of Congress have left to become key foreign-affairs cabinet members, including current secretary of state John Kerry.[6]

executive agreement

An agreement between the president and another country that has the force of a treaty but does not require the Senate's "advice and consent"

Interest Groups

Far and away the most important category of nonofficial player is the interest group—that is, the interest groups to whom one or more foreign policy issues are of long-standing and vital relevance. The type of interest group with the reputation for the most influence is the economic interest group. Yet the heft of the myths about these groups' influence far outweighs the reality. The influence of organized economic interest groups in foreign policy varies enormously from issue to issue and year to year. Most of these groups are *single-issue* groups and are therefore most active when their particular issue is on the agenda. On many of the broader and more sustained policy issues, such as the NAFTA or the general question of American involvement in international trade, the larger interest groups find it difficult to maintain tight enough control of their many members to speak with a single voice. The most systematic study of international trade policies and their interest groups concluded that the leaders of these large, economic interest groups

spend more time maintaining consensus among their members than lobbying Congress or pressuring major players in the executive branch.[7] The economic interest groups more successful in influencing foreign policy are the narrower, single-issue groups such as the tobacco industry, which over the years has successfully kept American foreign policy from putting heavy restrictions on international trade in and advertising of tobacco products. Likewise, the computer hardware and software industries have successfully hardened the American attitude toward Chinese piracy of intellectual property rights.

Another type of interest group with a well-founded reputation for influence in foreign policy is made up of people with strong attachments and identifications to their country of origin. The interest group with the reputation for greatest influence is Jewish Americans, some of whom maintain family and emotional ties to Israel that may make them particularly concerned with U.S. policies toward Israel. Similarly, some Americans of Irish heritage, despite having resided in the United States for two, three, or four generations, still maintain vigilance about American policies toward Ireland and Northern Ireland. Many other ethnic and national interest groups wield similar influence over American foreign policy.

A third type of interest group, one with a reputation that has been growing in the past two decades, is the human rights interest group. Such groups are made up of people who, instead of having self-serving economic or

IN BRIEF

Makers and Shapers of Foreign Policy

✔ Makers

- The president
- The bureaucracy (secretaries of State, Defense, and the Treasury; the Joint Chiefs of Staff; and the director of the Central Intelligence Agency)
- Congress (Senate approves treaties; both chambers vote on financing; foreign-policy and military policy committees in each chamber)

✔ Shapers

- Interest groups (economic, cultural/ethnic groups, human rights groups, environmental groups)
- The media

Interest groups comprising citizens with strong attachments to their country of origin or heritage may influence foreign policy. The American Israel Public Affairs Committee (AIPAC) has been prominent in helping shape American foreign policy toward Israel.

ethnic interests in foreign policy, are genuinely concerned for the welfare and treatment of people throughout the world—particularly those who suffer under harsh political regimes. A relatively small but often quite influential example is Amnesty International, whose exposés of human rights abuses have altered the practices of many regimes around the world. In recent years, the Christian right has also been a vocal advocate for the human rights of Christians who are persecuted in other parts of the world, most notably in China, for their religious beliefs. For example, the Christian Coalition joined groups such as Amnesty International in lobbying Congress to cut trade with countries that permit attacks against religious believers.

A related type of group with a fast-growing influence is the ecological or environmental group, sometimes called the "greens." Groups of this nature often depend more on demonstrations than on the usual forms and strategies of influence in Washington—lobbying and using electoral politics, for example. Demonstrations in strategically located areas can have significant influence on American foreign policy. In recent years environmental activists staged major protests at the 2009 London and 2010 Toronto international economic summits.

Putting It Together

What can we say about who really makes American foreign policy? First, except for the president, whose influence is felt in virtually every area of foreign policy, the influence of players and shapers varies from case to case—this

is a good reason to look with some care at each example of foreign policy in this chapter. Second, because the one constant influence is the centrality of the president in foreign policy making, it is useful to evaluate other actors and factors as they interact with the president.[8] Third, the reason influence varies from case to case is that each case arises under different conditions and with vastly different constraints: for issues that arise and are resolved quickly, the opportunity for influence is limited. Fourth, foreign policy experts will often disagree about the level of influence any player or type of player has on policy making.

But just to get started, let's make a few tentative generalizations. When an important foreign policy decision has to be made under conditions of crisis—where "time is of the essence"—the influence of the presidency is at its strongest. Within those time constraints, access to the decision-making process is limited almost exclusively to the narrowest definition of the "foreign policy establishment." The arena for participation is tiny; any discussion at all is limited to the officially and constitutionally designated players. To put this another way, in a crisis, the foreign policy establishment works as it is supposed to.[9] As time becomes less restricted, even when the decision to be made is of great importance, the arena of participation expands to include more government players and more nonofficial, informal players—the most concerned interest groups and the most important journalists. In other words, the arena becomes more pluralistic and therefore less distinguishable from the politics of domestic policy making. Because there are so many other countries with power and interests on any given issue, there are severe limits on the choices the United States can make. As one author concludes, in foreign affairs, "policy takes precedence over politics."[10] Thus, even though foreign policy making in noncrisis situations may more closely resemble the pluralistic politics of domestic policy making, foreign policy making is still a narrower arena with fewer participants.

THE INSTRUMENTS OF MODERN AMERICAN FOREIGN POLICY

Any government has at hand certain instruments, or tools, to use in implementing its foreign policy. An instrument is neutral, capable of serving many goals. There have been many instruments of American foreign policy, and we can deal here only with those instruments we deem to be most important in the modern epoch: diplomacy, the United Nations,

the international monetary structure, economic aid, collective security, military force, and dispute arbitration. Each of these instruments will be evaluated in this section for its role in the conduct of American foreign policy, including its place in the history and development of American values.

Diplomacy

We begin this treatment of instruments with diplomacy because it is the instrument to which all other instruments should be subordinated, although they seldom are. Diplomacy is the representation of a government to other foreign governments. Its purpose is to promote national values or interests by peaceful means. According to Hans Morgenthau, "a diplomacy that ends in war has failed in its primary objective."[11]

diplomacy

The representation of a government to other foreign governments

The first effort to create a modern diplomatic service in the United States was made through the Rogers Act of 1924, which established the initial framework for a professional foreign-service staff. But it took World War II and the Foreign Service Act of 1946 to forge the foreign service into a fully professional diplomatic corps.

Although diplomacy is a powerful tool of foreign policy, by its very nature it is overshadowed by spectacular international events and dramatic initiatives. The traditional American distrust of diplomacy continues today, albeit in weaker form. Impatience with or downright distrust of diplomacy has been built into not only all the other instruments of foreign policy but also the modern presidential system itself.[12] So much personal responsibility has been heaped on the presidency that it is difficult for presidents to entrust any of their authority or responsibility in foreign policy to professional diplomats in the State Department and other bureaucracies.

In 2008, both parties' presidential candidates criticized the Bush administration for having failed to use diplomacy to secure greater international support for the Iraq War. Both promised to revitalize American diplomacy. President Obama appointed Hillary Clinton as his secretary of state in part to underline the importance he attached to diplomacy by appointing such a prominent figure as America's chief diplomat. In 2013, Obama appointed former senators John Kerry as secretary of state and Chuck Hagel as secretary of defense. Both promised continuity with their predecessors' policies. Obama also promised to work to develop a better relationship with China. Though America's chief trading partner, the two nations are deeply suspicious of each other. The United States views China as a growing threat, while China believes that the United States wants to undermine its influence. Both, unfortunately, are correct.

Chapter 14: Foreign Policy

The United Nations

The utility of the United Nations (UN) to the United States as an instrument of foreign policy can be too easily underestimated, because the UN is a very large and unwieldy institution with few powers and no armed forces to implement its rules and resolutions. Its supreme body is the UN General Assembly, comprising one representative of each of the 192 member states; each member representative has one vote, regardless of the size of the country. Important issues require a two-thirds majority vote, and the annual session of the General Assembly runs only from September to December (although it can call extra sessions). It has little organization that can make it an effective decision-making body, with only six standing committees, few tight rules of procedure, and no political parties to provide priorities and discipline. Its defenders are quick to add that although it lacks armed forces, it relies on the power of world opinion, and this is not to be taken lightly. The powers of the UN devolve mainly to its executive committee, the UN Security Council, which alone has the real power to make decisions and rulings that member states are obligated by the UN Charter to implement. The Security Council may be called into session at any time, and each member (or a designated alternate) must be present at UN Headquarters in New York at all times. It comprises 15 members: 5 are permanent (the victors of World War II), and 10 are elected by the General Assembly for two-year, nonrepeatable terms. The 5 permanent members are China, France, Russia, the United Kingdom, and the United States. Each of the 15 members has only 1 vote, and a 9-vote majority of the 15 is required on all substantive matters. But each of the 5 permanent members also has a negative vote, a veto, and 1 veto is sufficient to reject any substantive proposal.

The UN can be a useful forum for international discussions and an instrument for multilateral action. Most peacekeeping efforts to which the United States contributes, for example, are undertaken under UN auspices.

> **United Nations (UN)**
> An organization of nations founded in 1945 to be a channel for negotiation and a means of settling international disputes peaceably. The UN has had frequent successes in providing a forum for negotiation and on some occasions a means of preventing international conflicts from spreading. On a number of occasions, the UN has been a convenient cover for U.S. foreign-policy goals

The International Monetary Structure

Fear of a repeat of the economic devastation that followed World War I brought the United States together with its allies (except the USSR) to Bretton Woods, New Hampshire, in 1944 to create a new international economic structure for the postwar world. The result was two institutions: the International Bank for Reconstruction and Development (commonly called the World Bank) and the International Monetary Fund.

The World Bank was set up to finance long-term capital. Leading nations took on the obligation of contributing funds to enable the World Bank to

make loans to capital-hungry countries. (The U.S. quota has been about one-third of the total.)

International Monetary Fund (IMF)

An institution established in 1944 that provides loans and facilitates international monetary exchange

The International Monetary Fund (IMF) was set up to provide for the short-term flow of money. After the war, the dollar, instead of gold, was the chief means by which the currency of one country would be "changed into" currency of another country for purposes of making international transactions. To permit debtor countries with no international balances to make purchases and investments, the IMF was set up to lend dollars or other appropriate currencies to needy member countries to help them overcome temporary trade deficits. For many years after World War II, the IMF, along with U.S. foreign aid, in effect constituted the only international medium of exchange.

During the 1990s, the IMF returned to a position of enhanced importance through its efforts to reform some of the largest debtor nations and formerly communist countries, to bring them more fully into the global capitalist economy. For example, in the early 1990s, Russia and 13 other former Soviet republics were invited to join the IMF and the World Bank with the expectation of receiving $10.5 billion from these two agencies, primarily for a currency-stabilization fund. Each republic was to get a permanent IMF representative, and the IMF increased its staff by at least 10 percent to provide the expertise necessary to cope with the problems of these emerging capitalist economies.[13]

The IMF, with $93 billion, has more money to lend poor countries than do the United States, Europe, or Japan (the three leading IMF shareholders) individually. It makes its policy decisions in ways that are generally consonant with the interests of the leading shareholders.[14] For example, two weeks after September 11, 2001, the IMF approved a $135 million loan to economically troubled Pakistan, a key player in the war against the Taliban government of Afghanistan because of its strategic location. Turkey, also because of its strategic location in the Middle East, was likewise put back in the IMF pipeline.[15] In 2010, the IMF organized a $40 billion loan package to rescue the Greek government, which faced the threat of default on its debt. The United States and major European governments feared that a Greek default might spark a worldwide economic crisis. The future of the IMF, the World Bank, and all other private sources of international investment will depend in part on extension of more credit to the Third World and other developing countries, because credit means investment and productivity. But the future may depend even more on reducing the debt that is already there from previous extensions of credit.

Economic Aid and Sanctions

Every year, the United States provides nearly $30 billion in economic assistance to other nations. Some aid has a humanitarian purpose, such as helping to provide health care, shelter for refugees, or famine relief. A good deal

of American aid, however, is designed to promote American security interests or economic concerns. For example, the United States provides military assistance to a number of its allies in the form of advanced weapons or loans to help them purchase advanced weapons. Such loans generally stipulate that the recipient must purchase the designated weapons from American firms. In this way, the United States hopes to bolster its security and economic interests with one grant. For years the two largest recipients of American military assistance have been Israel and Egypt, American allies that fought two wars against each other. The United States believes that its military assistance allows both to feel sufficiently secure to remain at peace with each other.

Aid is an economic carrot. Sanctions are an economic stick. Economic sanctions that the United States employs against other nations include trade embargoes, bans on investment, and efforts to prevent the World Bank or other international institutions from extending credit to a nation against which the United States has a grievance. Sanctions are most often employed when the United States seeks to weaken what it considers a hostile regime or when it is attempting to compel some particular action by another regime. Thus, for example, in order to weaken the Castro government, the United States has long prohibited American firms from doing business with Cuba, though President Obama has called for a relaxation of current trade and travel restrictions. In recent years, the United States has maintained economic sanctions against Iran and North Korea in an effort to prevent those nations from pursuing nuclear-weapons programs.

Unilateral sanctions by the United States usually have little effect, since the target can usually trade elsewhere, sometimes even with foreign affiliates of U.S. firms. If, however, the United States is able to convince its allies to cooperate, sanctions have a better chance of success. International sanctions applied to Libya, for example, played a role in the regime's decision to enter into negotiations with the United States over Libyan responsibility for a number of terrorist attacks. Similarly, international sanctions applied to Iran weakened that nation's economy and slowed its nuclear-weapon project.

Collective Security

In 1947, most Americans hoped that the United States could meet its world obligations through the UN and economic structures alone. But most foreign-policy makers recognized that was a vain hope even as they were permitting and encouraging Americans to believe it. They had anticipated the need for military entanglements at the time of drafting the original UN Charter by insisting on language that recognized the right of all nations to provide for their mutual defense independent of the UN. And almost immediately after enactment of the Marshall Plan, designed to promote European

economic recovery, the White House and a parade of State and Defense Department officials followed up with an urgent request to the Senate to ratify, and to both houses of Congress to finance, mutual-defense alliances.

At first quite reluctant to approve treaties providing for national-security alliances, the Senate ultimately agreed with the executive branch. The first collective-security agreement was the Rio Treaty (ratified by the Senate in September 1947), which created the Organization of American States (OAS). This was the model treaty, anticipating all succeeding collective-security treaties by providing that an armed attack against any of its members "shall be considered as an attack against all the American States," including the United States. A more significant break with U.S. tradition against peacetime entanglements came with the North Atlantic Treaty (signed in April 1949), which created the North Atlantic Treaty Organization (NATO). ANZUS, a treaty tying Australia and New Zealand to the United States, was signed in September 1951. Three years later, the Southeast Asia Treaty created the Southeast Asia Treaty Organization (SEATO).

In addition to these multilateral treaties, the United States entered into a number of bilateral treaties—treaties between two countries. As one author has observed, the United States has been a *producer* of security, whereas most of its allies have been *consumers* of security.[16]

This pattern has continued in the post–Cold War era, and its best illustration is in the Persian Gulf War. The United States provided the initiative, the leadership, and most of the armed forces, even though its allies were obliged to reimburse over 90 percent of the cost.

It is difficult to evaluate collective security and its treaties, because the purpose of collective security as an instrument of foreign policy is prevention, and success of this kind has to be measured in terms of what did *not* happen. Critics have argued that U.S. collective-security treaties posed a threat of encirclement to the Soviet Union, forcing it to ensure its own collective security, particularly the Warsaw Pact.[17] Nevertheless, no one can deny the counterargument that more than 60 years have passed without a world war.

In 1998, the expansion of NATO took its first steps toward former Warsaw Pact members, extending membership to Poland, Hungary, and the Czech Republic. Most of Washington embraced this expansion as the true and fitting end of the Cold War, and the U.S. Senate echoed this with a resounding 80-to-19 vote to induct these three former Soviet satellites into NATO. The expansion was also welcomed among European member nations, which quickly approved the move, hailing it as the final closing of the book on Yalta, the 1945 treaty that divided Europe into Western and Soviet spheres of influence after the defeat of Germany. Expanded membership seems to have made NATO less threatening and more acceptable to Russia. Russia became a partner when the NATO-Russia Council was formed in 2002. Finally, although the expanded NATO membership (now 28 coun-

North Atlantic Treaty Organization (NATO)

A treaty organization comprising the United States, Canada, and most of Western Europe, formed in 1949 to counter the perceived threat from the Soviet Union

bilateral treaty

A treaty made between two nations

In August 2013, Secretary of State John Kerry made a forceful case for U.S. military strikes against Syria, in response to the Syrian government's use of chemical weapons during the civil war there. The United States also used diplomacy to seek international support for military action in Syria.

tries) reduces the threat to Russia, it also reduces the utility of NATO as a military alliance. The September 11 attack on the United States was the first time in its 50-plus-year history that Article 5 of the North Atlantic Treaty had to be invoked; it provides that an attack on one country is an attack on all the member countries. In fighting the war on terror, the Bush administration recognized that no matter how preponderant American power was, some aspects of its foreign policy could not be achieved without multilateral cooperation. On the other hand, the United States did not want to be constrained by its alliances. The global coalition initially forged after September 11 numbered over 170 countries. Not all joined the war effort in Afghanistan, but most if not all provided some form of support for some aspect of the war on terrorism, such as economic sanctions and intelligence. The war in Iraq, however, put the "coalition of the willing" to a test. The Bush administration was determined not to make its decision to go to war subject to the UN or NATO or any other international organization. The breadth of the U.S. coalition was deemed secondary to its being nonconstraining. As a result, other than the British government, no major power supported U.S. actions.

Military Force

The most visible instrument of foreign policy is, of course, military force. The United States has built the world's most imposing military, with army, navy, marine, and air force units stationed across the globe. The United States spends nearly as much on military might as the rest of the world combined (Figure 14.1). The famous Prussian military strategist Carl von Clausewitz

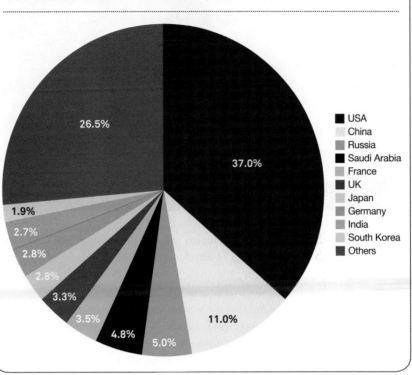

Figure 14.1

SHARES OF WORLD MILITARY EXPENDITURES BY TEN LARGEST SPENDERS, 2013

- 26.5%
- 37.0%
- 1.9%
- 2.7%
- 2.8%
- 2.8%
- 3.3%
- 3.5%
- 4.8%
- 5.0%
- 11.0%

- ■ USA
- □ China
- ■ Russia
- ■ Saudi Arabia
- ■ France
- ■ UK
- ■ Japan
- ■ Germany
- ■ India
- ■ South Korea
- ■ Others

NOTE: 2013 total military spending: $1.75 trillion
SOURCE: Stockholm International Peace Research Institute, "Trends in World Military Expenditure, 2013," http://books.sipri.org/files/FS/SIPRIFS1404.pdf (accessed 11/22/14).

called war "politics by other means." By this he meant that nations use force not simply to demonstrate their capacity for violence. Rather, force or the threat of force is a tool nations must sometimes use to achieve their foreign-policy goals. Military force may be needed to protect a nation's security interests and economic concerns. Ironically, force may also be needed to achieve humanitarian goals. For example, without international military protection, the Africans who took refuge in Darfur refugee camps would have been at the mercy of the violent Sudanese regime.

Though force is sometimes necessary, military force is generally seen as a last resort and avoided if possible because of a number of problems commonly associated with its use. First, the use of military force is extremely costly in both human and financial terms. In the past 50 years, tens of thousands of Americans have been killed and hundreds of billions of dollars spent in America's military operations. Before they employ military force to

achieve national goals, policy makers must be certain that achieving these goals is essential and that other means are unlikely to succeed.

Second, the use of military force is inherently fraught with risk. However carefully policy makers and generals plan for military operations, results can seldom be fully anticipated. Variables ranging from the weather to unexpected weapons and tactics deployed by opponents may upset the most careful calculations and turn military operations into costly disasters. Maneuvers that were expected to be quick and decisive may turn into long, drawn-out, expensive struggles. For example, American policy makers expected to defeat the Iraqi army quickly and easily in 2003—and they did. Policy makers did not anticipate, however, that American forces would still be struggling years later to defeat the insurgency that arose in the war's aftermath.

Finally, in a democracy, any government that chooses to address policy problems through military means is almost certain to encounter political difficulties. Generally speaking, the American public will support relatively short and decisive military engagements. If, however, a conflict drags on, producing casualties and expenses with no clear outcome, the public loses patience, and opposition politicians point to the government's lies and ineptitude. Korea, Vietnam, and Iraq are all examples of protracted conflicts whose domestic political repercussions included dissipating public support.

Thus, military force remains a major foreign policy tool, and the United States currently possesses a more powerful and effective set of military forces than any other nation. Nevertheless, even for the United States, the use of military force is fraught with risk and is not to be undertaken lightly.

Arbitration

The final foreign policy tool we consider is dispute arbitration. Arbitration means referring an international disagreement to a neutral third party for resolution. Arbitration is sometimes seen as a form of "soft power" as distinguished from military force, economic sanctions, and other coercive foreign policy instruments. The United States will occasionally turn to international tribunals to resolve disputes with other countries. For example, in February 2008, the U.S. government asked the International Court of Justice to resolve a long-standing dispute with Italy over American property confiscated by the Italian government more than 40 years ago. To take another example, in 1981 the United States and Iran established an arbitral tribunal to deal with claims arising from Iran's seizure of the U.S. embassy in Tehran in 1979.

More important, the United States relies heavily on the work of arbitral panels to maintain the flow of international trade on which America's economy depends. American firms would be reluctant to do business abroad if

International Court of Justice

The UN's chief judicial agency, located in The Hague, Netherlands. The ICJ settles legal disputes submitted by UN member states

they could not be certain that their property and contractual rights would be honored by other nations. Arbitration helps produce that certainty. Almost every international contract contains an arbitration clause requiring that disputes between the parties will be resolved not by foreign governments but by impartial arbitral panels accepted by both sides. By the terms of the New York Convention, virtually every nation in the world has agreed to accept and enforce arbitral verdicts. The United States has incorporated the terms of the New York Convention into federal law, and U.S. courts vigorously enforce arbitral judgments. The United States may not be happy with the outcome of every proceeding, but the arbitral system is essential to America's economic interests.

WHAT IS AMERICA'S ROLE IN THE WORLD?

The nineteenth-century British statesman Lord Palmerston famously said, "Nations have no permanent friends or allies; they only have permanent interests." Palmerston's comment illustrates what is sometimes known as the "realist" view of foreign policy. The realist school holds that foreign policies should be guided by the national interest—mainly security and economic interest—and that policy makers should steel themselves to the necessity of making decisions that might be viewed from the outside as cold and ruthless, as long as those decisions serve the nation's interests. Although many public officials have denounced such views in public—especially if they were running for office—many have become realists once in power. Every one of America's post–World War II presidents, liberals and conservatives, Democrats and Republicans alike, have been willing to order young Americans into battle and to visit death and destruction on the citizens of foreign states if they believed the national interest required it. As we saw in this chapter's introduction, the long and continuous history of these battles may belie their very justification: ensuring peace.

The harsh rationality of foreign policy often clashes with America's history and ideals. Our democratic and liberal traditions lead us to hope for a world in which ideals rather than naked interests govern foreign policy and in which our leaders pay heed to ideals. The ideals that Americans have historically espoused (though not always lived by) assert that our foreign policies should have a higher purpose than the pursuit of interest and that America is to use force only as a last resort. Since the realities of our foreign policy often clash with these historic ideals, our policy makers often struggle to explain their actions and avoid admitting to motivations that don't embody those ideals.

What should the United States' role be in world politics? American foreign policy is often controversial both within the United States and around the world. These Palestinian protesters objected to American policy toward Israel and the Palestinian territories.

"I have previously stated and I repeat now that the United States plans no military intervention in Cuba," said President John F. Kennedy in 1961 as he planned military action in Cuba. "As president, it is my duty to the American people to report that renewed hostile actions against United States ships on the high seas in the Gulf of Tonkin have today required me to order the military forces of the United States to take action in reply," said President Lyndon Johnson in 1964 referring to a fabricated incident used to justify expansion of American involvement in Vietnam. "We did not, I repeat, did not trade weapons or anything else [to Iran] for hostages, nor will we," said President Ronald Reagan in November 1986, four months before admitting that U.S. arms had been traded to Iran in exchange for Americans being held hostage there. "Simply stated, there is no doubt that Saddam Hussein now has weapons of mass destruction," said Vice President Dick Cheney in 2002. When it turned out that these weapons did not exist, Assistant Defense Secretary Paul Wolfowitz explained, "For bureaucratic reasons, we settled on one issue, weapons of mass destruction [as justification for invading Iraq], because it was the one reason everyone could agree on."[18] These false statements may hide discrepancies between our historic ideals and rationality, but they do not resolve them.

The ever-present conflicts between ideals and harsh realities manifested themselves again in 2009. As a candidate for the presidency, Barack Obama was praised for denouncing the Bush administration's treatment of enemy combatants. Obama was especially critical of the Guantánamo detention facility, where some alleged enemy combatants were incarcerated, and the creation of military tribunals, outside the regular court system, to hear their

cases. Once in office, however, Obama did not rush to close the Guantánamo facility—though he continued to plan for the facility's eventual closure. As for the tribunals, the Obama administration indicated in 2010 that it might employ them in some cases after all, not wishing to bring the most important enemy combatant cases to the regular courts. Ideals seemed to have given way to interests again. In 2011, the United States watched from the sidelines as a popular revolution ousted Egyptian president Hosni Mubarak. On the one hand, Americans sympathized with the democratic aspirations of the Egyptian people. On the other hand, Mubarak was a longtime and useful American ally. American policy makers seemed frozen by indecision as they watched events unfold and in 2011 scurried to mend fences with the new Egyptian government.

Must America always choose between its ideals and its interests? The Founders of the Republic believed that America would be different from other nations. They believed that its ideals would be its source of power, that its ideals would allow it to inspire and lead others as a "shining beacon." If, in the interest of national power and security, our political leaders always choose narrow interests over transcendent ideals, might they be robbing America of its true source of international power and global security?

For Further Reading

Selections highlighted in red are included in *Readings in American Politics: Analysis and Perspectives,* Third Edition.

Bacevich, Andrew. *The Limits of Power: The End of American Exceptionalism.* New York: Metropolitan Books, 2008.

Berman, Paul. *Terror and Liberalism.* New York: Norton, 2004.

Herring, George. *From Colony to Superpower.* New York: Oxford University Press, 2011.

Jentleson, Bruce. *American Foreign Policy—The Dynamics of Choice in the 21st Century.* 5th ed. New York: Norton, 2013.

Johnson, Chalmers. *The Sorrows of Empire.* New York: Holt, 2004.

Kagan, Robert. Dangerous Nation. New York: Knopf, 2006.

Maddow, Rachel. *Drift: The Unmooring of American Military Power.* New York: Crown, 2012.

Mandelbaum, Michael. *The Case for Goliath: How America Acts as the World's Government in the Twenty-First Century.* Washington, DC: PublicAffairs Press, 2005.

Mayer, Jane. *The Dark Side: The Inside Story of How the War on Terror Turned into a War on American Ideals.* New York: Doubleday, 2008.

Mead, Walter Russell. Special Providence: American Foreign Policy and How It Changed the World. New York: Routledge, 2002.

Reid, T. R. *The United States of Europe—The New Superpower and the End of American Supremacy.* New York: Penguin, 2004.

Appendix

The Declaration of Independence

In Congress, July 4, 1776

When in the course of human events, it becomes necessary for one people to dissolve the political bands which have connected them with another, and to assume among the Powers of the earth, the separate and equal station to which the Laws of Nature and of Nature's God entitle them, a decent respect to the opinions of mankind requires that they should declare the causes which impel them to the separation.

We hold these truths to be self-evident, that all men are created equal, that they are endowed by their Creator with certain unalienable rights, that among these are Life, Liberty, and the pursuit of Happiness. That to secure these rights, Governments are instituted among Men, deriving their just powers from the consent of the governed. That whenever any Form of Government becomes destructive of these ends, it is the Right of the People to alter or to abolish it, and to institute new Government, laying its foundation on such principles and organizing its powers in such form, as to them shall seem most likely to effect their Safety and Happiness. Prudence, indeed, will dictate that Governments long established should not be changed for light and transient causes; and accordingly all experience hath shown, that mankind are more disposed to suffer, while evils are sufferable, than to right themselves by abolishing the forms to which they are accustomed. But when a long train of abuses and usurpations, pursuing invariably the same Object evinces a design to reduce them under absolute Despotism, it is their right, it is their duty, to throw off such Government, and to provide new Guards for their future security.—Such has been the patient sufferance of these Colonies; and such is now the necessity which constrains them to alter their former Systems of Government. The history of the present King of Great Britain is a history of repeated injuries and usurpations, all having in direct object the establishment of an absolute Tyranny over these States. To prove this, let Facts be submitted to a candid world.

He has refused his Assent to Laws, the most wholesome and necessary for the public good.

He has forbidden his Governors to pass Laws of immediate and pressing importance, unless suspended in their operation till his Assent should be obtained; and when so suspended, he has utterly neglected to attend to them.

He has refused to pass other Laws for the accommodation of large districts of people, unless those people would relinquish the right of Representation in the Legislature, a right inestimable to them and formidable to tyrants only.

He has called together legislative bodies at places unusual, uncomfortable, and distant from the depository of their public Records, for the sole purpose of fatiguing them into compliance with his measures.

He has dissolved Representative Houses repeatedly, for opposing with manly firmness his invasions on the rights of the people.

He has refused for a long time, after such dissolutions, to cause others to be elected; whereby the Legislative powers, incapable of Annihilation, have returned to the People at large for their exercise; the State remaining in the mean time exposed to all dangers of invasion from without, and convulsions within.

He has endeavored to prevent the population of these States; for that purpose obstructing the Laws of Naturalization of Foreigners; refusing to pass others to encourage their migrations hither, and raising the conditions of new Appropriations of Lands.

He has obstructed the Administration of Justice, by refusing his Assent to Laws for establishing Judiciary powers.

He has made Judges dependent on his Will alone, for the tenure of their offices, and the amount and payment of their salaries.

He has erected a multitude of New Offices, and sent hither swarms of Officers to harass our People, and eat out their substance.

He has kept among us, in times of peace, Standing Armies without the Consent of our legislature.

He has affected to render the Military independent of and superior to the Civil Power.

He has combined with others to subject us to a jurisdiction foreign to our constitution, and unacknowledged by our laws; giving his Assent to their Acts of pretended Legislation:

For quartering large bodies of armed troops among us:

For protecting them, by a mock Trial, from Punishment for any Murders which they should commit on the Inhabitants of these States:

For cutting off our Trade with all parts of the world:

For imposing taxes on us without our Consent:

For depriving us in many cases, of the benefits of Trial by jury:

For transporting us beyond Seas to be tried for pretended offences:

For abolishing the free System of English Laws in a neighboring Province, establishing therein an Arbitrary government, and enlarging its Boundaries so as to render it at once an example and fit instrument for introducing the same absolute rule into these Colonies:

For taking away our Charters, abolishing our most valuable Laws, and altering fundamentally the Forms of our Governments:

For suspending our own Legislatures, and declaring themselves invested with Power to legislate for us in all cases whatsoever.

He has abdicated Government here, by declaring us out of his Protection and waging War against us.

He has plundered our seas, ravaged our Coasts, burnt our towns, and destroyed the lives of our people.

He is at this time transporting large armies of foreign mercenaries to compleat the works of death, desolation, and tyranny, already begun with circumstances

of Cruelty & perfidy scarcely paralleled in the most barbarous ages, and totally unworthy the Head of a civilized nation.

He has constrained our fellow Citizens taken Captive on the high Seas to bear Arms against their Country, to become the executioners of their friends and Brethren, or to fall themselves by their Hands.

He has excited domestic insurrections amongst us, and has endeavored to bring on the inhabitants of our frontiers, the merciless Indian Savages, whose known rule of warfare, is an undistinguished destruction of all ages, sexes, and conditions.

In every stage of these Oppressions We have Petitioned for Redress in the most humble terms: Our repeated Petitions have been answered only by repeated injury. A Prince, whose character is thus marked by every act which may define a Tyrant, is unfit to be the ruler of a free people.

Nor have We been wanting in attention to our British brethren. We have warned them from time to time of attempts by their legislature to extend an unwarrantable jurisdiction over us. We have reminded them of the circumstances of our emigration and settlement here. We have appealed to their native justice and magnanimity, and we have conjured them by the ties of our common kindred to disavow these usurpations, which, would inevitably interrupt our connections and correspondence. They too must have been deaf to the voice of justice and of consanguinity. We must, therefore, acquiesce in the necessity, which denounces our Separation, and hold them, as we hold the rest of mankind, Enemies in War, in Peace Friends.

WE, THEREFORE, the Representatives of the UNITED STATES OF AMERICA, in General Congress, Assembled, appealing to the Supreme Judge of the world for the rectitude of our intentions, do, in the Name, and by Authority of the good People of these Colonies, solemnly publish and declare, That these United Colonies are, and of Right ought to be FREE AND INDEPENDENT STATES; that they are Absolved from all Allegiance to the British Crown, and that all political connection between them and the State of Great Britain, is and ought to be totally dissolved; and that as Free and Independent States, they have full Power to levy War, conclude Peace, contract Alliances, establish Commerce, and to do all other Acts and Things which Independent States may of right do. And for the support of this Declaration, with a firm reliance on the Protection of Divine Providence, we mutually pledge to each other our Lives, our Fortunes, and our sacred Honor.

The foregoing Declaration was, by order of Congress, engrossed, and signed by the following members.

John Hancock

NEW HAMPSHIRE	MASSACHUSETTS BAY	RHODE ISLAND
Josiah Bartlett	Samuel Adams	Stephen Hopkins
William Whipple	John Adams	William Ellery
Matthew Thornton	Robert Treat Paine	
	Elbridge Gerry	

CONNECTICUT
Roger Sherman
Samuel Huntington
William Williams
Oliver Wolcott

NEW YORK
William Floyd
Philip Livingston
Francis Lewis
Lewis Morris

NEW JERSEY
Richard Stockton
John Witherspoon
Francis Hopkinson
John Hart
Abraham Clark

PENNSYLVANIA
Robert Morris
Benjamin Rush
Benjamin Franklin
John Morton
George Clymer
James Smith
George Taylor
James Wilson
George Ross

DELAWARE
Caesar Rodney
George Read
Thomas M'Kean

MARYLAND
Samuel Chase
William Paca
Thomas Stone
Charles Carroll,
of Carrollton

VIRGINIA
George Wythe
Richard Henry Lee
Thomas Jefferson
Benjamin Harrison
Thomas Nelson, Jr.
Francis Lightfoot Lee
Carter Braxton

NORTH CAROLINA
William Hooper
Joseph Hewes
John Penn

SOUTH CAROLINA
Edward Rutledge
Thomas Heyward, Jr.
Thomas Lynch, Jr.
Arthur Middleton

GEORGIA
Button Gwinnett
Lyman Hall
George Walton

Resolved, That copies of the Declaration be sent to the several assemblies, conventions, and committees, or councils of safety, and to the several commanding officers of the continental troops; that it be proclaimed in each of the United States, at the head of the army.

The Articles of Confederation

Agreed to by Congress November 15, 1777;
ratified and in force March 1, 1781

To all whom these Presents shall come, we the undersigned Delegates of the States affixed to our Names send greeting. Whereas the Delegates of the United States of America in Congress assembled did on the fifteenth day of November in the Year of our Lord One Thousand Seven Hundred and Seventy seven, and in the Second Year of the Independence of America agree to certain articles of Confederation and perpetual Union between the States of Newhampshire, Massachusetts-bay, Rhodeisland and Providence Plantations, Connecticut, New-York, New-Jersey, Pennsylvania, Delaware, Maryland, Virginia, North-Carolina, South-Carolina and Georgia in the Words following, viz. "Articles of Confederation and perpetual Union between the states of Newhampshire, Massachusetts-bay, Rhodeisland and Providence Plantations, Connecticut, New-York, New-Jersey, Pennsylvania, Delaware, Maryland, Virginia, North-Carolina, South-Carolina and Georgia.

Art. I. The Stile of this confederacy shall be "The United States of America."

Art. II. Each state retains its sovereignty, freedom and independence, and every Power, Jurisdiction and right, which is not by this confederation expressly delegated to the United States, in Congress assembled.

Art. III. The said states hereby severally enter into a firm league of friendship with each other, for their common defence, the security of their Liberties, and their mutual and general welfare, binding themselves to assist each other, against all force offered to, or attacks made upon them, or any of them, on account of religion, sovereignty, trade, or any other pretence whatever.

Art. IV. The better to secure and perpetuate mutual friendship and intercourse among the people of the different states in this union, the free inhabitants of each of these states, paupers, vagabonds and fugitives from Justice excepted, shall be entitled to all privileges and immunities of free citizens in the several states; and the people of each state shall have free ingress and regress to and from any other state, and shall enjoy therein all the privileges of trade and commerce, subject to the same duties, impositions and restrictions as the inhabitants thereof respectively, provided that such restriction shall not extend so far as to prevent the removal of property imported into any state, to any other state of which the Owner is an inhabitant; provided also that no imposition, duties or restriction shall be laid by any state, on the property of the united states, or either of them.

If any Person guilty of, or charged with treason, felony, or other high misdemeanor in any state, shall flee from Justice, and be found in any of the united states, he shall upon demand of the Governor or executive power, of the state

from which he fled, be delivered up and removed to the state having jurisdiction of his offence.

Full faith and credit shall be given in each of these states to the records, acts and judicial proceedings of the courts and magistrates of every other state.

Art. V. For the more convenient management of the general interests of the united states, delegates shall be annually appointed in such manner as the legislature of each state shall direct, to meet in Congress on the first Monday in November, in every year, with a power reserved to each state, to recall its delegates, or any of them, at any time within the year, and to send others in their stead, for the remainder of the Year.

No state shall be represented in Congress by less than two, nor by more than seven Members; and no person shall be capable of being a delegate for more than three years in any term of six years; nor shall any person, being a delegate, be capable of holding any office under the united states, for which he, or another for his benefit receives any salary, fees or emolument of any kind.

Each state shall maintain its own delegates in a meeting of the states, and while they act as members of the committee of the states.

In determining questions in the united states, in Congress assembled, each state shall have one vote.

Freedom of speech and debate in Congress shall not be impeached or questioned in any Court, or place out of Congress, and the members of congress shall be protected in their persons from arrests and imprisonments, during the time of their going to and from, and attendance on congress, except for treason, felony, or breach of the peace.

Art. VI. No state without the Consent of the united states in congress assembled, shall send any embassy to, or receive any embassy from, or enter into any conference, agreement, or alliance or treaty with any King, prince or state; nor shall any person holding any office or profit or trust under the united states, or any of them, accept of any present, emolument, office or title of any kind whatever from any king, prince or foreign state; nor shall the united states in congress assembled, or any of them, grant any title of nobility.

No two or more states shall enter into any treaty, confederation or alliance whatever between them, without the consent of the united states in congress assembled, specifying accurately the purposes for which the same is to be entered into, and how long it shall continue.

No state shall lay any imposts or duties, which may interfere with any stipulations in treaties, entered into by the united states in congress assembled, with any king, prince or state, in pursuance of any treaties already proposed by congress, to the courts of France and Spain.

No vessels of war shall be kept up in time of peace by any state, except such number only, as shall be deemed necessary by the united states in congress assembled, for the defence of such state, or its trade; nor shall any body of forces be kept up by any state, in time of peace, except such number only, as in the judgment of the united states, in congress assembled, shall be deemed requisite to garrison the forts necessary for the defence of such state; but every state shall always keep up a well regulated and disciplined militia, sufficiently armed and accoutred, and shall provide and constantly have ready for use, in public

stores, a due number of field pieces and tents, and a proper quantity of arms, ammunition and camp equipage.

No state shall engage in any war without the consent of the united states in congress assembled, unless such state be actually invaded by enemies, or shall have received certain advice of a resolution being formed by some nation of Indians to invade such state, and the danger is so imminent as not to admit of a delay, till the united states in congress asssembled can be consulted; nor shall any state grant commissions to any ships or vessels of war, nor letters of marque or reprisal, except it be after a declaration of war by the united states in congress assembled, and then only against the kingdom or state and the subjects thereof, against which war has been so declared, and under such regulations as shall be established by the united states in congress assembled, unless such state be infested by pirates; in which case vessels of war may be fitted out for that occasion, and kept so long as the danger shall continue, or until the united states in congress assembled shall determine otherwise.

Art. VII. When land-forces are raised by any state for the common defence, all officers of or under the rank of colonel, shall be appointed by the legislature of each state respectively by whom such forces shall be raised, or in such manner as such state shall direct, and all vacancies shall be filled up by the state which first made the appointment.

Art. VIII. All charges of war, and all other expences that shall be incurred for the common defence or general welfare, and allowed by the united states in congress assembled, shall be defrayed out of a common treasury, which shall be supplied by the several states, in proportion to the value of all land within each state, granted to or surveyed for any Person, as such land and the buildings and improvements thereon shall be estimated according to such mode as the united states in congress assembled, shall from time to time direct and appoint. The taxes for paying that proportion shall be laid and levied by the authority and direction of the legislatures of the several states within the time agreed upon by the united states in congress assembled.

Art. IX. The united states in congress assembled, shall have the sole and exclusive right and power of determining on peace and war, except in the cases mentioned in the sixth article—of sending and receiving ambassadors—entering into treaties and alliances, provided that no treaty of commerce shall be made whereby the legislative power of the respective states shall be restrained from imposing such imposts and duties on foreigners, as their own people are subjected to, or from prohibiting the exportation of any species of goods or commodities whatsoever—of establishing rules for deciding in all cases, what captures on land or water shall be legal, and in what manner prizes taken by land or naval forces in the service of the united states shall be divided or appropriated—of granting letters of marque and reprisal in times of peace—appointing courts for the trial of piracies and felonies committed on the high seas and establishing courts for receiving and determining finally appeals in all cases of captures, provided that no member of congress shall be appointed a judge of any of the said courts.

The united states in congress assembled shall also be the last resort on appeal in all disputes and differences now subsisting or that hereafter may arise between two or more states concerning boundary, jurisdiction or any other

cause whatever; which authority shall always be exercised in the manner following. Whenever the legislative or executive authority or lawful agent of any state in controversy with another shall present a petition to congress stating the matter in question and praying for a hearing, notice thereof shall be given by order of congress to the legislative or executive authority of the other state in controversy, and a day assigned for the appearance of the parties by their lawful agents, who shall then be directed to appoint by joint consent, commissioners or judges to constitute a court for hearing and determining the matter in question: but if they cannot agree, congress shall name three persons out of each of the united states, and from the list of such persons each party shall alternately strike out one, the petitioners beginning, until the number shall be reduced to thirteen; and from that number not less than seven, nor more than nine names as congress shall direct, shall in the presence of congress be drawn out by lot, and the persons whose names shall be so drawn or any five of them, shall be commissioners or judges, to hear and finally determine the controversy, so always as a major part of the judges who shall hear the cause shall agree in the determination: and if either party shall neglect to attend at the day appointed, without shewing reasons, which congress shall judge sufficient, or being present shall refuse to strike, the congress shall proceed to nominate three persons out of each state, and the secretary of congress shall strike in behalf of such party absent or refusing; and the judgment and sentence of the court to be appointed, in the manner before prescribed, shall be final and conclusive; and if any of the parties shall refuse to submit to the authority of such court, or to appear to defend their claim or cause, the court shall nevertheless proceed to pronounce sentence, or judgment, which shall in like manner be final and decisive, the judgment or sentence and other proceedings being in either case transmitted to congress, and lodged among the acts of congress for the security of the parties concerned: provided that every commissioner, before he sits in judgment, shall take an oath to be administered by one of the judges of the supreme or superior court of the state, where the cause shall be tried, "well and truly to hear and determine the matter in question, according to the best of his judgment, without favour, affection or hope of reward:" provided also that no state shall be deprived of territory for the benefit of the united states.

All controversies concerning the private right of soil claimed under different grants of two or more states, whose jurisdictions as they may respect such lands, and the states which passed such grants are adjusted, the said grants or either of them being at the same time claimed to have originated antecedent to such settlement of jurisdiction, shall on the petition of either party to the congress of the united states, be finally determined as near as may be in the same manner as is before prescribed for deciding disputes respecting territorial jurisdiction between different states.

The united states in congress assembled shall also have the sole and exclusive right and power of regulating the alloy and value of coin struck by their own authority, or by that of the respective states—fixing the standard of weights and measures throughout the united states—regulating the trade and managing all affairs with the Indians, not members of any of the states, provided that the legislative right of any state within its own limits be not infringed or violated—establishing

and regulating post-offices from one state to another, throughout all the united states, and exacting such postage on the papers passing thro' the same as may be requisite to defray the expences of the said office—appointing all officers of the land forces, in the service of the united states, except regimental officers—appointing all the officers of the united states—making rules for the government and regulation of the said land and naval forces, and directing their operations.

The united states in congress assembled shall have the authority to appoint a committee, to sit in the recess of congress, to be denominated "A Committee of the States," and to consist of one delegate from each state; and to appoint such other committees and civil officers as may be necessary for managing the general affairs of the united states under their direction—to appoint one of their number to preside, provided that no person be allowed to serve in the office of president more than one year in any term of three years; to ascertain the necessary sums of Money to be raised for the service of the united states, and to appropriate and apply the same for defraying the public expences—to borrow money, or emit bills on the credit of the united states, transmitting every half year to the respective states an account of the sums of money so borrowed or emitted,—to build and equip a navy—to agree upon the number of land forces, and to make requisitions from each state for its quota, in proportion to the number of white inhabitants in such state; which requisition shall be binding, and thereupon the legislature of each state shall appoint the regimental officers, raise the men and cloath, arm and equip them in a soldier like manner, at the expence of the united states, and the officers and men so cloathed, armed and equipped shall march to the place appointed, and within the time agreed on by the united states in congress assembled: But if the united states in congress assembled shall, on consideration of circumstances judge proper that any state should not raise men, or should raise a smaller number than its quota, and that any other state should raise a greater number of men than the quota thereof, such extra number shall be raised, officered, cloathed, armed and equipped in the same manner as the quota of such state, unless the legislature of such state shall judge that such extra number cannot be safely spared out of the same, in which case they shall raise, officer, cloath, arm and equip as many of such extra number as they judge can be safely spared. And the officers and men so cloathed, armed and equipped, shall march to the place appointed, and within the time agreed on by the united states in congress assembled.

The united states in congress assembled shall never engage in a war, nor grant letters of marque and reprisal in time of peace, nor enter into any treaties or alliances, nor coin money, nor regulate the value thereof, nor ascertain the sums and expences necessary for the defence and welfare of the united states, or any of them, nor emit bills, nor borrow money on the credit of the united states, nor appropriate money, nor agree upon the number of vessels of war, to be built or purchased, or the number of land or sea forces to be raised, nor appoint a commander in chief of the army or navy, unless nine states assent to the same: nor shall a question on any other point, except for adjourning from day to day be determined, unless by the votes of a majority of the united states in congress assembled.

The congress of the united states shall have power to adjourn to any time within the year, and to any place within the united states, so that no period of

adjournment be for a longer duration than the space of six Months, and shall publish the Journal of their proceedings monthly, except such parts thereof relating to treaties, alliances or military operations as in their judgment require secresy; and the yeas and nays of the delegates of each state on any question shall be entered on the Journal, when it is desired by any delegate; and the delegates of a state, or any of them, at his or their request shall be furnished with a transcript of the said Journal, except such parts as are above excepted to lay before the legislatures of the several states.

Art. X. The committee of the states, or any nine of them, shall be authorised to execute, in the recess of congress, such of the powers of congress as the united states in congress assembled, by the consent of nine states, shall from time to time think expedient to vest them with; provided that no power be delegated to the said committee, for the exercise of which, by the articles of confederation, the voice of nine states in the congress of the united states assembled is requisite.

Art. XI. Canada acceding to this confederation, and joining in the measures of the united states, shall be admitted into, and entitled to all the advantages of this union: but no other colony shall be admitted into the same, unless such admission be agreed to by nine states.

Art. XII. All bills of credit emitted, monies borrowed and debts contracted by, or under the authority of congress, before the assembling of the united states, in pursuance of the present confederation, shall be deemed and considered as a charge against the united states, for payment and satisfaction whereof the said united states and the public faith are hereby solemnly pledged.

Art. XIII. Every state shall abide by the determinations of the united states in congress assembled, on all questions which by this confederation are submitted to them. And the Articles of this confederation shall be inviolably observed by every state, and the union shall be perpetual; nor shall any alteration at any time hereafter be made in any of them; unless such alteration be agreed to in a congress of the united states, and be afterwards confirmed by the legislatures of every state.

AND WHEREAS it hath pleased the Great Governor of the World to incline the hearts of the legislatures we respectively represent in congress, to approve of, and to authorize us to ratify the said articles of confederation and perpetual union. KNOW YE that we the undersigned delegates, by virtue of the power and authority to us given for that purpose, do by these presents, in the name and in behalf of our respective constituents, fully and entirely ratify and confirm each and every of the said articles of confederation and perpetual union, and all and singular the matters and things therein contained: And we do further solemnly plight and engage the faith of our respective constituents, that they shall abide by the determination of the united states in congress assembled, on all questions, which by the said confederation are submitted to them. And that the articles thereof shall be inviolably observed by the states we respectively represent, and that the union shall be perpetual. In Witness whereof we have hereunto set our hands in Congress. Done at Philadelphia in the state of Pennsylvania the ninth Day of July in the Year of our Lord one Thousand seven Hundred and Seventy-eight and in the third year of the independence of America.

The Constitution of the United States of America

Annotated with references to *The Federalist Papers*

Federalist Paper
Number (Author)

[PREAMBLE]

We the People of the United States, in Order to form a more perfect Union, establish Justice, insure domestic Tranquility, provide for the common defence, promote the general Welfare, and secure the Blessings of Liberty to ourselves and our Posterity, do ordain and establish this Constitution for the United States of America.

84 (Hamilton)

ARTICLE I

Section 1

[LEGISLATIVE POWERS]

All legislative Powers herein granted shall be vested in a Congress of the United States, which shall consist of a Senate and House of Representatives.

10, 45 (Madison)

Section 2

[HOUSE OF REPRESENTATIVES, HOW CONSTITUTED, POWER OF IMPEACHMENT]

The House of Representatives shall be composed of Members chosen every second Year by the People of the several States, and the Electors in each State shall have the Qualifications requisite for Electors of the most numerous Branch of the State Legislature.

39, 45, 52–53, 57 (Madison)

No Person shall be a Representative who shall not have attained to the Age of twenty-five Years, and been seven Years a Citizen of the United States, and who shall not, when elected, be an inhabitant of that State in which he shall be chosen.

52 (Madison)

60 (Hamilton)

Representatives and *direct Taxes*[1] shall be apportioned among the several States which may be included within this Union, according to their respective Numbers, *which shall be determined by adding to the whole Number of free Persons, including those bound to Service for a Term of Years,* and excluding Indians not taxed, *three-fifths of all other Persons.*[2] The actual Enumeration shall be made within three Years after the first Meeting of the Congress of the United States, and within every subsequent Term of ten Years, in such Manner as they shall by Law direct. The Number of Representatives shall not exceed one for every thirty Thousand, but each State shall have at Least one Representative; *and until such enumeration shall be made, the State of New*

54, 58 (Madison)

55–56 (Madison)

---

1   Modified by Sixteenth Amendment.

2   Modified by Fourteenth Amendment.

Hampshire shall be entitled to chuse three, Massachusetts eight, Rhode-Island and Providence Plantations one, Connecticut five, New-York six, New Jersey four, Pennsylvania eight, Delaware one, Maryland six, Virginia ten, North Carolina five, South Carolina five, and Georgia three.[3]

When vacancies happen in the Representation from any State, the Executive Authority thereof shall issue Writs of Election to fill such Vacancies.

79 (Hamilton)

The House of Representatives shall chuse their Speaker and other Officers; and shall have the sole Power of Impeachment.

Section 3
[THE SENATE, HOW CONSTITUTED, IMPEACHMENT TRIALS]

39, 45 (Madison)
60 (Hamilton)

The Senate of the United States shall be composed of two Senators from each State, *chosen by the Legislature thereof,*[4] for six Years; and each Senator shall have one Vote.

62–63 (Madison)
59, 68 (Hamilton)

Immediately after they shall be assembled in Consequence of the first Election, they shall be divided as equally as may be into three Classes. The Seats of the Senators of the first Class shall be vacated at the Expiration of the second Year, of the second Class at the Expiration of the fourth Year, and of the third Class at the Expiration of the sixth Year, so that one third may be chosen every second Year: *and if vacancies happen by Resignation, or otherwise, during the Recess of the Legislature of any State, the Executive thereof may make temporary Appointments until the next Meeting of the Legislature, which shall then fill such Vacancies.*[5]

62 (Madison)
64 (Jay)

No person shall be a Senator who shall not have attained to the Age of thirty Years, and been nine Years a Citizen of the United States, and who shall not, when elected, be an Inhabitant of that State for which he shall be chosen.

The Vice-President of the United States shall be President of the Senate, but shall have no Vote, unless they be equally divided.

The Senate shall chuse their other Officers, and also a President pro tempore, in the Absence of the Vice-President, or when he shall exercise the Office of President of the United States.

39 (Madison)
65–67, 79 (Hamilton)

The Senate shall have the sole Power to try all Impeachments. When sitting for that Purpose, they shall be on Oath or Affirmation. When the President of the United States is tried, the Chief Justice shall preside: And no Person shall be convicted without the Concurrence of two-thirds of the Members present.

84 (Hamilton)

Judgment in Cases of Impeachment shall not extend further than to removal from Office, and disqualification to hold and enjoy any Office of honor, Trust or Profit under the United States: but the Party convicted shall nevertheless be liable and subject to Indictment, Trial, Judgment and Punishment, according to Law.

Section 4
[ELECTION OF SENATORS AND REPRESENTATIVES]

59–61 (Hamilton)

The Times, Places and Manner of holding Elections for Senators and Representatives, shall be prescribed in each State by the Legislature thereof; but the

---

3   Temporary provision.

4   Modified by Seventeenth Amendment.

5   Modified by Seventeenth Amendment.

Congress may at any time by Law make or alter such Regulations, except as to the Places of chusing Senators.

The Congress shall assemble at least once in every Year, and such Meeting shall be on the first Monday in December, unless they shall by Law appoint a different Day.[6]

Section 5
[QUORUM, JOURNALS, MEETINGS, ADJOURNMENTS]

Each House shall be the Judge of the Elections, Returns and Qualifications of its own Members, and a Majority of each shall constitute a Quorum to do Business; but a smaller Number may adjourn from day to day, and may be authorized to compel the Attendance of absent Members, in such Manner, and under the Penalties as each House may provide.

Each House may determine the Rules of its Proceedings, punish its Members for disorderly Behavior, and, with the Concurrence of two-thirds, expel a Member.

Each House shall keep a Journal of its Proceedings, and from time to time publish the same, excepting such Parts as may in their Judgment require Secrecy; and the Yeas and Nays of the Members of either House on any questions shall, at the Desire of one-fifth of the present, be entered on the Journal.

Neither House, during the Session of Congress, shall, without the Consent of the other, adjourn for more than three days, nor to any other Place than that in which the two Houses shall be sitting.

Section 6
[COMPENSATION, PRIVILEGES, DISABILITIES]

The Senators and Representatives shall receive a Compensation for their Services, to be ascertained by Law, and paid out of the Treasury of the United States. They shall in all Cases, except Treason, Felony and Breach of the Peace, be privileged from Arrest during their Attendance at the Session of their respective Houses, and in going to and returning from the same; and for any Speech or Debate in either House, they shall not be questioned in any other Place.

No Senator or Representative shall, during the time for which he was elected, be appointed to any civil Office under the authority of the United States, which shall have been created, or the Emoluments whereof shall have been encreased during such time; and no Person holding any Office under the United States, shall be a Member of either House during his Continuance in Office.

55 (Madison)
76 (Hamilton)

Section 7
[PROCEDURE IN PASSING BILLS AND RESOLUTIONS]

All Bills for raising Revenue shall originate in the House of Representatives; but the Senate may propose or concur with Amendments as on other Bills.

66 (Hamilton)

Every Bill which shall have passed the House of Representatives and the Senate, shall, before it become a Law, be presented to the President of the United States; if he approve he shall sign it, but if not he shall return it, with his Objections to that House in which it shall have originated, who shall enter the Objections at large on their Journal, and proceed to reconsider it. If after such Reconsideration

69, 73 (Hamilton)

---

6   Modified by Twentieth Amendment.

two-thirds of that House shall agree to pass the Bill, it shall be sent, together with the Objections, to the other House, by which it shall likewise be reconsidered, and if approved by two-thirds of that House it shall become a Law. But in all such Cases the Votes of both Houses shall be determined by Yeas and Nays, and the Names of the Persons voting for and against the Bill shall be entered on the Journal of each House respectively. If any Bill shall not be returned by the President within ten Days (Sundays excepted) after it shall have been presented to him, the Same shall be a Law, in like Manner as if he had signed it, unless the Congress by their Adjournment prevent its Return, in which Case it shall not be a Law.

69, 73 (Hamilton)

Every Order, Resolution, or Vote to which the Concurrence of the Senate and House of Representatives may be necessary (except on a question of Adjournment) shall be presented to the President of the United States; and before the Same shall take Effect, shall be approved by him, or being disapproved by him, shall be repassed by two-thirds of the Senate and House of Representatives, according to the Rules and Limitations prescribed in the Case of a Bill.

Section 8
[POWERS OF CONGRESS]

The Congress shall have Power

To lay and collect Taxes, Duties, Imposts and Excises, to pay the Debts and

30–36 (Hamilton)
41 (Madison)

provide for the common Defence and general Welfare of the United States; but all Duties, Imposts and excises shall be uniform throughout the United States;

To borrow Money on the Credit of the United States;

56 (Madison)
42, 45, 56
(Madison)

To regulate Commerce with foreign Nations, and among the several States, and with the Indian Tribes;

32 (Hamilton)

To establish an uniform Rule of Naturalization, and uniform Laws on the subject of Bankruptcies throughout the United States;

42 (Madison)

To coin Money, regulate the Value thereof, and of foreign Coin, and fix the Standard of Weights and Measures;

42 (Madison)

To provide for the Punishment of counterfeiting the Securities and current Coin of the United States;

42 (Madison)

To establish Post Offices and post Roads;

42 (Madison)
42, 43 (Madison)

To promote the Progress of Science and useful Arts, by securing for limited Times to Authors and Inventors the exclusive Right to their respective Writings and Discoveries;

81 (Hamilton)

To constitute Tribunals inferior to the supreme Court;

42 (Madison)

To define and Punish Piracies and Felonies committed on the high Seas, and Offences against the Law of Nations;

41 (Madison)

To declare War, grant Letters of Marque and Reprisal, and make Rules concerning Captures on Land and Water;

23, 24, 26 (Hamilton)

To raise and support Armies, but no Appropriation of Money to that Use shall be for a longer Term than two Years;

41 (Madison)

To provide and maintain a Navy;

To make Rules for the Government and Regulation of the land and naval forces;

29 (Hamilton)

To provide for calling for the Militia to execute the Laws of the Union, suppress Insurrections and repel Invasions;

To provide for organizing, arming, and disciplining, the Militia, and for governing such Part of them as may be employed in the Service of the United States, reserving to the States respectively, the Appointment of the Officers, and the Authority of training the Militia according to the discipline prescribed by Congress;

29 (Hamilton)
56 (Madison)

To exercise exclusive Legislation in all Cases whatsoever, over such District (not exceeding ten Miles square) as may, by Cession of particular States, and the Acceptance of Congress, become the Seat of the Government of the United States, and to exercise like Authority over all Places purchased by the Consent of the Legislature of the State in which the Same shall be, for the Erection of Forts, Magazines, Arsenals, dock-Yards, and other needful Buildings;—And

32 (Hamilton)
43 (Madison)

To make all Laws which shall be necessary and proper for carrying into Execution the foregoing Powers, and all other Powers vested by this Constitution in the Government of the United States, or in any Department or Officer thereof.

29, 33 (Hamilton)
44 (Madison)

Section 9
[SOME RESTRICTIONS ON FEDERAL POWER]

The Migration or Importation of such Persons as any of the States now existing shall think proper to admit, shall not be prohibited by the Congress prior to the Year one thousand eight hundred and eight, but a Tax or Duty may be imposed on such Importation, not exceeding ten dollars for each Person.[7]

42 (Madison)

The privilege of the Writ of *Habeas Corpus* shall not be suspended, unless when in Cases of Rebellion or Invasion the public Safety may require it.

83, 84 (Hamilton)

No Bill of Attainder or ex post facto Law shall be passed.

84 (Hamilton)

No Capitation, or other direct, Tax shall be laid, unless in Proportion to the Census or Enumeration herein before directed to be taken.[8]

No Tax or Duty shall be laid on Articles exported from any State.

No Preference shall be given by any Regulation of Commerce or Revenue to the Ports of one State over those of another; nor shall vessels bound to, or from, one State, be obliged to enter, clear, or pay Duties in another.

32 (Hamilton)

No Money shall be drawn from the Treasury, but in Consequence of Appropriations made by Law; and a regular Statement and Account of the Receipts and Expenditures of all public Money shall be published from time to time.

No Title of Nobility shall be granted by the United States: And no Person holding any Office of Profit or Trust under them, shall, without the Consent of the Congress, accept of any present, Emolument, Office or Title, of any kind whatever, from any King, Prince, or foreign State.

39 (Madison)
84 (Hamilton)

Section 10
[RESTRICTIONS UPON POWERS OF STATES]

No State shall enter into any Treaty, Alliance, or Confederation; grant Letters of Marque and Reprisal; coin Money; emit Bills of Credit; make any Thing but gold and silver Coin a Tender in Payment of Debts; pass any Bill of Attainder, ex post facto Law, or Law impairing the Obligation of Contracts, or grant any Title of Nobility.

33 (Hamilton)
44 (Madison)

---

7   Temporary provision.

8   Modified by Sixteenth Amendment.

No State shall, without the Consent of the Congress, lay any Imposts or Duties on Imports or Exports, except what may be absolutely necessary for executing its inspection Laws: and the net Produce of all Duties and Imposts, laid by any State on Imports or Exports, shall be for the Use of the Treasury of the United States; and all such Laws shall be subject to the Revision and Control of the Congress.

No State shall, without the Consent of Congress, lay any Duty of Tonnage, keep Troops, or Ships of War in time of Peace, enter into any Agreement or Compact with another State, or with a foreign Power, or engage in War, unless actually invaded, or in such imminent Danger as will not admit of Delay.

ARTICLE II

Section 1
[EXECUTIVE POWER, ELECTION, QUALIFICATIONS OF THE PRESIDENT]

The executive Power shall be vested in a President of the United States of America. *He shall hold his Office during the Term of four years and, together with the Vice-President, chosen for the same Term, be elected, as follows:*[9]

Each State shall appoint, in such Manner as the Legislature thereof may direct, a Number of Electors, equal to the whole Number of Senators and Representatives to which the State may be entitled in the Congress: but no Senator or Representative, or Person holding an Office of Trust or Profit under the United States, shall be appointed an Elector.

The electors shall meet in their respective States, and vote by ballot for two Persons, of whom one at least shall not be an Inhabitant of the same State with themselves. And they shall make a List of all the Persons voted for, and of the Number of Votes for each; which List they shall sign and certify, and transmit sealed to the Seat of the Government of the United States, directed to the President of the Senate. The President of the Senate shall, in the Presence of the Senate and House of Representatives, open all the Certificates, and the Votes shall then be counted. The Person having the greatest Number of Votes shall be the President, if such Number be a Majority of the whole Number of Electors appointed; and if there be more than one who have such Majority and have an equal Number of Votes, then the House of Representatives shall immediately chuse by Ballot one of them for President; and if no person have a Majority, then from the five highest on the List the said House shall in like Manner chuse the President. But in chusing the President, the Votes shall be taken by States, the Representation from each State having one Vote; A quorum for this Purpose shall consist of a Member or Members from two-thirds of the States, and a Majority of all the States shall be necessary to a Choice. In every Case, after the Choice of the President, the person having the greatest Number of Votes of the Electors shall be the Vice-President. But if there should remain two or more who have equal vote, the Senate shall chuse from them by Ballot the Vice-President.[10]

The Congress may determine the Time of chusing the Electors, and the Day on which they shall give their Votes; which Day shall be the same throughout the United States.

---

9 Number of terms limited to two by Twenty-Second Amendment.

10 Modified by Twelfth and Twentieth Amendments.

Margin references:

32 (Hamilton)
44 (Madison)

39 (Madison)
70, 71, 84 (Hamilton)
68, 69, 71, 77 (Hamilton)
39, 45 (Madison)

66 (Hamilton)

No Person except a natural born Citizen, or a Citizen of the United States, at the time of the Adoption of this Constitution, shall be eligible to the Office of President; neither shall any Person be eligible to that Office who shall not have attained to the Age of thirty-five Years, and been fourteen Years a Resident within the United States.

64 (Jay)

In Case of the Removal of the President from Office, or his Death, Resignation, or Inability to discharge the Powers and Duties of the said Office, the same shall devolve on the Vice-President, and the Congress may by Law provide for the Case of Removal, Death, Resignation, or Inability, both of the President and Vice-President, declaring what Officer shall then act as President, and such Officer shall act accordingly, until the Disability be removed, or a President shall be elected.

The President shall, at stated Times, receive for his Services, a Compensation, which shall neither be encreased nor diminished during the Period for which he shall have been elected, and he shall not receive within that Period any other Emolument from the United States, or any of them.

73, 79 (Hamilton)

Before he enter on the Execution of his Office, he shall take the following Oath or Affirmation:—"I do solemnly swear (or affirm) that I will faithfully execute the Office of President of the United States, and will to the best of my Ability, preserve, protect and defend the Constitution of the United States."

Section 2
[POWERS OF THE PRESIDENT]

The President shall be Commander in Chief of the Army and Navy of the United States, and of the Militia of the several States, when called into the actual Service of the United States; he may require the Opinion, in writing, of the principal Officer in each of the executive Departments, upon any Subject relating to the Duties of their respective Offices, and he shall have Power to grant Reprieves and Pardons for Offences against the United States, except in Cases of Impeachment.

69, 74 (Hamilton)

He shall have Power, by and with the Advice and Consent of the Senate, to make Treaties, provided two-thirds of the Senators present concur; and he shall nominate, and by and with the Advice and Consent of the Senate, shall appoint Ambassadors, other public Ministers and Consuls, Judges of the Supreme Court, and all other Officers of the United States, whose Appointments are not herein otherwise provided for, and which shall be established by Law: but the Congress may by Law vest the Appointment of such inferior Officers, as they think proper, in the President alone, in the Courts of Law, or in the Heads of Departments.

42 (Madison)
64 (Jay)
66, 69, 76, 77
(Hamilton)

The President shall have Power to fill up all Vacancies that may happen during the Recess of the Senate, by granting Commissions which shall expire at the End of their next Session.

67, 76
(Hamilton)

Section 3
[POWERS AND DUTIES OF THE PRESIDENT]

He shall from time to time give to the Congress Information of the State of the Union, and recommend to their Consideration such Measures as he shall judge necessary and expedient; he may, on extraordinary Occasions, convene both Houses, or either of them, and in Case of Disagreement between them, with Respect to the Time of Adjournment, he may adjourn them to such Time

69, 77, 78
(Hamilton)
42 (Madison)

as he shall think proper; he shall receive Ambassadors and other public Ministers; he shall take Care that the Laws be faithfully executed, and shall Commission all the Officers of the United States.

Section 4
[IMPEACHMENT]

39 (Madison)
69 (Hamilton)

The President, Vice-President and all civil Officers of the United States shall be removed from Office on Impeachment for, and Conviction of, Treason, Bribery, or other high Crimes and Misdemeanors.

ARTICLE III

Section 1
[JUDICIAL POWER, TENURE OF OFFICE]

65, 78, 79, 81, 82
(Hamilton)

The judicial Power of the United States, shall be vested in one supreme Court, and in such inferior Courts as the Congress may from time to time ordain and establish. The Judges, both of the supreme and inferior Courts, shall hold their Offices during good Behavior, and shall, at stated Times, receive for their Services, a Compensation, which shall not be diminished during their Continuance in Office.

Section 2
[JURISDICTION]

80 (Hamilton)

The judicial Power shall extend to all Cases, in Law and Equity, arising under this Constitution, the Laws of the United States, and Treaties made, or which shall be made, under their Authority;—to all Cases affecting Ambassadors, other public Ministers and Consuls;—to all Cases of admiralty and maritime Jurisdiction;—to Controversies to which the United States shall be a party;—to Controversies between two or more States;—*between a State and Citizens of another State;*—between Citizens of different States,—between Citizens of the same State claiming Lands under Grants of different States, *and between a State,* or the Citizens thereof, *and foreign States, Citizens or Subjects.*[11]

81 (Hamilton)

In all Cases affecting Ambassadors, other public Ministers and Consuls, and those in which a State shall be Party, the supreme Court shall have original Jurisdiction. In all the other Cases before mentioned, the supreme Court shall have appellate Jurisdiction, both as to Law and Fact, with such Exceptions, and under such Regulations as Congress shall make.

83, 84 (Hamilton)

The Trial of all Crimes, except in Cases of Impeachment, shall be by Jury; and such Trial shall be held in the State where the said Crimes shall have been committed; but when not committed within any State, the Trial shall be at such Place or Places as the Congress may by Law have directed.

---

11 Modified by Eleventh Amendment.

The Constitution of the United States of America

Section 3
[TREASON, PROOF, AND PUNISHMENT]

    Treason against the United States, shall consist only in levying War against them, or in adhering to their Enemies, giving them Aid and Comfort. No Person shall be convicted of Treason unless on the Testimony of two Witnesses to the same overt Act, or on Confession in open Court.

43 (Madison)
84 (Hamilton)

    The Congress shall have Power to declare the Punishment of Treason, but no Attainder of Treason shall work Corruption of Blood, or Forfeiture except during the Life of the Person attained.

43 (Madison)
84 (Hamilton)

ARTICLE IV

Section 1
[FAITH AND CREDIT AMONG STATES]

    Full Faith and Credit shall be given in each State to the public Acts, Records, and judicial Proceedings of every other State. And the Congress may by general Laws prescribe the Manner in which such Acts, Records and Proceedings shall be proved, and the Effect thereof.

42 (Madison)

Section 2
[PRIVILEGES AND IMMUNITIES, FUGITIVES]

    The Citizens of each State shall be entitled to all Privileges and Immunities of Citizens in the several States.

80 (Hamilton)

    A person charged in any State with Treason, Felony or other Crime, who shall flee from Justice, and be found in another State, shall on Demand of the executive Authority of the State from which he fled, be delivered up to be removed to the State having Jurisdiction of the Crime.

    No person held to Service or Labour in one State, under the Laws thereof, escaping into another, shall, in Consequence of any Law or Regulation therein, be discharged from such Service or Labour, but shall be delivered up on Claim of the Party to whom such Service or Labour may be due.[12]

Section 3
[ADMISSION OF NEW STATES]

    New States may be admitted by the Congress into this Union; but no new State shall be formed or erected within the Jurisdiction of any other State; nor any State be formed by the Junction of two or more States, or Parts of States, without the Consent of the Legislatures of the States concerned as well as of the Congress.

43 (Madison)

    The Congress shall have Power to dispose of and make all needful Rules and Regulations respecting the Territory or other Property belonging to the United States; and nothing in this Constitution shall be so construed as to Prejudice any Claims of the United States, or of any particular State.

43 (Madison)

---

12 Repealed by Thirteenth Amendment.

Section 4
[GUARANTEE OF REPUBLICAN GOVERNMENT]

39, 43
(Madison)

The United States shall guarantee to every State in this Union a Republican Form of Government, and shall protect each of them against Invasion; and on Application of the Legislature, or of the Executive (when the Legislature cannot be convened) against domestic Violence.

ARTICLE V
[AMENDMENT OF THE CONSTITUTION]

39, 43 (Madison)
85 (Hamilton)

The Congress, whenever two-thirds of both Houses shall deem it necessary, shall propose Amendments to this Constitution, or, on the Application of the Legislatures of two-thirds of the several States, shall call a Convention for proposing Amendments, which, in either Case, shall be valid to all Intents and Purposes, as Part of this Constitution, when ratified by the Legislatures of three-fourths of the several States, or by Conventions in three-fourths thereof, as the one or the other Mode of Ratification may be proposed by the Congress; *Provided that no Amendment which may be made prior to the Year One thousand eight hundred and eight shall in any Manner affect the first and fourth Clauses in the Ninth Section of the first Article;*[13] and that no State, without its Consent, shall be deprived of its equal Suffrage in the Senate.

ARTICLE VI
[DEBTS, SUPREMACY, OATH]

43 (Madison)

All Debts contracted and Engagements entered into, before the Adoption of this Constitution, shall be as valid against the United States under this Constitution, as under the Confederation.

27, 33 (Hamilton)
39, 44 (Madison)

This Constitution, and the Laws of the United States which shall be made in Pursuance thereof; and all Treaties made, or which shall be made, under the Authority of the United States, shall be the supreme Law of the Land; and the Judges in every State shall be bound thereby, any Thing in the Constitution or Laws of any State to the Contrary notwithstanding.

27 (Hamilton)
44 (Madison)

The Senators and Representatives before mentioned, and the Members of the several State Legislatures, and all executive and judicial Officers, both of the United States and of the several States, shall be bound by Oath or Affirmation, to support this Constitution; but no religious Test shall be required as a Qualification to any Office or public Trust under the United States.

ARTICLE VII
[RATIFICATION AND ESTABLISHMENT]

39, 40, 43
(Madison)

The Ratification of the Conventions of nine States, shall be sufficient for the Establishment of this Constitution between the States so ratifying the Same.[14]

---

13 Temporary provision.

14 The Constitution was submitted on September 17, 1787, by the Constitutional Convention, was ratified by the conventions of several states at various dates up to May 29, 1790, and became effective on March 4, 1789.

Done in Convention by the Unanimous Consent of the States present the Seventeenth Day of September in the Year of our Lord one thousand seven hundred and Eighty seven and of the Independence of the United States of America the Twelfth. *In Witness* whereof We have hereunto subscribed our Names,

G:^{0} WASHINGTON—
Presidt, and Deputy
from Virginia

NEW HAMPSHIRE
John Langdon
Nicholas Gilman

MASSACHUSETTS
Nathaniel Gorham
Rufus King

CONNECTICUT
Wm Saml Johnson
Roger Sherman

NEW YORK
Alexander Hamilton

NEW JERSEY
Wil: Livingston
David Brearley
Wm Paterson
Jona: Dayton

PENNSYLVANIA
B Franklin
Thomas Mifflin
Robt Morris
Geo. Clymer
Thos. FitzSimons
Jared Ingersoll
James Wilson
Gouv Morris

DELAWARE
Geo Read
Gunning Bedfor Jun
John Dickinson
Richard Bassett
Jaco: Broom

MARYLAND
James McHenry
Dan of St Thos Jenifer
Danl Carroll

VIRGINIA
John Blair—
James Madison Jr.

NORTH CAROLINA
Wm Blount
Richd Dobbs Spaight
Hu Williamson

SOUTH CAROLINA
J. Rutledge
Charles Cotesworth Pinckney
Charles Pinckney
Pierce Butler

GEORGIA
William Few
Abr Baldwin

Amendments to the Constitution

Proposed by Congress and Ratified by the Legislatures of the Several States, Pursuant to Article V of the Original Constitution

Amendments I–X, known as the Bill of Rights, were proposed by Congress on September 25, 1789, and ratified on December 15, 1791. *The Federalist Papers* comments, mainly in opposition to a Bill of Rights, can be found in number 84 (Hamilton).

AMENDMENT I
[FREEDOM OF RELIGION, OF SPEECH, AND OF THE PRESS]

Congress shall make no law respecting an establishment of religion, or prohibiting the free exercise thereof; or abridging the freedom of speech, or of the press; or the right of the people peaceably to assemble, and to petition the Government for a redress of grievances.

AMENDMENT II
[RIGHT TO KEEP AND BEAR ARMS]

A well regulated Militia, being necessary to the security of a free State, the right of the people to keep and bear Arms, shall not be infringed.

AMENDMENT III
[QUARTERING OF SOLDIERS]

No Soldier shall, in time of peace be quartered in any house, without the consent of the Owner, nor in time of war, but in a manner to be prescribed by law.

AMENDMENT IV
[SECURITY FROM UNWARRANTABLE SEARCH AND SEIZURE]

The right of the people to be secure in their persons, houses, papers, and effects, against unreasonable searches and seizures, shall not be violated, and no Warrants shall issue, but upon probable cause, supported by Oath or affirmation, and particularly describing the place to be searched, and the persons or things to be seized.

AMENDMENT V
[RIGHTS OF ACCUSED PERSONS IN CRIMINAL PROCEEDINGS]

No person shall be held to answer for a capital, or otherwise infamous crime, unless on a presentment or indictment of a Grand Jury, except in cases arising in the land or naval forces, or in the Militia, when in actual service in time of

War or in public danger; nor shall any person be subject for the same offence to be twice put in jeopardy of life or limb; nor shall be compelled in any Criminal Case to be a witness against himself, nor be deprived of life, liberty, or property, without due process of law; nor shall private property be taken for public use, without just compensation.

AMENDMENT VI
[RIGHT TO SPEEDY TRIAL, WITNESSES, ETC.]

In all criminal prosecutions, the accused shall enjoy the right to a speedy and public trial, by an impartial jury of the State and district wherein the crime shall have been committed, which district shall have been previously ascertained by law, and to be informed of the nature and cause of the accusation; to be confronted with the witnesses against him; to have compulsory process for obtaining Witnesses in his favor, and to have the Assistance of Counsel for his defence.

AMENDMENT VII
[TRIAL BY JURY IN CIVIL CASES]

In suits at common law, where the value in controversy shall exceed twenty dollars, the right of trial by jury shall be preserved, and no fact tried by a jury shall be otherwise re-examined in any Court of the United States, than according to the rules of the common law.

AMENDMENT VIII
[BAILS, FINES, PUNISHMENTS]

Excessive bail shall not be required, nor excessive fines imposed, nor cruel and unusual punishments inflicted.

AMENDMENT IX
[RESERVATION OF RIGHTS OF PEOPLE]

The enumeration in the Constitution, of certain rights, shall not be construed to deny or disparage others retained by the people.

AMENDMENT X
[POWERS RESERVED TO STATES OR PEOPLE]

The powers not delegated to the United States by the Constitution, nor prohibited by it to the States, are reserved to the States respectively, or to the people.

AMENDMENT XI
[Proposed by Congress on March 4, 1794; declared ratified on January 8, 1798]
[RESTRICTION OF JUDICIAL POWER]

The Judicial power of the United States shall not be construed to extend to any suit in law or equity, commenced or prosecuted against one of the United States by Citizens of another State, or by Citizens or Subjects of any Foreign State.

AMENDMENT XII

[Proposed by Congress on December 9, 1803; declared ratified on September 25, 1804.]

[ELECTION OF PRESIDENT AND VICE-PRESIDENT]

The Electors shall meet in their respective states, and vote by ballot for President and Vice-President, one of whom, at least, shall not be an inhabitant of the same state with themselves; they shall name in their ballots the person voted for as President, and in distinct ballots the person voted for as Vice-President, and they shall make distinct lists of all persons voted for as President, and of all persons voted for as Vice-President, and of the number of votes for each, which lists they shall sign and certify, and transmit sealed to the seat of the government of the United States, directed to the President of the Senate;—The President of the Senate shall, in presence of the Senate and House of Representatives, open all the certificates and the votes shall then be counted;—The person having the greatest number of votes for President, shall be the President, if such number be a majority of the whole number of Electors appointed; and if no person have such majority, then from the persons having the highest numbers not exceeding three on the list of those voted for as President, the House of Representatives shall choose immediately, by ballot, the President. But in choosing the President, the votes shall be taken by states, the representation from each state having one vote; a quorum for this purpose shall consist of a member or members from two-thirds of the states, and a majority of all states shall be necessary to a choice. And if the House of Representatives shall not choose a President whenever the right of choice shall devolve upon them, before the fourth day of March next following, then the Vice-President, shall act as President, as in the case of the death or other constitutional disability of the President. The person having the greatest number of votes as Vice-President, shall be the Vice-President, if such a number be a majority of the whole number of Electors appointed, and if no person have a majority, then from the two highest numbers on the list, the Senate shall choose the Vice-President; a quorum for the purpose shall consist of two-thirds of the whole number of Senators, and a majority of the whole number shall be necessary to a choice. But no person constitutionally ineligible to the office of President shall be eligible to that of Vice-President of the United States.

AMENDMENT XIII

[Proposed by Congress on January 31, 1865; declared ratified on December 18, 1865]

Section 1

[ABOLITION OF SLAVERY]

Neither slavery nor involuntary servitude, except as a punishment for crime whereof the party shall have been duly convicted, shall exist within the United States, or any place subject to their jurisdiction.

Section 2

[POWER TO ENFORCE THIS ARTICLE]

Congress shall have power to enforce this article by appropriate legislation.

AMENDMENT XIV

[Proposed by Congress on June 13, 1866; declared ratified on July 28, 1868]

Section 1

[CITIZENSHIP RIGHTS NOT TO BE ABRIDGED BY STATES]

All persons born or naturalized in the United States, and subject to the jurisdiction thereof, are citizens of the United States and of the State wherein they reside. No state shall make or enforce any law which shall abridge the privileges or immunities of citizens of the United States; nor shall any State deprive any person of life, liberty, or property, without due process of law; nor deny to any person within its jurisdiction the equal protection of the laws.

Section 2

[APPORTIONMENT OF REPRESENTATIVES IN CONGRESS]

Representatives shall be apportioned among the several States according to their respective numbers, counting the whole number of persons in each State, excluding Indians not taxed. But when the right to vote at any election for the choice of electors for President and Vice-President of the United States, Representatives in Congress, the Executive and Judicial officers of a State, or the members of the Legislature thereof, is denied to any of the male inhabitants of such State, being twenty-one years of age, and citizens of the United States, or in any way abridged, except for participation in rebellion, or other crime, the basis of representation therein shall be reduced in the proportion which the number of such male citizens shall bear to the whole number of male citizens twenty-one years of age in such State.

Section 3

[PERSONS DISQUALIFIED FROM HOLDING OFFICE]

No person shall be a Senator or Representative in Congress, or elector of President and Vice-President, or hold any office, civil or military, under the United States, or under any State, who, having previously taken an oath, as a member of Congress, or as an officer of the United States, or as a member of any State legislature, or as an executive or judicial officer of any State, to support the Constitution of the United States, shall have engaged in insurrection or rebellion against the same, or given aid or comfort to the enemies thereof. But Congress may by a vote of two-thirds of each House, remove such disability.

Section 4

[WHAT PUBLIC DEBTS ARE VALID]

The validity of the public debt of the United States, authorized by law, including debts incurred for payment of pensions and bounties for services in suppressing insurrection or rebellion, shall not be questioned. But neither the United States nor any State shall assume or pay any debt or obligation incurred

in aid of insurrection or rebellion against the United States, or any claim for the loss or emancipation of any slave; but all such debts, obligations and claims shall be held illegal and void.

Section 5
[POWER TO ENFORCE THIS ARTICLE]

The Congress shall have power to enforce, by appropriate legislation, the provisions of this article.

AMENDMENT XV
[Proposed by Congress on February 26, 1869; declared ratified on March 30, 1870]

Section 1
[NEGRO SUFFRAGE]

The right of citizens of the United States to vote shall not be denied or abridged by the United States or by any State on account of race, color, or previous condition of servitude.

Section 2
[POWER TO ENFORCE THIS ARTICLE]

The Congress shall have power to enforce this article by appropriate legislation.

AMENDMENT XVI
[Proposed by Congress on July 12, 1909; declared ratified on February 25, 1913]
[AUTHORIZING INCOME TAXES]

The Congress shall have power to lay and collect taxes on incomes, from whatever source derived, without apportionment among the several States, and without regard to any census or enumeration.

AMENDMENT XVII
[Proposed by Congress on May 13, 1912; declared ratified on May 31, 1913]
[POPULAR ELECTION OF SENATORS]

The Senate of the United States shall be composed of two Senators from each State, elected by the people thereof, for six years; and each Senator shall have one vote. The electors in each State shall have the qualifications requisite for electors of the most numerous branch of the State Legislature.

When vacancies happen in the representation of any State in the Senate, the executive authority of such State shall issue writs of election to fill such vacancies: Provided, That the Legislature of any State may empower the executive thereof to make temporary appointment until the people fill the vacancies by election as the Legislature may direct.

This amendment shall not be so construed as to affect the election or term of any Senator chosen before it becomes valid as part of the Constitution.

AMENDMENT XVIII

[Proposed by Congress December 18, 1917; declared ratified on January 29, 1919]

Section 1
[NATIONAL LIQUOR PROHIBITION]

After one year from the ratification of this article the manufacture, sale, or transportation of intoxicating liquors within, the importation thereof into, or the exportation thereof from the United States and all territory subject to the jurisdiction thereof for beverage purposes is hereby prohibited.

Section 2
[POWER TO ENFORCE THIS ARTICLE]

The Congress and the several states shall have concurrent power to enforce this article by appropriate legislation.

Section 3
[RATIFICATION WITHIN SEVEN YEARS]

This article shall be inoperative unless it shall have been ratified as an amendment to the Constitution by the legislatures of the several states, as provided in the Constitution, within seven years from the date of the submission hereof to the states by the Congress.[15]

AMENDMENT XIX

[Proposed by Congress on June 4, 1919; declared ratified on August 26, 1920]
[WOMAN SUFFRAGE]

The right of the citizens of the United States to vote shall not be denied or abridged by the United States or by any state on account of sex.

Congress shall have power to enforce this article by appropriate legislation.

AMENDMENT XX

[Proposed by Congress on March 2, 1932; declared ratified on February 6, 1933]

Section 1
[TERMS OF OFFICE]

The terms of the President and Vice-President shall end at noon on the 20th day of January, and the terms of the Senators and Representatives at noon on the 3rd day of January, of the years in which such terms would have ended if this article had not been ratified; and the terms of their successors shall then begin.

Section 2
[TIME OF CONVENING CONGRESS]

The Congress shall assemble at least once in every year, and such meeting shall begin at noon on the 3rd day of January, unless they shall by law appoint a different day.

---

15 Repealed by Twenty-First Amendment.

Section 3

[DEATH OF PRESIDENT-ELECT]

If, at the time fixed for the beginning of the term of the President, the President-elect shall have died, the Vice-President-elect shall become President. If a President shall not have been chosen before the time fixed for the beginning of his term, or if the President-elect shall have failed to qualify, then the Vice-President-elect shall act as President until a President shall have qualified; and the Congress may by law provide for the case wherein neither a President-elect nor a Vice-President-elect shall have qualified, declaring who shall then act as President, or the manner in which one who is to act shall be selected, and such person shall act accordingly until a President or Vice President shall have qualified.

Section 4

[ELECTION OF THE PRESIDENT]

The Congress may by law provide for the case of the death of any of the persons from whom the House of Representatives may choose a President whenever the right of choice shall have devolved upon them, and for the case of the death of any of the persons from whom the Senate may choose a Vice-President whenever the right of choice shall have devolved upon them.

Section 5

[AMENDMENT TAKES EFFECT]

Sections 1 and 2 shall take effect on the 15th day of October following ratification of this article.

Section 6

[RATIFICATION WITHIN SEVEN YEARS]

This article shall be inoperative unless it shall have been ratified as an amendment to the Constitution by the legislatures of three-fourths of the several States within seven years from the date of its submission.

AMENDMENT XXI

[Proposed by Congress on February 20, 1933; declared ratified on December 5, 1933]

Section 1

[NATIONAL LIQUOR PROHIBITION REPEALED]

The eighteenth article of amendment to the Constitution of the United States is hereby repealed.

Section 2

[TRANSPORTATION OF LIQUOR INTO "DRY" STATES]

The transportation or importation into any State, Territory, or Possession of the United States for delivery or use therein of intoxicating liquors, in violation of the laws thereof, is hereby prohibited.

Section 3
[RATIFICATION WITHIN SEVEN YEARS]

This article shall be inoperative unless it shall have been ratified as an amendment to the Constitution by conventions in the several States, as provided in the Constitution, within seven years from the date of the submission hereof to the States by the Congress.

AMENDMENT XXII
[Proposed by Congress on March 21, 1947; declared ratified on February 26, 1951]

Section 1
[TENURE OF PRESIDENT LIMITED]

No person shall be elected to the office of President more than twice, and no person who has held the office of President or acted as President for more than two years of a term to which some other person was elected President shall be elected to the Office of the President more than once. But this Article shall not apply to any person holding the office of President when this Article was proposed by the Congress, and shall not prevent any person who may be holding the office of President, or acting as President, during the term within which this Article becomes operative from holding the office of President or acting as President during the remainder of such term.

Section 2
[RATIFICATION WITHIN SEVEN YEARS]

This Article shall be inoperative unless it shall have been ratified as an amendment to the Constitution by the legislatures of three-fourths of the several states within seven years from the date of its submission to the States by the Congress.

AMENDMENT XXIII
[Proposed by Congress on June 21, 1960; declared ratified on March 29, 1961]

Section 1
[ELECTORAL COLLEGE VOTES FOR THE DISTRICT OF COLUMBIA]

The District constituting the seat of Government of the United States shall appoint in such manner as the Congress may direct:

A number of electors of President and Vice-President equal to the whole number of Senators and Representatives in Congress to which the District would be entitled if it were a State, but in no event more than the least populous State; they shall be in addition to those appointed by the States, but they shall be considered, for the purposes of the election of President and Vice-President, to be electors appointed by a State; and they shall meet in the District and perform such duties as provided by the twelfth article of amendment.

Section 2
[POWER TO ENFORCE THIS ARTICLE]

The Congress shall have power to enforce this article by appropriate legislation.

AMENDMENT XXIV

[Proposed by Congress on August 27, 1963; declared ratified on January 23, 1964]

Section 1
[ANTI-POLL TAX]

The right of citizens of the United States to vote in any primary or other election for President or Vice-President, for electors for President or Vice-President, or for Senator or Representative of Congress, shall not be denied or abridged by the United States or any State by reasons of failure to pay any poll tax or other tax.

Section 2
[POWER TO ENFORCE THIS ARTICLE]

The Congress shall have power to enforce this article by appropriate legislation.

AMENDMENT XXV

[Proposed by Congress on July 7, 1965; declared ratified on February 10, 1967]

Section 1
[VICE-PRESIDENT TO BECOME PRESIDENT]

In case of the removal of the President from office or his death or resignation, the Vice-President shall become President.

Section 2
[CHOICE OF A NEW VICE-PRESIDENT]

Whenever there is a vacancy in the office of the Vice-President, the President shall nominate a Vice-President who shall take the office upon confirmation by a majority vote of both houses of Congress.

Section 3
[PRESIDENT MAY DECLARE OWN DISABILITY]

Whenever the President transmits to the President pro tempore of the Senate and the Speaker of the House of Representatives his written declaration that he is unable to discharge the powers and duties of his office, and until he transmits to them a written declaration to the contrary, such powers and duties shall be discharged by the Vice-President as Acting President.

Section 4
[ALTERNATE PROCEDURES TO DECLARE AND TO END PRESIDENTIAL DISABILITY]

Whenever the Vice-President and a majority of either the principal officers of the executive departments, or of such other body as Congress may by law provide, transmit to the President pro tempore of the Senate and the Speaker of the House of Representatives their written declaration that the President is unable to discharge the powers and duties of his office, the Vice-President shall immediately assume the powers and duties of the office as Acting President.

Thereafter, when the President transmits to the President pro tempore of the Senate and the Speaker of the House of Representatives his written declaration that no inability exists, he shall resume the powers and duties of his office unless the Vice-President and a majority of either the principal officers of the executive departments, or of such other body as Congress may by law provide, transmit within four days to the President pro tempore of the Senate and the Speaker of the House of Representatives their written declaration that the President is unable to discharge the powers and duties of his office. Thereupon Congress shall decide the issue, assembling within 48 hours for that purpose if not in session. If the Congress, within 21 days after receipt of the latter written declaration, or, if Congress is not in session, within 21 days after Congress is required to assemble, determines by two-thirds vote of both houses that the President is unable to discharge the powers and duties of his office, the Vice-President shall continue to discharge the same as Acting President; otherwise, the President shall resume the powers and duties of his office.

AMENDMENT XXVI
[Proposed by Congress on March 23, 1971; declared ratified on June 30, 1971]

Section 1
[EIGHTEEN-YEAR-OLD VOTE]

The right of citizens of the United States, who are eighteen years of age or older, to vote shall not be denied or abridged by the United States or by any State on account of age.

Section 2
[POWER TO ENFORCE THIS ARTICLE]

The Congress shall have power to enforce this article by appropriate legislation.

AMENDMENT XXVII
[Proposed by Congress on September 25, 1789; ratified on May 7, 1992]

No law varying the compensation for the services of the Senators and Representatives shall take effect until an election of Representatives shall have intervened.

Federalist Papers

NO. 10: MADISON

Among the numerous advantages promised by a well-constructed Union, none deserves to be more accurately developed than its tendency to break and control the violence of faction. The friend of popular governments never finds himself so much alarmed for their character and fate as when he contemplates their propensity to this dangerous vice. He will not fail, therefore, to set a due value on any plan which, without violating the principles to which he is attached, provides a proper cure for it. The instability, injustice, and confusion introduced into the public councils have, in truth, been the mortal diseases under which popular governments have everywhere perished, as they continue to be the favorite and fruitful topics from which the adversaries to liberty derive their most specious declamations. The valuable improvements made by the American constitutions on the popular models, both ancient and modern, cannot certainly be too much admired; but it would be an unwarrantable partiality to contend that they have as effectually obviated the danger on this side, as was wished and expected. Complaints are everywhere heard from our most considerate and virtuous citizens, equally the friends of public and private faith and of public and personal liberty, that our governments are too unstable, that the public good is disregarded in the conflicts of rival parties, and that measures are too often decided, not according to the rules of justice and the rights of the minor party, but by the superior force of an interested and overbearing majority. However anxiously we may wish that these complaints had no foundation, the evidence of known facts will not permit us to deny that they are in some degree true. It will be found, indeed, on a candid review of our situation, that some of the distresses under which we labor have been erroneously charged on the operation of our governments; but it will be found, at the same time, that other causes will not alone account for many of our heaviest misfortunes; and, particularly, for that prevailing and increasing distrust of public engagements and alarm for private rights which are echoed from one end of the continent to the other. These must be chiefly, if not wholly, effects of the unsteadiness and injustice with which a factious spirit has tainted our public administration.

By a faction I understand a number of citizens, whether amounting to a majority or minority of the whole, who are united and actuated by some common impulse of passion, or of interest, adverse to the rights of other citizens, or to the permanent and aggregate interests of the community.

There are two methods of curing the mischiefs of faction: the one, by removing its causes; the other, by controlling its effects.

There are again two methods of removing the causes of faction: the one, by destroying the liberty which is essential to its existence; the other, by giving to every citizen the same opinions, the same passions, and the same interests.

It could never be more truly said than of the first remedy that it was worse than the disease. Liberty is to faction what air is to fire, an aliment without which it instantly expires. But it could not be a less folly to abolish liberty, which is essential to political life, because it nourishes faction than it would be to wish the annihilation of air, which is essential to animal life, because it imparts to fire its destructive agency.

The second expedient is as impracticable as the first would be unwise. As long as the reason of man continues fallible, and he is at liberty to exercise it, different opinions will be formed. As long as the connection subsists between his reason and his self-love, his opinions and his passions will have a reciprocal influence on each other; and the former will be objects to which the latter will attach themselves. The diversity in the faculties of men, from which the rights of property originate, is not less an insuperable obstacle to a uniformity of interests. The protection of these faculties is the first object of government. From the protection of different and unequal faculties of acquiring property, the possession of different degrees and kinds of property immediately results; and from the influence of these on the sentiments and views of the respective proprietors ensues a division of the society into different interests and parties.

The latent causes of faction are thus sown in the nature of man; and we see them everywhere brought into different degrees of activity, according to the different circumstances of civil society. A zeal for different opinions concerning religion, concerning government, and many other points, as well of speculation as of practice; an attachment to different leaders ambitiously contending for pre-eminence and power; or to persons of other descriptions whose fortunes have been interesting to the human passions, have, in turn, divided mankind into parties, inflamed them with mutual animosity, and rendered them much more disposed to vex and oppress each other than to co-operate for their common good. So strong is this propensity of mankind to fall into mutual animosities that where no substantial occasion presents itself the most frivolous and fanciful distinctions have been sufficient to kindle their unfriendly passions and excite their most violent conflicts. But the most common and durable source of factions has been the various and unequal distribution of property. Those who hold and those who are without property have ever formed distinct interests in society. Those who are creditors, and those who are debtors, fall under a like discrimination. A landed interest, a manufacturing interest, a mercantile interest, a moneyed interest, with many lesser interests, grow up of necessity in civilized nations, and divide them into different classes, actuated by different sentiments and views. The regulation of these various and interfering interests forms the principal task of modern legislation and involves the spirit of party and faction in the necessary and ordinary operations of government.

No man is allowed to be judge in his own cause, because his interest would certainly bias his judgment and, not improbably, corrupt his integrity. With equal, nay with greater reason, a body of men are unfit to be both judges and parties at the same time; yet what are many of the most important acts of legislation

but so many judicial determinations, not indeed concerning the rights of single persons, but concerning the rights of large bodies of citizens? And what are the different classes of legislators but advocates and parties to the causes which they determine? Is a law proposed concerning private debts? It is a question to which the creditors are parties on one side and the debtors on the other. Justice ought to hold the balance between them. Yet the parties are, and must be, themselves the judges; and the most numerous party, or in other words, the most powerful faction must be expected to prevail. Shall domestic manufacturers be encouraged, and in what degree, by restrictions on foreign manufacturers? are questions which would be differently decided by the landed and the manufacturing classes, and probably by neither with a sole regard to justice and the public good. The apportionment of taxes on the various descriptions of property is an act which seems to require the most exact impartiality; yet there is, perhaps, no legislative act in which greater opportunity and temptation are given to a predominant party to trample on the rules of justice. Every shilling with which they overburden the inferior number is a shilling saved to their own pockets.

It is in vain to say that enlightened statesmen will be able to adjust these clashing interests and render them all subservient to the public good. Enlightened statesmen will not always be at the helm. Nor, in many cases, can such an adjustment be made at all without taking into view indirect and remote considerations, which will rarely prevail over the immediate interest which one party may find in disregarding the rights of another or the good of the whole.

The inference to which we are brought is that the *causes* of faction cannot be removed and that relief is only to be sought in the means of controlling its *effects*.

If a faction consists of less than a majority, relief is supplied by the republican principle, which enables the majority to defeat its sinister views by regular vote. It may clog the administration, it may convulse the society; but it will be unable to execute and mask its violence under the forms of the Constitution. When a majority is included in a faction, the form of popular government, on the other hand, enables it to sacrifice to its ruling passion or interest both the public good and the rights of other citizens. To secure the public good and private rights against the danger of such a faction, and at the same time to preserve the spirit and the form of popular government, is then the great object to which our inquiries are directed. Let me add that it is the great desideratum by which alone this form of government can be rescued from the opprobrium under which it has so long labored and be recommended to the esteem and adoption of mankind.

By what means is this object attainable? Evidently by one of two only. Either the existence of the same passion or interest in a majority at the same time must be prevented, or the majority, having such coexistent passion or interest, must be rendered, by their number and local situation, unable to concert and carry into effect schemes of oppression. If the impulse and the opportunity be suffered to coincide, we well know that neither moral nor religious motives can be relied on as an adequate control. They are not found to be such on the injustice and violence of individuals, and lose their efficacy in proportion to the number combined together, that is, in proportion as their efficacy becomes needful.

From this view of the subject it may be concluded that a pure democracy, by which I mean a society consisting of a small number of citizens, who assemble and administer the government in person, can admit of no cure for the mischiefs of faction. A common passion or interest will, in almost every case, be felt by a majority of the whole; a communication and concert results from the form of government itself; and there is nothing to check the inducements to sacrifice the weaker party or an obnoxious individual. Hence it is that such democracies have ever been spectacles of turbulence and contention; have ever been found incompatible with personal security or the rights of property; and have in general been as short in their lives as they have been violent in their deaths. Theoretic politicians, who have patronized this species of government, have erroneously supposed that by reducing mankind to a perfect equality in their political rights, they would at the same time be perfectly equalized and assimilated in their possessions, their opinions, and their passions.

A republic, by which I mean a government in which the scheme of representation takes place, opens a different prospect and promises the cure for which we are seeking. Let us examine the points in which it varies from pure democracy, and we shall comprehend both the nature of the cure and the efficacy which it must derive from the Union.

The two great points of difference between a democracy and a republic are: first, the delegation of the government, in the latter, to a small number of citizens elected by the rest; secondly, the greater number of citizens and greater sphere of country over which the latter may be extended.

The effect of the first difference is, on the one hand, to refine and enlarge the public views by passing them through the medium of a chosen body of citizens, whose wisdom may best discern the true interest of their country and whose patriotism and love of justice will be least likely to sacrifice it to temporary or partial considerations. Under such a regulation it may well happen that the public voice, pronounced by the representatives of the people, will be more consonant to the public good than if pronounced by the people themselves, convened for the purpose. On the other hand, the effect may be inverted. Men of factious tempers, of local prejudices, or of sinister designs, may, by intrigue, by corruption, or by other means, first obtain the suffrages, and then betray the interests of the people. The question resulting is, whether small or extensive republics are most favorable to the election of proper guardians of the public weal; and it is clearly decided in favor of the latter by two obvious considerations.

In the first place it is to be remarked that however small the republic may be the representatives must be raised to a certain number in order to guard against the cabals of a few; and that however large it may be they must be limited to a certain number in order to guard against the confusion of a multitude. Hence, the number of representatives in the two cases not being in proportion to that of the constituents, and being proportionally greatest in the small republic, it follows that if the proportion of fit characters be not less in the large than in the small republic, the former will present a greater option, and consequently a greater probability of a fit choice.

In the next place, as each representative will be chosen by a greater number of citizens in the large than in the small republic, it will be more difficult for unworthy candidates to practise with success the vicious arts by which elections are too often carried; and the suffrages of the people being more free, will be more likely to center on men who possess the most attractive merit and the most diffusive and established characters.

It must be confessed that in this, as in most other cases, there is a mean, on both sides of which inconveniencies will be found to lie. By enlarging too much the number of electors, you render the representative too little acquainted with all their local circumstances and lesser interests; as by reducing it too much, you render him unduly attached to these, and too little fit to comprehend and pursue great and national objects. The federal Constitution forms a happy combination in this respect; the great and aggregate interests being referred to the national, the local and particular to the State legislatures.

The other point of difference is the greater number of citizens and extent of territory which may be brought within the compass of republican than of democratic government; and it is this circumstance principally which renders factious combinations less to be dreaded in the former than in the latter. The smaller the society, the fewer probably will be the distinct parties and interests composing it; the fewer the distinct parties and interests, the more frequently will a majority be found of the same party; and the smaller the number of individuals composing a majority, and the smaller the compass within which they are placed, the more easily will they concert and execute their plans of oppression. Extend the sphere and you take in a greater variety of parties and interests; you make it less probable that a majority of the whole will have a common motive to invade the rights of other citizens; or if such a common motive exists, it will be more difficult for all who feel it to discover their own strength and to act in unison with each other. Besides other impediments, it may be remarked that, where there is a consciousness of unjust or dishonorable purposes, communication is always checked by distrust in proportion to the number whose concurrence is necessary.

Hence, it clearly appears that the same advantage which a republic has over a democracy in controlling the effects of faction is enjoyed by a large over a small republic—is enjoyed by the Union over the States composing it. Does this advantage consist in the substitution of representatives whose enlightened views and virtuous sentiments render them superior to local prejudices and to schemes of injustice? It will not be denied that the representation of the Union will be most likely to possess these requisite endowments. Does it consist in the greater security afforded by a greater variety of parties, against the event of any one party being able to outnumber and oppress the rest? In an equal degree does the increased variety of parties comprised within the Union increase this security? Does it, in fine, consist in the greater obstacles opposed to the concert and accomplishment of the secret wishes of an unjust and interested majority? Here again the extent of the Union gives it the most palpable advantage.

The influence of factious leaders may kindle a flame within their particular States but will be unable to spread a general conflagration through the other

States. A religious sect may degenerate into a political faction in a part of the Confederacy; but the variety of sects dispersed over the entire face of it must secure the national councils against any danger from that source. A rage for paper money, for an abolition of debts, for an equal division of property, or for any other improper or wicked project, will be less apt to pervade the whole body of the Union than a particular member of it, in the same proportion as such a malady is more likely to taint a particular county or district than an entire State.

In the extent and proper structure of the Union, therefore, we behold a republican remedy for the diseases most incident to republican government. And according to the degree of pleasure and pride we feel in being republicans ought to be our zeal in cherishing the spirit and supporting the character of federalist.

PUBLIUS

NO. 51: MADISON

To what expedient, then, shall we finally resort, for maintaining in practice the necessary partition of power among the several departments as laid down in the Constitution? The only answer that can be given is that as all these exterior provisions are found to be inadequate the defect must be supplied, by so contriving the interior structure of the government as that its several constituent parts may, by their mutual relations, be the means of keeping each other in their proper places. Without presuming to undertake a full development of this important idea I will hazard a few general observations which may perhaps place it in a clearer light, and enable us to form a more correct judgment of the principles and structure of the government planned by the convention.

In order to lay a due foundation for that separate and distinct exercise of the different powers of government, which to a certain extent is admitted on all hands to be essential to the preservation of liberty, it is evident that each department should have a will of its own; and consequently should be so constituted that the members of each should have as little agency as possible in the appointment of the members of the others. Were this principle rigorously adhered to, it would require that all the appointments for the supreme executive, legislative, and judiciary magistracies should be drawn from the same fountain of authority, the people, through channels having no communication whatever with one another. Perhaps such a plan of constructing the several departments would be less difficult in practice than it may in contemplation appear. Some difficulties, however, and some additional expense would attend the execution of it. Some deviations, therefore, from the principle must be admitted. In the constitution of the judiciary department in particular, it might be inexpedient to insist rigorously on the principle: first, because peculiar qualifications being essential in the members, the primary consideration ought to be to select that mode of choice which best secures these qualifications; second, because the permanent tenure by which the appointments are held in that department must soon destroy all sense of dependence on the authority conferring them.

It is equally evident that the members of each department should be as little dependent as possible on those of the others for the emoluments annexed to their offices. Were the executive magistrate, or the judges, not independent of the legislature in this particular, their independence in every other would be merely nominal.

But the great security against a gradual concentration of the several powers in the same department consists in giving to those who administer each department the necessary constitutional means and personal motives to resist encroachments of the others. The provision for defense must in this, as in all other cases, be made commensurate to the danger of attack. Ambition must be made to counteract ambition. The interest of the man must be connected with the constitutional rights of the place. It may be a reflection on human nature that such devices should be necessary to control the abuses of government. But what is government itself but the greatest of all reflections on human nature? If men were angels, no government would be necessary. If angels were to govern men, neither external nor internal controls on government would be necessary. In framing a government which is to be administered by men over men, the great difficulty lies in this: you must first enable the government to control the governed; and in the next place oblige it to control itself. A dependence on the people is, no doubt, the primary control on the government; but experience has taught mankind the necessity of auxiliary precautions.

This policy of supplying, by opposite and rival interests, the defect of better motives, might be traced through the whole system of human affairs, private as well as public. We see it particularly displayed in all the subordinate distributions of power, where the constant aim is to divide and arrange the several offices in such a manner as that each may be a check on the other—that the private interest of every individual may be a sentinel over the public rights. These inventions of prudence cannot be less requisite in the distribution of the supreme powers of the State.

But it is not possible to give to each department an equal power of self-defense. In republican government, the legislative authority necessarily predominates. The remedy for this inconveniency is to divide the legislature into different branches; and to render them, by different modes of election and different principles of action, as little connected with each other as the nature of their common functions and their common dependence on the society will admit. It may even be necessary to guard against dangerous encroachments by still further precautions. As the weight of the legislative authority requires that it should be thus divided, the weakness of the executive may require, on the other hand, that it should be fortified. An absolute negative on the legislature appears, at first view, to be the natural defense with which the executive magistrate should be armed. But perhaps it would be neither altogether safe nor alone sufficient. On ordinary occasions it might not be exerted with the requisite firmness, and on extraordinary occasions it might be perfidiously abused. May not this defect of an absolute negative be supplied by some qualified connection between this weaker branch of the stronger department, by which the latter may be led to support the constitutional rights of the former, without being too much detached from the rights of its own department?

If the principles on which these observations are founded be just, as I persuade myself they are, and they be applied as a criterion to the several State constitutions, and to the federal Constitution, it will be found that if the latter does not perfectly correspond with them, the former are infinitely less able to bear such a test.

There are, moreover, two considerations particularly applicable to the federal system of America, which place that system in a very interesting point of view.

First. In a single republic, all the power surrendered by the people is submitted to the administration of a single government; and the usurpations are guarded against by a division of the government into distinct and separate departments. In the compound republic of America, the power surrendered by the people is first divided between two distinct governments, and then the portion allotted to each subdivided among distinct and separate departments. Hence a double security arises to the rights of the people. The different governments will control each other, at the same time that each will be controlled by itself.

Second. It is of great importance in a republic not only to guard the society against the oppression of its rulers, but to guard one part of the society against the injustice of the other part. Different interests necessarily exist in different classes of citizens. If a majority be united by a common interest, the rights of the minority will be insecure. There are but two methods of providing against this evil: the one by creating a will in the community independent of the majority— that is, of the society itself; the other, by comprehending in the society so many separate descriptions of citizens as will render an unjust combination of a majority of the whole very improbable, if not impracticable. The first method prevails in all governments possessing an hereditary or self-appointed authority. This, at best, is but a precarious security; because a power independent of the society may as well espouse the unjust views of the major as the rightful interests of the minor party, and may possibly be turned against both parties. The second method will be exemplified in the federal republic of the United States. Whilst all authority in it will be derived from and dependent on the society, the society itself will be broken into so many parts, interests and classes of citizens, that the rights of individuals, or of the minority, will be in little danger from interested combinations of the majority. In a free government the security for civil rights must be the same as that for religious rights. It consists in the one case in the multiplicity of interests, and in the other in the multiplicity of sects. The degree of security in both cases will depend on the number of interests and sects; and this may be presumed to depend on the extent of country and number of people comprehended under the same government. This view of the subject must particularly recommend a proper federal system to all the sincere and considerate friends of republican government, since it shows that in exact proportion as the territory of the Union may be formed into more circumscribed Confederacies, or States, oppressive combinations of a majority will be facilitated; the best security, under the republican forms, for the rights of every class of citizen, will be diminished; and consequently the stability and independence of some member of the government, the only other security,

must be proportionally increased. Justice is the end of government. It is the end of civil society. It ever has been and ever will be pursued until it be obtained, or until liberty be lost in the pursuit. In a society under the forms of which the stronger faction can readily unite and oppress the weaker, anarchy may as truly be said to reign as in a state of nature, where the weaker individual is not secured against the violence of the stronger; and as, in the latter state, even the stronger individuals are prompted, by the uncertainty of their condition, to submit to a government which may protect the weak as well as themselves; so, in the former state, will the more powerful factions or parties be gradually induced, by a like motive, to wish for a government which will protect all parties, the weaker as well as the more powerful. It can be little doubted that if the State of Rhode Island was separated from the Confederacy and left to itself, the insecurity of rights under the popular form of government within such narrow limits would be displayed by such reiterated oppressions of factious majorities that some power altogether independent of the people would soon be called for by the voice of the very factions whose misrule had proved the necessity of it. In the extended republic of the United States, and among the great variety of interests, parties, and sects which it embraces, a coalition of a majority of the whole society could seldom take place on any other principles than those of justice and the general good; whilst there being thus less danger to a minor from the will of a major party, there must be less pretext, also, to provide for the security of the former, by introducing into the government a will not dependent on the latter, or, in other words, a will independent of the society itself. It is no less certain than it is important, notwithstanding the contrary opinions which have been entertained, that the larger the society, provided it lie within a practicable sphere, the more duly capable it will be of self-government. And happily for the *republican cause,* the practicable sphere may be carried to a very great extent by a judicious modification and mixture of the *federal principle.*

PUBLIUS

Glossary

administrative legislation Rules made by regulatory agencies and commissions

affirmative action A policy or program designed to redress historic injustices committed against specific groups by making special efforts to provide members of these groups with access to educational and employment opportunities

agency representation The type of representation according to which representatives are held accountable to their constituents if they fail to represent them properly. That is, constituents have the power to hire and fire their representatives

agenda-setting effect The power to bring attention to particular issues and problems

amicus curiae "Friend of the court," an individual or group that is not party to a lawsuit but seeks to assist the court in reaching a decision by presenting an additional brief

Antifederalists Those who favored strong state governments and a weak national government and who were opponents of the constitution proposed at the American Constitutional Convention of 1787

appeasement The effort to forestall war by giving in to the demands of a hostile power

Articles of Confederation and Perpetual Union America's first written constitution. Adopted by the Continental Congress in 1777, the Articles of Confederation and Perpetual Union were the formal basis for America's national government until 1789, when they were superseded by the Constitution

Australian ballot An electoral format that presents the names of all the candidates for any given office on the same ballot. Introduced at the end of the eighteenth century, the Australian ballot replaced the partisan ballot and facilitated split-ticket voting

authoritarian government A system of rule in which the government recognizes no formal limits but may nevertheless be restrained by the power of other social institutions

autocracy A form of government in which a single individual rules

bicameral legislature A legislative assembly composed of two chambers, or houses

bicameralism The division of a legislative assembly into two chambers, or houses

bilateral treaty A treaty made between two nations

Bill of Rights The first 10 amendments to the U.S. Constitution, adopted in 1791. The Bill of Rights ensures certain rights and liberties to the people

block grants Federal funds given to state governments to pay for goods, services, or programs, with relatively few restrictions on how the funds may be spent

brief A written document in which an attorney explains—using case precedents—why the Court should rule in favor of his or her client

budget deficit The amount by which government spending exceeds government revenue in a fiscal year

bureaucracy The complex structure of offices, tasks, rules, and principles of organization that are employed by all large-scale institutions to coordinate the work of their personnel

bureaucratic drift The oft-observed phenomenon of bureaucratic implementation that produces policy more to the liking of the bureaucracy than faithful to the original intention of the legislation that created it, but without triggering a political reaction from elected officials

Cabinet The secretaries, or chief administrators, of the major departments of the federal government. Cabinet secretaries are appointed by the president with the consent of the Senate

casework An effort by members of Congress to gain the trust and support of constituents by providing personal services. One important type of casework consists of helping constituents obtain favorable treatment from the federal bureaucracy

categorical grants-in-aid Funds given by Congress to states and localities and that are earmarked by law for specific categories, such as education or crime prevention

caucus (political) A normally closed meeting of a political or legislative group to select candidates, plan strategy, or make decisions regarding legislative matters

causation A relationship or association between two variables such that one causes the other

census A comprehensive enumeration of all individuals in a population

checks and balances The mechanisms through which each branch of government is able to participate in and influence the activities of the other branches

chief justice The justice on the Supreme Court who presides over the Court's public sessions

civil law A system of jurisprudence, including private law and govermental actions, for settling disputes that do not involve criminal penalties

civil liberties The protections of citizens from improper governmental action

civil rights The legal or moral claims that citizens are entitled to make on the government

class-action suit A lawsuit in which a large number of persons with common interests join together under a representative party to bring or defend a lawsuit, as when hundreds of workers join together to sue a company

clientele agency A department or bureau of government whose mission is to promote, serve, or represent a particular interest

closed primary A primary election in which only those voters who registered with the party a specified period before the primary election day can participate

closed rule The provision by the House Rules Committee that prohibits the introduction of amendments during debate

cloture A rule allowing a supermajority of the members of a legislative body to set a time limit on debate over a given bill

Cold War The period of struggle between the United States and the former Soviet Union between the late 1940s and about 1990

commander in chief The power of the president as commander of the national military and the state national guard units (when called into service)

commerce clause The clause found in Article I, Section 8, of the Constitution, which delegates to Congress the power "to regulate Commerce with foreign Nations, and among the several States, and with the Indian Tribes." This clause was interpreted by the Supreme Court to favor national power over the economy

concurrence An opinion agreeing with the decision of the majority but not with the rationale provided in the majority opinion

concurrent powers The authority possessed by *both* state and national governments, such as the power to levy taxes

conference committee A joint committee created to work out a compromise for House and Senate versions of a piece of legislation

conservative Today this term refers to those who generally support the social and economic status quo and are suspicious of efforts to introduce new political formulas and economic arrangements. Many conservatives also believe that a large and powerful government poses a threat to citizens' freedoms

constituency The district making up the area from which an official is elected

constitutional government A system of rule in which formal and effective limits are placed on the powers of the government

containment A policy designed to curtail the political and military expansion of a hostile power

contracting power The power of government to set conditions on companies seeking to sell goods or services to government agencies

contributory program A social program financed in whole or in part by taxation or other mandatory contributions by its present or future recipients. The most important example is Social Security, which is financed by a payroll tax

cooperative federalism A type of federalism existing since the New Deal era, in which grants-in-aid have been used strategically to encourage states and localities (without commanding them) to pursue nationally defined goals. Also known as intergovernmental cooperation

correlation A relationship or association between two variables

court of appeals (or appellate court) A court that hears the appeals of trial-court decisions

criminal law The branch of law that deals with disputes or actions involving criminal penalties (as opposed to civil law)

de facto segregation Racial segregation that is not a direct result of law or government policy but is, instead, a reflection of residential patterns, income distributions, or other social factors

de jure segregation Racial segregation that is a direct result of law or official policy

delegate A representative who votes according to the preferences of his or her constituency

delegated powers Constitutional powers assigned to one government agency but exercised by another agency with the express permission of the first

democracy A system of rule that permits citizens to play a significant part in the governmental process, usually through the selection of key public officials

deregulation The policy of reducing or eliminating regulatory restraints on the conduct of individuals or private institutions

deterrence The development and maintenance of military strength as a means of discouraging attack

devolution The policy of removing a program from one level of government by deregulating it or passing it down to a lower level, such as from the national government to the state and local governments

diplomacy The representation of a government to other governments

discretionary spending Federal spending on programs that are controlled through the regular budget process

dissenting opinion A decision written by a justice who voted with the minority opinion in a particular case in which the justice fully explains the reasoning behind his or her opinion

distributive tendency The tendency of Congress to spread the benefits of a policy over a wide range of members' districts

divided government The condition in American government in which the presidency is controlled by one party while the opposing party controls one or both houses of Congress

dual federalism The system of government that prevailed in the United States from 1789 to 1937 in which fundamental governmental powers were shared between the federal and state governments, with the states exercising the most important powers

due process Proceeding according to law and with adequate protection for individual rights

electoral college The presidential electors from each state who meet in their respective state capitals after the popular election to cast ballots for president and vice president

eminent domain The right of the government to take private property for public use, with reasonable compensation awarded for the property

entitlement The eligibility for benefits by virtue of a category defined by law. Categories can be changed only by legislation; deprivation of individual benefits can be determined only through due process in court

equal protection clause The provision of the Fourteenth Amendment guaranteeing citizens "the equal protection of the laws." This clause has been the basis for the civil rights of African Americans, women, and other groups

equal time rule The requirement that broadcasters provide candidates for the same political office an equal opportunity to communicate their messages to the public

establishment clause The First Amendment clause that says, "Congress shall make no law respecting an establishment of religion." This law means that a wall of separation exists between church and state

exclusionary rule The ability of courts to exclude evidence obtained in violation of the Fourth Amendment

executive agreement An agreement between the president and another country that has the force of a treaty but does not require the Senate's "advice and consent"

executive orders A rule or regulation issued by the president that has the effect and formal status of legislation

executive privilege The claim that confidential communications between the president and the president's close advisers should not be revealed without the consent of the president

expressed powers The powers enumerated in the Constitution that are granted to the federal government

externalities The differences between the private cost and the social cost of economic behavior

fairness doctrine An FCC requirement that broadcasters that air programs on controversial issues provide time for opposing views

federal funds rate The interest rate on loans among banks that the Federal Reserve Board influences by affecting the supply of money available

Federal Reserve System (the Fed) A system of 12 Federal Reserve banks that facilitates exchanges of cash, checks, and credit; regulates member banks; and uses monetary policies to fight inflation and deflation

federalism The system of government in which a constitution divides power between a central government and regional governments

Federalists Those who favored a strong national government and supported the constitution proposed at the American Constitutional Convention of 1787

fighting words Speech that directly incites damaging conduct

filibuster A tactic used by members of the Senate to prevent action on legislation they oppose by continuously holding the floor and speaking until the majority backs down. Once given the floor, senators have unlimited time to speak, and it requires a cloture vote of three-fifths of the Senate to end a filibuster

fiscal policy Policies to regulate the economy through taxing and spending powers

food stamps The largest in-kind benefits program, administered by the Department of Agriculture, for individuals and families who satisfy a means test. Food stamps can used to buy food at most grocery stores

formula grants Grants-in-aid in which a formula is used to determine the amount of federal funds a state or local government will receive

framing The power of the media to influence how events and issues are interpreted

free riding Enjoying the benefits of some good or action while letting others bear the costs

frequency In statistics and probability, the number of times a specific behavior or value of a variable occurs or the percent of the observations in which it occurs

full faith and credit clause The provision in Article IV, Section 1, of the Constitution requiring that each state normally honors the public acts and judicial decisions that take place in another state

gender gap A distinctive pattern of voting behavior reflecting the differences in views between women and men

General Agreement on Tariffs and Trade (GATT) An international trade organization, in existence from 1947 to 1995, that set many of the rules governing international trade

gerrymandering The apportionment of voters in districts in such a way as to give unfair advantage to one political party

going public The act of launching a media campaign to build popular support

government The institutions and procedures through which a land and its people are ruled

grand jury A jury that determines whether sufficient evidence is available to justify a trial. Grand juries do not rule on the accused's guilt or innocence

grants-in-aid A general term for funds given by Congress to state and local governments

grassroots lobbying A lobbying campaign in which a group mobilizes its membership to contact government officials in support of the group's position

Great Compromise An agreement reached at the Constitutional Convention of 1787 that gave each state an equal number of senators regardless of its population but linked representation in the House of Representatives to population

gross domestic product (GDP) The total value of goods and services produced within a country

home rule The power delegated by the state to a local unit of government to manage its own affairs

impeachment The charging of a government official (president or otherwise) with "Treason, Bribery, or other high Crimes and Misdemeanors" and bringing him or her before Congress to determine guilt

implementation The efforts of departments and agencies to translate laws into specific bureaucratic routines

implied powers Powers derived from the necessary and proper clause (Article I, Section 8) of the Constitution. Such powers are not specifically expressed but are implied through the expansive interpretation of delegated powers

incumbency Holding the political office for which one is running

indexing The process of periodically adjusting social benefits or wages to account for increases in the cost of living

informational benefits Special newsletters, periodicals, training programs, conferences, and other information provided to members of groups to entice others to join

inherent powers Powers claimed by a president that are not expressed in the Constitution but are inferred from it

initiative A process by which citizens may petition to place a policy proposal on the ballot for public vote

in-kind benefits Goods and services provided to needy individuals and families by the federal government, as contrasted with cash benefits. The largest in-kind federal welfare program is food stamps

institutions The rules and procedures that provide incentives for political behavior, thereby shaping politics

interest group An organized group of individuals or organizations that makes policy-related appeals to government

intermediate scrutiny The test used by the Supreme Court in gender discrimination cases. Intermediate scrutiny places the burden of proof partially on the government and partially on the challengers to show that the law in question is constitutional

International Court of Justice (ICJ) The UN's chief judicial agency. Located in The Hague, Netherlands, the ICJ settles legal disputes submitted by UN member states

International Monetary Fund (IMF) An institution established in 1944 that provides loans and facilitates international monetary exchange

isolationism The desire to avoid involvement in the affairs of other nations

issue voting An individual's propensity to select candidates or parties based on the extent to which the individual agrees with one candidate more than others on specific issues

judicial activism The judicial philosophy that posits that the Court should see beyond the text of the Constitution or a statute to consider broader societal implications for its decisions

judicial restraint The judicial philosophy whose adherents refuse to go beyond the text of the Constitution in interpreting its meaning

judicial review The power of the courts to declare actions of the legislative and executive branches invalid or unconstitutional. The Supreme Court asserted this power in *Marbury v. Madison* (1803)

jurisdiction The domain over which an institution or member of an institution has authority

legislative initiative The president's inherent power to bring a legislative agenda before Congress

legislative supremacy The preeminent position assigned to Congress by the Constitution

Lemon test Rule articulated in *Lemon v. Kurtzman* according to which governmental action in respect to religion is permissible if it is secular in purpose, does not lead to "excessive entanglement" with religion, and neither promotes nor inhibits the practice of religion

libel A written statement made in "reckless disregard of the truth" and considered damaging to a victim because it is "malicious, scandalous, and defamatory"

liberal A liberal today generally supports political and social reform; government intervention in the economy; the expansion of federal social services; more vigorous efforts on behalf of the poor, minorities, and women; and greater concern for consumers and the environment

line-item veto The power of the executive to veto specific provisions (lines) of a bill passed by the legislature

lobbying An attempt by a group to influence the policy process through persuasion of government officials

logrolling A legislative practice wherein reciprocal agreements are made between legislators, usually in voting for or against a bill. In contrast to bargaining, logrolling unites parties that have nothing in common but their desire to exchange support

majority leader The elected leader of the party holding a majority of the seats in the House of Representatives or the Senate. In the House, the majority leader is subordinate in the party hierarchy to the Speaker

majority party The party that holds the majority of legislative seats in either the House or the Senate

majority rule A type of electoral system in which, to win a seat in a representative body, a candidate must receive a majority (50 percent plus one) of all the votes cast in the relevant district

mandatory spending Federal spending that is made up of "uncontrollables," budget items that cannot be controlled through the regular budget process. Some uncontrollables, such as interest on the debt, are beyond the power of Congress because the terms of payments are set in contracts

material benefits Special goods, services, or money provided to members of groups to entice others to join

mean The average value of a variable

means testing A procedure that determines eligibility for government public-assistance programs. A potential beneficiary must show a need and an inability to provide for that need

median The numerical value separating the higher half of a sample or population from the lower half; also called the fiftieth percentile

Medicaid A federally financed, state-operated program for medical services to low-income people

Medicare National health insurance for the elderly and the disabled

minority leader The elected leader of the party holding less than a majority of the seats in the House or Senate

Miranda rule The convention derived from the Supreme Court's 1966 ruling in the case of *Miranda v. Arizona* whereby persons under arrest must be informed of their legal rights, including their right to counsel, before undergoing police interrogation

monetary policy Policies to regulate the economy through the manipulation of the supply of money, the price of money (interest rate), and the availability of credit

money bill A bill concerned solely with taxation or government spending

monopoly The existence in a market of a single firm that provides all the goods and services of that market; the absence of competition

mootness A criterion used by courts to avoid hearing cases that no longer require resolution

most favored nation status An agreement to offer a trading partner the lowest tariff rate offered to other trading partners

National Security Council (NSC) A presidential foreign policy advisory council composed of the president; the vice president; the secretaries of state, defense, and the treasury; the attorney general; and other officials invited by the president

necessary and proper clause Article I, Section 8, of the Constitution, which enumerates the powers of Congress and provides Congress with the authority to make all laws "necessary and proper" to carry them out; also referred to as the elastic clause

nomination The process by which political parties select their candidates for election to public office

noncontributory program A social program that assists people based on demonstrated need rather than contributions they have made; also known as a public assistance program

non-state actor A group other than a nation-state that attempts to play a role in the international system. Terrorist groups are one type of non-state actor

North American Free Trade Agreement (NAFTA) A trade treaty among the United States, Canada, and Mexico to lower and eliminate tariffs among the three countries

North Atlantic Treaty Organization (NATO) A treaty organization comprising the United States, Canada, and most of Western Europe, formed in 1949 to counter the perceived threat from the Soviet Union

oligarchy A form of government in which a small group of landowners, military officers, or wealthy merchants controls most of the governing decisions

open primary A primary election in which voters can choose on the primary election day itself which party's primary to vote in

open rule The provision by the House Rules Committee that permits floor debate and the addition of amendments to a bill

open-market operations The process whereby the Open Market Committee of the Federal Reserve buys and sells government securities, and so on, to help finance government operations and to reduce or increase the total amount of money circulating in the economy

opinion The written explanation of the Supreme Court's decision in a particular case

oral argument The stage in Supreme Court proceedings in which attorneys for both sides appear before the Court to present their positions and answer questions posed by the justices

oversight The effort by Congress, through hearings, investigations, and other techniques, to exercise control over the activities of executive agencies

party activist A partisan who contributes time, energy, and effort to support a party and its candidates

party caucus, or party conference A normally closed meeting of a political or legislative group to select candidates or leaders, plan strategy, or make decisions regarding legislative matters

party identification An individual's attachment to a particular political party, which might be based on issues, ideology, past experience, or upbringing

party vote A roll-call vote in the House or Senate in which at least 50 percent of the members of one party take a particular position and are opposed by at least 50 percent of the members of the other party. Party votes are less common today than they were in the nineteenth century

patronage The resources available to higher officials, usually opportunities to make partisan appointments to offices and confer grants, licenses, or special favors to supporters

pluralism The theory that all interests are and should be free to compete for influence in the government. The outcome of this competition is compromise and moderation

plurality rule A type of electoral system in which victory goes to the individual who gets the most votes in an election, but not necessarily a majority of the votes cast

pocket veto A veto that is effected when Congress adjourns during the time a president has to approve a bill and the president takes no action on it

political action committee (PAC) A private group that raises and distributes funds for use in election campaigns

political party An organized group that attempts to influence government by electing its members to office

politics Conflict, struggle, cooperation, and collaboration over the leadership, structure, and policies of government

pork-barrel legislation The appropriations made by legislative bodies for local projects that often are not needed but are created so that local representatives can carry their home district in the next election

precedents Prior cases whose principles are used by judges as the bases for their decisions in present cases

preemption The willingness to strike first in order to prevent an enemy attack

preventive war The policy of striking first when a nation fears that a foreign foe is contemplating hostile action

priming The process of preparing the public to take a particular view of an event or a political actor

principal-agent relationship The relationship between a principal and his or her agent. This relationship may be affected by the fact that each is motivated by self-interest, yet their interests may not be well aligned

prior restraint An effort by a government agency to block the publication of material it deems libelous or harmful in some other way: censorship. In the United States, the courts forbid prior restraint except under the most extraordinary circumstances

privatization The act of moving all or part of a program from the public sector to the private sector

privileges and immunities clause The provision in Article IV, Section 2, of the Constitution stating that a state cannot discriminate against someone from another state or give its own residents special privileges

progressive taxation Taxation that hits the upper income brackets more heavily

project grants Grant programs in which state and local governments submit proposals to federal agencies and for which funding is provided on a competitive basis

proportional representation A multiple-member district system that allows each political party representation in proportion to its percentage of the vote

prospective voting Voting based on the imagined future performance of a candidate

public good A good that, first, may be enjoyed by anyone if it is provided and, second, may not be denied to anyone once it has been provided

public law Cases involving the action of public agencies or officials

public opinion Citizens' attitudes about political issues, leaders, institutions, and events

public policy A law, rule, statute, or edict that expresses the government's goals for rewards and punishments to promote their attainment

purposive benefits Selective benefits of group membership that emphasize the purpose and accomplishments of the group

recall The removal of a public official by popular vote

referendum A measure proposed or passed by a legislature that is referred to the vote of the electorate for approval or rejection

regressive taxation Taxation that hits the lower income brackets more heavily

regulated federalism A form of federalism in which Congress imposes legislation on the states and localities requiring them to meet national standards

regulatory agency A department, bureau, or independent agency whose primary mission is to eliminate or restrict certain behaviors defined as negative in themselves or negative in their consequences

regulatory review The Office of Management and Budget function of reviewing all agency regulations and other rule making before they become official policy

reserve requirement The amount of liquid assets and ready cash that the Federal Reserve requires banks to hold to meet depositors' demands for their money

reserved powers Powers, derived from the Tenth Amendment to the Constitution, that are not specifically delegated to the national government or denied to the states; these powers are reserved to the states

retrospective voting Voting based on the past performance of a candidate

right of rebuttal An FCC regulation giving individuals the right to have the opportunity to respond to personal attacks made on a radio or TV broadcast

right to privacy The right to be left alone, which has been interpreted by the Supreme Court to entail individual access to birth control and abortions

ripeness A case that is ready for litigation and does not depend upon hypothetical future events

roll-call votes Votes in which each legislator's yes or no vote is recorded

sample A small group selected by researchers to represent the most important characteristics of an entire population

senatorial courtesy The practice whereby the president, before formally nominating a person for a federal district judgeship, finds out whether the senators from the candidate's state support the nomination

seniority The priority or status ranking given to an individual on the basis of length of continuous service on a congressional committee

"separate but equal" rule The doctrine that public accommodations could be segregated by race but still be equal

separation of powers The division of governmental power among several institutions that must cooperate in decision making

signing statement An announcement made by the president when a bill is signed into law

single-member district An electorate that is allowed to elect only one representative from each district—the typical method of representation in the United States

slander An oral statement made in "reckless disregard of the truth" and considered

damaging to a victim because it is "malicious, scandalous, and defamatory"

Social Security A contributory welfare program into which working Americans place a percentage of their wages and from which they receive cash benefits after retirement

socialization A process through which individuals assimilate community preferences and norms through social interactions

solidary benefits Selective benefits of group membership that emphasize friendship, networking, and consciousness raising

Speaker of the House The chief presiding officer of the House of Representatives. The Speaker is elected at the beginning of every Congress on a straight party vote. He or she is the most important party and House leader

speech plus Speech accompanied by activities such as sit-ins, picketing, and demonstrations. Protection of this form of speech under the First Amendment is conditional, and restrictions imposed by state or local authorities are acceptable if properly balanced by considerations of public order

standing The right of an individual or an organization to initiate a court case

standing committee A permanent legislative committee that considers legislation within its designated subject area; the basic unit of deliberation in the House and Senate

state sovereign immunity A legal doctrine holding that states cannot be sued for violating an act of Congress

states' rights The principle that states should oppose increases in the authority of the national government. This view was most popular before the Civil War

strict scrutinity The most stringent standard of judicial review of a government's actions in which the government must show that the law serves a "compelling state interest"

subsidy A government grant of cash or other valuable commodities, such as land, to an individual or an organization; used to promote activities desired by the government, to reward political support, or to buy off political opposition

Supplemental Security Income (SSI) A program providing a minimum monthly income to people who pass a means test and are 65 years old or older, blind, or disabled. SSI is financed from general revenues that are not Social Security contributions

supremacy clause A clause of Article VI of the Constitution that states that all laws passed by the national government and all treaties are the supreme laws of the land and superior to all laws adopted by any state or any subdivision

supreme court The highest court in a particular state or in the United States. This court primarily serves an appellate function

survey A study of a relatively small subset of individuals that is used to make inferences about an entire population

Temporary Assistance for Needy Families (TANF) Federal funds for children in families that fall below state standards of need

Three-Fifths Compromise An agreement reached at the Constitutional Convention of 1787 stipulating that for purposes of the apportionment of congressional seats, every slave would be counted as three-fifths of a person

totalitarian government A system of rule in which the government recognizes no formal limits on its power and seeks to absorb or eliminate other social institutions that might challenge it

trial court The first court to hear a criminal or civil case

trustee A representative who votes based on what he or she thinks is best for his or her constituency

unfunded mandates National standards or programs imposed on state and local governments by the federal government without accompanying funding or reimbursement

United Nations (UN) An organization of nations founded in 1945 to be a channel for negotiation and a means of settling international disputes peaceably. The UN has had frequent successes in providing a forum for negotiation and on some occasions a means of preventing international conflicts from spreading. On a number of occasions, the UN has been a convenient cover for U.S. foreign policy goals

variable A categorization or numerical representation of all values of a given characteristic

veto The president's constitutional power to turn down acts of Congress within 10 days of their passage while Congress is in session. A presidential veto may be overridden by a two-thirds vote of each house of Congress

veto power The ability to defeat something even if it has made it on to the agenda of an institution

War Powers Resolution A resolution of Congress declaring that the president can send troops into action abroad only by authorization of Congress or if U.S. troops are already under attack or seriously threatened

whip system A communications network in each house of Congress. Whips poll the membership to learn their intentions on specific legislative issues and assist the majority and minority leaders in various tasks

World Trade Organization (WTO) An international group promoting free trade that grew out of the General Agreement on Tariffs and Trade

writ of *certiorari* A formal request by an appellant to have the Supreme Court review a decision of a lower court. *Certiorari* is from a Latin word meaning "to make more certain"

writ of *habeas corpus* A court order demanding that an individual in custody be brought into court and shown the cause for detention. *Habeas corpus* is guaranteed by the Constitution and can be suspended only in cases of rebellion or invasion

Endnotes

CHAPTER 1

1 Thomas Hobbes, *Leviathan, or The Matter, Forme, and Power of a Common Wealth, Ecclesiasticall and Civil* (1651; repr., New York: Macmillan, 1947), p. 82.

2 The most instructive treatment of the phenomenon of public goods and the free rider is Mancur Olson, Jr., *The Logic of Collective Action: Public Goods and the Theory of Groups* (1965; repr., Cambridge, MA: Harvard University Press, 1971), pp. 33–43, esp. n. 53.

3 Harold Lasswell, *Politics: Who Gets What, When, How* (New York: Meridian Books, 1958).

4 Quoted in John Cannon, *Parliamentary Reform, 1640–1832* (Cambridge: Cambridge University Press, 1973), p. 216.

5 For a review and analysis of the detrimental consequences of the "opening up" of American democracy since the 1960s, see Morris P. Fiorina, "Parties, Participation, and Representation in America: Old Theories Face New Realities," in *Political Science: State of the Discipline*, Ira Katznelson and Helen V. Milner, eds. (New York: Norton, 2002). For a more general and provocative analysis of the detrimental effects of too much democracy, see Fareed Zakaria, *The Future of Freedom: Illiberal Democracy at Home and Abroad* (New York: Norton, 2003).

CHAPTER 2

1 James Madison, *The Federalist*, no. 62 in *The Federalist Papers*, Clinton Rossiter, ed., (New York: New American Library, 1961), p. 381.

2 Alexei Anishchuk, "Medvedev Says Poor Rule of Law Holds Russia Back," Reuters, May 20, 2011, www.reuters.com (accessed 8/16/11).

3 Randall Peerenboom, *China's Long March toward Rule of Law* (Cambridge, UK: Cambridge University Press, 2002).

4 The social makeup of colonial America and some of the social conflicts that divided colonial society are discussed in Jackson Turner Main, *The Social Structure of Revolutionary America* (Princeton, NJ: Princeton University Press, 1965).

5 See Carl Becker, *The Declaration of Independence* (New York: Vintage, 1942).

6 See Merrill Jensen, *The Articles of Confederation* (Madison: University of Wisconsin Press, 1963).

7 There is no verbatim record of the debates, but James Madison, a Virginia delegate, was present during nearly all of the deliberations and kept full notes on them. Madison's notes are included in Max Farrand, ed., *The Records of the Federal Convention of 1787*, rev. ed., 4 vols. (New Haven, CT: Yale University Press, 1966).

8 Farrand, *Records of the Federal Convention*, vol. 1, p. 476.

9 Alexander Hamilton, *The Federalist*, no. 70, p. 424.

10 Max Farrand, *The Framing of the Constitution of the United States* (New Haven, CT: Yale University Press, 1962), p. 49.

11 Richard E. Neustadt, *Presidential Power* (New York: Wiley, 1960), p. 33.

12 An excellent analysis of the ratification campaigns is William H. Riker, *The Strategy of Rhetoric: Campaigning for the American Constitution* (New Haven, CT: Yale University Press, 1996).

13 *The Federalist*, esp. nos. 10 and 51.

14 The Fourteenth Amendment is included in this table as well as in Tables 2.3 and 2.4 because it seeks not only to define citizenship but seems to intend also that this definition of citizenship

included, along with the right to vote, all the rights of the Bill of Rights, regardless of the state in which the citizen resided. A great deal more is said about this in Chapter 4.

15 See Farrand, *Records of the Federal Convention*, vol. 1, p. 132.

16 *The Federalist*, no. 10.

CHAPTER 3

1 The notion that federalism requires separate spheres of jurisdictions in which lower and higher levels of government are uniquely decisive is developed fully in William H. Riker, *Federalism: Origin, Operation, Significance* (Boston: Little, Brown, 1964). This American version of federalism is applied to the emerging federal arrangements in the People's Republic of China during the 1990s in a paper by Barry R. Weingast, "The Economic Role of Political Institutions: Market-Preserving Federalism and Economic Development," *Journal of Law, Economics, and Organization* 11 (1995): 1–32.

2 For a good treatment of these conflicts of interests between states, see Forrest McDonald, *E Pluribus Unum—The Formation of the American Republic, 1776–1790* (Boston: Houghton Mifflin, 1965), chap. 7, especially pp. 319–38.

3 See David O'Brien, *Constitutional Law and Politics* (New York: Norton, 1997), vol. 1, pp. 602–3.

4 *United States v. Windsor*, 570 U.S. __ (2013).

5 *Hicklin v. Orbeck*, 437 U.S. 518 (1978).

6 *Sweeny v. Woodall*, 344 U.S. 86 (1953).

7 Marlise Simons, "France Won't Extradite American Convicted of Murder," *New York Times*, December 5, 1997, p. A9.

8 Patricia S. Florestano, "Past and Present Utilization of Interstate Compacts in the United States," *Publius* 24 (Fall 1994): 13–26.

9 A good discussion of the constitutional position of local governments is in York Y. Willbern, *The Withering Away of the City* (Bloomington: Indiana University Press, 1971). For more on the structure and theory of federalism, see Thomas R. Dye, *American Federalism: Competition among Governments* (Lexington, MA: Lexington Books, 1990), chap. 1; and Martha Derthick, "Up-to-Date in Kansas City: Reflections on American Federalism," *PS: Political Science & Politics* 25 (December 1992): 671–5.

10 *McCulloch v. Maryland*, 4 Wheaton 316 (1819).

11 *Gibbons v. Ogden*, 9 Wheaton 1 (1824).

12 In *Wabash, St. Louis, and Pacific Railway Company v. Illinois*, 118 U.S. 557 (1886), the Supreme Court struck down a state law prohibiting rate discrimination by a railroad. In response, Congress passed the Interstate Commerce Act of 1887, creating the Interstate Commerce Commission (ICC), the first federal regulatory agency.

13 *Hammer v. Dagenhart*, 247 U.S. 251 (1918).

14 *National Labor Relations Board v. Jones & Loughlin Steel Company*, 301 U.S. 1 (1937).

15 *Wickard v. Filburn*, 317 U.S. 111 (1942).

16 Kenneth T. Palmer, "The Evolution of Grant Policies," in *The Changing Politics of Federal Grants*, by Lawrence D. Brown, James W. Fossett, and Kenneth T. Palmer (Washington, DC: Brookings Institution, 1984), p. 15.

17 Palmer, "The Evolution of Grant Policies," p. 6.

18 Morton Grodzins, "The Federal System," in *Goals for Americans: The President's Commission on National Goals* (Englewood Cliffs, NJ: Prentice Hall, 1960), p. 265. In a marble cake, the white cake is distinguishable from the chocolate cake, but the two are streaked rather than in distinct layers.

19 The concept and the best discussion of this modern phenomenon will be found in Donald F. Kettl, *The Regulation of American Federalism* (Baltimore: Johns Hopkins University Press, 1983 and 1987), especially pp. 33–41.

20 See John DiIulio, Jr., and Donald F. Kettl, *Fine Print: The Contract with America, Devolution, and the Administrative Realities of American Federalism* (Washington, DC: Brookings Institution, 1995), p. 41.

21 Paul Posner, "Unfunded Mandate Reform: How Is It Working?" *Rockefeller Institute Bulletin* (Albany, NY: Nelson A. Rockefeller Institute of Government, 1998): 35.

22 Posner, "Unfunded Mandate Reform," p. 36.

23 *United States v. Darby Lumber Co.*, 312 U.S. 100 (1941).

24 W. John Moore, "Pleading the 10th," *National Journal*, July 29, 1995, p. 1940.

25 *United States v. Lopez*, 514 U.S. 549 (1995).

26 *Seminole Indian Tribe v. Florida*, 517 U.S. 44 (1996).

27 *Printz and Mack*, 521 U.S. 898, 117 S. Ct. 2365 (1997).

28 *Gonzales v. Oregon*, 546 U.S. 243 (2006).

29 *Arizona v. United States*, 567 U.S. __ (2012).

30 *Arizona et. al. v. Inter Tribal Council of Arizona, Inc.*, 570 U.S. __ (2013).

31 Alexander Hamilton, James Madison, and John Jay, *The Federalist Papers*, Clinton L. Rossiter, ed. (New York: New American Library, 1961), no. 47, p. 302.

32 *The Federalist Papers*, no. 48, p. 308.

33 Richard E. Neustadt, *Presidential Power* (New York: Wiley, 1960), p. 33.

34 *Marbury v. Madison*, 1 Cranch 137 (1803).

35 C. Herman Pritchett, *The American Constitution* (New York: McGraw-Hill, 1959), pp. 180–6.

36 *Immigration and Naturalization Service v. Chadha*, 462 U.S. 919 (1983). (See Chapter 7.)

37 Cass R. Sunstein, "Taking Over the Courts," *New York Times*, November 9, 2002, p. A19.

38 Sunstein, "Taking Over the Courts."

39 *Youngstown Sheet & Tube Co. v. Sawyer*, 343 U.S. 579 (1952).

40 *United States v. Nixon*, 418 U.S. 683 (1974).

41 *Clinton v. Jones*, 520 U.S. 681 (1997).

42 *Clinton v. City of New York*, 524 U.S. 417 (1998).

43 *Hamdi v. Rumsfeld*, 542 U.S. 507 (2004); *Rasul v. Bush*, 542 U.S. 466 (2004).

44 Not everybody will agree that divided government is so much less productive than government in which the same party controls both branches. See David Mayhew, *Divided We Govern: Party Control, Law Making and Investigations, 1946–1990* (New Haven, CT: Yale University Press, 1991). For another good evaluation of divided government, see Charles O. Jones, *Separate but Equal Branches—Congress and the Presidency* (Chatham, NJ: Chatham House, 1995).

CHAPTER 4

1 *Dred Scott v. Sandford*, 60 U.S. 393 (1857).

2 It would be useful at this point to review all the provisions of the Bill of Rights (in the Appendix) to confirm this distinction between the wording of the First Amendment and the rest of the Bill of Rights. For a spirited and enlightening essay on the extent to which the entire Bill of Rights was about equality, see Martha Minow, "Equality and the Bill of Rights," in Meyer and Parent, eds., *The Constitution of Rights*, pp. 118–28.

3 *Barron v. Mayor and City of Baltimore*, 32 U.S. 243 (1833).

4 The Fourteenth Amendment also seems designed to introduce civil rights. The final clause of the all-important Section 1 provides that no state can "deny to any person within its jurisdiction the equal protection of the laws." It is not unreasonable to conclude that the purpose of this provision was to obligate the state governments as well as the national government to take *positive* actions to protect citizens from arbitrary and discriminatory actions, at least those based on race. This will be explored in the second half of the chapter.

5 The Slaughter-House Cases, 16 Wallace 36 (1873); the Civil Rights Cases, 109 U.S. 3 (1883).

6 *Chicago, Burlington and Quincy Railroad Company v. Chicago*, 166 U.S. 266 (1897).

7 *Gitlow v. New York*, 268 U.S. 652 (1925).

8 *Near v. Minnesota*, 283 U.S. 697 (1931); *Hague v. C.I.O.*, 307 U.S. 496 (1939).

9 All of these were implicitly identified in *Palko v. Connecticut*, 302 U.S. 319 (1937), as "not incorporated" into the Fourteenth Amendment as limitations on the powers of the states.

10 *Brown v. Board of Education of Topeka, Kansas*, 347 U.S. 483 (1954).

11 *NLRB v. Jones & Laughlin Steel Corp.*, 301 U.S. 1 (1937).

12 The one exception was the right to public trial (Sixth Amendment), but a 1948 case (*In re Oliver*, 33 U.S. 257) did not actually mention the right to public trial as such; this right was cited in a 1968 case (*Duncan v. Louisiana*, 391 U.S. 145) as a precedent establishing the right to public trial as part of the Fourteenth Amendment.

13 *Gideon v. Wainwright*, 372 U.S. 335 (1963); Anthony Lewis, *Gideon's Trumpet* (New York: Random House, 1964).

14 *Mapp v. Ohio*, 367 U.S. 643 (1961).

15 *Miranda v. Arizona*, 384 U.S. 436 (1966).

16 *Benton v. Maryland*, 395 U.S. 784 (1969).

17 *NAACP v. Alabama ex rel. Patterson*, 357 U.S. 449 (1958).

18 This section is taken from Benjamin Ginsberg, Theodore J. Lowi, Margaret Weir, and Caroline J. Tolbert, *We the People: An Introduction to American Politics*, 9th ed. (New York: Norton, 2013).

19 For a lively and readable treatment of the possibilities of restricting provisions of the Bill of Rights without actually reversing prior decisions, see David G. Savage, *Turning Right: The Making of the Rehnquist Supreme Court* (New York: Wiley, 1992).

20 *Abington School District v. Schempp*, 374 U.S. 203 (1963).

21 *Engel v. Vitale*, 370 U.S. 421 (1962).

22 *Wallace v. Jaffree*, 472 U.S. 38 (1985).

23 *Lynch v. Donnelly*, 465 U.S. 668 (1984).

24 *Lemon v. Kurtzman*, 403 U.S. 602 (1971).

25 *Elk Grove Unified School District v. Newdow*, 542 U.S. 1 (2004).

26 *Van Orden v. Perry*, 545 U.S. 677 (2005).

27 *McCreary v. ACLU*, 545 U.S. 844 (2005).

28 *Employment Division v. Smith*, 494 U.S. 872 (1990).

29 *City of Boerne v. Flores*, 521 U.S. 507 (1997).

30 *United States v. Carolene Products Company*, 304 U.S. 144 (1938), 384. This footnote is one of the Court's most important doctrines. See Alfred H. Kelly, Winfred A. Harbison, and Herman Belz, *The American Constitution: Its Origins and Development*, 7th ed. (New York: Norton, 1991), vol. 2, pp. 519–23.

31 *Snyder v. Phelps*, 09-751 (2011).

32 *Brandenburg v. Ohio*, 395 U.S. 444 (1969).

33 *Buckley v. Valeo*, 424 U.S. 1 (1976).

34 *McConnell v. Federal Election Commission*, 540 U.S. 93 (2003).

35 *Federal Election Commission v. Wisconsin Right to Life*, 551 U.S. 449 (2007).

36 *Citizens United v. Federal Election Commission*, 558 U.S. 310 (2010).

37 *McCutcheon v. Federal Election Commission*, 133 S. Ct. 1242 (2013).

38 *United States v. O'Brien*, 391 U.S. 367 (1968).

39 *Texas v. Johnson*, 491 U.S. 397 (1989).

40 *Virginia v. Black*, 538 U.S. 343 (2003).

41 *Near v. Minnesota ex rel. Olson*, 283 U.S. 697 (1931).

42 *Reno v. ACLU*, 521 U.S. 844 (1997).

43 *United States v. American Library Association*, 539 U.S. 194 (2003).

44 *United States v. Williams*, 553 U.S. 285 (2008).

45 *Chaplinsky v. State of New Hampshire*, 315 U.S. 568 (1942).

46 *R.A.V. v. City of St. Paul*, 506 U.S. 377 (1992).

47 *Capital Broadcasting Company v. Acting Attorney General*, 405 U.S. 1000 (1972).

48 Louis Fisher, *American Constitutional Law*, 7th ed. (Durham, NC: Academic Press, 2007), vol. 2, p. 546.

49 *Lorillard Tobacco v. Reilly*, 533 U.S. 525 (2001).

50 *District of Columbia v. Heller*, 554 U.S. 570 (2008).

51 *McDonald v. Chicago*, 561 U.S. 3025 (2010).

52 *Horton v. California*, 496 U.S. 128 (1990).

53 For a good discussion of the issue, see Fisher, *American Constitutional Law*, pp. 884–9.

54 E. S. Corwin and Jack Peltason, *Understanding the Constitution*, 13th ed. (Fort Worth, TX: Harcourt Brace, 1994), p. 286.

55 For a full account of the story of the trial and release of Clarence Earl Gideon, see Lewis, *Gideon's Trumpet*.

56 *Escobedo v. Illinois*, 378 U.S. 478 (1964).

57 *Wiggins v. Smith*, 539 U.S. 510 (2003).

58 *Furman v. Georgia*, 408 U.S. 238 (1972).

59 *Roe v. Wade*, 410 U.S. 113 (1973).

60 *Bowers v. Hardwick*, 478 U.S. 186 (1986). The dissenters were quoting an earlier case, *Olmstead v. United States*, 277 U.S. 438 (1928), to emphasize the nature of their disagreement with the majority in the *Bowers* case.

61 *Lawrence and Garner v. Texas*, 539 U.S. 558 (2003).

62 *Gonzales v. Oregon*, 546 U.S. 243 (2006).

63 Woman Suffrage, *Collier's New Encyclopedia*, 1921 edition, http://en.Wikisource.org/wiki/Collier%27s_New_Encyclopeida_%281921%29/Woman_suffrage.

64 V.O. Key, *Southern Politics in State and Nation* (New York: Alfred A. Knopf, 1949).

65 Bernard Taper, *Gomillion v. Lighfoot: The Tuskegee Gerrymander Case* (New York: McGraw-Hill, 1962).

66 *Smith v. Allwright*, 321 U.S. 649 (1944).

67 *Gomillion v. Lightfoot*, 364 U.S. 339 (1960).

68 *Shelby County v. Holder*, 570 U.S. ___ (2013).

69 *Plessy v. Ferguson*, 163 U.S. 537 (1896).

70 *Missouri ex rel. Gaines v. Canada*, 305 U.S. 337 (1938).

71 *Sweatt v. Painter*, 339 U.S. 629 (1950).

72 *Smith v. Allwright* (1944).

73 *Shelley v. Kraemer*, 334 U.S. 1 (1948).

74 The District of Columbia case came up too, but since the District of Columbia is not a state, it did not directly involve the Fourteenth Amendment and its equal protection clause. It confronted the Court on the same grounds, however—that segregation is inherently unequal. Its victory in effect was "incorporation in reverse," with equal protection moving from the Fourteenth Amendment to become part of the Bill of Rights. See *Bolling v. Sharpe*, 347 U.S. 497 (1954).

75 *Brown v. Board of Education* (1954)

76 The two most important cases were *Cooper v. Aaron*, 358 U.S. 1 (1958), which required

Little Rock, Arkansas, to desegregate, and *Griffin v. Prince Edward County School Board*, 337 U.S. 218 (1964), which forced all the schools of that Virginia county to reopen after five years of being closed to avoid desegregation.

77 *Swann v. Charlotte-Mecklenberg Board of Education*, 402 U.S. 1 (1971).

78 For a good evaluation, see Gary Orfield, *Must We Bus? Segregated Schools and National Policy* (Washington, DC: Brookings Institution, 1978), pp. 144–6. See also Bob Woodward and Scott Armstrong, *The Brethren: Inside the Supreme Court* (New York: Simon & Schuster, 1979), pp. 426–7; and J. Anthony Lukas, *Common Ground* (New York: Random House, 1986).

79 *Parents Involved in Community Schools v. Seattle School District No. 1*, 551 U.S. 701 (2007).

80 *Franklin v. Gwinnett County Public Schools*, 503 U.S. 60 (1992).

81 Jennifer Halperin, "Women Step Up to Bat," *Illinois Issue* 21 (September 1995): 11–14.

82 *United States v. Virginia*, 518 U.S. 515 (1996).

83 Judith Havemann, "Two Women Quit Citadel over Alleged Harassment," *Washington Post*, January 13, 1997, p. A1.

84 See especially *Katzenbach v. McClung*, 379 U.S. 294 (1964).

85 *Griggs v. Duke Power Company*, 401 U.S. 24 (1971).

86 *Ledbetter v. Goodyear Tire and Rubber Co.*, 550 U.S. 618 (2007).

87 This and the next five sections are drawn in part from Ginsberg et al., *We the People*, 9th ed.

88 See Jane J. Mansbridge, *Why We Lost the ERA* (Chicago: University of Chicago Press, 1986); and Gilbert Steiner, *Constitutional Inequality* (Washington, DC: Brookings Institution, 1985).

89 See *Frontiero v. Richardson*, 411 U.S. 677 (1973).

90 See *Craig v. Boren*, 423 U.S. 1047 (1976).

91 *Meritor Savings Bank v. Vinson*, 477 U.S. 57 (1986).

92 *Harris v. Forklift Systems*, 510 U.S. 17 (1993).

93 *Burlington Industries v. Ellerth*, 524 U.S. 742 (1998); and *Faragher v. City of Boca Raton*, 524 U.S. 775 (1998).

94 New Mexico had a different history because not many Anglos settled there initially. (*Anglo* is the term for a non-Hispanic white of European background.) Mexican Americans had considerable power in territorial legislatures between 1865 and 1912. See Lawrence H. Fuchs, *The American Kaleidoscope* (Hanover, NH: University Press of New England, 1990), pp. 239–40.

95 On the La Raza Unida Party, see Carlos Muñoz, Jr., and Mario Barrera, "La Raza Unida Party and the Chicano Student Movement in California," in *Latinos and the Political System*, F. Chris Garcia, ed. (Notre Dame, IN: University of Notre Dame Press, 1988), pp. 213–35.

96 *Mendez v. Westminster*, 161 F2d 744 (Ninth Cir., 1947).

97 *United States v. Wong Kim Ark*, 169 U.S. 649 (1898).

98 *Lau v. Nichols*, 414 U.S. 563 (1974).

99 Dick Kirschten, "Not Black and White," *National Journal*, March 2, 1991, p. 497.

100 See the discussion in Robert A. Katzmann, *Institutional Disability: The Saga of Transportation Policy for the Disabled* (Washington, DC: Brookings Institution, 1986).

101 For example, after pressure from the Justice Department, one of the nation's largest rental car companies agreed to make special hand controls available to any customer requesting them. See "Avis Agrees to Equip Cars for Disabled," *Los Angeles Times*, September 2, 1994, p. D1.

102 Quoted in Joan Biskupic, "Gay Rights Activists Seek a Supreme Court Test Case," *Washington Post*, December 19, 1993, p. A1.

103 *Romer v. Evans*, 517 U.S. 620 (1996).

104 *United States v. Windsor*, 570 U.S. ___ (2013). That same day the Court also cleared the way for the legalization of same-sex marriage in California in the case *Hollingsworth v. Perry*, 570 U.S. ___ (2013).

105 *Regents of the University of California v. Bakke*, 438 U.S. 265 (1978).

106 *United Steelworkers of America v. Weber*, 443 U.S. 193 (1979); and *Fullilove v. Klutznick*, 448 U.S. 448 (1980).

107 *Martin v. Wilks*, 490 U.S. 755 (1989).

108 *Adarand Constructors v. Pena*, 515 U.S. 200 (1995).

109 *Hopwood v. State of Texas*, 78 F3d 932 (Fifth Cir., 1996).

110 *Gratz v. Bollinger*, 539 U.S. 244 (2003).

111 *Grutter v. Bollinger*, 539 U.S. 306 (2003).

CHAPTER 5

1 Alexander Hamilton, James Madison, and John Jay, *The Federalist Papers*, Clinton L. Rossiter, ed. (New York: New American Library, 1961), no. 47, p. 378.

2 See Richard F. Fenno, Jr., *Home Style: House Members in Their Districts* (Boston: Little, Brown, 1978). Essays elaborating on Fenno's classic are found in Morris P. Fiorina and David W. Rhode, eds., *Home Style and Washington Work* (Ann Arbor: University of Michigan Press, 1989).

3 For more on political careers generally, see John R. Hibbing, "Legislative Careers: Why and How We Should Study Them," *Legislative Studies Quarterly* 24 (1999): 149–71. See also Cherie D. Maestas, Sarah Fulton, L. Sandy Maisel, and Walter J. Stone, "When to Risk It? Institutions, Ambitions, and the Decision to Run for the U.S. House," *American Political Science Review* 100, no. 2 (May 2006): 195–208.

4 Constituents are not a legislative agent's only principals. Her or she may also be beholden to party leaders and special interests, as well as to members and committees in the chamber. See Forrest Maltzman, *Competing Principles* (Ann Arbor: University of Michigan Press, 1997).

5 See Linda L. Fowler and Robert D. McClure, *Political Ambition: Who Decides to Run for Congress* (New Haven, CT: Yale University Press, 1989); and Alan Ehrenhalt, *The United States of Ambition: Politicians, Power, and the Pursuit of Office* (New York: Times Books, 1991).

6 On the thesis of "strategic candidacy," see Gary C. Jacobson, *The Politics of Congressional Elections*, 7th ed. (New York: Pearson Longman, 2008).

7 See James D. Savage, *Funding Science in America: Congress, Universities, and the Politics of the Academic Pork Barrel* (New York: Cambridge University Press, 1999); and Diana Evans, *Greasing the Wheels: Using Pork-Barrel Projects to Build Majority Coalitions in Congress* (New York: Cambridge University Press, 2004).

8 Norman J. Ornstein, Thomas E. Mann, and Michael J. Malbin, *Vital Statistics on Congress, 1995–1996* (Washington, DC: CQ Press, 1996), pp. 60–61 (see also subsequent editions); Robert S. Erickson and Gerald C. Wright, "Voters, Candidates, and Issues in Congressional Elections," in *Congress Reconsidered*, 5th ed., Lawrence C. Dodd and Bruce I. Oppenheimer, eds. (Washington, DC: CQ Press, 1993), p. 99; John R. Alford and David W. Brady, Personal and Partisan Advantage in U.S Congressional Elections, 1846–1990," in *Congress Reconsidered*, 5th ed., pp. 141–57.

9 Stephen Ansolabehere and James Snyder, "Campaign War Chests and Congressional Elections," *Business and Politics*, no. 2 (2000): 9–34.

10 Gary W. Cox and Eric Magar, "How Much Is Majority Status in the U.S. Congress Worth?" *American Political Science Review* 93, no. 2 (June 1999): 299–309.

11 Kenneth Bickers and Robert Stein. "The Electoral Dynamics of the Federal Pork Barrel," *American Journal of Political Science* 40 (1996): 1300–26.

12 See Barbara C. Burrell, *A Woman's Place Is in the House: Campaigning for Congress in the Feminist Era* (Ann Arbor: University of Michigan Press, 1994), Chap. 6; and David Broder, "Key to Women's Political Parity: Running," *Washington Post*, September 8, 1994, p. A17.

13 See John H. Aldrich, *Why Parties? The Origin and Transformation of Political Parties in America* (Chicago: University of Chicago Press, 1995); and Gary W. Cox and Mathew D. McCubbins, *Legislative Leviathan: Party Government in the House* (Berkeley: University of California Press, 1993).

14 Richard Fenno, Jr., *Home Style: House Members in Their Districts* (Boston: Little, Brown, 1978).

15 John Gilmour, *Strategic Disagreement* (Pittsburgh: University of Pittsburgh Press, 1995).

16 16 See John W. Kingdon, *Congressmen's Voting Decisions* (New York: Harper & Row, 1973), chap. 3; and R. Douglas Arnold, *The Logic of Congressional Action* (New Haven, CT: Yale University Press, 1990). See also Joshua Clinton, "Representation in Congress: Constituents and Roll Calls in the 106th House," *Journal of Politics* 68 (2006): 397–409.

17 See Kenneth W. Kollman, *Outside Lobbying: Public Opinion and Interest Group Strategies* (Princeton, NJ: Princeton University Press, 1998).

18 See Janet M. Grenke, "PACs and the Congressional Supermarket: The Currency Is Complex," *American Journal of Political Science* 33, no. 1 (February 1989): 1–24. More generally, see Jacobson, *The Politics of Congressional Elections*. See also Stephen Ansolabehere, John de Figueiredo, and James Snyder, "Why Is There So Little Money in U.S. Politics?" *Journal of Economic Perspectives* 17 (2003): 105–30.

19 See Sven E. Feldmann and Morten Bennedsen, "Informational Lobbying and Political Contributions," *Journal of Public Economics* 90 (2006): 631–56.

20 A recent analysis of how floor time is allocated is found in Gary W. Cox and Mathew D. McCubbins, *Setting the Agenda: Responsible Party Government in the U.S. House of Representatives* (New York: Cambridge University Press, 2005).

21 David Broder, "At 6 Months, House GOP Juggernaut Still Cohesive," *Washington Post*, July 17, 1995, p. A1.

22 Carl Hulse, "Even Some in G.O.P. Call for More Oversight of Bush," *New York Times*, May 31, 2004, p. A13.

23 *U.S. v. Pink*, 315 U.S. 203 (1942). For a good discussion of the problem, see James W. Davis, *The American Presidency* (New York: Harper & Row, 1987), chap. 8.

CHAPTER 6

1 Quoted from the dissenting opinion of Justice Robert Jackson in *Korematsu v. United States*, 323 U.S. 214 (1944).

2 *Authorization for Use of Military Force*, Public Law 107-40, *U.S. Statutes at Large* 115 (2001): 224.

3 Alexander Hamilton, James Madison, and John Jay, *The Federalist Papers*, Clinton L. Rossiter, ed. (New York: New American Library, 1961), no. 39, p. 309.

4 David Fahrenthold, "Senator Obama vs. President Obama," *Washington Post*, June 26, 2011, p. A3.

5 *In re Neagle*, 135 U.S. 1 (1890).

6 James G. Randall, *Constitutional Problems under Lincoln* (New York: Appleton, 1926), chap. 1.

7 Edward S. Corwin, *The President: Office and Powers*, 4th rev. ed. (New York: New York University Press, 1957), p. 229.

8 These statutes are contained mainly in Title 10 of the U.S. Code, Sections 331, 332, and 333.

9 An excellent study covering all aspects of the domestic use of the military is that of Adam Yarmolinsky, *The Military Establishment* (New York: Harper & Row, 1971).

10 In *United States v. Pink*, 315 U.S. 203 (1942), the Supreme Court confirmed that an executive agreement is the legal equivalent of a treaty, despite the absence of Senate approval.

11 *United States v. Nixon*, 418 U.S. 683 (1974).

12 Another extension of executive power by President George W. Bush was the "signing statement," which is discussed later in this chapter.

13 *Clinton v. City of New York*, 524 U.S. 417 (1998).

14 For the complete list of presidential vetoes, see www.senate.gov/reference/Legislation /Vetoes/BushGW.htm (accessed 9/20/11).

15 Charles M. Cameron, *Veto Bargaining: Presidents and the Politics of Negative Power* (New York: Cambridge University Press, 2000). See also David W. Rohde and Dennis Simon, "Presidential Vetoes and Congressional Response: A Study of Institutional Conflict," *American Journal of Political Science* 29 (1985): 397–427.

16 Theodore J. Lowi, *The Personal President: Power Invested, Promise Unfulfilled* (Ithaca, NY: Cornell University Press, 1985).

17 Timothy Groseclose and Nolan McCarty, "The Politics of Blame: Bargaining before an Audience," *American Journal of Political Science* 45 (2001): 100–19.

18 This point is developed in both Kenneth R. Mayer, *With the Stroke of a Pen: Executive Orders and Presidential Power* (Princeton, NJ: Princeton University Press, 2001); and William G. Howell, *Power without Persuasion: The Politics of Direct Presidential Action* (Princeton, NJ: Princeton University Press, 2003).

19 Richard Neustadt, *Presidential Power: The Politics of Leadership* (New York: Wiley, 1960).

20 Charles M. Cameron, "Bargaining and Presidential Power," in *Presidential Power: Forging the Presidency for the Twenty-First Century*, Robert Y. Shapiro, Martha Joynt Kumar, and Lawrence R. Jacobs, eds. (New York: Columbia University Press, 2000), p. 47.

21 For related appraisals, see Jeffrey Tulis, *The Rhetorical Presidency* (Princeton, NJ: Princeton University Press, 1988), Stephen Skowronek, *The Politics Presidents Make: Presidential Leadership from John Adams to George Bush* (Cambridge, MA: Harvard University Press, 1993), and Robert Spitzer, *President and Congress: Executive Hegemony at the Crossroads of American Government* (New York: McGraw-Hill, 1993).

22 *National Labor Relations Board v. Jones & Laughlin Steel Corporation*, 301 U.S. 1 (1937).

23 See George Krause, "The Secular Decline in Presidential Domestic Policymaking: An Organizational Perspective," *Presidential Studies Quarterly* 34 (2004): 779–92. On the general issue, see James P. Pfiffner, ed., *The Managerial Presidency*, 2nd ed. (College Station: Texas A&M University Press, 1999).

24 Article I, Section 3, provides that the vice president "shall be President of the Senate, but shall have no Vote, unless they be equally divided."

25 Samuel Kernell, *Going Public: New Strategies of Presidential Leadership*, 3rd ed. (Washington, DC: CQ Press, 1997); also Jeffrey Tulis, *The Rhetorical Presidency* (Princeton, NJ: Princeton University Press, 1987).

26 Quoted in Sidney M. Milkis, *The President and the Parties* (New York: Oxford University Press, 1993), p. 97.

27 Kernell, *Going Public*, p. 79.

28 Theodore J. Lowi, *The Personal President: Power Invested, Promise Unfulfilled* (Ithaca, NY: Cornell University Press, 1985).

29 Kernell, *Going Public*, p. 114

30 The classic critique of this process is Theodore J. Lowi, *The End of Liberalism* (New York: Norton, 1979).

31 Kenneth Culp Davis, *Administrative Law Treatise* (St. Paul, MN: West Publishing, 1958), p. 9.

32 Elena Kagan, "Presidential Administration," *Harvard Law Review* 2245 (2001): 2265.

33 For example, Douglas W. Kmiec, "Expanding Power," in *The Rule of Law in the Wake of Clinton*, Roger Pilon, ed. (Washington, DC: Cato Institute Press, 2000), pp. 47–68.

34 A complete inventory is provided in Harold C. Relyea, "Presidential Directives:

Background and Review," The Library of Congress, *Congressional Research Service Report 98–611*, November 9, 2001.

35 *Youngstown Sheet & Tube Co. v. Sawyer*, 346 U.S. 579 (1952).

36 Mark Killenbeck, "A Matter of Mere Approval: The Role of the President in the Creation of Legislative History," 48 *University of Arkansas Law Review* 239 (1995).

37 Philip J. Cooper, *By Order of the President: The Use and Abuse of Executive Direct Action* (Lawrence: University Press of Kansas, 1998), p. 201.

38 Edward S. Corwin, *The President: Office and Powers*, 4th ed. (New York: New York University Press, 1957), p. 283.

39 Cooper, *By Order of the President*, p. 201.

40 *Ameron, Inc. v. U.S. Army Corps of Engineers*, 610 F.Supp. 750 (D.N.J. 1985).

41 *Lear Siegler, Inc. v. Lehman*, 842 F.2nd 1102 (1988).

CHAPTER 7

1 William A. Niskanen, *Bureaucracy and Representative Government* (Chicago: Aldine, 1971).

2 Stephen Peter Rosen, *Winning the Next War* (Ithaca, NY: Cornell University Press, 1991).

3 Harold Seidman, *Politics, Position, and Power: The Dynamics of Federal Organization*, 5th ed. (New York: Oxford University Press, 1998), chap. 8.

4 James Q. Wilson, *Bureaucracy: What Government Agencies Do and Why They Do It* (New York: Basic Books, 1989), p. 91.

5 When bureaucrats engage in interpretation, the result is what political scientists call bureaucratic drift. Bureaucratic drift occurs because, as we've suggested, the "bosses" (in Congress) and the "agents" (within the bureaucracy) don't always share the same purposes. Bureaucrats also have their own agendas to fulfill.

6 See Mathew D. McCubbins and Thomas Schwartz, "Congressional Oversight Overlooked: Police Patrols versus Fire Alarms," *American Journal of Political Science* 28 (1984): 165–79.

7 32 Stat. 825; 15 USC 1501.

8 For a detailed account of the creation of the Department of Commerce and Labor and its split into two separate departments, see Theodore J. Lowi, *The End of Liberalism* (New York: Norton, 1979), pp. 78–84.

9 The departments of Education and of Health and Human Services until 1979 were joined in a single department, the Department of Health, Education, and Welfare (HEW), which had been established by Congress in 1953.

10 Alexander Hamilton, James Madison, and John Jay, *The Federalist Papers*, Clinton L. Rossiter, ed. (New York: New American Library, 1961), no. 51.

11 Niskanen, *Bureaucracy and Representative Government*.

12 John Brehm and Scott Gates, *Working, Shirking, and Sabotage: Bureaucratic Response to a Democratic Public* (Ann Arbor: University of Michigan Press, 1997). For detailed insight about the motivations for government service combining the personal and the patriotic, consider the case of Henry Paulson, who became George W. Bush's Treasury secretary. Paulson's story is described well in Andrew Ross Sorkin, *Too Big to Fail* (New York: Viking, 2009), chap. 2.

13 For an expanded view of bureaucratic autonomy and insulation with historical application to the U.S. Department of Agriculture and the Post Office Department, see Daniel P. Carpenter, *The Forging of Bureaucratic Autonomy: Reputations, Networks, and Policy Innovation in Executive Agencies, 1862–1928* (Princeton, NJ: Princeton University Press, 2001).

14 See John Micklethwait, "Managing to Look Attractive," *New Statesman*, November 8, 1996, p. 24.

15 See Aaron Wildavsky, *The New Politics of the Budgetary Process*, 2nd ed. (New York: HarperCollins, 1992), pp. 15–6.

16 Morris S. Ogul, *Congress Oversees the Bureaucracy: Studies in Legislative Supervision* (Pittsburgh, PA: University of Pittsburgh Press, 1976); and Peter Woll, *American Bureaucracy*, 2nd ed. (New York: Norton, 1977).

17 See McCubbins and Schwartz, "Congressional Oversight Overlooked."

18 This is just under 99 percent of all national government employees. About 2 percent work for the legislative branch and for the federal judiciary. U.S. Bureau of the Census, *Statistical Abstract of the U.S. 2011*.

19 U.S. Bureau of the Census, *Statistical Abstract of the U.S. 2011*. (accessed 11/12/14)

20 Public Law 101-510, Title XXIX, Sections 2,901 and 2,902 of Part A (Defense Base Closure and Realignment Commission).

21 Ellen Nakashima, "Defense Balks at Contract Goals; Essential Services Should Not Be Privatized, Pentagon Tells OMB," *Washington Post*, January 30, 2002, p. A21.

CHAPTER 8

1 Justices in many state and local courts are elected.

2 *United States v. Nixon*, 418 U.S. 683 (1974).

3 Edward Corwin, *The President: Office and Powers,* 4th rev. ed. (New York: New York University Press, 1957), p. 16.

4 Terry M. More and William G. Howell, "The Presidential Power of Unilateral Action," *The Journal of Law, Economics and Organization,* 15 (1) (1999): 151–2.

5 Thomas E. Cronin and Michael A. Genovese, *The Paradoxes of the American Presidency* (New York: Oxford University Press, 1998), p. 271.

6 C. Herman Pritchett, *The American Constitution* (New York: McGraw-Hill, 1959), p. 138.

7 *Marbury v. Madison,* 1 Cranch 137 (1803).

8 For an analysis of the Court's use of judicial review to nullify acts of Congress, see Ryan Emenaker, "Constitutional Interpretation and Congressional Overrides: Changing Trends in Court–Congress Relations," presented at the annual meeting of the Western Political Science Association, Hollywood, CA, March 28–30, 2013.

9 This review power was affirmed by the Supreme Court in *Martin v. Hunter's Lessees,* 1 Wheaton 304 (1816).

10 56 Stat. 23 (January 30, 1942).

11 *Chevron v. Natural Resources Defense Council,* 467 U.S. 837 (1984).

12 *Hamdi v. Rumsfeld,* 542 U.S. 507 (2004).

13 *Hamdan v. Rumsfeld,* 548 U.S. (2006).

14 Walter F. Murphy, "The Supreme Court of the United States," in *Encyclopedia of the American Judicial System,* Robert J. Janosik, ed. (New York: Scribner's, 1987).

15 Gregory A. Caldeira and John R. Wright, "Organized Interests and Agenda Setting in the U.S. Supreme Court," *American Political Science Review* 82 (1988): 1109–27.

16 *Adarand Constructors, Inc. v. Peña,* 515 U.S. 200 (1995); *Missouri v. Jenkins,* 515 U.S. 70 (1995); *Miller v. Johnson,* 515 U.S. 900 (1995).

17 Robert Scigliano, *The Supreme Court and the Presidency* (New York: Free Press, 1971), p. 162. For an interesting critique of the solicitor general's role during the Reagan administration, see Lincoln Caplan, "Annals of the Law," *New Yorker,* August 17, 1987, pp. 30–62.

18 Quoted in Adam Liptak and Peter Baker, "Justices Cast Doubt on Benefits Ban in U.S. Marriage Law," *New York Times,* March 27, 2013, p. A1.

19 *Smith v. Allwright,* 321 U.S. 649 (1944).

20 *South v. Peters,* 339 U.S. 276 (1950).

21 *Gray v. Sanders,* 372 U.S. 368 (1963).

22 Warren Richey, "Dissenting Opinions as a Window on Future Rulings," *Christian Science Monitor,* July 1, 2002, p. 1.

23 Adam Liptak, "Supreme Court Upholds Health Care Law, 5–4, in Victory for Obama," *New York Times,* June 28, 2012, www.nytimes.com /2012/06/29/us/supreme-court-lets-health -law-largely-stand.html?pagewanted=all (accessed 7/15/13).

24 C. Herman Pritchett, *The Roosevelt Court* (New York: Macmillan, 1948).

25 William N. Eskridge, Jr., "Overriding Supreme Court Statutory Interpretation Decisions," *Yale Law Journal* 101 (1991): 331–55.

26 A full strategic analysis of the maneuvering among the legislative, executive, and judicial branches in the separation-of-powers arrangement choreographed by the U.S. Constitution may be found in William Eskridge and John Ferejohn, "The Article 1, Section 7 Game," *Georgetown Law Review* 80 (1992): 523–65. The entire issue of this journal is devoted to the theme of strategic behavior in American institutional politics.

27 Toni Locy, "Bracing for Health Care's Caseload," *Washington Post,* August 22, 1994, p. A15.

28 See "Developments in the Law—Class Actions," *Harvard Law Review* 89 (1976): 1318.

29 See Donald Horowitz, *The Courts and Social Policy* (Washington, DC: Brookings Institution, 1977).

30 *Moran v. McDonough,* 540 F. 2nd 527 (1 Cir., 1976; cert denied 429 U.S. 1042 [1977]).

31 David Van Drehle, "Court That Liberals Savage Proves to Be Less of a Target," *Washington Post,* June 29, 2003, p. A18.

CHAPTER 9

1 Alan Monroe, "Consistency between Public Preferences and National Policy Decisions," *American Politics Quarterly* 7 (1979): 3–18. See also Alan D. Monroe, "Public Opinion and Public Policy, 1980–1993," *Public Opinion Quarterly* 62, no. 1 (1998): 6–18.

2 Benjamin I. Page and Robert Y. Shapiro, "Effects of Public Opinion on Policy," *American Political Science Review* 77 (1983): 175–90. See also Jeff Manza, Fay Cook, and Benjamin Page, eds., *Navigating Public Opinion* (New York: Oxford University Press, 2002), Part I.

3 Carol Glynn, Susan Herbst, Garret O'Keefe, Robert Shapiro, and Mark Lindeman, *Public Opinion,* 2nd ed. (Boulder, CO: Westview, 2004), p. 293.

4 Lawrence R. Jacobs and Robert Y. Shapiro, *Politicians Don't Pander* (Chicago: University of Chicago Press, 2000), p. xv.

5   Dick Morris, *Behind the Oval Office* (Los Angeles: Renaissance, 1999). Quoted in Jacobs and Shapiro, *Politicians Don't Pander*, p. xv.

6   Michael Graetz and Ian Shapiro, *Death by a Thousand Cuts: The Fight over Taxing Inherited Wealth* (Princeton, NJ: Princeton University Press, 2005).

7   Jacob S. Hacker and Paul Pierson, *Off Center: The Republican Revolution and the Erosion of American Democracy* (New Haven, CT: Yale, 2005), chap. 2.

8   See Louis Hartz, *The Liberal Tradition in America: An Interpretation of American Political Thought since the Revolution* (New York: Harcourt, Brace, 1955).

9   For a discussion of political beliefs of Americans, see Everett Carl Ladd, *The American Ideology* (Storrs, CT: Roper Center, 1994).

10 Jordy Yeager, "House Limits Constituent E-mail to Prevent Crash," *The Hill*, September 30, 2008, http://thehill.com/leading-the-news/house-limits-constituent-e-mails-to-prevent-crash-2008-09-30.html (accessed 3/24/09).

11 The American Values Survey is available at www.people-press.org/values-questions.

12 Rawi Abdelal, Yoshiko M. Herrera, Alastair Iain Johnston, and Rose McDermott, "Identity as a Variable" *Perspectives on Politics* 4, no. 4 (2006): 695–711.

13 Pew Research Center for the People and the Press, "The Black and White of Public Opinion," October 31, 2005, http://people-press.org/commentary/?anaysisid=121 (accessed 3/24/09).

14 Pew Research Center, September 2014, "Wide Partisan Differences Over the Issues That Matter in 2014," www.people-press.org/files/2014/09/09-12-14-Midterms-Release1.pdf (accessed 12/16/14).

15 Gabriel R. Sanchez, "The Role of Group Consciousness in Latino Public Opinion," *Political Research Quarterly* 59, no. 3 (2006): 435–446. Pamela Johnston Conover, "The Influence of Group Identifications on Political Perception and Evaluation," *Journal of Politics* 46, no. 3 (1984): 760–85.

16 Taeku Lee, "Race, Immigration, and the Identity-to-Politics Link," *Annual Review of Political Science* 11 (2008): 457–78.

17 For data, see Center for American Women and Politics, Eagleton Institute of Politics, Rutgers, State University of New Jersey, www.cawp.rutgers.edu/fast_facts/voters/turnout.php (accessed 4/30/09).

18 Pew Research Center for the People and the Press, "Pragmatic Americans Liberal and Conservative on Social Issues: Most Want Middle Ground on Abortion," August 3, 2006, http://people-press.org/report/283/pragmatic-americans-liberal-and-conservative-on-social-issues (accessed 3/24/09).

19 An outstanding research paper along these lines is Ebonya Washington, "Female Socialization: How Daughters Affect Their Legislator Fathers' Voting on Women's Issues," *American Economic Review* 98 (2008): 311–32.

20 Angus Campbell, Philip E. Converse, Warren E. Miller, and Donald E. Stokes, *The American Voter* (Chicago: The University of Chicago Press, 1960).

21 Rene R. Rocha, and Rodolfo Espino, "Racial Threat, Residential Segregation, and the Policy Attitudes of Anglos," *Political Research Quarterly* 62, no. 2 (2009): 415–26.

22 Being a numerical majority is not necessary. For over a century, blacks in South Africa were oppressed by Afrikkaners, even though the white population accounted for only about 10 percent of all people in the country.

23 Paula D. McClain, Jessica D. Johnson Carew, Eugene Walton, Jr., and Candis S. Watts, "Group Membership, Group Identity, and Group Consciousness: Measures of Racial Identity in American Politics?" *Annual Review of Political Science* 12 (2009): 471–85.

24 Philip E. Converse, "The Nature of Belief Systems in Mass Publics," in *Ideology and Discontent*, David E. Apter, ed. (New York: Free Press, 1964).

25 Anthony Downs, An *Economic Theory of Democracy* (New York: Harper & Row, 1957).

26 For a discussion of the role of information in democratic politics, see Arthur Lupia and Mathew D. McCubbins, *The Democratic Dilemma: Can Citizens Learn What They Need to Know?* (New York: Cambridge University Press, 1998).

27 One of the most detailed analyses of the distribution of the tax burden in advanced industrial democracies in the past half-century is Thomas Piketty and Emmanuel Saez, "How Progressive Is the U.S. Federal Tax System? Historical and International Perspectives," working paper 12404, National Bureau of Economic Research, 2006. www.nber.org/papers/w12404 (accessed 3/25/09).

28 Jacob Hacker and Paul Pierson, *Winner Take All Polities* (New York: Simon & Shuster, 2010).

29 Larry M. Bartels, "Homer Gets a Tax Cut: Inequality and Public Policy in the American Mind," *Perspectives on Politics* 3 (2005): 15–31.

30 See Andrea Louise Campbell, "What Americans Think of Taxes," in *The New Fiscal Sociology: Taxation in Comparative and Historical Perspective*, Isaac William Martin, Ajay K. Mehrotra, and Monica Prasad, eds. (New York: Cambridge University Press, 2009).

31 Gerald F. Seib and Michael K. Frisby, "Selling Sacrifice," *Wall Street Journal*, February 5, 1993, p. 1.

32 Joshua Green, "The Other War Room," *Washington Monthly*, April 2002.

33 Michael Calderone, "White House News Strategy Causes Concerns about Access," February 15, 2011, http://news.yahoo.com/s/yblog _thecutline/20110215/bs_yblog_thecutline/white -house-media-strategy-causes-concerns-about -access (accessed 8/22/11).

34 Cynthia Gorney, "Gambling with Abortion," *Harper's Magazine*, November 2004, pp. 33–46.

35 See David Vogel, "The Power of Business in America: A Reappraisal," *British Journal of Political Science* 13 (January 1983): 19–44.

36 See David Vogel, "The Public Interest Movement and the American Reform Tradition," *Political Science Quarterly* 96 (Winter 1980): 607–27.

37 See Stephen Ansolabehere, Roy Behr, and Shanto Iyengar, *The Media Game* (New York: Macmillan, 1993).

38 These figures are tracked regularly by the Nielsen Corporation, www.nielsen-online.com/pr/pr _040318.pdf (accessed 3/25/09).

39 "The 10 Most Endangered Newspapers in America," *Time*, March 9, 2009, www.time .com/time/business/article/0,8599,1883785,00 .html (accessed 6/8/09).

40 *Near v. Minnesota ex rel.*, 283 U.S. 697 (1931).

41 See Matthew Baum, *Soft News Goes to War* (Princeton, NJ: Princeton University Press, 2006).

42 The seminal work on priming and framing in public policy and politics is Shanto Iyengar and Donald Kinder, *News That Matters* (Chicago: University of Chicago Press, 1987).

43 Page and Shapiro, "Effects of Public Opinion on Policy."

44 Robert A. Erikson, Gerald Wright, and John McIver, *Statehouse Democracy: Public Opinion and Democracy in the American States* (New York: Cambridge University Press, 1994).

45 The results of separate studies by the political scientists Lawrence Jacobs, Robert Shapiro, and Alan Monroe were reported by Richard Morin in "Which Comes First, the Politician or the Poll?" *Washington Post National Weekly Edition*, February 10, 1997, p. 35.

46 David S. Broder, *Democracy Detailed: Initiative Campaigns and the Power of Money* (New York: Harcourt, 2000).

47 In its 2013 term, the U.S. Supreme Court reaffirmed a lower court ruling which had the effect of reversing Proposition 8. *Hollingsworth v. Perry*, 570 U.S. __ (2013).

CHAPTER 10

1 Alexander Hamilton, James Madison, and John Jay, *The Federalist Papers*, Clinton Rossiter, ed. (New York: New American Library, 1961), no. 57.

2 Walter Lippman, *The Essential Lippman*, Clinton Rossiter and James Lare, eds. (New York: Random House, Vintage Books, 1965), p. 12.

3 Senate Committee on the Judiciary, *Hearings before the Subcommittee on Constitutional Amendments on S.J. Res. 8, S.J. Res. 14 and S.J. Res. 78, Relating to Lowering the Voting Age to 18*. 90th Cong., 2nd sess., 1968 (Washington, DC: U.S. Government Printing Office, 1968), p. 12.

4 Senate Committee, *Hearings*, p. 3.

5 Benjamin Ginsberg and Robert Weissberg, "Elections as Legitimizing Institutions," *American Journal of Political Science* 22, no. 1 (February 1978): 31–55.

6 In addition there is the restriction that those currently serving sentences for felonies cannot vote; some states prohibit ex-felons from voting.

7 There are further restrictions in some states that prohibit ex-felons from voting and impose residency requirements.

8 Sidney Verba, Kay Schlozman, and Henry Brady, *Voice and Equality: Civic Volunteerism in America* (Cambridge, MA: Harvard University Press, 1995).

9 See Walter Dean Burnham, "The Changing Shape of the American Political Universe," *American Political Science Review* 59, no. 1 (March 1965): 7–28. It should be noted that other democracies, such as India and Switzerland, have even lower turnout rates, as do some of the new democracies in eastern Europe.

10 See statistics of the U.S. Bureau of the Census and the Federal Election Commission. For voting statistics for 1960 to 2004, see "National Voter Turnout in Federal Elections: 1960–2004," at www.infoplease.com/ipa/A0781453.html (accessed 3/26/09).

11 Not all states report such figures in their certified tally of the vote. In fact, 11 states do not report the number of ballots cast, and researchers must substitute the total votes for all candidates for the presidency or another office on the top of the ballot. So, for example, if an individual voter in one of these states does not cast a vote for president but does turn out to vote on other questions on the ballot, this voter might not be counted in the total. However, since nearly all voters who turn out do vote on the races at the top of the ticket, counting those totals is a reasonably accurate substitute for official turnout records.

12 Michael McDonald and Samuel Popkin, "The Myth of the Vanishing Voter," *American Political Science Review* 95 (December 2001): 963–74.

13 These figures exclude undocumented, illegal immigrants, of which there are estimated to be another 12 million persons.

14 Helen Dewar, "'Motor Voter' Agreement Is Reached," *Washington Post*, April 28, 1993, p. A6.

15 Stephen Ansolabehere and Eitan Hersh, "Validation: What Big Data Tell Us about the Actual Electorate," *Political Analysis* (2012).

16 Stephen Ansolabehere and Nathaniel Persily, "Vote Fraud in the Eye of the Beholder," *Harvard Law Review* 121 (2008): 1737; Stephen Ansolabehere, "Effects of Identification Requirements on Voting: Evidence from the Experiences of Voters on Election Day," *PS* (January 2009): 127–130.

17 Jerold G. Rusk, "The Effect of the Australian Ballot Reform on Split Ticket Voting, 1876–1908," *American Political Science Review* 64, no. 4 (December 1970): 1220–38.

18 The exceptions are Maine and Nebraska, which choose the House electors in individual House districts and the Senate electors in a statewide vote.

19 For definitions of these units, see Bureau of the Census, Geographic Area Reference Manual, www.census.gov/geo/www/garm.html (accessed 6/17/09).

20 Over the centuries, many systems for voting and determining electoral outcomes have been devised. For an excellent analysis of voting systems and a complete classification, see Gary Cox, *Making Votes Count* (New York: Cambridge University Press, 1997).

21 *Hollingsworth et. al. v. Perry et. al.*, 570 U.S. ___ (2013).

22 This point is developed in Mordon Bennedsen and Sven Fledmann, "Lobbying Legislatures," *Journal of Political Economy* 110 (2002).

23 The most reliable source of information about the demographics of voting is the Current Population Survey, conducted by the Census Bureau. For these and other statistics, see U.S. Census Bureau, "Voting and Registration in the Election of November 2012," www.census.gov/hhes/www /socdemo/voting/publications/p20/2012 /tables.html (accessed 7/17/13).

24 The classic study in this area is Raymond Wolfinger and Steven Rosenstone, *Who Votes?* (New Haven, CT: Yale University Press, 1978). See also Steven Rosenstone and John Mark Hansen, *Participation, Mobilization and American Democracy* (New York: Macmillan, 1993).

25 This is the wording used by the Gallup Poll. Others ask "In politics today . . ." or offer "or another party" instead of "or what."

26 For an excellent treatment of the meanings of party identification and analysis of the implications of different theories, see Donald Green, Bradley Palmquist, and Eric Schickler, *Partisan Hearts and Minds* (New Haven, CT: Yale University Press, 2003).

27 For a detailed assessment of the political use of information-economizing devices such as party labels, see Arthur Lupia and Mathew D. McCubbins, *The Democratic Dilemma: Can Citizens Learn What They Need to Know?* (New York: Cambridge University Press, 1998).

28 The partitioning of the incumbency effect into officeholder advantages and challenger qualities begins with the important work of Gary C. Jacobson; see, for example, his excellent text *Congressional Elections*. Estimating exactly what fraction of the incumbency effect is due to officeholder benefits is tricky. See Stephen Ansolabehere, James M. Snyder, Jr., and Charles H. Stewart III, "Old Voters, New Voters, and the Personal Vote," *American Journal of Political Science* 44 (2000).

29 See Stephen Ansolabehere, Jonathan Rodden, and James M. Snyder, Jr., "Issue Voting," *American Political Science Review* (May 2008).

30 The classic study showing this is Philip Converse, "The Nature of Belief Systems in Mass Publics," in *Ideology and Discontent*, David Apter, ed. (New York: Free Press, 1964).

31 The FEC's website is an excellent resource for those interested in U.S. campaign finance, www.fec.gov.

32 *Buckley v. Valeo*, 424 U.S. 1 (1976).

33 *Citizens United v. Federal Election Commission*, 558 U.S. 310 (2010).

34 *McConnell v. Federal Election Commission*, 540 U.S. 93 (2003).

35 See Stephen Ansolabehere and James M. Snyder, Jr., "The Incumbency Advantage in U.S. Elections: An Analysis of State and Federal Offices, 1942–2000," *Election Law Journal* 1 (2002): 315–38.

CHAPTER 11

1 This distinction is from John H. Aldrich, *Why Parties? The Origin and Transformation of Party Politics in America* (Chicago: University of Chicago Press, 1995).

2 See Adam Nagourney, "Eyeing '08: Democrats Nurse Freshmen at Risk," *New York Times*, December 22, 2006.

3 For an excellent analysis of the parties' role in recruitment, see Paul Herrnson, *Congressional Elections: Campaigning at Home and in Washington* (Washington, DC: CQ Press, 1995).

4 For a discussion of some of the effects of primary elections, see Peter F. Galderisi and Benjamin

Ginsberg, "Primary Elections and the Evanescence of Third Party Activity in the United States," in *Do Elections Matter?* Benjamin Ginsberg and Alan Stone, eds. (Armonk, NY: M. E. Sharpe, 1986), pp. 115–30.

5 Maurice Duverger, *Political Parties* (New York: John Wiley and Son, 1951).

6 Don Gonyea, "Obama's Winning Streak on Hill Unprecedented," NPR, January 11, 2010, www.npr.org/templates/story/story .php?storyId=122436116 (accessed 10/28/11).

7 For what is perhaps still the best discussion of the bases of party identification, see Arthur S. Goldberg, "Social Determinism and Rationality as Bases of Party Identification," *American Political Science Review* 63, no. 1 (March 1969): 5–25. For a more recent article weighing in on economic versus social determinants of party attachments, see Larry M. Bartels, "What's the Matter with *What's the Matter with Kansas?" Quarterly Journal of Political Science* 1 (2006): 201–26.

8 A recent formulation of the Pluralist model of parties is Kathleen Bawn, Martin Cohen, David Karol, Seth Masket, Hans Noel, and John Zaller, "A Theory of Political Parties: Groups, Policy Demands, and Nominations in American Politics," *Perspectives on Politics* 10 (2012): 571–97.

9 For a useful discussion, see John Bibby and Thomas Holbrook, "Parties and Elections," in *Politics in the American States: A Comparative Analysis*, 6th ed., Virginia Gray and Herbert Jacob, eds. (Washington, DC: CQ Press, 1996), pp. 78–121.

10 See Aldrich, *Why Parties?* chap. 8.

11 See Paul S. Herrnson, *Party Campaigning in the 1980s* (Cambridge, MA: Harvard University Press, 1988).

12 See William E. Gienapp, *The Origins of the Republican Party, 1852–1856* (New York: Oxford University Press, 1994).

13 See David W. Rohde, *Parties and Leaders in the Post-Reform House* (Chicago: University of Chicago Press, 1991). An elaboration of this argument is presented in Gary W. Cox and Mathew D. McCubbins, *Setting the Agenda: Responsible Party Government in the U.S. House of Representatives* (New York: Cambridge University Press, 2005). See also Nolan McCarty, Keith Poole, and Howard Rosenthal, *Polarized America: The Dance of Inequality and Unequal Riches* (Cambridge, MA: MIT Press, 2006).

14 For a discussion of third parties in the United States, see Daniel A. Mazmanian, *Third Parties in Presidential Elections* (Washington, DC: Brookings Institution, 1974).

15 See Maurice Duverger, *Political Parties: Their Organization and Activity in the Modern State*, trans. Barbara North and Robert North (New York: Wiley, 1954).

CHAPTER 12

1 Mary Williams Walsh, "Major Changes Raise Concerns on Pension Bill," *New York Times*, March 10, 2006, p. A1.

2 Thomas Ferguson, *Golden Rule: The Investment Theory of Party Competition and the Logic of Money-Driven Political Systems* (Chicago: University of Chicago Press, 1995).

3 Alexander Hamilton, James Madison, and John Jay, *The Federalist Papers*, Clinton Rossiter, ed. (New York: New American Library, 1961), no. 10, p. 78.

4 *The Federalist*, no. 10, p. 83.

5 *The Federalist*, no. 10.

6 Betsy Wagner and David Bowermaster, "B.S. Economics," *Washington Monthly*, November 1992, pp. 19–22.

7 Mancur Olson, *The Logic of Collective Action* (Cambridge, MA: Harvard University Press, 1971).

8 Kay Lehman Schlozman and John T. Tierney, *Organized Interests and American Democracy* (New York: Harper & Row, 1986), p. 60.

9 John Herbers, "Special Interests Gaining Power as Voter Disillusionment Grows," *New York Times*, November 14, 1978.

10 Andrea Campbell, *How Policies Make Citizens: Senior Citizen Activism and the American Welfare State* (Princeton, NJ: Princeton University Press, 2003).

11 For discussions of lobbying, see John Wright, *Interest Groups and Congress* (New York: Longman, 2009).

12 Daniel Franklin, "Tommy Boggs and the Death of Health Care Reform," *Washington Monthly*, April 1995, p. 36.

13 Marie Hojnacki, "Interest Groups' Decisions to Join Alliances or Work Alone," *American Journal of Political Science* 41 (1997): 61–87; Kevin W. Hula, *Lobbying Together: Interest Group Coalitions in Legislative Politics* (Washington, DC: Georgetown University Press, 1999).

14 An excellent example is the mobilization of corporate executives in the tax reform efforts in the mid-1980s. See Jeff Birnbaum, *Showdown at Gucci Gulch: Lawmakers, Lobbyists, and the Unlikely Triumph of Tax Reform* (New York: Random House, 1987).

15 Peggy Kerns, "Revolving Door Laws," National Conference of State Legislators, www .ncsl.org/legislatures-elections/ethicshome /legisbrief-revolving-door.aspx (accessed 3/4/13).

16 David Kirkpatrick, "In Daschle's Tax Woes, a Peek into Washington," *New York Times*, February 2, 2009, p. A1.

17 Jacob Straus, *Lobbying the Executive Branch: Current Practices and Options for Change* (Congressional Research Service, December 6, 2010), Report 7-5700, pp. 3–4.

18 John P. Heinz et al., *The Hollow Core: Private Interests in National Policy Making* (Cambridge, MA: Harvard University Press, 1993).

19 For an excellent discussion of the political origins of the Administrative Procedure Act, see Martin Shapiro, "APA: Past, Present, Future," 72 *Virginia Law Review*, 377 (March 1986): 447–92.

20 *Griswold v. Connecticut*, 381 U.S. 479 (1965); *Eisenstadt v. Baird*, 405 U.S. 438 (1972); *Roe v. Wade*, 410 U.S. 133 (1973).

21 *Webster v. Reproductive Health Services*, 492 U.S. 490 (1989).

22 *Brown v. Board of Education of Topeka*, 347 U.S. 483 (1954).

23 *Scheidler v. National Organization for Women et al.*, 547 U.S. 9 (2006).

24 Pendleton Herring, *Group Representation before Congress* (1928; repr.: New York: Russell & Russell, 1967). See also Kenneth W. Kollman, *Outside Lobbying: Public Opinion and Interest Group Strategies* (Princeton, NJ: Princeton University Press, 1998).

25 Natasha Singer, "Harry and Louise Return, with a New Message," *New York Times*, July 16, 2009, www.nytimes.com/2009/07/17/business /media/17adco.html?_r=1&ref=media (accessed 11/7/11).

26 Jane Fritsch, "The Grass Roots, Just a Free Phone Call Away," *New York Times*, June 23, 1995, pp. A1, A22.

27 See Stephen Ansolabehere, John M. de Figueiredo, and James M. Snyder, Jr., "Why Is There So Little Money in U.S. Politics?" *Journal of Economic Perspectives* 17, no. 1 (2003): 105–30.

28 *Buckley v. Valeo*, 424 U.S. 1 (1976).

29 *Citizens United v. Federal Election Commission*, 558 U.S. 310 (2010).

30 Donald Green and Alan Gerber, *Get Out the Vote: How to Increase Voter Turnout*, 2nd ed. (Washington, DC: Brookings Institution Press, 2008).

31 Elisabeth R. Gerber, *The Populist Paradox* (Princeton, NJ: Princeton University Press, 1999).

32 Ansolabehere, de Figueiredo, and Snyder, "Why Is There So Little Money in U.S. Politics?"

33 John M. de Figueiredo and Brian S. Silverman, "Academic Earmarks and the Returns to Lobbying" working paper 9064, National Bureau of Economic Research, 2002; substantially rev., 2003, http: //web.mit.edu/jdefig/www/papers/academic _earmarks.pdf (accessed 4/7/09).

34 John M. de Figueiredo and Brian S. Silverman, "Academic Earmarks and the Returns to Lobbying," *Journal of Law and Economics* 42 (October 2006): 597–626.

CHAPTER 13

1 Matthew A. Crenson and Benjamin Ginsberg, *Downsizing Democracy: How America Sidelined Its Citizens and Privatized Its Public* (Baltimore: Johns Hopkins University Press, 2002), chaps. 7 and 9.

2 Lester M. Salamon, "Economic Regulation," in *The Tools of Government: A Guide to the New Governance*, Lester M. Salamon, ed. (New York: Oxford University Press, 2002), p. 146.

3 Adam Carasso, Eugene Steuerle, and Elizabeth Bell, "Making Tax Incentives for Home Owners More Equitable and Efficient," Tax Policy Center Discussion Paper No. 21, The Urban Institute, Washington, DC, 2005.

4 Inman News, "Survey: 85% Oppose Mortgage Interest Deduction Elimination," December 22, 2005, www.inman.com/news/2005/12/4/survey -85-oppose-mortgage-interest-deduction -elimination (accessed 10/28/11).

5 Compare with Gabriel Kolko, *The Triumph of Conservatism* (New York: Free Press, 1963), chap. 6.

6 Farm Subsidy Database: A Project of Environmental Working Group, www.ewg.org /farm (accessed 10/28/11).

7 A congressional act of 1956 officially designated the interstate highways the National System of Interstate and Defense Highways. It was indirectly a major part of President Eisenhower's defense program. But it was just as obviously a pork-barrel policy as any rivers and harbors legislation.

8 Center on Budget and Policy Priorities, "Tax Cuts: Myths and Realities," updated May 9, 2008, www.cbpp.org/cms/?fa=view&id=692 (accessed 4/20/09).

9 "Bush Urges Permanent Tax Cuts Amid 'Economic Uncertainty,'" *New York Times*, January 8, 2008.

10 Of course, it should be underscored that "relatively uncontrollable" is itself a policy decision made by the president and Congress. It is not carved in granite; it can be undone. To undo some things, such as not making a promised payment on the national debt, would have horrible consequences in credit markets. A modest across-the-board reduction in outlays for hospital assistance under

Medicare, on the other hand, though painful (literally and figuratively), might nevertheless be accommodated (with hospitals and patients sharing the burden in various ways—for example, by deferring elective procedures or delaying a salary increase). That is, things that are alleged to be off the table can be put right back on the table.

11 James Dao, "The Nation: Big Bucks Trip Up the Lean New Army," *New York Times*, February 10, 2002, sec. 4, p. 5.

12 The figures cited are for 2011.

13 Edward J. Harpham, "Fiscal Crisis and the Politics of Social Security Reform," in *The Attack on the Welfare State*, Anthony Champagne and Edward J. Harpham, eds. (Prospect Heights, IL: Waveland Press, 1984), p. 13.

14 David Kassabian, Anne White, and Erika Huber, "Welfare Rules Databook: State TANF Policies as of July 2011," The Urban Institute, August 2012. Available at www.urban.org/Uploaded PDF/412641 -Welfare-Rules-Databook-2011.pdf (accessed 7/24/13).

15 *Goldberg v. Kelly*, 397 U.S. 254 (1970).

16 See U.S. House of Representatives, Committee on Ways and Means, *Where Your Money Goes: The 1994–95 Green Book* (Washington, DC: Brassey's, 1994), pp. 325, 802.

17 *1998 Green Book*, Overview of Entitlement Programs, http://aspe.hhs.gov/98gb/intro .htm (accessed 7/15/09).

18 Robert Pear, "House Democrats Propose Making the '96 Welfare Law an Antipoverty Weapon," *New York Times*, January 24, 2002, p. A22.

19 Robin Toner, "Welfare Chief Is Hoping to Promote Marriage," *New York Times*, February 19, 2002, p. A1.

CHAPTER 14

1 Geoffrey Perret, *A Country Made by War* (New York: Random House, 1989), p. 558.

2 Rupert Smith, *The Utility of Force: The Art of War in the Modern World* (New York: Vintage, 2008).

3 D. Robert Worley, *Shaping U.S. Military Forces: Revolution or Relevance in a Post–Cold War World* (Westport, CT: Praeger Security International, 2006).

4 This was done quietly in an amendment to the Internal Revenue Service Reform Act (PL 105–206), June 22, 1998. But it was not accomplished easily. See Bob Gravely, "Normal Trade with China Wins Approval," *Congressional Quarterly Weekly Report*, July 25, 1998; and Richard Dunham, "MFN by Any Other Name Is . . . NTR?," *Business Week* online news flash, June 19, 1997.

5 Alexander Hamilton and James Madison, *Letters of Pacificus and Helvidius* (New York: Scholars Facsimiles and Reprints, 1999).

6 For example, under President Clinton, Senator Lloyd Bentsen and Representative Les Aspin left Congress to become the secretaries of the Treasury and Defense, respectively.

7 Raymond A. Bauer, Ithiel de Sola Pool, and Lewis Anthony Dexter, *American Business and Public Policy: The Politics of Foreign Trade*, 2nd ed. (Chicago: Aldine-Atherton, 1972).

8 A very good brief outline of the centrality of the president in foreign policy will be found in Paul E. Peterson, "The President's Dominance in Foreign Policy Making," *Political Science Quarterly* 109, no. 2 (Summer 1994): 215, 234.

9 One confirmation of this will be found in Theodore Lowi, *The End of Liberalism*, 2nd ed. (New York: Norton, 1979), pp. 127–30; another will be found in Stephen Krasner, "Are Bureaucracies Important?" *Foreign Policy* 7 (Summer 1972): 159–79. However, it should be added that Krasner was writing his article in disagreement with Graham T. Allison, "Conceptual Models and the Cuban Missile Crisis," *American Political Science Review* 63, no. 3 (September 1969): 689–718.

10 Peterson, "The President's Dominance in Foreign Policy Making," p. 232.

11 Hans Morgenthau, *Politics among Nations*, 2nd ed. (New York: Knopf, 1956), p. 505.

12 See Theodore Lowi, *The Personal President: Power Invested, Promise Unfulfilled* (Ithaca, NY: Cornell University Press, 1985), pp. 167–9.

13 "IMF: Sleeve-Rolling Time," *Economist*, May 2, 1992, pp. 98–99.

14 James Dao and Patrick E. Tyler, "U.S. Says Military Strikes Are Just a Part of Big Plan," *The Alliance*, September 27, 2001; and Joseph Kahn, "A Nation Challenged: Global Dollars," *New York Times*, September 20, 2001, p. B1.

15 "Official Says Turkey Is Advancing in Drive for I.M.F. Financing," *New York Times*, October 6, 2001, p. A7.

16 George Quester, *The Continuing Problem of International Politics* (Hinsdale, IL: Dryden Press, 1974), p. 229.

17 The Warsaw Pact was signed in 1955 by the Soviet Union, the German Democratic Republic (East Germany), Poland, Hungary, Czechoslovakia, Romania, Bulgaria, and Albania. Albania later dropped out. The Warsaw Pact was terminated in 1991.

18 Benjamin Ginsberg, *The American Lie* (Boulder, CO: Paradigm, 2007), p. 3.

Photo Credits

CHAPTER 1

Page 2: Jeff Malet Photography/Newscom; p. 9: Library of Congress; p. 14: Charlie Cullen-DoD/CNP/Photolink.net; p. 15: AP Photo.

CHAPTER 2

Page 24: Library of Congress; p. 33: Rue des Archives/The Granger Collection; p. 39: Granger Collection; p. 41: Xinhua/eyevine/Redux; p. 54: Photo/Roger L. Wollenberg/Landov.

CHAPTER 3

Page 58: Katherine Taylor/The New York Times/Redux; p. 64: Justin Sullivan/Getty Images; p. 68: Joshua Lott/Reuters/Landov; p. 78: Olivier Douliery/Pool/Landov; p. 82 (left): Zoonar/Maranso/Agefotostock; (right): Bob Daemmrich/Polaris/Newscom.

CHAPTER 4

Page 84: AP Photos; p. 96: Reuters/Corbis; p. 101: Roger L. Wollenberg/UPI/Newscom; p. 110: Culver Pictures/The Art Archive at Art Resource; p. 113: Elliott Erwitt/Magnum Photos; p. 123: Reuters/Shannon Stapleton/Landov.

CHAPTER 5

Page 130: AP Photo; p. 137: AP Photo; p. 140: Photo courtesy Alaska Department of Transportation and Public Facilities; p. 153: AP Photo; p. 156: Jeff Malet Photography/Newscom; p. 162: Scott J. Ferrell/Congressional Quarterly/Getty Images.

CHAPTER 6

Page 168: William Auth-Pool/Getty Images; p. 173: Jim Watson/AFP/Getty Images; p. 181: AP Photo; p. 189: Tobias Hase/EPA/Newscom; p. 192: AP Photo.

CHAPTER 7

Page 204: AP Photo; p. 210: Nicole Bengiveno/The New York Times/Redux; p. 214: George Frey/Reuters/Landov; p. 221: AP Photo; p. 225: AP Photo; p. 233: AP Photo; p. 235: Chris Maddaloni/Roll Call/Getty Images.

CHAPTER 8

Page 238: AP Photo; p. 245: AP Photo; p. 247: Granger Collection; p. 249: Mark Wilson/Getty Images; p. 257: Jonathan Ernst/Reuters/Newscom; p. 263: AP Photo.

CHAPTER 9

Page 274: AP Photo; p. 281: Jorge Cruz/Landov; p. 298: Scott Olson/Getty Images; p. 305 (left): Jason Moore/ZUMA Press/Newscom; (right): Michael S. Wirtz/MCT/Newscom; p. 309: EPA/Jim Lo Scalzo/Landov.

CHAPTER 10

Page 312: Fred Prouser/Reuters; p. 317: Joe Raedle/Getty Images; p. 322: Joe Skipper/Reuters/Landov; p. 352: Rick Wilking/Pool/EPA/Newscom.

CHAPTER 11

Page 358: Kevin Dietsch/UPI/Landov; p. 364: D. Lopez/San Antonio Express/ZUMA Press/Newscom; p. 367: AP Photo; p. 379: Jeff Haynes/Reuters/Landov; p. 388: Lee Balterman/Time & Life Pictures/Getty Images; p. 391 (left): Brenda Smialowski/AFP/Getty Images; (right): AP Photo.

CHAPTER 12

Page 394: AP Photo; p. 401: AP Photo; p. 405: Courtesy The Environmental Defense Fund; p. 412: AP Photo; p. 418: AP Photo.

CHAPTER 13

Page 426: Win McNamee/Getty Images; p. 431: iStockphoto; p. 437: AP Photo; p. 448: Photos 12/Alamy; p. 452: Steve Debenport Imagery/iStockphoto.com.

CHAPTER 14

Page 458: AP Photo; p. 466: Xinhua/Polaris/Newscom; p. 470: Jewel Samad/AFP/Getty Images; p. 474: Mandel Ngan/AFP/Getty Images; p. 481: Jason Reed/Reuters/Landov; p. 485: Ashraf Amra/APA Images/Polaris/Newscom.

Index

Page numbers in *italics* refer to figures and tables.

American Israel Public Affairs
Committee (AIPAC),
474
American Medical Association,
399, 403
American National Election
Studies (ANES), 19, 206,
297, 335
American Recovery and
Reinvestment Act, 411
American Revolution, 27–29,
31, 383
Americans with Disabilities Act
(ADA), 124
American Voter, The, 284
America's Party, *382, 390*
amicus curiae, 261, 262
Amnesty International, 474
Amtrak, 212
anarchy, 8
Anderson, John, 389
Anderson, Rocky, *390*
ANES (American National
Election Studies), 19, 206,
335
Animal and Plant Health and
Inspection Service
(APHIS), 218
Annapolis Convention, 61
Antifederalists, 46–47, 55, 62
Anti-Masonics, *382*
Antitrust Division of Department
of Justice, 216
antiwar movements, 404
ANZUS, 480
APHIS (Animal and Plant Health
and Inspection Service),
218
appeasement, 462
appellate courts, 244, 245,
246–47, 248, 256
appointments, 195
appropriations bill, 136
arbitration, 483–84
Arizona, 3–4, 77
Arizona, Miranda v., *90*, 92
*Arizona v. Inter Tribal Council of
Arizona, Inc.*, 77
Arkansas, 116, 173–74
Armed Services Committee,
472

Articles of Confederation, 34,
35, 61, 171, 324
adoption of, 29–30
Constitution *vs.*, 42
flaws of, 30–31, 36
Asian Americans, 121–22, 123,
353, 371
Asian Law Caucus, 123
Aspin, Les, A70*n*6
assembly, freedom of, *90*, 91, 98
Astroturf lobbying, 417
AT&T, 433
Australia
ANZUS and, 480
voting in, 316
Australia ballot, 322–23
authoritarian governments, 6, 7
autocracy, 6

Baird, Eisenstadt v., 414
Bakke, Allan, 126–27
Bakke case, 126–27, 128
ballots, *322*, 322–23
Baltimore, Barron v., 87–89, 91
Bank of the United States, 65,
436
Barr, Roseanne, *390*
Barron v. Baltimore, 87–89, 91
Bayh, Birch, 314
BCRA (Bipartisan Campaign
Reform Act), 97, 419
"beaker-ready" project proposals,
446
benefit seekers, 360
see also interest groups
Benton v. Maryland, *90*, 92
Bentsen, Lloyd, A70*n*6
Bernanke, Ben, *437*
bias, organizational, 205–6
bicameralism, 36, 131, 136–38
Biden, Joe, 132, 189, *189*
bilateral treaties, 480
Bill of Rights, 44, 45, 48, 84–128,
423
Antifederalist demand for,
46
nationalization of, 87–89, *90*,
91–93
purpose of, 49, *50*
recent court rulings on,
93–105

state v. national, 87–89, *90*,
91–93
see also specific amendments
bin Laden, Osama, 470, 471
Bipartisan Campaign Reform Act
(BCRA), 97, 419
Black Americans, *see* African
Americans
Blackmun, Harry, 267, *269*
block grants, 72–73
*Board of Education of Topeka,
Brown v.*, 91–92, 112–13,
114, 118, 121, 414
Boehner, John, *78*, 367
Bolling v. Sharpe, A59*n*74
Bollinger, Gratz v., 127–28
Bollinger, Grutter v., 128
Bosnia, 181, 469
Boston, 27–28
Boston Gazette, 326
Boston Marathon bombing
(2013), 58, 245
Boston Tea Party, 27–28
bourgeoisie, 11
Bowers v. Hardwick, 104, 125
BP oil spill, 174
Brady Bill, 77, 308
Brandenburg, Charles, 96–97
branding in political parties,
364–65
Brennan, William J., *269*
Breyer, Stephen G., 94, 249, *250*,
266, *268, 269*
briefs, 261–62
broadcast media, 301–2, *302*,
304–5, *305*
Brookings Institution, 399
Brown, Linda, 112–13
Brown, Oliver, 112–13, 116
*Brown v. Board of Education of
Topeka*, 91–92, 112–13,
114, 118, 121, 414
Bryan, William Jennings, 386
Buchanan, James, 201
Buckley v. Valeo, 97, 419
budget, Congress and,
131–32
Budget and Accounting Act,
223
budget deficit, 442–45, *443*
Bull Moose, *382*

citizenship, dual, 87–89
Citizens United, 419
*Citizens United v. Federal Election
    Commission*, 97, 419
City of Boerne v. Flores, 95
City of St. Paul, R.A.V. v., 100
civil law, 241, 242
civil liberties, 84–128
    definition of, 84, 85
    nationalization of, 87–89, *90*,
        91–93
    recent court rulings on, 93–105
    see also Bill of Rights
civil rights, 84–85, 105–28, 364,
        404, A58*n*4
    of African Americans, 85–86,
        111–15, *113*, *114–15*
    of Americans with disabilities,
        124
    of Asian Americans, 121–22,
        123
    Brown v. Board of Education and,
        112–15, *114*
    definition of, 84, 85
    of Department of Justice, 216
    education and, 112–18, *117*
    of gays and lesbians, 124–26,
        297
    immigration and, 122–24
    of Latino Americans, 121, 123
    of women, 117–18, 119–21
    see also affirmative action;
        voting rights
Civil Rights Act (1875), 111
Civil Rights Act (1964), 82, *114*,
        115, 116, 117, 118, 119,
        198, 293
civil unions, 125
    see also same-sex marriage
Civil War, U.S., 7, 85, 86, 89, 172,
        289, 385
Clark, Louise Caire, 416
class-action suits, 271
class in party identity, 372
Clausewitz, Carl von, 481–82
Clay, Henry, 384
clientele agencies, 214–16
Clinton, Bill, 53, 181, 192, 193,
        198, 210, 295, 339
    executive privilege claimed
        by, 240

foreign policy and, 467
gay rights and, 124–25
Gore and, 189
health care initiative of, 155,
        415–16
impeachment of, 164
judicial appointees of, 248,
        249, 250, *250*
management strategy of, 223
military base closings proposed
        by, 217
National Performance Review
        and, 223, 235
as "new Democrat," 366
regulatory review and, 195
scandals of, 81, 164, 303
signing statements and, 200
veto and, 177
voter registration bill signed
        by, 319
Clinton, George, 46
Clinton, Hillary, 223, 419
    in 2008 primary, 341
    as secretary of state, 476
closed primary, 362–63
closed rule, 152
cloture, 153
CNN (Cable News Network),
        300, 301, 304
coercion
    means of, 6, 7–8
    states and power of, 62
    trade-off between freedom
        and, 14–15
COLAs (cost-of-living
        adjustments), 449, 453
Cold War, 229, 337, 372,
        461–63
collecting revenue, means of, 6, 8
collective goods, *see* public goods
collective security, 479–81
Colorado, 351
Colorado, Wolf v., *90*
comity clause, 63–64
commander in chief, 172
Commerce, Department of, 215,
        467
Commerce and Labor,
        Department of, 214–15
commerce clause, 66, 67
commerce in Constitution, 61

commercial speech, 100
*Committee for Industrial
        Organization, Hague v.*, *90*
Committee on Administrative
        Management, 222–23
committee system, 147–49, *148*,
        158, 367
    conference committees,
        153
    deliberation in, 150, 152
    gatekeeping authority of,
        155–56
    interest groups and, 155–56
    oversight of, 162–63
    see also specific committees
Common Cause, 299, 399, 403,
        404
Communications Decency Act
        (CDA), 99
competition, market economy
        and, 432
Concerned Senators for the Arts,
        150
concurrence, 264
concurrent powers, 62–63
Conference Board, 339
conference committee, 153
Congress, U.S., 130–67, *168*
    Affordable Care Act and,
        451–52
    under Articles of
        Confederation, 30
    Bank of the United States
        and, 65
    budget and, 131–32, 221,
        442–43
    bureaucracy and, 223, 224–25,
        226–27, 235, 236, 447
    Case Act passed by, 163–64
    caucuses, 150
    civil rights and, *115*
    "committee on committees"
        in, 367–68
    committee system, 147–49,
        148, 225, 367
    constituency in, 154–55
    in Constitution, 37, 38–39
    constitutional amendments
        and, 48, 51, 85, 88
    decision-making process of,
        154–58, *157*, *159*, 160–61

delegated powers and, 171–72, 179–80, 185

distributive tendency in, 166

districts of, *144*, 144–45

economic policy and, 432–33

electoral districts and, 324, *325*, 326, *328*, 328–29, *329*

electoral system and, 138–41, *141*, *144*, 144–45

executive branch *vs.*, 202–3

Fed created by, 219

first (in 1789), 140

First Amendment and, 50

foreign policy and, 130–31, 472

grants-in-aid and, 68–71

grassroots campaigns and, 415, 416–17

Great Compromise and, 32

gun control and, 399

impeachment power of, 164

incumbency and, 139–41, *141*, 144

interest groups and, 155–56, 397, 405, 406–7, *410*, 410–11, 413, 415, 416–17, 418–19

interstate commerce and, 65–67

judicial review and, 252–53, *253*

logrolling in, 160, 161

Nixon and, 176

111th, 140

organization of, 145–50, *148*

oversight and, 162–63, 224–25

PACs and, 417–18

party discipline and, 156–58, *157*, *159*, 160, 161

party system and, 367–68, 381

presidential appointees and, *196*, 196–97, *197*

presidential nomination by, 171

presidential power and, 40, 170, 171–72, 173, 182, 190, 201

procedural rules of, 150, *151*, 152–54

regulatory agencies and, 212, 213, 218

religious freedom and, 93, 95

representation in, 133–34, *134*, *135*, 136–41, 144–45

seniority rule in, 149

on September 11, 2001, terrorist attacks, 169

staff system in, 149

Supreme Court size decided by, 41

Supreme Court's relationship with, *253*, 267, 270

taxes and, 130, 211, 276, 438

unfunded mandates and, 72

veto and, 154, 178–79

voter registration and, 319

voter turnout and, 316

war powers of, 25, 181

welfare reform and, 455

whip system in, 158, 160, 161

women in, 142–43

see also House of Representatives, U.S.; Senate, U.S.

Congressional Black Caucus, 150

Congressional Budget Office (CBO), 72, 149, 442–43

congressional campaign committees, 378

Congressional Caucus for Women's Issues, 150

Congressional Government (Wilson), 183

Congressional Quarterly, 389

Connecticut

privacy rights in, 103

ratification of Constitution, 46

Virginia Plan and, 32

Connecticut, Griswold v., *90*, 103, 414

Connecticut, Palko v., A58*n*9

Connecticut Compromise, *see* Great Compromise

Conscience of a Conservative, The (Goldwater), 387

conscription, military, 7–8

consent approach, 314–15

conservatism, 282–83, 365, 388

constituency, 131, 133–34, 136, 154–55

Constitution, U.S., 3, 4, 24–27, 52–55, 396

Article I, 37, 38–39, 42, 49–50, 61–62, 64, 65–66, 81, 85, 92, 130, 174, 177, A62*n*24

Article II, 37, 39–40, 42, 163, 170–72, 174, 176, 177, 196

Article III, 37, 40–41, 42, 244, 247, 257

Article IV, 37, 41, 43, 63–64, 173, 253

Articles of Confederation *vs.*, 42

Article V, 37, 43, 47–48, *48*

Article VI, 37

Article VII, 37, 43

commerce clause in, 66

equality and, 56

executive branch in, 37, 39–40, 42, 170–82

expressed powers in, 61–62

full faith and credit clause in, 63, 64

implied powers in, 62

institutions in, 10

interest and principle in, 55

judicial branch in, 37, 40–41, 42, 238–39

legislative branch in, 37, 38–39, 42

local government and, 64–65

national government restrained by, 44–45

necessary and proper clause in, 39, 65

president in, 169, 174

privileges and immunities clause in, 63–64

public opinion and, 277

ratification of, 37, 43, 46–47

Senate in, 163

slavery in, 33, 36

supremacy clause in, 43

war powers in, 25, 61

see also Antifederalists; Bill of Rights; federalism; Federalists; separation of powers

constitutional amendments, 37, 43, 47–52, *53*, 84

Eighteenth, 25, 48, 49, 51

Eighth, 49, 50, 88, 102, 103–4

Democratic Party, 18, 351,
365–66, 370, *371*
African Americans and, 285,
351, 353, 371, *373*
age and, *373*
2011 agendas of, *142*
Asian Americans and, 353
candidate recruitment by, 361
class and, 372
congressional campaign
committees and, 378
education and, *373*
2006 elections and, 178
2008 elections and, 337
2010 elections and, 350
2012 elections and, 336, *336*,
348, 351–53, *352*, *390*
gender and, 287, 335, 352–53,
371, *373*
history of, *382*, 384–89, 390
income and, 373
Latino Americans and, 287,
351, 353, 366, 371, *373*
New Deal and, 372
"new Democrats" in, 366
Obama and, 190
partisanship and, 335–37,
336
primary elections, 330–31
redistricting and, 329, *329*
religion and, 289, 365, 372,
373, *374*, 374–75, *375*
Republicans' differences with,
365
taxes and, 438, 442
two-party system and, 358,
359, 360
welfare reform and, 455
women and, 335, 352–53, 371,
373
Democratic-Republicans, *382*,
383
Democratic Republic of Congo,
469
Democratic Senatorial Campaign
Committee (DSCC), 378
Department of Agriculture, *see*
Agriculture, Department
of
Department of Commerce, 215,
467

Department of Commerce and
Labor, 214–15
Department of Defense (DOD),
217, 471
Department of Education (ED),
216
Department of Energy (DOE),
216
Department of Health and
Human Services (HHS),
216, 218, 219, A63*n*9
Department of Homeland
Security (DHS), 2, 175,
179, 188, 194, 214, 217,
471
Department of Housing and
Urban Development
(HUD), 216, 437
Department of Interior, 214, 216
Department of Justice (DOJ),
119, 177, 212, 215, 216,
261, 316
Department of Labor, 214, 218
Department of Transportation
(DOT), 216
deregulation, 230
descriptive representation, 284
desegregation, 112–16, *117*,
173–74, 272, A59*n*76
see also racial discrimination;
segregation
deterrence, 462
devolution, *231*, 231–32
DHS (Department of Homeland
Security), 2, 175, 179, 188,
194, 214, 217
diplomacy, 476
direct lobbying, 407, *410*, 410–13
disabilities, 124
discretionary spending, 444
discrimination
in employment, 119, 123
gender, 117–18, 119–21
outgroups and, 290
racial, 111–15, *113*, *114–15*,
121, 123, 385
dispute resolution, 210–11
disputes, types of, 241–43
dissenting opinion, 264–65
distributive tendency, 166
District of Columbia, A59*n*74

District of Columbia v. Heller, 101
districts, congressional, *144*,
144–45
divided government, 80
Dixiecrats, *382*
DNC (Democratic National
Committee), 377–78
DOD, 217, 471
Dodd-Frank Wall Street Reform
and Consumer Protection
Act, 214
DOE (Department of Energy),
216
DOJ (Department of Justice),
119, 177, 212, 215, 216,
261, 316
Dole, Bob, 76
DOMA (Defense of Marriage
Act), 63, 124–25, 126,
263, 294
"Don't Ask, Don't Tell" policy,
125
DOT (Department of
Transportation), 216
double jeopardy, 87, *90*, 92
Douglas, Stephen A., 384
Douglas, William O., 103, 264–65
drafts, military, 7–8
Dred Scott v. Sandford, 80, 86
DSCC (Democratic Senatorial
Campaign Committee),
378
dual citizenship, 87–89
dual federalism, 59, 65–68, *70*,
76, 81
due process of law, 91, 102, 245
Duncan, Richard, *390*

Early, Stephen, 191–92
earmarks, 140, 422
East India Company, 27, 28
East Timor, 469
economic aid, international,
478–79
economic policy, 427
goals of, 432–35
income gap and, *440*, 440–41,
441
tools of
fiscal policies, *see* fiscal
policies

foreign policy, 130–31, 458–86
  arbitration and, 483–84
  bureaucracy and, 471
  collective security and, 479–81
  Congress and, 130–31, 472
  diplomacy and, 476
  economic aid and sanctions,
    478–79
  goals of, 460–63, 466–69
    economic prosperity, 466–67
    international humanitarian
      policies, 467–69
    security, 461–63, 466
  interest groups and, 472–74
  International Monetary Fund
    and, 477–78
  military force and, 481–83,
    482
  president and, 470–71
  role of America in world
    politics, 484–86
  United Nations and, 477
Foreign Relations Committee,
  472
Foreign Service Act, 476
Forest Service, 210
formula grants, 69
Fourteenth Amendment, 51,
  51, *53*, 103, 116, A58*n*4,
  A59*n*74
  Bill of Rights and, 86, 89, *90*,
    91, 92
  Brown v. Board of Education and,
    113
  Plessy v. Ferguson and, 112, 113
  racial discrimination after,
    111–15, *113*, *114–15*
Fourth Amendment, 49, 50, *52*,
  88, 92, 102, 103
fourth party system, 386
Fox, 300, 301
framing, 307
France, 64, 462
Frankfurter, Felix, 264, 267
Franklin, Benjamin, 28
*Franklin v. Gwinnett County Public
  Schools*, 118
Frazier, Lynn, 332
freedom, *see* liberty
freedom of assembly, *90*, 91,
  98

Freedom of Information Act
  (FOIA), 211
freedom of petition, 98
freedom of religion, *90*, 93–95
freedom of speech, *90*, 91,
  95–100
  see also First Amendment
freedom of the press, *90*, 91, 95,
  98, 99, 305–6, 307
free exercise clause, 95
free rider problem, 9, 363,
  399–400, 401, 423
Free-Soilers, *382*
free trade, 467
Frémont, John C., 385
Friends of the Earth, 299
FTC (Federal Trade
  Commission), 100, 214,
  218
full faith and credit clause, 63, 64
Furman v. Georgia, 280

Gallup polls, 294
Garrity, W. Arthur, 272
gas industries, tax subsidies for, 3
gatekeeping, 155–56
Gates, Robert, 223
GATT (General Agreement on
  Tariffs and Trade), 467
gay and lesbian movement,
  124–26, 272, 296–97
  see also same-sex marriage
GDP (gross domestic product),
  229
gender
  partisan loyalty and, 335,
    352–53, *354*, 371, *373*
  public opinion and, 287–88,
    288
gender discrimination, 117–18,
  119–21
gender gap, 287–88, 352–53, 371
General Accounting Office, 123,
  149
General Agreement on Tariffs
  and Trade (GATT), 467
Genêt, Edmond, 175
Geneva Conventions, 255
geography and public opinion,
  289
George III, 171

Georgia
  ratification of Constitution, 46
  slavery in, 33
  sodomy laws in, 104
  voting in, 327
Georgia, Furman v., 280
Gerber, Alan, 420, 421
Germany
  during the 1940s, 461
  voting in, 316
Gerry, Elbridge, 326
gerrymandering, 145, 326–27
Gibbons, Thomas, 66
Gibbons v. Ogden, 66
Gideon, Clarence Earl, 103
Gideon v. Wainwright, *90*, 92,
  103
Gingrich, Newt, 350
Ginsburg, Ruth Bader, 249, *250*,
  263, *268*, *269*
Gitlow v. New York, *90*
GNP (gross national product),
  433–34
going public strategy, 415–16,
  421
Goldberg v. Kelly, 453–54
Goldwater, Barry, 387
Gomillion v. Lightfoot, 111
Gonzales v. Oregon, 77, 105
Goode, Virgil, *390*, *391*
*Goodyear Tire and Rubber Co.,
  Ledbetter v.*, 119
Google, 407, 433
Google News, 301
Gore, Al, 189, 391, 450
government, 6, 427
  complexity of, 2–3
  definition of, 6
  democratic, expansion of,
    11–13
  divided, 80
  forms of, 6, 7
  foundations of, 6–8
  limits on power of, 11, 82
  parties' influence on, 365–66
  purpose of, 8–10
  as restrained by Constitution,
    44–45
  see also bureaucracy; federalism;
    *and specific branches of
    government*

Joint Chiefs of Staff (JCOS), 471

Joint Committee on Taxation, 211

Joint Select Committee on Deficit Reduction, 464

Jones, Charles O., 192

Jones & Louhglin Steel Company, 67–68, 185

judges, 239, 240, 248–51, *250*, *251*

judicial activism, 80, 266–67

judicial branch, 238–72
  bureaucracy and, 236
  in Constitution, 37, 40–41, 42, 50, 88, 238–39
  executive branch *vs.*, *45, 79*
  legislative branch *vs.*, *45, 79*
  see also courts; Supreme Court

judicial restraint, 266–67

judicial review, 41, 252–56
  of Congress, 252–53, *253*
  definition of, 252
  of federal agency actions, 254–55
  lawmaking and, 256
  presidential power and, 255–56
  of state actions, 253–54

Judiciary Act, 252, 253

jurisdiction
  of congressional committees, 147
  definition of, 244
  federal, 244–51, *250, 251*

Justice, Department of (DOJ), 119, 177, 212, 215, 216, 261, 316

Justice Party, *390*

Kagan, Elena, 249, *249, 250*, 266

Kansas, 112–13

Kansas-Nebraska Act, 384

Katrina, Hurricane, 174, 223

Kelly, Goldberg v., 453–54

Kennan, George F., 462

Kennedy, Anthony M., 249, *250*, 263, 266, *268, 269*

Kennedy, Edward, 395

Kennedy, John F.
  civil rights and, *115*

Cuban missile crisis and, 463, 485
  election of, 189, 289

Kentucky, 109

Kerry, John, 472, 476, *481*

King, Martin Luther, Jr., *114*, 115, *115*

Korean War, 80, 483
  drafts during, 7
  Truman and, 180–81, 198

Kosovo, 282, 469

Kraemer, Shelley v., 112

Ku Klux Klan, 96–97

Kurtzman, Lemon v., 94

Kyoto Protocol, 468

Labor, Department of, 214, 215, 218

labor force, market economy and, 431

labor unions, 399, 419–20

Labour Party, British, 330

Lambda Legal Defense and Education Fund, 124

La Raza Unida Party, 121

Lasswell, Harold, 10

Latino Americans, 285, 287, *287*
  civil rights of, 121
  immigration and, 4, 123, 281, 285
  party identity of, 287, *287*, 335, 351, 353, 366, 371
  voting and, 284, 285

Lau v. Nichols, 122

law, categories of, 241–43

lawmaking, judicial review and, 256

Lawrence v. Texas, 104, 125

layer cake federalism, 70

League of United Latin American Citizens (LULAC), 121

League of Women Voters, 363

Lebanon, 469

Ledbetter v. Goodyear Tire and Rubber Co., 119

Lee, Richard Henry, 46

legal precedents, 241

legislative branch
  from 1800-1933, 183–84

in Constitution, 37, 38–39, 42, 78
  executive branch *vs.*, *45, 79*
  judicial branch *vs.*, *45, 79*
  supremacy of, 78, 79
  see also Congress, U.S.

legislative initiative, 181–82

legislative service organizations (LSOs), 150

Lemon test, 94

Lemon v. Kurtzman, 94

lesbians, 124–26

Leviathan (Hobbes), 8

Lewinsky, Monica, 81, 164

Libby, Lewis "Scooter," 175

libel, 99

Liberal Democrats, British, 330

liberalism, 282, 365

Liberal Party, *382*

Libertarian Party, *382, 390*

liberty
  Constitution and, 55–56
  trade-off between coercion and, 14–15

Libya, 170, 203, 313, 469, 471, 479

Lightfoot, Gomillion v., 111

Lincoln, Abraham, 385
  executive orders of, 168, 172
  as strong president, 183, 201

line-item veto, 81, 177

Lippman, Walter, 313

literacy tests, 319

Livingston, Robert, 28

lobbying, 406, 421
  Astroturf, 417
  of Congress, 407, *410*, 410–11
  definition of, 407
  direct, 407, *410*, 410–13
  of executive branch, 412
  going public strategy of, 415–16
  grassroots, 415, 416–17
  influence of, *408*, 408–9, *409*
  of president, 411
  regulation of, 412–13
  schools and, 422–23
  see also interest groups

Supreme Court (*continued*)
segregation and, 111–15, 116, 122, 414
Sixth Amendment and, 103
Tenth Amendment and, 73, 76–77
voting rights and, 111
war on terrorism and, 255
writs and, 258–60, *259*, *260*
see also judicial review; *specific cases*
surveys, 19
Switzerland, A66*n*9
symbolic speech, 98
Syria, 181, 481

takings clause, 102–3
Taliban, 478
Taney, Roger Brooke, 240
TANF (Temporary Assistance to Needy Families), 219, 452, 453, 454
taxation bill, 136
taxes, 438, *439*, 442
collection of, growth in, 8
in colonial America, 27
Congress and, 130, 211, 438
in Constitution, 51, 61
estate, 276
G. W. Bush and, 293, 438
income, 51
mortgage-interest deduction, 427–28
Obama and, 293
progressive, 438
public opinion and, 292–93
regressive, 438
between states, 61
subsidies, 3
types of, federal revenues by, *439*
Tea Act, 28
Teamsters, 399, 403
Tea Party, 132, 350, 361, 404
Telecommunications Act, 99, 305
television, 301–2, *302*, 304
Temporary Assistance to Needy Families (TANF), 219, 452, 453, 454
Tenth Amendment, 50, 62, 73, 76–77, 88

terrorism, 60
see also September 11, 2001, terrorist attacks; war on terrorism
Texas
flag burning and, 98
House seats gained by, 144–45
Mexican Americans in, 121
redistricting in, *328*, 328–29
Texas, Lawrence v., 104, 125
Third Amendment, 49, 50, 88, 103
third party system, 359, *382*, 385, 389–92, *390*
Thirteenth Amendment, 51, *53*, 86
Thomas, Clarence, 249, *250*, 262, 266, *268*, *269*
Three-Fifths Compromise, 33, 36
Thurmond, Strom, *153*
Time, 304
tort cases, 242
torture, 200
totalitarian governments, 6, 7
trade, free, 467
Transportation, Department of (DOT), 216
Transportation Security Administration (TSA), 214, 217
Travel and Tourism Caucus, 150
Treasury Department, 132, 216, 471
treaties, 130–31
trial courts, 244, 246
Truman, Harry S., 80, 160, 176
desegregation of armed services, 198
Korean War and, 180–81, 198
signing statements and, 200
trustees, 133
TSA (Transportation Security Administration), 214, 217
Tsarnaev, Dzhokhar, 245
Turkey, 478
Twelfth Amendment, *52*
Twentieth Amendment, *52*
Twenty-Fifth Amendment, *52*
Twenty-First Amendment, 25, 48, 49

Twenty-Fourth Amendment, *51*
Twenty-Second Amendment, *52*
Twenty-Seventh Amendment, 51
Twenty-Sixth Amendment, *51*, 313–14
Twenty-Third Amendment, *51*
Twitter, 433
interest groups and, 405
Obama and, 298
two-party system, 358–60, 381
see also party systems; political parties

UAW (United Auto Workers), 420
UMRA (Unfunded Mandates Reform Act), 72
unfunded mandates, 72
Unfunded Mandates Reform Act (UMRA), 72
UN General Assembly, 477
Uniform Code of Military Justice, 255
Union Labor Party, *382*
Union of Concerned Scientists, 399, 403
unions, 363, 419–20
United Auto Workers (UAW), 420
United Kingdom
party systems in, 367, 368
United Nations and, 477
United Mine Workers, 399, 403
United Nations, 282, 469, 477, 479–80, 481
United Nations Framework Convention on Climate Change, 468
United States, Mack v., 77
United States, Olmstead v., A59*n*60
United States, Printz v., 77
United States v. Lopez, 76
United States v. Nixon, 80–81, 176, 240, 255
United States v. O'Brien, 98
United States v. Pink, A62*n*10
United States v. Williams, 99
United States v. Wong Kim Ark, 122

United We Stand Party, *382*
University of California, 127
UN Security Council, 477
UPN, 300
USA PATRIOT Act, 60, 175

Valeo, Buckley v., 97, 419
values, 277, 279, 280–81
Van Buren, Martin, 384
van Lohuizen, Jan, 298
Van Orden v. Perry, 94
Ventura, Jesse, 389
Vermont, 126
veto, 40, 81, 154, 177–79, *178*,
    183
vice presidency, 188–89, A62*n*24
Vietnam War, 163, 181, 228, 372,
    387, 483
    drafts during, 7
    Johnson and, 485
    media and, 295
    protests against, 98
Virginia
    Constitutional Convention
        and, 34
    ratification of Constitution, 46
    slavery in, 33
    Virginia Plan and, 32
Virginia Military Institute, 118
Virginia Plan, 32, 34, 35
voter registration, 319–21,
    363
voter turnout, 202, 316–17, 321,
    334–35, 356
    measuring, 317–19
    in presidential elections, 317,
        318
voting, 108, 316–17, 333
    African Americans and,
        326–27, 351, 353
    ballots and, *322*, 322–23
    compulsory, 316–17
    decisions in, 333–42, *336*,
        340
    facilitating electoral choice in,
        364–65
    identification and, 321,
        369–71, *370*
    income and, 20–22, *355*
    issues and policy preferences
        in, 338–39, 341

Latino Americans and, 121,
    285, 351, 353, 366
nonvoters and, 334–35
partisanship and, 284, 333,
    335–38, *336*, 341
prospective, 339
requirements for, 313, 316–17,
    319–21, A66*n*7
retrospective, 339
secret ballots and, 322–23
shifts between 2008 and 20012
    in, *354–55*
split-ticket, 323
voting rights, 105
    African Americans and,
        110–11
    struggle for, 108–11
    women and, 109–10, *110*
Voting Rights Act, 110, 111, *115*,
    122, 145, 284, 293, 326,
    388

*Wabash, St. Louis, and Pacific
    Railway Company v. Illinois*,
    A57*n*12
Wade, Roe v., see *Roe v. Wade*
Wagner Act, *see* National Labor
    Relations Act
Wainwright, Gideon v., *90*, 92, 103
Wallace, George, 388, *388*, 389,
    390
Wallace, Henry, 390
wall of separation, 94
Wall Street Journal, 304
war
    in Constitution, 25, 61
    declaration of, 61, 173, 180–81
    gender and public opinion on,
        288
    see also specific wars
War Department, 217
War of 1812, 383
War on Poverty, *115*
war on terrorism, 82, 170, 175,
    181, 255, 282, 463, 481
    see also Afghanistan war; Iraq
        war
War Powers Resolution, 181
Warren, Earl, 267
Warsaw Pact, 480, A70*n*17
    (ch. 14)

Washington, George, 39
    on alliances with foreign
        powers, 461
    Constitution and, 24
    Genêt received by, 175
    House request refused by, 176
    partisan politics and, 358–59,
        381
Washington Post, 303
Watergate scandal, 97, 176, 418
WB, 300
WCBS (radio station), 302
weapons of mass destruction
    (WMDs), 188, 275, 308
*Webster v. Reproductive Health
    Services*, 414
welfare agencies, 219
welfare system, 447–55, *451*
    Medicare, 190, 449, 450–52,
        A69*n*10
    public assistance programs,
        452–54
    reform, 454–55
    Social Security, 219, *439*, 447,
        448–50, *451*
Westboro Baptist Church,
    96–97
Westminster, Mendez v., 121
Whig Party, *382*, 384, 389
whip system, 158, 160, 161
white Americans, 285, *286*
White House Communications
    Office, 192, 194
White House Live, 304
White House staff, 186, 188,
    368
Wickard v. Filburn, 68
Williams, United States v., 99
Wilson, James Q., 206
Wilson, Woodrow, 183, 190, 223,
    462
Wisconsin, 321, 334–35
*Wisconsin Right to Life, Federal
    Election Commission v.*, 97
WMDs (weapons of mass
    destruction), 188, 275, 308
Wolf v. Colorado, *90*
women
    education and, 117–18
    party identity and, 335,
        352–53, 371, *373*